*"**Money, Possessions, and Eternity** has affected my life and ministry more than any other book besides the Bible. My heart's desire is that every believer would read and reread what God has put upon Randy's heart. If that happened, there would never ever be a lack of finances in any legitimate ministry anyplace in the world. Knowing Randy as I do, I know that this message is his life and his life is this message. It's a privilege to endorse this book."*

Ronald W. Blue, founder and CEO, Ron Blue and Company

*"For the last thirteen years, **Money, Possessions, and Eternity** has been my textbook on how I should manage my finances and giving. This book has helped me determine how best to help the poor, how to keep from hoarding, how to maintain right priorities, and how to understand what the Bible says about eternal rewards. Randy Alcorn is a very perceptive guide. I welcome this fresh revision of a life-changing book."*

Hugh Maclellan Jr, president, The Maclellan Foundation

*"**Money, Possessions, and Eternity** is a book destined to impact generations. It is a classic study of what God wants us to know about handling money with eternity in mind. I heartily recommend it."*

Howard Dayton, CEO, Crown Financial Ministries

POSSESSIONS
AND
ERNITY

Randy Alcorn

Tyndale House Publishers, Inc.
WHEATON, ILLINOIS

Visit Tyndale's exciting Web site at www.tyndale.com

Money, Possessions, and Eternity

Copyright © 1989, 2003 by Eternal Perspective Ministries (Revised and Updated Edition 2003). All rights reserved.

Cover illustration © 2002 by Raul Colon. All rights reserved.

Designed by Timothy R. Botts

Edited by Dave Lindstedt

Library of Congress Cataloging-in-Publication Data

Alcorn, Randy C.
  Money, possessions, and eternity / Randy C. Alcorn.
    p. cm.
  Includes bibliographical references and indexes.
  ISBN 0-8423-5360-7
  1. Wealth—Religious aspects—Christianity. 2. Wealth—Biblical teaching. I. Title.
BR115.W4 A436 2003
241'.68—dc21   2002015642

ISBN 0-8423-5360-7

Printed in the United States of America

07 06 05 04 03
6   5   4   3   2   1

To our precious daughters,
Karina Elizabeth Alcorn
and
Angela Marie Alcorn,
with the prayer and
expectation
that your dreams will not be
the fleeting dreams
of a materialistic culture,
but the eternal dreams
of the Risen Christ.

I wrote the above dedication
in 1988, when our girls were
seven and nine. Since then
I've walked them down the
aisle and given them away in
marriage. God has graciously
answered our prayers about
their dreams being Christ's.
We're so proud of them, and
delighted to see them in their
new season of life. Nanci and
I want to expand this
dedication to include their
husbands:

To our wonderful sons,
Dan Franklin
and
Dan Stump:
May you continue to follow
the Lord wholeheartedly,
loving our daughters as
Christ loves His church,
and loving Him above all.
We thank God—and your
parents—for you.

CONTENTS

Appendixes

ACKNOWLEDGMENTS

I want to express my deepest thanks to some who significantly influenced this book. When I wrote the original work, I received the kind assistance of Wendell Hawley and Ken Petersen at Tyndale House. I thank Ken Taylor for sharing encouraging words about the book's impact. For this new edition, I'm grateful to Tyndale publisher Ron Beers, who asked me to do the update and revision so it could be repackaged and delivered into many new hands.

Thanks to Dave Lindstedt and MaryLynn Layman at Tyndale House Publishers for fine-tuning the revised manuscript and preparing it for publication.

Thanks to great insights I've gained from my many friends in the generous giving community, including Hugh Maclellan, Howard Dayton, Darryl Heald, Todd Harper, Tony Cimmarrusti, David Wills, and Ron Blue. Particular thanks to Ron for sharing his expertise on wealth transfer.

Thanks also to my friend and pastor Barry Arnold, especially for our long discussions on ministry fund-raising ethics, as well as his insights on church debt and gambling. Also, thanks to my best buddy Steve Keels, who didn't really do anything related to this book, but who loves to see his name in print.

Years ago, Rod Morris encouraged me to write on this subject. Larry Gadbaugh offered helpful suggestions on early drafts of that manuscript. Thanks to Bruce Wilkinson for sharing his insights on eternal rewards fifteen years ago at Western Seminary.

Kathy Norquist, world's best ministry assistant, and our outstanding EPM staffers, Bonnie Hiestand and Janet Albers, are of great help in everything I do. Thanks to the EPM board for their partnership and encouragement.

Special thanks is due my wonderful wife, Nanci, my loyal partner in the adventure of living and giving. Thanks, sweetheart, for having such an open heart to giving.

Finally, I offer my heartfelt thanks to my beloved Savior, Jesus Christ. He is the Audience of One, whose opinion of this book—and everything else—is the only one that ultimately matters.

Preface to the Revised & Updated Edition

MUCH HAS CHANGED since 1988 when I finished the original edition of this book. For instance, I had to delete present tense references to the Iron Curtain! What hasn't changed is that wealth has continued to increase in the Western world, despite some economic downturns, while at the same time poverty has increased in underdeveloped nations. Meanwhile, in the United States, watching others compete to make money has turned into a national pastime. The television program *Who Wants to Be a Millionaire?* set ratings records, followed closely by the various installments of *Survivor* (sort of a *"Gilligan's Island* meets *The Millionaire"*). And, since 1988, state lotteries have collected billions of dollars from citizens seeking a big payoff.

Something else that hasn't changed is the need among Christians for a biblical perspective on money and possessions in light of eternity. The Barna Research Group reported that the mean per capita donation to churches dropped by 19 percent in 2000, as compared to 1999, down from $806 to $649. Seventeen percent of American adults claim to tithe, but only 6 percent actually do. One-third of adults who said they were born again also said they tithed in 2000, but a comparison of household income and actual giving revealed that only one out of eight—that's 12 percent of professing born-again Christians—actually did. Younger adults were even less likely to give money to a church. In fact, 23 percent of Christians gave *nothing* in 2000, a 44 percent rise in non-givers.[1]

But if I had any doubts about whether people are genuinely interested in learning about and applying God's perspective on finances, they ended late in 2001 when my little book *The Treasure Principle: Discovering the Secret of Joyful Giving* was published. It immediately went through five printings and sold 100,000 copies within five months.[2] Amazed observers asked, "Are people really that interested in giving?"

The answer is yes.

The Treasure Principle addresses only one aspect of stewardship (which I will cover in this book, along with many other principles), but we desperately need to see the full biblical picture to inform and correct our faulty view of the world. *Money, Possessions, and Eternity* attempts what no small book could ever accomplish—to present a comprehensive biblical and practical treatment of Christian stewardship.

The amazing response to the first edition of Money, Possessions, and Eternity has been a continuous encouragement. I have received countless letters and emails telling me how people have been liberated to a new joy in their Christian lives. One man told me that the book helped him choose to move from his position as CEO of a major company to work in a missions organization. Another man told me he has given millions of dollars to God's kingdom as a result of God speaking to him through the book. Pastors have written to say how their lives and their churches have been changed. This is a tribute not to my insight but to the power of the Scriptures that are the cornerstone of this book.

Some churches have used the book for group study. Several use it to train new church members. However, despite the availability of excellent steward- ship study materials—including publications from Crown Financial Ministries[3]—only 10 percent of churches have active programs to teach biblical financial and stewardship principles. Only 15 percent of pastors say they have been equipped by their denomination or seminary to teach biblical financial principles. Only 2–4 percent of seminaries offer courses, seminars, or Bible studies to teach stewardship principles, and only 1–2 percent of Christian col- leges offer such training.[4]

It's remarkable that something so central to the teaching of Scripture is so neglected by schools dedicated to teaching the Scriptures and preparing students to train others. I hope this new edition might serve as a textbook to assist in such vital training.

This is a thorough revision. Not a single page of the original has been left unchanged. People have used it as a desktop reference over the years, but they've been hindered by the lack of an index. We have added both scriptural and topical indexes, making it much more accessible as a reference. The revised thirteen-week study guide in the back will facilitate group discussion.

There's much that I would like to have included that I couldn't. Some of that material is available at the Eternal Perspective Ministries Web site, www. epm.org, and I encourage readers to freely make use of it.

I've learned a great deal more in these past fourteen years than I knew when writing the original. But what's most important hasn't changed at all— God and his Word, which have a power and authority far beyond my own. I cite Scripture often throughout the book, so that even if my opinions are incor- rect, readers can draw their own conclusions from the truth itself. I cannot be certain of all my insights, but I am absolutely certain of God's.

My revision includes updating of time-sensitive illustrations, adding new insights, and adjusting—in some cases correcting—things I wrote fourteen years ago. God's Word requires no updates or adjustments, unlike some of what I wrote in the original edition. I believe that my life experiences and interactions I've had with many people over the years have helped to make this a better book.

When I wrote the original book I was a local church pastor, but for the past thirteen years I've directed a parachurch ministry. In 1988, I knew that this subject matter had gripped me and changed my family's life—but I had no idea what would happen less than a year after the book came out. Our belief in the truths presented in the book was tested in ways we never could have predicted. More about that later, but for now suffice it to say we found those truths to be rock solid.

I pray your heart will be touched and your life forever changed, as mine has been, through studying and applying Scripture's exciting perspectives on money, possessions, and eternity.

INTRODUCTION

The man of pseudo faith will fight for his verbal creed but refuse flatly to allow himself to get into a predicament where his future must depend upon that creed being true. He always provides himself with secondary ways of escape so he will have a way out if the roof caves in. What we need very badly these days is a company of Christians who are prepared to trust God as completely now as they know they must do at the last day. A. W. TOZER

This book trespasses on enemy territory. It invades the turf of a powerful adversary, attempting to cross a war zone laced with mines. It seeks to recover strategic territory that rightly belongs to the true King.

Satan is the Lord of Materialism. "Mammon" is but an alias of the Prince of Darkness, who has a vested interest in whether or not we understand and obey Christ's commands concerning money and possessions. The Enemy will not give ground without a fight. Because of the spiritual warfare that surrounds this great subject of money and possessions, if this book is to be read with eternal benefit, it must be read with prayer. Our use of money and possessions is a decisive statement of our eternal values. What we do with our money loudly affirms which kingdom we belong to. Whenever we give of our resources to further God's kingdom, we cast a ballot for Christ and against Satan, for heaven and against hell. Whenever we use our resources selfishly and indifferently we further Satan's goals.

The key to a right use of money and possessions is a right perspective—an eternal perspective. Each of our lives is positioned like a bow, drawn across the strings of a cosmic violin, producing vibrations that resound for all eternity. The slightest action of the bow produces a sound, a sound that is never lost. What I do today has tremendous bearing on eternity. Indeed, it is the stuff of which eternity is made. The everyday choices I make regarding money and possessions are of eternal consequence.

The game becomes only more serious as the stakes are raised—or when we begin to realize how high the stakes already are. Far too many evangelical Christians have succumbed to the heresy that this present life may be lived disobediently without serious effects on their eternal state. Never have so many

Christians believed the lie that their money and possessions are theirs to do with as they please. Never have so many thought that as long as they affirm with their lips a certain doctrinal statement, they may live their lives indifferent to human need and divine command, and all will turn out well in the end.

There is something in this book to offend everyone. Some of it offends me—and I wrote it. Please understand that it is not my intention to insult or irritate anyone. Any offenses are simply the by-product of trying to be faithful to the principles of Scripture—which have an annoying tendency to take issue with the way we prefer to think and live.

I have undoubtedly erred in some of my conclusions. I invite you to examine carefully the hundreds of passages cited, searching the Scriptures like the Bereans, to see whether these words are true (Acts 17:11).

God's Word is grain; our word is straw. His Word is the fire that consumes and the hammer that breaks Jeremiah 23:28-29). This book should be judged not in the light of prevailing opinion, but in the light of God's Word. A. W. Tozer said, "Listen to no man who has not listened to God." To the degree that my words do not match up to Scripture, they are worthless. To the degree that they stand up under the scrutiny of God's Word, they should be taken seriously.

The best way to check our heart's attitude regarding material possessions is to allow all the principles of God's Word to penetrate our innermost being. "The word of God is living and active. Sharper than any double-edged sword, it penetrates even to dividing soul and spirit, joints and marrow; it judges the thoughts and attitudes of the heart" (Hebrews 4:12).

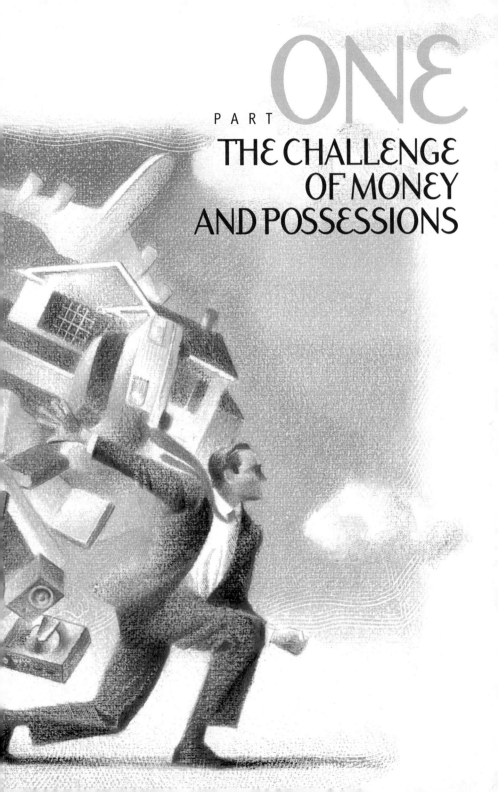

PART ONE

THE CHALLENGE
OF MONEY
AND POSSESSIONS

CHAPTER 1

Money: Why Is It So Important to God?

He who has God and everything has no more
than he who has God alone.   C. S. LEWIS

Jesus Christ said more about money than about any other
single thing because, when it comes to a man's real nature,
money is of first importance. Money is an exact index
to a man's true character. All through Scripture there is
an intimate correlation between the development of a
man's character and how he handles his money.

RICHARD HALVERSON

Were we the Bible's editors, we might be tempted to cut out much of what it says about money and possessions. Anyone can see it devotes a disproportionate amount of space to the subject, right? When it comes to money and possessions, the Bible is sometimes redundant, often extreme, and occasionally shocking. It turns many readers away, making it a hard sell in today's marketplace. It interferes with our lives and commits the unpardonable sin—it makes us feel guilty. If we want to avoid guilt feelings, it forces us to invent fancy interpretations to get around its plain meanings.

If the Bible were written today and judged by what it says about money and possessions, it would never be published. If it were published, it would be mercilessly panned by its reviewers and not see a second printing.

We come to the Bible for comfort, not financial instruction. If we want to know about money, we're more apt to pick up *The Wall Street Journal* or *Fortune, Forbes,* or *Money.* Scripture should concern itself with what's spiritual and heavenly. Money is physical and earthly. The Bible is religious; money is secular. Let God talk about love and grace and brotherhood, thank you. Let the rest of us talk about money and possessions—and do whatever we want with them.

How could the Bible's Author and Editor justify devoting twice as many verses to money (about 2,350 of them) than to faith and prayer combined?

How could Jesus say more about money than about both heaven and hell? Didn't he know what was really important?

Sixteen years ago, when I was a pastor, I planned a three-week sermon series on money. I began by compiling a cross section of Bible passages. I spent weeks on it. Every passage led to another and another. By the time I was done, I had before me a full-fledged book, a book from within The Book. It turns out the Bible had a staggering amount to say about money, how we are to view it, and what we are to do with it. Why hadn't I noticed? Perhaps because I'd never had a single course on this subject in Bible college or seminary, though I'd had courses on subjects about which the Bible has a great deal less to say. While researching that series of messages, I became convinced that God cares a great deal about our money—a great deal more than most of us imagine.

The sheer enormity of Scripture's teaching on this subject screams for our attention. And the haunting question is this—why? Why does God give us so much instruction on money and possessions? Considering everything else he could have told us that we really want to know, why did the Savior of the world spend 15 percent of his recorded words on this one subject? Why did he say more about how we are to view and handle money and possessions than about any other single thing?

Why? What did he know about money and possessions that we don't?

MONEY AND SALVATION

When Zacchaeus said he would give half his money to the poor and pay back fourfold those he had cheated, Jesus did not merely say, "Good idea." He said, "Today salvation has come to this house" (Luke 19:9). This is amazing. Jesus judged the reality of this man's salvation based on his willingness—no, his cheerful eagerness—to part with his money for the glory of God and the good of others.

Then there's the counterpart to Zacchaeus—the rich young ruler (Matthew 19:16-30; Luke 18:18-30). This earnest, decent, hardworking young professional asked Jesus what good thing he could do to get eternal life. When Jesus recited God's commandments, the man said he had kept them all. Then the Lord delivered his bottom line: "Go, sell your possessions and give to the poor, and you will have treasure in heaven. Then come, follow me" (Matthew 19:21).

We would certainly handle the situation differently! First, we would probably commend the rich young ruler for his interest in spiritual things. Then we might tell him, "Just believe, that's all; ask God into your life—you don't really have to do anything."

When he said, "Okay, I believe" (which no doubt he would, since it cost nothing), we would consider him a follower of Christ. Think how blessed we would feel, knowing that God's kingdom was greatly enhanced by the conversion of this well-known wealthy man! Soon there would be articles and books about him. He'd be on TV and radio talk shows. He'd be put on mission and church boards, speak at rallies, and receive invitations to share his testimony in churches and conferences across the country, likely making him into a richer young ruler.

Lacking our sophisticated, twenty-first century knowledge of how to close a conversion, Jesus said something that cost him a valuable convert: "Sell your possessions, give to the poor, and follow me." We might surmise by the results that this was the wrong thing to say: "When the young man heard this, he went away sad, because he had great wealth" (Matthew 19:22).

After losing this potential follower, a man so sincere that he was grieved to turn away, Jesus said to his disciples, "I tell you the truth, it is hard for a rich man to enter the kingdom of heaven" (Matthew 19:23). He said it was harder than for a camel to go through a needle's eye (which, contrary to some modern interpretations, was no easier then than it is now). This statement left the disciples "greatly astonished" (Matthew 19:23-25). They did not understand the barrier that wealth presents to genuine spiritual birth and growth. Apparently, neither do we.

Notice that Jesus didn't tell the young man to give 10 percent to the poor. (If he was truly an obedient Jew, he already did that.) Neither did Jesus say, "Set up a trust fund, keep the principal intact, and give the interest to the poor." The young man would have gladly done that. Instead, Jesus stopped him dead in his tracks by telling him to give up everything and follow him.

As we'll see in a later chapter, Jesus did not and does not call all his disciples to liquidate their possessions, give away all their money, and leave home. But Jesus knew that money was the rich young man's god. He also knew that none of us can enthrone the true God unless in the process we dethrone our other gods. If Christ is not Lord over our money and possessions, then he is not our Lord. Just as Jesus gauged Zacchaeus's true spiritual condition by his willingness to part with his money, so he gauged the rich young ruler's true spiritual condition by his unwillingness to part with his money. Jesus sees our hearts and souls and he knows us just as well as he knew those two men. He will call us to take action that breaks our bondage to money and possessions and frees us to live under his exclusive lordship.

None of us can enthrone the true God unless in the process we dethrone our other gods.

The principle is timeless: There is a powerful relationship between our true spiritual condition and our attitude and actions concerning money and possessions.

Zacchaeus and the rich young ruler are not isolated cases. When people asked John the Baptist what they should do to bear the fruit of repentance, he told them first to share their clothes and food with the poor. Then he told the tax collectors not to collect and pocket extra money. Finally he told the soldiers not to extort money and to be content with their wages (Luke 3:7-14).

No one asked John about money and possessions. They just asked him what they should do to bear the fruit of spiritual transformation. Yet all his answers relate to money and possessions. Those two things were of such high priority, so close to the heart of what it takes to follow God, that John couldn't talk about spirituality without talking in terms of how we handle our money and possessions.

In the story recounted in Acts 19:18-20, the Ephesian occultists demonstrated the reality of their spiritual conversions by their willingness to burn their magic books, which were worth the vast sum of 50,000 days' wages, the equivalent of perhaps six million dollars in today's economy. The depth of transformation in the lives of the early Christians was most clearly evident in their willingness to surrender their money and possessions to meet each other's needs (Acts 2:44-45; 4:32-35).

There is a powerful relationship between our true spiritual condition and our attitude and actions concerning money and possessions.

It was no more natural for the Christians in the book of Acts to cheerfully liquidate and disburse assets they had spent their lives accumulating than it would be for us. And that's the whole point. Conversion and the filling of the Holy Spirit are supernatural experiences that produce supernatural responses—whether in the first century or the twenty-first. Although private ownership of property was still practiced by the early Christians, the joyful giving and sharing of this property became the new norm of supernatural living.

If John the Baptist (or a first-century Christian) were to visit us today and gauge our spiritual condition by our attitudes and actions regarding money and possessions, what conclusions would he come to?

When you look around our Christian communities today, what do you see in our handling of money and possessions that can only be explained by the supernatural work of God?

A POOR WOMAN AND A RICH MAN

Play the role of financial counselor. Today you have two appointments, first with an elderly woman and then a middle-aged man.

The woman's husband died six years ago. She says, "I'm down to my last two dollars. I have no more money. The cupboards are bare. These two dollars are all I have to live on, yet I feel as if God wants me to put them in the offering. What do you think?"

What would you tell her? (Don't read on until you think about it.)

Likely you'd say something like this: "That's very generous of you, dear, but God gave you common sense. He knows your heart—that you want to give—but he wants you to take care of yourself. He knows you need to eat. I'm sure God would have you keep those two dollars and buy food for tomorrow. He wants your needs to be met. You can't expect him just to send down food from heaven if you give up the little money he's already provided, can you? God wants us to do the sensible thing."

Your next appointment is with a successful, hardworking, middle-aged farmer whose crop production has been excellent. He tells you, "I'm planning to tear down my old barns to build bigger ones so I can store up more crops and goods and have plenty saved up for the future. Then I can take it easy, retire early, and maybe do some traveling and golfing. What do you think?"

What's your answer?

Perhaps something like this: "Sounds good to me! You've worked hard and the Lord has blessed you with good crops. It's your business, crops, and money. If you can save up enough to take care of yourself for the rest of your life, by all means go for it. Maybe one day I'll be in a position to do the same!"

Doesn't our advice to this poor widow and this rich man seem reasonable? But what would God say? We needn't speculate—Scripture tells us exactly what he says.

In Mark 12 we meet a poor widow. She put two tiny copper coins in the temple offering box. This was the only money she had. Jesus called his disciples together to teach them a lesson. Did he question the woman's wisdom? Did he say she should have been more sensible than to surrender her only remaining resources? No. He gave her an unqualified commendation: "I tell you the truth, this poor widow has put more into the treasury than all the others. They all gave out of their wealth; but she, out of her poverty, put in everything—all she had to live on" (Mark 12:43-44).

Jesus regarded the woman as wise. He set her up as a model for his disciples to follow. He enshrined her example in the Word of God so that future generations might emulate her faith and sacrificial generosity. (And yet, if she'd come to us for advice, we would have tried to talk her out of doing what Jesus commended her for.)

In Luke 12 we meet a rich man. We're not told that he gained his wealth dishonestly or that he wasn't religious. He probably attended synagogue weekly, visited the temple three times a year, tithed, and prayed, as most Jews did. He worked diligently to build his business. Now, like any good business-man, he wanted to expand by building bigger barns. His purpose was to accumulate enough wealth to retire early and have a good time. Sounds like the American dream, doesn't it?

So what did God have to say to this man? "You fool! This very night your life will be demanded from you. Then who will get what you have prepared for yourself?"

Jesus added, "This is how it will be with anyone who stores up things for himself but is not rich toward God" (Luke 12:20-21).

By our standards, both outside and inside the Church, the widow's actions seem unwise and the rich man's seem wise. But God, who knows the hearts of both and sees from the vantage point of eternity, regards the poor woman as eternally wise and the rich man as eternally foolish.

This shows that our beliefs about money are not only radically different from God's but diametrically opposed to them.

If we take these passages seriously, we must ask some probing questions. Who are featured more frequently in Christian magazines and talk shows—poor widows or rich fools? Who receives the most respect and attention in many Christian organizations? Who is more highly esteemed in most churches? Who typically serves on our boards and determines the direction of our ministries? Today, don't we have a scarcity of poor widows and a surplus of rich fools?

THE STORY MONEY TELLS

The study of Zacchaeus, the rich young ruler, the poor widow, the rich fool, and many other Bible characters shows that our handling of money is a litmus test of our true character. It's an index of our spiritual life. Our stewardship of our money and possessions becomes the story of our lives.

If this is true of all people in all ages, doesn't it have a special application to us who live in a time and place of unparalleled affluence? who live in a society where almost everyone enjoys comforts and conveniences that King Solomon never dreamed of? who live in a country where the "poverty level" exceeds the average standard of living of nearly every other society in human history, past or present?

Take for example a man or woman who works from age twenty-five to sixty-five and makes "only" $25,000 a year. Forget for the moment the huge additional value of health and retirement benefits, interest, pay raises, and other income sources, including inheritance or Social Security. Even without these extras, this person of modest income (by our standards) will receive a million dollars. He or she will manage a fortune. Because we all will eventually give an account of our lives to God (Romans 14:12; 2 Corinthians 5:10), one day everyone must answer these questions: Where did it all go? What did I spend it on? What has been accomplished for eternity through my use of all this wealth?

In the account of the poor widow, Mark writes, "Jesus sat down opposite the place where the offerings were put and watched the crowd putting their money into the temple treasury" (Mark 12:41). Notice that it doesn't say, "Jesus happened to see . . ." No, he deliberately watched to observe what people were giving.

How close was Jesus to the offering box? Close enough to see that some people put in large amounts. Close enough even to see two tiny coins in a shriveled old hand and to identify them as copper (Mark 12:41-42).

Jesus was interested enough in what people were giving to make an object lesson for his disciples (Mark 12:43-44).

This passage should make all of us who suppose that what we do with our money is our own business feel terribly uncomfortable. It's painfully apparent that God considers it his business. He does not apologize for watching with intense interest what we do with the money he's entrusted to us. If we use our imagination, we might even peer into the invisible realm to see him gathering some of his subjects together this very moment. Perhaps you can hear him using your handling of finances as an object lesson.

The question is this: What kind of example are you?

HITTING CLOSE TO HOME

Can we put Christ before all, deny ourselves, take up our crosses and follow him (Matthew 10:38; Mark 8:34; Luke 14:27), with no apparent effect on what we do with our money and possessions?

What are we to think of all the current teaching on money and possessions that emphasizes what does not apply to us? Confident voices assure us that the Old Testament practice of tithing doesn't apply to us, that the New Testament practice of sacrificial giving by liquidating assets and giving to the poor doesn't apply to us, that the biblical prohibitions of interest and the restriction of debt don't apply to us, that the commands not to hoard and stockpile assets don't apply to us, and so on. It's time to ask, "What does apply to us?"

Not only are our spiritual lives at stake but also the wholeness of our families. Half of all marriages end in divorce, and 80 percent of divorced people indicate that financial issues played a primary role in ending their marriage.[1] If we could get it right when it comes to money, how many other areas of our life would fall into place?

Sometimes more can be learned from the passages of Scripture we ignore than those we underline. The Bible contains an arsenal of such verses on the subject of money and possessions, and they just keep firing away at us. No wonder C. S. Lewis called God "The Transcendental Interferer." God has this annoying habit of stepping into our lives even when we've pulled in the welcome mat and bolted the door. He can throw a great party but he also knows how to spoil one.

The more we allow ourselves to grapple with these unsettling passages, the more we are pierced. Jesus wounds us with his words about money. Then, just when we think we're healed, we run into another sharp passage, and God's Word pierces us again. Our only options, it seems, are to let Jesus wound us until he accomplishes what he wishes, or to avoid his words and his gaze altogether by staying away from his Word. The latter option is easier in the short run. But no true disciple can be content with it.

By now some readers are long gone and others who remain are uncomfortable. I must admit that I share your discomfort. You may be thinking, *I'd rather not deal with these issues; I'm content with what I'm doing.* But are you really content? Are any of us who know Christ, who have his Spirit living within us, really content when we haven't fully considered our Savior's words? when we haven't completely opened ourselves to what he has for us? Comfortable, perhaps. Complacent, certainly. But not content.

I, for one, hate to live with that nagging feeling deep inside that when Jesus called people to follow him he had more in mind than I am experiencing. I don't want to miss out on what he has for me. And if he has really touched your life, I don't think you do either.

The fear of dealing with what God expects me to do with my money is exceeded by the fear of not dealing with it. I don't want to stand before him one day and try to give an answer for how I could call myself a disciple without ever coming to grips with money and possessions. Not when even a cursory reading of the New Testament shows this issue to be right at the heart of discipleship.

You may be thinking, *I'd rather not deal with these issues; I'm content with what I'm doing. But are you really content?*

I might feel a little better trying to squirm out of responsibility for some minor or obscure teaching of Scripture. "I just didn't understand it, Lord. It was unclear. You really didn't give us much to go on." But I can't help but feel that if I plead ignorance concerning money and possessions, God is liable to say, "What more would you have wanted me to say than what I said? Was your problem that these passages were unclear . . . or that they were too clear?"

I must quickly add that for me the process of discovering God's will about money and possessions has been exciting and liberating. My growth in financial stewardship has closely paralleled my overall spiritual growth. In fact, it has propelled it. I have learned more about faith, trust, grace, commitment, and God's provision in this area than in any other.

I have also learned why Paul said, "God loves a cheerful giver" (2 Corinthians 9:7). I have found that cheerful givers love God and love him more deeply each time they give. To me, one of the few experiences comparable to the joy of leading someone to Christ is the joy of making wise and generous choices with my money and possessions. Both are supreme acts of worship. Both are exhilarating. Both are what we were made for.

I write this book not as a critic but as an excited learner. I feel like a child who has found a wonderful trail hidden in the woods. Countless others have gone before and blazed the trail, but to the child it's as new and fresh as if it had never been walked before. The child is invariably anxious for others to join in the great adventure. It's something that can only be understood by actual experience. Those who've begun the journey, and certainly those who've gone further than I, will readily understand what I'm saying.

My hope is that even if you have come to this book as a spectator, you will finish as a participant. I pray you will join a multitude of God's people, past and present, in not just talking about God's grace, but experiencing it at the deepest level of your heart.

MY BACKGROUND AND PERSPECTIVE

I am not a professional financial counselor, and this is not a typical book about money.

For fourteen years I was a pastor. For the past thirteen years I've been a ministry director. My background is not in economics, investments, or accounting. It's in biblical studies, theology, teaching, biblical counseling, and writing. I wrote this book because I have discovered that the Bible, my interactions with others, and my personal experience all speak with one voice in affirming something profound and revolutionary. They substantiate what the greatest Theologian, Teacher, and Counselor knew only too well—that the issue of money and possessions lies at the very heart of the Christian life.

How we view our money and possessions is of the utmost importance. What we do with our money will—and I choose these words deliberately—influence the very course of eternity.

My study of this subject has reinforced the reality that we were made for only one person and one place. Jesus is the person and heaven is the place. Our purpose should pervade our approach to money. If it does, the door will be unlocked to exhilarating Christian discipleship, where "following Christ" is not merely a comforting but meaningless cliché; instead it is an electrifying, life-changing reality.

This book won't tell you how to achieve your financial goals. But it will provide the light in which your financial goals should be set. It will lay the foundation on which they should be built. And it will set forth the principles that should govern your attempts to achieve your goals.

I'm leery of most books that tell us how to accomplish our financial goals. Such advice is valuable only if the goals we set are right, only if they are biblically based and Christ-centered. Much financial counsel, from secular and sometimes Christian sources, serves the same purpose as instruction on how to maneuver a canoe heading toward a waterfall. It's not only important to know how to get the canoe down the river, it's also essential to know where the river is taking you.

Before we learn the fine art of building a sturdy boat or the skill of staying in the boat as we head down the rapids, we should make certain that our

11

desired destination is really downstream rather than upstream. Because if it's upstream, we would do better to get off the river altogether, forget the boat, and plot our course by land. It may be a harder trip, but isn't the whole point to arrive at the correct destination?

I believe that most of the financial matters we typically discuss are on the fringes of what's important, light years away from the core of the issue. We tend to focus on things that belong at the tail end of stewardship discussions, not the beginning. In effect we're trying to install the gutters before we've laid the foundation and started the framing. We must realize that many of the things our society considers to be at the heart of financial planning (such things as insurance, the stock market, and retirement, for instance) never existed before the modern era and still don't exist in much of the world. That doesn't mean they're wrong—only that they are secondary.

A friend who edited a Christian magazine in Kenya for years told me that most financial material coming from the United States, Christian as well as secular, is irrelevant to most Africans, because so much of our American economic structure is exclusive to our isolated segment of twenty-first century Western civilization. We can talk all day about what we consider the great financial issues of our time without ever touching upon the timeless financial principles that the Bible considers important.

My interactions with people as a pastor, teacher, counselor, and researcher—as well as my observation of my own tendencies—have convinced me that in the Christian community today there is more blindness, rationalization, and unclear thinking about money than anything else.

"Do not conform any longer to the pattern of this world, but be transformed by the renewing of your mind" (Romans 12:2). If we prefer to think as the world thinks about money and possessions, we needn't change a thing. Conformity is as natural as swimming downstream. But if we're committed to thinking about money and possessions as God does, it's a different matter. We need to set aside the bookshelves and magazine racks filled with advice on how to make, spend, and invest our money and blow the dust off our Bibles. The Bible is the only book worthy of the title chosen by a popular financial counselor for his own book: *The Only Investment Guide You'll Ever Need*.

STARTING AT GROUND LEVEL

To build the proper foundation, we must understand the following things about money:

- what it is (it's more than coins and currency)
- whose it is
- how God views it
- its potential use for two different kingdoms

These four issues are what this book is about.

You may be surprised to find that several chapters don't deal exclusively with money but instead discuss the larger issue of what eternity holds for us and how that relates to our money. I believe this is the primary missing ingredient in most Christian books on finances. When we look at money only as money, and not in light of its impact on eternity, we walk away with a cloudy and shortsighted vision that results in cloudy and shortsighted financial decisions and lifestyles.

That's why the central focus of this book is not insurance as much as *assurance*, not securities but *security*, not trusts but *trust*, not principal but *principles*, not real estate but our *real* estate. You will not find in these pages any net-worth calculations (which we easily mistake for self-worth calculations), but you will see how God measures your life's worth on another basis. You will not learn here about the dangers of inflation but you will see the dangers of a much truer enemy of financial stewardship, a lion who seeks to devour us.

> When we look at money only as money, and not in light of its impact on eternity, we walk away with a cloudy and shortsighted vision.

You won't find in this book any advice about tax planning, where to put your IRA, or whether to buy term insurance or whole life. There is a place for such things—but only after a close and careful look at what God has to say about money.

In these pages you won't find budget sheets, expenditure lists, or telephone numbers to help you place an order for gold bullion. But you will find many practical helps that relate directly to biblical principles. These include such varied applications as transferring ownership to God, choosing a strategic lifestyle, evaluating ministry fund-raising techniques, and examining the Christian's role in multilevel marketing.

You will find an analysis of religious materialism and the scandals it has created, as well as a critique of the Christian prosperity doctrine—the health and wealth gospel that has been so widely adopted. We'll consider the question of whether capitalism is more or less Christian than socialism, what Scripture says about private property, how we really can help the poor and reach the lost with our money, whether tithing is for us today, and how much and to whom the Bible calls us to give.

We will see what the Bible says about lending and borrowing, and explore the alarming philosophy that often underlies our decisions to assume debt. We will look at the implications of credit card use for Christians and mortgage debt for churches. We'll address true contentment and how to keep our needs in focus in an economy based on wants. And we will uncover some of the most persistent spending myths that allow us to rationalize poor financial stewardship.

We will discuss the importance of wise counsel, whether it's right to have certain kinds of insurance, and if it's appropriate for Christians to risk money in investments. We will examine the difference between Scripture's injunctions to save and its warnings against stockpiling. We'll also look at the stewardship of our money and possessions at death: What should we leave to our children and what shouldn't we? And speaking of our children: How can we raise them to see money and possessions as instruments of eternal value rather than substitutes for them? What practical steps can we parents take to raise wise and generous financial stewards rather than grabby materialists? All along, we will try to examine these things under the bright sun of our eternal future, not the fading penlight of our passing present.

In our pursuit of the biblical truth about money, we'll repeatedly come back to the practicalities of the present. But I hope we'll come back armed with convictions that will help us take the tough steps of true discipleship, leading to incomparable rewards.

As we explore together the exciting issues ahead, let's determine not to be rich fools disguised as disciples. Instead, let's commit ourselves to developing the heart of the poor widow, learning to boldly put all our resources at God's disposal as he has put all his resources at ours.

May we learn together the truth that Martin Luther recognized when he said that for each of us there must be not only the conversion of the heart and mind but also the conversion of the purse.

CHAPTER 2

The Weakness of
Asceticism

*If silver and gold are things evil in themselves, then those
who keep away from them deserve to be praised. But if they
are good creatures of God, which we can use both for the
needs of our neighbor and for the glory of God, is not a
person silly, yes, even unthankful to God, if he refrains
from them as if they were evil?*   MARTIN LUTHER

*Away, then, with that inhuman philosophy which, while
conceding only a necessary use of creatures, not only
malignantly deprives us of the lawful fruit of God's
beneficence but cannot be practiced unless it robs a man of
all his senses and degrades him to a block.*   JOHN CALVIN

At times I crave an audible voice from heaven that would tell me exactly what
I'm supposed to do with my money and possessions. Philip Yancey expresses
my own dilemma when it comes to money:

> Many Christians have one issue that haunts them and never falls silent:
> for some, it involves sexual identity; for others, a permanent battle
> against doubt. For me, the issue is money. It hangs over me, keeping
> me off balance, restless, uncomfortable, nervous.
>
> I feel pulled in opposite directions over the money issue. Sometimes
> I want to sell all that I own, join a Christian commune, and live out my
> days in intentional poverty. At other times, I want to rid myself of guilt
> and enjoy the fruits of our nation's prosperity. Mostly, I wish I did not
> have to think about money at all. But I must somehow come to terms
> with the Bible's very strong statements about money.[1]

God gives us principles in his Word, principles that will change us if we believe them. Yet we are left with a lot of latitude. I appreciate freedom, but it
raises a lot of questions. In light of global needs and the tendency to be distracted

from the things of God, should I own a house? a car? two cars? If so, what kind of house or car? Is it all right to own a nice suit? Can I own one, but not two or three? How many pairs of shoes are too many? Is it all right to golf once in a while but too extravagant to belong to a club? Can I go out for dinner? If so, where and how often? Should I take a vacation that costs three hundred dollars but not one that costs three thousand? How can I be sure I'm pleasing God in my financial decisions?

Materialism is money-centered and thing-centered rather than God-centered. It has no place in the Christian life. But is there an opposite extreme? Can the pendulum swing away from materialism and go too far in the other direction? I believe the answer is yes. That other extreme is *asceticism*. Asceticism is a way of thinking that sees money and things as evil. To the ascetic, the less you own, the more spiritual you are. If something isn't essential, you shouldn't have it.

Materialism and asceticism are rooted in equally wrong views of money and possessions. In subsequent chapters, we will take a close look at materialism, including materialism in the Church. In this chapter we'll consider the question of whether money is evil or good. Then we'll examine asceticism in light of history and Scripture.

UNDERSTANDING THE NATURE OF MONEY

If we are to understand our proper relationship to money, we must first understand what money is.

Money is more than just metal disks or colored paper. It is a tool that simplifies trade. The farmer needs lumber more than beef, milk, and eggs. He has plenty of those. The lumberman needs beef, milk, and eggs more than his many stacks of boards. By trading their goods, both get what they want.

Money is a tool that can expedite such a trade and widen its circle to include others. Rather than trading two pigs for a plow and three sacks of grain, one person can give another the agreed-upon worth of the two pigs in the form of money. This saves time and energy. Who wants to carry around pigs and plows?

God encouraged the people of Israel to take advantage of money's convenience. He told them that if their place of worship was too far from their home, they should exchange the tithes of their crops and livestock for silver, then convert it back to the goods of their choice once they arrived (Deuteronomy 14:24-26).

Money allows much more flexibility than a direct exchange of goods. If I get fifty dollars for my pigs, I can use the money to buy the exact plow I want, two sacks of grain instead of three, or whatever I prefer and can afford. Instead of grain, I can buy coffee, a saddle, a lamp, or books.

Money is one person's promise of goods or services, granted in return for actual goods or services. In a sense, money is no more than a widely recognized IOU. Realizing its convenience, people consent to participate in an economic system in which money is the transferable object that makes it all possible. Of course, it's only the widespread participation of others in this same system that gives meaning to money. Without the mutual agreement that money means something, money means nothing.

Because money has no inherent value, only ascribed value, money is not wealth. It merely symbolizes wealth. You can't eat money and you can't plow a field with it. You can use a one hundred dollar bill to light a cigar or wad up your gum, but that's about it. Practically speaking, gold is much less valuable than some other metals. In and of itself, it's little more than a pretty paper-weight or doorstop. Gold, silver, platinum, coins, and currency are only worth something in a society where other people have agreed to attach a certain value to them. That they do so is proven by their willingness to give goods and services in exchange for them.

Money is nothing more than a pledge of assets, a means of payment, a medium of exchange. It is morally neutral. Puritan William Ames put it this way: "Riches . . . are morally neither good nor bad, but things indifferent which men may use either well or ill."[2]

THE TWO FACES OF MONEY

Money has social and economic benefits that can be used for the betterment of people. As a plow can be used for honest labor and a sack of grain for feeding a family, so money, which simply represents their value, can be used for good. If my neighbor's barn burns down, I may give him some grain out of compassion for his loss. Or I may sell the grain and give him money to use as he wishes, perhaps to buy meat, lumber, or tools. The grain and the money amount to the same thing, except that the money can be used for other goods besides grain.

Christian compassion can accomplish great good through the giving of grain, lumber, or money to alleviate suffering. Money can be used to feed, clothe, and provide shelter. It can fund the translation and printing of Bibles, provide for missionaries, or build houses of worship. In this sense, money may appear to be good. But it's really the giver who is doing good. People may be moral or immoral, but things are morally neutral. The money is an instrument of good, not good itself. Money is no more responsible for doing good than a computer is responsible for writing a book or a baseball bat for hitting a home run.

Money can be used to buy a slave or a whip to be used on a slave. Money can purchase sex, bribe a judge, buy cocaine, and fund terrorist acts. But in each case the evil resides in people, not money, just as in other cases the good resides in people, not money.

Money is nothing more than a pledge of assets, a means of payment, a medium of exchange. It is morally neutral.

Water is a gift of God. Used properly, it gives life. Out of control, it floods, drowns, and destroys. Fire is a gift of God. Out of control, it brings horrible destruction and death. The greater a thing's potential for good when used rightly, the greater its potential for evil when used wrongly. So it is with money—it has vast potential to be used for either good or evil.

If this were a morally neutral world, we would expect money to be used in a morally neutral way. But the world is not neutral—it is sinful and under a curse (Romans 8:20-22). This is the problem with money. In a sinful world, money becomes something other than a neutral means of barter. It becomes an instrument of power. In the hands of sinful people, power is perverted into oppression, and money becomes an object of worship, a false god. In rejecting a God they don't wish to serve, sinful people instead come to serve—and serve themselves with—the god of money.

Although there's nothing inherently wrong with money, there's something desperately wrong with devotion to money. "People who want to get rich fall into temptation and a trap and into many foolish and harmful desires that plunge men into ruin and destruction. For the love of money is a root of all kinds of evil" (1 Timothy 6:9-10).

Given all the error, deception, and abuse of money, Richard Foster argues that money is not neutral, but "a 'power' that is demonic in character."[3] I believe this is an overstatement that logically leads to asceticism or even dualism, yet it's certainly true that money can be used for demonic purposes.

Since money can be used for either good or evil, if those using it are more evil than good, it will most often be used for evil. The problem is human sinfulness—and so it will be until Christ returns and we live on the new earth, where there will be no more curse and no more evil (Revelation 21:1-5).

USING MONEY FOR GOOD PURPOSES

Jesus said to his disciples, "I tell you, use worldly wealth to gain friends for yourselves, so that when it is gone, you will be welcomed into eternal dwellings" (Luke 16:9).

I'll deal with the precise meaning of these words later, but my point now is simply that Jesus tells us to do something good with "worldly wealth" (literally, "the mammon of unrighteousness"). It's as if he's saying, "Take this thing that is commonly used for evil and use it for good. Look at this worn currency; smell in it the foul purposes for which it was used—perhaps to buy drugs or sex or injustice. It may have once been stolen, perhaps even killed for. But now that it's in your hands, use it wisely and well; use it for eternal purposes."

Jesus clearly said that we can and should use money for good purposes, both for this life and the next. Human hearts can be redeemed by Christ, and in the hands of the redeemed, money can serve redemptive purposes.

But lest we forget money's dangers, Jesus also said, "No servant can serve two masters. Either he will hate the one and love the other, or he will be devoted to the one and despise the other. You cannot serve both God and Money" (Luke 16:13).

Once we allow money to have lordship over our lives, it becomes Money with a capital M, a god that jealously dethrones all else. Money makes a terrible master, yet it makes a good servant to those who have the right master—God.

To regard money as evil, and therefore useless for purposes of righteousness, is foolish. To regard it as good and therefore overlook its potential for spiritual disaster is equally foolish. Use it, Jesus said, but don't serve it.

The goal, then, is not that money be put to death, but that it be trained and handled with discipline, as a lion we are seeking to tame. Money may be temporarily under our control, but we must always regard it as a wild beast, with power to turn on us and others if we drop our guard.

Money must not call the shots. We may have plenty of money to buy a new car, but we must not take our direction from Money. If we serve God, we will buy the car only if we believe he wants us to—and we must base that belief on more than preference.

Likewise, if we believe God is leading us to go to the mission field or to help a brother in need, we do not say, "There's no money, so I can't." That also would be serving Money. If God is our master, all money is at his disposal. We must concern ourselves not with what Money says, but with what God says. The need for money may be a factor in our decisions, but it is never the factor. God, not Money, is sovereign. Money—whether by its presence or absence—must never rule our lives.

> Once we allow money to have lordship over our lives, it becomes Money with a capital M, a god that jealously dethrones all else.

Money is neither a disease nor a cure. It is what it is, nothing less and nothing more. We may use it well or poorly. Either way, how we use money is always of critical importance to our spiritual lives. It has a lasting impact on two worlds—this one and the next.

TWO RESPONSES TO MONEY AND POSSESSIONS

Two equally incorrect beliefs about money are that it is always evil, or that it is always good. Both views have the advantage of all unbalanced positions—they require no discernment. Unfortunately, they also both result in excesses that undermine rather than further kingdom purposes.

Two extreme philosophies and lifestyles that stem from these two incorrect beliefs about money are asceticism and materialism. Martin Luther compared humanity to a drunkard who falls off his horse to the right, then gets back on and falls off to the left. Asceticism is falling off the horse on one side and materialism off the other.

Some, including Eugene Peterson and Dallas Willard, use "asceticism" in a positive way, linking it to spiritual disciplines, including meditation, prayer, and fasting.[4] I certainly agree with their emphasis on these spiritual disciplines and believe that the Church desperately needs to revive them. What I am calling asceticism, following the term's more popular usage, is what might be regarded as extreme, false, or dualistic asceticism.

Ascetics practice strict self-denial, depriving themselves of all but the essential basics of the material world. Often, asceticism is rooted in the concept of dualism, a philosophy championed by Plato that sees the spiritual world as good but the physical world as evil.

> The Jews saw material things as gifts from God's hand, as a Father's loving provision for his children.

It's easy to see why dualists who value spiritual things would become ascetics. By avoiding physical pleasures and conveniences, they think they're avoiding sin. Ascetics in Church history have denied themselves nearly every possession and pleasure. St. Francis of Assisi objected to friars having books besides the Scriptures because they were unnecessary. In stark contrast, Paul valued not only the Scriptures but also his other books and asked them to be brought to him in prison (2 Timothy 4:13). Francis taught that money should be shunned as the devil himself. He and his disciples refused even to touch money. They glorified poverty and saw begging for food as a virtue, a way of earning merit with God.

Many ascetics in Church history refrained from marriage, and some who did marry abstained from sexual relations with their spouse, believing that abstinence made them more spiritual. Others, including the Church father Origen, attempting to obey Christ's words in Matthew 5:29-30 and 19:12, emasculated themselves to avoid the evils of lust, fornication, and adultery. Some literally beat their bodies; others spent most of their lives atop towers, seeking to avoid the world's defilements.

SCRIPTURE AND ASCETICISM

The entire fabric of Old Testament teaching and Hebrew thought argues against dualism and asceticism, by inference and example. There are not two gods, a god of the spiritual and a god of the physical. There is one God who is God of both. The same God created the spiritual and physical worlds, and he created both for us to enjoy.

Except for one small sect, the Essenes, the Jews did not labor under the notion that the physical world was bad. On the contrary, they saw material things as gifts from God's hand, as a Father's loving provision for his children. They saw God as the Lord of the harvest. As his grateful children, they celebrated national feasts to recognize and rejoice in his material provision (Deuteronomy 16:15). These feasts were parties. By God's command, a portion of the holy tithes was set aside to underwrite these celebrations (Deuteronomy 14:22-27). The Israelites worshiped, fellowshipped, and celebrated and in the process had a great deal of fun.

Similarly, the Jews understood sex as a gift from God, to be shunned outside of marriage but thoroughly enjoyed within it (Proverbs 5:18-19). In fact, much of the Song of Solomon—as inspired by God as the book of Romans—is a celebration of a married couple's sexual pleasure. The rabbi-turned-apostle Paul not only ordered the materialistic Corinthians to avoid immorality but also commanded the ascetics in the church to stop withholding themselves from sexual relations with their spouses (1 Corinthians 7:3-5). Satan is the master of extremes. As Luther said, Satan doesn't care which side of the horse we fall off, as long as we don't stay in the saddle.

Scripture portrays the relationship between the material and the spiritual not as either/or but both/and. The material must not take precedence over the spiritual, but it's nonetheless a necessary and legitimate part of our existence, intended for us to enjoy.

Tim Hansel addresses the ascetic Christian's misreading of Scripture:

> Irony of ironies, his commitment to Jesus Christ has become a prison rather than a blessing. So blinded by religious observations and reservations, he fails to see the festivity that was so central in the life of Jesus. He forgets that Jesus, despite the sad world he inhabited, was the prime host and the prime guest of the party. Jesus let himself be doused with perfume. He attended to wedding wine and wedding garments. The Bible is full of merriment. The feast outruns the fast. It is crammed with spitted kids and lambs and fatted calves, grapes, pomegranates, olives, dates, milk, and honey.[5]

Paul warned Timothy that there would be those who "abandon the faith and follow deceiving spirits and things taught by demons" (1 Timothy 4:1). Those responsible for these teachings are described as "hypocritical liars, whose consciences have been seared as with a hot iron" (1 Timothy 4:2). Paul issued a "wanted poster" on these theological criminals. Here's how he describes them:

> They forbid people to marry and order them to abstain from certain foods, which God created to be received with thanksgiving by those who believe and who know the truth. For everything God created is good, and nothing is to be rejected if it is received with thanksgiving, because it is consecrated by the word of God and prayer. (1 Timothy 4:3-5)

The phrase "everything God created is good" is the theological death knell for asceticism. From a biblical perspective, everything is fair game to have and to enjoy, as long as we partake thankfully and prayerfully—unless, of course, what we partake in violates God's Word.

Eden was Paradise, and the new heavens and new earth will be an even greater paradise with much for us to enjoy (Revelation 21–22). In my novels, I attempt to give a biblically based glimpse into what heaven may be like. My nonfiction book In Light of Eternity: Perspectives on Heaven explores the tangible pleasures that Scripture either teaches directly or implies will be ours in heaven.[6] In our new bodies, without sin to twist and warp us, we will enjoy God's provisions and take full pleasure and delight in him and his gifts. The delights of heaven—including feasting together at banquets (Matthew 8:11)—are proof that the material world and physical pleasures are good, not evil.

A BRIGHTER SIDE TO ASCETICISM

It would be wrong to cast all ascetics in the same light. Richard Foster has shown us the other side of some of these ascetics.[7] Some were godly people, deeply devoted to the Lord. St. Francis and his band were filled with the love of life. They bubbled with humor and humanity, singing merrily as they went about their simple tasks. Although some ancient ascetics were morose and regarded pleasure a sin, as some do today, others delighted all the more in what little they had. They enjoyed scraps of bread and cups of cold water as feasts.

It's hard to know what to think of saints who retreated to the desert to meet God when so many of us today who retreat to the desert won't go without suntan oil and golf clubs. In fact, it's difficult for Westerners to imagine a good time without corks popping, bands playing or—in Christian circles—casseroles, punch, and cookies. But some of these followers of Christ found more joy in their simple celebrations of life than we do with all our modern conveniences and pleasures that dull our senses to delights such as fresh bread and clear, cold water.

We should be careful not to dismiss the lessons we could learn by observing the ascetics who walked before us in Church history. After all, the pursuit of materialism has surely led more people into darkness than has the practice of asceticism.

THE MODEL OF MOTHER TERESA

We needn't only look back to ancient times for examples of individuals who have chosen an ascetic lifestyle. Mother Teresa of Calcutta, who died in 1997, and her order, the Missionaries of Charity, are perhaps the best-known modern examples. Through their vow of poverty, they seek to identify with the poor, homeless, diseased, and dying people to whom they minister. I have seen their work firsthand and commend them for it. The sisters, who are still at work around the world, are an example of what it means to serve.

With all the respect due Mother Teresa and her coworkers, however, their view of material things may not be entirely biblical. In a moving documentary about her life and work, Mother Teresa is shown instructing workers to downgrade a modest facility that had been donated to the mission. She directed them to remove carpets and a hot-water hookup that were already in place. There was no indication that the carpet was sold and the proceeds distributed to the poor. The point seemed only to be that because they *could* do without the carpet, they *should* do without it, even if no one else would benefit from their sacrifice.

This selfless gesture may appear to be spiritual precisely because of its selflessness. But does it really square with the biblical teaching on material things? Couldn't the readily available hot water have been immensely helpful in caring for the many sick people in the facility? Wouldn't the carpet have helped keep the building warm and brought some comfort to the suffering? By choosing to forgo what had already been provided, the workers either had to do without the benefits of hot water or take the time and effort to heat the water on stoves or over a wood fire. What harm was the carpet in the building? What good was it once it had been thrown out on the street?

Are all conveniences and modern amenities wrong? If carpets and hot water are to be avoided as luxuries, why do the Missionaries of Charity use medicine to care for the sick? Why did Mother Teresa ride in trucks and fly in airplanes? If technology is undesirable, why do many of the sisters in the order wear glasses? Surely they could get along without them, just as the facility could get along without hot water and carpet.

My desire is not to criticize such devotion and sacrifice, but only to point out the necessary inconsistency of asceticism. Ultimately, every form of asceticism is selective and arbitrary. The Amish, for example, who forgo electricity, nevertheless use gas engines, pulleys, wheels, and other technologies that were once as modern as electricity. Is an oil lamp more spiritual than one lit by electricity? Is either lamp less spiritual than a candle, a match, or no light at all? If pleasures are unspiritual, we can always eat a little less and get along with a little less sleep. If material things are truly bad, we would have to eat, drink, and wear nothing to avoid being tainted. Because the body itself is material, both masochism and suicide are logical conclusions of pure asceticism. Without daily compromising one's position, a true ascetic's lifespan would be short indeed.

THE INADEQUACIES OF ASCETICISM

The Reformers, including Luther, rejected asceticism as taught by the Catholic Church. The Puritans, who are often—but wrongly—viewed as ascetics, made statements such as these:

> These earthly things are the good gifts of God, which no man can simply condemn, without injury to God's disposing hand and providence, who hath ordained them for natural life.[8]

23

Riches are consistent with godliness, and the more a man hath, the more advantage he hath to do good with it, if God give him an heart to it.[9]

Puritan William Ames rejected the monks' vow of poverty as "madness, a superstitious and wicked presumption, being that they sell this poverty for a work of perfection . . . which will much prevail for satisfaction and merit before God."[10]

These are some perspectives we must bring to our understanding of asceticism:

Poverty is not piety. Nowhere does Scripture consider poverty inherently virtuous. Certainly, God cares for the poor—but out of his compassion, not based on their merit. It is just as erroneous to view poverty as a sign of spirituality as to view wealth that way. "The Lord sends poverty and wealth; he humbles and he exalts" (1 Samuel 2:7).

> We must be careful not to stereotype sainthood and judge righteousness by outward appearances.

Scripture says that the ideal state is somewhere between poverty and riches: "Give me neither poverty nor riches, but give me only my daily bread. Otherwise, I may have too much and disown you and say, 'Who is the Lord?' Or I may become poor and steal, and so dishonor the name of my God" (Proverbs 30:8-9).

Wealth and poverty both can tempt us to sin. Richard Baxter, a seventeenth-century pastor wrote, "Poverty also hath its temptations. . . . For even the poor may be undone by the love of that wealth and plenty which they never get; and they may perish for over-loving the world, that never yet prospered in the world."[11]

Spirituality is a matter of the heart, not one's material circumstances. Someone can have few possessions yet still be a materialist at heart, just as one can be an alcoholic without a bottle in hand. Ascetics may trust in their self-denial rather than in Christ. The poor may be as proud of not having things as the rich may be of their possessions. The one who owns little may not pray at all, whereas the one with much may pray earnestly. (Common sense and experience, however, suggest that it's more often the other way around.)

We must be careful not to stereotype sainthood and judge righteousness by outward appearances. Hearing the word *saint*, our minds must not be so narrow as to envision only St. Francis living in austerity. Our perspective must be broad enough to include C. S. Lewis debating an issue with colleagues as he smoked his pipe and drank his ale at Oxford's Eagle and Child Pub, or R. G. LeTourneau daydreaming the design of his next earthmover. Saints come in many different trappings. We err when we draw too many conclusions from the trappings themselves.

Asceticism can be an attempt to win favor with God or man. It's one thing to wish to please God but another to try to earn one's standing before him through self-denial. The ascetic lifestyle can be a bid to impress God and others with our spirituality. Christ condemned the Pharisees for trying to impress people with their public self-denial of giving, prayer, and fasting (Matthew 6:1-18). Impure motives can drive ascetics as strongly as materialists.

Some ascetics choose to suffer in order to cope with feelings of guilt. They may feel guilty for their own sins or because others have lived in poverty while they have not. But we must realize that only suffering that is divinely ordained—and therefore purposeful—is godly, not suffering per se. God is glorified when our suffering is brought about by our faithfulness to Christ (1 Peter 2:20), not when we bring it upon ourselves by attempting to appear faithful. He is glorified by outwardly focused self-denial for the good of others, not by inwardly focused self-deprivation for our own benefit (including attempts to remove our guilt feelings). God is looking for those who are willing to become martyrs for his purposes, not those eager to be martyrs for their own purposes.

A sacramental view of suffering would put God in our debt, from which he would then bless us with salvation or save others through our suffering rather than Christ's. However, neither suffering in general, nor poverty in particular, has any intrinsic merit or atoning power. Although Satan, the other fallen angels, and unredeemed humanity will suffer in hell for eternity, their suffering will have no atoning value. God may use our suffering to extend his grace and build our character, and in that sense purify us (Romans 5:3-4), but not to atone for our guilt.

The Roman Catholic concept of purgatory infiltrates the thinking of many Christian ascetics. But self-inflicted punishment is not only unbiblical, it is also prideful and self-righteous. What an inflated opinion of myself I must have to believe that my suffering could remove my guilt before a Holy God. Only Christ's suffering has redemptive value. God calls me to *accept* the atonement, not to repeat it.

Asceticism can lead to unfair condemnation of others who choose a different lifestyle. Our standard of living can become a yardstick by which we measure others. We may see others as unspiritual if they own a house and we don't, or if their house is bigger than ours, or if their car is newer than ours. (One man wrote me a letter condemning a friend's choice to frequent a local coffee shop, while at the same time he saw no problem with his own decision to spend money on skiing. Neither choice is inherently wrong, and it would be equally unfair for the coffee lover to criticize the skier based solely on his personal preferences.) An ascetic's attempts to deny the flesh often become just another way of feeding and indulging it. We are called to pursue God, not sainthood—or the appearance of sainthood.

Modern conveniences can free up time to pursue spiritual aims as well as enhance ministry. Because most of the day in Bible times was devoted to tending crops or herds, earning money, and preparing meals, some would suggest that we should shun the use of modern conveniences. But can't a microwave oven or a dishwasher be God's provision to free up time for prayer, hospitality, and a variety of ministries in the home, neighborhood, and church?

Do we imagine Jesus using his bare hands to cut wood, or can we assume he used the best affordable tools in his carpentry? And if our Lord were living in today's society, wouldn't he take advantage of the current technology in his trade? Would he abstain from using power saws, believing that handsaws are more spiritual? Would he hesitate to travel in a car any more than he did a boat? Would he avoid using a microphone even if it would allow the crowds to hear him better?

It would be disastrous if every believer dropped out of society's mainstream and stopped making money. If everyone took a vow of poverty, who would support the Missionaries of Charity? Who would provide the medical advances that their ministries utilize, or make the glasses they wear, or build the trucks and repair the planes used to deliver their supplies? St. Francis and his band refused to touch money and often begged for food, but someone had to earn the money required to care for them. Generating income is a necessary part of life, not something unspiritual. It would be inconsistent to describe those who produce material goods as "worldly" or "secular," while spiritualizing those who don't produce anything but depend on those who do.

We should commend those who choose to live simply or strategically and devote the larger portion of their income to help the needy. But we shouldn't go so far as to disdain the production of income or withdraw from "the system," as if economics were sinful, and end up contributing to poverty rather than helping to alleviate it.

Many forms of asceticism are not conducive to evangelism. If every Christian adopted the monastic practice of retreating from society to escape material temptations, how would people in most walks of life be reached with the gospel? Mother Teresa served in the midst of a crowded city, but many ascetics withdraw from society and thereby diminish their opportunities to minister to others.

Paul makes it clear that part of our calling in this world is to rub shoulders with non-Christians, regardless of their sins and lifestyles. We must be actively involved in the lives of others, and therefore present in their world (1 Corinthians 5:9-10). As Jesus said, we must remain in the world but at the same time not be of it (John 17:15-16).

There's much good in regularly retreating from the world. But the purpose of these times should be to draw near to God and then come back to our troubled, materialistic society and reach out to those troubled materialists for whom Christ died. We must all battle materialism. But the most difficult and rewarding battle is not to withdraw from society but to serve God faithfully within it.

Asceticism doesn't deliver what it promises. Many people expect to find peace, purity, and holiness in an ascetic lifestyle. Yet Paul warned against the inaccurate assumptions underlying asceticism and the abuses it fosters (1 Timothy 4:1-5). He also warned that asceticism does not accomplish its purpose: "Such regulations indeed have an appearance of wisdom, with their self-imposed worship, their false humility and their harsh treatment of the body, but they lack any value in restraining sensual indulgence" (Colossians 2:23). Union with Christ, not self-deprivation, is the foundation of holiness (Colossians 3:1-17).

History confirms that withdrawing from society doesn't eliminate or even curb our sinful nature. According to one writer, "the monastic orders . . . did not really escape from the problem of a Christian attitude toward the handling of wealth. The members of these orders did not own property as individuals. But the orders entered at once into the field of creating and accumulating wealth. In many cases the monks in their group relationships fell into all of the sins of avarice which had formerly characterized individuals who were dominated by covetousness."[12]

Our Lord lived simply, but he was not an ascetic. In fact, some people condemned Jesus for associating with gluttons and drunkards (Matthew 11:19; Luke 7:34). He not only drank wine, he *made* wine for a wedding celebration (John 2:1-11). He moved with equal ease among the poor, such as John the Baptist and Bartimaeus, and the wealthy, such as Mary, Martha, Lazarus, Nicodemus, Zacchaeus, and Joseph of Arimathea (Matthew 27:57-61; John 19:38-42). Jesus accepted material support from wealthy women (Luke 8:2-3), and he gratefully accepted the extravagant anointing of his body with an expensive perfume (Matthew 26:6-12; Luke 7:36-50; John 12:1-8).

Christ's birth attracted poor shepherds and rich kings. A poor thief (on an adjacent cross) and a rich man (who donated a tomb for his burial) attended his death. His life on earth drew many—both poor and rich. And regardless of their means, he was pleased to accept into his kingdom all who would bow their knee before the Messiah.

QUESTIONS TO CONSIDER

Is it possible to learn from those who have chosen asceticism without adopting their lifestyle? Can we follow the example of the many Christians, both past and present, who have chosen a more simple and uncluttered lifestyle than our own? Would we consider giving up enough of our things to detach ourselves from the things we have, yet hold onto enough to use for our good and the good of others? Can we do what Jesus commanded us—to *use* money but not *serve* it? Can we discover what it means to invest money for eternal purposes? Is it possible to live in a materialistic culture without being tainted by materialism? These are some of the challenges and opportunities set before us as we seek to follow the clear-thinking, simple-living Galilean who was and is the Son of God.

CHAPTER 3

The Nature of Materialism

*For over a hundred years, a large part of the American
people has imagined that the virtual meaning of life lies
in the acquisition of ever-increasing status, income,
and authority.*   ROBERT BELLAH

*The lust for affluence in contemporary society has become
psychotic; it has completely lost touch with reality.*
RICHARD FOSTER

*Where riches hold the dominion of the heart, God has
lost His authority.*   JOHN CALVIN

The comic strip "Cathy" depicted a young man and woman discussing various items they'd acquired:

"Safari clothes that will never be near a jungle."

"Aerobic footwear that will never set foot in an aerobics class."

"Deep-sea dive watch that will never get damp."

"Keys to a four-wheel-drive vehicle that will never experience a hill."

"Architectural magazines we don't read filled with pictures of furniture we don't like."

"Financial strategy software keyed to a checkbook that's lost somewhere under a computer no one knows how to work."

"Art poster from an exhibit we never went to of an artist we never heard of."

Finally, as both characters stand with blank stares, one says to the other: "Abstract materialism has arrived." To which the other replies: "We've moved past the things we want and need and are buying those things that have nothing to do with our lives."

Shopping has become our most popular weekday out-of-home entertainment. In the United States there are sixteen-and-a-half square feet of mall space for every man, woman, and child. More people visit Minnesota's Mall of

America each year than Disneyland, the Grand Canyon, and the Grand Ole Opry combined.[1] But it's no longer even necessary to fight through the crowds at the mall—or even to pick up a catalog. Today all that's needed to "shop till you drop" is a credit card, a telephone, and access to the Home Shopping Network or one of its spin-offs. Or you can bid day and night on eBay. Many of us act as if we believe the words of the old bumper sticker: "He who dies with the most toys wins."

A STUDY IN MATERIALISM

In 1955, Fortune magazine interviewed a large number of twenty-five-year-olds who were starting to build their careers. The study portrayed the group as dedicated to family and community service. In 1980, Fortune repeated the same exercise with a new crop of twenty-five-year-olds. This time, however, the results were strikingly different. Over the span of twenty-five years, materialism had made remarkable inroads. Writer Gwen Kinkead summarized the attitudes of those she interviewed:

> They believe that business offers the fastest means of gratifying their frankly materialistic requirements. Deferred success, the traditional basis of the work ethic, holds little appeal. They expect to enjoy immediately a relatively high level of material comfort. Terry Michel, a management trainee at Connecticut General Life Insurance Company, echoes the consensus: "I like to spend money. I don't feel like giving up any luxuries. I grew up with lots of land, private schools, horses, dogs, a car at sixteen."
>
> To a stranger from another generation, they sometimes seem a grabby bunch.
>
> It seems that, almost unprincipled, this class flaunts its ambitions. Why bother with goals, they ask, if you don't shoot for the top?
>
> Worries about marketability have turned this group into congenital scale-watchers who tote up their chances of promotion, weigh their salaries against the going market rate, and never, never do anything that won't enhance their records. . . .
>
> Dwight Billingsly, a utilities consultant in a Washington, D.C., firm, strikes a common chord: "I plan to set up my own business, be independent, report to no one," he says. "Though I have more money now than I ever thought possible, I'd like all the money in the world, and to own a major-league baseball or football team." . . .
>
> They are unabashed materialists who crave the latest labor-saving and electronic hardware, along with frequent entertainment and travel. Scarcely any twenty-fives have children at present. Most of those who doubt they will ever be parents say they can't spare the time. Explains

Edward Beam, a planning officer at Chicago Northern Trust Company, "I love kids, but I don't want any. I'm too selfish to give what's necessary to raise them properly. Eventually, I'd resent their taking me away from my interests, just as I'd be upset that I wasn't devoting enough attention to them."

Some already view owning a home (and having two incomes to cover the mortgage) as more desirable than having children. Later the choice may be between having children and an even higher standard of living—or greater job mobility.

One woman in the group stated, "With our lifestyle, we can't afford good child care and all the things we like."

Few devote time to public service or volunteer work or express concerns about social problems. Organized religion, favored by the 1955 group as a social and family adhesive, appears too proscriptive or irrelevant to today's secular twenty-fives. The majority call themselves agnostic or privately spiritual.[2]

In the more than two decades since the 1980 *Fortune* interviews, America has continued to drink deeply of materialism. However, in recent years we've begun to see a backlash, as typified by the PBS television special "Affluenza," which addressed what it called the "modern-day plague of materialism." The program highlighted several symptoms of this new "plague," including the following statistics:

- The average American shops six hours a week but spends only forty minutes playing with his or her children.
- By the age of twenty, the average television viewer has seen one million commercials.
- Recently, more Americans declared bankruptcy than graduated from college.
- In 90 percent of divorce cases, arguments about money play a prominent role.[3]

The remarkable thing about this public television program is that it doesn't argue against materialism on a moral basis but a pragmatic one. The producers' main objection to materialism is simply that material wealth *doesn't make us happy.*

THE ORIGIN OF MATERIALISM

One look at the treasures of King Tut should convince us that materialism didn't first arise in the latter twentieth century, or even with the industrial revolution or the establishment of Western capitalism. Materialism was rampant in the time of Christ, but it didn't begin there either. The genesis of materialism was in the Garden of Eden, when the first man and woman chose to follow their appetites rather than God, seeking fulfillment in the one thing he had told them was forbidden. A. W. Tozer describes the ongoing results of their sin and ours:

> Before the Lord God made man upon the earth, He first prepared for him a world of useful and pleasant things for his sustenance and delight. . . . They were made for man's use, but they were meant always to be external to the man and subservient to him. In the deep heart of the man was a shrine where none but God was worthy to come. Within him was God; without, a thousand gifts which God had showered upon him.
>
> But sin has introduced complications and has made those very gifts of God a potential source of ruin to the soul.
>
> Our woes began when God was forced out of His central shrine and things were allowed to enter. Within the human heart things have taken over. Men have now by nature no peace within their hearts, for God is crowned there no longer, but there in the moral dusk stubborn and aggressive usurpers fight among themselves for the first place on the throne. This is not a mere metaphor, but an accurate analysis of our real spiritual trouble. There is within the human heart a tough, fibrous root of fallen life whose nature is to possess, always to possess. It covets things with a deep and fierce passion. The pronouns my and mine look innocent enough in print, but their constant and universal use is significant. They express the real nature of the old Adamic man better than a thousand volumes of theology could do. They are verbal symptoms of our deep disease. The roots of our hearts have grown down into things, and we dare not pull up one rootlet lest we die. Things have become necessary to us, a development never originally intended. God's gifts now take the place of God, and the whole course of nature is upset by the monstrous substitution.[4]

WHAT IS MATERIALISM?

Webster's *New Collegiate Dictionary* defines *materialism* as "a theory that physical matter is the only or fundamental reality and that all being and processes and phenomena can be explained as manifestations or results of matter." Two other definitions flow from the first: "A doctrine that the only or the highest value or objectives lie in material well-being and in the furtherance of material progress," and "a preoccupation with or stress upon material rather than intellectual or spiritual things."[5] In short, a materialist attaches the wrong price tags to the things of this world and the things of God.

Materialism begins with our beliefs. Not merely what we *say* we believe—not our doctrinal statement—but the philosophy of life by which we actually live. So even though true Christians would deny belief in the philosophical underpinnings of materialism (they couldn't be Christians if they didn't), they may nonetheless be preoccupied with material things. Materialism is first and foremost a matter of the heart.

God created us to love people and use things, but materialists love things and use people. Take for example our society's tendency to treat people as objects. In the marketplace we refer to *consumers*—economic units that are of value to a company only insofar as they contribute to its profits. Products are marketed to "consumers" without regard to the fact that they may become addicted, depressed, obese, or diseased—taking years off their lives—as a result of consuming those products.

The genesis of materialism was in the Garden of Eden, when the first man and woman chose to follow their appetites rather than God.

We have every reason to be alarmed about our country's materialism but no reason to be surprised by it. We cannot reject the Creator and his truth without rejecting the respect for human dignity that naturally flows from it. We cannot teach and believe that human beings are merely the product of time, chance, and natural forces without ultimately treating each other that way. When young people are taught that they're no different in kind than animals, it shouldn't surprise us when they act like the animals we've told them they are.

Materialism drives not just the "bad apples" of society, not just the abandoned street kids or reform schoolers. It drives "the best and the brightest," those from the finest homes and schools, those who become government and business leaders, physicians, and attorneys. Materialists are simply living out what they've learned at home, at school, from the media, from their friends—and sometimes, sadly, even from our churches. Every person values something. What other values than materialistic ones would we expect from a generation of materialists? As a society, we are reaping exactly what we have sown.

Materialism can never be corrected by high-sounding courses in ethics or the campaign speeches of politicians calling on us to restore the moral fiber of our nation. Moral fiber must come from somewhere. It cannot simply be grabbed out of the sky in the midst of a moral vacuum. Materialism can only be corrected by changing our view of God. This change, in turn, can only come from a belief in and study of the Scriptures, which tell us about God, and which alone give us the context to understand ourselves and the proper place of money and possessions.

Materialism results from a failure to realize that we were made for only one person (Jesus) and one place (heaven). Those of us who know Christ will one day be with him in heaven. Until then, nothing else can satisfy us. Materialism is a lie that Satan whispers in our ears: "If you had this thing or this person, you'd finally be happy." As long as we live by the lie, regardless of what we *say* we believe, we will be practicing materialists.

WARNINGS FROM THE WORD

Materialism fills the pages of Scripture. Achan's lust for money and possessions brought death to himself, his family, and dozens of men in battle (Joshua 7). The prophet Balaam cursed God's people in return for Balak's payment (Numbers 22:4-35). Delilah betrayed Samson to the Philistines for a fee (Judges 16). Solomon's lust for more and more wealth led him to disobey flagrantly God's prohibitions against accumulating large quantities of horses, gold, silver, and wives (Deuteronomy 17:16-17). To gain wealth, Gehazi lied to Naaman and then to Elisha, for which he was afflicted with leprosy (2 Kings 5:20-27). In the ultimate act of treachery, Judas asked the chief priests, "What are you willing to give me if I hand him over to you?" Judas then betrayed the Son of God for thirty pieces of silver (Matthew 26:14-16, 47-50; 27:3-10).

In the midst of God's powerful work right after the Church was born, Ananias and Sapphira withheld money they said was given to the Lord and were struck dead for it (Acts 5:1-11). It's no accident that this happened so early in Church history and that God acted in such a powerful and memorable way. It was as if he was saying, "The Church will not be immune to materialism, greed, and deceit, but I will bring strong judgment on those who poison my Church with them." The subsequent story of Simon Magus sends the same message (Acts 8:18-21).

Jesus Christ sounded a sober warning against materialism in any form and in any age: "Watch out! Be on your guard against all kinds of greed; a man's life does not consist in the abundance of his possessions" (Luke 12:15).

Greed surfaces in possessiveness and covetousness. Possessiveness relates to what we have, covetousness to what we want. Possessiveness is being selfish with what we own, not quick to share. To covet is to long for and to be preoccupied with having what God hasn't given us. It's the passion to possess what is not ours.

Greed isn't a harmless pastime but a serious offense against God. As one who lusts is an adulterer (Matthew 5:28) and one who hates is a murderer (1 John 3:15), so one who is greedy is an idolater (Colossians 3:5). Greed is money worship, a violation of the first and most fundamental commandment: "I am the Lord your God. . . . You shall have no other gods before me" (Exodus 20:2-3). The eighth commandment is a prohibition against stealing (Exodus 20:15), another product of greed, and the tenth commandment is a warning against covetousness (Exodus 20:17). Remarkably, the ten great laws of God, written in stone, contain three prohibitions against materialism

Greed is considered the source of almost every destructive force imaginable, including war (James 4:1-3). The lust for money and possessions is considered the root of a thousand social evils, the most basic of which is apostasy, running away from the true God (1 Timothy 6:10).

Materialists come from every walk of life. There are communist materialists just as there are capitalist materialists; Republican materialists and Democrat materialists; materialists in management and in labor; secular and religious materialists. Greed transcends all economic philosophies, social systems, political parties, religions, and financial situations. It's part of our basic sinful nature.

What will happen to the affluent person or society that does not rectify its materialism? The basic laws of physics give us the answer. The greater the mass, the greater the hold that mass exerts. This explains why the largest planets are capable of holding so many satellites in orbit. Similarly, the more things we own—the greater their total mass—the more they grip us, hold us, set us in orbit around them. Finally, like a black hole, a gargantuan cosmic vacuum cleaner, they mercilessly suck us into themselves, until we become indistinguishable from our things, surrendering ourselves to the inhuman gods we have idolized. This is the final end of materialism.

We must understand that materialism is not simply wrong. It is stupid.

In the face of this grim prognosis, Jesus Christ brings us good news. He calls us to adopt a mind-set of generous giving, a habit of life that changes the equation of our lives. Generous giving frees us from the hold of our possessions, breaking us out of their orbit. Through generous giving we can escape the gravity of things on earth by establishing a new orbit around treasures we store up in heaven.

THE STUPIDITY OF MATERIALISM

We must understand that materialism is not simply wrong. It is stupid. As Jesus once asked his profit-conscious audience, "What good will it be for a man if he gains the whole world, yet forfeits his soul? Or what can a man give in exchange for his soul?" (Matthew 16:26).

The parable of the rich fool portrays a man who thought of himself as a successful businessman (Luke 12:16-21). The essence of foolishness is that we either don't recognize the truth or we choose to ignore it. The rich fool of the parable thought he was captain of his fate. He made his plans without taking into account God's plans. He failed to come to grips with three fundamental facts—the mortality of his present life, the eternality of his future life, and the reality that today's choices were forging his future life.

The rich fool was a materialist. He acted irrationally, as if he could escape death or delay it indefinitely. He neglected to number his days and therefore failed to gain a heart of wisdom (Psalm 90:12).

Scripture describes our lives as "like grass" and our achievements as "the flowers of the field." The grass withers and the flowers fall—in the eyes of eternity this earthly life comes and goes in the blink of an eye (Isaiah 40:6-8). "But man, despite his riches, does not endure; he is like the beasts that perish" (Psalm 49:12). "Man is a mere phantom as he goes to and fro: He bustles about, but only in vain; he heaps up wealth, not knowing who will get it" (Psalm 39:6).

A Greek philosopher said, "All men think it is only the other man who is mortal." The way we scurry about accumulating things is testimony to our unspoken doctrine that we are exceptions to the law of death. The events of September 11, 2001, were a shocking reminder to millions of Americans of something we should have already understood—our mortality.

The rich fool was "not rich toward God" (Luke 12:21); that is, he did not handle money in a God-centered way. He was self-centered, hoarding and stockpiling money and possessions rather than releasing them to serve God and meet the needs of others. He was too self-sufficient and independent to ask God's counsel on how much to keep and how much to give, too preoccupied with the business of "success" to open his heart in love to meet the needs of those around him.

The Talmud says, "Man is born with his fist clenched but dies with his hands wide open." The Scriptures say, "Naked a man comes from his mother's womb, and as he comes, so he departs. He takes nothing from his labor that he can carry in his hand" (Ecclesiastes 5:15). But the rich fool was too busy being "successful" to care.

When one of the wealthiest men in history, John D. Rockefeller, died, his accountant was asked, "How much did John D. leave?"

The accountant's reply was classic: "He left all of it."

You can't take it with you. Or as someone put it, "You'll never see a hearse pulling a U-Haul."

Perhaps we need to read the obituaries to remind ourselves how short our time on earth is. Perhaps we need to visit a junkyard to remind ourselves where all the things we work for and chase after will one day end up. The wise man thinks ahead. The foolish man acts as if there is no eternal tomorrow.

THE REVERSAL DOCTRINE

Luke 16:19-31 tells us the story of another rich man and a poor man named Lazarus. The rich man dressed well, lived in luxury, and was apparently healthy. Lazarus was a beggar, diseased, dirty, and "longing to eat what fell from the rich man's table" (Luke 16:21). If I asked, "Who would you rather be, the rich man or Lazarus?" you would presumably reply, "The rich man, of course."

We aren't told that this rich man was dishonest or irreligious or that he was worse than your average person. We don't know that he despised poor Lazarus; we only know that he ignored him. He lived his life as if the poor man didn't exist. He didn't use his God-provided wealth to care for another man in need.

Both men die. Lazarus goes to heaven and the rich man goes to hell. When the rich man begs Abraham from across the gulf to send Lazarus to relieve his suffering, Abraham replies, "Son, remember that in your lifetime you received your good things, while Lazarus received bad things, but now he is comforted here and you are in agony" (Luke 16:25).

Now that you've heard the rest of the story, who would you rather be, the rich man or Lazarus? You'd probably like to switch places, wouldn't you? But that's Abraham's point: After death, it's too late to switch.

This parable represents a strong and often overlooked New Testament teaching, which we might call "the reversal doctrine." It teaches that in eternity many of us will find ourselves in opposite conditions from our current situation on earth.

In this life, the rich man "lived in luxury every day," while Lazarus begged at his gate, living in misery. At the moment of death, their situations reversed—the rich man was in hell's torment and the poor man in heaven's comfort.

It would be both simplistic and theologically inaccurate to conclude that heaven is earned by poverty and hell is earned by wealth. But this parable is not isolated—it corroborates a host of other teachings by Jesus, as well as those of the apostles.

> **In eternity many of us will find ourselves in opposite conditions from our current situation on earth.**

In the song she composed in anticipation of Christ's birth, Mary said, "He has filled the hungry with good things but has sent the rich away empty" (Luke 1:53).

"Blessed are you who are poor," Jesus said, and "Woe to you who are rich," precisely because their status will one day be reversed (Luke 6:20, 25). The poor in spirit, those who mourn, those who are meek, those who hunger and thirst for righteousness and are persecuted will be relieved and fulfilled and have a great reward in heaven (Matthew 5:3-12). Those praised in this world will not be highly regarded in the next, and vice versa (Matthew 6:1-4, 16-18). Those who are exalted in this life will often be humbled in the next; those who are humbled here on earth will be exalted in heaven (Matthew 23:12).

Those who are poor in this world will often be rich in the next, and those who are rich in this world will often be poor in the next (James 1:9-12). The poor are reassured that the hoarding and oppressing rich will one day be punished and the honest poor will be relieved (James 5:1-6). In Revelation 18:7, a voice from heaven says of materialistic Babylon, "Give her as much torture and grief as the glory and luxury she gave herself."

Some of these passages may present us with theological difficulties, but all of them remind us that temporal sacrifices will pay off in eternity and temporal indulgences will cost us in eternity. These are the verses that encouraged Christian slaves and should have served warning to the plantation owners who were profiting from slavery. The reversal doctrine is comforting to the poor and weak, and threatening to the rich and powerful. But it's a consistent teaching of

37

the New Testament—one that confirms the premise that materialism is not only wrong but stupid. Conversely, trusting God, giving and caring and sharing are not only right but smart.

Someday this upside-down world will be turned right side up. Nothing in all eternity will turn it back again. If we are wise, we will spend our brief lives on earth positioning ourselves for the turn.

RECOGNIZING MATERIALISM
John Wesley said:

> Wherever true Christianity spreads, it must cause diligence and frugality, which, in the natural course of things, must beget riches! And riches naturally beget pride, love of the world, and every temper that is destructive of Christianity. Now, if there be no way to prevent this, Christianity is inconsistent with itself and, of consequence, cannot stand, cannot continue long among any people; since, wherever it generally prevails, it saps its own foundation.[6]

After one of our church's missionaries had been home for a month, he said, "I've been overwhelmed with the materialism here." When another missionary was returning to the field after a year's furlough, we asked him, "What struck you the most in the time you were home with us?" His matter-of-fact reply was sobering: "What struck me the most was how people use their houses to make statements to each other; their houses aren't just places to keep warm and dry, but showcases to display their wealth and impress each other."

Both these men were from other cultures. The sad thing is that if either had stayed in the United States for another year or two, he might no longer have noticed. Like the frog that boiled to death by degrees, we tend to gradually acclimate to our materialism, becoming desensitized to it. Finally, we regard it as normal rather than an aberration.

The hardest part of dealing with our materialism is that it has become so much a part of us. Like people who have lived in darkness for years, we have been removed from the light so long that we don't know how dark it really is. Many of us have never known what it is not to be materialistic. This is why we need so desperately to read the Scriptures, to grapple with these issues, bring them to God in prayer, discuss them with our brothers and sisters, and look for and learn from those rare models of nonmaterialistic living in our Christian communities.

If we were to gain God's perspective, even for a moment, and were to look at the way we go through life accumulating and hoarding and displaying our things, we would have the same feelings of horror and pity that any sane person has when he views people in an asylum endlessly beating their heads against the wall.

For years, the argument against materialism, among Christians, has been that materialism is wrong. Materialism *is* wrong, but since this line of argument has proven itself ineffective, perhaps it's time for a new approach: "Materialism is stupid; in fact, materialism is insane."

Seeking fulfillment in money, land, houses, cars, clothes, boats, campers, hot tubs, world travel, and cruises has left us bound and gagged by materialism—and like drug addicts, we pathetically think that our only hope lies in getting more of the same. Meanwhile, the voice of God—unheard amid the clamor of our possessions—is telling us that even if materialism did bring happiness in this life, which it clearly does not, it would leave us woefully unprepared for the next life.

4

The Dangers of Materialism

The soul is a spiritual thing, riches are of an earthly extract, and how can these fill a spiritual substance? How man does thirst after the world, but, alas, it falls short of his expectation. It cannot fill the hiatus and longing of his soul.
THOMAS WATSON

The type of man most likely to grow very, very rich is the type of man least likely to enjoy it. MAX GUNTHER

The poorest man I know is the man who has nothing but money. JOHN D. ROCKEFELLER

Surrounded by wealthy socialites, a beautiful young woman sat at a dinner party on a luxury boat. To her surprise, a millionaire sitting near her passed her a note asking, "Would you go to bed with me tonight for ten thousand dollars?"

Blushing, the woman paused for a moment and then wrote back, "Yes."

A few minutes later the two left the party. When they were alone the man asked the woman, "Would you go to bed with me for ten dollars?"

Outraged, she asked him, "What kind of woman do you think I am?"

Matter-of-factly he replied, "We've already determined what kind of woman you are. Now we're just trying to find your price."

IDOLATRY AND ADULTERY

Satan works on the assumption that every person has a price. Often, unfortunately, he is right. Many people are willing to surrender themselves and their principles to whatever god will bring them the greatest short-term profit.

The Old Testament portrays Israel as a bride who has turned into a prostitute. She abandons her rightful husband, God, and sells herself to the highest bidder. The prophets develop this metaphor to embarrassing extents (Isaiah 57:3-9; Jeremiah 3:1-10; Ezekiel 16:1-48). The nauseating descriptions of Israel's waywardness exemplify God's hurt and horror at the spiritual adultery of his people as they chase after other gods.

The New Testament tells us that "greed . . . is idolatry" (Colossians 3:5). Idolatry is worshiping and serving anything other than the one true God. Everything material we have, including money, is either a tool or an idol. If we fail to use it as a tool for God's intended purposes, it mutates into an idol. For the Church, the bride of Christ, idolatry is the same as adultery—a wanton betrayal of a husband who loves us enough to die for us.

Herbert Schlossberg addresses the idolatrous nature of materialism:

The common expression that describes such a value system as "the pursuit of the almighty dollar" is soundly based in the recognition that the exaltation of possessions to the level of ultimacy is the end of a religious quest, one that seeks and ascribes ultimate meaning. Like all idolatries, it finds ultimate meaning in an aspect of the creation rather than in the Creator. And like all idolatries it finds outlet in destructive pathologies that wreck human lives.[1]

Scripture speaks of these destructive pathologies:

People who want to get rich fall into temptation and a trap and into many foolish and harmful desires that plunge men into ruin and destruction. For the love of money is a root of all kinds of evil. Some people, eager for money, have wandered from the faith and pierced themselves with many griefs. (1 Timothy 6:9-10)

Note the self-destructive nature of money love. It's a life of self-mutilation in which we repeatedly pierce ourselves with grief after grief. The good we seek destroys us. We load our idols with expectations they cannot deliver. The happiness we try to wrest from them can only be found elsewhere.

Jesus said the rich are at a spiritual disadvantage (Matthew 19:23-24). The problem, of course, is not that God doesn't love the rich. The problem is that the rich don't love God. They simply have too much else to love. Who needs God, we think, when we've got everything? This is why Jesus didn't say, "You should not serve both God and Money," but "You cannot serve both God and Money" (Matthew 6:24, italics mine). Why? For the same reason a woman cannot have two husbands. When we carry on a love affair with the world, we commit spiritual adultery. We place God in the role of the jilted husband. He loves us and longs for our return but will not allow us in his intimate chambers when we are prostituting ourselves to another. God will not be a half husband. He will not be comforted by the fact that we call him "Savior" when we refuse to follow him as Lord.

Materialism consists of the two things God hates most—idolatry and adultery. The magnitude of God's abhorrence for materialism surfaces in the final act prior to the return of Christ—the destruction of the money-loving system of this world, called "Babylon the Great." It's said of this Babylon, "The kings of the earth committed adultery with her, and the merchants of the earth grew rich from her excessive luxuries." A voice from heaven pleads with God's people—a voice that we would do well to heed today:

> Come out of her, my people, so that you will not share in her sins, so that you will not receive any of her plagues; for her sins are piled up to heaven, and God has remembered her crimes. Give back to her as she has given; pay her back double for what she has done. Mix her a double portion from her own cup. Give her as much torture and grief as the glory and luxury she gave herself. (Revelation 18:4-7)

The images of the World Trade Center—that towering symbol of our financial prosperity—falling to the ground are forever etched in our memories. As terrible a tragedy as it was, the collapse was a reminder of the truth that, one day, God in his justice will bring down all the centers of human achievement and prosperity that do not humble themselves before him. When financial Babylon comes down, the merchants who gained their wealth from this corrupt materialistic philosophy will say, "Woe, O great city, dressed in fine linen, purple and scarlet, and glittering with gold, precious stones and pearls! In one hour such great wealth has been brought to ruin!" (Revelation 18:16-17).

Materialism consists of the two things God hates most—idolatry and adultery.

We might expect all heaven to mourn at this devastation. But in fact, all heaven will rejoice at the destruction of materialism's stronghold: "Rejoice over her, O heaven! Rejoice, saints and apostles and prophets! God has judged her for the way she treated you" (Revelation 18:20). God will eventually break the stronghold of materialism, but we must seek for it to be broken now.

I was scheduled to preach on giving at my church. I was overwhelmed with a sense that many people would not be ready to hear the message because of Mammon's grip on their lives. I was scheduled to begin this series the week after Easter Sunday, when more than one hundred people had come to Christ in our services. During one of the Easter services, Nanci and I had been part of a prayer group in a little room off the front of the auditorium. We experienced God's power through prayer. We learned how the prayers that morning dramatically affected what happened in people's hearts. A week later, I couldn't imagine getting up to preach without knowing that people would be in that little room praying. A friend recruited fifty-five people to pray, divided among the six services I'd be preaching.

Why was prayer just as important that weekend as the weekend before when the gospel was being shared? Because there's a battle over ownership and lordship of our lives that's just as intense as the battle for salvation. The grace that saves us is also the grace that sanctifies and empowers us. God's power isn't just needed by unbelievers to be converted. It's needed by believers to be obedient and joyful. The grace that has freed us from bondage to sin is desperately needed to free us from our bondage to materialism.

WHAT WE REALLY LONG FOR

We cannot be delivered from materialism or any other idolatry until we can accurately answer these questions: "What is it we really long for? What's the deepest desire and need of our hearts?" Scripture gives us a clear answer:

> As the deer pants for the water brooks, so my soul pants for Thee, O God, . . . for the living God. (Psalm 42:1-2, NASB).

> My soul thirsts for Thee, my flesh yearns for Thee, in a dry and weary land where there is no water. (Psalm 63:1, NASB)

> How priceless is your unfailing love! Both high and low among men find refuge in the shadow of your wings. They feast on the abundance of your house; you give them drink from your river of delights. For with you is the fountain of life; in your light we see light. (Psalm 36:7-9)

> Taste and see that the Lord is good. (Psalm 34:8)

> Blessed are those who hunger and thirst for righteousness, for they will be filled. (Matthew 5:6)

> Jesus stood and said in a loud voice, "If anyone is thirsty, let him come to me and drink. Whoever believes in me, as the Scripture has said, streams of living water will flow from within him." (John 7:37-38)

> I am the Alpha and the Omega, the Beginning and the End. To him who is thirsty I will give to drink without cost from the spring of the water of life. (Revelation 21:6)

> The Spirit and the bride say, "Come!" And let him who hears say, "Come!" Whoever is thirsty, let him come; and whoever wishes, let him take the free gift of the water of life. (Revelation 22:17)

The Westminster Shorter Catechism of 1647 says, "Man's chief end is to glorify God and enjoy him forever." God calls us to find our primary joy in him. When we seek to find our primary joy in anything or anyone else, we commit idolatry. Idolatry is not only wrong—it's always unsuccessful. It simply doesn't work. Nothing and no one but God can bear the weight of our worship or give us lasting joy.

Reflecting back on his former life of immorality and materialism, St. Augustine prayed,

> How sweet all at once it was for me to be rid of those fruitless joys which I had once feared to lose! You drove them from me, you who are the true, the sovereign joy. You drove them from me and took their place, you who are sweeter than all pleasure.[2]

HOW MATERIALISM BRINGS US TO RUIN

What does materialism actually do to us? The remainder of this chapter offers ten answers to that question.

1. Materialism prevents or destroys our spiritual life.

Jesus rebuked the Laodicean Christians because although they were materially wealthy, they were desperately poor in the things of God (Revelation 3:17-18). Materialism blinds us to our own spiritual poverty. Puritan Richard Baxter said, "When men prosper in the world, their minds are lifted up with their estates, and they can hardly believe that they are so ill, while they feel themselves so well."[3]

In his Confessions, Augustine writes, "Thou hast made us for Thyself, O God, and the heart of man is restless until it finds its rest in Thee." Along the same lines, philosopher Blaise Pascal made the following observation:

> There was once in man a true happiness of which there now remain to him only the mark and empty trace, which he in vain tries to fill from all his surroundings, seeking from things absent the help he does not obtain in things present. But these are all inadequate, because the infinite abyss can only be filled by an infinite and immutable object, that is to say, only by God Himself.[4]

Materialism is a fruitless attempt to find meaning outside of God. When we try to find ultimate fulfillment in a person other than Christ or a place other than heaven, we become idolaters. According to Scripture, materialism is not only evil; it is tragic and pathetic:

> "Has a nation ever changed its gods? (Yet they are not gods at all.) But my people have exchanged their Glory for worthless idols. Be appalled at this, O heavens, and shudder with great horror," declares the Lord. "My people have committed two sins: They have forsaken me, the spring of living water, and have dug their own cisterns, broken cisterns that cannot hold water." (Jeremiah 2:11-13)

Imagine people dying of thirst and frantically digging cisterns that cannot hold water. In their last desperate attempts to quench their thirst, driven mad by the scorching sun, they shovel sand into their mouths, choking and retching as death overtakes them. Imagine that all the while, just a stone's throw away, there is a spring of cold, fresh water, pure and life-giving. This is the picture that God paints through the prophet Jeremiah. Every attempt to find life in anyone or anything but God is vain. Materialism is a dead-end street. It is not only wrong—it is utterly self-destructive.

2. Materialism blinds us to the curses of wealth.

John Steinbeck wrote a letter to Adlai Stevenson, which was recorded in the January 28, 1960 edition of the *Washington Post*. "A strange species we are," Steinbeck said. "We can stand anything God and nature can throw at us save only plenty. If I wanted to destroy a nation, I would give it too much, and I would have it on its knees, miserable, greedy, sick."[5]

During the days of the Iron Curtain, a persecuted Romanian pastor told a group of us, "In my experience, 95 percent of the believers who face the test of persecution pass it, while 95 percent who face the test of prosperity fail it." This was Thomas Carlyle's point when he said, "Adversity is sometimes hard upon a man, but for one man who can stand prosperity, there are a hundred that will stand adversity."[6]

Ezekiel says, "By your wisdom and understanding you have gained wealth for yourself and amassed gold and silver in your treasuries. By your great skill in trading you have increased your wealth, and because of your wealth your heart has grown proud" (Ezekiel 28:4-5). We commit pride or conceit—the devil's sin (1 Timothy 3:6)—when we begin crediting ourselves with the skills, opportunities, and providential blessings that are in reality God's gifts, unearned and undeserved. Hosea put it this way: "When I fed them, they were satisfied; when they were satisfied, they became proud; then they forgot me" (Hosea 13:6).

Scripture suggests that the possession of riches is almost always a spiritual liability.

One of life's great ironies is the change that occurs when a poor and humble person who walks with God is rewarded with prosperity. Often the person's attention gradually turns away from the Lord. Unless corrected, the believer will ultimately be transformed into a proud rich person who comes under God's judgment. Some wonder why God still blesses with wealth many of the Western nations that have departed from their godly heritage. Perhaps the "blessing" is no longer a true blessing but a curse in disguise. The greatest blessing would be one that would return us to following God wholeheartedly—and our entanglement with wealth is certainly not accomplishing that. In the midst of prosperity, the challenge for believers is to handle wealth in such a way that it acts as a blessing, not a curse.

Scripture suggests that the possession of riches is almost always a spiritual liability (Mark 10:23-25). If Jesus was serious when he said how hard it is for a rich man to enter God's kingdom, and if being part of the kingdom of heaven is the highest blessing a person can receive, then how can we imagine that having riches is always a blessing from God? Was God blessing the rich fool? the rich man who neglected Lazarus? the wealthy and wicked kings of Israel, Babylon, and Assyria? Is he really blessing the wealthy rulers of modern nations who raid their national treasuries while their people live in squalor?

After the exodus from Egypt, God sent quail as a loving provision for the children of Israel. But after they grumbled and complained about their circumstances, he said he would send quail again, "until it comes out of your nostrils and you loathe it" (Numbers 11:18-20). Material prosperity can begin as God's blessing, but when we treat it as a substitute for God, it becomes a curse. Given the lessons of Scripture and history, if God were going to curse someone, what more effective means could he use than to heap on the wealth?

3. Materialism brings us unhappiness and anxiety.

Many lives are an endless string of materialistic "if onlys." If only I could get a raise; if only I could get a better-paying job; if only I could buy a new car; if only I could get that boat, country cottage, dress, rifle, or toy, then I would be happy. Here's another version of the same theme: "If only I had more money, I'd give more." Unfortunately, those who give little when they have little almost never increase their percentage of giving when they become wealthy.

In *The Lion, the Witch and the Wardrobe*, C. S. Lewis tells of young Edmund who sampled the Witch's Turkish Delight, then sacrificed his integrity to get more of it—only to find that the more he gorged himself on it, the sicker and less satisfied he became. Similarly, the bait of wealth hides the hook of addiction and slavery.

Who is it we desire to be like? Do we really want to be like the rich people we've observed? The string of broken families and broken lives among the rich should tell us something. Consider the pitiful life of Howard Hughes, who with all his money and power became miserable and crazed. Consider the testimonies of five other men of wealth:

John D. Rockefeller: "I have made many millions, but they have brought me no happiness."

W. H. Vanderbilt: "The care of $200 million is enough to kill anyone. There is no pleasure in it."

John Jacob Astor: "I am the most miserable man on earth."

Henry Ford: "I was happier when doing a mechanic's job."

Andrew Carnegie: "Millionaires seldom smile."[7]

Dr. Aaron Beck conducted a ten-year study of patients hospitalized with suicidal intentions. He published the results in *The American Journal of Psychiatry*.

One of the fifteen major risk factors contributing to a suicidal frame of mind was listed simply as "financial resources." The doctor's terse commentary was this: "Risk increases with resources."[8] The risk of financial resources is well illustrated by the suicides and emotional breakdowns that commonly occur during significant drops in the stock market. It's also demonstrated in the epidemic levels of high blood pressure and hypertension among today's "successful" professionals.

I once took a test designed to predict a person's lifespan (barring accidents). It was based on statistical probabilities and included instructions to add so many years if I exercised regularly, subtract so many years if I smoked, and so on. One statement was particularly striking: "Subtract two years from your life if your family income is over $50,000 a year."[9]

Materialism is the mother of anxiety. No wonder Christ's discourse on earthly and heavenly treasures is immediately followed by his admonitions not to worry about material things (Matthew 6:25-34). People lay up treasures on earth rather than in heaven not only because of greed and selfishness, but also because of fear and insecurity. Yet putting our hope in earthly treasures does nothing but multiply anxiety. Why? Because earthly treasures are so temporary and uncertain.

The hopes of a person with primary investments in the stock market will rise and fall with the market. The one whose greatest riches are deposited in the bank will be destroyed when the banks fail, as will the farmer whose greatest asset is in crops when the crops fail or when the commodity markets fall. In contrast, the one whose hope is in God will be devastated only if God fails— and he never does.

To set our heart on earthly riches not only deprives God of glory, others of help, and ourselves of reward, it also destines us to perpetual insecurity. Materialism has no upside.

Paul said that the rich should not "put their hope in wealth, which is so uncertain, but . . . in God, who richly provides" (1 Timothy 6:17). Solomon made a profound observation when he noted, "The sleep of the laborer is sweet, whether he eats little or much, but the abundance of a rich man permits him no sleep" (Ecclesiastes 5:12). The more we have, the more we have to worry about.

4. Materialism ends in ultimate futility.
The book of Ecclesiastes is the most powerful exposé of materialism ever written. Solomon recounts his attempts to find meaning in pleasure, laughter, alcohol, folly, building projects, and the pursuit of personal interests, as well as in amassing slaves, gold and silver, singers, and a huge harem to fulfill his sexual desires (Ecclesiastes 2:1-11). He achieved the ultimate in material success and international fame living by this philosophy: "I denied myself nothing my eyes

desired; I refused my heart no pleasure" (Ecclesiastes 2:10). The more Solomon had, the more he was tempted to indulge. His indulgence led to sin, and his sin brought misery.

What follows are Solomon's statements in Ecclesiastes 5:10-15. The italicized paraphrases after each statement are mine.

"Whoever loves money never has money enough."

The more you have, the more you want.

"Whoever loves wealth is never satisfied with his income."

The more you have, the less you're satisfied.

"As goods increase, so do those who consume them."

The more you have, the more people (including the government) come after it.

"And what benefit are they to the owner except to feast his eyes on them?"

The more you have, the more you realize it doesn't meet your real needs.

"The sleep of a laborer is sweet, whether he eats little or much, but the abundance of a rich man permits him no sleep."

The more you have, the more you have to worry about.

"I have seen a grievous evil under the sun: wealth hoarded to the harm of its owner."

The more you have, the more you can hurt yourself by holding onto it.

"or wealth lost through some misfortune."

The more you have, the more you have to lose.

"Naked a man comes from his mother's womb, and as he comes, so he departs. He takes nothing from his labor that he can carry in his hand."

The more you have, the more you'll leave behind.

After his years as the world's richest man, Solomon said, "When I surveyed all that my hands had done and what I had toiled to achieve, everything was meaningless, a chasing after the wind; nothing was gained under the sun" (Ecclesiastes 2:11). The more Solomon had, the more meaningless his life became. Most people chase their mirages with money, but they run out of money before they run out of mirages. So they still believe the lie that *"if only I had more money, then I'd be happy."* But Solomon had it all. He had more money than he could possibly spend. He chased down every mirage. He ran out of mirages before he ran out of money.

Consider this statement, "Whoever loves money never has money enough; whoever loves wealth is never satisfied with his income" (Ecclesiastes 5:10). The repeated word *never* is emphatic—there are no exceptions. There's an unspoken corollary to this statement: *To become satisfied, you must change your attitude toward wealth.*

Money itself is never the answer. What we need is a radically different perspective on money and a genuine opportunity to do something with it that will make our lives meaningful instead of meaningless. As we'll see in chapter 7, that's exactly what Jesus offers us.

5. Materialism obscures many of the best things in life, which are free— including the gift of salvation.

Some of life's greatest blessings are just as available to the poor as to the rich, and often they are far more appreciated by the poor, whose lives are less cluttered and distracted by material wealth. The greatest blessing that God offers is available to all: "Come, all you who are thirsty, come to the waters; and you who have no money, come, buy and eat! Come, buy wine and milk without money and without cost" (Isaiah 55:1). The same invitation is repeated in the final chapter of the Bible: "Whoever is thirsty, let him come; and whoever wishes, let him take the free gift of the water of life" (Revelation 22:17). The only thing worth buying cannot be bought with money. God's Son bought us our salvation, and he freely gives himself to all who seek him. Money cannot buy salvation, and it cannot buy rescue from judgment. "Wealth is worthless in the day of wrath" (Proverbs 11:4). As Tertullian put it in A.D. 200, "Nothing that is God's is obtainable by money."

John Piper helps us envision the final irony of materialism:

> Picture 269 people entering eternity in a plane crash in the Sea of Japan. Before the crash there is a noted politician, a millionaire corporate executive, a playboy and his playmate, a missionary kid on the way back from visiting grandparents. After the crash they stand before God utterly stripped of MasterCards, checkbooks, credit lines, image clothes, how-to-succeed books, and Hilton reservations. Here are the politician, the executive, the playboy, and the missionary kid, all on level ground with nothing, absolutely nothing, in their hands, possessing only what they brought in their hearts. How absurd and tragic the lover of money will seem on that day—like a man who spends his whole life collecting train tickets and in the end is so weighed down by the collection he misses the last train.[10]

6. Materialism spawns independence and self-sufficiency, which are deadly to faith.

Why have faith in God when you have faith in yourself? Why trust God when you have all your bases covered? Why pray when you have everything under control? Why ask for your daily bread when you own the bakery? Self-sufficiency is the great enemy of faith and prayer, which are the heartbeat of the Christian life. We pride ourselves on our "financial independence," but where would we be without God, from whom our every breath is a gift? The very expression "financial independence" may be blasphemy.

Alexander Maclaren writes of God's providential care in terms that those of us who pride ourselves in our independence may find disturbing:

Up to the very edge we are driven before He puts out His hand to help us. It is best for us that we should be brought to desperation, to say, "My foot slips" and then, just as our toes feel the ice, help comes and His mercy holds us up. At the last moment—never before it, never until we have discovered how much we need it, and never too late—comes the Helper.

If we want to get our needs supplied, our weakness strengthened, and wisdom to dispel our perplexity, we must be where all the provision is stored. If a man chooses to sit outside the provision shop, he may starve on its threshold. If a woman will not go into the bank, her pockets will remain empty though there may be bursting vaults to which she has a right. If we will not ascend the hill of the Lord and stand in His holy place by simple faith, God's amplest provision will be nothing to us, and we will be empty in the midst of affluence.[11]

What is it that keeps us from these "bursting vaults" and the "simple faith" needed to access them? Prosperity—or the illusion of prosperity. Wealth insulates us from our need. More accurately, it insulates us from discerning the true depth of our need.

7. Materialism leads to pride and elitism.

The Bible is full of references proving that our tendency in prosperity is to believe we deserve the credit for what we have and to grow proud and thankless (Deuteronomy 6:1-15; 31:20; 32:15-18; 2 Chronicles 26:6-16; Psalm 49:5-6; 52:7; Proverbs 30:8-9; Hosea 13:4-6). Paul asks the prideful Christians of Corinth, "For who makes you different from anyone else? What do you have that you did not receive? And if you did receive it, why do you boast as though you did not?" (1 Corinthians 4:7). Paul tells Timothy, "Command those who are rich in this present world not to be arrogant" (1 Timothy 6:17). After all, God is the one who has given us our intellect (Daniel 2:21), our abilities (Romans 12:6), and our capacity to earn money (Deuteronomy 8:18).

> Wealth insulates us from discerning the true depth of our need.

One of the uglier manifestations of pride is elitism, an illusion of superiority over others that's held by a privileged class. Elitism is at the heart of racism, nationalism, and denominationalism. It is sometimes the driving force behind private clubs, restaurants, hotels, schools, fraternities, sororities, certain churches, and countless affiliations.

While waiting in a doctor's office, I browsed through a beautiful publication that described itself as "a magazine like no other, intended for an elite group of subscribers." It then said, "In order to maintain the high quality of our magazine we must limit its printing. We cannot accept more than 100,000 subscribers."

Why would accepting more subscribers lower the quality of the magazine, since the next 100,000 copies would be printed and mailed exactly like the first? The idea, of course, is elitism. Snob appeal. *I'm one of the privileged who receives this magazine, and you're not. (So there!)*

Jesus came to die for every person of every social and economic level. Paul reminded the proud Corinthians that the Church is made up of the dregs of this world (1 Corinthians 1:26-31). Elitism boosts our egos by making us think we are somehow more worthy than others. Few things are more repugnant to the Lord than the rich despising the poor (Job 12:5). Yet our clubs and social circles, sometimes even our churches, foster this very attitude.

8. Materialism promotes injustice and exploitation.

Money is power. Power is not intrinsically evil, of course, but it is intrinsically dangerous. Only God is all-powerful, and only our all-good God can afford to be. Among sinful human beings, an endless string of despots have proven the old adage correct: Power corrupts and absolute power corrupts absolutely.

James condemns the rich, virtually assuming that anyone who is rich practices injustice to the poor and will come under God's judgment as a result (James 5:1-6). The Old Testament prophets spoke out so consistently against the oppression of the poor by the rich that they left the distinct impression that a righteous rich man is rare (Isaiah 10:1-3; Jeremiah 5:27-28; 15:13; Hosea 12:8; Amos 5:11, 24; Micah 6:12).

The rich man will usually be materialistic. The materialistic man will always be unjust. The wealthier the man, the greater his opportunity for injustice. Of course, the wealthy man is no more inherently sinful than the poor— he simply has more means and opportunity to subsidize and impose his sins upon others.

In Philippi, Paul was permitted to preach the gospel openly, until he cast out a future-predicting demon from a suffering slave girl, who "earned a great deal of money for her owners by fortune-telling" (Acts 16:16). The girl was freed from a horrible burden, but her owners didn't care about her. They'd lost their meal ticket: "When the owners of the slave girl realized that their hope of making money was gone, they seized Paul and Silas and dragged them into the marketplace to face the authorities" (Acts 16:19).

Before we self-righteously decry this injustice, we shouldn't forget that only a short time ago slavery was a standard practice in America, and people in both the North and the South profited from it. But we need not go back 150 years to find notorious examples of exploitation. Consider today's profit-based abortion business, which is lucrative for the abortionist and financially advantageous to parents who do not wish to interrupt their careers, jeopardize their house and car payments, or dissipate their income to care for a child. It's a tragic fact that many abortions are procured by married couples for purely financial reasons. A young couple at our church came very close to killing their preborn child because they needed both of their incomes to make their house payment. In the interest of having a beautiful family home, they nearly killed a family member.

Perhaps the most obvious examples of the exploitation of people for financial gain in America are the tobacco corporations.

Consider also the industries of alcohol, drugs, pornography, prostitution, sensationalist tabloid journalism, and—to a degree—television and motion pictures, none of which hesitates to exploit human beings for financial gain. Although I believe in the legitimacy of a strong military defense, certain companies profit immensely by the production of weapons. Some of these companies welcome wars anywhere in the world in order to turn a profit and are willing to produce and sell weapons indiscriminately at the cost of human lives.

Perhaps the most obvious examples of the exploitation of people for financial gain in America are the tobacco corporations. For fifty years now, they have defended their multibillion-dollar industry in the face of incontrovertible evidence that millions of people suffer terrible disease and death because of smoking. The tenacity with which the tobacco industry hires lobbyists and propagandists to juggle and explain away the research and statistics and defend the indefensible, at the cost of untold human suffering, is a clear sacrifice of moral principle on the altar of the almighty dollar. Whether or not the leaders in this industry attend church and tithe isn't relevant. They clearly embody materialism, with its elevation of financial profit over human welfare.

9. Materialism fosters immorality and the deterioration of the family.

"Motives having to do with money or sex account for 99 percent of the crimes committed in the United States, but those with money as their object outpoint sexual offenses by a ratio of four to one."[12]

Materialism underlies the vast majority of illegal activities. But most forms of materialism are perfectly legal, and many enjoy the highest status, evoking admiration and envy.

In Deuteronomy 17:14-20, the future kings of Israel are specifically warned not to accumulate horses (power), wives (pleasure), and gold (possessions). Why? Because these would then become the center of the king's gravity. Instead, he was instructed to inaugurate his reign by writing out with his own hand (not delegating the task to a scribe) all the words of the law, becoming intimately familiar with it. He was to place himself under the law with no special privileges of rank. He was to be as much a servant to the law as the poorest, lowliest citizen. King Solomon violated all of these warnings, and he and his country paid the price. The biggest temptation for leaders, whether business, political, or spiritual, is to think they're an exception to the rule, that they're entitled to certain privileges.

Those who enjoy prosperity, power, and privilege also commonly indulge in sexual immorality. Solomon had seen his father's bad example. Prosperous King David, spoiled by getting everything he wanted, did not deny himself one more possession—another man's wife (2 Samuel 11). For years, studies have shown that "among both men and women the incidence of marital infidelity rises in conjunction with an increase in income." Indeed, of men whose income isn't far above minimum wage, 31 percent conduct adulterous affairs but of those with triple that income the number committing adultery increases to 70 percent.[13]

The point is not the income itself, but the lifestyle it underwrites. A Christian can make a million dollars a year, give generously, live modestly, and avoid much of the added temptation to immorality. It's not how much we make that matters. It's how much we keep. In light of such statistics, we shouldn't be surprised by the frequency of immorality among Christians—including Christian leaders—who live in wealth. After all, those who indulge their material appetites are not likely to curb their sexual appetites.

A look at the people who occupy our attention through the media tells us something of the connection between materialism and sexual immorality:

> Much can be determined about a nation's ideals and future welfare by the character of its models. Who are the most admired people in America? Spiritual leaders, civil leaders, altruistic social reformers? Hardly.
>
> The heroes and idols of America are actors and actresses, jet setters and yacht owners, entertainers and rock stars. With a glass of wine or a joint in one hand and somebody else's mate in the other, they prance, jiggle, curse, and swindle their way into the heart of Americans. Our homage to such celebrities tells us as much about us—and our probable destiny—as it does them.[14]

A consequence of adultery is often divorce, and the consequences of divorce in the lives of children are inestimable. Even when adultery doesn't result in divorce, it destroys the fabric of marriage and prevents the home from being a moral sanctuary from the corruption of the world. Anything that contributes to an increase in immorality, as materialism clearly does, directly contributes to the breakdown of families and the deterioration of society.

John Piper is on target again when he points out the emptiness of materialism and the immorality it fosters:

> Who do you think has the deepest, most satisfying joy in life, the man who pays $140 for a fortieth-floor suite downtown and spends his

evening in the half-lit, smoke-filled lounge impressing strange women with ten-dollar cocktails, or the man who chooses the Motel 6 by a vacant lot of sunflowers and spends his evening watching the sunset and writing a love letter to his wife?[15]

The same principle that links wealth to sexual immorality links it to almost any temptation. A famous athlete was asked why he turned to drugs. His answer was simple: "Because I had so much money I didn't know what to do with it." His money, while not sinful itself, provided him greater temptation and opportunity to sin.

10. Materialism distracts us from our central purpose.

John Wesley complained that too few preached against the sin of loving money, which he believed hindered revival:

> Wesley noted that in the old days of Methodism, the people were poor. But, he observed . . . many Methodists had become 20, 30, or even 100 times richer than they were at first. With this increase in wealth had come a decrease in godliness. It seemed to him the more money the Methodists had, the less they loved the Lord.[16]

When Jesus described the various kinds of people who respond to the gospel, he said that some seed "fell among thorns, which grew up and choked the plants" (Matthew 13:7). He later explained to the disciples, "The one who received the seed that fell among the thorns is the man who hears the word, but the worries of this life and the deceitfulness of wealth choke it, making it unfruitful" (Matthew 13:22). Notice the clear relationship between wealth and worry.

My wife and I have lived in the same house for twenty-five years. For the first nine years, we had an ugly, old, orange carpet. We didn't care what happened to it. Finally it wore through to the floor, so we replaced it. The first day we got our new carpet, there was an accident that burned a hole in it. Any day previous to that one we wouldn't have cared. But now our emotional energy was poured into regret and anxiety about the carpet. It takes time to hover over our things, and that time must come from elsewhere—from time we might spend cultivating intimacy with God, from time in his Word and prayer, time with family, time visiting the needy, time with people who need Christ. Every item I add to my possessions is one more thing to think about, talk about, clean, repair, display, rearrange, and replace when it goes bad.

I can't just buy a television. I have to hook up an antenna or subscribe to a cable service. Then I buy a DVD player and start renting or buying movies. Then I get surround-sound speakers and a recliner so I can watch everything in comfort. By then my neighbor has purchased a bigger screen TV, so it's my turn to upgrade. This all costs money and also takes immense amounts of time, energy, and attention. It isn't just the bad television programs that interfere with God's will for my life. Even if I could find only good programs to watch, the time I devote to my TV and its accessories means less time for communicating with my family, reading the Word, praying, opening our home, or ministering to the needy.

Acquiring a possession may also push me into redefining my priorities and make me unavailable for ministry. If I buy a boat, the problem isn't just the money. I must now justify my purchase by using the boat, which may mean frequent weekends away from church, making me unavailable to teach a Sunday school class, or work in the nursery, or lead a small group, or . . . fill in the blank. As Jesus said, worries and wealth can choke me, making me unfruitful.

Suppose I buy rental property. First there's the big down payment, then monthly payments that go on and on. There are bills to pay, taxes that always go up, and repairs that have to be made. The financial drain is substantial, but the drain on my mental energy and my time may be even greater. There's the hassle of finding the right renters, the anxiety that they may mistreat the home, the concerns when their payments are late, the worry about possible vandalism and weather damage, the compulsion to drive by just to make sure everything is all right. Then, every few years, I have to go in, clean up the place, and start over looking for renters. And when I hear there's an expressway that may go through and reduce the value of my property, suddenly I'm circulating petitions and attending meetings to persuade the city council to build it near someone else's property. All this is in addition to the never-ending concerns related to the home I actually live in!

I'm certainly not suggesting it is wrong for Christians to own rental property. The question is whether I own the property or it owns me.

At the airport, Hugh Maclellan Jr. saw an acquaintance who looked troubled. "What's the matter?" Hugh asked.

The man sighed. "I thought I was finally going to have a weekend to myself. But now I have to go supervise repairs on my house in Florida." Dejected, he sat waiting to take off in his private jet.[17]

Here's a man with everything he needs, and with resources that most people only dream of, yet he can't even enjoy his weekend because he is enslaved by his possessions.

What is true of rental property or a second home is true of everything we own, to a lesser or greater extent. What I'm pointing out is a law of life—the tyranny of things. The central issue is not the things themselves, but the depletion of the resources of time, energy, enthusiasm, and money that might otherwise have been invested in the kingdom of God. The key question is not, "Should a Christian own this or that?" but, "Does God want me to own this or that in light of the drain on my resources it will create?" Will owning this new thing keep me from doing other things that God wants me to do? Do the benefits for God's kingdom outweigh the liabilities that ownership always brings? Will this commitment of my resources—*God's* resources—contribute to or detract from my devotion to and service for my Lord? The answer to these questions may be different for two different believers. But in every case the questions should be asked before the decisions are made.

Like the circus plate spinner who runs frantically from one plate to the next, quickly spinning each one again before it can fall and crash, many of us center our lives around possessions, concerns, and activities that demand our constant attention and thereby draw attention away from what God has called us to be and do.

Paul told Timothy, "No one serving as a soldier gets involved in civilian affairs—he wants to please his commanding officer" (2 Timothy 2:4). Notice that Paul did not say civilian concerns are wrong, just that they are distracting. The believer lives to please his Commander. He or she recognizes that involvement in peripheral things is bound to tap resources that need to be wholly devoted to the overriding cause, the spiritual battle for the kingdom of God. If one is to be a true soldier, not just show up for an occasional weekend drill, it's important to avoid not only the entanglements of sin but also the entanglements in "legitimate things" that result in preoccupation with the peripheral. Everything accumulated is one more thing that can potentially take our attention away from God.

> Will owning this new thing keep me from doing other things that God wants me to do?

In the parable of the great banquet, Jesus describes invitations that went out to three men (Luke 14:16-24). All three declined. One said he had to go look at his newly bought field. Another had just gotten married and didn't have the time. The third man had just purchased five yoke of oxen and was anxious to try them out. The master is angered by these excuses, and he orders his servants to "go out quickly into the streets and alleys of the town and bring in the poor, the crippled, the blind and the lame." Speaking of those originally invited, who were preoccupied with other concerns, Jesus said, "I tell you, not one of those men who were invited will get a taste of my banquet" (Luke 14:24).

There was nothing wrong with what any of the three men was involved in. They didn't stay away from the banquet because they were stealing or committing adultery. They stayed away because they had more pressing concerns—a new field, a new wife, a new herd. But regardless of their reasons—good or bad—the bottom line was the same: They were so preoccupied with their new treasures that they said no to the banquet giver and missed the banquet. Significantly, those without material resources were available to accept the invitation.

For what seemingly good, legitimate, and compelling reasons are *you* saying no to God? Are your possessions and other pressing concerns causing you to miss the banquet? How would you benefit, and how would God's kingdom be furthered, if you gave away those possessions?

After striking a large deposit of gold, two miners in the Klondike gold rush were so excited about unearthing more and more gold each day that they neglected to store up provisions for the winter. Then came the first blizzard. Nearly frozen, one of the miners scribbled a note explaining their foolishness. Then he lay down to die, having come to his senses too late. Months later, a prospecting party discovered the note and the miners' frozen bodies lying on top of a huge pile of gold.

For what seemingly good, legitimate, and compelling reasons are *you* saying no to God?

Obsessed with their treasure, these men hadn't taken into account that the fair weather wouldn't last and winter was coming. Hypnotized by their wealth, they failed to prepare for the imminent future. The gold that seemed such a blessing proved to be a deadly curse.

Dazzled by riches and the prospect of having more, materialists live out their life on earth as if this were all there is. They fail to prepare for the long life ahead. One day, sooner than expected, materialists will find out they were wrong. They will discover the truth that all the wealth in the world can do nothing for them. If they don't make that discovery until they die, it will be too late to go back and change the way they lived.

CHAPTER 5

Materialism in the Church

*Experience shows that it is an easy thing in the midst of
worldly business to lose the life and power of religion, that
nothing thereof should be left but only the external form,
as it were the carcass or shell, worldliness having eaten
out the kernel, and having consumed the very soul of
life and godliness.*   RICHARD MATHER

*We always pay dearly for chasing after what
is cheap.*   ALEKSANDR SOLZHENITSYN

"God loves you and has a wonderful plan for your bank account" read the bold
caption of an advertisement in a Christian magazine. Another ad in several
Christian magazines featured a stylishly dressed man, standing in front of a
beautiful home, leaning against a brand-new, shiny automobile. The text of the
ad tells readers how they, too, can become wealthy in their spare time through
a Christian ministry opportunity. When it comes to materialism, it is increasingly difficult to tell where the world ends and the Church begins.

RELIGIOUS MATERIALISM IN SCRIPTURE AND HISTORY

The father of "Christian" materialism was Simon Magus (Acts 8:18-21). When he
saw the power of the Holy Spirit he saw dollar signs. He wanted to bottle the Holy
Spirit and sell him for profit. If Simon were with us today, he would no doubt be
merchandising the Spirit via radio, television, the Internet, and direct mail.

Once Simon began to lose followers to Philip, he became interested in
"buying into" the Christian faith, which looked like a promising venture. Although he initially appeared to be a genuine convert, Simon's attitude toward
God and money gave him away. Peter said to Simon, "May your money perish
with you, because you thought you could buy the gift of God with money!"
(Acts 8:20). The message was clear: God is not selling anything, and he himself is not for sale.

Swarms of "Simons" have infiltrated the Church in every age. In the early sixteenth century, Pope Leo X raised funds by selling the forgiveness of sins in the form of indulgences. For a fee, a person could supposedly deliver a deceased loved one from purgatory—or even pay against his or her own future sins. In order to buy from the pope the office of archbishop of Mainz, Albert of Brandenburg borrowed a huge sum of money from the bank, and with Leo's authorization began to sell indulgences in Germany in order to repay the debt.

Albert's chief salesman was Johann Tetzel, who traveled from town to town selling forgiveness as if it were a sack of potatoes. Tetzel's catchy chant went like this: "As soon as the coin in the coffer rings, the soul from Purgatory springs." When Tetzel brought his act to Wittenberg, a German priest named Martin Luther was outraged. He responded with his Ninety-five Theses, which he nailed to the Wittenberg Church door on October 31, 1517. This marked the beginning of the Protestant Reformation, with its return to the authority of the Scriptures and the doctrine of salvation by faith. It all came about because one man stood up to oppose the swelling tide of religious materialism.

RELIGIOUS MATERIALISM TODAY

Wealth is not synonymous with materialism, but it always constitutes a temptation to materialism. Although the evangelical movement began when some believers walked away from liberal mainline denominations and left behind land and buildings and lifetimes of financial investments, today evangelicalism has moved into prosperity while many liberal denominations are in decline. Michael Hamilton details this striking development in *Christianity Today*:

> In most American neighborhoods today, nearly all the new large church buildings have been built by evangelicals. The new wealth of evangelicalism is even more pronounced in the parachurch world. The largest charitable organization in the nation—with an annual budget of over $2 billion—is the Salvation Army, a unique combination of holiness denomination and parachurch agency devoted to human services. Of the nine largest parachurch organizations in the U.S. devoted to spreading the gospel, eight are evangelical, with combined 1998 budgets of $729 million. Of the seven largest communications media agencies, six are evangelical, with total budgets of $625 million. In foreign ministry and missions, evangelical parachurch agencies raise $1.5 billion per year, while evangelical denominations raise another $1 billion. Mainline denominations and the independent agencies associated with them together raise less than $500 million.[1]

Over the past twenty years, an amazing array of novelties and trinkets has flooded the religious market. Jesus jewelry, wristbands, T-shirts, bumper stickers, angel figurines, nativity sets, anointing oil key chains, Scripture tea, Scripture cookies, Scripture soap, Bible belt buckles, prayer and praise pots, Christian dolls, and even a soft plastic toy called Scapegoat on which Christians can physically take out their frustrations. These things aren't necessarily wrong, but they do reflect our tendency to replace secular things with religious things. Instead of rejecting the world's materialism, the Church creates its own "spiritualized" version. If godliness is popular, someone will find a way to market it.

A full-page ad in Christian magazines advertises Prayer of Jabez jewelry. It's an ostentatious display of "six gorgeous medallions" in the form of a "14K gold-plated bracelet with two full microns of real gold." The ad reads, "God desires to give you more than you could ever dare to dream or imagine and the remarkable Prayer of Jabez not only shows you how to release God's blessings, but also His power and protection in your life."

This ad is *not* from the publisher of the book *The Prayer of Jabez*. It's a case of Christian entrepreneurs capitalizing on the book's popularity. The fundamental problem isn't that the ad and the jewelry make money. The problem is that they pervert a prayer of Scripture, turning it into a magic formula to secure personal prosperity, symbolized by the jewelry.

Each day the mailboxes of a million Christians are full of pleas for money. I've received letters from Christian organizations labeled "personal" and "confidential" that are posted as bulk mail, meaning that thousands received the same "confidential" letter, asking them each "personally" to send their "essential" gift to keep this "vital" ministry afloat.

Knowing that many don't bother opening such mail, some religious organizations no longer identify themselves on the envelope. Others package their mailings to look like checks, notifications of sweepstakes winnings, or important notices from the IRS—anything to trick the recipient into opening the letter.

One evangelist wrote requesting $27 from everyone on his mailing list. He promised to pray over all their letters accompanying their checks, in effect selling his prayers and God's answers. He said the $27 had to be in his hand by a certain date and he promised to tell any givers the secret of why the Lord chose the odd amount of $27.

Each day the mailboxes of a million Christians are full of pleas for money.

To those who sent in their $27, he responded by asking for a special offering of $48 to pay his television bills. I can only guess how much more money he requested from those who sent in the $48. The same evangelist promised that for $100 he would embroider the giver's name on his pillowcase.

One woman was thrilled to receive a "personal" letter from a Christian leader, indicating that her face had been brought to his mind in a vision. He wrote that God had told him to write to her personally and to ask for money. He didn't mention the thousands of others who had also been "personally" called—not by God, but by the organization's computer—and sent the identical letter. Believing the letter was written only to her and that God had inspired it, she sent the leader some money. He never explained how, after seeing her face in the vision, he had managed to come up with her name and address.

Some Christian radio and television ministries sell their booklets and blessings at $25 a whack. Others send out holy water, talismans, sacred crosses, and healing handkerchiefs touched by their evangelists. Within a six-month period, one evangelist sent everyone on his mailing list a packet of water from the Sea of Galilee, a "holy cloth" dipped in water from the Jordan River, two coins from Jerusalem, and "communion grape juice from the Holy Land." He also sent them all a plastic-coated mustard seed, telling them to carry it with them wherever they go because it will "cause you to be blessed in everything you undertake."

Enclosing a prayer cloth with a picture of Jesus, the same evangelist asked the recipients to cut off the bottom of the cloth (on the dotted line) and send it back with an offering, promising he would touch their cloth with his own hands and pray for them individually. Some mailings from "ministries" imply a promise to secure in prayer the salvation of one's loved ones if a certain amount of money is sent (shades of Johann Tetzel!).

One evangelist wrote, "The Lord told me to cut up seventy of my neckties that I've worn in my miracle crusades, and send the cloths to 300 of my closest friends." In another letter he claimed he needed $300,000 more to make it through the month and said he was personally going to borrow $100 to give to his ministry. He suggested that his supporters do the same. Another mailing came from the man's mother, saying what a fine boy he really is and explaining why everyone should send him money.

Still another tactic, used by various organizations, is a letter that says, "Satan is attacking our ministry through the postal system, and our mailings are apparently being stolen. We must know if you've received this mailing. Please notify us by sending back the enclosed envelope with your offering."

Materialism shows itself in other ways besides money. Theological liberalism, for instance, is a man-centered, earth-centered system that denies eternal realities. The "good news" is that somehow a God without holiness helps a man without sin by a Christ without a cross. God is not taken seriously but is simply used to promote a human agenda. The fact that this agenda may include some benevolent causes doesn't eliminate its exclusive focus on the present life and the consequent materialistic focus. Denying the heart and soul of the gospel, liberalism's attempts to help the world without addressing its ultimate spiritual problem have the same effect as rearranging the furniture on the Titanic.

MATERIALISM AND THE CHRISTIAN LEADER

With just a few hundred dollars, enterprising individuals can produce a brochure, letterhead and business cards, put up a Web site, and suddenly be a "ministry." They can buy a mailing list from another ministry, and they're on their way, accountable to no one, and free to tap and dissipate the resources that God has entrusted to his Church. They may credit their success to the Holy Spirit, but often their real power comes from their mailing lists and the gifts of sincere but gullible people.

Some big-name Christian celebrities fly first class around the country charging ten thousand dollars for each speaking engagement or musical performance. Some have egos even bigger than their bank accounts and are respected most by those who know them least. Some on the speaking and singing circuits are fine men and women of God, but others are sadly lacking in character. They foist themselves upon an undiscerning Christian community with nothing to commend them but an ability to speak or perform, a busy schedule, a CD they recorded, or a book they wrote (often a book they didn't write but that has their name on it).

In some circles, pastors routinely have mail-order and honorary doctorate degrees hanging on their walls and delight in being addressed as "Doctor." I saw a catalog of an unaccredited seminary where the faculty members average four "doctorates" apiece.

Some pastors play the numbers game of grossly exaggerating their church attendance. Others hang huge pictures of themselves in the church foyer and put their names in a large, bold font on every piece of literature printed by the church.

One magazine advertised an upcoming rally in the southern United States. The woman bringing the most visitors, the magazine promised, would be crowned queen. Along with her ten runner-up "princesses," she would have her picture taken with a well-known evangelical preacher. Another preacher was available after a speaking engagement to shake hands with anyone willing to pay $100 to his ministry. This blatant appeal to ego and its elevation of God's servants as celebrities is just one more form of religious materialism.

How many senior pastors have been pedestalized, fawned over, and spoken of as if the church belonged to them, not Christ? How many large church pastors are given periodic "love offerings," even though their salaries are already five times higher than the struggling youth pastor's? Is it any wonder these men begin to believe they are something special, that they grow arrogant and fall into immorality and disgrace?

As a former pastor and someone with very close relationships with other pastors, I can tell you that Satan is delighted when pastors are underpaid and underappreciated—and he's just as delighted when they're overpaid and overappreciated. For the devil's tastes, let pastors be crucified or worshiped. He

> How many senior pastors have been pedestalized, fawned over, and spoken of as if the church belonged to them, not Christ?

cringes only when they are given the respect they're due and the accountability they need, no more and no less.

One Christian leader told of a pastor who offered him $1,000 to come meet with his board and share some biblical principles. When he declined, saying he needed to spend more time with his family, the pastor replied, "We'll pay you $2,000." After he declined again and the ante was upped to $3,000, the leader made it clear he didn't appreciate someone trying to buy him away from his family.

How often does the same thing happen when pulpit committees approach a potential pastor? He may say, "Thanks for asking, but I've prayed about it and I believe God would have me stay in my present ministry." Then the pulpit committee comes back with a better offer, with an additional $10,000 in salary and promises of a new car and other benefits. Since this is using money to persuade a man to violate his stated conviction, what can it be called but bribery? The fact that it happens among God's people doesn't make it better, it makes it worse.

We can thank God that he has countless faithful servants in the ministry, some in radio and television and other highly visible ministries. But their job is made far more difficult by the religious materialists, who cast a shadow on their profession and raise doubts about their credibility.

A number of Christian organizations have been called to account for their financial improprieties and unreported or exaggerated revenues. These infractions are particularly disturbing when one considers that God's first disciplinary act in Church history was striking dead Ananias and Sapphira for deliberately misrepresenting their financial transactions (Acts 5:1-11). Although we should be thankful that God is not striking dead large segments of his Church today, we should not be lulled into thinking he's lowered his standards of financial integrity.

As we look at examples of ministry abuses, we must be careful not to overlook the potential for corruption in our own lives. Our purpose is not to point an accusing finger at others but to understand our own materialism, with a view toward changing our thinking and behavior. The truth is, if our hearts were not captive to materialism, we would neither subsidize nor tolerate materialism in churches, nonprofit ministries, and for-profit businesses.

MULTILEVEL MATERIALISM

I am about to tread on some sensitive territory and more than a few toes. Many readers were offended by this next section in the earlier edition of the book, and some readers will no doubt be offended this time around as well. Nevertheless, I ask that you consider what I have to say with an open mind and evaluate my words on their merits.[2]

Many multilevel marketing businesses are an example of how a large organization can foster materialism in the lives of individuals, families, and churches. Hundreds of thousands of Christians have at one time or another been part of multilevel sales organizations, some of which explicitly claim to be Christian.[3]

First, some clarifications are in order. There is absolutely nothing wrong with selling products or making a profit. Every Christian needs to work for a living, and sales is a legitimate and respectable profession. Some multilevel sales organizations, both Christian and secular, offer good products at a fair price. Furthermore, I recognize that many good Christians are only nominally involved in multilevel sales and do not aggressively recruit others. Some of those who are heavily involved are innocent of the kinds of attitudes and actions I will address. However, I urge such people to consider whether they may be unconsciously contributing to serious problems in other people's lives.

Here's a common scenario: Someone is warmly approached by fellow Christians who appear to be genuinely interested in friendship. Typically, these people will work something into the conversation about their involvement with a particular line of cleaning products or vitamins or cosmetics, then make a pitch to enlist the other's involvement. Or, they might call and say, "We have a tremendous money-making opportunity to share with you and want you to come over to discuss it," but refuse to disclose exactly what the opportunity is. In several cases I know of, callers have actually lied rather than reveal their true purpose.

Over the years, many people have told me similar stories of their experiences with multilevel marketers, with varying degrees of hurt or anger. I have experienced it enough times myself to know that it really happens. I have received "the call" from a fellow alumnus from Bible college or seminary. First, he'll ask about me and my family, saying pleasant and flattering things, before he finally moves on to his real reason for calling. When I politely say no to his proposition, sometimes he will persist and I must get firmer. Suddenly, all his interest in my family and me is transferred to the next person on his contact list, which consists of every person he has ever met whose name he can remember.

With inspiration from silver-tongued success speakers, positive thinking gurus, pop psychologists, and pop theologians whose repertoire of Scripture verses is limited to the prosperity passages, some multilevel sales organizations are so materialistically oriented as to make a secularist blush. Of course, interspersed with the promise of luxury cars and trips around the world are spirit-soothing reminders that the Christian will be able to give more to God and others than ever before. Often, the most effective appeals to the flesh are made under the guise of the Spirit.

The distinctive element of multilevel sales is that people are not just potential customers but also potential distributors who would come "under" their recruiter (who from that point forward would receive a percentage of their profits). Not only is every occasion a potential sales pitch and every person a potential sale, but every person is a potential salesman, making money for the "upline." If I work to establish a multilevel network, people naturally become hot items—objects, not subjects. Their personal welfare may be a concern to

Often, the most effective appeals to the flesh are made under the guise of the Spirit.

me, but it is not the main concern. No matter how much I might deny it, my interest in them is primarily utilitarian— what can they do for *me*? After all, how interested was I in them before they became part of the blueprint for my prosperity? And how interested will I be if they flatly turn down my business proposition?

I know a man and woman who were invited to dinner by two close friends who'd recently become involved in multilevel sales. Before dinner was served, the man noticed out of the corner of his eye that his host had deliberately tipped over the gravy bowl, spilling it onto the tablecloth. Saying something like "clumsy me," he marched into the kitchen and then reappeared with a bottle of cleaning fluid. He proceeded to demonstrate its amazing ability to get gravy stains out of tablecloths and then launched into a sales pitch for his organization and its wonderful products. The visiting couple was deeply hurt and shaken by this deception and manipulation. It wasn't only the end of the evening, but the end of a long friendship. The man told me, "It's no problem if someone asks me to buy something—I can just say yes or no. But when people set you up like that, and especially good Christian friends, . . . something is really wrong."

Something is really wrong. This is the same exploitative and manipulative approach we identified in the previous chapter as one of the prime characteristics of materialism. Sadly, it is far more common in the Christian community than many would like to believe.

A woman visited our church one Sunday, took a church directory, and immediately started calling people straight down the list, offering her services with a particular multilevel sales company. When she called my wife, this woman shared how much she enjoyed our fellowship, saying that her family had decided ours would be their new church home. After some more pleasantries, she tried to sell her product. When my wife politely said she wasn't interested, the woman's previously sweet tone changed. She asked if there were others in the church already selling her product. When my wife said, "Yes, there's a number," there was a quiet "Oh," and the conversation ended. So did the relationship with our church—she did not come back again, moving on to "greener pastures" at a church with less sales competition and more profit potential.

Unfortunately, multilevel marketing lends itself to ulterior motives. Because an up-front and to-the-point sales approach may be quickly dismissed, more covert strategies are often adopted. Instead of openly relating as brothers and sisters in Christ, people come with hidden agendas and unspoken purposes, calculating how to produce a desired response. People become targets. Strategies are developed to overcome sales resistance—including the strategy of keeping prospects in the dark to get them to a meeting they would otherwise never attend.

As people start catching on to these indirect sales strategies, a loss of trust occurs. Nobody likes to find out that an apparent friendship is nothing more than a head-hunting recruitment strategy. How many of us, due to our past experiences with such people, now instinctively ask, "Why is he being so nice to me? What's his angle? What's he leading up to?" That we have to ask such questions in society is sad enough. That we have to ask them inside the Church is tragic.

It's particularly regrettable when pastors and lay leaders use their contacts with people as a platform for their personal financial growth. When a leader calls or knocks on the door, people don't know whether he's there to minister or make a sale (or recruit a salesperson). Sometimes even the caller may not know. These conflicts of interest can undermine the integrity of an entire ministry.

How does the multilevel marketing phenomenon work out in the Church? Sometimes, no doubt, it works out fine. But sometimes it produces people who use the body of Christ and whose "ministry" is their devotion to sales and recruitment. Sometimes it produces people who seem capable of thinking and talking about nothing other than their lucrative business and how they will soon be able to quit their other job, buy their dream home, and retire in paradise. Sometimes it produces people who use church social gatherings and home Bible studies to share their "testimonies" of how this company or this product · has transformed their lives. (I've heard such testimonies myself.) Sometimes it produces people who move from church to church to get more customers, who exaggerate or lie about their profits, and who go into debt to pursue materialistic lifestyles as proof of their success and God's blessing—the "fake it till you make it" approach.

Many of these organizations entice new prospects by touting extravagant incomes. But the statistics refute the claims. In her book *Amway Motivational Organizations: Behind the Smoke and Mirrors*, Ruth Carter maintains that of the five million or so Americans who've been involved with this company over its forty-year history, fewer than one percent have made a profit, and fewer than one-tenth of one percent have established the large incomes that the company claims are achievable by all.[4] Furthermore, the few who succeed—and Ruth Carter was one of them—often pay a terrible personal and relational price.

Even though I know it will offend some readers, I must say what I believe is true: Deep involvement in multilevel sales changes people and often not for the best. Some end up fueling the greed of their brothers and sisters in Christ, tampering with their priorities, and encouraging them to pursue a path of materialism. Some go so far as to restrict their friendships to those who work under them or over them, or buy their products, or are useful in some other way. Some become evangelists who spread tapes and literature far and wide, anxious to pass on "the good news" of their wonderful organization and moneymaking opportunity. Sometimes, their "gospel" becomes a cheap substitute for the real gospel. Most of us can only handle one gospel—when there are two we end up sharing the one that is most to our immediate advantage

Deep involvement in multilevel sales changes people and often not for the best.

Besides the well-known larger multilevel sales organizations, there are numerous smaller ones that have come and gone through the years. Some garages are filled five years later with products that were supposed to "sell themselves."

But why do multilevel sales plans find such a presence in the Christian community in the first place? The Church is an ideal climate for such a system because there's already an established level of trust—"He's a good churchgoer and my brother in Christ"—and a well-established network of people (sometimes known as contacts) who are already linked by having something important in common (Christ and the Church).

Although there's nothing wrong with businesspeople having customers from their own church—this is natural and healthy when it develops on its own—it's another thing for salespeople to use church contacts to actively recruit customers. When that occurs, something ugly starts to happen to people and their view of others. They begin using the body of Christ to further their own purposes for financial gain. Those who see no danger in this are, by their very failure to see it, living proof of how dangerous it really is.

MODERN MONEY CHANGERS AND AN ANGRY CARPENTER

When Christ walked the earth, religion had been turned into big business in Jerusalem by money changers who made their profits exchanging currency and selling "convenience" animals for sacrifice in the temple. They charged an excessive price and probably engaged in loud haggling that destroyed the climate of worship (John 2:13-17). Jesus was outraged that people would see the community of saints as an opportunity to make a profit. After driving the salesmen and their animals out with a whip and overturning the money tables, the strong-armed carpenter from Galilee rebuked the stunned materialists with words that could be heard in the streets: "Get these out of here! How dare you turn my Father's house into a market!" (John 2:16).

Is Christ any less outraged by materialism in the Church today? Are we less deserving of his wrath than those two thousand years ago? Will God hesitate to turn the whip on us any more than he did on them? Christ is jealous for his bride. The Church is his, not ours. Those who would exploit the bride of Christ for material ends do so at their own peril.

In the 1990s and early 2000s, many ministries and churches were rocked by moral scandals. But it was back in 1987 and 1988 that the public gained an unprecedented look at the inner workings of three of the major Christian television ministries. What happened then still has much to teach us. These scandals may represent the whip of the outraged Son of God disciplining and purging the modern Christian community for our materialism.

In each of the three scandals I'm about to refer to, I believe the Christian leaders involved were originally sincere and honestly devoted to the Lord. But that does not take away from the force of what happened to them or the seriousness of the wrong thinking that characterized their lives and ministries. If their attitudes and actions were no longer a part of the Christian landscape today, I would gladly let the scandals rest. Unfortunately, the same seeds of self-destruction that took them down are still being widely planted today.

For years, the PTL network, headed by Jim and Tammy Faye Bakker, maintained a superficial wealth-oriented emphasis, replete with heavy makeup, large flashy jewelry, expensive clothes, and frequent mention of trips to exotic places. The Bakkers had their lavish homes, limousines, and endless fringe benefits from viewer contributions, including a heated and air-conditioned doghouse and chandeliers in their walk-in closets. Yet all the while they made frequent pleas, sometimes in tears: "Please send more money for our ministry."

The message was evangelical, but the lifestyle and values were Hollywood—a baptized Hollywood dressed in a Sunday suit. Many observers couldn't help but believe that beneath the surface of this ego-feeding opulence and showiness was a serious spiritual and moral erosion just waiting to be revealed. It was revealed, in a story involving adultery, payoffs, addictions, power struggles, and opulence even beyond what was imagined.

All this is the stuff of which soap operas are made, but this time the soap opera was sponsored and funded by the evangelical community, which was pouring $100 million a year into the PTL network, not including revenues from the Heritage Theme Park, "a Christian Disneyland," and Tammy Faye's books and records.

Meanwhile, television evangelist Oral Roberts stepped into the show, defending the Bakkers, telling the Christian public to "send more money than ever to PTL," and rebuking a third television evangelist for supposedly plotting a takeover of PTL. (Interestingly, when Oral Roberts came on television to defend Jim Bakker, a thunderstorm suddenly cut off the telecast. Was God trying to get a word in edgewise?)

The man who revealed Jim Bakker's exploits to Assembly of God officials was well-known televangelist Jimmy Swaggart. This was significant for several reasons, including the fact that a year earlier Swaggart had similarly exposed prominent New Orleans pastor and televangelist Martin Gorman, who admitted to one adulterous affair but filed a lawsuit against Swaggart for accusing him of other immoral relationships (this became an important factor later in the story). Swaggart, accused of trying to eliminate his television competitors and take over the PTL empire, publicly decried Bakker's perversions and stated, "Jim Bakker is a cancer on the body of Christ."

Only days before his questionable intervention in this scandal, Oral Roberts had received a $1.3 million gift from a wealthy dog racer (his fortune made in the same gambling arena that Roberts publicly opposed for years). This strange benefactor then told the press that Roberts "needs psychiatric help."

The "life-saving" $1.3 million from the dog racer climaxed what might be the most bizarre fund-raising attempt in television history (which is no small claim). Oral Roberts had publicly announced that God had told him he would take his life unless by a certain date he could raise $8 million for a medical scholarship program.

In a materialistic system, if it "works," if it makes money, then it's okay.

The implications of this fund-raising scenario were far-reaching. As a world without Christ looked on, God was cast in the role of a ruthless money-loving gangland figure, who was holding Oral Roberts for ransom and threatening to kill him if someone didn't cough up the dough. A Celestial Loan Shark, God the Father (or was it the Godfather?) was portrayed as even more capricious and vindictive than the Mafia, since Oral Roberts, presumably, was not a double-crossing weasel, but one of God's faithful "boys," one of his own gang!

The only thing that can be said for this fund-raising technique is that, unfortunately, it worked. And that is the scariest thing of all; for in a materialistic system, if it "works," if it makes money, then it's okay.

Unfortunately, the Oral Roberts story did not end there. Less than a year later, Roberts called off the medical scholarship program he had been ready to die for. Apparently, either God or Oral had changed his mind. After the bad publicity this generated, Oral—or was it God? —changed his mind once again and said that God had called eighty thousand followers to give $100 each to raise the $8 million per year the program required. Finances eventually got so bad that Roberts had to sell his $3.25 million Beverly Hills mansion.

Meanwhile, after receiving an anonymous tip, former pastor and televangelist Martin Gorman, still outraged at Swaggart for exposing his adultery, hired a private detective to follow him. Swaggart, his castigation of Jim Bakker's perversions still fresh in the public mind, was then confronted with pictures of himself with a prostitute. Swaggart confessed that he paid her to perform pornographic acts, and that he had an obsession with pornography going back to his childhood. In an issue that sold out in five days, one prostitute posed for Penthouse and recounted her raunchy involvements with Swaggart. Seeming to express genuine repentance, yet defying his denomination's attempt at discipline, Swaggart was back in television ministry only three months later. (Oral Roberts assured the public that he had—over the phone—healed Swaggart of his lust problem.)

By this time it was hard to tell the difference between ministries and mini-series. To those who understand the ingredients of unchecked materialism, such scandals were predictable, if not inevitable, long before they surfaced. The combination of human depravity and the staggering financial incomes and lack of accountability of these ministries spelled nothing but temptation and could produce nothing but disaster.

ARE WE ALSO TO BLAME?

The point is not that all media ministries are bad. Christian publishing is a media ministry with its own share of spiritual accomplishments and scandals. But without it this book wouldn't be in your hands. In fact, you wouldn't even have a Bible. There are many fine ministries in television and radio, as well. In no way do I intend to lump them all together or to throw out the good with the bad. Still, a fundamental question remains. Of the most obviously shallow, superficial, egocentric, and materialistic "ministries," many of which are still in business, we must ask, "Why did the Christian community support them in the first place? And why do we continue to support them?"

Part of the answer may be that there are many non-Christian contributors trying to "buy into" salvation as one might buy into a real estate deal. But the great majority are at least professing Christians. This forces us to a sobering conclusion—namely, that it is not that these people are superficial and materialistic and we are not. It is that we too are superficial and materialistic and *they are giving us precisely what we want.* After all, it's primarily donations by Christians that subsidize this rampant materialism and moral failure. If supporters would refuse to tolerate wrongful behavior, these ministries would cease to exist, because the money would dry up.

Why haven't people seen through these organizations and invested their money, time, and prayers instead in the many faithful servants of God who elevate Christ's name rather than their own?

How is my life resisting materialism in the Church rather than contributing to it?

"But I don't support such ministries and I never have," someone may say. Scripture doesn't let us off so easily. There is one body of Christ, and we're all members of it. I can't separate myself from the rest of the Church. I must ask, how is my life resisting materialism in the Church rather than contributing to it? How am I providing a model that's a clear alternative to the materialism undermining the integrity of the Christian community?

Because we allow (at best) and endorse (at worst) a false or superficial form of Christian faith, people without Christ judge the Church by the three-ring circus they see on television and walk away with one of two responses.

Either they feel worse ("Obviously these Christians don't have the answer, and I was hoping they did because I really need an answer"), or they feel better ("Just as I suspected, they're all a bunch of hypocrites anyway, and I should feel fine because I'm as good as or better than they are"). Either way, the Church's folly is the world's loss.

The only thing worth counterfeiting is what's valuable. People make counterfeit currency and jewels, not counterfeit bottle caps or garbage. Because the truth of the gospel is priceless, we should expect it to be continuously counterfeited. Bank employees are taught to identify counterfeit bills by handling the real thing—not by studying all the possible counterfeits. If you're not acquainted with the original, you can easily be deceived by an imitation. But once you're familiar with the genuine article, you will be able to spot a counterfeit. Still, no matter how many counterfeit bills someone might run across, he should never conclude, "There's no such thing as real money." What the world needs is the genuine gospel, lived and proclaimed by a genuine Church. Then it will reveal the counterfeits for what they are.

PROSPERITY, THE CHURCH, AND ITS LEADERS

People were amazed that the apostles were plain, ordinary men, with no great education or social status (Acts 4:13). Peter said to the crippled man, "Silver or gold I do not have, but what I have I give you. In the name of Jesus Christ of Nazareth, walk" (Acts 3:6). To see God's power and truth coming through uneducated men who weren't wealthy challenged the observers' most basic beliefs. Gene Getz points out:

> The religious leaders in Jerusalem were the rich people. In many instances, their wealth was overwhelming. And many of the poor people felt that this wealth was a result of God's special blessing on their leaders.
>
> By contrast, here were two former fishermen with very little but who had the power to heal and the message of salvation that could give eternal life. The contrast had to be startling in the eyes of those who observed this event. For the first time, many moved from a purely human perspective on religion to a divine perspective and responded to the gospel. It is understandable why this antagonized the religious leaders in Jerusalem.[5]

Although the leaders of the early Church and many of its first members were uneducated and poor, or perhaps middle class, before long some churches became wealthy, and their pastors became educated and moved to the socioeconomic status once reserved for the Pharisees. There's nothing wrong with education or money, but certain temptations accompany the status that goes with both. The higher our social standing and the more silver and gold we have, the harder it is for others (and sometimes for us) to believe our message that Christ is our greatest asset and the center of our lives.

It's easy for many evangelical Christians to write off religious materialism as characterizing other groups, denominations, fellowships, and traditions, but not *ours*. Yet many evangelical Bible-teaching ministries sponsor a variety of expensive events for their donors, including luxury cruises. The object is to raise funds for their ministry, but is a luxurious setting really the most God-honoring context in which to raise money for a ministry? What would evangelicals of even a generation ago have thought of this?

I recently received an invitation from a good, Christ-centered, Bible-teaching ministry that does missions work in some very poor countries. The invitation began by sharing the "good news" of a chance to hear some wonderful Bible teaching, and the "even better news" that the conference would be held in an exclusive top-rated resort in the Bahamas. The luxurious accommodations were then described. All one needed to do was pay plane fare, and the lodging would be provided at no charge—in the hopes that those taking advantage of the deal would contribute generously to the ministry.

Is this an appropriate setting to raise funds for evangelizing and discipling people, some of whom live in abject poverty? Isn't there something disingenuous about appealing to people's most materialistic cravings to motivate them to support missions? By subsidizing a conference at an exclusive resort, doesn't a ministry put its stamp of approval on the lifestyle choices it represents? Inviting people to contribute sacrificially would offer them the opportunity to practice giving as an alternative to materialism. Instead, to get people to contribute, we seem willing and eager to appeal to and foster their materialism.

> It's easy for many evangelical Christians to write off religious materialism as characterizing other groups, denominations, fellowships, and traditions, but not *ours*.

HOW DID WE GET HERE?

Is the Church really different from the world in its treatment of money and possessions? We have our philanthropists, to be sure, but so does the world. We have charities and relief funds, but so does the world. The world is full of consumers who live for the short term and ignore the long term. The Church should be full of strategic and generous stewards, living for the long term and seeing the short term as a temporary opportunity for eternal investment. Sadly, too often the Church looks suspiciously like the world.

Why does the Christian community in the Western world bear so little resemblance to the Church described in the early chapters of Acts? It's not that we haven't addressed the issues of money and possessions. On the contrary, innumerable Christian financial teachers, writers, investment counselors, and seminar leaders have ridden the crest of the wave of our national prosperity. Some take pains to be biblical, but many simply parrot their secular colleagues. Other than beginning and ending with prayer, mentioning Christ, and sprinkling in some Bible verses, there's no fundamental difference. They reinforce people's materialistic attitudes and lifestyles. They suggest a variety of profitable plans in which people can spend or stockpile the bulk of their resources. In short, to borrow a term from Jesus, some Christian financial experts are helping people to be the most successful "rich fools" they can be.

Not wanting to come across as negative—the unpardonable sin of our day—or to spoil the party for ourselves or others, we've failed to take materialism as a serious threat to godliness. We've rationalized and justified our lust for money and possessions. Worse, we have baptized our materialism, couched it in religious terms and affirmed it as God's plan for our lives. This prosperity theology, the gospel of health and wealth, is the subject of our next chapter.

Meanwhile, a sobering question remains, one that will not go away, one that every Christian must ask in light of our values and lifestyles: Can a materialistic world ever be won to Christ by a materialistic Church?

CHAPTER **6**

Prosperity Theology: The Gospel of Wealth

Religion begat prosperity and the daughter devoured the mother.   COTTON MATHER

The figure of the Crucified invalidates all thought that takes success for its standards.   DIETRICH BONHOEFFER

A "man of God" stands before his audiences and rebukes the "spirit of poverty," assuring them of material prosperity. He sends a Christmas letter concerning "the urgent need you have to get into true biblical prosperity as the wise men did. The money they brought literally met the financial needs of Mary, Joseph, and the child in that desperate hour." By sending money to this evangelist in his desperate hour, according to the letter, one may expect to become materially prosperous, just like the wise men who gave generously to the baby Jesus.

This man represents a large and visible segment of American evangelicalism that subscribes to what is called "prosperity theology," or the "health and wealth gospel." This worldview thrives, in churches and in parachurch ministries, only because such men have willing supporters, eager to get their share of the prosperity pie. This chapter isn't about some position "out there" in the world, but "in here" in the Church. It addresses the attitudes and lifestyles of millions of mainstream Christians who, to varying degrees and sometimes without realizing it, have bought into the lie of prosperity theology.

THE OLD TESTAMENT AND PROSPERITY
What makes every heresy dangerous is an element of truth. Without a sugar-coating of truth, the lies would never be swallowed. The portion of truth that makes prosperity theology credible is that some Old Testament passages link material prosperity with God's blessing. For instance, God gave material wealth to Abraham (Genesis 13:1-7), Isaac (Genesis 26:12-14), Jacob (Genesis 30:43), Joseph (Genesis 39:2-6), Solomon (1 Kings 3:13), and Job (Job 42:10-17)

because he approved of them. He promised the Israelites he would reward them materially for faithful financial giving (Deuteronomy 15:10; Proverbs 3:9-10; 11:25; Malachi 3:8-12).

In Deuteronomy 28:1-13, God tells the Israelites that he would reward their obedience by giving them children, crops, livestock, and victory over their enemies, but he also tacks on fifty-four more verses describing the curses that would come upon the nation if they didn't obey him—including diseases, heat and drought, military defeat, boils, tumors, madness, and blindness. The teaching is double-edged: prosperity for obedience, adversity for disobedience (Deuteronomy 28:14-68).

The Old Testament also warns against the dangers of wealth—especially the possibility that in our prosperity we may forget the Lord (Deuteronomy 8:7-18). Furthermore, the Bible recognizes frequent exceptions to the prosperity/adversity doctrine, noting that the wicked often prosper more than the righteous. The psalmist said, "I have seen a wicked and ruthless man flourishing like a green tree in its native soil" (Psalm 37:35), and "I envied the arrogant when I saw the prosperity of the wicked. . . . This is what the wicked are like— always carefree, they increase in wealth" (Psalm 73:3, 12). Solomon saw "a righteous man perishing in his righteousness, and a wicked man living long in his wickedness" (Ecclesiastes 7:15). Jeremiah, a righteous man who lived in constant adversity, framed the question this way: "You are always righteous, O Lord, when I bring a case before you. Yet I would speak with you about your justice: Why does the way of the wicked prosper? Why do all the faithless live at ease?" (Jeremiah 12:1).

Are material wealth, achievement, fame, victory, or success reliable indicators of God's reward or approval? If so, then he is an evil God, for history is full of successful madmen and prosperous despots. Was God on the side of Hitler, Stalin, Mao, and other prosperous butchers of history during their rise to power and at the apex of their regimes when they were surrounded by material wealth? Is God also on the side of wealthy cultists, dishonest business executives, and immoral rock stars? If wealth is a dependable sign of God's approval and lack of wealth shows his disapproval, then Jesus and Paul were on God's blacklist, and drug dealers and embezzlers are the apple of his eye.

CHRIST AND PROSPERITY

Many in Old and New Testament times believed in a direct cause-and-effect relationship between righteousness and prosperity on the one hand, and sin and adversity on the other. Health and wealth meant that God approved; sickness and poverty meant he did not. Job's "comforters" thought there must be hidden sin in his life to account for his loss of prosperity, but they were wrong. God approved of Job (Job 1:8; 42:7), yet he permitted Satan to destroy everything of earthly value that Job possessed.

The well-to-do Pharisees lived and breathed a prosperity theology, labeling everyone beneath their social caste as "sinners" (Luke 15:1-2; John 9:34). Christ's disciples betrayed their own assumptions when they asked, "Rabbi, who sinned, this man or his parents, that he was born blind?" (John 9:2). Jesus responded by saying their presupposition was entirely wrong: "Neither this man nor his parents sinned, . . . but this happened so that the work of God might be displayed in his life" (John 9:3). In other words, God had a higher purpose for this man's adversity that simply didn't fit in the neat little categories of "Do good and you'll be well off" and "Do bad and you'll suffer."

Consider their response when Christ told his disciples, "It is hard for a rich man to enter the kingdom of heaven," and "It is easier for a camel to go through the eye of a needle than for a rich man to enter the kingdom of God" (Matthew 19:23-24). When the disciples heard this, they were greatly astonished and asked, "Who then can be saved?" (Matthew 19:25).

Why the astonishment? It was because they were accustomed to thinking of wealth as a sign of God's approval. If the wealthy, of whom God obviously approves (why else would he make them wealthy?), have a hard time going to heaven, how could the poor (whom God obviously disdains) ever make it? The disciples hadn't yet grasped the significance of their Lord's lifestyle. The one whose Father said, "This is My beloved Son, in whom I am well pleased" (Matthew 3:17, NKJV) was the same Son of Man who didn't have a place to lay his head and owned nothing but a robe and sandals (Matthew 8:20).

> The well-to-do Pharisees lived and breathed a prosperity theology, labeling everyone beneath their social caste as "sinners."

Jesus said of his Father, "He causes his sun to rise on the evil and the good, and sends rain on the righteous and the unrighteous" (Matthew 5:45). God extends common grace to all. The air breathed by every person—sinner or saint—is God's gift, regardless of the person's morality. What we call prosperity is often incidental: An evil person may have good soil and a large crop, while the good person has poor soil and a small crop. As Christ's account of the rich man and Lazarus demonstrates, an evil person may live a long life, suffer little, and prosper, while the righteous person may have life cut short, suffer considerably, and live in poverty (Luke 16:19-31). Jesus says things will be turned around in eternity, but often not until then (Luke 6:20-25).

The New Testament goes one step further. Not only may the righteous suffer despite their righteousness, but often they will suffer *because* of their righteousness. "Everyone who wants to live a godly life in Christ Jesus will be persecuted" (2 Timothy 3:12). The early Christians continually suffered for their faith and were assured that "your brothers throughout the world are undergoing the same kind of sufferings" (1 Peter 5:9). A materialistic world system, with its emphasis on personal peace and prosperity, does not look with favor upon a true disciple of Christ (John 15:18-20).

These examples from Scripture should disturb any of us whose goal is to be hailed a success by the standards of this world. If we fit in so well with the world, is it because we are living by the world's standards, not Christ's?

LIVE LIKE THE KING'S KID?

There's great irony in a popular saying heard in "health and wealth" circles: "Live like a King's kid." The "King's kid" was Jesus, who lived a life exactly opposite of what is meant by the phrase today. The King we serve was stripped down for battle. At the end of the age he will don the royal robes of victory, and so will his faithful servants with him; but now is the time for battle garb, not regalia.

How did the King send his "kid" into this world? Born in lowly Bethlehem, raised in despised Nazareth, part of a pious but poor family that offered two doves because they couldn't afford a lamb (Leviticus 12:6-8; Luke 2:22-24), Christ wandered the countryside dependent on others to open their homes, because he didn't have one of his own. "Live like a king's kid"? Whatever king's kid the prosperity proponents are speaking of, it obviously isn't Jesus!

Prosperity theology sees as our model the ascended heavenly Lord rather than the descended earthly servant. Jesus warned his disciples not to follow a lordship model, but his own servant model (Mark 10:42-45). In this life, we are to share in his cross—in the next life we will share in his crown (2 Timothy 2:12).

In verses you'll never see embroidered, framed, or posted on refrigerators, the King promised persecution, betrayal, flogging, and being dragged before courts and tried for our faith (Matthew 10:16-20). He warned, "In this world you will have trouble" (John 16:33) and said, "Any of you who does not give up everything he has cannot be my disciple" (Luke 14:33).

This is not the stuff of which prosperity sermons are made.

PAUL AND PROSPERITY

Other than the life and teachings of Christ, the most powerful refutation of prosperity theology can be seen in the life and writings of Paul. As the health gospel tries to experience the full redemption of the body in this life, so the wealth gospel tries to experience heaven's rewards on earth. Because these are two inseparable sides of the prosperity gospel coin, we'll look at Paul's life in terms of health and wealth and other trappings of success.

Raised a Pharisee and therefore a believer in prosperity theology, Paul was one of those who could not believe that Jesus was Messiah, because of Jesus' obvious lack of success. God's disapproval of the man Jesus was surely self-evident in his questionable parentage, his disreputable place of upbringing, his lack of formal education, his poverty, and above all, his shameful death. But when Paul bowed his knee to the Carpenter from Galilee, he forever turned his back on prosperity theology. As his Lord said, "I will show him how much he must suffer for my name" (Acts 9:16).

In his letter to the Philippians—written from a prison, not a plush office or the Rome Marriott—Paul says, "It has been granted to you on behalf of Christ not only to believe on him, but also to suffer for him" (Philippians 1:29). He depicts Christ as the suffering Servant, whose prosperity came after his life on this earth, not during it (Philippians 2:5-11). Had Jesus laid claim to prosperity in this life, there would have been no crucifixion, no atonement, no gospel, and no hope for any of us.

In Philippians 3, Paul discusses his credentials of success, his diplomas, and awards. These he once highly valued, but now he says, "Whatever was to my profit I now consider loss for the sake of Christ. What is more, I consider everything a loss compared to the surpassing greatness of knowing Christ Jesus my Lord, for whose sake I have lost all things. I consider them rubbish, that I may gain Christ" (Philippians 3:7-8). Actually, this translation is too delicate. Paul did not call his credentials and possessions "rubbish," but *dung*. Excrement. That's how he viewed the things he once valued, when stacking them up against Christ. Contrast that with today's prosperity preachers, their heavy jewelry swaying as they strut across the stage.

As a result of following Christ, Paul lost everything.

As a result of following Christ, Paul lost everything. What little money and possessions might have passed through his hands he considered a loss. He describes his daily adversity, persecution for Christ, and nearness to death (2 Corinthians 4:7-12). Two chapters later, Paul refers to his troubles, hardships, distresses, beatings, imprisonments, riots, sleepless nights, and hunger, as well as the experience of nearly dying, and being sorrowful and poor (2 Corinthians 6:3-10).

Perhaps the most graphic portrayal of Paul's life comes later in the same letter:

> I have worked much harder, been in prison more frequently, been flogged more severely, and been exposed to death again and again. Five times I received from the Jews the forty lashes minus one. Three times I was beaten with rods, once I was stoned, three times I was shipwrecked, I spent a night and a day in the open sea, I have been constantly on the move. I have been in danger from rivers, in danger from bandits, in danger from my own countrymen, in danger from Gentiles; in danger in the city, in danger in the country, in danger at sea; and in danger

from false brothers. I have labored and toiled and have often gone without sleep; I have known hunger and thirst and have often gone without food; I have been cold and naked. Besides everything else, I face daily the pressure of my concern for all the churches. Who is weak, and I do not feel weak? Who is led into sin, and I do not inwardly burn? (2 Corinthians 11:23-29)

Paul seems to make a case for what might be called "adversity theology," or the "sickness and poverty gospel." I wonder if in his dreams the apostle ever heard a faint chorus of voices from the future saying, "Paul,

Paul seems to make a case for what might be called "adversity theology," or the "sickness and poverty gospel."

you don't have to live like this—why don't you trust God and live like a king's kid?" The truth is, Paul heard some of these voices in his own day. In fact, Paul had to defend himself against the "super apostles," well-off ministers who berated him because he couldn't claim their wealth and prestige (1 Corinthians 4:8-13). He said to them, "Already you have all you want! Already you have become rich! You have become kings" (1 Corinthians 4:8). He added, "We are weak, but you are strong! You are honored, we are dishonored!" (1 Corinthians 4:10). Paul faced off with these prosperity preachers, pointing out that they'd jumped the gun on reigning with Christ by living now as kings rather than as servants. Paul's point is clear: Don't try to reign prematurely! Dress like a servant. Let God put robes of honor on you when he brings you to his kingdom. Don't put them on yourself now!

After explaining that God had given him some special revelations, Paul adds:

To keep me from becoming conceited . . . there was given me a thorn in my flesh, a messenger of Satan, to torment me. Three times I pleaded with the Lord to take it away from me. But he said to me, "My grace is sufficient for you, for my power is made perfect in weakness." Therefore I will boast all the more gladly about my weaknesses, so that Christ's power may rest on me. That is why, for Christ's sake, I delight in weaknesses, in insults, in hardships, in persecutions, in difficulties. For when I am weak, then I am strong. (2 Corinthians 12:7-10)

Paul knew that God had a definite purpose in his illness or disability. We don't know what the disease was, but among other things it apparently caused his deteriorating eyesight (Galatians 6:11). His affliction, Paul said, was "given" to him in order to keep him from being conceited.

Moreover, God had a specific purpose for not removing the disease—to teach Paul that God's grace was sufficient. Paul wasn't to trust in his own strength but in God's. His disease was a day-by-day reminder of his need to trust in the Lord rather than his own gifts and accomplishments.

A physician sponsors a frequent ad on our local Christian radio station. He says, "Helping you get well is all that matters." Well, actually, it isn't—there's a great deal more that matters, and a great deal that matters more! I speak as an insulin-dependent diabetic who has seen God do greater things through my sickness than through my health.

Instead of assuming that God wants us healthy, we need to realize that he may accomplish higher purposes through our sickness than through our health. We may pray for healing when we're sick, which is exactly what Paul did. But notice that he prayed only three times. When God chose not to heal him, he didn't "name it and claim it" and demand that God heal him. Instead, he acknowledged God's spiritual purpose in his adversity.

Today's health and wealth preachers bypass the rest of this passage and say, "Paul called this disease a 'messenger of Satan.' It's from the devil, not God. The devil wants us sick, but God wants us well." Yes, Paul called the ailment a messenger of Satan. But God is bigger than all, and Satan is just one more agent he can use to accomplish his own purpose. After all, whose purpose and plan is the passage talking about? Satan would never give anyone something to keep him from being conceited. **Like many** God is the one who intended the disease for Paul's good. It **of God's** wasn't Satan but God who refused to remove the disease, despite Paul's pleadings. **servants in**

If you've prayed for healing and not received it, take **the early** heart—you're in good company! Not only was Paul himself **Church, Paul** not healed, but he also had to leave Trophimus in Miletus be- **was neither** cause of sickness (2 Timothy 4:20). His beloved friend **healthy nor** Epaphroditus was gravely ill (Philippians 2:24-30). His son in **wealthy.** the faith, Timothy, had frequent stomach disorders, for which Paul didn't tell him to "claim healing" but to drink a little wine for medicinal purposes (1 Timothy 5:23). Those who claim "anyone with enough faith can be healed" apparently have greater faith than Paul and his missionary associates.

Like many of God's servants in the early Church, Paul was neither healthy nor wealthy. It's clear that God didn't intend for him to be healthy or wealthy. Paul is now enjoying perfect health and wealth for all eternity. But when he was on this earth, it was God's higher plan that for much of his life he would be poor and sick.

When Paul was taken in chains from his filthy Roman dungeon and beheaded at the order of the opulent madman Nero, two representatives of humanity faced off, one of the best and one of the worst. One lived for prosperity on earth, the other didn't. One now lives in prosperity in heaven, the other doesn't. We remember both men for what they truly were, which is why we name our sons Paul and our dogs Nero.

THE NEW TESTAMENT UNDERSTANDING OF WEALTH

How can we explain the apparent contradiction between the words and lifestyle of Jesus and the apostles, and the Old Testament prosperity passages? The answer lies in the fundamental differences between the Old and New Covenants, which we will explore further in chapter 11. For now, suffice it to say that the New Testament reflects a fundamental change in its understanding of true wealth.

In the New Testament, the Greek word *ploutos* is used six times for material riches put to evil purposes (Matthew 13:22; Mark 4:19; Luke 8:14; 1 Timothy 6:17; James 5:2; Revelation 18:17). Yet the same word is used eleven times in the positive sense, each time referring to spiritual, not material, riches (Romans 11:33; Ephesians 1:18; Philippians 4:19; Colossians 1:27). Once we experience those riches, we find them so profoundly satisfying that we can never again elevate earthly and material riches to the place of importance they once held.

DIDN'T CHRIST PROMISE PROSPERITY IN THIS LIFE?

The most popular New Testament proof text for prosperity theology comes on the heels of Christ's disciples pointing out that they had left everything behind to follow him:

> "I tell you the truth," Jesus replied, "no one who has left home or
> brothers or sisters or mother or father or children or fields for me
> and the gospel will fail to receive a hundred times as much in this
> present age (homes, brothers, sisters, mothers, children and fields—
> and with them, persecutions) and in the age to come, eternal life."
> (Mark 10:29-30)

Referring to this passage in a letter to his supporters, a famous evangelist said, "To my knowledge, God's people have never received their hundredfold return. It's been there in God's Reward System, but never understood or received—until now!"

According to this man and other prosperity preachers, the people of God can now tap into what Jesus intended from the beginning—that all his followers would be materially prosperous in this life.

But is this really what Jesus meant?

First, no matter what Jesus was saying in these passages, it surely does not contradict Scripture's direct teaching and repeated example that followers of Christ will often—indeed *usually*—not be wealthy in this life. This was undeniably true of the apostles, who were the ones to whom Jesus was speaking.

Second, almost none of those who claim the *benefits* of this passage have actually fulfilled the *conditions* of the promise. Unlike the disciples, they haven't given up their material goods or left their families to follow Christ.

Third, the phrase "in this present age" does indeed refer to this world, but in what sense does it mean we are to receive "many times" or "a hundred times" as much in terms of homes, brothers, sisters, parents, children, and fields? The only words of a material nature are *fields* and possibly *homes.* Yet even the word for home (*oikia*) may mean not the house itself but the household or inhabitants of the house—that is, the family (Matthew 12:25; John 4:53; 1 Corinthians 16:15).

Even if Christ was referring to a physical house, is he promising that all believers who give up the roof over their head will literally own many other houses in this life? Clearly not, because everything we know about the apostles to whom he was speaking, from biblical and extrabiblical sources, suggests none of them were wealthy. To put it in terms that proponents of a health and wealth gospel would understand, none of the apostles owned a Jerusalem condo, a split-level in suburban Bethany, a cabin in the mountains at Carmel, or a summer beach house near Caesarea. Indeed, if the hundredfold blessing was a literal promise of houses, those receiving it would have to own a hundred houses, and a hundred fields, not just a measly half dozen or so.

If Jesus literally meant to say that the faithful believer would own large numbers of homes and fields, did he also mean to say that the disciples would have a hundred children and that hundreds of older folks would become their literal parents? Obviously not!

Christ was saying that those who would follow him, in leaving behind what was theirs, would become part of the larger family of faith, where relationships are deep and possessions are freely shared. Everywhere the apostles went they would find "homes" that were theirs for as long as they wished to stay, meals prepared from the harvest of the "fields" freely shared with them. They would have "brothers" and "sisters" to fellowship with, "parents" to give them wisdom and guidance and love, and "children" who would learn at their feet, and whom they would guide into Christlikeness. This same rich reservoir of relationships and possessions is available today to all who will follow the Lord. I've experienced it myself and likely you have too.

Paul had no permanent home (though his prison cells nearly qualified), no fields, no close family, and no literal offspring, but he proudly called Timothy, the Thessalonians, and others his beloved children. After acknowledging his lack of health and wealth, Paul demonstrated the real meaning of Mark 10:29-30 (and the parallel passage in Luke 18:29-30) by describing himself as "having nothing, and yet possessing everything" (2 Corinthians 6:10). Paradoxically, Paul "had it all" while possessing very little.

Finally, it's striking that the prosperity preachers who quote Mark 10:30

almost never comment on the phrase "and with them, persecutions." When was the last time you heard a sermon on God's promise of hundredfold persecutions?

I'm not suggesting that no New Testament promises of blessing apply in a literal, material way. Jesus said, "Give, and it will be given to you. A good measure, pressed down, shaken together and running over, will be poured into your lap. For with the measure you use, it will be measured to you" (Luke 6:38). Both Scripture and experience demonstrate God's frequent material blessing upon those who generously share what he has entrusted to them. I am a firm believer in this. In refuting the excesses of prosperity theology, I don't minimize the fact that God is a giver by nature, that he loves to give to his children, and that he rewards our generosity. Often those rewards may include financial and material blessings. (We'll take a closer look at this topic in chapter 13.)

WHEN GOD PROSPERS US, WHY?

I have no argument with anyone who says that God often chooses to prosper his people in material ways. But the great question is this: "Why does he prosper us?" When he blesses us financially, what does he expect us to do with the abundance?

> When God blesses us financially, what does he expect us to do with the abundance?

Health and wealth preachers suggest that we may do whatever we please with God's provision. We may buy beautiful homes and cars, take dream vacations, and live in wealth and prosperity—as long as we give God the credit. Whether God wants the credit for some of these lifestyles is another question. Some prosperity preachers go so far as to say that God expects us—or even commands us—to live in luxury, in order that we would not be "bad witnesses" by appearing to be poor! By this standard, Jesus and Paul were terrible witnesses.

It seems as if these preachers would have us believe that Jesus said, "By this all men will know that you are my disciples, if you have lots of money and fabulous possessions." (To see what Jesus actually said, read John 13:35.)

In the context of financial giving Paul says, "God is able to make all grace abound to you, so that in all things at all times, having all that you need [not want], you will abound in every good work" (2 Corinthians 9:8). In other words, Paul says that God provides us with abundance precisely so we can use it to do good works. He also said that the God who "supplies seed to the sower" will "increase your store of seed" (2 Corinthians 9:10). Why? So we can stockpile seed or eat it? No, so we can scatter it, spread it out, so it can produce life and bear fruit. Why does God make many of us rich? We don't have to wonder, because Scripture directly answers the question: "You will be made rich in every way *so that* you can be generous on every occasion, and through us your generosity will result in thanksgiving to God" (2 Corinthians 9:11, italics mine). God entrusts riches to us not so we can keep them, but so that we can generously *give*. Paul made this same point earlier:

> Our desire is not that others might be relieved while you are hard pressed, but that there might be equality. At the present time your plenty will supply what they need, so that in turn their plenty will supply what you need. Then there will be equality. (2 Corinthians 8:13-14)

This passage argues against the notion that we who have more than enough should store up as much as possible for the future, so we'll never have to rely on the gifts of others. That may fit our individualistic spirit of American pride, but it doesn't fit the teaching of Scripture. We're told to give of our plenty now, realizing that someday—perhaps even partly because we've given to others—we will be in a position to receive from others. Maybe that would be healthy for both others and us. Giving away money puts us in a position of financial weakness. We don't like that—we prefer being in a position of financial strength. But giving away our excess does something for us that keeping or spending it doesn't. It makes us dependent on God, and keeps us open to the possibility that at some point we may need to depend on others, just as they are currently depending on us.

Our ministry has the privilege of giving away my book royalties to support worthy ministries. In a year when we'd been able to give away more than one hundred thousand dollars in the first five months, suddenly we had a shortfall in our revenues. We had to make some quick and significant cutbacks. The next thing we knew, one of the missions organizations we regularly support sent us $500. This was the first time I'd ever received a financial gift from a missions organization! For a moment it felt very uncomfortable. Then I smiled, realizing what a blessing it was to us and to them. They moved from recipient to donor, and we moved from donor to recipient, exactly as 2 Corinthians 8:13-14 describes.

It's fun to have our prayers answered. And it's fun to be the answer to someone else's prayer. I recently recommended to a group of ministry CEOs that they choose several other ministries and make periodic gifts to them. We can say "we're not in competition" with other ministries, but nothing tests that sentiment—and nothing actually cultivates cooperation—like choosing to give other ministries what we could have spent or saved for ourselves.

God has richly blessed us financially not so that we can show ourselves to be his children by living above the standards of others, but so that we can show ourselves to be his children by coming down a few rungs on the ladder of affluence and bringing others up a few rungs, that there might be true, from-the-heart equality.

God could have distributed goods equally in the first place, but he wants to rely on his people to share freely in his name. He wants us to be the conduit through which he meets the needs of others for whom he cared enough to die.

John Piper identifies the purpose of God's abundant provision:

God is not glorified when we keep for ourselves (no matter how thankfully) what we ought to be using to alleviate the misery of unevangelized, uneducated, unmedicated, and unfed millions. The evidence that many professing Christians have been deceived by this doctrine is how little they give and how much they own. God has prospered them. And by an almost irresistible law of consumer culture (baptized by a doctrine of health, wealth, and prosperity) they have bought bigger (and more) houses, newer (and more) cars, fancier (and more) clothes, better (and more) meat, and all manner of trinkets and gadgets and containers and devices and equipment to make life more fun. They will object: Does not the Old Testament promise that God will prosper his people? Indeed! God increases our yield, so that by giving we can prove our yield is not our god. God does not prosper a man's business so he can move from a Ford to a Cadillac. God prospers a business so that 17,000 unreached peoples can be reached with the gospel. He prospers the business so that 12 percent of the world's population can move a step back from the precipice of starvation.[1]

Prosperity theology encourages spending on ourselves. But this not only forges the chains of materialism for us, it constitutes a lost opportunity to give to what could count for eternity. Christ said, "Do to others what you would have them do to you" (Matthew 7:12). If you and your children were hungry, what would you want prosperous Christians to do for you? If your answer is that you'd want them to share from their abundance, then say no to prosperity theology, obey Christ, and share your abundance with others.

How different John Wesley sounded than today's prosperity preachers:

Do not you know that God entrusted you with that money (all above what buys necessities for your families) to feed the hungry, to clothe the naked, to help the stranger, the widow, the fatherless; and, indeed, as far as it will go, to relieve the wants of all mankind? How can you, how dare you, defraud your Lord, by applying it to any other purpose?[2]

GOD THE GREAT GENIE

Teaching the "seed faith" and "hundredfold return" principles, one pastor triumphantly told of a woman in his church whose still-new car was about to be repossessed. As an act of faith, claiming God's "promise" of a hundredfold return, she put $20 in the offering. Sure enough, the next day she received $2,000 in the mail and was able to catch up on her payments, keep her car, and gain some extra spending money.

That's a nice testimony, but it raises some questions. Did it occur to the woman (or the pastor) that perhaps she should not have gone into debt in the first place, that her beautiful car might be a luxury God didn't approve of, or that God might want her to give up her car and invest the $2,000 in his kingdom (and not expect a check in the mail for $200,000 to compensate her for doing so)? It apparently didn't occur to them that many unrighteous people also received checks in the mail that day, while many righteous people didn't.

Prosperity teaching raises the very question that Satan asked God: "Does Job fear God for nothing?" (Job 1:9). Though Job's faith was proved genuine, many other people are less interested in God himself than in the fringe benefits we claim that he offers. The world comes to a prosperous Church with mixed motives. As Sir Robert L'Estrange, a seventeenth-century British journalist, observed, "He that serves God for money will serve the devil for better wages."[3]

The central problem with the health-and-wealth gospel is that it's man-centered, not God-centered. When approached from a "prosperity" posture, prayer degenerates into coercion, by which we "name it and claim it," pulling God's leash until he follows our whims. We attempt to arm-twist the Almighty into increasing our comforts and underwriting lifestyles about which we've not bothered to consult him in the first place.

The central problem with the health-and-wealth gospel is that it's man-centered, not God-centered.

"Faith" becomes a crowbar to break down the door of God's reluctance, rather than a humble attempt to lay hold of his willingness. When we claim the blood of Christ, believing that God must take away this illness or handicap or financial hardship, are we asking him to remove the very things he has put into our lives to make us more Christlike?

We treat God as an object, a tool, a means to an end. God's blessing on financial giving is turned into a money-back guarantee whereby he is obligated to do precisely what we want. A Florida man heard a pastor say that if the man gave a hundred dollars, God would give him a thousand dollars back. When the thousand never came, he filed a lawsuit against the church.

In prosperity theology, God is seen as a great no-lose lottery in the sky, a cosmic slot machine into which you put in a coin and pull the lever, then stick out your hat and catch the winnings while your "casino buddies" (or fellow Christians) whoop and holler (or say "Amen") and wait their turn in line.

God's reason for existing, apparently, is to give us what we want. If we had no needs, God would probably just disappear. After all, what purpose would he serve? This feeble theology reduces prayer to an endless "wish list" that we take before our Santa God. Many healthy and wealthy Christians view God as little more than a wish-granting fairy. We call him "Master" but treat him like a genie. Instead of rubbing a lamp, we quote a verse or say "Praise the Lord" three times, and presto-change-o, abracadabra, the smoky God with the funny hat and big biceps is indebted to act out the script we've written for him. Consider God's role in relation to us in these words of a prominent preacher of prosperity: "Put God to work for you and maximize your potential in our divinely ordered capitalist system."[4]

WHO'S WORKING FOR WHOM?

Our pragmatic use of God demonstrates a clear lack of interest in God himself. After all, who cares what a genie is like? Genies serve one purpose—to grant us our wishes and make us prosperous and happy. Instead of being the great subject of our faith, for many of us God is merely an object—which explains the glut of sermons, books, articles, seminars, and conversations about us and the dearth of those about God. He is introduced and dismissed at our convenience. "You can go now, God—I'll call you back when I think of something else I want."

The Bible shows us a very different picture of God, in which he is central, his glory is the focal point of the universe, and his sovereign purpose entitles him to do what he wills, even when it violates what we want and expect.

When righteous Job lost everything, even his own sons and daughters, he fell to the ground and worshiped God, saying, "The Lord gave and the Lord has taken away; may the name of the Lord be praised." We're told, "In all this, Job did not sin by charging God with wrongdoing" (Job 1:21-22).

In contrast, when advocates of a prosperity gospel lose their health and wealth, they often lose their faith. They conclude that they must have committed some unknown sin. If they could only find it and confess it, they would get their health and wealth back. The only other alternative is that God's promises are not true, that God is undependable, or that he's forsaken them. Job's wife said, "Curse God and die." Job's response was a simple question that exposes the shallowness of prosperity theology: "Shall we accept good from God, and not trouble?" (Job 2:9-10).

WHAT WE'RE SAYING TO THE WORLD

When unbelievers witnessed the generosity of the early Christians, they saw how they loved one another and cared for each other. As a consequence, these believers were "enjoying the favor of all the people." There was something attractive about running counterculture to the self-centered prosperity theology that dominated Jerusalem's religious landscape. Not coincidentally, many came to faith partly through the power and integrity of this refreshing alternative to materialism: "The Lord added to their number daily *those who were being saved*" (Acts 2:45-47, italics mine).

This is in stark contrast to the health and wealth gospel featured on some Christian television programs, which most unbelievers see as self-serving hucksterism. Unfortunately, they're often right. This baptized materialism does not draw the world to Christ. On the contrary, it pushes the world away from him. In fact, the only unbelievers who are drawn to the Church by prosperity theology are drawn for all the wrong reasons.

PROSPERITY AND PROVINCIALISM

I've thought a lot about prosperity theology. I thought about it as I walked through the streets of Cairo's Garbage Village, shaking the grimy hands of Christians living in abject poverty. I thought about it when I worshiped alongside faithful believers on a rough backless bench in a dirt-floor church in Kenya. I thought about it again when I sat in a dim room with pastors behind the Iron Curtain. I thought of it when I walked down muddy backstreets in Cambodia and squeezed into tiny homes in China. I thought about it as I was flown across the United States, put up in a plush hotel room, and picked up in a limousine that drove me to a Christian television studio for a twenty-minute interview.

I've thought about prosperity theology and Scripture enough to reach a conclusion about what God thinks of it. Although some have tried to justify their prosperity theology by using isolated proof texts, in reality it is the product of the materialistic and success-driven psychology that dominates industrialized nations. The health-and-wealth gospel will thrive in North America, Western Europe, Korea, Japan, Singapore, and other economically progressive countries. But where does it fit in Bangladesh, Ethiopia, Laos, Haiti, or Afghanistan? Far from being a reflection of biblical teaching, prosperity theology is a product of our place and time, a reflection of our materialism and self-absorption.

> Prosperity theology is a product of our place and time, a reflection of our materialism and self-absorption.

My novel *Safely Home* is the story of a U.S. businessman and his Chinese roommate who graduated from Harvard together twenty-five years before. They haven't communicated with each other for two decades but are suddenly reunited in China. The one who has followed Christ is experiencing adversity and joy. The one who turned from Christ is experiencing prosperity and emptiness. The contrast between these two old friends is the contrast between biblical Christianity and prosperity theology.

My novel is, of course, a work of fiction, but a similar contrast can be seen in the real-life testimonies of two men:

In America, a sharp-looking businessman stands up at a luncheon to give his testimony: "Before I knew Christ, I had nothing. My business was in bankruptcy, my health was ruined, I'd lost the respect of the community, and I'd almost lost my family. Then I accepted Christ. He took me out of bankruptcy and now my business has tripled its profits. My blood pressure has dropped to normal and I feel better than I've felt in years. Best of all, my wife and children have come back, and we're a family again. God is good—praise the Lord!"

In China, a disheveled former university professor gives his testimony: "Before I met Christ, I had everything. I made a large salary, lived in a nice house, enjoyed good health, was highly respected for my credentials and profession, and had a good marriage and a beautiful son. Then I accepted Christ as my Savior and Lord. As a result, I lost my post at the university, lost my beautiful house and car, and spent five years in prison. Now I work for a subsistence wage at a factory. I live with pain in my neck, which was broken in prison. My wife rejected me because of my conversion. She took my son away and I haven't seen him for ten years. But God is good, and I praise him for his faithfulness."

Both men are sincere Christians. One gives thanks because of what he's gained. The other gives thanks in spite of what he's lost.

Material blessings and restored families are definitely worth being thankful for. The brother in China would be grateful to have them again; indeed, he gives heartfelt thanks each day for the little he does have. And while the American brother is certainly right to give thanks, he and the rest of us must be careful to sort out how much of what he has experienced is part of the gospel and how much is not. For any gospel that is more true in America than in China is not the true gospel.

And whether a message be proclaimed by an angel, a television evangelist, a pastor, or a fund-raising letter, Scripture makes clear what our response must be to any gospel other than the true one:

> I am astonished that you are so quickly deserting the one who called you by the grace of Christ and are turning to a different gospel—which is really no gospel at all. Evidently some people are throwing you into confusion and are trying to pervert the gospel of Christ. But even if we or an angel from heaven should preach a gospel other than the one we preached to you, let him be eternally condemned! As we have already said, so now I say again: If anybody is preaching to you a gospel other than what you accepted, let him be eternally condemned!
>
> Am I now trying to win the approval of men, or of God? Or am I trying to please men? If I were still trying to please men, I would not be a servant of Christ. (Galatians 1:6-10)

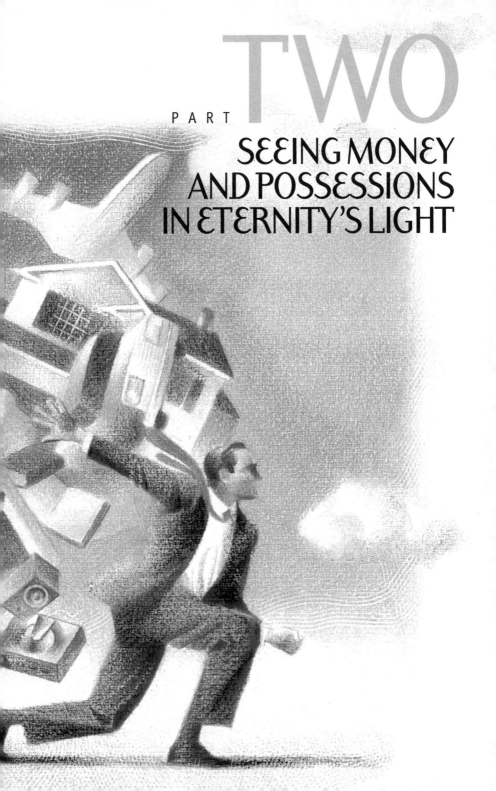

PART TWO

SEEING MONEY AND POSSESSIONS IN ETERNITY'S LIGHT

CHAPTER 7

Two Treasuries, Two Perspectives, Two Masters

I have held many things in my hands and I have lost them all. But whatever I have placed in God's hands, that I still possess.   MARTIN LUTHER

He is no fool who gives what he cannot keep to gain what he cannot lose.   JIM ELLIOT

In the greatest message ever preached, Jesus addresses the believer's proper relationship to money and possessions:

> Do not store up for yourselves treasures on earth, where moth and rust destroy, and where thieves break in and steal. But store up for yourselves treasures in heaven, where moth and rust do not destroy, and where thieves do not break in and steal. For where your treasure is, there your heart will be also.
>
> The eye is the lamp of the body. If your eyes are good, your whole body will be full of light. But if your eyes are bad, your whole body will be full of darkness. If then the light within you is darkness, how great is that darkness!
>
> No one can serve two masters. Either he will hate the one and love the other, or he will be devoted to the one and despise the other. You cannot serve both God and Money. (Matthew 6:19-24)

Jesus always had two kingdoms in mind. He spoke here of the two treasuries, two perspectives, and two masters of those two kingdoms.

Each couplet presents two options and demands one choice. There's a default choice if "no choice" is made. Unless the right choice is deliberately made and tenaciously clung to, the wrong choice will naturally be implemented. In that case, as if on automatic pilot, people will spend their lives investing in the wrong treasury, adopting the wrong perspective, and serving the wrong master.

TWO TREASURIES

What is our treasure? A. W. Tozer suggested we may discover the answer by responding to four basic questions:

> What do we value most? What would we most hate to lose? What do our thoughts turn to most frequently when we are free to think of what we will? And finally, what affords us the greatest pleasure?[1]

Based on these four questions, what's *your* treasure?

Most people would list people and relationships as their treasures. But if we're honest, we'd also include money and possessions. However, by juxtaposing the storing up of treasures on earth with treasures in heaven, Jesus suggests there's an eternal use for money and possessions.

When spent on earthly treasure, money is only of temporary value—unless it's spent with a view toward heavenly treasure. Moths destroy fabric, rust destroys "precious" metals, and thieves can steal almost anything. Jesus could have gone on—fires consume, floods destroy, governments seize, enemies attack, investments go sour. No earthly treasure is safe.

But when money and possessions are spent on heavenly treasure, the equation changes radically. The investment takes on eternal value. (Since God, his Word, and people are eternal, what will last is what is used wisely for God, his Word, and his people.)

Jesus invites us to choose our treasury. Will we invest our treasures on earth and lose them when we die? Or will we invest our treasures in heaven, where they will be ours for eternity?

Aggressive Investing

In reading Matthew 6, many people see something negative and miss the positive. They think that Jesus is categorically against the storing up of treasures. In fact, Jesus didn't tell us not to store up treasures. On the contrary, he commanded us to. He simply said, "Stop storing them up in the wrong place, and start storing them up in the right place."

Christ's primary argument against amassing material wealth isn't that it's morally wrong, but simply that it's a poor investment. Material things just won't stand the test of time. Even if they escape moths and rust and thieves, they cannot escape the coming fire of God that will consume the material world (2 Peter 3:7).

Jesus isn't saying it's wrong to invest. He's saying, "Don't make a stupid investment, make a smart one."

John Wesley said, "I value all things only by the price they shall gain in eternity." David Livingstone said, "I place no value on anything I possess, except in relation to the kingdom of God." God's kingdom was the reference point for these men. They saw all else in light of that kingdom. They were compelled to live as they did, not because they treasured no things, but because they treasured the right things.

When we think of missionaries, we often visualize simple people with no aspirations for treasures or greatness. We miss something in missionary martyr Jim Elliot's famous words, "He is no fool who gives what he cannot keep to gain what he cannot lose." We focus on his willingness to sacrifice and serve, but we neglect his passion for personal gain. Reread his words and you'll see that Jim Elliot was a profit seeker! What separated him from the common Christian wasn't that he didn't want treasure, but that he wanted true and *lasting* treasure. He wasn't satisfied with treasure that would be lost, only treasure that would last.

Christ's position on wealth is not that it should be rejected, but that it should be pursued. It's an understatement to say that God doesn't object to an investment mentality. According to this passage, God *has* an investment mentality. Christ agrees wholeheartedly with us: wealth is worth seeking. The question is, what constitutes true wealth?

Discovering True Wealth

Jesus vividly described what it's like when we discover true wealth: "The kingdom of heaven is like treasure hidden in a field. When a man found it, he hid it again, and then in his joy went and sold all he had and bought that field" (Matthew 13:44).

This man, like most of us, was probably quite attached to his possessions. Yet, having seen the value of this great treasure in the field, he "sold all he had" to obtain it. Did the sacrifice pain him? Should we feel sorry for him that the treasure cost him everything? No! "In his joy," he sold all to obtain the treasure. Why? It was a simple question of relative value. Until he found the treasure, all his possessions seemed valuable. But compared to the dazzling beauty and incalculable worth of what he had discovered, everything he had owned and treasured to that point seemed worthless.

John White said this about the man in the parable who gives up everything for this one great treasure:

> The choice he faces lies between his worthless bits
> and pieces and the field with buried treasure. There is
> nothing noble about his sacrifice. There would, on the
> other hand, be something incredibly stupid about not
> making it. Anyone but a fool would do exactly as the
> man did. Everyone will envy him his good fortune and
> commend him not on his spiritual character but on his
> common sense.[2]

> The kingdom of heaven is like treasure hidden in a field. When a man found it, he hid it again, and then in his joy went and sold all he had and bought that field.
>
> MATTHEW 13:44

95

The greatest treasure is Christ himself. To Paul, gaining Christ made everything else seem comparatively worthless (Philippians 3:7-11). But part of gaining Christ was looking forward to eternal reward, Christ's stamp of approval on his faithful service while on earth. This prospect of eternal reward from his Master's hand was Paul's consuming motivation throughout his life (1 Corinthians 9:24-27) and his greatest anticipation at his death (2 Timothy 4:6-8).

Christ offers us the incredible opportunity to trade temporary goods and currency for eternal rewards. By putting our money and possessions in his treasury while we're still on earth, we assure ourselves of eternal rewards beyond comprehension.

Consider the implications of this offer. We can trade temporal possessions we can't keep to gain eternal possessions we can't lose. This is like a child trading bubble gum for a new bicycle, or a man offered ownership of the Coca-Cola company in exchange for a sack of bottle caps. Only a fool would pass up the opportunity.

What we keep we will lose. What we give and share and do in Christ's name will ultimately come back to us in heaven, in a far better and permanent form.

Anything we try to hang onto here will be lost. But anything we put into God's hands will be ours for eternity (and insured for infinitely more than $100,000 by the real FDIC: the Father's Deposit Insurance Corporation).

If we give instead of keep, if we invest in the eternal instead of the temporal, we store up in heaven treasures that will never stop paying dividends.

Whatever treasures we store up on earth will be left behind when we leave. Whatever treasures we store up in heaven will be waiting for us when we arrive.

The reality of eternal rewards inevitably fosters an investment mentality. For instance, with $15,000 I may be able to buy a new car. With the same money, I could help translate the Scriptures for an unreached people group, support church planting, feed the hungry in the name of Christ, get gospel literature distributed in Southeast Asia, or send out multiple Nigerian or Indian missionary families, and support them full-time for a year. If I have an investment mentality, I ask myself, *What's the better investment for eternity?*

Of course, it may be God's will for me to buy a car. True, a car used for his purposes can also be an investment in the kingdom. But I must be careful not to rationalize. A used car or no car at all may serve his kingdom purposes equally well or far better—and allow me to make an investment in heaven that will never get scratched, dented, stolen, or totaled. And if I invest the money in his kingdom and ask him to provide a car at little or no expense, might he choose to do that? Why wouldn't I give him the chance?

A Safe Place for Your Money?

Note that the central focus of Matthew 6:19-24 is the accumulation of heavenly treasures, not the renunciation of earthly treasures. We're to avoid storing up treasures on earth not as an end in itself, but as part of a life strategy to lay up treasures in heaven. A person may give up all earthly treasures without ever investing in heavenly treasures. Jesus is not looking for ascetics or hermits, but eternity-wise investors. Jesus is not speculating, he's speaking of sure things. When he warns us not to store up treasures on earth, it's not just because wealth might be lost. It's that wealth will definitely be lost. Either it leaves us while we live, or we leave it when we die.

"Naked a man comes from his mother's womb, and as he comes, so he departs. He takes nothing from his labor that he can carry in his hand" (Ecclesiastes 5:15).

You can't take it with you.

"Do not be afraid when a man becomes rich, when the glory of his house is increased; for when he dies he will carry nothing away; his glory will not descend after him" (Psalm 49:16-20, NASB).

You can't take it with you.

King Tut thought that by surrounding himself with treasures, they would be his in the afterlife. He was wrong. They didn't go with him. When Howard Carter discovered Tut's tomb in 1922, the treasures were still there. Today those treasures sit in a Cairo museum. They're still here, but Tut is long gone.

You can't take it with you.

When Jesus speaks of moths and rust and thieves taking our earthly treasures, he is saying in effect: "You can't take it with you." But then he adds something breathtaking, something revolutionary, a brand-new corollary to the old adage: "You can't take it with you, but . . . you can send it on ahead."

Jesus said there's only one safe place to put our money: the kingdom of God.

What a stunning qualification. Who would have dared to think such a thing possible—that we creatures of dust could make choices today that would result in possessing eternal treasures in heaven? Moses prayed, "Make permanent the works of my hands" (Psalm 90:17, literal translation). Jesus says, "Here's how you can do that: Take treasures you could have stored up on earth (only to eventually lose them) and instead store them up in heaven, where they'll remain intact for eternity."

People are always looking for safe places to put their money. Jesus says there's ultimately only one safe place to put our money: the kingdom of God. By wisely and generously using our earthly resources, which will mean forgoing some earthly treasures, we can lay up treasures in heaven.

Returning to the question posed earlier, What is your treasure? Is it your house? car? boat? library? gun collection? Is your treasure in art, coins, or gold? Is it in savings, a retirement program, insurance policies, annuities, real estate, or commodities? Is your treasure five hundred shares of AT&T or Microsoft? Some people may own these items without them necessarily being their treasure. But every possession we hold onto presents a constant temptation that it will become our treasure.

Paul told the rich in this world that through their generosity and good deeds they may "lay up treasure for themselves as a firm foundation for the coming age" (1 Timothy 6:18-19). Christians throughout the ages have taken these passages literally and have been far less serious than we are about earthly treasures and far more serious about heavenly treasures.

John Bunyan wrote *Pilgrim's Progress* from an English prison cell to which he had been condemned for unlicensed preaching of the gospel. This is how he interpreted the words of Christ and Paul:

> Whatever good thing you do for Him, if done according to the Word,
> is laid up for you as treasure in chests and coffers, to be brought out
> to be rewarded before both men and angels, to your eternal comfort.[3]

Is this a biblical concept? Absolutely. Paul spoke about the Philippians' financial giving and explained, "Not that I am looking for a gift, but I am looking for what may be credited to your account" (Philippians 4:17). God keeps an account open for us in heaven, and every gift given for his glory is a deposit in that account. Not only God, not only others, but we are the eternal beneficiaries of our giving. Have you been making regular deposits?

"For yourselves." Does it seem strange that Jesus commands us to do what's in our own best interest? Isn't that selfish? No—God expects and commands us to act out of enlightened self-interest. Our generosity is not only for God's glory, not only for others' good, but also for our good.

Selfishness is when we pursue gain at the expense of others. But God doesn't have a limited number of treasures to distribute. When you store up treasures for yourself in heaven, it doesn't reduce the treasures available to others. In fact, it is by serving God and others that we store up heavenly treasures. Everyone gains; no one loses.

MONEY BELTS AND INEXHAUSTIBLE TREASURE

Is Jesus speaking metaphorically when he refers to "treasures"? Or is storing up treasures in heaven instead of on earth a reference to financial giving? I believe it is. Although Christ's words can be applied in principle to investing in God's kingdom the treasures of our time and talents, the primary meaning relates to giving our money and possessions.

The first indicator that Jesus is talking about our money is the *context* of his remarks. He begins this segment of his message by addressing the spiritual disciplines of giving, praying, and fasting. Because he has been talking about giving, his audience would naturally understand that the recommendation to "store up treasures for yourself in heaven" is an elaboration on the subject of giving.

Second, the word *treasure* has an obvious literal meaning. His listeners knew that "treasures on earth" were money, gems, gold, land, houses, livestock, and other valued possessions. When Jesus told them not to store up their treasures on earth but in heaven, they would naturally conclude he was saying to invest them in purposes close to God's heart.

Third, his audience was very familiar with giving, which was an important part of the instruction of the Old Testament that they were taught in homes and synagogues. He adds a new dimension to the subject, but they would not be surprised for him to address it.

Fourth, the clincher is Luke 12:33, where Jesus unmistakably connects giving with providing "treasure in heaven":

> Sell your possessions and give to the poor. Provide purses [some translations say money belts] for yourselves that will not wear out, a treasure in heaven that will not be exhausted, where no thief comes near and no moth destroys.

The use of thief and moth and treasure, and the injunction to provide money belts "for yourselves," shows that this passage in Luke is more than just a parallel passage to Matthew 6:19. It's another way of saying the same thing, but it was spoken on another occasion—and because most of his teachings aren't repeated, the repetition emphasizes its importance. This passage unmistakably connects selling one's possessions with giving them away, thereby providing treasures in heaven. The purpose is not asceticism—no longer having money— but ministry, helping the poor and needy.

The picture of the "money belt" or "purse" (either translation has merit) that doesn't wear out further develops the concept of heavenly treasures. Our giving is the conduit, container, or means that safely delivers the treasures to heaven. We provide assets for ourselves in heaven by giving away our assets on earth.

Jesus adds another insight in Luke 12 that is not present in Matthew 6. Not only is heavenly treasure not subject to thieves and moths, not only will the heavenly money belt not wear out, but there is "a treasure in heaven that will not be exhausted." This refinement is significant because it says not simply that these heavenly treasures are safe and indestructible, as Matthew 6 suggests, but that they are also inexhaustible. That is, they can be used in heaven without ever being used up. In other words, a boy who gives a little girl a drink of water out of kindness on earth will receive for this a reward that can be enjoyed without being consumed. On earth, his mother might see his good deed and bake him a cake, which he would gratefully eat. But then it would be gone. But in heaven we can enjoy and use our rewards, our heavenly treasures—whatever they may be—without ever exhausting them.

Not only will there be rewards in heaven for the cup of water given on earth, but those rewards will never disappear. The act of kindness will be remembered forever and its reward will always last. Hence, eternal rewards are not only "rewards we will receive in eternity," but rewards that are themselves eternal, imperishable, inexhaustible (1 Peter 1:4).

To say that something cannot ever be used up is more than to say it cannot be stolen or spoiled. Something could be safe and untainted, such as a meal or an admission ticket, yet once used or consumed it's gone. But our treasures in heaven are inexhaustible.

Moses prayed the oldest psalm, "Establish the work of our hands for us" (Psalm 90:17). The literal translation is "*Make permanent the work of our hands.*" This is our heart's desire—that we would do things here and now that would survive this world, that would bear fruit forever in the world to come. That is exactly what Christ promises.

CONFEDERATE CURRENCY

I use this analogy in my book *The Treasure Principle: Discovering the Secret of Joyful Giving:*

> Imagine you're alive at the end of the Civil War. You're living in the South, but you're a Northerner. You plan to move home as soon as the war's over. While in the South you've accumulated lots of Confederate currency. Now, suppose you know for a fact the North's going to win the war, and the end is imminent. What will you do with your Confederate money?
>
> If you're smart, there's only one answer. You should immediately cash in your Confederate currency for U.S. currency—the only money that will have value once the war's over. Keep only enough Confederate currency to meet your short-term needs.[4]

As believers, we have inside knowledge of a coming change in the worldwide economic situation. The currency of this world will be worthless at our death or Christ's return, both of which are imminent.

The currency of this world will be worthless at our death or Christ's return, both of which are imminent.

This knowledge should radically affect our investment strategy. For us to accumulate vast earthly treasures in the face of the inevitable future is equivalent to stockpiling Confederate money. It's not just wrong. It's stupid.

Kingdom currency, backed by the eternal treasury, is the only medium of exchange recognized by the Son of God, whose government will last forever. The currency of his kingdom is our present faithful service and sacrificial use of our resources for him. The payoff in eternity will be what Paul called "a firm foundation," consisting of treasures beyond our wildest dreams.

In the financial world, there are experts known as "market timers." When they read the signs that the stock market is about to take a downward turn, they recommend switching funds immediately into more dependable or consistent investments, such as treasury bills, money market funds, or certificates of deposit. In Matthew 6, Jesus functions as the foremost investment advisor, the ultimate expert in the economics of earth and heaven. His strategy is simple. He tells us to switch investment vehicles once and for all. He says we should transfer our funds from earth—which is volatile and ready to take a permanent dive—to heaven, which is totally dependable and is coming soon to forever replace earth's economy.

In Wall Street terms, Christ is bearish when it comes to investing on earth. His financial forecast for this world is ultimately bleak. But he's unreservedly bullish about investing in heaven, where every market indicator is eternally positive!

WHERE IS YOUR HEART?

Christ's words were direct and profound: "Where your treasure is, there your heart will be also" (Matthew 6:21). What we do with our possessions is a sure indicator of what's in our hearts. Jesus is saying, "Show me your checkbook, your credit card statement, and your receipts for cash expenditures, and I'll show you where your heart is." What we do with our money doesn't lie. It is a bold statement to God of what we truly value.

But what we do with our money doesn't simply *indicate* where our heart *is*. According to Jesus, it *determines* where our heart *goes*. This is an amazing and exciting truth. If I want my heart to be in one particular place and not in another, then I need to put my money in that place and not in the other.

I've heard people say, "I want more of a heart for missions." I always respond, "Jesus tells you exactly how to get it. Put your money in missions, and your heart will follow."

Do you wish you had a greater heart for the poor and lost? Then give your money to help the poor and reach the lost. Do you want your heart to be in your church? Put your money there. Your heart will always be where your money is and not where your money isn't. If most of your money is in mutual funds, retirement, your house, or your hobby, that's where your heart's going to be.

Suppose you're giving to help African children with AIDS, or you're sponsoring a child in Haiti. When you see an article on the subject, you're hooked. If you're sending money to plant churches in India and an earthquake hits India, you watch the news and fervently pray. Why? Because your heart is where your treasure is.

"My heart isn't in all the things of God." Is it because your treasure isn't in the things of God? Put your resources, your assets, your money and possessions, your time and talents and energies into the things of God. As surely as the compass needle follows north, your heart will follow your treasure. Money leads; hearts follow.

TWO PERSPECTIVES

After discussing the two treasures, Jesus speaks of two perspectives: "The eye is the lamp of the body. If your eyes are good, your whole body will be full of light. But if your eyes are bad, your whole body will be full of darkness" (Matthew 6:22-23).

Physical vision is used here as a metaphor for *perspective*, the way we look at life. Unbelievers look at life as a brief interval that begins at birth and ends at death. In looking to the future, they look no further than their own life span, if even that. Their vision is pitifully short and narrow, restricted to the horizons of the world. Like a myopic horse with blinders on, the person without Christ can see neither far nor wide. Bereft of eternal perspective, unbelievers are bound to take all the wrong turns and come to all the wrong conclusions, thinking, "If this life is all there is, why deny myself any pleasure or possessions?" Given this premise, why would they come to any other conclusion? People only *live* for a higher purpose when they *see* a higher purpose.

As believers in Christ, our theology gives us perspective. It tells us that this life is the preface—not the book. It's the preliminaries—not the main event. It's the tune-up—not the concert.

When you're on a long airplane flight, you naturally talk to people, socialize, eat, read, pray, sleep, or maybe talk about where you're going. But what would you think if a passenger by the window seat started hanging curtains over the window, taped photographs to the seat in front of him, painted murals, and put up wall hangings? You'd think, *Hey, it's not that long of a trip. Once we get to the destination, none of this will matter.* Even a long plane flight is short compared to the span of your entire life.

I think of our lives in terms of a dot and a line, signifying two phases. Our present life on earth is the dot. It begins. It ends. It's brief. However, from the dot, a line extends that goes on forever. That line is eternity, which Christians will spend in heaven.

Right now we're living in the dot. But what are we living for? The short-sighted person lives for the dot. The person with perspective lives for the line. This earth, and our time here, is the dot. Our beloved Bridegroom, the coming wedding, the Great Reunion, and our eternal home in the New Heavens and New Earth . . . *they're all on the line.*

The person who lives for the dot lives for treasures on earth that end in junkyards. The person who lives for the line lives for treasures in heaven that never end.

The Dot: The Line:
Life on earth   Life in heaven

Giving is living for the line.

We'll each part with our money. The only question is when. We have no choice but to part with it later. But we do have the choice of whether to part with it now. We can keep earthly treasure for the moment, and we may get some temporary enjoyment from it. But if we give it away, we'll enjoy eternal treasures that will never be taken from us.

Foolish people live for the dot. Wise people live for the line.

It's all about perspective. The believer's view of reality should be radically different than the nonbeliever's. We should live differently because we see differently. We witness the same current events, but interpret them differently. We eat the same food, exchange the same currency, but live according to two different purposes. These purposes are based squarely on two different perspectives—one that looks at life in the short run and the other that looks at life in the long run.

When our eyes are set on eternity, the news that someone has come to know the Savior means a great deal more than the news of a salary raise or the prospect of getting the latest high-tech gadget. Of course, the salary raise, and perhaps the gadget, can be used for the kingdom of God. But the point is that neither one in itself is ultimately important, whereas new birth, which affects the eternal destiny of a precious human being, is vitally important.

The Christian who accumulates land and houses and bank accounts but doesn't invest in eternity isn't depicted by Jesus in his sermon as unrighteous, greedy, or selfish—though he might be any or all of these. Rather, he's depicted as shortsighted. Blind. Unwise is too weak a word—this person is stupid, stupid on the grandest scale, as stupid as the rich fool of Luke 12. As stupid as the man who found the treasure in the field would have been to hold on to his paltry possessions instead of trading them in for what was of far greater value.

The believer's view of reality should be radically different than the nonbeliever's.

The one with good eyes, the one with an eternal perspective, is accurate in his or her appraisal of what is important. Like the poor widow in Mark 12, this person is eternally wise. With vision corrected by biblical "laser surgery," this person sees life through the eyes of eternity. Unlike the average person, the believer stares through the haze and peers beyond the horizons of this world to another.

MOMENTARY SACRIFICE, ETERNAL GAIN

The patriarchs lived as "aliens and strangers on earth," spending their days "longing for a better country—a heavenly one" (Hebrews 11:13-16). Peter encouraged Christians to find joy by focusing not on the trial that will go on only "a little while," but on their heavenly inheritance that will never perish (1 Peter 1:4-9; 5:10). Paul said, "I consider that our present sufferings are not worth comparing with the glory that will be revealed in us" (Romans 8:18). "For our light and momentary troubles are achieving for us an eternal glory that far outweighs them all" (2 Corinthians 4:17).

Note the contrasts: "light" versus that which will "far outweigh," "momentary" versus "eternal," and "troubles" versus "glory." Paul is teaching us how to have a proper perspective: "View the present in light of the future; see time in light of eternity; look beyond sacrifice to reward; bear the cross while anticipating the crown." Paul speaks not of a glory achieved for Christ but for us. Likewise, Jesus didn't say, "Store up for God treasures in heaven"; he said, "Store up for *yourselves* treasures in heaven" (Matthew 6:20, italics mine). Christ will be glorified as the sole object of our worship in heaven. Scripture teaches that we will not only behold his glory but also participate in it. This gives the believer an incentive to do what the Philippian Christians did in giving to Paul's missionary work—withdrawing funds from their earthly accounts in order to have them credited to their heavenly account (Philippians 4:17).

Suppose you disliked split pea soup but I told you that if you would eat split pea soup for a week, I would provide you and your family with all the groceries you needed for the rest of your lives. Wouldn't this promise change your perspective on eating split pea soup? You still might not like it, but you would gladly eat it in light of the promised rewards (and you might even develop a taste for it). This is an example of delayed gratification. Soldiers, athletes, and farmers all know that short-term sacrifices are justifiable in light of their long-term benefits (2 Timothy 2:3-6). This same principle applies to those who adopt an eternal perspective.

Suppose I offer you $1,000 to spend today however you want. Not a bad deal. But suppose I give you a choice—you can either have that $1,000 today, or you can have ten million dollars if you'll wait one year—then ten million more every year thereafter.

Only a fool would take the $1,000 today. Yet that's what we do whenever we grab onto what will last for only a moment, forgoing something far more valuable we could enjoy later for much longer. A year may seem a long time to wait. But after it's done—as when our lives here are done—it will seem like it passed quickly.

The money God entrusts to us is eternal investment capital. Every day is an opportunity to buy up more shares in his kingdom.

You can't take it with you, but you can send it on ahead.

It's a revolutionary concept that changed my life and my family's. If you embrace it, I guarantee it will change your life as well.

THE MOST HIGH YIELDS

Financial planners have a hard time convincing people to look ahead instead of focusing on today, this week, or this year. "Don't think this year," they'll tell you. "Think thirty years from now." Then they'll share ways to prepare for thirty years from now by planning, budgeting, saving, contributing to an IRA, investing in this mutual fund or that real estate partnership. But the truth is, thinking thirty years ahead is only slightly less shortsighted than thinking thirty days ahead. Wise people think ahead not just to the retirement years, not merely to the end of their earthly life, but to eternity. We shouldn't say, "Think thirty years ahead," but "Think thirty million years ahead."

Financial counselors point out the difference between investing the same yearly amounts in an Individual Retirement Account starting at age twenty-five or age forty. At retirement, the bottom-line difference is huge. This is good insight for the Christian who is storing up for eternity: The sooner you get started, the more you'll have awaiting you.

A financial counselor will say, "You can't go back at age sixty-five and snap your fingers to compensate for forty years of poor planning." But what's far more important is that you can't reach the end of your life, snap your fingers, and compensate for a lifetime of poor planning to meet God. The rich fool is proof of that.

God's eternal prospectus bears a careful look in light of its guaranteed rate of interest. Jesus promises an ultimate return of a hundred times—a 10,000 percent rate of interest that lasts forever (Matthew 19:29). What earthly investment compares to that?

Based on Christ's words, let me assume the role of "eternal financial counselor" and offer some advice: Choose your investments carefully, compare rates of interest, and evaluate how your investments will be working for you a few million years from now.

Unbelievers see with what Jesus called the "bad eye." The Christian's view of finances, seen through a "good eye," should be radically different. True, we may participate in some of the same earthly investments as unbelievers. Occasionally our short-term goals will appear similar. But our long-term goals and purposes should be fundamentally different.

TWO MASTERS

Having already spoken of two treasuries and two perspectives, Jesus now speaks of two masters. He says that although we might *have* both God and money, we cannot *serve* both God and Money.

I might have two jobs, three sisters, or five friends, but only one spouse. Some relationships by their very nature are exclusive. The most basic of these is our relationship with God. There's a throne in each life only big enough for one. Christ may be on that throne. Money may be on that throne. But both cannot occupy that throne.

Mammon is a false god. It is antichrist in the true meaning of the word. The Greek preposition *anti-* does not fundamentally mean "against" but "instead of."

105

Hence, antichrist is not just "one who is against Christ" but "one who is a substitute for Christ." When he named it Mammon, Christ personified money to portray its danger. Mammon is a god-substitute, a false messiah.

The four chapters that follow develop in more detail the concepts of eternity and eternal rewards. Although this subject is almost never dealt with in books on money and possessions, I believe it provides the essential perspective that allows us to see our money and possessions the way God sees them—through the eyes of eternity. Only when we gain an eternal perspective will we eagerly follow our Lord's command to devote our brief lives on earth to the pursuit of eternal treasure.

> Only when we gain an eternal perspective will we eagerly follow our Lord's command to devote our brief lives on earth to the pursuit of eternal treasure.

Are you investing in the right treasury? Are you adopting the right perspective? Are you serving the right master?

There's nothing wrong with having money. We need it to live on while we're still in this foreign land away from home, and God graciously provides it for us. Still, we must understand its limits. Like Confederate money near the end of the Civil War, it's only good for a very short period of time, and that time is running out. It will be worthless once we get home. We're here on earth on a short-term visa. One day soon it's going to expire.

Jesus gave us a choice—a life wasted in the pursuit of wealth on earth, or a life invested in the pursuit of wealth in heaven. Every heartbeat brings us one moment closer to eternity. Every day, the person whose treasure is on earth is headed *away* from his treasure. Every day, the person whose treasure is in heaven is headed *toward* his treasure. Whoever spends his life heading away from his treasure has reason to despair. Whoever spends his life headed toward his treasure has reason to rejoice.

Where's your treasure? Are you heading toward it or away from it? Do you have reason to despair or reason to rejoice?

Is it time to start relocating your treasure?

CHAPTER 8

The Steward's Eternal Destiny

It ought to be the business of every day to prepare for our last day. MATTHEW HENRY

He who provides for this life but takes not care for eternity is wise for a moment but a fool forever.
JOHN TILLOTSON

An ancient story goes like this: A slave travels with his master to Baghdad. Early one morning, while milling through the marketplace, the slave sees Death in human form. Death gives him a threatening look. The slave recoils in terror, convinced that Death intends to take him that day.

The slave runs to his master and says, "Help me. I have seen Death, and his threatening look tells me he intends to take my life this very day. I must escape him. Please, master, let me leave now and flee on camel so that by tonight I can reach Samara, where Death cannot find me."

His master agrees, and the terrified servant rides like the wind for the fifteen-hour journey to Samara.

A few hours later, the master sees Death among the throngs in Baghdad. He boldly approaches Death and asks him, "Why did you give my servant a threatening look?"

"That was not a threatening look," Death replies. "That was a look of surprise. You see, I was amazed to see your servant today in Baghdad, for I have an appointment with him tonight in Samara."

While the story's imagery is problematic (it's our righteous Master, not Death, who has the power to call us home at his appointed time), the moral is on target. The time of our death is unknown. The way of our death is unpredictable. But the fact of our death is inescapable. The statistics are unwavering: 100 percent of those who are born die. We may spend our lives running from death and denying death, but that won't stop death from coming at its appointed time. "No man has power over the wind to contain it; so no one has power over the day of his death" (Ecclesiastes 8:8).

Talking about death won't bring it a moment sooner. But it will give us opportunity to prepare for what lies ahead. If life's greatest certainty is death, wouldn't it be foolish not to prepare for what lies beyond this life? Any life that leaves us unprepared for death is a wasted life.

What does this have to do with our attitude toward money and possessions? It has *everything* to do with it. Without a doubt, the single greatest contributor to our inability to see money and possessions in their true light is our persistent failure to see our present lives through the lens of eternity.

THE LOST SENSE OF THE ETERNAL

A startling thing has happened among Western Christians. Many of us habitually think and act as if there were no eternity—or as if what we do in this present life has no eternal consequences.

Many of us habitually think and act as if there were no eternity.

How many sermons about heaven or hell have most of us heard lately? How many modern gospel booklets even mention the words *heaven* or *hell*? The trend is to focus on our present circumstances instead of our eternal future. Yet Scripture states that eternal realities should influence the character of our present life, right down to every word we speak and every action we take (James 2:12; 2 Peter 3:11-12).

In those rare times when we do seriously consider the afterlife, it seems strange or dreamlike, so otherworldly as to be unreal. So we come back to "reality"—our present lives and possessions that we can see, hear, touch, feel, and taste. Things are real. *Now* is real. So we return to the pressing business of the day, that which is immediately relevant, those all-important matters of the present. These might include what's happening in Hollywood, on Wall Street, in Washington or London, or the NFL or NBA; or what new self-help technique can make us beautiful or happy; or how we can decorate our house, or what kind of car we want to buy; or where we can get a low-interest loan. We live as if these shadowlands were the real world, the ultimate reality. But Scripture tells us they are not.

Our devotion to the newspaper and neglect of the Bible is the ultimate testimony to our interest in the short-range over the long-range. We fail to ask how expensive clothes, cruises, face-lifts, breast implants, and liposuctions will serve eternal purposes. Such questions are fit for theologians and pious old ladies, perhaps, but not for us—which would be true enough if only theologians and old ladies died, met their Maker, and spent eternity somewhere!

Being oblivious to eternity leaves us experts in the trivial and novices in the significant. We can name that tune, name that starting lineup, name that actor's movie debut, and detail the differences between computers or four-wheel drives. None of this is wrong, of course, but it's certainly revealing when we consider that most Christians, let alone the general public, do not even have an accurate picture of what the Bible says will happen to us after we die. We major in the momentary and minor in the momentous.

What does God have to say about our lives here? He says this life is so brief that we are like grass that grows up in the morning and wilts in the afternoon (Isaiah 40:6-8). Our life here is but "mist that appears for a little while and then vanishes" (James 4:14).

When my friend Leona Bryant discovered she had only a short time to live, she told me of radical changes in her perspective. "The most striking thing that's happened," she said, "is that I find myself totally uninterested in all the conversations about material things. Things used to matter to me, but now I find my thoughts are never on possessions, but always on Christ and people. I consider it a privilege that I can live each day, knowing I will die soon. What a difference it makes!"

David likewise sought to gain God's perspective in light of the brevity of life:

> Show me, O Lord, my life's end and the number of my days; let me know how fleeting is my life. You have made my days a mere hand-breadth; the span of my years is as nothing before you. Each man's life is but a breath. Man is a mere phantom as he goes to and fro: He bustles about, but only in vain; he heaps up wealth, not knowing who will get it. But now, Lord, what do I look for? My hope is in you. (Psalm 39:4-7)

Because this life is so brief, we might easily conclude it's inconsequential. Our lives may seem like pebbles dropped in a pond. They create ripples for a moment, tiny wrinkles that smooth out, then are gone forever. Abandoned tombstones with names no one remembers are a stark reminder of our eventual anonymity in this world. What do you know about your great-grandfather? What will your great-grandchildren know about you?

Our brief stay here may seem unimportant, but nothing could be further from the truth. The Bible tells us that although others may not remember us or care what our lives here have been, God will remember perfectly and cares very much—so much that the door of eternity swings on the hinges of our present lives.

The Bible tells us that this life lays the foundation upon which eternal life is built. Eternity will hold for us what we have invested there during our life on earth.

Scripture makes clear that the one central business of this life is to prepare for the next!

THE LONG TOMORROW: WHAT LIES AHEAD?

As no piece of a puzzle can be understood apart from the greater context of the full puzzle, so our present lives—including what we should do with all our money and possessions—cannot be understood apart from the greater context of eternity. In the rest of the chapter, I'll try to paint the backdrop of what A. W. Tozer called "the long tomorrow," against which the question of money—and all questions of life—must be properly viewed.

Many have been taught a few things about the Tribulation and the Antichrist and have certain beliefs that fit their particular cosmic eschatology. But we tend to be very vague about our personal eschatologies, the eternal futures awaiting each of us. The only certainty seems to be that if we know Christ as Savior we'll be in heaven. We might say, "Just knowing I'll be in heaven is good enough for me." Apparently, however, it isn't good enough for God. His Word tells us specifically about other aspects of our personal futures. And many readers will find them quite different than what they've supposed.

DEATH AND JUDGMENT

We spoke already of the next item on our eternal agenda—death. "Man is destined to die once, and after that to face judgment" (Hebrews 9:27). The old saying, "Nothing is certain but death and taxes," is only half true, since there are tax evaders, but no death evaders. Those alive at the return of Christ may not technically die, but the result will be the same—their earthly lives will abruptly end, and they will move immediately to the afterlife.

Hebrews 9:27 continues our written-in-stone itinerary—man is destined to die "and after that to face judgment." This judgment is for all men, not some. Whether we go to Christ in death or he comes to us in his return, we face judgment. This doctrine is as old as the Church itself. The statement, "Christ will come again to judge the living and the dead," found its way into the Apostles' Creed (A.D. 250), the Nicene Creed (A.D. 325), and the Athanasian Creed (A.D. 400).

There seems to be built into every person, society, and religion, a basic belief that good deserves reward and evil deserves punishment. There seems to be built into every person, society, and religion, a basic belief that good deserves reward and evil deserves punishment, and both will ultimately get what they deserve. God has written his moral law on human hearts (Romans 2:12-16). This includes an inborn sense that one day we will be judged in the light of that law.

Scripture confirms this inbred human expectation of judgment. It says that God will judge everyone (Acts 17:31), and he will judge fairly (Genesis 18:25). Specifically, he will judge us according to our deeds: "I the Lord search the heart and examine the mind, to reward a man according to his conduct, according to what his deeds deserve" (Jeremiah 17:10).

"Does not he who weighs the heart perceive it? Does not he who guards your life know it? Will he not repay each person according to what he has done?" (Proverbs 24:12).

"They will be paid back with harm for the harm they have done" (2 Peter 2:13).

All men should live each day with this awesome awareness: "But they will have to give an account to him who is ready to judge the living and the dead" (1 Peter 4:5).

God will judge us with total knowledge: "Nothing in all creation is hidden from God's sight. Everything is uncovered and laid bare before the eyes of him to whom we must give account" (Hebrews 4:13).

Because his knowledge is total, his judgment is comprehensive and detailed: "Men will have to give account on the day of judgment for every careless word they have spoken" (Matthew 12:36).

His judgment extends to what is hidden to others: "God will bring every deed into judgment, including every hidden thing, whether it is good or evil" (Ecclesiastes 12:14). He even knows the motives of men's hearts and judges us in that light (1 Corinthians 4:5).

We are all sinners and the wages of sin is death (Romans 3:23; 6:23). But an all-holy God, out of love for us, judged Jesus for our sins (Isaiah 53:9-10). Only by embracing Christ's atonement for our sins can we escape the everlasting punishment due us (Romans 6:23; 2 Corinthians 5:21). God's justice was satisfied, but only at the cost of his own blood. To purchase our redemption, Jesus experienced an eternity of hell in a few hours on the cross.

Our Lord said, "To him who is thirsty I will give to drink without cost from the spring of the water of life" (Revelation 21:6). Without cost to us, but at unimaginable cost to him—a cost that will be visible for eternity, as we behold his nail-scarred hands and feet (John 20:24-29). Bonhoeffer was right: grace is free, but it is not cheap.

THE UNBELIEVER'S JUDGMENT IN HELL

Hell is a place of punishment designed for Satan and the fallen angels (Matthew 25:41-46; Revelation 20:10). However, it will also be inhabited by those who do not accept God's gift of redemption in Christ (Revelation 20:12-15).

Hell is an actual place, clearly and graphically spoken of by Jesus (Matthew 10:28; 13:40-42; Mark 9:43-44). Hell is as literal as heaven (Psalm 11:4-6), and despite recent claims to the contrary (even among some evangelicals), as eternal as heaven (Matthew 25:46). Hell is a horrible place of suffering and everlasting destruction (Matthew 13:41-42; 2 Thessalonians 1:9). In hell, people are fully conscious and retain all of their capacities and desires with no hope for any fulfillment for all eternity (Luke 16:22-31).

Hell is indescribably dreadful. If we trust the Bible, we must realize that hell is undeniably real. Hell is something most of us do not want to believe in, but who are we to tell God he's wrong? He so wants us not to go to hell that he paid the ultimate price so we wouldn't have to. Nevertheless, apart from trusting Christ for salvation, any person's eternal future will be spent in hell.

Because God is fair, hell won't be the same for everyone. The severity of punishment will vary with the degree of truth known and the nature and number of sins committed. This concept is foreign to most Christians, but is clearly taught in Scripture (Matthew 11:20-24; Luke 20:45-47; Romans 2:3-5). This is no consolation, however, since the "best" of hell will still be hell—eternal exclusion from the presence of God and the soothing light of his grace.

THE BELIEVER'S EXPERIENCE IN HEAVEN

I've written novels that develop themes of eternal perspective and portray conversations and events in heaven.[1] People often ask me why I portray heaven as such a real and tangible place. First, because every time Scripture speaks of heaven it portrays it as a real place inhabited by real people, not by ghosts or pale, neutered Milquetoasts floating in the clouds. Second, because we desperately need an antidote to all the vague, dull, and notoriously unbiblical concepts about heaven that cause us not to long for it but to dread it.

In my nonfiction book In Light of Eternity: Perspectives on Heaven, I quote believers who admit they have feared heaven, then suggest why this may be:

> Because of pervasive distortions of what heaven is like, it's common for Christians to not look forward to heaven—or even to dread it. I think there's only one explanation for how these appalling viewpoints have gripped so many of God's children: Satan. Demonic deception.
>
> Jesus said of the devil, "When he lies he speaks his native language, for he is a liar and the father of lies" (John 8:44). Some of Satan's favorite lies are about heaven. Revelation 13:6 tells us the satanic beast "opened his mouth to blaspheme God, and to slander his name and his dwelling place and those who live in heaven." Our enemy slanders three things: God's person, God's people, and God's place—heaven.
>
> After being forcibly evicted from heaven (Isaiah 14:12-14), the devil is bitter not only toward God, but toward us and the place that's no longer his. (It must be maddening for him to realize we're now entitled to the home he was kicked out of.) What better way for demons to attack than to whisper lies about the very place God tells us to set our hearts and minds on (Colossians 3:1-2)?[2]

Jesus commands us to store up for ourselves treasures in heaven. Yet because we've bought into misconceptions of heaven, failing to look at what Scripture tells us, we cling to earth as our home.[3] Naturally, then, we tend to lay up our treasures here rather than there. Because we cannot devote our lives to laying up treasures in a heaven we're not looking forward to, it's critical that we take time here to address the question of what heaven is like.

As he was about to leave this world, Jesus said to his disciples, "There are many rooms in my Father's home, and I am going to prepare a place for you. . . . When everything is ready, I will come and get you, so that you will always be with me where I am" (John 14:2-3, NLT).

We were made for a person and a place. Jesus is the person. Heaven is the place. And Jesus is the one building that place for us.

Before our children were born, my wife, Nanci, and I prepared a place for them. The quality of the place we prepared for our daughters was limited only by our skills, resources, and imaginations.

A good carpenter envisions what he wants to build. He plans and designs. Then he does his work, carefully and skillfully fashioning it to exact specifications. He takes pride in the work he's done and loves to show it off. And Jesus isn't just any carpenter—we already know he's the Creator of the world and he built everything we see. Heaven is his greatest building project.

We were made for a person and a place. Jesus is the person. Heaven is the place.

For Christians, heaven is our home. Paul said, "As long as we are at home in the body we are away from the Lord. . . . We . . . would prefer to be away from the body and at home with the Lord" (2 Corinthians 5:6-8). Paul said we'd prefer to be in heaven, our true home. Home is the place of acceptance, security, rest, refuge, deep personal relationships, and great memories.

God's people, aliens and strangers on earth, spend their lives "looking forward to a country they can call their own" and "looking for a better place, a heavenly homeland" (Hebrews 11:14, 16, NLT). The capital of this heavenly country will be a "city with eternal foundations, a city designed and built by God" (Hebrews 11:10, NLT). This city will have all the freshness, vitality, and openness of the country with all the vibrancy, interdependence, and relationships of a city. A city without crime, litter, smog, sirens, seaminess, or slums.

Heaven will have an endless supply of fresh water and delicious food. No famine or drought. Christ promised we would eat and drink with him—along with Abraham and others (Matthew 8:11). We'll meet and converse with other inhabitants of heaven. Not only Abraham, Isaac, and Jacob, but Moses, David, Ruth, Esther, Mary, and Peter. I look forward to conversations with C. S. Lewis, A. W. Tozer, Jonathan Edwards, and Amy Carmichael.

We'll converse with angels. Because angels are "ministering spirits" who serve us (Hebrews 1:14), we'll get to know those who protected us during our years on earth.

We'll enjoy and share with others the treasures we laid up for ourselves in heaven while we lived on earth (Matthew 6:19-21). We'll open our dwelling places to entertain people (Luke 16:9).

God gave Adam and Eve creativity in their unfallen state that was twisted but remained when they fell. He will surely not give us less creativity in heaven but *more*, unmarred by sin, unlimited by mortality. We will compose, write, paint, carve, build, plant, and grow.

There will be no temple, no church buildings. Christ will be the focus of all. Worship will be unaffected, without pretense or distraction. We'll be lost in our worship, overcome by God's magnificence and the privilege of being his children.

In Revelation 5 we're told of a choir of angels numbering ten thousand times ten thousand—that's 100 million! And then we're told that the whole rest of creation adds its voices to these 100 million. The 100 million are merely an ensemble on the stage. Can you imagine the power of the song?

Will we learn in heaven? Definitely. We're told that in the coming ages God will continuously reveal to us the "incomparable riches of his grace" (Ephesians 2:7). When we die, we'll know a lot more than we do now, but we'll keep learning about God and his creation and each other throughout eternity.

Will we remember our lives and relationships on earth? Of course. (We'll be smarter in heaven, not dumber!) Remembrance is important to God, which is why the heavenly city has memorials of people and events of earth (Revelation 21:12-14). It's also why God keeps in heaven "a scroll of remembrance," written in God's presence, "concerning those who feared the Lord and honored his name" (Malachi 3:16). The pain of the past will be gone. But memories of being together in the trenches, walking with Christ, and experiencing intimate times with family and friends will remain.

Will we know our loved ones in heaven? Certainly. We'll know even those we didn't know on earth, just as Peter, James, and John recognized Moses and Elijah when they joined Jesus (Luke 9:28-33), though they could not have known what they looked like. After entering heaven, the martyrs look down on earth and clearly remember their lives, fully aware of what's happening there (Revelation 6:9-11). Heaven isn't characterized by ignorance of events on earth but by perspective on them.

Heaven will offer much-needed rest to the weary (Revelation 14:13). What feels better than putting your head on the pillow after a hard day's work or kicking back to read a good book with a cold drink by your side?

But rest renews us, revitalizes us to become active again. Heaven will offer refreshing activity, productive and unthwarted—like Adam and Eve's work in Eden before sin brought the curse on the ground.

In heaven, we're told, "his servants will serve him" (Revelation 22:3). This means we'll be active, because to "serve" means to work, to expend effort, to do something. Service involves responsibilities, duties, effort, planning, and creativity to do work well.

We'll lead and exercise authority in heaven, making important decisions. We'll reign with Christ (2 Timothy 2:12; Revelation 3:21), not temporarily but "for ever and ever" (Revelation 22:5). "Reigning" implies specific delegated responsibilities for those under our leadership (Luke 19:17-19). We'll rule over the world and even over angels (1 Corinthians 6:2-3).

When God brings heaven down to the new earth, he "will wipe every tear from their eyes" (Revelation 21:4). What an intimate picture—God's hands will touch the face of each individual child, removing every tear. The same verse says, "There will be no more death or mourning or crying or pain." As the Irish poet Thomas Moore put it, "Earth has no sorrow that Heaven cannot heal."

No hospitals. No cemeteries. No sin. No evil. No fear. No abuse, rape, murder, drugs, drunkenness, bombs, guns, or terrorism.

Heaven will be deeply appreciated by the disabled, who will be liberated from ravaged bodies and minds, and by the sick and elderly who will be free from their pains and restrictions. They will walk and run and see and hear, some for the first time. Hymn writer Fanny Crosby said, "Don't pity me for my blindness, for the first face I ever see will be the face of my Lord Jesus."

God is the Creator of diversity. People of every tribe and nation and tongue will worship the Lamb together (Revelation 7:9-10).

Heaven will be the home of relentless joy. The greatest joy will be marrying our bridegroom, Jesus Christ. If we love Christ, we long to be with him. The next greatest joy will be reuniting with our departed loved ones. I don't like to be away from my family, but what keeps me going is the anticipation of reunion. The longer the separation, the sweeter the reunion. I haven't seen my mom for twenty years, my childhood friend Jerry for nine years, my dad for five. Some will be reunited with parents they've not seen for fifty years and with children lost long ago. For Christians, death is never the end of a relationship but only an interruption to be followed by glorious reunion.

Heaven is the Christian's certain hope, a hope that can and should sustain us through life's darkest hours. But this doesn't happen automatically. We must choose to think about heaven and center our lives around it: "Set your sights on the realities of heaven, where Christ sits at God's right hand. . . . Let heaven fill your thoughts" (Colossians 3:1-2, NLT).

THE BELIEVER'S JUDGMENT IN HEAVEN

Heaven will be a wonderful place. But Scripture plainly tells us there is a judgment of believers that will determine for all eternity our positions or roles in heaven.

The Bible teaches two eternal judgments, one for unbelievers and one for believers (John 5:28-29). All true believers will pass the judgment of faith in Christ. All unbelievers will fail the judgment of their faith in Christ at the great white throne, since their names are not written in the Book of Life (Revelation 20:11-15).

But faith is not the only thing judged. Scripture repeatedly states that all men, not just unbelievers, will be judged for their works (Proverbs 24:12; Ecclesiastes 12:14). The unbeliever's judgment of works comes at the great white throne (Revelation 20:11-12). The believer will not be condemned at the great white throne, but nonetheless he or she still faces a judgment of works, at what is called the "judgment seat of Christ."

Scripture teaches with unmistakable clarity that all believers in Christ will give an account of their lives to their Lord.

The Lord's evaluation of the seven churches in Revelation 2 and 3 makes clear that he is watching us, evaluating us. He is "keeping score." As an instructor gives grades to his students, Christ gives grades to his churches. To Christians, Jesus says, "I am he who searches hearts and minds, and I will repay each of you according to your deeds" (Revelation 2:23).

Scripture teaches with unmistakable clarity that all believers in Christ will give an account of their lives to their Lord (Romans 14:10-12). We will be judged by him according to our works, both good and bad (2 Corinthians 5:10). The result of this will be the gain or loss of eternal rewards (1 Corinthians 3:12-15; 2 Corinthians 5:9-10; Romans 14:10-12).

God's Word treats this judgment with great sobriety. It does not portray it as a meaningless formality or going through the motions before we get on to the real business of heavenly bliss. Rather, Scripture presents it as a monumental event in which things of eternal significance are brought to light and things of eternal consequence are put into effect.

> If any man builds on this foundation [the foundation of Christ] using gold, silver, costly stones, wood, hay or straw, his work will be shown for what it is, because the Day will bring it to light. It will be revealed with fire, and the fire will test the quality of each man's work. If what he has built survives, he will receive his reward. If it is burned up, he will suffer loss; he himself will be saved, but only as one escaping through the flames. (1 Corinthians 3:12-15)

Our works are what we have done with our resources—time, energy, talents, money, possessions. The fire of God's holiness will reveal the quality of these works, the eternal significance of what we've done with our God-given assets and opportunities. The fate of the works will be determined by their nature. If they are made of the right stuff (gold, silver, costly stones), they'll withstand and be purified by the fire. But no matter how nice our works of wood, hay, and straw may look in the display case of this world, they will not withstand the incendiary gaze of God's Son in the next.

"We must all appear before the judgment seat of Christ, that each one may receive what is due him for the things done while in the body, whether good or bad" (2 Corinthians 5:10).

"Whether good or bad" in the above verse may be the most disturbing phrase in the New Testament. It's so disturbing, in fact, that I've found any honest attempts to deal with it are met with tremendous resistance. Equally disturbing is the direct statement to Christians that not only will they receive reward from Christ for their good works, but "anyone who does wrong will be repaid for his wrong, and there is no favoritism" (Colossians 3:25). Since Christ has paid the price for our sins, if we have confessed and received forgiveness of our sins, what can this mean?

Our sins are totally forgiven when we come to Christ, and we stand justified in him. Nevertheless, Scripture speaks about a coming judgment of our works, not our sins. When we commit sins or neglect doing righteous acts we should have done, we are not doing what we could to lay up precious stones on the foundation of Christ. Therefore, these sins contribute to our "suffering loss." Through this loss of reward, the believer is considered to be receiving his "due" for his works "whether good or bad." So what we do as believers, both good and bad, will have eternal effects.

In light of this, the writer of Hebrews says, "Therefore, since we are surrounded by such a great cloud of witnesses, let us throw off everything that hinders and the sin that so easily entangles, and let us run with perseverance the race marked out for us" (Hebrews 12:1). Sin entangles our feet, puts us out of the competition, and results in losing the race and the prize.

God is for us, not against us (Romans 8:31). He has assured us we won't face the Great White Throne Judgment. He wants to commend us at the judgment seat of Christ. He doesn't want the works of our lifetime to go up in smoke. He wants us to have eternal rewards—and he has given us every resource in Christ to live the godly life that will result in those eternal rewards (2 Peter 1:3).

For those who have served Christ faithfully, the judgment seat will be a time of commendation and celebration. He will reward us for acts of love that no one else even noticed.

DOES GOD REALLY CARE ABOUT OUR WORKS?

The five-hundred-year-old play *Everyman* is a picture of all people. As Everyman faces Death, he looks among his friends for a companion. Only one friend would accompany him on the journey through death to final judgment. His name? Good Deeds.

Some balk at such a picture. Yet it's explicitly biblical: "Then I heard a voice from heaven say, 'Write: Blessed are the dead who die in the Lord from now on.' 'Yes,' says the Spirit, 'they will rest from their labor, for their deeds will follow them'" (Revelation 14:13).

In Revelation 19:7-8, we're told "the wedding of the Lamb has come, and his bride has made herself ready. Fine linen, bright and clean, was given her to wear. (Fine linen stands for the righteous acts of the saints.)"

Note that the parenthetical statement in the preceding verse is not mine, but God's! This passage offers several surprises. We might have expected to be told that Christ makes the bride ready, rather than she herself. We could also have expected that the fine linen would stand for the righteousness of Christ, or perhaps the righteous faith of the saints. But what we are told is that it stands for the righteous *acts* or works of the saints. If we will indeed be clothed according to our works for Christ, this verse suggests that some Christians will be scantily clad!

If we will indeed be clothed according to our works for Christ, some Christians will be scantily clad!

We've been deceived into thinking that *works* is a dirty word. Not true. God condemns works done to earn salvation and works done to impress others. But our Lord enthusiastically commends works done for the right reasons. Immediately after saying our salvation is "not by works," Paul adds: "For we are God's workmanship, created in Christ Jesus to do good works, which God prepared in advance for us to do" (Ephesians 2:8-10).

God has a lifetime of good works for each of us to do. Many of these works he intends to do with our money and possessions. He will reward us according to whether or not we do them. Scripture ties God's reward-giving to his character: "God is not unjust; he will not forget your work and the love you have shown him as you have helped his people and continue to help them" (Hebrews 6:10). The verses that follow in Hebrews 6 tell us that if we are to inherit God's promised blessings we must not become lazy but diligent in our God-given works.

James repeatedly states that good works are essential to the Christian life (James 2:17-18, 22, 24, 26). "Who is wise and understanding among you? Let him show it by his good life, by deeds done in the humility that comes from wisdom" (James 3:13).

God gives us eternal rewards for doing good works (Ephesians 6:8; Romans 2:6, 10), persevering under persecution (Luke 6:22-23), showing compassion to the needy (Luke 14:13-14), and treating our enemies kindly (Luke 6:35). He also grants us rewards for generous giving: "Go, sell your possessions and give to the poor, and you will have treasure in heaven" (Matthew 19:21).

We know Christ will say to some (but not all) believers, "Well done, good and faithful servant!" (Matthew 25:21). Not "Well said," or "Well believed," but "Well done." What separates the sheep from the goats is what they did and didn't do with their God-entrusted resources of time, money, and possessions.

Peter says, "If you do these things, [then] you will never fall, and you will receive a rich welcome into the eternal kingdom of our Lord and Savior Jesus Christ" (2 Peter 1:10-11). What a powerful encouragement this is to saints who sacrifice in this life to prepare for the next! In heaven a great welcoming committee awaits them and a hearty "Well done!" But this isn't automatic—the conditional "if, then" makes it clear that if we don't do what Peter prescribed, then we won't receive this rich welcome when we enter heaven.

Where we spend eternity, whether heaven or hell, depends on our faith. Our further condition in either place will be determined by our works. John Bunyan said, "Consider, to provoke you to good works, that you shall have from God, when you come to glory, a reward for everything you do for him on earth."

A SECOND CHANCE?

My God-given resources, including money and possessions, have immense potential. They are the levers, positioned on the fulcrum of this life, by which I can move the mountains of eternity.

Evangelicals reject the doctrine of a second chance for unbelievers. We recognize that there's no opportunity to come to Christ after death. But it's equally true that after death there's no second chance for believers. There's no more opportunity for us to walk by faith and serve our Lord in this fallen world.

We can't do life here over again. There's no retaking the course once we've failed it. There's no improving a D to an A. No rescheduling the final exams. Death is the deadline. There's no extension.

A basketball game is over at the final buzzer. Shots taken late don't count. When the trumpet heralds Christ's return, our eternal future begins and our present opportunity ends. If we have failed by then to use our money, possessions, time, and energy for eternity, then we have failed—period.

"But we'll be in heaven and that's all that matters." On the contrary, Paul spoke of the loss of reward as a great and terrible loss. The fact that we're still saved is a clarification, not a consolation—"if it is burned up, he will suffer loss; he himself will be saved, but only as one escaping through the flames" (1 Corinthians 3:15). Receiving reward from Christ is unspeakable gain with eternal implications. Forfeiting reward is a terrible loss with equally eternal implications. How dare we say that being in heaven is all that matters to us, when so much else matters to God?

What we do in this life is of eternal importance. You and I will never have another chance to move the hand of God through prayer to heal a hurting soul, share Christ with one who can be saved from hell, care for the sick, give a cup of water to the thirsty, comfort the dying, invest money to help the helpless, rescue the unborn, further God's kingdom, open our homes, and share our clothes and food with the poor and needy.

What you do with your resources in this life is your autobiography. The book you've written with the pen of faith and the ink of works will go into eternity unedited, to be seen and read as is by the angels, the redeemed, and God himself. When we view today in light of the long tomorrow, the little choices become tremendously important. Whether I read my Bible today, pray, go to church, share my faith, and give my money—graciously empowered not by my flesh but by his Spirit—is of eternal consequence, not only for other souls, but mine.

At death we put the signature to our life's portrait. The paint dries. The portrait's done. Those who've dabbled in photography understand the "fixer." In developing a photograph, the negatives are immersed in different solutions. The developing solution parallels this life. As long as the photograph is in the developer it's subject to change. But once it's dropped into the fixer or "stop bath," it's permanently fixed. The photograph is done. What you see is what you get. So it will be when we die and enter eternity—the lives we lived on earth will be fixed as is, never to be altered or revised.

At the end of the movie *Schindler's List*, there's a heart-wrenching scene in which Oskar Schindler—who bought from the Nazis the lives of many Jews—looks at his car and his gold pin and regrets that he didn't give more of his money and possessions to save more lives. Schindler had used his opportunity far better than most. But in the end, he longed for a chance to go back and make better choices.

This life is our opportunity. Scripture does not teach what most of us seem to assume—that heaven will transform each of us into equal beings with equal possessions and equal responsibilities and equal capacities. It does not say our previous lives will be of no eternal significance. It says exactly the opposite.

Beyond the new heavens and new earth—which themselves are populated and structured according to what has been done in this life—there is no record of change. We might hope that what happens at the judgment seat will be of only temporary concern to the Judge, and that all of our disobedience and missed opportunities will make no difference. Will God make all souls equal in heaven and thereby consider as equally valid a life of selfishness and indifference to others' needs as compared to a life spent kneeling in prayer and feeding the hungry and sharing the gospel? The Bible clearly answers no.

Donald Gray Barnhouse put it this way:

Let us live, then, in the light of eternity. If we do not, we are weighting the scales against our eternal welfare. We must understand that "whatsoever a man soweth" must be taken in its widest meaning, and that every thought and intent of the heart will come under the scrutiny of the Lord and His coming. We can be sure that at the Judgment Seat of Christ there will be a marked difference between the Christian who has lived his life before the Lord, clearly discerning what was for the glory of God, and another Christian who was saved in a rescue mission at the tag end of a depraved and vicious life, or a nominal Christian saved on his deathbed after a life of self-pride, self-righteousness, self-love, and self-sufficiency. All will be in heaven, but the differences will be eternal. We may be sure that the consequences of our character will survive the grave and that we shall face those consequences at the Judgment Seat of Christ.[4]

If we really believed that what we do with our money and possessions—and everything else—will have an irreversible effect on eternity . . . wouldn't we live differently?

There lies ahead for each of us, at the end of the term, a final examination. It will be administered by a fair yet strict Headmaster. How seriously we take this clear teaching of Scripture is demonstrated by how seriously we are preparing for that day.

When we took courses in college, we asked questions about the teacher: "What are his tests like? Does he take attendance? Is he a hard grader? What does he expect in your papers?" If we're to do well in the course, we must know what the instructor expects of us. We must study the course syllabus, God's Word, to find out the answers to these questions. Once we find out, we should be careful to plot our lives accordingly—in light of the long tomorrow.

> What you do with your resources in this life is your autobiography.

I spent a day with a missionary friend in the ruins of ancient Corinth. For an hour we sat on the same judgment seat that Paul stood before in Acts 18, the one he used to help the Corinthians visualize Christ's future judgment of Christians. Together we read Scriptures that speak of that day when we will stand before the Lord's judgment seat and give an account for what we have done with all he has given us. We discussed the implications and prayed that when that day comes he might find us faithful and say to us, "Well done." We prayed knowing that our hourly and daily choices, empowered by our Lord, will determine what transpires on that day. It was one of the most sobering hours of my life.

Alfred Nobel was a Swedish chemist who made his fortune by inventing dynamite and other powerful explosives that governments bought to produce weapons. When Nobel's brother Ludvig died, a French newspaper accidentally printed Alfred's obituary instead. He was described as a man who became rich from enabling people to kill each other in unprecedented quantities. Shaken by this assessment, Nobel resolved to use his fortune to reward accomplishments that benefited humanity, including what we now know as the Nobel Peace Prize. He invested nine million dollars in this attempt to edit his role in history.

Nobel had a rare opportunity to look at the assessment of his life at its end—yet while he was still alive and had an opportunity to change that assessment.

Put yourself in Nobel's place. Read your own obituary, not as written by an uninformed or biased reporter, but as an onlooking angel might write it from heaven's point of view. Look at it carefully. Then use the rest of your life to edit that obituary into what you want it to be.

When you leave this world, will you be known as one who accumulated treasures on earth that you couldn't keep? Or will you be recognized as one who invested treasures in heaven that you couldn't lose?

Martin Luther said that on his calendar there were only two days: "today" and "that Day." May we invest our money and possessions today in light of that day.

CHAPTER 9

The Steward's Eternal Rewards

*It is my happiness that I have served Him who never fails
to reward His servants to the full extent of His promise.*
JOHN CALVIN

*Whatever good thing you do for Him, if done according
to the Word, is laid up for you as treasure in chests and
coffers, to be brought out to be rewarded before both men
and angels, to your eternal comfort.*   JOHN BUNYAN

Two men owned farms side by side. One was a bitter atheist, the other a devout Christian. Constantly annoyed at the Christian for his trust in God, the atheist said to him one winter, "Let's plant our crops as usual this spring, each the same number of acres. You pray to your God, and I'll curse him. Then come October, let's see who has the bigger crop."

When October came the atheist was delighted because his crop was larger. "See, you fool," he taunted, "what do you have to say for your God now?"

"My God," replied the other farmer, "doesn't settle all his accounts in October."

A CLOSER LOOK AT REWARDS

A day of judgment is coming upon all men. God promises great reward for all who have served him faithfully (Revelation 11:18). He will reward every loyal servant for works done in this life: "At that time each will receive his praise from God" (1 Corinthians 4:5).

God rewards generously, promising a return of "a hundred times" (Matthew 19:29). This is ten thousand percent interest, a return far out of proportion to the amount invested.

God rewards us for doing good works (Ephesians 6:8; Romans 2:6, 10), denying ourselves (Matthew 16:24-27), showing compassion to the needy

(Luke 14:13-14), and treating our enemies kindly (Luke 6:35). He also grants us rewards for generous giving: "Go, sell your possessions and give to the poor, and you will have treasure in heaven" (Matthew 19:21).

Rewards are promised to those who endure difficult circumstances while trusting in God (Hebrews 10:34-36), and to those who persevere under persecution (Luke 6:22-23). A life of godliness will be richly rewarded (2 Peter 3:11-14). When we extend hospitality and give a meal to those too poor or incapacitated to pay us back, Christ promises, "you will be blessed. Although they cannot repay you, you will be repaid at the resurrection of the righteous" (Luke 14:14).

Paul reminds us there's a timetable for the harvest: "Let us not become weary in doing good, for at the proper time we will reap a harvest if we do not give up" (Galatians 6:9). The believer's compensation, just like the unbeliever's, is usually deferred. God doesn't settle all his accounts in October.

THE REWARD OF RULERSHIP

Believers will reign with Christ over the world (Revelation 20:6). We'll even rule over angels (1 Corinthians 6:3). Some will be put "in charge of many things" (Matthew 25:21-23). Christ spoke of granting some followers rulership over cities—eleven cities for one, five for another, and none for a third, in proportion to their faithful service (Luke 19:17-24).

It's apparent from these passages that although all believers will be with Christ, not all will reign with him, at least not with equal responsibility and authority. There are conditions for reigning: "If we endure, we will also reign with him" (2 Timothy 2:12). Christ promises, "To him who overcomes, I will give the right to sit with me on my throne" (Revelation 3:21). He says, "To him who overcomes and does my will to the end, I will give authority over the nations . . . just as I have received authority from my Father. I will also give him the morning star" (Revelation 2:26-28).

Jesus promised to give faithful believers "the morning star." This was the name for the planet Venus. Is it possible that Christ will have his servants reign not only in the new earth but in places throughout the new heavens?

CROWNS AS REWARDS

Crowns are a common symbol of ruling power, though they may symbolize other rewards as well. Five crowns are mentioned in the New Testament:

1. The Crown of Life—given for faithfulness to Christ in persecution or martyrdom (James 1:12; Revelation 2:10).

2. The Incorruptible Crown—given for determination, discipline, and victory in the Christian life (1 Corinthians 9:24-25).

3. The Crown of Rejoicing—given for pouring oneself into others in evangelism and discipleship (1 Thessalonians 2:19; Philippians 4:1).

4. The Crown of Glory—given for faithfully representing Christ in a position of spiritual leadership (1 Peter 5:1-4). (Note that a prerequisite is being "not greedy for money, but eager to serve." A Christian leader's preoccupation with money can forfeit this reward.)

5. The Crown of Righteousness—given for joyfully purifying and readying oneself to meet Christ at his return (2 Timothy 4:6-8).

There's nothing in this list that suggests it is exhaustive. There may be innumerable crowns and types of crowns and rewards unrelated to crowns. But all are graciously given by the Lord Jesus in response to the faithful efforts of the believer.

These crowns bring glory to Christ as they are laid before his feet (Revelation 4:10), showing that our rewards are given not merely for our recognition but for God's glory. Although God's glory is the highest reason for any action, Scripture sees no contradiction between God's eternal glory and our eternal good. On the contrary, glorifying God will always result in our greatest eternal good. Likewise, pursuing our eternal good, as he commands us to do, will always glorify God. False humility that says, "I want no reward," effectively means, "I want nothing to lay at Christ's feet to bring him glory."

We are to guard our crowns carefully (Revelation 3:11). Why? Because we can be disqualified from receiving them (1 Corinthians 9:27). We can lose them (1 Corinthians 3:15). They can be taken from us (Matthew 25:28-29). We can seek our rewards from men, thereby forfeiting them from God (Matthew 6:5-6). John warns, "Watch out that you do not lose what you have worked for, but that you may be rewarded fully" (2 John 8). We can fail to earn rewards, and we can forfeit rewards already in our account.

ETERNAL DIFFERENCES IN HEAVEN?

This is an unpopular subject, but Scripture is clear. Not all Christians will hear the master say, "Well done, good and faithful servant" (Matthew 25:23). Not all of us will have treasure in heaven (Matthew 6:19-21). Not all of us will have the same position of authority in heaven (Luke 19:17, 19, 26). We will have differing levels of reward in heaven (1 Corinthians 3:12-15). There is no hint that, once given or withheld, rewards are anything other than eternal and irrevocable.

Not all Christians will hear the master say, "Well done, good and faithful servant."

Scripture suggests that some Christians will be ashamed at Christ's coming (1 John 2:28). Although it seems incomprehensible that such shame would continue in heaven, the doctrine of eternal rewards has sobering implications. The tangible results of those who have faithfully served Christ in this life and those who haven't will be evident for all eternity. They will be exemplified in eternal possessions and positions that will differ significantly from person to person.

125

Scripture is clear that there's a payback in eternity according to what was done during our time on earth, and that there will be differences among our rewards in heaven (Proverbs 24:11-12; Matthew 19:27-30; Luke 14:12-14). In other words, our experiences in heaven will not be the same. (Obviously, in heaven there will be no conceit, pettiness, jealousy, or unhealthy comparisons, but there nonetheless will be differences in reward and position.)

We saw in the last chapter that hell will be terrible for all, but it will be more terrible for some than others, depending on their works on earth (Matthew 11:20-24; Luke 20:45-47). Doesn't it follow that although everyone's experience in heaven will be wonderful, it will be more wonderful for some than others, depending on their works on earth?

Perhaps it's a matter of differing capacities. Two jars can both be full, but the one with greater capacity contains more. Likewise, all of us will be full of joy in heaven, but some may have more joy because their capacity for joy will be larger, having been stretched through trusting God in this life. John Bunyan put it this way:

> And why shall he that doth most for God in this world, enjoy most of him in that which is to come? But because by doing and acting, the heart, and every faculty of the soul is enlarged, and more capacitated, whereby more room is made for glory. Every vessel of glory shall at that day be full of it; but every one will not be capable to contain a like measure; and so if they should have it communicated to them, would not be able to stand under it; for there is 'an eternal weight in the glory that saints shall then enjoy' (2 Corinthians 4:17), and every vessel must be at that day filled—that is, have its heavenly load of it. . . . He that is best bred, and that is most in the bosom of God, and that so acts for him here; he is the man that will be best able to enjoy most of God in the kingdom of heaven.[1]

No matter how we attempt to explain it, no matter how uneasy it makes us, it's a fact that the doctrine of differing rewards and differing positions in heaven means we will have different experiences in heaven. These eternal experiences are presently being forged in the crucible of this life. What I do with my money and possessions here and now will significantly affect my eternal experience in heaven.

UNDERSTANDING SALVATION AND REWARDS

Whenever we speak of rewards, particularly because we speak of them so rarely, it's easy to confuse God's work and man's. Many mistakenly believe that heaven is our reward for doing good things. This is absolutely not the case. Our presence in heaven is in no sense a reward for our works, but a gift freely given by God in response to faith (Romans 6:23; Ephesians 2:8-9; Titus 3:5).

The following chart distinguishes the difference between regeneration and rewards:

REGENERATION	REWARDS
Past (1 John 3:2)	Future (Revelation 22:12)
Free (Ephesians 2:8-9)	Earned (1 Corinthians 3:8)
Can't be lost (John 10:28-29)	Can be lost (2 John 8)
Same for all Christians (Romans 3:22)	Differ between Christians (1 Corinthians 3:12-15)
For those who believe (John 3:16)	For those who work (1 Corinthians 9:27)

This next chart puts rewards in the larger context of the believer's life:

JUDGMENT	TIME	RELATIONSHIP	SCRIPTURE
Condemnation to New life	Past (Regeneration)	As a Sinner	2 Corinthians 5:21; Romans 6:1-23
Discipline or Rewards	Present (Sanctification)	As a Son	Hebrews 12:5-11; James 1:2-4
Loss or Rewards	Future (Glorification)	As a Steward	1 Corinthians 3:10-15; 2 Corinthians 5:10

As sinners, we were under condemnation for our sin until we accepted the provisions of Christ, who took this condemnation on himself. At that point, we were moved from condemnation to regeneration.

As a son or daughter, we presently make choices that are either righteous or sinful. When they're sinful, our Father disciplines us for our own good to make us holy and fruitful. His discipline is intended to turn us back to the path of righteousness. When we make right choices, we experience the immediate reward of God's approval and a variety of short-term benefits, as well as long-term rewards in eternity. Of course, we may also forfeit certain temporal benefits—perhaps even our life. Eternal rewards are guaranteed, whereas temporal rewards, at least in their outward form, are not.

Our works done as stewards or servants will someday be evaluated by our Master. He will reward us accordingly. The works worthy of reward are those done with faithfulness (1 Corinthians 4:2) and right motives (1 Corinthians 4:5), which only God is qualified to judge. To the degree that our life hasn't been characterized by good works, or to the degree these works have been done with improper motives, we will lose or forfeit our reward (1 Corinthians 3:12-15).

Salvation is about God's work on behalf of humanity. Conversely, rewards are a matter of our work for God. When it comes to salvation, our work for God is no substitute for God's work for us. God *saves* us because of Christ's work, not ours. Likewise, when it comes to rewards, God's work for humanity is no substitute for our work for God. God *rewards* us for our work, not Christ's.*

Let me be sure this is perfectly clear. Christ paid the eternal price (hell) for all our sins, once and for all (Hebrews 10:12-18). If we have trusted him for that provision, we will not pay the eternal price; that is, we will not go to hell. He has fully forgiven our sins and we are completely secure in the love of Christ (Psalm 103:8-18; Romans 8:31-39). Our salvation is sure, and we will not undergo the judgment of condemnation (John 5:24; Romans 8:1).

But although the forgiveness of our sins has every bearing on our eternal destination, it has no automatic bearing on our eternal rewards. The Bible teaches not only forgiveness of sins, but consequences of our choices that apply despite forgiveness. Forgiveness means that God eliminates our eternal condemnation. But it does not mean that our actions in this life have no consequences on earth. (Forgiven people can still contract AIDS or suffer the death penalty, for example.) Neither does it mean our choices have no consequences in eternity. Forgiven people can still lose their rewards and forfeit eternal positions of responsibility they could have had.

With our salvation, the work was Christ's. With our rewards, the work is ours. It's imperative that we trust in Christ, lean on him, and draw upon him for power, for apart from him we can do nothing. But if we hope to receive a reward, we must still do the necessary work. As our forefathers put it, we must bear the cross if we are to wear the crown.

Belief (trust, faith) determines our eternal destination: *where* we will be. Behavior (obedience) determines our eternal rewards: *what* we will have there. Works do not affect our destination (in other words, our redemption is secured by the work of Christ). However, works *do* affect our reward experienced at that destination. Just as there are eternal consequences to our faith, so there are eternal consequences to our works.

A STEWARD'S MOTIVATION

"Why should I follow Scripture's teaching on money and possessions when it's so much fun to have all the nice things I want and do whatever I please with my money? I'm a Christian, and I know I'm going to heaven anyway, so why get radical about the whole money thing? Why not have the best of both worlds, this one and the next?"

Though few of us are bold enough to openly ask such questions, they accurately reflect a prevailing attitude in our society. That's why I'm convinced it's necessary to deal with the subject of eternal rewards in this book.

The missing ingredient in the lives of many Christians today is motivation.

---

* Of course, even our reward-earning works are empowered by the Holy Spirit, not the flesh. Note the integration of God's work and man's in Colossians 1:29, "To this end I labor, struggling with all his energy, which so powerfully works in me."

Given our false assumption that what we do in this life won't have eternal consequences (apart from our decision to place our trust in Christ for salvation), it's no wonder we're unmotivated to follow God's directions regarding money and possessions (and everything else). When it comes down to it, what difference will it make? According to the prevailing theology, everything comes out in the wash, so it won't make any difference at all. But according to the Bible, it will make a tremendous difference! The doctrine of eternal rewards for our obedience is the neglected key to unlocking our motivation.[2]

Moses "regarded disgrace for the name of Christ as of greater value than the treasures of Egypt, because he was looking ahead to his reward" (Hebrews 11:26). Motivated by long-term reward, he chose short-term disgrace.

Paul ran his life's race with his eyes on the prize, which motivated him to run hard and long. He strove not to get a crown of laurel leaves that would rot, but "to get a crown that will last forever" (1 Corinthians 9:24-25). Paul was unashamedly motivated by the prospect of eternal reward, which he affirmed freely and frequently (2 Corinthians 4:16-18; 5:9-10; 2 Timothy 4:7-8). He encouraged all believers to be motivated by rewards (Galatians 6:9-10; 1 Timothy 6:17-19; 2 Timothy 2:5, 12). Slaves, for instance, were to obey their masters in order to receive eternal reward (Ephesians 6:5-9; Colossians 3:22-25).

The missing ingredient in the lives of many Christians today is motivation.

Another model of motivation by reward is Christ himself. He endured the cross "for the joy set before him" (Hebrews 12:2). He humbled himself, knowing that he would ultimately be exalted (Philippians 2:9).

Jesus said, "But when you give a banquet, invite the poor, the crippled, the lame, the blind, and you will be blessed. Although they cannot repay you, you will be repaid at the resurrection of the righteous" (Luke 14:13-14). Our instinct is to give to those who will give us something in return and not to those who won't. Christ appealed not only to our compassion but to our eternal self-interest: If we do a compassionate act that goes unrewarded by others in this life, God will pay us back in the next life.

What a motivation this is when we feel our labors are unappreciated by others! We can be freed from the burden of concern about whether others overlook our deeds, because God assures us that he will not overlook them. When we understand what it means to be promised a reward from God, any prospect of reward from others—or any bitterness for not being rewarded by them—will shrink in comparison.

"Love your enemies, and do good, and lend, expecting nothing in return; and your reward will be great, and you will be sons of the Most High" (Luke 6:35, NASB). Once again, Christ sought to motivate us to do good works by the promise of rewards.

Despite prevailing opinions to the contrary, the prospect of rewards is a

129

proper motivation for the Christian's obedience (Matthew 6:19-21)—including the generous sharing of our money and possessions. If we maintain that it's wrong to be motivated by rewards, we bring a serious accusation against Christ. We imply he is tempting us to sin every time he offers rewards for obedience! Since God does not tempt his children, it's clear that whatever he lays before us as a motivation is legitimate. It's not wrong for us to be motivated by the prospect of reward. Indeed, something is seriously wrong if we are not motivated by reward.

THE POWER OF INCENTIVES

Businesspeople work in a world of incentives. So do homemakers, school children, and every other human being, regardless of age, nationality, or wealth. Every effective manager, every qualified leader knows the importance of incentives. These are tangible motivators that may be personal, social, spiritual, physical, or financial. Unfortunately, too many Christians consider incentives to be "secular" or "unspiritual."

Most of us use rewards to motivate our children. So why are we surprised that God uses rewards to motivate us? By God's own design, all of us need incentives to motivate us to do our jobs and do them well. Motivation by reward is not a result of the fall, but God's original design for humanity.

To say, "I don't do anything for the reward—I do it only because it's right," may appear to take the spiritual high road. But in fact it's pseudospiritual. It goes against the grain of the way God created us and the way he tries to motivate us.

Back when our daughters lived in our home, suppose I'd told one of them, "If you do a full day of yard work Saturday, I'll pay you $50 and take you out to a nice dinner." Would it be wrong for her to want to earn the $50? Would it be wrong for her to look forward to going out to a nice dinner with her dad? Of course it wouldn't be wrong! I'm her father, I made the offer, and I want her to want those things!

Now, it would be inappropriate if my daughter refused to work without my granting rewards. But because it was my idea, not hers, she would have every right to be motivated by the rewards I offered her. In fact, my own joy would be lessened if she didn't want the rewards I offered her.

"But God doesn't owe us anything," you might argue. "He has the right to expect us to work for him with no thought of reward." True, he owes us absolutely nothing. And yes, we should be willing and happy to serve him, even if there was no payoff. If we came to God and said, "You owe us—we want to be paid," we would be dead wrong. But there is a payoff! And here's the kicker—it wasn't our idea that God would reward us. It was his idea! Satan didn't make up the idea of incentives. God did. He made us the way we are. He made us to need incentives to motivate us to do our jobs and do them well.

If my daughter did the yard work joylessly and then said, "No, Dad, I refuse the money and I don't want to go to dinner with you," how would that make me feel? We flatter ourselves—and insult God—when we say, "I don't care about reward." As if we have the right not to care about what God graciously promises us for obeying him!

God will reward the child who gave to the missions offering the money she'd saved for a softball mitt. He'll reward the teenager who kept himself pure despite all the temptations. He'll reward the man who tenderly cared for his wife with Alzheimer's, the mother who raised the child with cerebral palsy, the child who rejoiced in his heart despite his handicap. He'll reward the unskilled person who was faithful and the skilled person who was meek and servant-hearted. He'll reward the parents who modeled Christ to their children and the children who followed him despite their parents' bad example. He'll reward those who suffered while trusting him, and those who helped the ones who were suffering. He doesn't *have* to. He *wants* to! And make no mistake, he will. "For the Son of Man is going to come in his Father's glory with his angels, and then he will reward each person *according to what he has done*" (Matthew 16:27, italics mine).

CHOICES AND CONSEQUENCES

Every major choice involves a major consequence. Scripture brims with promises and warnings of the consequences for our choices—this punishment for that sin; that reward for this obedience. Some of these incentives or consequences are short-term or temporal (Proverbs 3:9-10; Malachi 3:10-12); others are long-term or eternal (Luke 12:32-33; Matthew 6:20); and still others involve both temporal and eternal incentives (Mark 10:29-30).

Of course, reward is not our only motivation. We should be motivated by gratitude to serve God (Hebrews 12:28). We should be motivated by our ambition "to please him" (2 Corinthians 5:9). But these motives are never in scriptural conflict with the motive of reward. The same Bible that calls upon us to obey God out of our love for him as Father and Redeemer (Deuteronomy 7:9; 11:1; 30:20) also calls upon us to obey out of our fear of him as Creator and Judge (Genesis 2:17; Deuteronomy 28:58-67; Hebrews 10:30-31) and out of our hope in him as Rewarder of those who serve him (Deuteronomy 28:2-9; Hebrews 11:6). Each of these motivations is legitimate, and each complements the other. Sometimes we need the combined persuasiveness of all these incentives to do what is pleasing to the Lord. This isn't a matter of mixed motives (some good, some bad), but of multiple motives—multiple *righteous* motives.

We should evangelize out of our love for God. But if that isn't enough, our love for other people should motivate us. Scripture tells us we should also be motivated to evangelize out of our fear of God. We will stand before the judgment seat and be recompensed for our works, Paul says, and therefore, since we know the fear of God, "we try to persuade men" (2 Corinthians 5:10-11). Love is one motivator, fear another, reward yet another. If one or two don't suffice, the three together should.

Our delightful daughters are grown and married now. When they were children, they loved me, and sometimes that was a sufficient incentive for obeying. But other times it wasn't enough. Fortunately, they also feared me, in the best sense. They knew I would punish wrongdoing. And they also knew I'd be very pleased when they did the right thing. They knew I would reward them for doing right, always with approving words, and sometimes in material ways too.

What is in God's best interests is also in others' best interests and in my best interests (not necessarily immediately, but always ultimately). Something that is good will be good for everyone—not good for God and bad for me, or good for me and bad for my neighbor. What's good is good for all. Every time I obey God, I'm doing what's ultimately best for all. Every time I disobey him, I'm doing what's ultimately worst for all. The Master and steward are both pleased when the steward does well. Both are displeased when he doesn't do well.

The prospect of being praised by others is a strong motivator. Children are motivated by the hope of being praised by their parents. Why would it be different with the children of God? The prospect of hearing my Father say to me, "Well done," should be tremendously motivating. The Pharisees "loved praise from men more than praise from God" (John 12:43). Their problem wasn't that they were motivated by praise. It's that they were content with praise from the wrong source—men, rather than God.

How should we respond to adversity for the sake of Christ? "Rejoice in that day and leap for joy." Why should we leap for joy? "Because great is your reward in heaven" (Luke 6:23).

The believer who knows God's Word knows its promise of reward for obedience. God has set up a system that rewards obedience and punishes disobedience and that rewards others-centered sacrifice and punishes self-centered indulgence. What's right is always smart, because it will be rewarded. What's wrong is always stupid, because it will be punished. This is the way God has made it. This system—not personal preference—should be our reference point in deciding what to do with our money and possessions. If it's not, we lose.

Consider these words: "Do not wear yourself out to get rich; have the wisdom to show restraint. Cast but a glance at riches, and they are gone, for they will surely sprout wings and fly off to the sky like an eagle" (Proverbs 23:4-5).

What a picture. Next time you buy a prized possession, imagine it sprouting wings and flying off. Sooner or later, it'll disappear. Our instinct is to think of this as a moral warning. It isn't. It's a pragmatic one. If riches satisfied us and if riches lasted, a case could be made for pursuing them. But they don't satisfy and they don't last. Hence, pursuing riches just doesn't make sense. We're not told to "have the *righteousness* to show restraint," but to "have the *wisdom* to show restraint." Don't pursue wealth, not merely because it's wrong, but because it's stupid.

PLEASURE, POSSESSIONS, AND POWER

God has created each of us with certain desires that correspond to certain motivations. Each of us has built-in desires for pleasure, possessions, and power. At first this may sound unbiblical, because we've come to think of these things as temptations. Satan does indeed tempt us in each of these areas. The desire for pleasure can degenerate into hedonism, desire for possessions into materialism, and desire for power into egotism. We might relate the desire for pleasure to the "lust of the flesh," the desire for possessions to the "lust of the eyes," and the desire for power to "the pride of life" (1 John 2:16, KJV).

Satan approached Christ on all three of these levels during his wilderness temptation. He tempted Jesus to make bread for the pleasure of eating, to worship Satan for the possession of all the world's kingdoms, and to cast himself from the highest point of the temple for the power of commanding angelic intervention (Luke 4:1-13).

So if the desires for pleasure, possessions, and power make us vulnerable to temptation, how can they be good? How can they properly motivate us? We must understand that the evil one can only appeal to our desire for these things because our Creator built that desire into us. This is how God designed us to be.

Next time you buy a prized possession, imagine it sprouting wings and flying off. Sooner or later, it'll disappear.

The draw to pleasure, possessions, and power cannot be rooted in our sin nature, because Satan appealed to these desires in Adam and Eve before they were sinful (Genesis 3:1-7). Christ had no sin nature. Satan knew this, yet he sought to tempt Jesus on these same three grounds—pleasure, possessions, and power. Why? Because Christ was human, and to be human is to have desires for these things. We want pleasure, possessions, and power, not because we are sinful but *because we are human.*

If this argument seems unconvincing, there's a clincher: God himself appeals to each of these desires in us! He offers us the reward of power in his eternal kingdom (Matthew 20:20-28; Luke 12:42-44; 19:15-19), possessions in his eternal kingdom (Matthew 6:19-21; 19:16-22, 27-30), and pleasures in his eternal kingdom (Psalm 16:11).

God appeals to our human nature, but *never* to our sin nature. Power, possessions, and pleasures are legitimate objects of desire that our Creator has instilled in us *and* by which he can motivate us to obedience. The evil one counterattacks by tempting us to direct these legitimate desires to the wrong objects.

HOW TO GAIN ETERNAL PLEASURE, POSSESSIONS, AND POWER

The way of the world and the temptation of the devil is for us to try to gain pleasure, possessions, and power in the present world. The way of the Lord is to gain these things in the future—not by clinging to them in the present but by forgoing them in the present. It's at this point that prosperity theology is so misguided.

Consider the threefold disciplines of fasting, giving, and prayer, which Christ addresses in Matthew 6:1-18. Fasting is denying ourselves the pleasure of eating in order to gain pleasure in God. Giving is denying the possession of riches to gain possessions from God. Prayer is denying our own power in order to gain power from God. Eating, owning, and ruling are not inherently bad—but we temporarily abstain from them, as a matter of spiritual discipline, in order to accomplish a higher kingdom purpose.

If the desires for pleasure, possessions, and power make us vulnerable to temptation, how can they be good?

For centuries, monastic orders have tried to practice relinquishment through their vow of chastity (forgoing pleasure), vow of poverty (forgoing possessions), and vow of obedience (forgoing the power of living life one's own way).

But one need not forgo power because he hates power. He may forgo it now precisely because he wants it in a better world. Jesus didn't tell his disciples they shouldn't want to be great, but that they could become great in the next world by being a servant in this one (Mark 10:42-44). Likewise, one does not forgo possessions here because he hates possessions, but because he wants them in another world. Jesus didn't tell his disciples they shouldn't want to be rich. Rather, he told them they could become rich in the next world by giving away riches in this one (Matthew 6:19-21). It's not a matter of no gratification but delayed gratification. It's forgoing present, temporal gratification in order to achieve future, eternal gratification.

We admire Olympic athletes for their dedication and discipline, but we don't pretend they're not acting from self-interest. We are right to admire a missionary, someone who works with street children, or someone who feeds the poor. What they are doing is not selfish, but neither is it selfless in the way we often think. Their short-term sacrifices are in their eternal self-interest, because God promises to reward them. This is not self-denial for its own sake, but purposeful self-denial for God's glory and their own ultimate good. The key to this self-denial is faith, as described and exemplified in Hebrews 11:8-16. Faith is what motivates us to forgo something in this life for the promise that it—or an even higher form—will be ours in the next.

This concept is difficult for us to understand, because our sin nature has so tainted our pleasures, possessions, and power in this world. But in eternity we'll be able to manage these things rightly—as our sinless Lord did—because we'll be without sin.

Believers in prosperity theology don't realize that when we fail to limit our seeking of pleasures, possessions, and power in this world, where we're yet sinful, the results are disastrous. Look at the scandals that have rocked Christian organizations (several of which we examined in chapter 5). The lives of the two most prominent fallen evangelists—Jim Bakker and Jimmy Swaggart—consisted of three basic elements in extensive measure: power, possessions, and pleasures. Both men rose to tremendous power over people, amassed a great number of possessions, and indulged in many pleasures, which ultimately included sexual immorality. Like most of us, these men in their sinful human natures were incapable of handling such large portions of power, possessions, and pleasures.

CAN APPEAL TO OUR DESIRES REALLY BE SPIRITUAL?

God created us with certain desires, and he made us to be motivated by rewards that appeal to those desires. He calls us to act on the basis of those promised rewards. As we've seen, the Scriptures are full of exhortations to act in certain ways to gain certain rewards. Yet there persists a misguided belief that desire for power, possessions, and pleasure in the next life is crass and to pursue rewards is selfish or mercenary. Three godly Englishmen of three different centuries offer us a very different perspective, an explicitly biblical one.

John Bunyan, the seventeenth-century pastor who was imprisoned for preaching the gospel, said of eternal rewards, "They are such as should make us leap to think on, and that we should remember with exceeding joy, and never think that it is contrary to the Christian faith, to rejoice and be glad for [them]."[3]

William Wilberforce, through his tireless efforts in Parliament in the early nineteenth century, finally succeeded in abolishing England's slave trade. He devoted most of his fortune to the cause of Christ. This was his perspective on our God-given desires: "Christianity proposes not to extinguish our natural desires. It promises to bring the desires under just control and direct them to their true object."[4]

C. S. Lewis, a professor at Oxford and Cambridge in the mid-twentieth century, wrote prolifically on the Christian faith. He diverted most of his royalties to charitable causes and individual needs, living simply and thinking often of the world:

> The faint, far-off results of those energies which God's creative rapture implanted in matter when He made the worlds are what we now call physical pleasures; and even thus filtered, they are too much for our present management. What would it be to taste at the fountainhead that stream of which even these lower reaches prove so intoxicating? Yet

135

that, I believe, is what lies before us. The whole man is to drink joy from the fountain of joy.

The New Testament has a lot to say about self-denial, but not about self-denial as an end in itself. We are told to deny ourselves and to take up our cross in order to follow Christ— and nearly every description of what we shall ultimately find if we do so contains an appeal to desire. If there lurks in most modern minds the notion that it's a bad thing to desire one's own good and earnestly hope for enjoyment, it is because it has crept in from the teachings of Immanuel Kant and the ancient Stoics. Certainly, it has no part in the Christian faith. Indeed, if we consider the unblushing promises of rewards promised in the Gospels, it would seem that our Lord finds our desires not too strong, but too weak. We are half-hearted creatures, fooling about with drink and sex and ambition when infinite joy has been offered to us. We are far too easily pleased, like an ignorant child who goes on making mud pies in a slum because he cannot imagine what is meant by an offer of a holiday at the sea.[5]

> **We are half-hearted creatures, fooling about with drink and sex and ambition when infinite joy has been offered to us.**
>
> C. S. LEWIS

We must realize, once and for all, that fulfilling our desires and seeking rewards are not anti-Christian. What is anti-Christian is the self-centeredness that's unconcerned about God and our neighbor, and the preoccupation with the immediate fulfilling of desires that distracts us from finding our ultimate fulfillment in Christ. The person who gives life, money, and possessions to receive rewards from God—the greatest of which is to hear the resounding "Well done"—is one whose deepest thirsts will be eternally quenched by the Maker and Fulfiller of all desire. It is senseless to devote our lives to the "mud pies" of power, possessions, and pleasures of this world—when our Lord offers to us the power, possessions, and pleasures of the next world, our eternal home.

DREAMS OF ETERNAL DIMENSION

Every year in Portland, Oregon, builders showcase a row of big, beautiful houses called the "Street of Dreams." Although the houses are fun to look at, I'm struck by how sad it would be to have a dream as small as one of those houses.

When I was a pastor, a wonderful couple came to my office and told me they wanted to be able to give more money to the church and to missions, but they couldn't if they were going to keep saving to build their dream house. They said, "We've always had this dream for a beautiful home in the country, and we can't seem to shake it. Is that wrong?"

I told them I thought their dream of a perfect home was from God. I think they were surprised to hear that. Then I said, "It's just that your dream can't be fulfilled here, in this world."

Our dream house is coming; we don't have to build it ourselves. In fact, we can't. Any dream house on earth will eventually be ravaged by time, floods, earthquakes, tornadoes, carpenter ants, or freeway bypasses. Who would want to divert kingdom funds to build a dream house on earth if they understood that either it will leave them or they will leave it? Instead, why not use our resources to send building materials ahead to the Carpenter, our Bridegroom, who this very moment is building our dream house in heaven?

Writing in 1649, Pastor Richard Baxter asked a probing question:

> If there be so certain and glorious a rest for the saints, why is there no more industrious seeking after it? One would think, if a man did once hear of such unspeakable glory to be obtained, and believed what he heard to be true, he should be transported with the vehemency of his desire after it, and should almost forget to eat and drink, and should care for nothing else, and speak of and inquire after nothing else, but how to get this treasure. And yet people who hear of it daily, and profess to believe it as a fundamental article of their faith, do as little mind it, or labour for it, as if they had never heard of any such thing, or did not believe one word they hear.[6]

May we joyously believe. And then may we live as if we believe!

CHAPTER 10

The Steward and the Master

One more revival—only one more—is needed, the revival
of Christian stewardship, the consecration of the money
power to God. When that revival comes, the kingdom of
God will come in a day.   HORACE BUSHNELL

It is just as much a matter of discipline for a church
member practically to deny his stewardship as to deny
the divinity of Christ.   CHARLES FINNEY

A distraught man furiously rode his horse up to John Wesley, shouting, "Mr. Wesley, Mr. Wesley, something terrible has happened. Your house has burned to the ground!" Weighing the news for a moment, Wesley replied, "No. The Lord's house burned to the ground. That means one less responsibility for me."

Wesley's response wasn't the sanctimonious reply of someone who thought I'd be quoting his words hundreds of years later. We might say, "Get real," but his reaction didn't stem from a denial of reality. Rather, it sprang from life's most basic reality—that God is the owner of all things, and we are simply his stewards.

Jerry Caven had a successful restaurant chain, two banks, a ranch, a farm, and several real estate ventures. At age fifty-nine, he was searching for a nice lakeside retirement home. But the Owner had other plans.

"God led us to put our money and time overseas," Jerry said. "It's been exciting. Before, we gave token amounts. Now we put substantial money into missions. We often go to India."

What changed the Cavens' attitude toward giving?

"It was realizing God's ownership," Jerry explained. "Once we understood we were giving away God's money to do God's work, we discovered a peace and joy we never had back when we thought it was our money!"

John Wesley and Jerry Caven have something in common that all of us need to cultivate: a life-changing understanding of God's ownership and our stewardship.

STEWARDSHIP

The word *stewardship* has recently fallen on hard times. To many it's no longer relevant to the day in which we live. To some it's a religious cliché used to make fund-raising sound spiritual. It conjures up images of large red thermometers on church platforms, measuring how far we are from paying off the mortgage.

Because of these bland associations, I was tempted not to use the word in this book. But it's such a good word, both biblically and historically, that it deserves resuscitation rather than burial.

"A steward is someone entrusted with another's wealth or property and charged with the responsibility of managing it in the owner's best interest."[1] A steward is entrusted with sufficient resources and the authority to carry out his designated responsibilities.

> A steward's primary goal is to be found faithful by his master as the steward uses the master's resources to accomplish the tasks delegated to him.

Scripture tells us that God delegated to us authority over all his creation (Genesis 1:28). "You made him [man] ruler over the works of your hands; you put everything under his feet: all flocks and herds, and the beasts of the field" (Psalm 8:6-7). God expects us to use all the resources he gives us to best carry out our responsibilities. A steward's primary goal is to be found faithful by his master as the steward uses the master's resources to accomplish the tasks delegated to him (1 Corinthians 4:2).

Stewardship isn't a subcategory of the Christian life. Stewardship is the Christian life. After all, what is stewardship except that God has entrusted to us life, time, talents, money, possessions, family, and his grace? In each case, he evaluates how we regard what he has entrusted to us—and what we do with it.

Our use of money and possessions is only one aspect of stewardship, but all its aspects are overlapping circles. In Exodus 36:2-7, for instance, we see the tabernacle built by people giving their time, energy, skills, money, and possessions. How we view and handle our money will correspond with how we view and handle our time, energy, talents, family, church, vocation, and every facet of life.

Though it should be obvious from reading the Gospels, it surprises many people to hear that Jesus showed a keen interest in and familiarity with the subject of money. He spoke frequently in economic terms. Gene Getz provides a summary of Christ's teaching:

Evidently Jesus learned the carpenter trade from His father and maintained a relatively low profile in His hometown of Nazareth. However, when He began His ministry, He demonstrated an unusual awareness of all kinds of economic activity in Palestine. The main source for comprehending Jesus' knowledge of what kinds of business enterprises existed at that time is His parables, which He told to illustrate spiritual truth. In fact, a large number of these stories utilized various facets of economic life to make spiritual applications. More than a quarter of these parables (eleven out of thirty-nine) deal with finances and money directly:

- He referred to *investment* in jewels and treasures to illustrate the importance of investing in the kingdom of God (Matthew 13:44-45).

- He referred to *saving* new treasures as well as old treasures to illustrate the importance of storing up both old and new truth (Matthew 13:52).

- He used *indebtedness* to illustrate the importance of forgiveness (the parable of the unmerciful servant; Matthew 18:23-35).

- He referred to *hiring procedures* and *wage structures* to illustrate God's sovereignty and generosity in treating all with equality, forgiving sins, and rewarding people with eternal life (the parable of the workers in the vineyard; Matthew 20:1-16).

- He told a story about a fruit farmer who *leased* his property to illustrate the way the chief priests and Pharisees were rejecting God and His Son (the parables of the tenants; Matthew 21:33-46; Mark 12:1-12; Luke 20:9-19).

- He discussed *capital, investments, banking,* and *interest* to emphasize our human responsibility to utilize God's gifts in a prudent and responsible way (the parable of the talents, Matthew 25:14-30; the parable of the ten minas, Luke 19:11-27).

- He referred to *money lenders, interest,* and *debt cancellation* to illustrate the importance of love and appreciation to God for canceling our debt of sin (Luke 7:41-43).

- He spoke of building barns to *store grain* for the future while neglecting to store up spiritual treasures as a very foolish decision (the parable of the rich fool; Luke 12:16-21).

- He used *architectural planning, building construction,* and *cost analysis* to illustrate the importance of future planning and counting the cost before we make decisions in building our spiritual lives (Luke 14:28-30).

- He used the human joy that comes from *finding lost money* to illustrate the joy in the presence of angels when a lost soul believes in Christ (Luke 15:8-10).

- He used *wealth,* dividing up an *estate,* irresponsible *spending,* and a *change*

141

of heart to illustrate repentance and forgiveness (the parable of the prodigal son; Luke 15:11-32).

- He used bad financial management and dishonest debt reduction to illustrate that dishonest business people are sometimes wiser in their worldly realm than honest followers of Christ in the spiritual realm (the parable of the shrewd manager; Luke 16:1-12).
- He contrasted a rich man who died and went to hell with a poor beggar who died and went to heaven to illustrate how wealth and what it can provide may harden our hearts against spiritual truth (the parable of the rich man and Lazarus; Luke 16:19-31).
- He contrasted the proud Pharisee who fasted and tithed regularly with the humble tax collector who acknowledged his sin of dishonesty and greed to illustrate that God acknowledges humility and rejects self-exaltation (the parable of the Pharisee and the tax collector; (Luke 18:9-14).
- He used a grain-ripened field and harvesters to illustrate "spiritually ripened hearts" in Samaria and the part the apostles would have in "harvesting" people's souls (John 4:34-38).[2]

In the remainder of this chapter, I'll take a close look at one of Christ's parables, summarize two more, and compile a number of key lessons that set an agenda for all stewards who would faithfully serve their Master.

LESSONS FROM A SHREWD STEWARD

Christ's parable of the shrewd manager, often called the "unrighteous steward," concerns a wealthy owner who fires his business manager for wasting his assets (Luke 16:1-13). During the brief period before his termination becomes effective, the steward goes to his master's debtors and reduces their debt, thereby engendering their friendship. When the master learns of this, he praises the steward for his foresight in making friends that will be supportive to him now that his term of stewardship is over.

There are different interpretations of this passage that attempt to explain the owner's apparent approval of what seems to be a dishonest act. Here are three possibilities:

- The steward reduced long outstanding debts so that at least his master received some payment rather than none.
- Because stewards were sometimes paid from the interest charged on loans, what the steward deducted from the debts might have been what was due him, but which he needed to obtain now if he was ever to receive it.
- The steward had grossly overcharged the debtors in the first place, planning to pocket the excess, and now lets them pay for their goods at the true, uninflated price.

Regardless of the correct interpretation—and parables normally have one central point that should not be obscured by uncertainties about secondary issues—the master praised the steward for his shrewdness in using, with his own future well-being in mind, his master's money to invest in his relationships with people (Luke 16:8-9).

Clearly, Jesus intends to draw a parallel between the shrewd manager's position and our own. He encourages us to emulate the steward's wisdom by handling our Master's resources with our eternal future in mind.

The man's termination signifies that every steward's service will one day come to an end, and could at any time. We will be terminated from this life just as he was terminated from his job, and likely just as unexpectedly. As his master appointed a day for his service to end, so a day has been appointed for ours to end, a day in which we shall give an account of our stewardship, just as he did (Romans 14:12). Consequently, we should do exactly what the steward did—use wisely what little remaining time and influence we have before our term of stewardship (life on this earth) is done.

Eternal Friends and Houses

Jesus doesn't tell us to stay away from the mammon of unrighteousness or "worldly wealth," but to use it strategically. He says to use it "to gain friends for yourselves, so that when it is gone, you will be welcomed into eternal dwellings" (Luke 16:9). Money can be a tool of Christ. But it must be used as such now, before our period of service on earth ends. There will be no second chance to use the money for Christ later. After his termination was effective, after he could work no longer, the manager would have no more leverage. He used his final days of service to win friends who could take him into their dwellings when his work was done.

Jesus tells us that after we die, when our present assets of money, possessions, time, and life are gone, we may be welcomed by friends into eternal dwellings. Perhaps the welcoming committee of this parable will participate in the "rich welcome" some believers will receive upon entering heaven (2 Peter 1:11). Clearly, this welcoming will be contingent upon the wise use of our resources on earth to impact these "friends."

But who are these friends? The reference appears to be to believers in heaven who are there as a result of our ministry or whose lives we have touched in a significant way through the use of our material assets. Apparently they will have their own "eternal dwelling places" and will welcome us in so that we may have a place to stay as we move about the heavenly kingdom. That believers will have their own living quarters in heaven is substantiated by other texts. The New Jerusalem is a physical place, with exact measurements given (Revelation 21:16). To qualify as a "city," it presumably consists of individual residences (Revelation 21:2). Jesus says that he is preparing eternal dwelling places for us (John 14:2-3).

It's true—the Carpenter from Galilee is constructing residences for us. (He has qualities that come in handy in a building project, including omniscience and omnipotence!) If we integrate a similar analogy, 1 Corinthians 3:10-15 suggests that in this life we are providing the building materials for our Lord to use in this construction project, of which he himself is the foundation. If this is true, then the size and quality of our eternal dwelling is influenced by how we live our lives now. This certainly fits with the concept of reward being commensurate to service, as taught in 2 Corinthians 5:10 and all the stewardship parables.

The size and quality of our eternal dwelling is influenced by how we live our lives now.

If we follow through with the construction and residence imagery that Scripture itself employs, then all believers are engaged in a sort of eternal building project, the results of which will vary widely. We might imagine that some of us are sending ahead sufficient materials for pup tents, some for studio apartments, some for trailer homes, some for ranch houses, and others for great mansions. (I intend this only as an illustration, but remember it is Scripture—not me—that tells us we will have real dwelling places in heaven.) If we imagine that Jesus employs the angels in our heavenly building projects, we might envision asking them, "Why isn't my house larger than this?" To which they might reply, "We did the best we could with what you sent us."

Based on Christ's words in the parable, we might further imagine that the larger our dwelling place, the more we will be able to serve as (pardon the expression) heavenly hosts—those who entertain heavenly guests. Perhaps we will even have angels as our guests. Or perhaps we'll be invited into angels' quarters to visit with them in exchange for the hospitality we offered them on earth when we were unaware of their true identity (Hebrews 13:2).

If this seems too fantastic, remember that we are simply trying to understand Christ's own words. Obviously he meant something—if not this, then what? There is no indication in the text that Jesus intended a symbolic or allegorical meaning. Consequently, we should not spiritualize his words but take them in their plain, ordinary sense.

Why do these concepts seem foreign to us? Perhaps because we've become so preoccupied with our life here that we never stop to think about life in heaven. As I develop in my book In Light of Eternity: Perspectives on Heaven, we regularly overlook the fact that heaven is consistently described in the Bible not in ethereal, vague, or abstract terms but in very tangible and surprisingly earthly ways.[3]

If we take these passages at face value—as the weight of evidence suggests we should—we must conclude that each of us will have a specific individual location in heaven, an address of our own. We will live there, invite people in, and be invited to other places. We know that we will have actual bodies in heaven (Luke 24:39; John 20:27; 1 Corinthians 15:42-54), and that we will be recognizable (Matthew 17:3). We will have a place at a table to eat and drink (Matthew 8:11; Revelation 19:9). We will experience literal pleasure in heaven, just as those in hell will experience literal pain (Luke 16:22-31). Given the physical nature of our resurrection bodies, why should we be surprised to find that we will also have places to live, or that having such places we will be able to welcome others into them?

All this should prompt a self-evaluation. What kind of building materials are we sending ahead to heaven for our own dwelling place? Whom have we influenced spiritually to the point that they would welcome us into their eternal dwelling places? To which needy people have we sacrificially given our resources? Apparently those whom we have influenced for Christ, directly or indirectly, will know and appreciate us and desire our fellowship in heaven. What a thought! This is encouraging both in light of saved family members, friends, and others we have influenced, and for the many we do not even know who have been touched by our prayers, service, and financial giving.

Ray Boltz's song "Thank You" pictures us meeting people in heaven who explain how our giving touched their lives. They say, "Thank you for giving to the Lord, I am so glad you gave."[4] This is more than just a nice sentiment. It's something that will actually happen. Every time you give to world missions and famine relief and God's kingdom, you can dream about the day you will meet these precious people in heaven.

Jesus gives us a powerful incentive to invest our lives and assets in his kingdom while on earth. The greater our service and sacrifice for him and for others, the larger and more enthusiastic our welcoming committee will be in heaven, the more eternal residences we'll have opportunity to visit, and the more substantial our own places in heaven will be.

One day money will be useless. While it's still useful, Christians with foresight will use it for eternal good.

Trustworthy with a Little, Entrusted with a Lot

Continuing after the parable of the shrewd steward, Jesus says, "Whoever can be trusted with very little can also be trusted with much, and whoever is dishonest with very little will also be dishonest with much" (Luke 16:10). Jesus implies that all of us are being continually tested in little things. If a child can't be trusted to spend his father's money and return the change, neither can he be trusted to stay overnight alone at a friend's house. But if he can be trusted to clean his room and take out the garbage, he can be trusted with a dog or a bike.

This principle invalidates all of our "if onlys," such as, "If only I made more money, I'd help the poor," or, "If only I had a million dollars, then I'd give it to my church or missions." If I'm dishonest or selfish in my use of a few dollars, I would be dishonest or selfish in my use of a million dollars. The issue is not what I would do with a million dollars if I had it, but what I am doing with the hundred thousand, ten thousand, one thousand, one hundred, or ten dollars I *do* have. If we are not being faithful with what he has entrusted to us, why should he trust us with any more?

This thought raises a sobering question: What opportunities are we currently missing because we've failed to use our money and our lives wisely in light of eternity?

God pays a great deal of attention to the "little things." He numbers the hairs on our heads, cares for the lilies of the field, and is concerned with the fall of a single sparrow (Matthew 10:29). What we do with a little time, a little talent, and a little money tells God a lot. The little things are a major factor as he considers whether to commend and promote us—or reprimand and demote us—in his kingdom corporation.

Handling True Riches

"If you have not been trustworthy in handling worldly wealth, who will trust you with true riches?" (Luke 16:11). What are "true riches?" They're not just more of the same worldly wealth. True riches are those that are valuable to God, that will last for all eternity. What could those be but other human beings with eternal souls? Apparently, God tests us in the handling of money and possessions to determine the extent of our trustworthiness in handling people in personal ministry.

How many people, including pastors and other Christian leaders, have forfeited eternally significant ministry to eternal souls because they have failed to handle their money well? Through mismanagement of God's funds we can lose credibility with people as well as lose God's willingness to entrust us with more people to influence.

There are further implications related to our position of authority in eternity. Having been faithful in handling our resources in this life, we are granted leadership of others in the next (Luke 19:17, 19). "If you have not been trustworthy with someone else's property, who will give you property of your own?" (Luke 16:12). This passage implies that although we are currently stewards, responsible for handling the property of another, someday we will be owners. Jesus confirms this when he says, "Store up for yourselves treasures in heaven." He makes a clear distinction between handling someone else's property in the present and the prospect of having our own property in the future. The message seems to be that if we have not been good stewards with God's money while on earth, then we won't be property owners in heaven. But if we handle God's property well here on earth, he will give us property of our own in heaven.

THE STEWARDSHIP PARABLES

The parable of the shrewd manager (Luke 16:1-13), shows that each of us should carefully invest our financial assets, gifts, and opportunities to have an impact on people for eternity, thereby making preparations for our own eternal future.

The parable of the talents (Matthew 25:14-30) shows that we're each entrusted by God with different financial assets, gifts, and opportunities, and we'll be held accountable to God for how we've invested them in this life. We're to prepare for the Master's return by enhancing the growth of his kingdom through wisely investing his assets.

The parable of the ten minas (Luke 19:11-27) shows that those with comparable gifts, assets, and opportunities will be judged according to their faithfulness and industriousness in investing them in God's kingdom, and consequently will receive varying positions of authority in heaven.

LESSONS CONCERNING THE MASTER

Each of the stewardship parables has two major subjects, the master and the servants. The lessons concerning the master can be summarized as follows:

His ownership. The master is the true owner of all assets. The possessions, the money—even the servant—belong to the master. He has the right to do with everything as he wishes. (See the end of this chapter for an application of this critical point.)

His power. The master's will is authoritative, his decisions determinative. Behind his words there is ultimate power.

His trust. He has delegated to his servants significant financial assets and authority over his money and possessions. This indicates a level of trust in their ability to manage them. It also shows a willingness to take the risk of delegating responsibilities to people who may fail.

His expectations. The master has specific expectations of his stewards. They're not easy, but they're fair. He has every right to expect his stewards to do what he's told them.

His absence. The master is gone for a season. Because he's not physically present, there's a long-distance relationship—and, consequently, delayed accountability. It's a test of each servant to see if the master's standards are maintained even though he isn't there to give immediate reward or correction.

His return. The master will come back. It may be sooner, it may be later, but he could return at any time, likely when least expected.

His generosity. Although he has the right to expect the servant to do what he commanded without a reward, the master graciously promises reward and promotion to the steward who has been faithful.

His strictness. The master's instructions were reasonable, and he's not one to accept excuses. The servants know of his high standards and should not presume upon his grace by being lazy and disobedient. The master will take away whatever reward he would have given the servant who was unfaithful and will discipline the servant for poor stewardship.

LESSONS CONCERNING THE SERVANT

Stewardship. Servants should be acutely aware that they are not the owners, or the masters, but only caretakers or money managers. It's their job to take the assets entrusted (not given) to them and use them wisely to care for and expand the master's estate. If a servant does not fully grasp the implications of the master's ownership, it renders impossible the proper exercise of stewardship.

Accountability. Because they don't own these assets, the servants are accountable for them to the master. They will stand before him one day to explain why they invested as they did.

Faithfulness. Servants seek to be trustworthy, to handle their master's estate in a way that would please him. They do this until the master returns or until death, no matter how many years it may be. Stewardship is the life calling of the servant. Resignation isn't an option.

Industriousness. The servants must work hard, do well, and not slack off.

Wisdom in investing. Because they are managing the master's assets, servants must choose their investments carefully. They can neither afford to take undue risks nor let capital erode through idleness. The goal isn't merely to conserve resources but to multiply them. The servants must be intelligent, resourceful, and strategic thinkers regarding the best long-term investments.

Readiness for the master's return. A man went to visit the caretaker of a large estate that had an absentee owner. Noticing how meticulously the caretaker performed every chore, the visitor asked him, "When do you expect the owner to return?" The caretaker's reply: "Today, of course."

Like soldiers ready at any moment for a barracks inspection, the servants are constantly aware this could be the day of the master's return. If they knew the day or hour of that return, they could waste time. They might "borrow" some of the master's money, figuring to replace it before he comes back. When they cease to expect the master's return, embezzlement or squandering become a great temptation. But the stewards know that the master is a man of his word. He will keep his promise to return. The servants must live each day as if it were the day of the master's return. One day it will be.

> Servants should be acutely aware that they are not the owners, or the masters, but only caretakers or money managers.

Our death is equivalent to the master's return, for it marks the day our earthly service ends. Our service record "freezes" into its final form, to be evaluated as such by our Master at the judgment.

Fear of the master. The stewards know that the master is just. His instructions were explicit and his expectations high. If the stewards work wisely, they know they will fare well. The master's generosity indicates they will be handsomely rewarded.

But they also know that if they're unfaithful they will feel the master's wrath. This healthy fear motivates them to good stewardship.

Individual standing before the master. The master has a keen eye. An individual servant's efforts will not be sullied by the incompetence of others. The master may deal with other servants however he wishes. Each servant must do the job and be prepared to give account to one from whom nothing can be hidden (Hebrews 4:13).

Single-mindedness in service. The wise steward's life revolves around service for the master. All side interests are brought into orbit around this one consuming purpose in life—to serve the master well.

OVERALL LESSONS FROM THE STEWARDSHIP PARABLES

Drawing from all these parables concerning the master and the servants, several overriding principles stand out:

The long-term significance of today's behavior and choices. How we handle God's assets in our present daily life has tremendous bearing on eternal realities.

The inevitability of consequences for all our actions. The law of the eternal harvest is more certain than the laws of physics: "Do not be deceived: God cannot be mocked. A man reaps what he sows" (Galatians 6:7).

Our painstaking responsibility to choose wisely and live rightly. The master's absence is both a challenge and an opportunity to prove ourselves worthy to be elevated to greater responsibility.

Our clear-cut incentives and motivations. Unwise stewards are lazy, but wise stewards are diligent and highly motivated. They know their master well enough to know there will be lasting consequences for their labor, whether good or bad.

Our preoccupation with responsibilities, not rights. As stewards our rights are limited by our lack of ownership. Instead, we manage assets for the owner's benefit, and we carry no sense of entitlement to the assets we manage. It's our job to find out what the owner wants done with his assets, then carry out his will. If we focus on the master's rights, we will fulfill our responsibilities. But the moment we begin to focus on what we think we deserve, on what we think our master or others owe us, we lose perspective. The quality of our service deteriorates rapidly.

The meaninglessness of everyone else's evaluation of the steward compared to the judgment of our one and only master. In a context that leads to the statement that "each of us will give an account of himself to God," Paul asks, "Who are you to judge someone else's servant? To his own master he stands or falls" (Romans 14:3-4, 12). This principle is critical. In the day that we stand before our Master and Maker, it will not matter how many people on earth knew our name, how many called us great, and how many considered us fools. It will not matter whether schools and hospitals were named after us, whether our estate was large or small, whether our funeral drew ten thousand or no one. It will not matter what the newspapers or history books said or didn't say. What will matter is one thing and one thing only—what the Master thinks of us.

C. S. Lewis said it brilliantly in his essay "The World's Last Night":

We have all encountered judgments or verdicts on ourselves in this life. Every now and then we discover what our fellow creatures really think of us. I don't of course mean what they tell us to our faces: that we usually have to discount. I am thinking of what we sometimes overhear by accident or of the opinions about us which our neighbours or employees or subordinates unknowingly reveal in their actions: and of the terrible, or lovely, judgments artlessly betrayed by children or even animals. Such discoveries can be the bitterest or sweetest experiences we have. But of course both the bitter and the sweet are limited by our doubt as to the wisdom of those who judge. We always hope that those who so clearly think us cowards or bullies are ignorant and malicious; we always fear that those who trust us or admire us are misled by partiality. I suppose the experience of the Final Judgment (which may break in upon us at any moment) will be like these little experiences, but magnified to the Nth.

For it will be infallible judgment. If it is favorable we shall have no fear, if unfavorable, no hope, that it is wrong. We shall not only believe, we shall know, know beyond doubt in every fibre of our appalled or delighted being, that as the Judge has said, so we are: neither more nor less nor other. We shall perhaps even realise that in some dim fashion we could have known it all along. We shall know and all creation will know too: our ancestors, our parents, our wives or husbands, our children. The unanswerable and (by then) self-evident truth about each will be known to all. . . .

We can, perhaps, train ourselves to ask more and more often how the thing which we are saying or doing (or failing to do) at each moment will look when the irresistible light streams in upon it; that light which is so different from the light of this world—and yet, even now, we know just enough of it to take it into account. Women sometimes have the problem of trying to judge by artificial light how a dress will look by daylight. That is very like the problem of all of us: to dress our souls not for the electric lights of the present world but for the daylight of the next. The good dress is the one that will face that light. For that light will last longer.[5]

THE FULL IMPLICATIONS OF GOD'S OWNERSHIP

From beginning to end, Scripture repeatedly emphasizes God's ownership of everything:

"To the Lord your God belong the heavens, even the highest heavens, the earth and everything in it" (Deuteronomy 10:14).

"The land is mine and you are but aliens and my tenants" (Leviticus 25:23).

"Yours, O Lord, is the greatness and the power and the glory and the majesty and the splendor, for everything in heaven and earth is yours. Yours, O Lord, is the kingdom; you are exalted as head over all. Wealth and honor come from you; you are the ruler of all things" (1 Chronicles 29:11-12).

"Who has a claim against me that I must pay? Everything under heaven belongs to me" (Job 41:11).

"The earth is the Lord's and everything in it, the world, and all who live in it; for he founded it upon the seas and established it upon the waters" (Psalm 24:1-2).

"For every animal of the forest is mine, and the cattle on a thousand hills. I know every bird in the mountains, and the creatures of the field are mine. If I were hungry I would not tell you, for the world is mine, and all that is in it" (Psalm 50:10-12).

"'The silver is mine and the gold is mine,' declares the Lord Almighty" (Haggai 2:8).

Search and you won't find a single verse of Scripture that suggests that God has surrendered his ownership to us. God didn't die and leave the earth—or anything in it—to me, you, or anyone else. And if we should think, *Well, at least I own myself*, God says, "You are not your own; you were bought at a price" (1 Corinthians 6:19-20).

When teaching from 1 Corinthians 6 in a college class, I sometimes ask someone in the front row to lend me his pencil for a moment. When he hands me the pencil, I immediately take it, break it in half, throw it on the ground and crush it under my foot. The reaction of the students is shock and disbelief. What right do I have to break someone else's pencil? But then I explain that it's really my pencil, which I planted with that person before the session. Suddenly everything changes. If it's my pencil, but only if it's mine, then I have the right to do with it as I please—which is precisely Paul's point in his letter to the Corinthians. The believers in Corinth were doing what they pleased. And why not? They thought their lives were their own. But Paul said, "No, it's not your life. You own nothing, not even yourself. When you came to Christ you surrendered the title to your life. You belong to God, not to yourself. He is the only one who has the right to do what he wants with your life—your body, sexual behavior, money, possessions, everything."

God doesn't just own the universe. He owns you and me. We are twice his—first by creation, second by redemption.

> **When you came to Christ you surrendered the title to your life. You belong to God, not to yourself.**

151

Not only does God own everything, but he determines how much of his wealth he will entrust to us:

"Remember the Lord your God, for it is he who gives you the ability to produce wealth" (Deuteronomy 8:18).

"The Lord makes poor and makes rich; He brings low and lifts up" (1 Samuel 2:7, NKJV).

"Wealth and honor come from you; you are the ruler of all things" (1 Chronicles 29:12).

Stewardship is living in the light of these overriding truths. It's living with the awareness that we are managers, not owners; that we are caretakers of God's assets, which he has entrusted to us for this brief season here on earth. How we handle money and possessions demonstrates who we *really* believe is their true owner—God or us.

John Wesley posed four questions that will help us decide how to spend money. Notice how the last three flow directly out of the first one:

- In spending this money, am I acting as if I owned it, or am I acting as the Lord's trustee?
- What Scripture requires me to spend this money in this way?
- Can I offer up this purchase as a sacrifice to the Lord?
- Will God reward me for this expenditure at the resurrection of the just?[6]

If we really believe he is the owner of all that has been entrusted to us, shouldn't we regularly be asking him, "What do you want me to do with your money and your possessions?" And shouldn't we be open to the possibility that he may want us to share large portions of his assets with those whose needs are greater than ours?

HOW MY FAMILY LEARNED ABOUT GOD'S OWNERSHIP

In 1977, a group of us started the church I mentioned, where I served as one of the pastors. By 1990, the church was large, and I was making a good salary and earning royalties from my writing. Then something happened that turned our lives upside down.

I was on the board of a crisis pregnancy center and Nanci and I had opened our home to a pregnant teenager, helping her give up her baby for adoption. (We also had the joy of seeing this young woman come to Christ.) With a growing burden for children who were being aborted and after searching the Scriptures and praying, I began participating in peaceful, nonviolent rescues at abortion clinics. I was arrested several times and went to jail. An abortion clinic subsequently won a court judgment against me and twenty others. When the decision was handed down, I told the judge that normally I would pay anything I owed, but I couldn't hand over money to people who would use it to kill babies.

Soon after, I discovered that my church was about to receive a writ of garnishment, demanding that they surrender one-fourth of my wages each month to the abortion clinic. The church would either have to pay the abortion clinic or defy a court order. To avoid this, I had to resign.

The only way I could avoid garnishment was to make no more than minimum wage. (My wife could earn an income that wasn't restricted to minimum wage.) I had already divested myself of all book royalties. Fortunately, our family had been living on only a portion of my church salary, and we'd just made our final house payment, so we were out of debt.

Another court judgment followed, involving another abortion clinic. Although our actions were nonviolent, we were assessed the largest judgment ever against a group of peaceful protestors: $8.4 million. This time it seemed likely we'd lose our house. By all appearances, and certainly by the world's standards, our lives had taken a devastating turn. Right?

If God was the owner, I was the manager. More than ever before, I needed to adopt a steward's mentality toward the assets he'd entrusted— not given— to me.

Wrong. It was one of the best things that ever happened to us.

What others intended for evil, God intended for good (Genesis 50:20). We began Eternal Perspective Ministries. Nanci worked at a secretary's salary, supplementing my minimum wage. All of our assets, including the house, were hers. My name wasn't on bank accounts or checkbooks. Legally I don't own any of the books I've written. I own nothing at all. (I have access to plenty, but I still don't own anything.) I began to understand what God means when he says, "Everything under heaven belongs to me" (Job 41:11).

Ironically, I'd written extensively about God's ownership in the first edition of Money, Possessions and Eternity. Then, within a year of its publication, I no longer owned anything! God was teaching me, in the crucible of adversity, the life-changing implications of that truth.

I realized that our house belonged to God, not us. Why worry about whether or not we would keep it if it belonged to him anyway? He has no shortage of resources. He could easily provide us another place to live.

But learning about ownership was only half the lesson. If God was the owner, I was the manager. More than ever before, I needed to adopt a steward's mentality toward the assets he'd entrusted—not given—to me.

I thank him for his grace in teaching me the full implications of his ownership.

Despite the $8.4 million court judgment, we never lost our house. While paying me a minimum-wage salary (with generous benefits, including allowing my wife and me to drive ministry-owned cars), Eternal Perspective Ministries owned my books. Then something interesting happened. Suddenly the books were on the best-seller lists. Royalties increased. Our ministry has been able to give away all of those royalties to missions, famine relief, and pro-life work. In recent years, by God's grace, the ministry has given more than $500,000. Sometimes I think God sells the books just to raise funds for ministries close to his heart!

Nanci and I don't go to bed at night feeling that we've "sacrificed" that money, wishing somehow we could get our hands on it. We go to bed feeling joy, because there's nothing like giving. For me, the only feeling that compares is the joy of leading someone to Christ. Giving infuses life with joy. It interjects an eternal dimension into even the most ordinary day. That's just one reason you couldn't pay me enough not to give.

In 2001, when the ten-year judgment from the abortion clinic expired, some of our ministry board members suggested that Nanci and I could assume ownership of the books and royalties.

She and I talked and prayed about it—and we came to the same conviction. God had faithfully provided for us during the previous ten years. Why would we want to change that? We don't need a higher standard of living. We don't need a better house or car. We don't need a better retirement program or more insurance. So, with joy in our hearts, we said, "No thanks." (Six months later, we discovered that the abortion clinic had gotten the judgment extended for another ten years, but we're thankful we didn't know that when we made our decision!)

It's all about ownership and stewardship. They're not my book royalties—they're God's. Nanci and I have a certain amount we live on, and the rest goes to the kingdom. We're certainly comfortable. We don't need a million dollars or a hundred thousand dollars. We do fine on a lot less. God provides for us faithfully. And we get to experience one of life's greatest thrills—the joy of giving.

SETTING OUR OWN SALARIES

The Owner, God, has put each of our names on his account. We have unrestricted access to it, a privilege that is subject to abuse. As his money managers, God trusts us to set our own salaries. We draw needed funds from his wealth to pay our living expenses. One of our central spiritual decisions is determining what's a reasonable amount to live on. Whatever that amount is—and it will legitimately vary from person to person—we shouldn't hoard or waste the excess. After all, it's his, not ours. And he has something to say about where to put it.

The money manager has legitimate needs, and the Owner is generous—he doesn't demand that his stewards live in poverty, and he doesn't resent us for making reasonable expenditures on ourselves. But suppose the Owner sees us living luxuriously in a mansion, driving only the best cars, and flying first class? Isn't there a point where as stewards we can cross the line of reasonable expenses? Won't the Owner call us to account for squandering money that's not ours?

We're called God's servants, and we're told he requires us to "prove faithful" (1 Corinthians 4:2). We're God's errand boys and delivery girls. We should keep that in mind when we set our salaries. Let's not have an overinflated view of our own value. We don't own the store. We just work here!

Suppose you have something important you want to get to someone who needs it. You wrap it up and hand it over to the FedEx delivery person. What would you think if, instead of delivering the package, the driver took it home, opened it, and kept it?

When you confront him and he says, "If you didn't want me to keep it, why'd you give it to me in the first place?" You'd say, "You don't get it. The package doesn't belong to you. You're just the middleman. Your job is to get the package from me and deliver it to those I want to have it." Likewise, just because God puts his money in our hands doesn't mean he intends for us to keep it!

MODERN LESSONS IN OWNERSHIP AND STEWARDSHIP

As a lesson in stewardship, some churches have conducted reverse offerings, in which a plate is passed and each person takes five or ten dollars out of it. Receivers are entrusted with this amount from the church, and their job is to ask God to guide them and help them choose something in which they can make a spiritual investment. In one church, someone used the money to buy a meal for someone on the street and talked to him about Christ. Someone else bought a book to give to a neighbor who needed encouragement. Another person bought some inexpensive flowers and took them to a shut-in. One spent it on a long-distance call to rekindle a relationship with a friend she hadn't talked to for decades. Several who knew one particular woman pooled their funds and bought her an antibiotic and some rice she needed.

The great thing about this exercise is that it drives home the true nature of stewardship. The truth is, it isn't just that the church entrusts us with five or ten dollars on a particular Sunday. It's that all the money we have belongs to God and is entrusted to us by him every day, week, month, and year of our lives. He wants us to pray and ask him to guide us into choosing the best eternal investments, both small and large.

Over the years I have received many wonderful letters in response to this book. One seems particularly appropriate to quote here:

> This past July 26, our house burned to the ground. God graciously
> permitted it while we were elsewhere, 500 miles away. Your book
> has brought focus to my life. It was quite literally a God-send.
>
> I didn't have the same immediate reaction to my house burning as
> did John Wesley. But the Lord strengthened our faith, and our trust in

Him never wavered. We have fervently prayed that He would use us to show others Christ through this wonderful opportunity to witness.

I have been blessed by the Lord with much more wealth than most. The fire burned away the temporal wood, hay, and stubble in my life and illuminated the path to store up for ourselves treasures in heaven. We used to tithe, and gave a pittance over that to a few parachurch ministries, but since the fire and reading your book the scales have begun to drop from my eyes. I see now that I have been very miserly. With the Lord's help, that has all changed.

Now we live much more simply. The house that burned was a gorgeous 3,500 square foot stone house, replete with original oils, antiques, very expensive oriental rugs, etc., etc. We moved into our guesthouse, a comfortable 1,600-square-foot manufactured house. We are not rebuilding, but will continue to live here until the Lord moves us elsewhere. We continue to tithe, of course, but unlike pre-July 26, we live on much less, reinvest in our businesses as the Lord directs, and give the rest away.

I also learned that materialism can take unexpected forms. I always thought of materialism as meaning that one loves material possessions for their monetary value. As one with substantial inherited wealth, money was never that important to me. I loved certain possessions because I grew up with them, and they once belonged to my beloved parents. I didn't care how much they were worth, since I would never sell them. Being among them gave me a sense of love and security, a feeling that my parents were not completely gone but something of what they loved I could still see and touch. The Lord has disciplined me. I now understand that my love for those things had come between Him and me.

Now I have a much better understanding of what the Lord Jesus meant when He said that a man must be willing to give up his house, or father, or mother, for His sake and the Gospel's (Mark 10:30). Thank you so much for your book. It has resulted in more funds being directed to the building of God's kingdom.[7]

The writer sent me pictures of the home that had burned to the ground. It was a vivid reminder of what will happen to all things. When we realize they belong to God and not us, it removes from us the burden of worry or despair. What we value most, the treasures we will enjoy for eternity, are in heaven, not on earth.

TRANSFERRING THE TITLE DEED TO GOD

God owns all things, whether we recognize it or not. But life becomes much clearer—and in some respects much easier—when we consciously recognize it. The question isn't whether we theoretically affirm God's ownership. The question is whether we've deliberately transferred the ownership of ourselves and all our assets to him. Have we invited him to be what Scripture says he is— Creator, Owner, and Controller of us, family, possessions, and "our" money? Have we extended the invitation again after we've forgotten and taken things back into our hands? This self-surrender to God is the beginning of true stewardship.

John Wesley asked, "Can any steward *afford* to be an errant knave? To waste his Lord's goods? Can any servant *afford* to lay out his master's money any otherwise than his master appoints him?" A test of our stewardship is whether we ask God to show us what to do with his money. If we don't consult him, we act as if we were owners, not stewards.

> When I grasp that I'm a steward, not an owner, it totally changes my perspective.

When I grasp that I'm a steward, not an owner, it totally changes my perspective. Suddenly, I'm not asking, "How much of my money shall I, out of the goodness of my heart, give to God?" Rather, I'm asking, "Since all of 'my' money is really yours, Lord, how would you like me to invest your money today?"

When I realize that God has a claim not on a few dollars to throw in an offering plate, not on 10 percent or 50 percent but 100 percent of "my" money, it's revolutionary. Suddenly I'm God's money manager. I'm not God. Money isn't God. God is God. He's in his place, I'm in mine, money's in its.

Not only does God own everything, God controls everything. Again, the implications are enormous. I don't have to own everything. I don't have to control everything. It's in better hands than mine. When catastrophe strikes, I can honestly adopt the posture of John Wesley when he said, "The Lord's house burned down. That means one less responsibility for me."

God's ownership and sovereignty offer such a life-changing and freeing perspective when the house is robbed, the car is totaled, the bike is stolen . . . or when the diagnosis is terminal cancer.

To visualize and reinforce this vital concept in your mind, I suggest you sit down and draw up a title deed, or use the one on the following page.

When we come to Christ, God puts all his resources at our disposal. He also expects us to put all our resources at his disposal. This is what stewardship— and the Christian life—is all about.

TRANSFER OF TITLE

Date: _____

I hereby acknowledge God's ownership of me and all "my" money and possessions, and everything else I've ever imagined belonged to me—including my family and loved ones. Instead of seeing myself as the ultimate recipient, I will see myself as God's delivery boy or girl, enjoying what he intends me to keep and distributing what he intends to go elsewhere. From this point forward I will think of these assets as his to do with as he wishes. I will do my utmost to ask him and to prayerfully consider how he wishes me to invest his assets to further his kingdom. In doing so I realize I will surrender certain temporary earthly treasures but gain in exchange eternal treasures, as well as increased perspective and decreased anxiety.

Signed: _____

Witness: _____

CHAPTER 11

The Pilgrim Mentality

And so it is that when a man walks along a road, the lighter he travels, the happier he is; equally, on this journey of life, a man is more blessed if he does not pant beneath a burden of riches. TERTULLIAN

If a man have Christ in his heart, heaven before his eyes, and only as much of temporal blessing as is just needful to carry him safely through life, then pain and sorrow have little to shoot at. WILLIAM BURNS

Let temporal things serve your use, but the eternal be the object of your desire. THOMAS Á KEMPIS

A wealthy plantation owner invited John Wesley to his home. The two rode their horses all day, seeing just a fraction of all the man owned. At the end of the day the plantation owner proudly asked, "Well, Mr. Wesley, what do you think?" After a moment's silence, Wesley replied, "I think you're going to have a hard time leaving all this."

All of us form attachments. All of us have a place we call home. The question is, do we think and live as if this world, or the next world, is our home? Are our minds on earth or heaven? The plantation owner was attached to the world he was in. Wesley was attached to the world he was going to.

Perhaps you've heard it said, "He's so heavenly minded he's of no earthly good." Yet Scripture commands us to set our minds on heaven. It says, "Since, then, you have been raised with Christ, set your hearts on things above, where Christ is seated at the right hand of God. Set your minds on things above, not on earthly things" (Colossians 3:1-2).

When we're properly heavenly minded, we'll be of maximum heavenly and earthly good. But when we are too earthly minded, we will ultimately bring no good to heaven or earth. C. S. Lewis writes:

If you read history you will find that the Christians who did most for the present world were just those who thought most of the next.

The Apostles themselves, who set on foot the conversion of the Roman Empire, the great men who built up the Middle Ages, the English Evangelicals who abolished the slave trade, all left their mark on Earth, precisely because their minds were occupied with Heaven. It is since Christians have largely ceased to think of the other world that they have become so ineffective in this.[1]

Materialism would dupe us into believing this world is center stage, the destination rather than the road to the destination. From there it's a short step to racing off to earn, collect, accumulate, take, and consume, as if that's all there is to life. Then we wake up one day to realize how terribly unhappy we are or, just as likely, we never wake up at all. To escape the gravity of materialism we desperately need to redirect our minds toward heaven.

As usual, A. W. Tozer had something significant to say on the subject:

It has been cited as a flaw in Christianity that it is more concerned with the world to come than with the world that now is, and some timid souls have been fluttering about trying to defend the faith of Christ against this accusation as a mother hen defends her chicks from the hawk.

Both the attack and the defense are wasted. No one who knows what the New Testament is about will worry over the charge that Christianity is other-worldly. Of course it is, and that is precisely where its power lies. . . .

Let no one apologize for the powerful emphasis Christianity lays upon the doctrine of the world to come. Right there lies its immense superiority to everything else within the whole sphere of human thought or experience. When Christ arose from death and ascended into heaven He established forever three important facts: namely, that this world has been condemned to ultimate dissolution, that the human spirit persists beyond the grave and that there is indeed a world to come. . . .

The church is constantly being tempted to accept this world as her home, and sometimes she has listened to the blandishments of those who would woo her away and use her for their own ends. But if she is wise she will consider that she stands in the valley between the mountain peaks of eternity past and eternity to come. The past is gone forever and the present is passing as swift as the shadow on the sun dial of Ahaz. Even if the earth should continue a million years, not one of us could stay to enjoy it. We do well to think of the long tomorrow.[2]

TIME AND ETERNITY

Can we of the short today really comprehend the long tomorrow? God "has also set eternity in the hearts of men; yet they cannot fathom what God has done from beginning to end" (Ecclesiastes 3:11). We are made for heaven, but meanwhile we live on earth. Life's great disillusionments come as we try to force our round, made-for-eternity hearts into the rectangular hole of this earth. They just don't fit. We do not fit. No matter how far we stray from the narrow path of kingdom living, we remain children of eternity, not time.

Think about the special spiritual moments you've experienced—perhaps in prayer, at a baptism, in communion, a conversation with a loved one, a simple walk on the beach, or in the woods, gazing up into the bright stars of a night sky, or when you've done something you know God is pleased with. Have you ever had a sense of moving on the edge of eternity, briefly but really breaking into its circle, knowing in that moment that you were participating, catching a faint glimpse of what the universe must be about? Have you ever sensed that the world you were made for was not this one, but another? This was just a peek at eternity. It was the awakening of a desire that lies deep within, where God has set eternity in our hearts.

C. S. Lewis casts light on this desire:

> Creatures are not born with desires unless satisfaction for those desires exists. A baby feels hunger: well, there is such a thing as food. A duckling wants to swim: well, there is such a thing as water. Men feel sexual desire: well, there is such a thing as sex. If I find in myself a desire which no experience in this world can satisfy, the most probable explanation is that I was made for another world. If none of my earthly pleasures satisfy it, that does not prove that the universe is a fraud. Probably earthly pleasures were never meant to satisfy it, but only to arouse it, to suggest the real thing. If that is so, I must take care, on the one hand, never to despise, or be unthankful for, these early blessings, and on the other, never to mistake them for the something else of which they are only a kind of copy, or echo, or mirage. I must keep alive in myself the desire for my true country, which I shall not find till after death; I must never let it get snowed under or turned aside; I must make it the main object of life to press on to that other country and to help others to do the same.[3]

From childhood most of us learn to shut out our "true country," to stifle our thirst for the eternal, replacing it with the pursuit of the temporal. This is how we who were created to be spiritual end up being such accomplished materialists. But when we live with eternity in view, we'll do many things differently, and those we do the same will be done with transformed perspective—not only teaching and preaching and witnessing, but also washing dishes and pruning trees and repairing carburetors. Almost any honest activity—whether building a shed, driving a bus, or caring for a patient—can be an eternal contribution to people, an investment in God's eternal plan.

TWO COVENANTS, TWO COUNTRIES

In the Old Testament, material blessing was given for obedience (Deuteronomy 28:2), yet in the New Testament many of the saints were poor (Matthew 8:20; 2 Corinthians 11:27; James 2:5). Enjoying worldly wealth is emphasized in the Old Testament (Deuteronomy 28:11; Joshua 1:15; Proverbs 15:6), yet the New Testament talks of giving away possessions (Mark 10:17-21; 1 Timothy 6:17-18). By their obedience, the Israelites avoided persecution (Deuteronomy 28:7), but by their obedience Christians incur persecution (Matthew 5:11-12; 2 Timothy 3:12; 1 Peter 1:6).

Why this disparity? Because God was determined that New Testament saints would understand that their home is in another world. No book better demonstrates the relationship of Old and New Testaments, and the two worlds on which they center, than the book of Hebrews. The new covenant is said to be "founded on better promises" than the Old (Hebrews 8:6). The Old Testament is copy and type and shadow. Accordingly, the material blessings promised to Old Testament saints are to remind us of our future heavenly blessings—but never are they to replace them. The new covenant brings not the temporal inheritance promised Israel, but an eternal inheritance (Hebrews 9:15).

We no longer sacrifice animals, because the Lamb of God has come. We no longer worship in a temple, because we ourselves are temples of God's Holy Spirit. We no longer go to a priest, because Christ is our high priest, and we ourselves are a believing priesthood. We no longer look to material riches, because of the spiritual riches that are ours in Christ.

God demonstrated to the nations surrounding Israel his superiority to their gods by prospering the people of Israel when they obeyed him. Now he wishes to display Christ's lordship and presence to the world around us through a better faith and morality, not a higher standard of living.

The Israelites were citizens of the Promised Land (Deuteronomy 8:7-9; 11:8-12). Their destination was on this earth. But New Testament saints haven't yet arrived at their destination and won't until our lives here are done. We're told our citizenship is in heaven (Philippians 3:20; 1 Peter 2:11). The Promised Land was a foretaste of the glory that awaits us. We are to stake our claim in the ultimate Promised Land: "You have come to Mount Zion, to the heavenly Jerusalem, the city of the living God" (Hebrews 12:22). The earthly Jerusalem isn't our destination. It's only a signpost pointing the way, just as earthly blessings aren't our ultimate rewards, just foretastes of what's coming.

Hebrews speaks of promised blessings, a great inheritance of lasting possessions (Hebrews 6:12; 10:34; 11:13-16). These promises must be patiently awaited, because they come not in this world but the next (Hebrews 10:35-39; 11:13, 16). Our destination is as much superior to the Promised Land of Palestine as Christ's blood was superior to the blood of bulls and goats. The effect of prosperity theology is to promote "heaven on earth." But prior to Christ's return there can be no heaven on earth. When earth becomes our heaven—when we see God's blessings as being primarily immediate and temporal—we lose sight of who we are, why we are here, and what awaits us beyond the horizons of this world.

Much disappointment comes in expecting God to do in the present what he has promised for the future. The fallacy is not in thinking that God repays faithfulness. He does. The fallacy is in thinking that this payment takes place in the wrong way, in the wrong time, in the wrong place. God's primary means of payment isn't with this world's goods. His primary timing isn't now, it's later; it's not here, it's there. Every time we seek a short-term payday, we lose out on the long-term (Matthew 6:1-18). If we desire to look out for our own best interests, in the truest sense, we will seek our reward later, not now; and not here, but there.

AT HOME IN THIS WORLD?

Scripture spells out our identity and our role here on earth:

Our citizenship is in heaven, not earth (Philippians 3:20).

We are ambassadors representing Christ to the world (2 Corinthians 5:20).

We are aliens, strangers, and pilgrims on this earth (Hebrews 11:13).

These passages argue not only against prosperity theology but against a large proportion of evangelical teaching, preaching, and literature that is geared toward making us more at home in this world. James warns us of the dangers of worldliness: "You adulterous people, don't you know that friendship with the world is hatred toward God? Anyone who chooses to be a friend of the world becomes an enemy of God" (James 4:4).

Imagine an ambassador from the United States who goes to work in another country hostile to America. Naturally, he'll want to learn about this new place, see the sights, become familiar with the people and culture. But suppose eventually he becomes so comfortable in this foreign country that he begins to regard it as his true home. His allegiance wavers. He gradually compromises his position as an American ambassador. He becomes ineffective in representing the best interests of his mother country. His loyalties are transferred and eventually he defects. First he becomes useless to the cause of his own country. Then he betrays it.

> Much disappointment comes in expecting God to do in the present what he has promised for the future.

Peter writes, "Since you call on a Father who judges each man's work impartially, live your lives as strangers here in reverent fear" (1 Peter 1:17). Later he adds, "I urge you, as aliens and strangers in the world, to abstain from sinful desires, which war against your soul" (1 Peter 2:11). We are strangers and aliens here. We must never become too much at home in this world or we'll become useless to our true kingdom. We too may betray it.

Our earthly bodies are called "tents," temporary dwelling places for our eternal soul (2 Peter 1:13). Paul contrasts our brief time on earth with what he regarded as the real life, of which this is but a foreshadow: "While we are in this tent, we groan and are burdened, because we do not wish to be unclothed but to be clothed with our heavenly dwelling, so that what is mortal may be swallowed up by life" (2 Corinthians 5:4).

The writer of Hebrews explains what it means to be a pilgrim:

> By faith Abraham, when called to go to a place he would later receive as his inheritance, obeyed and went, even though he did not know where he was going. By faith he made his home in the promised land like a stranger in a foreign country; he lived in tents, as did Isaac and Jacob, who were heirs with him of the same promise. For he was looking forward to the city with foundations, whose architect and builder is God. (Hebrews 11:8-10)

Abraham didn't know where he was going, but he knew with whom he was going. He was able to live in this world and not receive the things promised, knowing there was an eternity in which promises would be fulfilled and a city awaiting him as far superior to an earthly city as its Architect and Builder is superior to men. (Note that the greatest Old Testament saints were those who ultimately saw beyond the temporal to the eternal; they became models for faith.)

> All these people were still living by faith when they died. They did not receive the things promised; they only saw them and welcomed them from a distance. And they admitted that they were aliens and strangers on earth. People who say such things show that they are looking for a country of their own. If they had been thinking of the country they had left, they would have had opportunity to return. Instead, they were longing for a better country—a heavenly one. Therefore God is not ashamed to be called their God, for he has prepared a city for them. (Hebrews 11:13-16)

Faith isn't insisting we get what we seek now. It's believing we'll get it later. This is in stark contrast to prosperity theology, which sees faith as a means of claiming immediate rather than eventual blessing. Following Christ is seeing and welcoming from a distance our eternal reward—not getting it now. The great people of faith were looking for a country "of their own," better than anything earth could offer.

If these saints had focused on their own possessions, their real estate on earth, they might have forfeited their *real* estate in heaven. If the great saints whose lives are recorded in "faith's hall of fame" in Hebrews 11 had gauged their lives by the short-term standards of the health and wealth gospel, today we wouldn't know their names. Instead, they longed for "a better country—a heavenly one." Because they lived on earth in light of their fixation on heaven, God was pleased with them, so pleased that "he has prepared a city for them" (Hebrews 11:16).

Moses also lived with an acute awareness of the eternal:

> By faith Moses, when he had grown up, refused to be known as the son of Pharaoh's daughter. He chose to be mistreated along with the people of God rather than to enjoy the pleasures of sin for a short time. He regarded disgrace for the sake of Christ as of greater value than the treasures of Egypt, because he was looking ahead to his reward. By faith he left Egypt, not fearing the king's anger; he persevered because he saw him who is invisible. (Hebrews 11:24-27)

Moses could forgo pleasures and possessions that wouldn't last because he anticipated pleasures and possessions that would last forever. He turned his back on Egypt's treasures to pursue heaven's treasures. He feared not the king of Egypt, but the King of Heaven.

THE PILGRIM, HIS MONEY AND POSSESSIONS

The Levites had no earthly inheritance, because God himself was their inheritance (Deuteronomy 18:1-2). Christians have been told that we are "a chosen people, a royal priesthood, a holy nation, a people belonging to God" (1 Peter 2:9). The priests had no earthly inheritance, and neither do we of the new covenant priesthood. We are both princes and priests. We are "heirs of God and co-heirs with Christ" (Romans 8:17), but ours is "an inheritance that can never perish, spoil or fade—kept in heaven for you" (1 Peter 1:4).

The more holdings we have on earth, the more likely we are to forget that we're citizens of another world, not this one, and that our inheritance lies there, not here. Pilgrims are unattached. They are travelers, not settlers, who are acutely aware that excessive things will distract and burden them. Material things are valuable to pilgrims, but only as they facilitate their mission. If you were traveling through a country on foot or on a bicycle, what would your attitude be toward possessions? You wouldn't hate them or think them evil—but you would choose them strategically. Unnecessary things would slow your journey or even force you to stop.

Many of us are called to stay in one place and we naturally become "settlers" in one sense, living in houses, building barns, owning furniture, tools, crops, and businesses. There's nothing wrong with this. But we must cultivate the pilgrim mentality of detachment, the traveler's utilitarian philosophy concerning

165

If you were traveling through a country on foot or on a bicycle, what would your attitude be toward possessions?

things. We need to be able to live in a house without owning it, or own a house without being owned by it. If God so directs us, as he has many of his disciples, we need to be able to leave behind a farm or a business or a house without going back.

The slaves in early America understood the pilgrim mentality. Without possessions, without rights, they lived for another world, a better one. This central theme permeated their spirituals. They sang, "I am a poor wayfarin' stranger, a travelin' far away from home," and "Soon I will be done with the troubles of the world, I'm goin' home to live with God." They sang, "Swing low, sweet chariot, comin' fo' to carry me home." They knew that home wasn't earth, but heaven.

Wealth entrenches us in the present world. Financial commitments and debts can be like spikes chained to our legs and driven into the ground, making us unresponsive to God's call to serve him elsewhere. God may never call me to move on from my home or business or country. But I must be in a position to say yes if he does. If not, I might wonder all my life if he may have had other plans for me—plans I didn't hear or respond to because I was so tied to where I was.

There are many roadblocks to giving: unbelief, insecurity, pride, idolatry, desire for power and control. The raging current of our culture—and often our churches—makes it hard to swim upstream. It's considered normal to keep far more than we give.

I'm convinced that the greatest deterrent to our giving is this: the illusion that earth is our home. Where we choose to store our treasures depends largely on where we think our home is. Those who think of earth as their real home will naturally want to pile up treasures here. Those who think of heaven as their real home will naturally want to pile up treasures there. It all comes down to the question, "Where's your home?" To the Christian, God gives a clear answer. The only question is whether we'll live as if that answer is true.

DOES THE PILGRIM MENTALITY FOSTER ASCETICISM?

How does a pilgrim's perspective differ from asceticism, the philosophy I critiqued in an earlier chapter? Doesn't the pilgrim mentality lead to a sour or cynical view of this present world? Precisely the opposite! It's the materialist, not the Christian pilgrim, who is the cynic. The typical citizen of this world doesn't derive true satisfaction from worldly things. Materialists can't fully appreciate the joys and wonders of creation. It's the believer who can see the Creator's handiwork everywhere, who truly sees the beauty of mountains, rivers, and waterfalls. No one appreciates creation like someone who knows the Creator. No one can appreciate a good meal like those who love the one who provided it. No one can enjoy marriage like the one who knows its

Architect and understands the greater reality that marriage foreshadows (Ephesians 5:31-32).

Those in love with this world never get the best it has to offer. They expect the world to deliver them from their internal emptiness, and when they find that it can't, they're forever disillusioned. Christian pilgrims have no such illusions about the world. They appreciate it for what it is—a magnificent creation of the God who alone can fill the emptiness of their heart. C. S. Lewis said, "Because we love something else more than this world, we love even this world better than those who know no other."[4]

When I travel, I find particular joy in those places that remind me of my lifelong home in Oregon. Likewise, one of the greatest joys that Christian pilgrims find in this world is in those moments when it reminds them of heaven, their true home. They have not seen heaven, but they have read about it and dreamed about it. They live with the exhilarating assurance that at this very moment their beloved Savior is making it ready for them (John 14:2-3).

In the truest sense, Christian pilgrims have the best of both worlds. We have joy whenever this world reminds us of the next. And we have comfort whenever it does not. We have the promise of a new heaven and new earth, where the worst elements of this world—sorrow, pain, death, and the tears they produce—will be gone forever (Revelation 21:4). Yet we also know that the best elements of this world—love, joy, wonder, worship, and beauty—will not be gone but intensified and perfected in the remade world. "Aim at heaven," C. S. Lewis says, "and you will get earth thrown in. Aim at earth and you will get neither."[5]

In The Last Battle, the final book of The Chronicles of Narnia, when Jewel the unicorn reaches Aslan's country, he exclaims, "I have come home at last! This is my real country! I belong here. This is the land I have been looking for all my life, though I never knew it till now. The reason why we loved the old Narnia is that it sometimes looked a little like this."[6]

> In the truest sense, Christian pilgrims have the best of both worlds. We have joy whenever this world reminds us of the next. And we have comfort whenever it does not.

EAGER TO POSSESS

This is the Christian attitude toward possessions, forged in the crucible of adversity: "You . . . joyfully accepted the confiscation of your property, because you knew that you yourselves had better and lasting possessions" (Hebrews 10:34).

This passage hinges on what follows the "because." We misread it if we conclude that God's people place no value on personal property. No. The passage tells us they were able to joyfully surrender their earthly property precisely *because* they did value property—real property that is "better and lasting."

They knew that earthly goods could rust, decay, and be stolen (Matthew 6:19-21). And they knew that even if by sweat and fretting they could manage to hold onto them, at most they would last but a short time and be destined for destruction. But listen to the promise that follows the guarantee of material destruction:

> The day of the Lord will come like a thief. The heavens will disappear with a roar; the elements will be destroyed by fire, and the earth and everything in it will be laid bare.
>
> Since everything will be destroyed in this way, what kind of people ought you to be? You ought to live holy and godly lives as you look forward to the day of God and speed its coming. That day will bring about the destruction of the heavens by fire, and the elements will melt in the heat. But in keeping with his promise we are looking forward to a new heaven and a new earth, the home of righteousness.
>
> So then, dear friends, since you are looking forward to this, make every effort to be found spotless, blameless and at peace with him.
> (2 Peter 3:10-14)

Here we see the immediate lifestyle implications of the return of Christ. He promises special reward to those who, uninfatuated with the present world, "have longed for his appearing" (2 Timothy 4:8).

We are told in several places that the Lord will return unexpectedly, like a thief in the night. After using that analogy, Paul says, "You, brothers, are not in darkness" (1 Thessalonians 5:2-4). In other words, Christ's sudden return will not take by surprise those who are prepared for it.

Although its central point is unexpectedness, the analogy of Christ's return to the arrival of a thief is interesting as it relates to money and possessions. The thief's design is to make his victims poorer by taking their treasures. If our treasures are on earth, Christ's return will indeed make us poorer, because it will take away our earthly treasures just as surely as a thief raiding a house.

But if we have stored up our treasures in heaven, Christ's return will bring treasures to us, rather than take them away—the very opposite of a thief's intent. Christ will turn the analogy on its head, because the faithful believer will not become poorer when Christ returns, but immeasurably richer!

In Hebrews, after a series of inspiring stories about the hardships faced by God's people with their eyes on heaven (Hebrews 11:35-40), the writer presents a challenge:

> Therefore, since we are surrounded by such a great cloud of witnesses,
> let us throw off everything that hinders and the sin that so easily

entangles, and let us run with perseverance the race marked out for us. Let us fix our eyes on Jesus, the author and perfecter of our faith, who for the joy set before him endured the cross, scorning its shame, and sat down at the right hand of the throne of God. (Hebrews 12:1-2)

The writer's concern is not only for the sin that entangles us, but for the morally neutral things that hinder us. No one runs a race carrying a television, stereo, computer, or recliner. If we're to have such things, we must be able to let go of them. If we can pass them through our hands to others, or leave them at a moment's notice, only then are they safe in our possession. Otherwise we fix our eyes on them rather than on Jesus, and we will either veer off course or stop running the race altogether.

Pilgrims of faith look to the next world, their eyes on a certain hope that will never forsake them. Eyes clear and unclouded, they see money and possessions for what they are—useful for kingdom purposes, but far too flimsy to bear the weight of trust and wholly unable to survive the coming holocaust of things.

The book of Hebrews ends with one more reminder to believers who are tempted to live in the light of this world and not the next: "For here we do not have an enduring city, but we are looking for the city that is to come" (Hebrews 13:14).

The hymn writer says it beautifully:

Turn your eyes upon Jesus,
Look full in His wonderful face,
And the things of earth will grow strangely dim
In the light of His glory and grace.

CINDERELLA WITH AMNESIA

All of us need to lock arms with a group of comrades who will inspire and encourage us and challenge us to greater accomplishments for God's kingdom causes. That's why we all desperately need to be part of a local church where God's Word is taught and God's Son is worshiped (Hebrews 10:25). Hebrews shows how today's churches can trace their heritage back to the ancient body of Christ and heroes of the faith throughout the ages.

Michael Griffiths wrote *God's Forgetful Pilgrims*, in which he maintains that the church has largely forgotten her wondrous identity in Christ and has settled for the world's substitute identities. I came across the original British edition of the book, which had a more striking title: *Cinderella with Amnesia*. As children of God, we are prized by the Prince, chosen by him to reign at his side (1 Peter 2:9). Yet, beautiful and beloved as we are to the Prince, we go right on—like Cinderella with amnesia—living in drudgery as citizens of a second-class country, forfeiting heavenly treasures by clinging to earthly ones.

Back in Kansas, with her experience in the land of Oz behind her, Dorothy said, "There's no place like home." How true! But how easily we forget where our home really is. At death, a Christian doesn't leave home. We *go* home: "We . . . prefer to be away from the body and at home with the Lord" (2 Corinthians 5:8). Consider the paradox—our true home is a place we've never been! (Had we been there we could hardly bear to live here.) Home is where our Father is. Though content to be about our Father's business here in these motel rooms we call bodies, we're never entirely at home. How can we be? Our true home is so far superior, the spiritual family there so vast and rich. The Great Reunion awaits us. We long for it.

When we understand what home really is, money and things lose their glitter. We finally see them as they have been all along: pale, insipid, cheap imitations of the true and vast wealth that is ours as children of God.

Perhaps we should say aloud, over and over, the words of the song: "This world is not my home." C. S. Lewis put it well: "Our Father refreshes us on the journey with some pleasant inns, but will not encourage us to mistake them for home."[7]

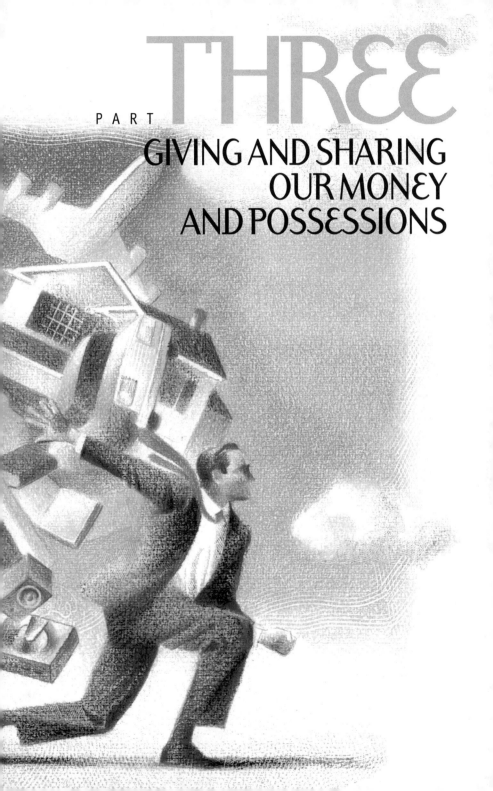

PART **THREE**

GIVING AND SHARING OUR MONEY AND POSSESSIONS

CHAPTER **12**

Tithing: The Training Wheels of Giving

The Jews were constrained to a regular payment of tithes;
Christians, who have liberty, assign all their possessions to
the Lord, bestowing freely not the lesser portions of their
property, since they have the hope of greater things.
IRENAEUS

Tithes are required as a matter of debt, and he who has
been unwilling to give them has been guilty of robbery.
Whosoever, therefore, desires to secure a reward for
himself, let him render tithes, and out of the nine parts
let him seek to give alms. AUGUSTINE

On the wall of President Lyndon Johnson's White House office hung a framed letter written by General Sam Houston to Johnson's great-grandfather, George W. Baines, more than a hundred years earlier. Baines had led Houston to Christ and the general was a changed man, no longer coarse and belligerent, but peaceful and content. After General Houston was baptized—an incredible event for those who knew him—he offered to pay half the local minister's salary. When someone asked him why, he said, "My pocketbook was baptized too." Sam Houston demonstrated the reality of God's grace to him by reciprocating that grace through giving.

According to the Christian Stewardship Association, in 1899—when the total number of books published was a tiny fraction of what we have today—a bibliography on "Tithing and Systematic Proportionate Giving" listed more than 500 titles. Today, although thousands of new Christian books are published annually, very few deal with money-related subjects—and even fewer take a close look at the scriptural teaching on this subject. The great majority of Bible colleges and seminaries have no courses, required or elective, devoted to a biblical study of stewardship or giving. Pastors are almost never trained to address these vital aspects of the Christian life.

The more America has gained wealth, the less the Church has addressed the subject of giving. Perhaps that's why the percentage of income Christians give away has been declining for thirty years. In fact, dollar for dollar, the average American gave more during the Great Depression than today.

In this section, we'll examine the biblical teaching on giving and sharing our money and possessions. Then we'll look at the acquisition and use of funds by churches and ministries.

THE MEANING OF TITHING

I begin with the subject of tithing, not to promote legalism, but to begin where God began historically. Although Christian giving goes far beyond tithing, the principle of tithing was ingrained in the beliefs and lifestyles of the early Christians, most of whom grew up in Jewish homes.

"A tithe of everything from the land, whether grain from the soil or fruit from the trees, belongs to the Lord; it is holy to the Lord" (Leviticus 27:30). The tithe "belongs to the Lord," not to people. It applied to "everything," not some things. It was "holy," to be set apart and given to God, not used for any other purpose.

The meaning of the word *tithe* is "a tenth part." Today the term tithing is often erroneously used of all giving. People talk about "tithing" fifty dollars, when they make two thousand dollars a month (a tithe of which is two hundred dollars, not fifty). You can *donate* 2 percent or 4 percent or 6 percent of your income, but you cannot *tithe* it, any more than you can "whitewash" a wall with red paint. The Israelites were warned that to present to their Creator anything less than the full 10 percent was to "rob God," since the first 10 percent belonged to him, not them:

> "Will a man rob God? Yet you rob me. But you ask, 'How do we rob you?' In tithes and offerings. You are under a curse—the whole nation of you—because you are robbing me. Bring the whole tithe into the storehouse, that there may be food in my house. Test me in this," says the Lord Almighty, "and see if I will not throw open the floodgates of heaven and pour out so much blessing that you will not have room enough for it." (Malachi 3:8-10)

God says, "Bring the *whole* tithe into the storehouse," not just part of it. The obedient Israelite didn't ask whether he could give 7 percent, or whether he could tithe on the "net" rather than the "gross." Whatever God provided, 10 percent belonged to him.

Actually, there was not just one tithe for Israelites, but three. One tithe supported the priests and Levites (Numbers 18:21, 24), another provided for a sacred festival (Deuteronomy 12:17-18; 14:23), and the third tithe supported orphans, widows, and the poor (Deuteronomy 14:28-29; 26:12-13).

The Levite and festival tithes were perpetual tithes, but the tithe for the poor was collected only every third year. This amounted to an average of 23 percent per year. Because Israel was a nation as well as a spiritual community, some of these funds would equate to taxes that we pay today. However, the first and most basic tithe was for religious purposes, specifically to support the spiritual leaders, freeing them to fulfill God's calling, and providing the resources necessary to do their job well.

The practice of tithing began long before the law of Moses. Abraham tithed to the high priest Melchizedek (Genesis 14:20). Jacob promised a tithe to the Lord (Genesis 28:22). We're not told that others tithed, or even that these two men tithed at other times, but neither are we told otherwise. Perhaps Abel and Enoch and Noah and others tithed prior to the law, just as they kept the Sabbath prior to the law. Records indicate that the Egyptians, Chaldeans, and Assyrians all tithed to their gods, as did some of the ancient Chinese, Greeks, Romans, and Arabians.

The obedient Israelite didn't ask whether he could give 7 percent, or whether he could tithe on the "net" rather than the "gross."

THE FIRSTFRUITS

"Honor the Lord with your wealth, with the firstfruits of all your crops" (Proverbs 3:9). Three times a year the children of Israel were to bring an offering of firstfruits before the Lord. God said, "No one is to appear before me empty-handed" (Exodus 23:15). The firstfruits offering included the first production of a vineyard (Leviticus 19:23-25) and the first annual production of grain, wine, olive oil, and sheared wool (Exodus 23:16; 34:22; Deuteronomy 18:4). The first of any coarse meal (Numbers 15:20-21), honey, and all the produce belonged to the Lord (2 Chronicles 31:5). A significant portion of the firstfruits went to the religious leaders and their ministry (Numbers 18:12).

The giving of firstfruits made an important statement: "We give of our first and best to you, Lord, because we recognize all good things come from you. In doing so, we recognize our responsibility to sustain the spiritual leadership provided for us."

Tithe denoted the amount of the offering, firstfruits the nature of the offering. In Israel, tangible goods were the natural things to tithe. The same principle applied to money. The first 10 percent of God's provision was returned to the Lord. God was regarded as the provider of the harvest. The firstfruits offering reminded people of God's ownership. They saw God as the source of all life and blessing. Parents hoped that their children, by witnessing this regular, systematic giving of wealth to the Lord, would grow up understanding their infinite debt to God, and their need to continuously honor him by their worshipful giving.

The firstfruits offering also said, "We trust you, God, to help us harvest the rest." To hold back any of the firstfruits, or to give anything less than the best, was to incur God's wrath. Hophni and Phinehas were priests who took what they wanted and left the residue for the Lord (1 Samuel 2:12-16). Scripture says, "Their sin was very great before the Lord." God sent fire from heaven to consume them for taking what belonged to him. Anyone who is tempted to hold back from God what is his need only remember Hophni and Phinehas!

The nature of firstfruits requires it be taken "off the top." It's both the best and the first.

The nature of firstfruits requires it be taken "off the top." It's both the best and the first. As soon as it's harvested or received, it's to be given to the Lord. It's not to be stored up, hidden, hoarded, or distributed in any other way. Those who kept the best and gave God the leftovers brought God's judgment on Israel. Giving back to the Lord what was rightfully his was a thermometer of faith. When Israel slid spiritually, they ceased to give as they should. When they ceased to give as they should, they slid spiritually. (Regardless of today's debate over tithing, these principles of giving are surely timeless, applying as much to the church as to Israel.)

VOLUNTARY OFFERINGS

The tithe was recognized as God's. Hence, people didn't *give* a tithe but *repaid* it to the Owner of all things. This is why the Old Testament speaks of "bringing," "taking," "presenting," or even "paying" tithes and firstfruits, rather than "giving" them. These payments were no more optional than paying taxes today. An Israelite paid tithes and firstfruits out of obedience, whether or not he wanted to.

The Old Testament also emphasizes "freewill offerings" (Leviticus 22:18-23; Numbers 15:3; Deuteronomy 12:6, 17). "All . . . who were willing brought to the Lord freewill offerings" (Exodus 35:29). These were voluntary contributions beyond the tithe or firstfruits. They constituted true giving, because the tithe was a debt repaid to God, not a gift per se.

When the temple needed to be rebuilt, people were asked to provide freewill offerings (Ezra 1:4, 6; 3:5; 7:16; 8:28). Such offerings amounted to "give as you wish" or "give as you are led." When "everyone whose heart God had moved" went to build the temple in Jerusalem, "their neighbors assisted them with articles of silver and gold, with goods and livestock, and with valuable gifts, in addition to all the freewill offerings" (Ezra 1:5-6).

We are wrong to think of Old Testament giving as a dreary, dutiful legalism. On the contrary, the Israelites got caught up in the thrill of giving:

All the skilled craftsmen who were doing all the work on the sanctuary left their work and said to Moses, "The people are bringing more than enough for doing the work the Lord commanded to be done." Then Moses gave an order and they sent this word throughout the camp: "No man or woman is to make anything else as an offering for the sanctuary." And so the people were restrained from bringing more, because what they already had was more than enough to do all the work. (Exodus 36:4-7)

The emphasis here is not on the amount of the offering or the cause for it, but the willingness of each person's heart. It wasn't a tithe, but giving entirely above and beyond it. It wasn't mandatory giving, but voluntary. This vital aspect of giving is ignored by those who suppose that Old Testament giving was all about tithing. Clearly it was not. Voluntary offering did not begin in the New Testament.

The tithe was explicit and objective. Though God desired his people to do it joyfully, it required no heart response. But the freewill offering was entirely different. It involved the joy of a heart touched by God's grace.

This account in Exodus 36 shows the results when people earnestly seek God's pleasure by giving freely: The amount collected was huge, far more than what was needed. Even after the need had been met, the people kept giving, out of joy. They recognized that giving wasn't simply to benefit the cause, but to benefit them as givers. It was an act of worship that defied logic. Theirs was an eager, childlike insistence on giving: "Daddy, can I please keep giving?" The giving was contagious, because the joy that resulted from giving was contagious.

We have no way of knowing what percentage of their assets the people gave in freewill offerings. The sky was the limit. Depending on the wealth God provided, some may have given 30, 50, 70, 90 percent, or more. If that was true of Old Testament believers, who were not indwelt by God's Spirit, how much more eager to give voluntarily should we be, who have been transformed by Christ's grace and are indwelt and empowered by his Spirit?

If Old Testament believers only started with the tithe but didn't stop there, why should Christians feel inclined to stop? Al Mueller wrote to me: "If we hadn't learned of God's ownership, we would have been content and comfortable giving 20 to 30 percent of our income away each year and feeling pretty generous, but doing whatever we wanted with the balance. Since then, we've tried to remember that we'll give an account of what we do with money we keep. We seek to have a steward mentality and an eternal perspective."

When the first Christians joyfully worshiped God and freely gave their possessions to the needy, some thought they were drunk. They *were* under the control of a foreign influence—God's Spirit. Some unbelievers will be drawn to Christ by the grace they see in giving Christians. One man told me, "A non-Christian couple saw how much our giving excited and changed us. Then they started giving too, even before knowing Christ. They saw the joy and they wanted in on it!"

Other unbelievers dismiss giving as irrational. I've seen that happen with Christians whose chief counselors are non-Christian attorneys and financial advisors. They respond to a substantial proposed increase in giving by saying it's unwise. By human standards, it doesn't make sense. By God's standards, though, it does. We should be careful to surround ourselves with biblically based advisors, who do not resist but embrace the promptings of God's Spirit to give.

SUMMARY OF OLD TESTAMENT GIVING

No one ever had to say, "I feel led to tithe," or ask, "Would you like me to give the firstfruits, Lord?" The answer had already been given in Scripture. Voluntary giving started after the firstfruits. The tithe was never a ceiling for giving, only a floor. It was a beginning point. Beyond it, God's children gave more, sometimes much more, as needs and opportunities arose. The tithe was a demonstration of obedience. Voluntary offerings were a demonstration of love, joy, and worship. As we've seen, people got carried away, literally having to be restrained from giving (Exodus 36:5-7). The grace of giving transformed a pack of gripers and whiners into joyful worshipers—and the same thing happens sometimes in churches today. (In fact, there's nothing wrong with many churches that couldn't be solved by a good dose of joyful giving!)

David said, "I now give my personal treasures of gold and silver for the temple of my God, over and above everything I have provided" (1 Chronicles 29:3). Then family and tribal leaders "gave willingly" and generously (1 Chronicles 29:6-8). "The people rejoiced at the willing response of their leaders, for they had given freely and wholeheartedly to the Lord" (1 Chronicles 29:9).

David also said to the Lord:

Who am I, and who are my people, that we should be able to give as generously as this? Everything comes from you, and we have given you only what comes from your hand. . . . It comes from your hand, and all of it belongs to you. . . . All these things have I given willingly and with honest intent. And now I have seen with joy how willingly your people who are here have given to you. O Lord, God of our fathers . . . keep this desire in the hearts of your people forever, and keep their hearts loyal to you. (1 Chronicles 29:14, 16-18)

David measured the people's loyalty to God by their willingness to freely give to God.

Imagine a boy's father who wants his son to take out his old friend's daughter on a date. The boy reluctantly agrees to do it because his father expects it of him. But when the boy actually meets the girl he enjoys her company so much that he asks to take her out again—and again and again. At this point the boy is no longer acting out of duty, but voluntarily. He doesn't have to take her out; he *wants* to.

The Israelites tithed because God told them to. They gave above and beyond in voluntary offerings because they *wanted* to. But just as the young man would never have fallen in love with the girl if he'd refused his father's prompting to date her, so if the Israelites hadn't first learned the discipline of tithing, they would never have discovered the joy of voluntary giving.

THE VALUE OF TITHING

By emphasizing the vitality of voluntary offerings, I don't want to demean tithing. This is where God started his first covenant people. It's a fine beginning. Tithing's stated purpose is "that you may learn to revere the Lord your God always" (Deuteronomy 14:23). Tithing is intended to train people to put God first in their lives. Because the giving of the 10 percent represents the other 90 percent, tithing symbolizes the giving of one's whole life to God.

Tithing gives perspective. It reminds us that all we are and all we have is from God. Tithing is not a tip thrown mindlessly down on a table after a meal, but a meaningful expression of dependence upon God and gratitude to him. Tithing requires calculation. When we deal specifically with the amounts God has provided, we assess God's goodness to us. We literally count our blessings, thanking him for his generosity. Tithing was, and can still be, a built-in reminder at every juncture of life of our unlimited debt to God.

Parting with money wasn't any easier for the people of Israel than for us. In fact, most of them were far poorer and worked a great deal harder for their money than we do. Yet tithing was so built into their lives that it became "natural" to them in the best sense. In times of national obedience, their fathers, mothers, brothers, sisters, and business partners—everyone around them—practiced tithing. It became a way of life.

When they went their own way and stopped tithing and withheld freewill offerings, God told them they were robbing him. Then he invited his people to test him by going back to tithing and giving voluntary offerings. The tithe was a divine invitation to test God's promises to provide (Malachi 3:8-12). Tithing begins as a duty but can become a delight, leading to joyful voluntary giving. For faithful Israelites, unclenching their fists and opening them to God had a thousand trickledown benefits. Is it any different for us today?

> **Parting with money wasn't any easier for the people of Israel than for us. In fact, most of them were far poorer and worked a great deal harder for their money than we do.**

THE STATE OF AMERICAN GIVING

Before considering whether Christians should tithe today, let's look at our current giving habits. In 2001, Barna Research revealed some significant trends in giving:

- Compared to 1999, the mean per capita donation to churches dropped by 19 percent in 2000.
- Among born-again adults, there was a 44 percent rise in those who gave nothing.
- The number of donors to any nonprofit or church organization declined by 7 percent.
- Four out of every ten adults gave nothing to churches . . . a rise of 15 percent among those refusing to support churches.
- One-third of born-again adults said they tithed in 2000, but a comparison of their giving versus their household income revealed that only one out of eight actually did.
- The average church donor contributed a mean of $649 in 2000, down from $806 in 1999. Married adults are more likely than single adults to donate some money to a church in a typical month (64 percent to 42 percent, respectively).
- Comparing giving habits of those in their twenties, forties, and sixties was revealing: "Busters are substantially less likely (36 percent) than are Boomers (58 percent), Builders (68 percent), or Seniors (68 percent) to give to a church in a given month." Between 30 and 50 percent of active church attenders give nothing. And because 70 percent of Christians have no wills at the time they die, they don't leave any money to their church or Christian ministries. Many of the remaining 30 percent who do have wills designate no money to God's work.[1]

There has been a gradual decline in giving that has continued for thirty years, down 6 to 8 percent annually from 1998 to 2000, and down a full 15 percent in 2000. Since 1975, total charitable giving by Americans has run between 1.6 percent and 2.16 percent of income.[2] According to the Gallup organization, those who attend weekly church services give 3.4 percent of income annually, whereas nonreligious people give 1.1 percent to 1.4 percent. Other estimates indicate the percentage of income given by professing Christians to church and kingdom causes at between 1.5 and 3.5 percent of income. The midpoint, 2.5 percent, is perhaps the most accurate figure.

Barna Research reports that the more money a person makes the less likely he or she is to tithe.[3] In fact, "those with annual earnings of more than $500,000 reduced their average donations from $47,432 in 1980 to $16,062 in 1988."[4]

GRACE, LAW, AND TITHING

I have mixed feelings on tithing. I detest legalism. I certainly don't want to pour new wine into old wineskins, imposing superseded first covenant restrictions on Christians. However, the fact is that every New Testament example of giving goes beyond the tithe. This means that none falls short of it. The strongest arguments made against tithing today are "law versus grace." But does being under grace mean we should stop doing all that was done under the law?

I'm a strong believer in the new covenant's superiority over the old (Romans 7; 2 Corinthians 3; Hebrews 8). On the other hand, I believe there's ongoing value to certain aspects of the old covenant. The model of paying back to God the firstfruits (tithing) and giving freewill offerings beyond that is among those. Because we are never told that tithing has been superseded, and because Jesus directly affirmed it (Matthew 23:23) and prominent church fathers taught it as a requirement for Christian living, it seems to me the burden of proof falls on those who say tithing is no longer a minimum standard for God's people. The question is not whether tithing is the whole of Christian giving or even at the center of it. Clearly it is not. Many people associate the command to tithe with the command to keep the Sabbath. New Testament Christians are not obligated to keep the Sabbath with all its legislated rules under the Mosaic covenant (Colossians 2:16). However, a weekly day of rest based on God's pattern of creation was instituted before the Law (Genesis 2:2-3). It's a principle never revoked in the New Testament. The special day of observance changed to Sunday, "the Lord's day," yet the principle of one special day set aside for worship remained intact.

Christ fulfilled the entire Old Testament, but he didn't render it irrelevant. Old Testament legislation demonstrated how to love my neighbor. Although the specific regulations don't all apply, the principles certainly do, and many of the guidelines are still as helpful as ever. Consider the command to build a roof with a parapet to protect people from falling off (Deuteronomy 22:8). When it comes to the Old Testament, we must be careful not to throw out the baby (ongoing principles intended for everyone) with the bathwater (detailed regulations intended only for ancient Israel).

We don't offer sacrifices anymore, so why should we tithe? Because sacrifices are specifically rescinded in the New Testament. As the book of Hebrews demonstrates, Christ has rendered inoperative the whole sacrificial system. But where in the New Testament does it indicate that tithing is no longer valid? There is no such passage. With a single statement, God could have easily singled out tithing like he did sacrifices and the Sabbath. But he didn't.

Some argue against tithing by saying, "The New Testament advocates voluntary offerings." Yes, but as we've seen, so does the Old Testament. Voluntary giving is not a new concept. Having a minimum standard of giving has never been incompatible with giving above and beyond that standard. If both mandatory and voluntary giving coexisted under the old covenant, why not the new? It's not a matter of either tithing or voluntary offering. The two have always been fully compatible.

The disciples gave all that they had because "much grace was upon them all" (Acts 4:33). It was obvious from the beginning that being under grace didn't mean that New Testament Christians would give less than their Old Testament brethren. On the contrary, it meant they would give more.

Being under grace does not mean living by lower standards than the law. Christ systematically addressed such issues as murder, adultery, and the taking of oaths and made it clear that his standards were much higher than those of the Pharisees (Matthew 5:17-48). He never lowered the bar. He always raised it. But he also empowers us by his grace to jump higher than the law demanded.

GRACE GIVING

Since writing the original edition of this book in 1989, I've heard Christians argue—often angrily—that tithing is legalism. They claim tithing is bondage, and we have been liberated to "grace giving." As we've seen, however, the Israelites' triple tithes amounted to 23 percent of their income—in contrast to the average 2.5 percent giving of American Christians. This statistic suggests that the law was about ten times more effective than grace! Even using 10 percent as a measure, the Israelites were four times more responsive to the Law of Moses than the average American Christian is to the grace of Christ. (Reread that last sentence and ask yourself if something isn't terribly wrong.)

Having a minimum standard of giving has never been incompatible with giving above and beyond that standard.

When we as New Testament believers, living in a far more affluent society than ancient Israel, give only a fraction of that given by the poorest Old Testament believers, we surely must reevaluate our concept of "grace giving." And when you consider that we have the indwelling Spirit of God and they didn't, the contrast becomes even more glaring.

I believe there's a timeless truth behind the concept of giving God the firstfruits. Whether or not the tithe is still the minimum measure of those firstfruits, I ask myself, does God expect his new covenant children to give less, the same, or more? I've found that, to many people, the term "grace giving" simply means "give whatever you feel like." (And obviously most people just don't feel like giving!) The assumption seems to be that God no longer expects his people to give substantially.

Many people do not give because they haven't been taught to give. As the law was a tutor to lead us to Christ (Galatians 3:24), so the tithe can be a tutor that leads us to giving. If we can learn to give without tithing, fine. But the giving track record of American Christians clearly indicates we have not learned to give. In fact, we've learned not to give. Our giving declines as our prosperity increases. And perhaps worst of all, we continue to lose ground, because our children are giving even less than we are. Although grace giving is a wonderful sounding term, it has come to disguise an underlying attitude that is twisted and unbiblical. It has dishonored us, our children, our churches, and above all, our Lord.

Whatever the Church is teaching about giving today, either it's not true to Scripture, the message isn't getting through, or we're being disobedient. The tithe is God's historical method to get people on the path of giving. In that sense, it can serve as a gateway to the joy of true "grace giving" today, just as it gave rise to the spontaneous, joyous, freewill giving we see in various Old Testament passages. It's unhealthy to view tithing as a place to stop with our giving, but it can still be a good place to start. Remember, even under the first covenant, tithing was never a maximum standard—it was merely a starting point.

Tithing isn't the finish line of giving; it's the starting blocks. But, clearly, most of us need help getting started!

Can tithing be legalistic? Of course. The holy habits of church attendance, prayer, and Bible reading can also degenerate into legalism—but that doesn't make them illegitimate. Anyone who stops going to church, praying, or reading Scripture for fear of being legalistic is approaching the problem from the wrong angle!

Some fine Bible teachers preach against tithing. They themselves may be strong givers, but I don't think they realize the effects of their words on those who have no concept of disciplined giving. I get mail from people who strenuously object—sometimes with name-calling—to the suggestion that tithing is a legitimate starting place for Christians. I listen to any Christian who says, "Tithing isn't meant for us today"—provided he gives regularly himself and that his giving exceeds the tithe. But I've learned that often there's a hidden agenda behind the protest.

The pro-grace or anti-legalism trump card rings hollow when it attempts to normalize wealthy Christians giving less than the poorest Israelite. While appearing to take the theological high ground, they are effectively saying that God has lowered his standards of giving and that the power of New Testament grace is less than that of the law. Such a view is an insult to the saving and empowering work of Christ. With some exceptions, I have found that most who argue against tithing use their arguments to justify their own lack of generous giving. My response is to gently suggest to such people that their reasons may be less biblical and theological than personal—they simply don't want to give that much.

We tend naturally to embrace arguments that serve our perceived self-interests. Our substandard giving suggests we have ulterior motives for adopting an anti-tithing theology. We should consider the converse of what Jesus said in Matthew 6:21: Where our treasure isn't shows where our heart isn't.

We must examine our hearts to discover whether when we say, "Tithing isn't for today," we are using grace as a license to clutch tighter to material wealth. The New Testament clearly demonstrates that Christians are called upon to be *more* sacrificial and generous, not less.

Some friends of ours, as young Christians, believed they were supposed to tithe. They did so faithfully, not legalistically, and God used tithing to remind them to put him first. Like the discipline of a regular quiet time, the discipline of tithing moved their thoughts toward God. However, when they started attending another church—a large Bible-teaching church—they heard from the pulpit "tithing is legalism" and "God has called us to grace giving." Unfortunately, the pastor did not suggest any starting place or guidelines for grace giving. As a result of this teaching, our newly "liberated" friends reduced their giving. Within a few years, they were giving almost nothing. Meanwhile, they floundered in their walk with God and incurred more and more debt. Finally, in a different church, they were reintroduced to the concept of tithing—not as a legalistic ritual, but as a simple starting place for giving. When they committed themselves to tithing again, they sensed God's blessing and experienced a peace they hadn't known for years. They attribute their several years of spiritual wandering directly to this high-sounding but misleading concept of "grace giving."

JESUS AND TITHING

Jesus was raised in a devout Jewish home, meaning that his parents tithed and instructed him to tithe. The Old Testament, the only Bible Jesus knew, also taught him to tithe. During his ministry, although Jesus was carefully scrutinized by his enemies and accused of every possible offense, including breaking the Sabbath, never once did they accuse him of violating the law of tithing. The Talmud forbade a strict keeper of the law from sitting down to dine with anyone who did not tithe. Yet on several occasions, the Pharisees ate at the same table with Jesus. Obviously, Christ tithed.

Furthermore, Jesus specifically said that while they should have paid attention to more important things, the Pharisees were correct in being careful to tithe: "You should have practiced the latter [justice, mercy, and faithfulness] without neglecting the former [tithing]" (Matthew 23:23).

With his emphasis on sacrificial giving Jesus never once suggested that the "floor" set by the tithe is now invalid, but simply that the ceiling of Christian giving is far above it. When Jesus told the disciples to go the second mile, he assumed they had already gone the first.

THE EARLY CHURCH AND TITHING

Because tithing and freewill offerings were so deeply embedded in the Jewish consciousness, the Jewish Christians who composed the early Church naturally gave their tithes and freewill offerings to the local assembly. Having been transformed by the grace of Jesus, their freewill offerings were no doubt greater than ever. But there is no suggestion that the early Church ever retreated from believing that the tithe was a mandatory minimum for giving.

That this was still the case within the first few hundred years of the Church is demonstrated in the words of the influential Church father Irenaeus: "The Jews were constrained to a regular payment of tithes; Christians, who have liberty, assign all their possessions to the Lord, bestowing freely not the lesser portions of their property, since they have the hope of greater things."[5] Note the key phrase, "not the lesser portions," in reference to the Jews. This is a direct indication that the tithe was considered a minimum standard in the early Christian community.

A few hundred years later, Augustine indicated that tithing was still practiced: "Tithes are required as a matter of debt, and he who has been unwilling to give them has been guilty of robbery. Whosoever, therefore, desires to secure a reward for himself . . . let him render tithes, and out of the nine parts let him seek to give alms."[6] Note the clear distinction between the mandatory tithe and the voluntary offering of almsgiving. Alms were to be given—above and beyond the tithe.

Jerome said, "If anyone shall not do this [pay tithes] he is convicted of defrauding and supplanting God."[7] Like Augustine, Jerome believed and taught that it is possible for New Testament Christians to "rob God" by withholding the tithe, just as it was for Old Testament believers. For the first four hundred years, the Church often, if not normally, considered the practice of tithing a minimum standard for giving.

THE BENEFITS OF TITHING

In most states, there's a mandatory seat-belt law. For many years wearing a seat belt wasn't a legal requirement. But even when it wasn't required, it was still a good idea. But suppose the seat-belt law was repealed. Would I stop wearing my seat belt? Would I tell my children or grandchildren, "Take off your seat belts. We're not under the law, and we're not going to be legalistic, so no more seat belts for us." Of course not. A good idea is a good idea, whether or not it's the law.

Even if you don't agree with me on the biblical arguments, please don't dismiss the practical arguments for tithing. For example, the concept of tithing is clear, consistent, and transferable—that is, it can easily be taught to others, including children. It increases the believer's sense of commitment to God's work. Tithing can also be a significant factor in spiritual growth. I just reread ten letters written to me by church families whose spiritual lives were revolutionized as they discovered how to give. Though a number of them now give more than the tithe, seven of the ten specifically mention that tithing was a spiritual breakthrough in their lives.

Over the years, I've interviewed many generous givers, some of whose stories I tell on our Web site (www.epm.org/givingstories). Though I never introduce the subject myself, a high percentage of these givers mention that they started with tithing. That was their introduction to the great adventure of giving. Though they've now gone far beyond it, they are quick to credit learning to tithe with their launch into giving. One Christian leader said, "As I reflect on my growth as a Christian across the years, the second most important gift of grace I have received has been the discipline of tithing. The first was the surrender of my will to Jesus Christ." He went on to say of himself and his wife, "The Lord got our hearts when we began to tithe."[8]

If Western Christians all practiced tithing, the task of world evangelism and feeding the hungry would be within reach.

If Western Christians all practiced tithing, the task of world evangelism and feeding the hungry would be within reach. Because many Christians, once they begin to tithe, also give freewill offerings beyond the tithe, the work of God could be multiplied in every corner of the world.

Many churches have demonstrated the spiritual power of tithing. The Southern Baptist denomination, which began in 1845, now has about 5,000 missionaries in 153 countries. Not only do the Southern Baptists emphasize missions, they also emphasize tithing as the means to underwrite missions, as well as to meet the needs of the local church. Church members understand that they are expected to tithe. Although I am not a Southern Baptist, I'm confident they would've had far less impact, both in their communities and in world evangelization, if they hadn't emphasized tithing.

TITHING: GROSS OR NET?

Business owners must pay for materials, rent, employee wages, and many other expenses. These costs are not included in their personal gross income and therefore would not be subject to tithing. But our personal income isn't merely what's left after taxes and bills are paid. The value we receive for company-paid retirement, life insurance, health insurance, etc., is all part of God's provision for us, isn't it? Scripture refers to "a tithe of everything."

Because taxes are withheld and insurance payments are made by their employers, many don't consider those dollars as income. But suppose your employer also withheld money for your house payment, groceries, and children's tuition. Would you consider those no longer part of your income and therefore not subject to tithing? If your employer paid all your bills, would that mean you wouldn't give anything to the Lord?

Tithing naturally applies not only to the cash we hold in our hands, but also to the value of everything that is accrued, paid, or provided for our benefit. When we tithe, Nanci and I try to take into consideration all of God's provisions, including those that are sometimes difficult to quantify, such as when someone graciously provides us a place to stay on vacation. Our freewill giving then starts beyond this amount. Although tithing itself is satisfying, for us the real fun begins when we move beyond it to freewill giving.

When asked "Should we tithe on the gross or the net?" it's appropriate to ask, "What do we want to be blessed on, the gross or the net?"

WHY NOT TITHE?

There can be serious problems with tithing. People can treat it as an unwanted tax or bill, robbing themselves of joy. In some churches, tithing is like paying membership dues. You pay to belong to a club and you pay to belong to the church. Tithing can lead to pride that we're part of a faithful remnant that really trusts God, in contrast to all those nontithing apostates.

One of the worst dangers of tithing is complacency. While arguing strongly for tithing, one writer adds this caution:

> The tithe can become an idol to set upon a pedestal to admire. It is often a dangerously tempting resting place rather than a minimal starting place. Much of the Christian community thinks of tithing as a high and lofty perch that only a few fanatical radicals have reached after years of struggle, rather than seeing it at the bottom or beginning place.[9]

Someone told me, "I wish I'd win a million dollars in the lottery. Then I'd give $100,000 to the Lord, and I could do whatever I want with the rest!" But tithing isn't something I do to clear my conscience so I can do whatever I want with the 90 percent—it also belongs to God! I must seek his direction and permission for whatever I do with the full amount. I may discover that God has different ideas than I do.

There are many common arguments against tithing, including the following:

"Tithing is legalism."

Any legitimate practice can be done with a legalistic attitude. In such cases, the fault lies with the attitude of our heart, not with the practice itself. If anything hits too close to home or starts meddling in our life, we can dismiss it simply by calling it "legalistic." Legalism can be a convenient label to cover our unwillingness to obey God.

Although most of the letters I received in response to the original edition of this book were positive, by far the majority of negative responses concerned tithing. Here's one example (with the writer's capitalization retained):

Dearest Teacher of the Gospel,
   I read what you said about tithing and here are my comments:
Adding to the Gospel of Christ comes from the devil . . . and you know

it. All the Blessings I receive from our MIGHTY GOD are free. Received by Faith—not by paying 10 percent to SATAN, may GOD REBUKE HIM.

Stop perverting the gospel of Christ. If you want to imitate Abraham [who tithed], I will be glad to circumcise you myself. Just come on down. I will also expect you to imitate him in offering sacrifices, the altar, the ram, the blood. And do not forget your firstborn, you hypocrite.

I do love you and pray that the Demon would depart from your wicked teachings. REPENT FOR THE KINGDOM OF HEAVEN IS NEAR!

After years of ministry, my instincts have been honed enough to surmise that the person who wrote this e-mail was upset. I'm just grateful for his assurance that he loves me. Think of what the letter might have said if he didn't! Although this response is extreme, it's only different in degree, not in kind, from many others. I'd like to think it's just because people hate legalism, which I also despise. Unfortunately, I've concluded it's also because many Christians are under the Holy Spirit's conviction because of their failure to give.

"I must pay off my debts rather than tithe."

Why am I in debt in the first place? Is God responsible for my unwise or greedy decisions that may have put me there? And even if I've come into debt legitimately, isn't my first debt to God? Isn't the tithe a debt to God since he says that it belongs to him and not to me? If we obey God and make good our financial debt to him, he'll help us as we seek to pay off our debts to others. But I must not rob God to pay men.

"If I'm going to tithe eventually, I'll need to move toward it slowly."

I'm often asked, "If I haven't been giving at all, won't God understand if I move toward it gradually, starting at 3 percent or 5 percent?" What if I told you I've had this bad habit of robbing convenience stores, knocking off about a dozen a year. But then I say to you "This year I'm only going to rob a half-dozen!" Is that better? Well, yes. But what would you advise me to do? The solution to robbing God is not to start robbing him less, it's to stop robbing him at all.

"I just can't afford to tithe."

Of course I can. If tithing is God's will and he promises to provide for those who trust and obey him, won't he allow me to get by on 90 percent rather than 100 percent? In fact, aren't I a lot safer living on less inside God's will than living on more outside it?

Here's an interesting hypothesis: No one benefits from a tithe he or she holds on to. We can't keep what belongs to God. If we don't give it to him, either the devil gets it or it just disappears. Whether or not this is true, many Christians testify that they live just as easily on the 90 percent as the 100 percent. Many others have said that their financial problems really began when they withheld the tithe, not when they tithed. We have it backwards!

If tithing is God's minimum expectation, can I afford not to tithe? Can I afford to rob God, or are there always consequences? Of course, there is one way to reduce my tithe, and that is to reduce my income. If my tithe seems to be a lot of money, I should praise God! It proves how abundantly he has provided. When people tell me, "I can't afford to tithe," I often ask, "If your income were reduced by 10 percent, would you die?" They always admit they wouldn't. Somehow, they would manage to get by. That's proof that they really can tithe. The truth is simply that they don't want to. An atheist could get by if he gave away 10 percent of his income. Even if they don't believe in God, people can afford to tithe. How much more should Christians be able to trust God and by faith step out in obedience and watch him provide?

Ironically, many people "can't afford" to give precisely because they're not giving (Haggai 1:9-11; Malachi 3:9). If you think this principle is restricted to the Old Testament, consider Christ's words: "Give, and it will be given to you. A good measure, pressed down, shaken together and running over, will be poured into your lap. For with the measure you use, it will be measured to you" (Luke 6:38).

If we pay our debt to God first, then we will incur his blessing to help us pay our debts to men. But when we rob God to pay men, we rob ourselves of God's blessing and thereby dig a deeper hole. No wonder we don't have enough. It's a vicious cycle, and it takes obedient faith to break out of it.

I receive many e-mails from people who say they can't tithe. I suggest that they are robbing themselves of blessing because they're robbing God. When we steal from him, we cannot expect him to bless us financially.

I find that most people sincerely believe that if they made more money they would start tithing. Yet, as the statistics cited earlier show, the richer someone becomes the less likely it is he or she will tithe.

Others believe their poverty exempts them from tithing. Yet by global standards, most of these people are easily in the top 10 percent of the world's wealthy. I've been with poor Africans who make less than $50 a year to care for their large families, and they wouldn't think of giving less than a tithe.

What's wrong with us?

God doesn't tell us to do something without empowering us. The tithe is a *proportion*, and a small one at that. It's not as if everyone is assigned a fixed amount, such as $5,000, to give each month. If our income is

> Consider Christ's words: "Give, and it will be given to you. A good measure, pressed down, shaken together and running over, will be poured into your lap. For with the measure you use, it will be measured to you" (LUKE 6:38).

189

small, our tithe is proportionally small. In some cases, those who say they "can't afford to tithe" live in very nice homes, regularly go out to eat, have a boat in the driveway, belong to a health club, and vacation at expensive resorts. We brought groceries to a man in our church to feed his family, only to find he had a $30,000 recreational vehicle sitting in his driveway.

When it comes to giving, we need a major reality check.

PROFILES OF CHRISTIANS WHO ROB GOD

The Situation: Bill and Donna are in their midthirties. Bill has steady work, but there's always too much month left at the end of their money. Bill and Donna sincerely intend to put in the offering box whatever's left at the end of the month. But between house payments, bills, and sticking a little into savings, there's never anything left. They feel bad, but what can they do when they're out of money?

The Problem: Bill and Donna don't understand "firstfruits." They should give to the Lord off the top, not out of what's left—or not left. They don't realize that the tithe belongs to God, and that there's a word for taking money that doesn't belong to them—*stealing.*

The Situation: Joan's a twenty-two-year-old, just finishing college. Her thirty-hour-a-week job pays just over minimum wage. She earns $800 a month. Joan's parents still provide room and board, but she has to take care of her tuition, books, and other expenses.

"I can't afford to give," says Joan. "I'm barely making it now. If I gave a tithe, it would be $80 a month, and I'd probably have to drop out of school. I'd like to give, but I just can't."

The Problem: Joan is not only robbing God, she's robbing herself of the opportunity to grow in faith. Right now she doesn't believe God's promise in Malachi 3 (confirmed in Matthew 6:33 and Luke 6:38) that he'll take care of her if she puts God first by giving him what's his. If God is capable of helping her get by on $800 a month, isn't he capable of helping her get by on $720 a month? Joan's God doesn't seem very big—he can't even compensate for an $80 shortfall.

The Situation: Bob and Elaine are in their early fifties. Elaine says, "For years we frittered away our income on all kinds of luxuries. Now we're twelve years from retirement and we don't have anything saved. On top of that, we've still got two kids in college."

"We'd like to give to the church," Bob explains, "but Scripture says we've got to provide for our family first. After we get our kids through school and get a nest egg started, then we'll start giving."

The Problem: Bob and Elaine are keeping what belongs to God in order to compensate for their poor planning and lack of discipline. Their first debt is not to their children's college education. Their first debt is to God. If it wasn't tuition costs, it would be something else. Since they have no standard of giving, they'll always find reasons not to give.

The Situation: Phil and Pam enjoy giving. With their little blue Santa's helper (credit card) they just gave each other a DVD player and a large-screen television. The kids got a new computer to keep them busy while their parents enjoy the city's finer restaurants. They're tired of their three-year-old Chevy, so they just bought a new model.

"Next year I've got a big promotion coming," says Phil. "Then we'll start giving. Right now the budget's tight. It's not that we don't ever give to God's work," Phil adds. "Why, when we were in Hawaii last month we attended a church service on the beach and I dropped $20 in the offering."

The Problem: Phil and Pam are blind. They say there's no money left to give—and they do their best to make sure of it! No matter what they say, their lifestyle proves that toys, trips, and cars are more important to them than God and others. They say they'll give when they earn more, but they won't. If Phil and Pam have been unfaithful with a little (more than a little), they'll be unfaithful with a lot. Their expenditures will always rise to meet their income. Making more money will only make them guilty of robbing God more. Phil and Pam don't understand that the tithe belongs to God, not them, and they should return to him the "firstfruits," not "last fruits" or "no fruits."

The Situation: Don and Sue believe that they aren't under law but grace, and that tithing lends itself to a pharisaical "letter of the law" approach. They believe that God's law is written in our hearts and we should give freely without compulsion. They are proud of their mature and liberating belief in "grace giving."

The Problem: Last year Don and Sue's "grace giving" amounted to $30 per month—about one-half of one percent of their income. While they laud grace and deplore the law, their actions suggest that grace is one-twentieth as effective as the law. If grace is as ineffective in motivating their sexual purity as it is their giving, they won't be married much longer. (The problem isn't grace, of course, but their belief that grace means God has lowered his standards and doesn't care how we live.)

The Situation: Ralph was laid off three months ago and collects $1500 a month in unemployment. Others in the church give him an average of $500 per month to supplement his income. Ralph says "amen" to the financial sermons and wishes he were in a position to give too. Ralph assumes that even though God says the tithe belongs to him, it surely doesn't apply to things like unemployment, social security, benefits, gifts, inheritances, or other "non-salary" forms of income.

The Problem: Scripture makes no such distinction between sources of revenue. If it comes in, it's income. God doesn't tag monies "tithe exempt." The source of material blessing is not the point. If I receive $500 to help get me through the month, the first $50 belongs to God. Why should it matter where it comes from? If it's provision, it comes from the Provider.

The Situation: "There's a lot more to stewardship than money," says Gina. "We can't all give—but we can teach Sunday school, clean the building, and open our homes to guests. I consider that to be my giving."

The Problem: Gina rightly believes that stewardship involves more than money—but she wrongly believes that stewardship ever fails to include money. Her argument is just as faulty as saying, "I can't give the church any of my time or my gifts and talents, so I'll just give my money instead." God expects *all* of these, not just some of them. We all can and should give, just as we all can and should pray. Gina is attempting to justify robbing God by "making up for it" with things she should be doing anyway.

The Situation: "I'm so far in debt that I can't give a dime to the church," says Tony. "What am I supposed to do, stop my car payments? What kind of testimony would that be? And it would be bad stewardship to sell my car—I'd have to take a $3,000 loss. God doesn't want me to be stupid, does he?"

The Problem: Tony has already been stupid. In buying his new car, he put himself in a position to disobey God's command to give. He violated Scripture by spending money he didn't have. His greedy and foolish misuse of credit is what put him in this fix. Tony apparently believes that God, his church, and needy people should pay for his foolish choices. Why not take a $3,000 loss in order to get into a position to obey God? Is there any stewardship more terrible than robbing your Creator and Savior?

Tony is another person who acts as if the tithe is his, not God's. Scripture doesn't say "firstfruits" are to be given to those to whom they will be the best testimony, but to God. If Tony ends up having a bad testimony, it's because of his foolish choices, which are only complicated by further disobedience. He needs to ask forgiveness and learn from the situation so he doesn't do it again. But it makes no sense to rob God in order to have a "better testimony" to men.

The Situation: Joe is an outspoken Christian known as a man of faith. He stands up at church business meetings and says he wants the church to build, raise the pastors' salaries, and expand into new ministries. Joe challenges the church to rise to the occasion and reads passages of Scripture about walking by faith. He inspires everyone. Everyone, that is, except God and the financial secretary, who know the truth: If everyone gave like Joe, the pastors would be laid off, the missionaries would have to leave the field, and the church would close its doors.

The Problem: Joe has great faith and vision when it comes to other people's obedience. It's his own obedience he has trouble with. He fails to ask himself, "If everyone gave like I do, where would this church be?" He's quick to commit other people's money but clings to his own. Joe is a hypocrite. He says one thing and does another. In doing so, he heaps up judgment for himself. He'll be held accountable to God, not only for his lack of giving, but also for his hollow words.

The Situation: Paula believes in giving but thinks that Scripture says giving should be voluntary. After all, "God loves a cheerful giver." However, Paula is not yet to the point that she really wants to give. "Given my financial obligations, right now I just can't give cheerfully," Paula says. "And if you can't give cheerfully, you shouldn't give at all."

The Problem: Paula is right that God wants us to give cheerfully. But she is wrong in thinking that she should only give if she feels like it. The tithe belongs to God. It is not Paula's to withhold, regardless of how she feels about it. Paula's point about cheerfulness may be relevant to freewill offerings (those beyond the tithe), but not to the tithe itself, since it doesn't belong to her in the first place. After becoming obedient, Paula will perhaps become more cheerful in her giving. But whether she does or not, she should still be obedient.

The Situation: Dan is a seminary student headed for the ministry. He and his wife, Karla, have sacrificed to attend seminary. Knowing that God commands them to give to his work, they believe that by giving their tithe to their own tuition they are investing in the ministry, even though they don't give to their church.

The Problem: Dan and Karla are not God, and they are not the church. Giving to themselves is not giving to God or the church, no matter how the money is spent. The people of Israel brought tithes to the storehouse for the spiritually qualified leaders of Israel to distribute, just as the first Christians laid gifts at the apostles' feet. The Israelites were not given the option of "tithing to themselves"—that is a contradiction in terms. It is not *their* tithe, it is God's.

Should church leaders or others decide to help Dan and Karla financially, that's up to them and God—not to Dan and Karla. They are robbing God, and it's hard to imagine him blessing them as they steal their way through seminary.

This final profile centers not on the amount of giving, but where it goes:

The Situation: Jim is a successful Christian businessman who wants his dollars to count. "I strongly believe in tithing," says Jim. "Part of my tithe goes to a missions organization, part to a student ministry, a radio broadcast, and a television ministry. I believe in giving where it matters. Too much of the church's money goes to salaries and buildings and maintenance. I don't want my money going to clean restrooms and mow lawns. I'm not that impressed with the church anyway. The services are too crowded, the building needs repairs, and we ought to be giving more money to missions. Why doesn't this church get on the ball?"

The Problem: Jim fails to understand the centrality of the local church in God's kingdom program. Jim is annoyed at the deterioration of the church facilities, yet he doesn't want his money going to buildings. He would be appalled at dirty restrooms, yet he doesn't want his money to clean them. He wants and expects his pastors to meet his needs, but he doesn't want to pay their salaries. He wants the church to give to missions, but he doesn't give to the church. The church will get on the ball when people like Jim get on the ball.

BEGINNING WHERE GOD BEGAN

Without guideposts, where do you start giving? Why not start where God started Israel? Why not start with the tithe? I view tithing as a child's first steps. His first steps aren't his last, neither are they his best, but they're a fine beginning. Tithing is the first toddler's step of stewardship. It's the training wheels on the bicycle of giving. It's not a home run, but it gets you on base—which is a lot further than many Christians ever get.

For those who still believe the tithe has no bearing on Christians, let me suggest that you figure out your pretax income from every source—all of it, including the dollar value of the benefits you receive—then multiply by 10 percent. If you discover that you have been regularly giving beyond 10 percent, then you're right—you don't need the tithe, any more than you need training wheels on a bike. Just go right on doing what you're doing and let God move you on in freewill giving. But if your giving adds up to 7 percent or 5 percent or 3 percent, it shows you really do need the tithe as training wheels to get you up on the bike of giving. If you fear legalism, fine, start at 11 percent or 12 percent. Choose your own percentage—but don't go below a standard you believe was superseded by the superior grace of Christ.

Begin with the tithe. It shows you're serious. As you continue to tithe, you'll sense God's approval. You'll experience the freedom and joy of acknowledging his lordship of your money and possessions, and thereby your whole life.

"I can see it's right to tithe, but I can't start right now." To procrastinate obedience is to disobey God. Trust him to help you begin this life-changing, eternity-impacting adventure of giving. Tithing isn't the end of giving—but it can be a good beginning.

CHAPTER 13

Giving: Reciprocating God's Grace

Money never stays with me. It would burn me if it did. I throw it out of my hands as soon as possible, lest it should find its way into my heart.   JOHN WESLEY

Grace and gratitude belong together like heaven and earth. Grace evokes gratitude like the voice an echo. Gratitude follows grace as thunder follows lightning.   KARL BARTH

The most striking characteristic of the early Christians is that they shared all they owned, liquidating their possessions to give to the needy (Acts 2:44-45; 4:32-37). In one verse we're told, "Much grace was upon them all," and in the next, "There were no needy persons among them." Compare this description with that of Christ's bickering disciples, jockeying for position and unwilling to wash each others' feet (Mark 9:33-34, 10:35-41; Luke 9:46, 22:24; John 13:3-16). Radical giving demonstrates the life-changing power of God.

There are two common errors made in evaluating the first Jerusalem church. One is to see it as a model to be followed by all Christians. The other is to reject it as irrelevant to us today.

Those who see the Jerusalem church as a detailed model fail to understand its unique historical context. Perhaps a million Jews had made the Passover pilgrimage to Jerusalem. The city was bursting at its seams. Many of the thousands coming to Christ wanted to stay in Jerusalem to learn as much as possible before going home. Others probably couldn't return to their homes at all. As a result of following Christ, they would have become "the victims of social and economic ostracism, ecclesiastical excommunication, and national disinheritance. Their business enterprises must in most cases have collapsed in ruins and family bonds been heart-breakingly severed."[1]

The result was thousands of homeless, jobless people. This was an emergency situation that called for unusual action. It cannot serve as a strict pattern for all Christian communities, because not all congregations are faced with such extreme situations. However, the first Christians' attitude toward money and possessions is a timeless model for all Christians. Second-century Church leader Justin Martyr writes: "We who formerly treasured money and possessions more than anything else now hand over everything we have to a treasury for all and share it with everyone who needs it."[2]

Some groups have followed a communal model and done well, whereas others have found it problematic. I don't oppose attempts to imitate the early Church. To hoard or withhold our resources from the needy is always unscriptural. But the graces of giving and sharing can legitimately take other forms than that of Acts 2 and 4. Although sacrificial giving is an integral part of all healthy churches, never again in the New Testament do we see it manifested in the same way as in Acts 2–4.

Some have taken these texts to indicate that the early Church rejected the private ownership of property. On the contrary, the liquidation of possessions took place not all at once but "from time to time" (Acts 4:34). It was strictly voluntary. Peter told Ananias and Sapphira that their property was theirs till they sold it, and once they sold it the money was still theirs to use as they wished (Acts 5:3-5). Their sin wasn't in failing to lay everything at the apostles' feet, but in claiming they were doing so when they weren't, just to impress others.

The early Church is not portrayed as utopian. In addition to the situation with Ananias and Sapphira, the Greek and Hebrew Christians quarreled over inequities in the distribution of food to the needy (Acts 6:1).

The "bread line" of Acts 6 is not a specific pattern for churches but a reflection of the ongoing effects of the emergency in the fledgling Church. However, it demonstrates the high priority of helping the needy and taking organizational steps to do so effectively (Acts 6:2-6). It would be a mistake to see Acts 2–4 as a socialistic model, but an even greater mistake to disregard the early Church's example of openhanded giving to the needy.

THE RELATIONSHIP OF MONEY AND POSSESSIONS

Giving involves money, but much more. We can give a meal, house, dress, shovel, bicycle, sewing machine, or any possession. I may give someone a car. Or I may freely loan it to others, or use it to give a ride to my elderly neighbor, or go buy groceries for a shut-in. There's a great deal of giving that can take place even when I retain ownership—as long as I remind myself that God is the true owner, and I'm only his asset manager.

Two cautions are in order. First, we can easily rationalize owning unnecessary things on the grounds that we share them with others. The fact that people often invite others out on their boat doesn't necessarily mean that owning a boat is the most strategic ministry use for the money required. We must also be careful that our ownership doesn't involve possessiveness. If we're the kind of people that others are afraid to borrow from because they know that a dent or scratch or break would bother us, we're not having much of a ministry no matter how "willing to share" we imagine ourselves to be.

As Americans, we routinely buy things for ourselves that we need very seldom, sometimes once in a lifetime. Three people who use a chain saw twice a year will each likely have their own. Someone who needs a pickup truck once a month for three hours might buy one at an incredible expense. Why should a friend, neighbor, or church member buy a one-hundred-foot extension cord to use once a year when he can borrow mine? And why should I buy or rent a hedge clipper when I can borrow his?

Some churches establish lists of possessions that members make freely available for the use of others. (Why not borrow something instead of buying it, then give to the church what you would have spent?) Not only does sharing our assets with others deepen our relationships, cultivate friendships, and lead to evangelism and edification, it also releases huge amounts of money that can be invested in the kingdom of God. Furthermore, it helps free us of possessiveness.

Why not borrow something instead of buying it, then give to the church what you would have spent?

I love books. For years, I spent lots of money on thousands of great books. I loaned some of them out, but most just sat on my shelves. However, it troubled me when my favorite books weren't returned or came back looking shabby.

In 1985, I decided to take all of my books out of my office and put them in our new church library. This saved the church a lot of money and made seldom-used great books available to others. I'll never forget standing in the library a few years later and looking at the names of those who had checked out many of my favorite books. Sometimes there were dozens of names per book. I realized that by releasing those books I had invested in others' lives. Suddenly, the more worn the book, the more delighted I was! My perspective totally changed. Although I still love books, my emotional attachment to possessing them is less than it's ever been. The body of Christ came out ahead on this arrangement, and so did I.

NEW TESTAMENT GUIDELINES FOR GIVING
1. Give.
Christians give. There are no exceptions. Not all will give the same, but all will give: *"Each man should give what he has decided in his heart to give"* (2 Corinthians 9:7, italics mine). It's a sad statistic that four out of ten church attenders give nothing, and another two or three out of ten give next to nothing.

The act of giving is a vivid reminder that our life is all about God, not about us. It says, "I am not the point, God is the point. He does not exist for me. I exist for him." God's money has a higher purpose than my affluence. Giving is a joyful surrender to a greater Person and a greater agenda. Giving affirms Christ's lordship. It dethrones me and exalts him. It breaks the chains of Mammon that would enslave me and transfers my center of gravity to heaven.

As long as I still have something, I believe I own it. But when I give it away, I relinquish the control, power, and prestige that come with wealth. At the moment of release, the light turns on. The magic spell is broken. My mind clears, and I recognize God as owner, myself as servant, and other people as intended beneficiaries of what God has entrusted to me.

Giving doesn't strip me of my vested interest; rather, it shifts my vested interest from earth to heaven—from self to God.

2. Give Generously.

When a grateful woman anointed Jesus with a costly ointment, some observers rebuked her (Mark 14:3-9). "'Leave her alone,' said Jesus. 'Why are you bothering her? She has done a beautiful thing to me'" (Mark 14:6). Some people may consider generous giving "fanatical," but Jesus called it "love." In fact, he was so moved by the woman's giving that he vowed "Wherever the gospel is preached throughout the world, what she has done will also be told, in memory of her" (Mark 14:9). Those who are most calculating usually give less. Love generates lavish giving.

How much is generous? There's no one-size-fits-all answer. When a friend was trying to figure out how much he should give monthly, he decided to give at least as much as his house payment. He told me, "If I can't afford to give that much, then I can't afford to live in a house this nice either."

If you've never tithed, start there—then begin to stretch your generosity. The first few steps beyond the tithe can be particularly exciting, as we give God his claim on the other 90 percent—which also belongs to him. If 10 percent, why not 12 percent? If 12 percent, why not 15 percent? If 15 percent, why not 20 or 30 or 50 or 90 percent or more? Countless people live on one-half or one-third of what many of us make, and I don't mean people who live in poverty. Why not choose to live at a particular income level and simply give everything above that to God? When Nanci and I have done this, we've never regretted it.

3. Give Regularly.

Many people don't give at all, but most who do give do so sporadically. They might give two months in a row, skip three months, give one, skip two more.

Some people don't give when they're on vacation. They don't give if they have the flu. Obviously they don't make it to the offering plate that week—but they don't ever make up for the giving they missed. If I'm out of town when my house payment is due, I may pay it early or even a few days late, but I pay it. Why should my giving to God be any less regular and disciplined? (And why should I get a financial bonus for missing church?)

For years our church had a weekend retreat attended by half our adults and two-thirds of our regular givers. We chose not to take an offering on this retreat, believing that regular givers would simply compensate for their missed week by giving the next week. But every year we discovered that only a fraction of the amount missed that Sunday was ever recovered. Just because people weren't by the offering boxes, they ended up keeping money they otherwise would have given.

It's this hit-and-miss approach to giving that Paul wished the Corinthians to avoid: "On the first day of every week, each one of you should set aside a sum of money in keeping with his income" (1 Corinthians 16:2). When Paul arrived to get the money for the needy, no last minute collections would have to be made from people who had already spent what they should have given. Systematic giving is central to biblical giving. If you give "the leftovers" to God rather than firstfruits, there's often little or nothing left to give.

We should plan our giving in advance—not simply give if we happen to be present or feel moved by the offertory. Can you imagine standing before the Lord and explaining why you disobeyed his command to give: "Lord, I could never find a pen before the plate got there." When we miss church, we can put our check in the mail or add it to next Sunday's giving.

Unless people give systematically, they rarely give substantially. They may give a few hundred or a few thousand dollars a couple of times a year and think of themselves as big givers. But the people who consistently give seventy dollars a week every week, or three hundred, or five hundred dollars a month every month, are the real backbone of the church. They end up giving far more than the "lump sum" givers, who just come through in late December to get their tax deduction. (End of the year giving is fine—but not as a substitute for regular giving.)

If you are paid weekly, you should give weekly. If you're paid monthly, then give monthly.

People who don't give systematically invariably overestimate how much they give. When our church financial secretary was handing out giving receipts one Sunday morning (to save postage), one man told her there must be a mistake, because his wasn't there. Although he was certain it had been only a few months since he'd given, it turned out he actually hadn't given for the entire year.

If you are paid weekly, you should give weekly. If you're paid monthly, then give monthly. If you are a farmer or nurseryman or salesman who receives windfalls a few times a year and little or no income the rest, then you should give just as regularly as your income comes in. If I receive a bonus or gift, I set aside my giving to God immediately.

If we have weekly income but wait until the end of the month to give, or have monthly income but wait until the end of the year, we end up robbing God. We may have every intention of paying him back, but meanwhile we're using money that's his, not ours. That's stealing.

The longer we wait to give, the higher the likelihood that the money will disappear. We will use it for this emergency or that indulgence. The great thing about giving immediately upon receiving is that it removes the temptation to rob God.

If someone asked me to pass twenty dollars on to a friend, I wouldn't put it in my wallet and mix it with my own money. I'd set it aside, perhaps putting it in an envelope with his name on it. Then I'd be sure it got where it was supposed to go as soon as possible. Why? Because I don't want to rob my friend. And it's even more important not to rob God.

The church's needs are monthly needs. A budget must be planned on the basis of regular income. Church members should ask themselves how well the church could operate if everyone gave as much or little, and as often or rarely, as they do.

Stewardship is not a once-a-year consideration, but a week-to-week, month-to-month commitment requiring discipline and consistency. When the Corinthian church expressed their desire to be financially involved in a worthy need-meeting project, Paul told them, "Now finish the work, so that your eager willingness to do it may be matched by your completion of it, according to your means" (2 Corinthians 8:11).

Barring an extraordinary economic turn, a church should meet its budget—assuming the budget has been developed in harmony with the giving levels of church members. We shouldn't be sending missionaries out, then dropping support because of insufficient funds. By regular, systematic giving, the church should ensure that it finishes well in carrying out God's work.

4. Give Deliberately.

I asked an older couple to write out their thoughts on giving. This was their response:

> Our life's purpose for giving is as follows: Help fulfill the Great
> Commission by giving 50 percent of our annual income to Christian
> causes that have the greatest leverage. To do this we must maximize our
> income, consult with people knowledgeable about ministry, and select
> the best organizations to support. We have averaged giving 33 percent
> for the last fifteen years, and in the most recent two years we have
> moved to 50 percent of our gross income.

Notice the clarity of their statement. It reflects thought and determination. If we would give that kind of attention to other areas of our lives, why not our giving?

A recent giving trend is automatic payroll reduction or predetermined monthly payments from a bank account. This has the advantage of convenience and consistency for the giver, and predictability for the recipient. Even if the giver "forgets," the money goes to his church or missionaries. This might result in more giving over the course of the year. Unfortunately, this strategy could also move giving to the back burner, so it's no longer conscious and deliberate. Whether it's paying the tithe or giving the freewill offering, God's children make choices and follow through on them. Automated giving could degenerate into a mindless convenience, detaching someone from the joy and sacrifice of giving. If I write out a monthly check to a missionary family, I'm likely to think of them and pray for them, and sense that I'm part of their team. If the bank sends it off on my behalf, I might not think of them for months at a time. (Of course, if I receive regular letters and examine the bank statement, that may be sufficient to keep me actively involved in the lives of those I support.)

Personally, I think we should avoid giving that is done automatically, without thought, prayer, and worship. I may give my wife flowers on her birthday or our anniversary, but it would not be the same to her or to me if I signed up for a program that would automatically send her a gift and flowers every year on that day. Giving is at its best when it's a conscious effort that's repeatedly made. There's something to be said for actually putting money in an offering plate, or writing a check and dropping it in the mail.

When one spouse balances the checkbook, it's important that the other participate in the giving. Some couples take turns writing the check. Nanci and I make our giving decision together. She writes out the check and I put it in the offering. We're both involved.

5. Give Voluntarily.

When the community of saints contributed to building the tabernacle, the words "willing" and "freewill" were continuously emphasized (Exodus 35:21, 26, 29; 36:3). Everyone "whose heart moved him" gave. Likewise, for the special offering to the needy saints, Paul said, "Each man should give what he has decided in his heart to give, not reluctantly or under compulsion" (2 Corinthians 9:7).

Based on these passages, people have told me we should give to the Lord only if we feel like it. But the believers in Exodus were never told all giving was voluntary. They didn't tithe if they felt led to; they tithed no matter how they felt, because it was their duty. But no one was commanded to give to the tabernacle. They gave to this worthy one-time need because they wanted to, because their hearts were moved by God.

When Paul says a man shouldn't give under compulsion, he isn't talking about the normal week-to-week operations and ministries of the church to which every member must contribute. He is talking about a one-time special offering (for the needs of poor saints in Jerusalem). Because this was above and beyond the regular needs of their local church, it called for a contribution above and beyond their regular giving. They weren't asked to give to the Jerusalem church instead of their own, but in addition to their own.

When churches have special offerings and general giving dips dramatically, there's no special giving involved—people are simply putting their giving in a different place. Is Paul saying that a believer should never feel any compulsion to give to the needs of his church, to the poor, or to world missions? Is he implying that if we are reluctant to part with our money that we shouldn't? No!

Do we share our faith only if we feel led, read our Bible only if we choose, love our spouse only when we feel inspired? Of course not. The principle is not "give voluntarily or don't give at all," but "as your heart is moved, give voluntarily above and beyond your regular giving."

Like many Christians today, the rich fool lived by the principle, "Only give when you feel like it." It just so happens that—like four out of ten churchgoers in America—he never felt like it. In contrast, the Macedonian believers "urgently pleaded with us for the privilege of sharing in this service to the saints" (2 Corinthians 8:4). When we catch a vision of God's grace, we will give *beyond* our duty.

6. Give Sacrificially.

Describing the Macedonian Christians, Paul writes, "Out of the most severe trial, their overflowing joy and their extreme poverty welled up in rich generosity. For I testify that they gave as much as they were able, and even beyond their ability" (2 Corinthians 8:2-3).

There are three levels of giving— less than our ability, according to our ability, and beyond our ability.

How do "severe trial," "overflowing joy," "extreme poverty," and "rich generosity" all fit together in one verse? Among other things, we see here that giving is not a luxury of the rich. It's a privilege of the poor.

There are three levels of giving—less than our ability, according to our ability, and beyond our ability. It's fair to say that 96 percent of Christians in the Western world give less than their ability. Perhaps another 3 percent or more give according to their ability, and less than 1 percent give beyond their ability.

What does it mean to give beyond our ability? It means to push our giving past the point where the figures add up. It means to give when the bottom line says we shouldn't. It means to give away not just the luxuries, but also some of the necessities. It means living with the faith of the poor widow. For most of us, giving according to our means would stretch us. Giving beyond our means would appear to break us. But it won't—because we know God is faithful.

Giving sacrificially also means giving the best. If we have two blankets and someone needs one of them, sacrificial giving hands over the better of the two. Sadly, much of our "giving" is merely discarding. Donating secondhand goods to church rummage sales and benevolence organizations is certainly better than throwing them away. But giving away something we didn't want in the first place isn't giving; it's selective disposal. It's often done because we want a newer or better version.

King David said, "I will not sacrifice to the Lord my God burnt offerings that cost me nothing" (2 Samuel 24:24). Sacrificial giving is parting with what we'd rather keep. It's keeping the old and giving away the new or giving away both. The giving of the first Christians was spontaneous, unguarded, and uncalculated.

Sacrificial giving appears to be unreasonable. In reality, though, it's perfectly reasonable. It brings God glory, meets others' needs, and ensures us eternal rewards. And all the while God takes care of our immediate needs.

Sacrificial giving makes no human sense. But we are to think like Christ, not the world.

A single man in our church came to Christ in his twenties, read the Scriptures, and got so excited that he decided to sell his house and give all the money to God. But when he shared this plan with older believers in his Bible study group, something tragic happened: they talked him out of it.

If we ever feel inclined to talk a young believer, including our own child, out of giving, we should restrain ourselves. Let's not quench God's Spirit and rob loved ones of the present joy and future rewards of giving. Instead, let's watch and learn. Then let's lay God's assets on the table and ask him which ones he wants us to give away.

We don't like risky faith. We like to have our safety net below us, a backup plan in case God fails. Our instinct for self-preservation leads us to hedge our bets. If we give at all, we will give as much as we can without really feeling it and no more. We take away the high stakes, and we also lose the high returns. We miss the adventure of seeing God provide when we've really stretched ourselves in giving.

A disciple does not ask, "How much can I keep?" but, "How much more can I give?" Whenever we start to get comfortable with our level of giving, it's time to raise it again.

7. Give Excellently.

Paul says, "See that you also excel in this grace of giving" (2 Corinthians 8:7). Like piano playing, giving is a skill. With practice, we get better at it. We can learn to give more, give more often, and give more strategically. We teach the pursuit of excellence in our vocations. Why not make giving something we study, discuss, and sharpen, striving for excellence? We have Bible studies on everything else. Why not giving?[3]

Paul is not just speaking to individuals. The church is to work together corporately to excel in giving. It's increasingly common for Christians to ask each other the tough questions: "How are you doing in your marriage?" "How much time have you been spending in the Word?" "How's your sexual purity?" "Have you been sharing your faith?" But how often do we ask, "Have you been robbing God?" or "Are you winning the battle against materialism?" or "How much are you giving to the Lord?"

When it comes to giving, churches operate under a "don't ask, don't tell" policy. We lack communication, accountability, and modeling. It's as if we have an unspoken agreement—"I won't talk about it if you won't"—so we can go right on living as we are. Ask the young people at your church if they can point out examples of prayer warriors in the congregation, people who have a lot to teach about prayer. Most can come up with names. Now ask them to point out the giving warriors, people who have a lot to teach about giving. The fact that the term *giving warrior* sounds so foreign says it all, doesn't it?

Think about it—how do young Christians in our churches learn how to give? Where can they go to see what giving looks like in the life of a believer captivated by Christ? Why are we surprised when, seeing no other example, they take their cues from a materialistic society? Statistics clearly indicate that young adults in the church give a much lower percentage of their income. Part of the reason is that older Christians have failed to pass on a vision for giving.

We're to "consider how we may spur one another on toward love and good deeds" (Hebrews 10:24). Shouldn't we be asking, "How can we spur on each other's giving? How can we help each other excel in giving?"

One way church leaders can inspire giving is by committing the church to give away a higher percentage of its own income. Does 15 percent of the church's income go to missions? Raise it to 25 percent next year and more the next. Does 5 percent go to helping the poor? Raise it to 15 percent. For the same reason that churches wanting to discourage their people from incurring debt should not incur debt, churches wanting to encourage giving should give. Giving shouldn't just be something churches talk about, but something they do.

When Paul said to "excel" in giving, he was referring to special giving to suffering believers facing famine in Jerusalem. Pastors shouldn't limit instruction on giving to times where they're raising funds for building projects. Why not preach on giving for four weeks, and then follow it not with an offering that will benefit the church but with a missions offering that will benefit others? If we want people to stretch themselves in their giving, the best way to model this is for the church to stretch itself in its giving.

8. Give Cheerfully.
"God loves a cheerful giver" (2 Corinthians 9:7). God takes delight in the believer who takes delight in giving. Seeing the temple was in need of repair,

Joash put a chest outside its gate. "All the officials and all the people brought their contributions gladly, dropping them into the chest until it was full" (2 Chronicles 24:10). Whenever the chest was filled they would empty it, return it, and soon it would be full again. The key word is "gladly." The people of God, when they see a worthy cause, give gladly.

There are many reasons for joy in giving. One is knowing that we're investing in eternity and that one day in the heavenly kingdom we'll see the tangible results of our giving. There's an ongoing drama of human request and divine response in which God the Director offers us the part of the giver. Just as the tide comes in and goes out, so one part of Christ's body channels its resources to a more needy part, then receives those resources back in other ways at other times. "At the present time your plenty will supply what they need, so that in turn their plenty will supply what you need" (2 Corinthians 8:14).

The giver senses his part in a great community of faith, extending beyond this world to the angelic hosts and "great cloud of witnesses" in heaven.

Ray Berryman, CEO of Berryman & Henigar, told me, "While we're still working we want to give 50 percent or more of our income, and before we die, with the exception of personal items going to our children, we want to give away all that we have to God's work. My joy in giving comes from serving God in a way that I know he's called me to, and also in realizing that what I give is impacting people for Christ. It's exciting to know we're part of evangelizing, discipling, helping, and feeding the needy. It feels so wonderful and fulfilling."

Notice that Ray's giving is more joy driven than duty driven. In my experience, there's nothing more exhilarating than joining with brothers and sisters in extending God's grace (giving) through our grace (giving) to others. From the day I came to Christ as a high school student, giving has been an integral part of my walk with God. I read Tortured for Christ, God's Smuggler, Foxe's Book of Martyrs, and many other books that gave me a vision for giving to help the needy and reach the lost. Many of the greatest joys of my life, and some of the closest times of intimacy with my Lord, have come in giving. There've been days when I've lost focus, then a need arises and God leads me to give. Suddenly I'm infused with energy, purpose, and joy.

Jesus said, "It is more blessed to give than to receive" (Acts 20:35).Why? Perhaps because when we give it blesses not just one but three people—us, the recipient, and God. We should not be content with the first blessing (which easily becomes a curse) that's ours when we spend money on ourselves. There is the second blessing of others receiving it, and the third blessing of God being pleased with it. Ironically, the blessing on us when we give is always greater than if we had kept it. Hence, by not giving, we rob not only God and others of blessing, we rob ourselves. How many blessings have we robbed ourselves of in the last year by failing to give as we could have? We can't know the answer, but we can give in such a way as to not miss out on God's blessing now.

How many blessings have we robbed ourselves of in the last year by failing to give as we could have?

Tom Conway, of the Generous Giving Advisory Council, writes, "I get great satisfaction by investing in God's kingdom. That's where I will live forever and I want to help as many people as possible get there. I have made other financial investments, some good and others not so good, but you can never make a mistake investing with God. To be able to share our resources in such a way that they produce eternal dividends for the kingdom is pure joy. The joy comes from participating with God in the building of his kingdom, knowing that it will last forever."

Hal Thomas, CEO of Corban Communications, told me about the blessings that giving brought to his life:

My marriage is stronger since it's not based on things of this world. My relationships are stronger since they're not based on things. My walk with God is more real because we have seen Him use us to supply what others need. Nothing in this world can satisfy one's desire more than to have God literally use you to build a church in a small village, bring food to an orphanage, or bring a doctor to a sick person. I have seen each of these happen. I have seen God working through me.

Giving provides me a sense of purpose in God's kingdom. All around my office and home are little knickknacks I have picked up while on mission trips around the world. Today, and more than forty trips since becoming a Christian, I have reminders of the people and places God has allowed me to participate in his work. Each of these reminders, wood carvings, photographs, etc., helps me to pray for the people I have met along the way. My path is a path of sharing, building, and providing for those God chooses for me to help. He has given us a company that generates resources for just such a purpose. Knowing that I am right in the middle of God's plan for my life is the most exciting aspect of being alive that I can ever imagine.

Do we lack joy? It's one of the great blessings of giving. Giving is becoming like our Father. It isn't just God's way of raising money—it's his way of raising children.

Someone told me, "God says not to give if you can't give cheerfully. I can't give cheerfully so I don't give!" God wants us to be cheerful, yes, but he also wants us to be obedient. The path to cheerfulness is not by abstaining from giving, but giving even when we don't feel like it. If we're not cheerful, the problem is our heart, and the solution is redirecting our heart, not withholding our giving. Our heart follows our treasures (Matthew 6:21). Put your treasures in God's kingdom, and a cheerful heart will eventually follow. God also loves an *obedient* giver.

9. Give Worshipfully.

Cornelius is described as "devout and God-fearing," one who "gave generously." When an angel of God appeared, he said to Cornelius, "Your prayers and gifts to the poor have come up as a memorial offering before God" (Acts 10:1-4). Cornelius worshiped God through giving. Because of that, God thought of him with special fondness.

When Paul describes the sacrificial giving of the Macedonian saints he writes, "They did not do as we expected, but they gave themselves first to the Lord and then to us in keeping with God's will" (2 Corinthians 8:5). Giving should be directed toward God before anyone else.

Challenging the Corinthians to give like the Macedonians, Paul points to the basis of all Christian giving: "For you know the grace of our Lord Jesus Christ, that though he was rich, yet for your sakes he became poor, so that you through his poverty might become rich" (2 Corinthians 8:9). The climax of two powerful chapters on giving isn't "Thanks for your philanthropy" but "Thanks be to God for his indescribable gift!" (2 Corinthians 9:15).

Giving is a response of the heart triggered by God's grace. We give because God first gave to us. Karl Barth said it beautifully: "Grace and gratitude belong together like heaven and earth. Grace evokes gratitude like the voice an echo. Gratitude follows grace as thunder follows lightning."[4]

Our giving is a reflexive response to God's grace. It doesn't come out of our altruism—it comes out of the transforming work of Christ in us. Giving is most worshipful not when it's a purely individual matter, as in responding to a mailing or a plea on television, but when it takes place in the gathering of the saints for worship. Jesus said if we're offering a gift at the altar and remember that we have wronged our brother, we are to go and be reconciled before we complete our worship through giving (Matthew 5:23-24). Christian giving is not just individual but corporate. Its relational implications are both vertical and horizontal.

Giving is worship, every bit as much as praying or singing a hymn. My own church has an offering box and passes a plate only on special occasions, but churches need not apologize for making giving a part of the worship service. Although dispensing with passing the plate avoids some of the intrusion of money-consciousness or the danger of showiness, there's also danger in disassociating giving from corporate worship.

If giving as an act of worship is one of the best motives, there are many candidates for the worst. One is giving to get a tax deduction. How would it affect giving if churches and Christian organizations lost their tax-exempt status? We may find out, because the United States is one of the few countries in the world that grants such a status in the first place, and even here it's being challenged. Of course, as long as we have the opportunity to stretch our giving dollars further, it's wise to take advantage of it. But we should never twist a heartfelt act of worship into a mere strategy to reduce our tax liability.

10. Give Proportionately.

When there was an impending famine, "the disciples, each according to his ability, decided to provide help for the brothers living in Judea" (Acts 11:29). God says when it comes to giving, "each one of you should set aside a sum of money in keeping with his income" (1 Corinthians 16:2).

The Old Testament tithe was proportionate, not fixed. If someone earned five hundred pieces of gold, he tithed fifty. But if he earned only twenty pieces, he was required to tithe only two. Tithing was proportionate to income.

But proportionate giving is not equal giving. It's a much greater sacrifice for someone who earns ten thousand dollars a year to give a thousand than it is for someone who earns eighty thousand to give eight thousand. Although it's true that the second person is giving away eight times as much as the other, he's also left with eight times more to live on.

It's easy for us to describe someone as a generous giver based solely on the amount given, but true generosity is determined by how much a person gives of what he or she has. A financial counselor wrote to me, saying, "I've worked with wealthy couples who are making a million dollars a year, with a net worth of $10 million, but they're giving $15,000 a year and feel very generous." Some people would think that anyone who gave $15,000 a year must be generous. But not necessarily. It all depends on what's left.

Seeing rich people throw large amounts in the temple treasury and the widow put in two tiny copper coins, Jesus called his disciples to him and said, "This poor widow has put more into the treasury than all the others. They all gave out of their wealth; but she, out of her poverty, put in everything—all she had to live on" (Mark 12:43-44).

The same logic that would automatically consider a gift of $20,000 or $200,000 as generous (a perspective that is prevalent among churches and ministries) would have to conclude, on the same basis, that the poor widow wasn't generous because she only gave two coins.

God looks not only at what we give, but also at what we keep. The less we have left, the more we have given. Consider the appropriateness of a graduated giving percentage that keeps sliding higher as income increases. Suppose a family makes $40,000 annually and gives 20 percent. Their giving would amount to $8,000, leaving them $32,000 to support their lifestyle. Now let's say that a few years later, their income rises to $80,000. Without factoring in cost-of-living and tax increases (remembering that giving, at least up to 50 percent of income, nullifies tax liability), they would be able to maintain their standard of living for $32,000, which would allow them to give $48,000. Now, instead of giving away 20 percent, they would be giving 60 percent, but their lifestyle would remain constant. In other words, they could dramatically increase their giving without increasing their true sacrifice. When our daughters finished college and got married, Nanci and I were able to give more without it affecting our standard of living. Our proportion and amount of giving increased, but our sacrifice didn't.

One person can give $25 in an act of great sacrifice, whereas another can give a million dollars and not sacrifice at all. If someone makes $10,000,000 a year, gives away $9,000,000 and spends "only" the other million on himself we may be impressed, and it may be a relatively wise eternal investment, but is it really sacrificial in God's eyes? This is one reason why it's unhealthy and misleading to publicly laud large donors in the Christian community. Often their sacrifice is far less than those whose names will never be known.

> God looks not only at what we give, but also at what we keep.

One study showed that American households with incomes under $10,000 gave 5.5 percent of their income to charities, whereas those earning more than $100,000 gave 2.9 percent.[5] This disparity shows that true sacrifice in giving typically decreases, not increases, as people make more money.

A. W. Tozer said that God weighs not the size of our gift but the significance of that size in proportion to our giving potential. In *That Incredible Christian*, he writes:

> Before the judgment seat of Christ, my service will be judged not by how much I have done, but by how much I could have done. In God's sight, my giving is measured not by how much I have given, but by how much I could have given and how much I had left after I made my gift.[6]

Believers, as they sense God's direction, can increase the proportion of their giving as God blesses them financially or as they learn to trust him more. Hence, over the years, many believers give a higher and higher percentage to the Lord. Nanci and I live comfortably, and we know we don't need more than a certain amount to live on. What comes in beyond that goes to God's kingdom.

11. Give Quietly.

Jesus says, "Be careful not to do your 'acts of righteousness' before men, to be seen by them. If you do, you will have no reward from your Father in heaven" (Matthew 6:1). The illustrations that follow include prayer and fasting, but begin with giving. When you give to the needy, he says, don't announce it, as do the hypocrites, who want to be honored by men. Instead, give quietly, not telling anyone, "so that your giving may be in secret. Then your Father, who sees what is done in secret, will reward you" (Matthew 6:4).

I read of a New York fund-raising dinner where people stood up to identify themselves and make pledges to a charitable cause. One man rose, gave his name, his wife's name, the name of his business, its location, and the kind of merchandise he sold, then loudly announced, "We want to give $5,000 anonymously."[7]

Showiness in giving is always inappropriate. But sometimes our acts of righteousness will be seen by men and even should be. The world will know we are Christians by our love for each other (John 13:35), but our acts of love must be visible, just as they were when the early Christians sold their property and gave away the proceeds to meet each other's need. Earlier in the same sermon where he says we're not to give in order to be seen by men, Christ commands us, "Let your light shine before men, that they may see your good deeds and praise your Father in heaven" (Matthew 5:16).

How can we reconcile these commands? We do so by realizing that Christ's point is about our motives: Don't do a righteous act in order to impress people. But when you do a good work, use that opportunity to bring praise to God. What Jesus objects to is not that men would know we give, but that we would give to impress men rather than to please God.

The same principle applies to prayer. Jesus tells us to pray in secret, and God will reward us for that (Matthew 6:6). Yet gathering for group prayer is certainly important (Matthew 18:19-20). God wants us to pray secretly sometimes but not others. He also wants us to give secretly sometimes but not others. It all comes down to the motives of our heart.

Studies show that people give more when they get public recognition—but in the Church is that the right thing to do? Many Christian organizations and churches put contributors' names on plaques, bricks, pews, and cornerstones. They publish donor lists and name schools and buildings after patrons. This surely encourages the very thing Jesus condemned. It's hard to understand how we could read this passage and still continue these practices. What are we thinking? By granting the reward of human recognition, we deprive givers of the one reward that would count for eternity: God's reward. (This practice will be considered more thoroughly in chapter 15.)

Studies show that people give more when they get public recognition—but in the Church is that the right thing to do? During a building project years ago, our church elders were considering whether to offer to put givers' names on individual bricks. One of the elders said, "If we do that, I hope those people really like bricks, because if that's why they give, it's the only reward they're going to get." Eventually we decided against the idea, because we thought it would tempt people to give for the wrong reasons—and would thereby remove God's blessing from that building project.

In some circles, "giving" is merely the price of admission for social status. Many people's businesses have flourished more than the value of their giving through the publicity their giving produces. If this is their motive, then their "giving" is merely a business expense.

210

I'm always amused at companies that purchase television airtime for $100,000 to make a big deal out of giving $10,000 to needy kids. Why not just give $110,000 to help the kids and shut up about it? What they're doing is not about giving—it's about self-promotion for the purpose of financial gain.

Some use giving to purchase recognition, while others use it to purchase control. They give with strings attached, pulling this string and that, leaving the recipient organization afraid not to comply since it will mean losing future gifts. This is the stockholder mentality. It's common in local churches where the wealthy can wave their money and lobby for what they want, or strike back by withholding their giving when they don't get their way. At a church where there was disagreement over who should serve as a new pastor, one board member said, "I've poured a lot of money into this church, and I intend to get the pastor I want." In the truest sense, of course, this man wasn't giving money to God or the church. He was spending money, under the guise of giving, to purchase control and ego enrichment. God wants quiet and humble givers, not self-serving power brokers.

The best way to avoid exalting givers is to avoid knowing who they are in the first place.

The best way to avoid exalting givers is to avoid knowing who they are in the first place. There are many reasons for keeping giving anonymous. Most churches have one or two financial secretaries who record donations for tax purposes. These people are the only ones who know who gives what. Other times one or more pastors, elders, or deacons are also aware of giving levels. In one church, the pastor personally sends his thanks for the exact amount given during the year, making a point of the fact that he knows exactly who has given how much. This is standard practice in Christian parachurch organizations where large donors receive personal letters, special mailings, phone calls, and other forms of reward and wooing. Of course, parachurch ministries are not entrusted with shepherding the flock, whereas local churches are.

There are several reasons why I believe that no one in church leadership should know who's giving what. If leaders know how much people give, they'll be tempted to show preference to big givers and neglect those who give less. This is the very trap Scripture warns against, calling it "favoritism" and "evil" (James 2:1-5). Also, it puts leaders in a position of judging others with incomplete knowledge. They may conclude that some people are unspiritual and others are spiritual, without knowing the whole story. (Again, this is different in parachurch ministries, because there is limited direct contact between most ministries and many of their supporters. Consequently, the circumstances do not exist for givers to be compared as readily as they might be in a church, and conclusions are rarely drawn about nongivers.) In some cases, church leaders' judgments may be accurate, but still unhealthy. Those who have served as financial secretaries carry the burden of knowing when vocal church members whom everyone admires give nothing to the church.

The most important reason for anonymous giving is to remove or at least minimize the temptation to give in order to impress others. If the pastor or the board knows how much I give, I may give in order to impress them. But if I do, Jesus says, I have my reward and will receive none from him. When I give at my church, I'm grateful there are only one or two people I could be tempted to impress. The fewer the better.

One of the great tests for Christian leaders is whether we can trust God to provide financially without courting or favoring big donors. And perhaps the greatest test for givers is whether we are able to give of ourselves and our resources without getting the credit, concerned only that God gets the glory.

For misrepresenting their giving, God struck Ananias and Sapphira dead (Acts 5:1-10). Keep in mind that they were generous donors. Many Christian ministries today would pay their way to a donors' conference in a gorgeous hotel in the Caribbean or name a new building after them. If we are tempted to exaggerate our giving or make it appear we're making more sacrifice than we are, we should take seriously what God did to Ananias and Sapphira!

The Master says, "Well done" to the servant, not for being well known or popular or for getting his name engraved on cornerstones and having buildings named after him. Rather he commends him for being "good" and "faithful." When we're true servants, it isn't about us. We're like the ox grinding out the corn. We don't own the corn, and we don't get credit for growing it. We just do our job and get to eat some of it, and we're grateful for that. Recognition isn't what it's about. Slaves think about their master's reputation, not their own.

I have no desire to lose my future reward from God by calling attention to myself now. Nevertheless, Scripture does show there is encouragement in believers seeing God at work in the giving of other believers (1 Chronicles 29:6-9; 2 Corinthians 8:1-7). I've been encouraged and stimulated to give as I've heard the giving testimonies of others. For this reason I sometimes tell our giving story, as I have at places in the book, hoping it will benefit others. If the reason for my giving is in order to get the readers' approval, however, I will forfeit my reward. (See appendix E, "Should Giving Always Be Kept Secret?")

GOD'S PROVISION FOR THE GIVER

In many cases God blesses us financially when we give generously (Proverbs 11:24-25). Jesus says, "Give, and it will be given to you. A good measure, pressed down, shaken together and running over, will be poured into your lap. For with the measure you use, it will be measured to you" (Luke 6:38). The apostle Paul says: "Whoever sows sparingly will also reap sparingly, and whoever sows generously will also reap generously" (2 Corinthians 9:6).

Whether or not you're a giver, you have considerable material blessings from God. Have you ever asked yourself, "*Why* has he provided so much?" You don't need to wonder. God tells us *exactly* why he provides us with more money than we need:

> Now he who supplies seed to the sower and bread for food will also supply and increase your store of seed and will enlarge the harvest of your righteousness. You will be made rich in every way so that . . . (2 Corinthians 9:10-11)

So that *what?* How will he finish this sentence? How *you* finish the sentence is one of the most important decisions you will ever make. Prosperity theology would finish it like this: ". . . so that we might live in wealth, showing the world how much God blesses those who love him."

But that isn't how Paul finishes it. He says, "You will be made rich in every way *so that you can be generous on every occasion*" (italics mine). God doesn't make us rich so we can indulge ourselves and spoil our children, or so we can insulate ourselves from needing God's provision. God gives us abundant material blessing so that we can give it away, and give it generously.

When God provides more money we often think, *This is a blessing.* Yes, but it would be just as scriptural to say, "This is a test."

Abundance isn't God's provision for me to live in luxury. It's his provision for me to help others live. God entrusts me with his money not to build my kingdom on earth, but to build his kingdom in heaven. Paul encouraged the church to give to the needy in Jerusalem: "At the present time your plenty will supply what they need, so that in turn their plenty will supply what you need. Then there will be equality, as it is written: 'He who gathered much did not have too much, and he who gathered little did not have too little'" (2 Corinthians 8:14-15).

Why does God give some of his children more than they need and others less than they need? He does it to teach his children to help each other. God distributes wealth unevenly, not because he loves some of his children more than others, but so his children can distribute it to their brothers and sisters on his behalf. He doesn't want us to have too little or too much (Proverbs 30:8-9). When those with too much give to those with too little, two problems are solved. When they don't, two problems are perpetuated.

God entrusts me with his money not to build my kingdom on earth, but to build his kingdom in heaven.

We need to envision what our gifts do for the recipients. One giver wrote to me, "My greatest joy in giving is seeing the fruit of the gift. Seeing people blessed, seeing Bibles printed and distributed, seeing missionaries going to the field. The giving itself is a blessing, but the deepest levels of joy come when I see the fruit." This is one reason that I recommend people take trips that allow them to see some of the faces and meet some of the people touched by their giving. Hugh Maclellan Jr. says he was hooked as a giver when he saw firsthand what God was really doing through missions work. Hugh says, "I knew that's where I wanted to put my money—where it would make a difference for eternity."

Are you eager to plant God's money in the field of a world that needs Christ? Does the thought of giving to what will count for eternity make your spine tingle? Does storing up treasures in heaven make your heart leap? If we understood the out-of-this-world returns on our investments in others, we'd join the Macedonians and beg for the privilege of giving.

R. G. LeTourneau understood God's purpose for blessing him financially. An inventor of earthmoving machines, LeTourneau reached the point of giving 90 percent of his income to the Lord. As he put it, "I shovel out the money, and God shovels it back—but God has a bigger shovel."

My family has experienced God's "bigger shovel," his abundant material provision to the giver. In some cases it's obvious—such as an unexpected check in the mail or being given something just when we thought we'd have to buy it. One time when we really needed it, it came in the form of discovering an error we had made in the figuring of our bank balance.

In other cases, God's provision is less obvious but equally real. A washing machine that should have stopped a decade ago keeps on working. A car with 200,000 miles on it runs for two years without so much as a tune-up. A checking account that should have dried up long before the end of the month somehow makes it through. As God miraculously stretched the oil and bread of the widow in Elisha's day, and as he made the clothes and sandals of the children of Israel last forty years in the wilderness, I'm convinced he sometimes graciously extends the life of things that would normally have to be replaced.

We often thank God for his behind-the-scenes provision, including preventing accidents and incidents that would have been costly. God provides not only in what he gives us, but at times in what he keeps from us. Have you ever noticed that excess money just seems to dissipate in a multitude of directions? When the Israelites were building their paneled houses and God's house was in ruins, God said to them, "Give careful thought to your ways. You have planted much, but have harvested little. . . . You earn wages, only to put them in a purse with holes in it" (Haggai 1:5-6). God said that because the nation of Israel had given to themselves and not to him, he had minimized and dissipated their profits so they didn't come out ahead (Haggai 1:9-11). We need to give careful thought to our ways, asking ourselves if we'd do better to give more to the Lord and ask him to maximize what we keep. That's so much better than trying to hang on to more, only to watch it leak out of our pockets.

In 1988, Nanci and I sensed God's leading to take our daughters, Karina and Angela, and spend two months visiting our church's missionary families in

Africa and Europe. Our church wanted to pay my way, but when we figured how much it would cost for the rest of the family, it was prohibitive. I felt strongly that my family should be with me, but there was just no way to do it. In another situation, we might have seen this as God's way of saying no; but in this case we sensed his direction to move forward. We deliberately didn't announce our intention to go for fear the announcement itself would bring funds in. We wanted to see God provide in other ways.

As we saved for the trip, remarkable amounts of money began to appear. Most of the funds came from unexpected sources. Beyond all this, every month we found we were saving far more than we should have been able to. There were no extra expenses draining our funds.

We'd determined not to reduce our giving. Although we would never touch the tithe, we were tempted to rationalize using some of our extra monthly freewill giving to pay for our trip—after all, it was for a missionary purpose! But this didn't seem right.

Two weeks before the trip, an amazing amount of money had come in, but we still lacked a thousand dollars. Meanwhile, there was a special missionary offering at church. We determined to give substantially to this offering, above and beyond our normal giving. It "didn't make sense," but we knew it was right. No one who has seen God work will be surprised to hear that within a week of the trip he gave back not only the money we had given but over a thousand dollars more, enough to give some back to him once more before getting on the plane.

We looked back at the trip and realized that, humanly speaking, we shouldn't have been able to accumulate the needed funds. But God provided abundantly.

As we learn to give, we draw closer to God. But no matter how far we move on in the grace of giving, Jesus Christ remains the matchless giver: "For you know the grace of our Lord Jesus Christ, that though he was rich, yet for your sakes he became poor, so that you through his poverty might become rich" (2 Corinthians 8:9). No matter how much we give, we can never outgive God.

IS IT APPROPRIATE TO TEACH GIVING TO THE POOR?

A fine brother who ministers faithfully in a poor country asked me this question:

> I wonder if people in this country would just tune me out if I spoke on the subject of giving. Pastors here don't really expect many people to tithe, because some people in their congregations only make between $4 and $9 per month. Is it cruel to preach to them about giving?

The biblical principles of giving are universal, timeless truths that God taught to the poorest Israelites and to the predominantly poor New Testament saints. Giving brings to people not only future reward, but also present fruits, purpose, and dignity.

In my experience, poor believers would never tune someone out for teaching about giving, any more than other biblical subjects. God knows exactly what's best for them, and he gave them the Bible. What God teaches about money and possessions was not written for wealthy Christians in North America, but for all people in all times in all places. Jesus didn't elevate the rich fool but the poor widow, setting her up as a model for giving.

Second Corinthians 8–9, the longest passage on giving in the Bible, starts by focusing on the Macedonians who lived in "extreme poverty," yet who gave not simply according to their means but "beyond their ability." Paul speaks of the "overflowing joy" connected with their generosity, and how they begged for "the privilege" of giving. This has direct application to the question asked by the missionary. We certainly should not deprive these poor believers of the privilege of giving by withholding from them the principles of giving that God intended for poor Christians just as much as for rich ones. Widows and the poor were not only recipients of gifts. The poor widow was Christ's model for giving.

So would it be cruel to preach about giving to poor people? On the contrary, it would be cruel not to preach about giving. If we withhold part of the whole counsel of God, we act as his editors rather than as his messengers. Remember, it's not the poor who are an anomaly among Christians. It's rich people—like us—who are the exception. Today's poor join ranks with most Christians down through the ages, in countless places, including many who have been persecuted.

If the people make only between $4 and $9 a month, then the tithe would be only 40 to 90 cents. That may seem like a lot, but God promises his blessing and provision. God blesses giving, and when we hang on to what is his, it's never in our best interest. We have it backwards. The poor are not hurt by giving; they are helped by giving. God says, "Test me in this, and watch me provide" (Malachi 3:10, my paraphrase). Jesus said, "Give, and it will be given to you. . . . For with the measure you use, it will be measured to you" (Luke 6:38). If we don't teach people about giving, we deprive them of what God would have provided if they had learned to become givers.

Of course, we need to carefully distinguish this teaching from the health and wealth gospel, making sure our illustrations and examples are commensurate with their means and opportunities within their economy. But God has called today's poor to give, just as he called the poor widow and the poverty-stricken Macedonians to give. Who are we to withhold God's promises and this wonderful privilege from those who need it most?

Brian Kluth taught stewardship and giving to evangelists and church leaders in India. At the end of the course, a thirty-seven-year-old Indian evangelist wrote this response:

Satan always tries to stop us from giving to God, because he does not want God's kingdom and people to prosper. Through our giving we must rebuke Satan and make it a financial priority to give to God first (even if we only have meager resources). We must also be very faithful in all of our financial matters. When a man loves money more than God, he always misuses God's money. That is why it is so important for us to make our first priority to give to God. We need to use the money God entrusts to us for the extension of his kingdom on the earth.

Nearly every testimony from those attending the conference—all of whom live way below America's poverty level—could have been spoken by Western Christians. Why? Because these are timeless truths and cross-cultural principles. The culture in which Scripture was written was much closer to today's Two-Thirds World cultures than to those in the United States, Canada, Britain, and other industrialized nations.

ASKING GOD ABOUT OUR GIVING

Hugh Maclellan Jr. directs the Maclellan Foundation, a third-generation effort that supports missions across the globe. Hugh seeks to give away a yearly minimum of 70 percent of his personal income. He breaks down his giving into different categories, starting with a tithe to his local church and widening out to other ministries. He makes substantial gifts that he believes have a chance to make a long-term kingdom impact. The Maclellan Foundation tries to put as much thought and research into where their money goes as mutual fund investors do. "Why not?" they reason, since they're seeking to invest not just on earth, but also in heaven, not just for a moment, but for eternity.

Hugh says, "I want my life to bear fruit that will last." He adds, "Meet with God to determine what his giving goals are for you. Not just your goals, but his goals for you to carry out as his steward. Then ask him to give you the particular passion to burden you for giving to certain kinds of ministries. Also ask yourself, 'What are the barriers that keep me from being a generous giver?' Ask God to deal with you in those areas. He will!"

We're told to examine ourselves and test ourselves (2 Corinthians 13:5). David prayed that God would search his heart and test him, then show him anything he needed to repent of and change (Psalm 139:23-24).

I'll end this chapter with forty questions that each of us can ask God about our giving. You may wish to read them through for their cumulative effect, or just read one or two at a time. Ask them honestly of God over a period of weeks. After taking these to the Lord, just between you and him, you may wish to discuss them with others. Perhaps, like me, you'll want to come back to these questions periodically.

FORTY QUESTIONS TO ASK GOD ABOUT YOUR GIVING

1. Father, with the financial assets and opportunities you've entrusted to me, have you raised me up for just such a time as this? (Esther 4:14). Have you called me to join a great team of your children in freeing up money and possessions to reach out to the needy and fulfill the great commission?

2. Is the fact that you've entrusted me with so many resources an indication that you have given me the gift of giving and want me to learn to exercise it more frequently and skillfully?

3. What am I holding on to that is robbing me of present joy and future reward? What am I keeping that's preventing me from having to depend on you? What am I clinging to that makes me feel like I don't have to depend on you to provide, like I used to before I had this much? What do you want me to release that could restore me to a walk of faith?

4. In light of 2 Corinthians 8:14 and 9:11, do you want me to assume that each financial blessing you entrust to me is not intended to raise my standard of living but to raise my standard of giving?

5. Am I being held in orbit around the mass of treasures I've stored up? Have I overaccumulated? Have you multiplied "my" assets not so I would stockpile them, but so I would distribute them to the needy?

6. Where in the world (and in my community) do you want me to go, to see, and participate in Christ-centered ministries meeting physical and spiritual needs?

7. Am I treating you as owner and CEO/CFO of "my" assets, or am I treating you merely as my financial consultant, to whom I pay a fee (of 10 percent or greater)?

8. When I make a list of all the assets you've entrusted to me and ask what you want me to give away, is there anything I'm leaving off the list? Is there anything I'm treating as if it were untouchable, as if it were mine and not yours? Do my retirement funds belong to you too? What doesn't?

9. Do you want me to set a basic level of income and assets to live on, then give away whatever you provide beyond that (regardless of whether that's 50 percent, 90 percent, 99 percent, or more)?

10. How can I be sure that the assets you've entrusted to me will serve you after my death? How do I know that those to whom I leave them, or those to whom they leave them, will use them for your glory? If I want money to go to your kingdom later and it's more than I presently need, why wouldn't I give it to your kingdom now?

11. If the world and everything in it will burn at your second coming (2 Peter 3:10-13), will my assets, accounts, and the holdings I've stored up on earth be wasted if you return in my lifetime? Once my present opportunity to give is lost, will I get a second chance? Do you want me to adopt a "use it or lose it" approach to my current opportunities for eternal investment?

12. Once they've finished college or are working on their own, would inheriting wealth (beyond items of special sentimental and heritage value) help my children's eternal perspective and walk with God? Or would it have a corrupting influence on their character, lifestyle, work ethic, or marriage?

13. If my children would resent my giving money to your kingdom instead of leaving it for them, does that indicate they're not qualified to receive it? If so, why would I give them your money? If my investment manager died, what would I think if he left my money to his children? Does the fact that you entrusted your money to me, not others, indicate that you want me, during my lifetime, to invest it in eternity? Will you, in turn, provide my children with the money you expect them to manage?

14. What's the eternal downside to giving now? What's the eternal downside of delaying giving until later? Am I really in danger of giving too much too soon? Or is the only real danger giving too little too late? If I give away most of my assets now, what will I have available to give later?

15. If I don't give something now, is it possible I may no longer have it to give later?

16. If I don't give something now, is it possible I may die before I get a chance to give it later? If my desire is to give it away before I die and I can't know when I'll die, should I give it now?

17. If I don't give it now, am I in danger of my heart getting further wrapped up in earthly treasure, rather than in heavenly treasure? (Matthew 6:21). Will the same heart that's prompting me to give today later persuade me to keep something because I ignored your prompting to give?

18. Because I have no choice but to leave money behind when I die, is it really "giving" to designate money to ministries in my will? (Although these may be the wisest places to leave my assets—and all of us will have some assets remaining at our death—it involves no sacrifice or need for faith.) Will I rob myself of joy and reward and rob you of my trust by holding on to significant assets until death that I could have given while I was still alive?

19. In James 4:13-17, you tell me I can't know how much money I can

make (or lose) tomorrow, or even whether I'll be here. Is it presumptuous of me to accumulate a large amount of "Confederate money" that may not be used for you in the future, when it could definitely be used for you in the present?

20. When I stand before your judgment seat, would you ever say to me, "You blew it—you sold those shares and gave them to feed the hungry and evangelize the lost, and then two years later the market peaked"? Or would you say, "Well done, my good and faithful servant"?

21. Can you produce higher eternal returns from money I give to you today than Wall Street can? Can anything match your promise of a hundredfold return (10,000 percent)?

22. Is it ever wrong to give to you now rather than wait until later? If Christ commended the poor widow in Mark 12 for giving to you everything she had—considering her faithful, not irresponsible— how much would I have to give away before you would consider me irresponsible?

23. Do you want me to set up a foundation or give money out as you bring it in? If I have a foundation, do you want me to give assets away now, or implement a phase-out plan so the principal doesn't end up wasted at your return?

24. Because you called the rich young ruler in Matthew 19:16-30 to give away all that he had and follow you in faith, is it possible you might call me to do the same? Do you want me to ask you?

25. Why do I want to hold on to my wealth? Am I trying to prove something? What am I trying to prove—and to whom? Is it pride? power? prestige? selfishness? insecurity? fear? Am I a control freak? Or is it just because possessiveness is normal in our society, and I'm merely going with the flow? Do you want me to go with the flow or do something different—maybe radically different?

26. Am I living to hear others say of me, "He [or she] is a great success" or to have you say to me, "Well done, my good and faithful servant"?

27. Instead of asking "Why should I give this away?" do you want me to ask "Why shouldn't I give this away?" Should I put the burden of proof on *keeping* rather than on *giving*? When money comes in, which should be the rule and not the exception: *giving* or *keeping*? Unless there's a compelling reason to keep, should I normally give?

28. Am I hanging on to money excessively as a backup plan in case you fail me? Is my fear of dire health catastrophes and old-age scenarios creating an inertia in my giving, because I imagine I must provide everything for myself if something goes wrong? Considering that

the vast majority of people in history and most in the world today have nothing stored up for retirement, am I preoccupied with putting too many treasures in retirement funds? Are you calling me to work without a net—or with less of a net—trusting you'll catch me in case of a fall?

29. Has Money become my idol? Are material assets competing with you for lordship over my life? Is generous giving your lifeline to rescue me from bondage, your leverage to allow me to tear down the idols? If materialism is the disease, is giving the only cure?

30. I want to submit everything to your review and ask you to guide me as to what I should do with your money and possessions. What specifically am I hanging on to that you want me to give away?

31. Am I giving your money to people of weak character and materialistic values? Although they may be good causes, are the Humane Society or opera as close to your heart as evangelism, church planting, and helping the poor? Do the ministries I'm supporting financially help the poor in Christ's name, not just in the name of humanitarianism? Is the gospel offered to dying people once they've been fed?

32. How can I better communicate with and pray with my spouse so we can walk together down this exhilarating road of giving, leading each other and not leaving the other behind?

33. What am I doing to train my children to be generous givers—not just donors, but disciples?

34. What handful of people in my unique sphere of influence do you want me to pray for and talk with about generous giving? Have you called me to mentor others in giving, that they may end up giving more than I do? In helping someone become a great giver, will I be like the man who led D. L. Moody to Christ?

35. What giving-oriented, mission-oriented, and eternity-oriented books and magazines can I pass on to those in my sphere of influence? What tapes or videos can we listen to and watch together?

36. What simple reminder of God's call to stewardship and giving can I make for myself, then pass on to others? Maybe I can give them something to put in their Day-Timer or on their PalmPilot, in their wallet or Bible, on their dashboard or refrigerator or exercise machine, such as a business card or a bookmark with central verses such as Deuteronomy 8:17-18 or Matthew 6:19-21.[8]

37. What can I set up to provide a discussion forum concerning stewardship and giving? A dinner? A weekly breakfast? A weekend retreat? A weekly study using *Money, Possessions and Eternity*, *The Treasure Principle*, or materials from Crown Ministries?[9]

38. What conferences can I invite others to attend? What ministries can I introduce others to? What vision and ministry trips can we go on together?

39. How can I help my pastor(s) encourage biblical training in steward-ship and giving and assist them in creating an open church dialogue regarding lifestyle choices and kingdom investments?

40. Five minutes after I die, what will I wish I would have given away while I still had the chance? Would you help me spend the rest of my life closing the gap between what I'll wish I'd given then and what I'm actually giving now?

CHAPTER 14

Helping the Poor and Reaching the Lost

That bread which you keep belongs to the hungry; that coat
which you preserve in your wardrobe, to the naked; those
shoes which are rotting in your possession, to the shoeless;
that gold which you have hidden in the ground, to the
needy. Wherefore, as often as you are able to help others,
and refuse, so often did you do them wrong.   AUGUSTINE

Obedience to the Great Commission has more consistently
been poisoned by affluence than by anything else.
RALPH WINTER

Mother Teresa devoted her life to helping the poorest of the poor. After observing her arduous work among the filth, disease, and suffering of Calcutta, a television commentator told her, "I wouldn't do what you're doing for all the money in the world." She replied, "Neither would I."

What we wouldn't do for all the money in the world, we are called to do out of obedience to Christ, compassion for others, and anticipation of eternal reward.

I am always amazed when I read about acts of philanthropy to Planned Parenthood, the world's largest abortion provider. It's alarming how easily giving can be wasteful, or even harmful. Bernard Marcus, founder of Home Depot, gave $200 million for an aquarium in Atlanta. I'm all for aquariums, but when I see a world full of lost and hungry people, I wonder, *Where are the huge gifts to Christian ministries that are devoted to reaching the lost and helping the needy in the name of Christ?*

Claude Rosenberg Jr. devoted years to researching America's giving habits and potential and put his findings into a book titled *Wealthy and Wise: How You and America Can Get the Most out of Your Giving.* According to Rosenberg, most of us give away less than 10 percent of what we could actually afford to give, even without making significant lifestyle changes. Does that sound incredible? If you look at it closely, you'll see that it's true. Rosenberg argues that Americans giving away 2 percent of their income could give away 20 percent, provided they simply made wiser choices with what they spend. He calculates that Americans could donate at least $100 billion *more* per year than we already do—and with a minimum of sacrifice or risk. This is without even going as far as the sacrificial giving we see in Scripture, and without calculating in the way God provides generously for givers.

According to Rosenberg, if we had a better grasp of what we actually own, most of us could double, triple, or quadruple the amount we now give.[1]

Why is this money tied up, inaccessible to God to use for his purposes? Partly it may stem from our failure to come to grips with the needs of the poor and the lost, as well as our neglect of strategic opportunities to make an eternal difference through our giving.

GIVING TO THE POOR
Who Is Responsible for the Poor?
In his essay on self-reliance, Ralph Waldo Emerson writes, "Do not tell me, as a good man did today, of my obligation to put all poor men in good situations. Are they my poor?"[2] Emerson's attitude reflects our national spirit of independence. Few of us wish harm to the poor. We just don't want to be held responsible for them. But Emerson's question is a valid one. Are the poor my poor? Am I responsible for their plight? More than one evangelical writer would have us believe that because we ourselves are not poor, because we have money and possessions others don't, we are at fault for their poverty.

This perspective is a "zero sum" philosophy, the belief that wealth cannot be created but only distributed, and that for every winner there must be a corresponding loser. For example, if there are eight people at a party and a pie is cut in eight pieces, and I take two or three pieces for myself, then I've taken what belongs to the others. They have less because I have more.

Those holding this position apply the pie analogy to the world. There's only so much wealth in the world, they say, and everyone's entitled to his share. If I have more than someone else, essentially I've stolen from him. Karl Marx taught this concept, dividing all men into "the oppressors and the oppressed." Those who have much are oppressors; those who don't are oppressed.

However, unlike a finite pie that cannot be made bigger, wealth is not limited—it *can* be produced and enlarged. Scripture tells us, "Remember the Lord your God, for it is he who gives you the ability to produce wealth" (Deuteronomy 8:18). Wealth is being produced every day as a result of ingenuity and hard work. One person's prosperity can take place at the expense of another, but it need not.

Is Capitalism to Blame for Poverty?
Some would claim that although we may not directly exploit the poor, we're voluntarily part of an economic system that exploits them. Therefore, we're culpable. In this view, capitalism is the supposed enemy of the poor.

Every discussion of the plight of the poor involves economics, so I need to address the subject at least briefly. Interested readers may turn to a number of fine books that explore the issues in depth.[3]

Capitalism is a free-market economic system that operates without exterior control. "Control" is left to what economist Adam Smith called "the invisible hand." According to this theory, the marketplace naturally orders itself around the needs and wants of the population. The principle of supply and demand determines what sells at what price. The greater the competition, the more goods there are to choose from and the more reasonable prices will be.

It's difficult to understand how one particular system (capitalism) can be blamed for a problem (poverty) that has existed in every country with every economic structure in human history. A capitalistic society can certainly foster greed and allow the poor to be exploited, but it can also give opportunity to the poor to do what many have done in free-market economies—work themselves out of poverty.

Capitalism results at times in exploitation, because no system can eliminate sin. But capitalism is not built on exploitation, it's built on common interest. In a truly free market, all parties will ultimately get what they want. For example, when you bought this book, presumably you were satisfied with the transaction—you profited from the exchange of currency for ideas and principles. Who else came out ahead on the transaction? One would hope the bookseller, the publisher, and the author, as well as loggers, the paper company, the printer, truckers, and others who took part in the process. When you buy milk, who profits? You do—you get the milk you wanted. But others profit as well, including your grocer and the dairy farmer. All parties involved can profit in the buying and selling of goods. One's profit is not at the expense of another.

The major alternative to capitalism is socialism. Some outspoken Christians still suggest it's a better alternative. Socialism is an economic system controlled by the state. It supposedly spreads out the goods to all, preventing the formation of a rich, land-grabbing elite that would oppress the poor. In socialism, economic power is centralized in the government so that no individual can become rich at the expense of others. Unfortunately, somebody has to run this system. And because power tends to corrupt, these caretakers of the system inevitably become the rich and oppressive elite. Under capitalism, a large number of the rich get richer—but so do some of the poor. Under socialism, a small number of the rich get richer, but the poor stay poor.

Those who laud socialism ignore the fact that historically the poor usually fare better in capitalist economies. They also fail to recognize that when the profit incentive is removed from labor, someone must find another way to motivate people to work. There's only one other way that works—and that's coercion. The capitalist says, "You scratch my back and I'll scratch yours." The socialist says, in effect, "You scratch my back or I'll break yours."

Can capitalism involve exploiting the poor? Of course. Does socialism lead to the oppression of the poor? Inevitably. The point isn't that capitalism is a perfect system, but that the alternatives are worse. It isn't a systemic problem, it's a sin problem. Any economic system will work where there's no sin. None will work ideally when there is sin, but some will work better than others.

Our Responsibility to Help the Poor

Neither God's Word nor an accurate understanding of economics supports the notion that the prosperous are automatically responsible for making others poor. As we're about to see, what Scripture does say is that we are responsible to help the poor. I may not be responsible for the existence of world hunger. But I am responsible to do what I can to relieve it.

Any economic system will work where there's no sin.

So, back to Emerson's question, "Are they my poor?" If by this he means, "Have I made them poor?" in most cases the answer is no. But if he means, "Am I responsible to help the poor?" then the answer is yes, they are indeed my poor.

Of course, many have exploited the poor and need to face up to it. They should adopt the posture of Zacchaeus, who determined to pay back fourfold those whom he had cheated (Luke 19:8).

We're not to feel guilty that God has entrusted an abundance to us. But we are to feel responsible to compassionately and wisely use that abundance to help the less fortunate. Consider the Good Samaritan (Luke 10:30-37). In contrast to the two religious leaders who passed by the poor man who had been stripped and beaten by robbers, when the Samaritan found him, he took pity on him and stopped to help. His reaction wasn't to feel guilt and remorse. He hadn't brutalized the man. But he took responsibility to care for him.

At great inconvenience to himself, he treated and bandaged the man's wounds, then "put the man on his own donkey, took him to an inn and took care of him" (Luke 10:34). The next day, he paid the innkeeper to watch over the man until he could come back and resume care for him himself. Although the Samaritan wasn't in any way responsible for hurting the man, he nevertheless took responsibility to help him however he could. "Go and do likewise," Jesus says (Luke 10:37). Every man is our neighbor, and we are to show mercy and care for him in his need.

The Roman emperor Julian had an interesting complaint about Christians: "The impious Galileans support not only their own poor but ours as well; everyone can see that our people lack aid from us."[4] The theologian Tertullian said, "It is our care of the helpless, our practice of loving kindness that brands us in the eyes of many of our opponents. 'Only look,' they say, 'look how they love one another!'"[5]

During the time of the plague, Christians were known for coming into the cities to help the dying, rather than fleeing from the cities to save their lives. Dionysius described this phenomenon:

> Most of our brother Christians showed unbounded love and loyalty; never sparing themselves and thinking only of one another. Heedless of the danger, they took charge of the sick, attending to their every need and ministering to them in Christ, and with them departed this life serenely happy; for they were infected by others with the disease, drawing on themselves the sickness of their neighbors and cheerfully accepting their pains. Many, in nursing and curing others, transferred their death to themselves and died in their stead.[6]

Helping the poor has always set Christians apart, showing the world that we operate on a radically different value system. John Wesley said, "Put yourself in the place of every poor man and deal with him as you would God deal with you." Wesley demonstrated this attitude in his own lifestyle choices:

> In 1776, the English tax commissioners inspected his return and wrote back, "[We] cannot doubt but you have plate for which you have hitherto neglected to make entry." They assumed that a man of his prominence certainly had silver dinnerware in his house, and they wanted him to pay the proper tax on it. Wesley wrote back, "I have two silver spoons at London and two at Bristol. This is all the plate I have at present, and I shall not buy any more while so many round me want bread."[7]

WHAT THE SCRIPTURES SAY ABOUT CARING FOR THE POOR

Caring for the poor is a central theme throughout Scripture. The Mosaic Law made many provisions for the poor, including the following:

> When you reap the harvest of your land, do not reap to the very edges of your field or gather the gleanings of your harvest. Do not go over your vineyard a second time or pick up the grapes that have fallen. Leave them for the poor and the alien. I am the Lord your God. (Leviticus 19:9-10)

> Give generously to [the poor] and do so without a grudging heart; then because of this the Lord your God will bless you in all your work and in everything you put your hand to. There will always be poor people in the land. Therefore I command you to be openhanded toward your brothers and toward the poor and needy in your land. (Deuteronomy 15:10-11)

Proverbs promises reward for helping the poor:

> He who is kind to the poor lends to the Lord, and he will reward him
> for what he has done. (Proverbs 19:17)

> A generous man will himself be blessed, for he shares his food with the
> poor. (Proverbs 22:9)

> He who gives to the poor will lack nothing, but he who closes his eyes
> to them receives many curses. (Proverbs 28:27)

The Old Testament prophets boldly proclaim God's commands to care for the
poor:

> I want you to share your food with the hungry and to welcome poor
> wanderers into your homes. Give clothes to those who need them, and
> do not hide from relatives who need your help. (Isaiah 58:7, NLT)

> Feed the hungry and help those in trouble. Then your light will shine
> out from the darkness, and the darkness around you will be as bright as
> day. The Lord will guide you continually, watering your life when you
> are dry and keeping you healthy, too. You will be like a well-watered
> garden, like an ever-flowing spring. (Isaiah 58:10-11, NLT)

Jesus came to preach the good news to the poor, the captives, the blind, and
the oppressed (Luke 4:18-19). Of course, the gospel is for the rich and the
sighted as well. It's just that the poor and handicapped understand bondage
enough to appreciate deliverance. They're quicker to recognize their spiritual
need, because it's not buried under layers of prosperity. Though he himself
had little, Jesus made a regular practice of giving to the poor (John 13:29). He
repeatedly commands care for the poor, promising eternal reward:

> Then Jesus said to his host, "When you give a luncheon or dinner,
> do not invite your friends, your brothers or relatives, or your rich
> neighbors; if you do, they may invite you back and so you will be
> repaid. But when you give a banquet, invite the poor, the crippled, the
> lame, the blind, and you will be blessed. Although they cannot repay
> you, you will be repaid at the resurrection of the righteous." (Luke
> 14:12-14)

Special offerings to help the poor were commonplace in the early Church:

> During this time, some prophets traveled from Jerusalem to Antioch.
> One of them named Agabus stood up in one of the meetings to predict
> by the Spirit that a great famine was coming upon the entire Roman
> world. (This was fulfilled during the reign of Claudius.) So the believers
> in Antioch decided to send relief to the brothers and sisters in Judea,

everyone giving as much as they could. This they did, entrusting their gifts to Barnabas and Saul to take to the elders of the church in Jerusalem. (Acts 11:27-30, NLT)

Tabitha "was always doing good and helping the poor" (Acts 9:36). Luke says of Cornelius the centurion, "He and all his family were devout and God-fearing; he gave generously to those in need and prayed to God regularly." An angel appears in a vision and tells him, "Your prayers and gifts to the poor have come up as a memorial offering before God" (Acts 10:2-4).

Early Church leaders emphasized giving to the poor: "All they asked was that we should continue to remember the poor, the very thing I was eager to do" (Galatians 2:10). "Religion that God our Father accepts as pure and fault-less is this: to look after orphans and widows in their distress and to keep one-self from being polluted by the world" (James 1:27). James also writes:

What good is it, my brothers, if a man claims to have faith but has no deeds? Can such faith save him? Suppose a brother or sister is without clothes and daily food. If one of you says to him, "Go, I wish you well; keep warm and well fed," but does nothing about his physical needs, what good is it? (James 2:14-16)

The apostle John writes:

This is how we know what love is: Jesus Christ laid down his life for us. And we ought to lay down our lives for our brothers. If anyone has material possessions and sees his brother in need but has no pity on him, how can the love of God be in him? Dear children, let us not love with words or tongue but with actions and in truth. This then is how we know that we belong to the truth, and how we set our hearts at rest in his presence. (1 John 3:16-19)

Caring for the poor and helpless is so basic to the Christian faith that those who don't do it aren't considered true Christians. Christ says if we feed the hungry, give drink to the thirsty, invite in the stranger, give clothes to the needy, care for the sick, and visit the persecuted, we are doing those things to him: "Come, you who are blessed by my Father, take your inheritance, the kingdom prepared for you since the creation of the world. For I was hungry and you gave me something to eat" (Matthew 25:34-35). Likewise, if we don't do these things, then we're turning our backs on Christ himself. To those who didn't help the poor and needy, Christ says, "Depart from me, you who are cursed, into the eternal fire prepared for the devil and his angels. For I was hungry and you gave me nothing to eat" (Matthew 25:41-42).

In the full context of Matthew 24–25, those we are to help in their need seem mainly to be Christians, Christ's "brothers," who are in need as a result of persecution for their faith. Our first priority is to care for the needs of those "of the household of faith" (Galatians 6:10, NASB). Although the passage's general principle can be applied to all the world's poor, we should especially seek to find ways to help suffering Christians, and particularly our persecuted brothers and sisters throughout the world in places such as Sudan, China, Indonesia, and the Middle East.[8]

> If Christ were on the other side of the street, or the city, or the other side of the world, and he was hungry, thirsty, and helpless, or imprisoned for his faith, would we help him?

When Saul was persecuting Christians, Jesus appeared to him and asked, "Why are you persecuting Me?" (Acts 9:4, NKJV). This shows how personally Jesus takes the suffering of his people. To persecute them is to persecute him. To help them is to help him.

We must ask, "If Christ were on the other side of the street, or the city, or the other side of the world, and he was hungry, thirsty, and helpless, or imprisoned for his faith, would we help him?" Any professing Christian would have to say yes. But we mustn't forget what Christ himself says in Matthew 25: He is in our neighborhood, community, city, country, and across the world, in the form of poor and needy people—and especially in those who are persecuted for their faith.

The rich man who passed by poor Lazarus is condemned not for a specific act of exploitation but for his lack of concern and assistance for a man in need (Luke 16:19-31). The passage suggests that the rich man should either have brought Lazarus to his table or joined him at the gate. Ignoring the poor is not an option for the godly. Likewise, in the account of the final judgment, the sin held against the "goats" is not that they did something wrong to those in need, but that they failed to do anything right for them (Matthew 25:31-46). Theirs is not a sin of commission, but of omission. Yet it's a sin of grave eternal consequence.

We cannot wash our hands of responsibility to the poor by saying, "I'm not doing anything to hurt them." We must actively be doing something to help them.

What Can We Really Do?

"But I'm just one person. And we're just a small church. How can we eliminate poverty?" The answer is, you can't. Jesus said the poor would always be with us (Mark 14:7). Then, should we give up? Of course not. I saw a relief organization poster that asked the question, "How can you help a billion hungry people?" The answer it gave was right on target: "One at a time." Just because I can't take care of all the world's poor doesn't mean I can't begin by helping one, then two, then five, ten, and so on. The logic that says, "I can't do everything, so I won't do anything" is from the pit of hell.

I must help the poor who are near, but also those who are far away. In fact, most of the truly poor, hungry, and persecuted people live in another part of the world. At this point, we usually hear another worn-out excuse: "Well, there's no sense giving my money to hunger relief organizations, because the people who need the food never get it anyway." This assertion is simply false. Yes, distribution is sometimes a major challenge, and some organizations are more efficient than others. And yes, corrupt officials or soldiers may confiscate some supplies. Nevertheless, a great deal of food does get to the hungry people. Our responsibility is to choose the best organizations we can find, give our money, pray, and trust God and our fellow servants in ministry that most of the food and supplies will get to the needy.

We should take some of our favorite excuses for not feeding the hungry and imagine stating them at the judgment seat of Christ. In light of his uncompromising command to feed the hungry, how many of our excuses will he accept?

"But feeding the hungry is just a short-term measure. They'll be starving again unless they are taught how to feed themselves." Many development organizations are dedicated to finding and implementing long-term solutions by teaching nationals the kinds of skills and getting them the kinds of equipment that can help them grow and harvest plenty of their own food. Are you and I giving our money, time, or prayers to help these groups accomplish their goals?

The poor need not only our provisions, but also social justice. The law says that no one should take advantage of a widow or an orphan, or God will surely punish the tyrant (Exodus 22:22-23). Likewise, aliens are not to be oppressed in any way (Exodus 23:9). God says, "Do not show favoritism to a poor man in his lawsuit," then three verses later adds, "Do not deny justice to your poor people in their lawsuits" (Exodus 23:3, 6).

The prophets were particularly concerned about the exploitation of the poor (Amos 2:6-7; 5:11-12; 8:4-6). James warns the church against courting and favoring the rich over the poor (James 2:1-13). Concern for the poor was built right into the land laws (Exodus 23:10). "I know that the Lord secures justice for the poor and upholds the cause of the needy" (Psalm 140:12).

Every church and Christian must ask, "What are we *doing* to feed the hungry and help the poor? What are we *doing* to secure justice for the poor? What are we *doing* to uphold the cause of the needy?" Sentiment is not enough. Why not determine a salary to live on, then give back to God every dime he entrusts to us beyond that, so every day we work and earn income is a day that will help the poor and reach the lost.

ARE WE HELPING OR SUBSIDIZING THE POOR?

The worst thing we can do to the poor is ignore them. The next worst thing is to subsidize them—that is, to help them only enough to keep them alive, but

231

not enough to assist them in developing the means by which they might move out of poverty. The poor are frequently lumped together into one group, as if they're all the same. They aren't.

The all-inclusive term "the poor" is used repeatedly by some evangelicals. We're told we must help "the poor" by doing this and that, as if it does not matter why they are poor. Yet neither Scripture nor experience indicates that all poor people are poor for the same reasons. Consequently, they cannot be truly helped by the same means.

A person may be poor for any one or a combination of the following ten reasons: insufficient natural resources; adverse climate; lack of knowledge or skill; lack of needed technology; catastrophes, such as earthquakes or floods; exploitation and oppression; personal laziness; wasteful self-indulgence; religion or worldview; and personal choices by some to identify with and serve the poor. For instance, the Hindu concept of Karma does not encourage people to initiate improving their circumstances, and their reverence for certain animals allows people to starve while one of their major God-given food sources (cattle) consumes another (grain).

So when we say, "This is what we should do to help the poor," it's like saying, "This is what we should do to cure sickness." To be effective, cures must be sought and applied for specific diseases, such as cancer, heart disease, diabetes, colitis, or asthma, not for "sickness" in general. It's as ludicrous to use one formula to "help the poor" as it is to give all sick people the same treatment for every disease and expect it to heal them.

If people are poor because their homes and businesses have been wiped out in a flood, the solution may be to give them the money, materials, and assistance to rebuild their homes and reestablish their businesses. If they're poor because of insufficient natural resources or adverse climate, we can share the knowledge, skills, and technology necessary to help them make the best of their situation. If this is impossible, we might help them relocate.

If people are poor due to oppression or injustice in our nation, then we can do what we can to remove or mitigate the oppression. For instance, we can petition and lobby for legal, social, and economic reforms. If the needy are in another country, we may be able to apply the pressure of international opinion to bring about change. And, of course, we can pray.

If people are poor due to their religion or worldview, the problem is especially thorny. Certainly we can try to convince them to change their religion and worldview. Sharing the gospel is basic to that. Sadly, we must realize that without a fundamental religious or philosophical change, all the short-term aid we can give will never help solve the long-term problem. This doesn't mean we should withhold aid—just that we must realize its limitations.

A person may also be poor because of self-indulgence. "He who loves pleasure will become poor" (Proverbs 21:17). Someone may make a decent income but waste it on drugs, alcohol, cigarettes, expensive convenience foods, costly recreation, or gambling (including lotteries). Some people manage to meet their family's needs on very low incomes. Others make several times as much money but are always "poor," always in a financial crisis. This isn't because their means are too little, but because they're living irresponsibly.

We once called a government agency to get the names of some needy families. Then we drove to their homes with sacks of food—only to find people living in better conditions than some who had contributed the food. I've seen people who perpetually have no money to buy groceries for their family but who own nice cars and expensive electronic equipment. The government may consider this poverty, but it certainly is not. Such a person needs only to liquidate his assets to feed his family, then learn to live within his means and not squander his income. Christians shouldn't subsidize the irresponsible but supplement the responsible.

Finally, a person may be poor due to laziness. God's Word explicitly says that the result of laziness will be poverty (Proverbs 24:30-34). "Lazy hands make a man poor, but diligent hands bring wealth" (Proverbs 10:4). "A sluggard does not plow in season; so at harvest time he looks but finds nothing" (Proverbs 20:4). "The fool folds his hands and ruins himself" (Ecclesiastes 4:5). Ultimately, the lazy man is poor by choice.

We shouldn't rescue lazy people from their poverty. Every act of provision removes their incentive to be responsible for themselves and makes them more dependent on others. Paul commands the Thessalonian church to stop taking care of the lazy and reminds them of the rule he issued when present with them: "If a man will not work, he shall not eat" (2 Thessalonians 3:10). In other words, it's a sin to feed the lazy. The point is not to let people starve; the point is that people who are faced with starvation will be motivated to work and support themselves as God intended. As it says in Proverbs 16:26, "The laborer's appetite works for him; his hunger drives him on."

Lazy and self-indulgent people do not need financial support; they need incentives to no longer be lazy and self-indulgent. "Laziness brings on deep sleep, and the shiftless man goes hungry" (Proverbs 19:15). It isn't our job to invalidate this principle of God's Word. It isn't our place to make exceptions to God's law of the harvest that says, "A man reaps what he sows" (Galatians 6:7). Any system that feeds the lazy is a corrupt system. It does them and the rest of society a grave disservice and opposes the God-ordained structure of life.

Of course, someone can be unemployed without being lazy. We need to help the unemployed, but all the while we need to help them find work. When employment isn't to be found, we need to provide it however we can. From time to time, only as a short-term measure, our church has helped the unemployed by giving them work on our grounds. It's important for their self-respect and motivation to associate income with work.

If money steadily comes in to the able-bodied person who isn't working, then money becomes disassociated from work. Such people come to believe that society or the Church owes them provision—which further encourages laziness and the destruction of self and family. A nation, social service organization, church, or individual that subsidizes the lazy spawns laziness. Rather than eliminating poverty, they perpetuate it.

The question is not simply, "What shall we do for the poor?" but "Which poor?" The truly poor must be helped. But they must be helped thoughtfully and carefully, according to the fundamental reasons for their poverty and according to their long-range best interests.

DISTRIBUTING FUNDS TO THE POOR

Indiscriminate distributions to the poor can be catastrophic. Often the "professionally poor" receive goods while the true poor—those who want to work but can't, or those who work but can't make enough money to provide for their own needs—are hesitant to take handouts. I've seen a man choose not to work for a year and receive unemployment benefits that are twice as much as another man earns for a forty-hour workweek. Worse yet, I've seen the same man grow accustomed over that one-year period to not having to work to live. That was more than twenty years ago, and he hasn't had a job since. He still lives off the misguided "help" of others. Meanwhile he's lost his self-respect and his family.

There's much to learn from the Old Testament practice of gleaning. The corners of the fields were left uncut so the poor could have food. But the grain wasn't cut, bundled, processed, ground, bagged, transported, and delivered to the poor. Provided they were able, the poor did the work themselves—and thereby were neither robbed of their dignity nor made irresponsible by a system requiring no work. The special tithe taken at the end of every third year went to the poor, including the Levites, travelers, the fatherless, and widows (Deuteronomy 14:28-29). It did not include able-bodied adults who simply preferred not to work.

Churches should help the needy. But "helping" means more than just giving them money or a sack of food.

Churches should help the needy. But "helping" means more than just giving them money or a sack of food. It requires personal attention—our time, skills, and interest. A widow doesn't just need a check; she needs someone to take her shopping, sit with her, pray with her. She may need someone to mow her lawn, fix her fence, drive her to church. She needs not only material support but also personal support. (And she needs the latter even if she has plenty of money.)

Many people don't need more money, but they need help in handling the money they have. Good financial counseling, including how to make a reasonable budget and stick to it, is a more valuable gift than five hundred dollars to bail someone out of a situation he should never have gotten into in the first place. Direction in how to find and keep a job is far more helpful than putting groceries on a shelf while someone sits home and watches television all day. When a middle-aged man is laid off his job, he not only needs to find a new one, but he may need support to avoid the paralytic depression that often accompanies such situations.

Churches need to develop a screening process that isn't impersonal or dehumanizing but that accurately determines whether a person is in need, and if so, why. Paul says to care for "those widows who are really in need" (1 Timothy 5:3) and goes on to say that not every widow qualifies for church support. For instance, the church is not to take over responsibilities that belong to family members:

> Give proper recognition to those widows who are really in need. But if a widow has children or grandchildren, these should learn first of all to put their religion into practice by caring for their own family and so repaying their parents and grandparents, for this is pleasing to God. The widow who is really in need and left all alone puts her hope in God and continues night and day to pray and to ask God for help. (1 Timothy 5:3-5)

In light of this principle, our church has approached relatives to encourage them to meet the material needs of a family member they may be neglecting. It's the church's role to help and encourage the family—not to take over its responsibilities.

To distribute funds to the needy, a church must have accurate information and ongoing accountability to determine who's needy and why, and what exactly they really need. Otherwise, we can be guilty of the very same thing our government does—trying to solve every problem by indiscriminately throwing money at it. In doing so, we often decrease incentives and increase dependence and hostility. Attempting to meet needs by giving money sometimes has the same effect as trying to put out a fire by throwing gasoline on it.

The Didache, written in the second century as a guidebook to Christian converts, says, "Let thine alms sweat in thy hands, until thou knowest to whom thou shouldst give." When in doubt, we should err on the side of helping the poor, even though we may have to swallow our pride, and sometimes others will take advantage of us. Martin Luther was so generous he was sometimes taken advantage of. In 1541, a transient woman, allegedly a runaway nun, came to their home. Martin and Katherine fed and housed her, only to discover she had lied and stolen. Yet Luther believed no one would become poor by practicing charity. "God divided the hand into fingers so that money would slip through," he said. [9]

FACING UP TO THE POOR

When asked, "What's the secret to happiness?" Tennessee Williams responded, "Insensitivity." Many follow this advice. We become calloused to the plight of the poor. We pretend their condition isn't so bad, that they're all irresponsible, that there's really nothing we can do to help them. Or we rationalize that we're already helping enough through paying taxes and occasionally giving to a charitable cause.

Jacques Ellul was right: "Each of us must face up to the poor."[10] We must do so now or later, when we stand before the Judge. "If a man shuts his ears to the cry of the poor, he too will cry out and not be answered" (Proverbs 21:13). God says that his willingness to answer our prayers is directly affected by whether we're giving ourselves to help the hungry, needy, and oppressed (Isaiah 58:6-10). Do you want to improve your prayer life? Give to the poor.

I must ask myself, Where are the poor in my budget? It's easy to verbalize concern for the poor but hard to implement it. For some it's a question of getting up the nerve to walk down the block and get to know the poor. For others it's a matter of having to drive twenty miles to find a poor person, and even then not knowing exactly where to look. That's why it's so easy in an affluent community to pretend the poor don't exist.

I must ask myself, *Where are the poor in my budget?* Our family gives regularly to relief ministries that bring material help and the gospel to the needy throughout the world. But this isn't enough. What current efforts am I making to find a materially needy person and help him or her? I cannot relate meaningfully to the poor when I'm isolated from the poor. Perhaps I must take regular trips away from the cozy suburbs where I live. Perhaps I need also to travel overseas, not as a tourist, but to meet needs.

Years ago, some of our church families brought warm clothes, space heaters, and supplies to help local Hispanic migrant workers through the cold winter. This led to the opening of homes and our church building to develop ongoing relationships. Some studied Spanish to further bridge the gap, deepen friendships, and share the gospel.

Whole churches have become involved in projects of helping the poor. Our church high school group has taken trips to Mexico to meet and minister to the poor. They've put on evangelistic Bible clubs for inner-city children. That's a beginning. Many churches can go to the inner city, the jails, the hospitals, and rest homes—wherever there's a need.

We need to examine our motives. It's becoming trendy for the middle and upper classes to help the poor. It makes us feel good, soothes our consciences to make a few token gestures to the poor, then return to our lives of materialism. The challenge is not to pat ourselves on the back for giving away a sack of groceries at Christmas. It's to integrate caring for the poor into our lifestyles.

236

Some seem to think that giving to a good cause is all that matters, and doing so is itself a sign of good motives. But Paul says, "If I give all I possess to the poor, . . . but have not love, I gain nothing" (1 Corinthians 13:3).

We must not just open our pocketbooks but also our homes (Romans 12:13). It's easy to be hospitable to "our own kind." But what about the poor and the needy? I say these things not as an expert in ministering to the poor. I'm just a beginner. I have very far to go. But if I'm to be a disciple of Jesus Christ, then go I must.

May God one day say of us what he said of King Josiah: "He defended the cause of the poor and needy, and so all went well. Is that not what it means to know me?" (Jeremiah 22:16)

GIVING AND THE GREAT COMMISSION

The apostle Paul gave us our top priority: "What I received I passed on to you as of first importance: that Christ died for our sins according to the Scriptures, that he was buried, that he was raised on the third day according to the Scriptures" (1 Corinthians 15:3).

The gospel, and therefore the spread of the gospel, is of first importance.

Church budgets often designate less than 10 percent of their income to missions. And what's called "missions" often includes ministries directed at reaching our own country or community. More than 90 percent of an average local church budget never leaves the country. According to the U.S. Center for World Missions, only 5.7 percent of giving to Christian causes goes to foreign missions. Of that, 87 percent goes for work among those who are already Christians, 12 percent for work among already evangelized non-Christians, and 1 percent for work among people groups who are unevangelized or unreached.[11] Americans spend far more on pet food—and chewing gum!—than on the cause of world missions.

Ninety percent of the world's Christian workers live in countries with 10 percent of the world's population. Here's a question corresponding to this statistic: If you saw ten people trying to lift a huge log and wanted to help them, and nine of the people were lifting at one end and one on the other, which end would you go to?

Some would say, "We have plenty of needs in our own country. People here are just as important as people off in some jungle. A soul is a soul—God doesn't care whether it comes from our country or another." But the gravity of needs of those without access to the gospel is obviously greater than that of those with churches in every community, a Bible on the shelf, gospel programs on the radio, and Christians living next door. (Why should some hear the gospel many times over when others have never heard it at all?)

Furthermore, although it's certainly true that we're surrounded by needs, our nation has vast resources. And almost every church and organization pours its funds back into our country, resulting in still greater resources. Our family and ministry gladly joined in contributing to help after the events of September 11, 2001. But given our extreme wealth, the truth is that America on its worst day was far better off than most nations on their best day.

We must realize that God is interested in more than the total number of souls in heaven. He *also* cares where they come from! The four living creatures will join the heavenly hosts in singing praise to the Lamb: "With your blood you purchased men for God from every tribe and language and people and nation. You have made them to be a kingdom and priests to serve our God, and they will reign on the earth" (Revelation 5:9-10). John was overwhelmed when he saw "a great multitude that no one could count, from every nation, tribe, people and language, standing before the throne and in front of the Lamb" (Revelation 7:9).

Christ is glorified not simply by the total number who worship him, but also by the fact that this number includes representatives from every tribe, language, people, and nation. Therefore, we must be making concerted efforts to see that missionaries, whether from our country or another, reach the "hidden" people who have not yet heard the gospel.

Shortly before he and his four friends were killed by the Auca Indians in their attempts to bring them the gospel, missionary Nate Saint wrote:

> As we weigh the future and seek the will of God, does it seem right that we should hazard our lives for just a few savages? As we ask ourselves this question, we realize it is the simple intimation of the prophetic Word that there shall be some from every tribe in His presence in the last day, and in our hearts we feel that it is pleasing to Him that we should interest ourselves in making an opening into the Auca prison for Christ.
>
> As we have a high old time this Christmas, may we who know Christ hear the cry of the damned as they hurtle headlong into the Christless night without ever a chance. May we be moved with compassion as our Lord was. May we shed tears of repentance for these we have failed to bring out of darkness. Beyond the smiling scenes of Bethlehem may we see the crushing agony of Golgotha. May God give us a new vision of His will concerning the lost and our responsibility.[12]

We are motivated first by the glory of God, but we're also moved by the eternal needs of people. Many of us decry the fact that religious liberals don't believe in hell. But there's a shame even greater—that we who do believe in hell make so little effort to keep others from going there.

"Everyone who calls on the name of the Lord will be saved." How, then, can they call on the one they have not believed in? And how can they believe in the one of whom they have not heard? And how can they hear without someone preaching to them? And how can they preach unless they are sent? (Romans 10:13-15)

Some of Christ's disciples must leave behind their money and possessions to go reach the thousands of unreached people groups of the world. Some of his disciples must stay where they are, reaching out to those around them and living lifestyles that allow them not only to pray for the others but to give generously to send and support them.

The opportunities for using our financial resources to spread the gospel and strengthen the church all over the world are greater than they've ever been. As God raised up Esther for just such a time as hers, I'm convinced he's raised us up, with all our wealth, to help fulfill the great commission. The question is, what are we doing with that money? Our job is to make sure it gets to his intended recipients.

Imagine Christ multiplying the five loaves and two fish, and the disciples accumulating the proceeds until they were buried underneath, while the masses went unfed. It's a bizarre scenario, yet how easily we bury ourselves in the resources God has handed to us, while the needs of the world go unmet. We assume that God has multiplied our assets so we can keep them, when in fact he has multiplied them so we can distribute them (2 Corinthians 8:14; 9:11).

> Imagine Christ multiplying the five loaves and two fish, and the disciples accumulating the proceeds until they were buried underneath, while the masses went unfed.

All the royalties from my books go to Christian ministries, and most go to missions, famine relief, and development work overseas. Our ministry makes available at no charge all my books to missionaries and international Bible colleges and seminaries that can use them to train and enrich those serving Christ. I don't believe God has called me (for now) to spend my life overseas, but it's our privilege here to earn money and give resources to help those who have been sent. As Jesus said, "Freely you have received, freely give" (Matthew 10:8).

Think of what Christian publishers could do overseas (some of them are doing this now) by giving away great books in English, giving away translation rights to worthy recipients, and helping to train nationals to become fluent writers in their own languages. Think of what your company might be able to offer at no charge to missionaries and needy national churches. Such giving should not be done indiscriminately but could be administered through existing faithful agencies that know best how to utilize such resources. (Although we do not receive these resources at Eternal Perspective Ministries, we would be happy to link you with qualified ministries who will gladly help you.)

Giving money to evangelism is no substitute for evangelizing, but it's an excellent supplement to it. There's no greater way to invest our money in eternity than in the cause of world missions. All of us should be giving regularly to our local churches, and we should encourage our leaders in turn to invest an even larger share of their church budgets in world missions. Beyond that most of us can invest substantially in the cause of world evangelization through many fine mission organizations.

Is it more important that starving people are fed or that they be reached with the gospel? The two are simultaneously critical, which is why Jesus commanded both. The dead do not hear the gospel; to allow people to die or suffer needlessly is unconscionable. On the other hand, people who don't hear the gospel can't go to heaven (Romans 10:13-14), so to feed them is right but to neglect sharing the gospel is wrong. That's why our ministry only supports famine relief organizations that are explicitly Christian and are committed to sharing Christ with those they help.[13] Some experts estimate that more than half the charitable giving done by Christians is to secular organizations. It's hard to understand why this is the case, when there are people doing almost every kind of charitable work in the name of Christ and who will bring people what they need more than anything: Jesus himself.

CHURCHES AND MISSIONS
Our church has a policy of substantially supporting our missionary families. We prefer to be one of a few churches—preferably in the same area—that make up the bulk of a missionary's support. Among other things, this concentration of support allows the missionaries to avoid the exhausting process of spending their furloughs visiting dozens of supporting churches and individuals across the country. By spending their furloughs with us and perhaps a few other supporting churches in the same area, they develop close relationships. This helps them not to become just a picture on a refrigerator. Furthermore, this personal contact dramatically increases the commitment and prayer support of the members of our congregation. (This is also a good reason for sending people from the church on short-term missions trips to visit and work alongside the missionaries who are supported by the church.)

If a missionary family is supported by one hundred individuals, they have no spiritual community or home base. Likewise, if a church supports one hundred missionaries at $40 a month, it has no missionaries to call its own.

Short-term Missions
I can think of nothing better than if some readers would feel their hearts being touched by God to spend the rest of their lives on the mission field. If there's anything I could do to encourage someone to that end, I would do it gladly. I'm a strong believer in missions, and in my travels I've seen firsthand God's wonderful work through missions and national churches. But I also encourage

those who do not feel God's leading into a lifetime of missions to take a few weeks and go out on a short-term mission. Nothing will touch and change your heart quite like seeing the work firsthand and getting involved in ministry. It will also motivate your prayer life and stimulate your giving to missions.

Some have asked me, wouldn't it be better just to take the money spent on short-term trips and send it to the mission field instead? In some cases, yes. Americans sometimes believe that our seeing ministry firsthand validates it. If a missions trip costs tens of thousands of dollars and involves minimal ministry impact, it's really nothing more than a fun cross-cultural experience— which wouldn't be enough to justify it. But many short-term missions trips are strategic and greatly help the national churches, missionaries, and indigenous people. They create "world Christians," who come back changed and who will pray for and fund missions the rest of their lives, thereby spreading their world vision and serving on missions task forces in ways they never would have if they'd stayed home. Also, many long-term missionaries have started with short-term experiences that have helped prepare them and move their hearts toward missions.

> **Wouldn't it be better just to take the money spent on short-term trips and send it to the mission field instead?**

It might cost a church $5,000, for instance, to send a pastor to Sudan to fellowship with believers, hear their stories, teach them the Bible, and above all learn from these persecuted Christians. But when that pastor comes back to his church, his visit might bear the fruit of hundreds of thousands of dollars given, many hours of prayer, and an ongoing relationship with fellow believers overseas that otherwise wouldn't have happened. Furthermore, if people don't go on short-term trips, the equivalent money will almost never be spent on missions but instead will go toward cars, vacations, or repaving the driveway. Many missions and vision trips are not funded out of missions dollars but from money that would have been spent other ways.

Our church sends out more than one hundred short-term missionaries a year. Consequently, our congregation is filled with world Christians who know our missionaries personally, pray for them regularly, and give to missions more generously. The eternal dividends far outweigh the short-term costs.

All That Matters

One day years ago, my Nigerian friend Samuel Kunhiyop and I were talking in my living room. We discovered we were the same age. After he shared what a privilege it was to be visiting our country, I said, "It surprises me that you have such a great appreciation for America. So many countries, even those we've helped, are anti-American. But many Nigerians were bought or stolen and shipped to America and sold as slaves, weren't they? With all the countries that resent us without good reason, I'd think you of all people would despise us. Why don't you?"

I'll never forget the chills I felt hearing Samuel's measured response, spoken slowly with his rich accent: "No matter what else you did, you brought us the gospel . . . and that is all that matters." (Yes, I do believe that other things matter besides preaching the gospel—among them character, integrity, and social justice. But Samuel was saying the same thing the apostle Paul said—that the gospel is more important than anything else.) Two generations ago, a wave of missionaries sent by American churches had won this man's village, including his parents, to Christ. As a result, while I was growing up in a non-Christian home in America, he was being raised in a Christian home in Nigeria.

David Bryant asks, "Who wouldn't like to end each day, putting our heads on our pillows, confidently saying, 'I know this day my life has counted strategically for Christ's global cause, especially for those currently beyond the reach of the gospel'?"[14]

The need is desperate. Isn't it time we emptied our pockets to help reach the world for Christ? Like those who pray, those who give are partners with those who go (Colossians 4:2-4; Philippians 1:4-5). Some can go. All can pray. All can give. Will you?

As you consider your answer, imagine for a moment the warm voice of someone from a different culture—perhaps with a different color of skin—coming to you in heaven, embracing you and whispering, "Thank you—you brought us the gospel, and that is all that matters."

Ministry Finances and Fund-Raising: Special Ethical Concerns

Whoever believes that giving is an easy matter, makes a mistake; it is a matter of very great difficulty, provided that gifts are made with wisdom, and are not scattered haphazard and by caprice.   SENECA

God's work done in God's way will never lack God's supply.   HUDSON TAYLOR

A distressed woman wrote to Horace Greeley, the famed journalist, saying her church was going bankrupt. She explained they'd tried fairs, festivals, suppers, mock weddings, and socials, but none had generated enough money to keep the church afloat. "Do you have any suggestions of what else we could do?" she asked. Greeley wrote back, "Why not try religion?"

Perhaps if churches would do what they're supposed to do, God and his people would come through and meet the financial needs.

This chapter will address the recipients of giving, fund-raising methods, the proper use of funds, and how to identify worthy ministries. It will also raise some disturbing and controversial questions related to various financial practices among evangelicals that are ethically troublesome and leave us vulnerable to criticism and ethical moral decline.

GIVING TO SECULAR ORGANIZATIONS

Many early American philanthropists sought to further Christian causes. Today, the most prominent philanthropists don't embrace a Christian worldview. The Rockefeller Foundation states as its purpose: "To promote the well-being of mankind throughout the world." For Christians, this statement doesn't go far enough. The command to "love your neighbor" is inseparable from the command to "love the Lord your God" (Matthew 22:37-38). Any philosophy of distributing wealth that fails to account for God's glory and his redemptive purposes for men falls short of the mark.

"Should Christians support secular organizations?" As good as they may be, are museums, art galleries, and public broadcasting as close to God's heart as evangelism, church planting, and helping the poor in Christ's name? Many Christians support secular universities, often their alma maters, that promote disbelief in a Creator as the only rational worldview. Others support "Christian" colleges that no longer believe the Scriptures. If God wants you to give his money to a school, shouldn't it be a school that believes, loves, and obeys him? How much of God's money today is going to schools that oppose rather than support biblical causes? What does God think of the fact that money managed by his children is funding not only non-Christian but anti-Christian causes?

> When there's a choice, why not support organizations characterized by prayer, biblical standards, and the supernatural work of God's Spirit?

For every secular organization, there's a Christian organization doing the same work but with an eternal perspective. When there's a choice, why not support organizations characterized by prayer, biblical standards, and the supernatural work of God's Spirit?

Can we love our neighbor without sharing our most precious possession with him? A secular organization can do good and relieve physical suffering, but humanity's deepest need is for a Savior. Those who don't offer Jesus Christ don't offer what people most desperately need.

FINANCES AND FUND-RAISING IN THE LOCAL CHURCH
Giving to the Local Church

Giving should start with your local Bible-believing, Christ-centered church, the spiritual community where you're fed and to which you're accountable. In the New Testament, giving was not directed to the Church at large, the universal body of Christ, but to the church, the local Christian assembly. Even gifts that were sent to other places were given through the local church. Whereas the Old Testament temple was a storehouse, the New Testament Church was a clearinghouse, a conduit of gifts to help the needy and reach the lost.

Normally, I think firstfruits, or the tithe, should go to the local church. But I don't believe in "storehouse tithing" if it means that a church hoards funds or spends them on frills or monuments to ego and prosperity. Freewill giving beyond the tithe also can go to worthy parachurch ministries.[1] For fourteen years I was a local church pastor, and for thirteen years I've directed a parachurch ministry. I believe that both types of ministry deserve support, but the church should always come first. That's why we give more to our church than to our ministry.

Our giving should go first to the local church because it's our primary spiritual community. ("Electronic churches" are a contradiction in terms. They're media programs—not churches.) No mission boards, youth organizations, or Bible colleges are mentioned in the New Testament. There's only the local church, which filled all these roles. But history has demonstrated there's much that local churches have been unable or unwilling to do. Parachurch groups have filled the gap. Many have done a remarkable job. They've been servants of Christ and the Church. Others, unfortunately, have competed with churches, draining their resources.

How can a ministry in Chicago or Dallas be accountable to donors living in Idaho or New York? How can supporters evaluate whether parachurch leaders are of reputable character? I hope that most church members see their pastors in real-life situations. But all they know about the parachurch leader is what they're told. From a distance, parachurch organizations with sharp brochures and attractive spokespeople often outshine the local church, where much of the giving supports mundane activities like paying the utility bills and the salary of a pastor who, though a man of integrity, may be ordinary. The church is small, the faucets leak, and the people are irritating. The custodian wears old overalls and putters about, jangling his mammoth key chain.

People think, *I don't want my money to pay the water or garbage bill; I want it to go 100 percent to evangelism.* The television ministers, with their straight teeth and makeup, tell stories of thousands of conversions. Why fiddle with the penny-ante local church when you can send your money to the big boys? So people give their money instead to a parachurch group, apparently without realizing that it too has irritating, ordinary people; garbage bills; and a custodian with old overalls and a jangly key chain.

Paul doesn't encourage individual believers to give to a needy cause on their own, but instead to give to and through the local church (1 Corinthians 16:2). When the early Christians sold their land and houses, they "brought the money from the sales and put it at the apostles' feet, and it was distributed to anyone as he had need" (Acts 4:34-35). They didn't discern on their own where the funds should go. They entrusted them to spiritually qualified church leaders, who distributed them wisely.

Writing in A.D. 390, John Chrysostom said this about the early Church's giving:

> They did not dare to put their offering into the hands of the needy,
> nor give it with lofty condescension, but they laid it at the feet of the
> apostles and made them masters and distributors of the gift. What a man
> needed was then taken from the treasurer of the community, not from
> the private property of individuals. Thereby the givers did not become
> arrogant.[2]

245

Most of the undiscerning giving among Christians today stems from our independence. If we were honest, we might have to say, "I give to this place and that place as I see fit, rather than giving to the church to have it distributed as the spiritual leaders see fit. Why? Because it's my money and I'll do with it what I want. Furthermore, I enjoy receiving recognition and ego strokes from those I send my money to."

If believers entrusted the distribution of their God-given funds to qualified local church leaders (I realize that some church leaders aren't qualified), the worthy parachurch ministries would thrive and the unworthy ones would fade away.

I'm often asked, "But how can I give to my church when I don't agree with how the money is spent?" Perhaps your church leaders are in a better position to judge this than you are. And if you actually saw some of these other ministries up close, you'd likely find as much or more to disagree with. If the Bible tells me to pay taxes (Romans 13:1-7), and I comply, even though some will be wasted and even used for bad purposes, surely I can give to God even when I don't feel comfortable with every use of the funds. Of course, I must draw the line somewhere. If my money—*God's* money—is going to Bible-denying seminaries and groups that promote immorality, it's time to speak to my church leaders. If I still cannot in good conscience give regularly and substantially to my church, perhaps it's time to ask God for help finding a church where I can give as he has directed.

Fund-Raising through Pledges and Faith Promises

Many fund-raising gimmicks are used by churches, including raffles, bingo, and other forms of gambling. One church raised funds for its building program by giving cash prizes to those bringing in the highest pledges from other church members.[3] But not all attempts at fund-raising are gimmicks. Pledges and faith promises are also common fund-raising methods. A "pledge" is a commitment made in light of known or anticipated income. A "faith promise" is a commitment to give a certain amount of money, even if the giver doesn't know where it will come from. In either case, individuals are asked to designate an amount of money to be given by a certain date, perhaps in regular monthly installments. Some pledges are merely statements of intention. Others are serious commitments that bring a follow-up reminder from the church. Too many misses and the phone call turns into a visit from the pastor or fund-raising chairman. Some pledges are actually legally binding contracts with legal liability in the event of a default. (When a pledge is simply an expression of desire or intent, or an agreement with God left for his Holy Spirit to enforce, it's not necessarily unscriptural. However, when it becomes a legal contract, we've strayed far from the principles of biblical giving examined in chapter 13.)

It's increasingly common, especially in building projects, to bring in professional fund-raisers or canvassing directors from outside the membership. No matter how well-intentioned, these programs communicate a sad message: The church leaders cannot share a compelling vision that the people will want to support, so they bring in a "hired gun" with an arsenal of ways to get money from people. Pledges are often the backbone of such campaigns.

The strength of the "faith promise" method is that it can prompt not only trust but discipline and ingenuity to earn and save money in order to give it to God. Having a tangible goal of, say, $500 or $5,000 encourages prayers for provision and acts of diligence. The weakness of this approach is that faith promises are highly subjective. They assume God has determined an exact amount of money to be given, and this amount can only be discerned through the person's "feeling." Because Scripture never says that God has determined or will reveal such an amount, to "trust God" for it is to obligate him to something he hasn't promised in the first place.[4] Committing to give a predetermined amount over a period of years may violate James 4:13-17, which tells us we cannot know how much money we will make tomorrow, much less months and years from now. If God leads me to relocate while I still have two years and $6,000 left on my faith promise, do I continue to give to my former church rather than my present one?

> It's increasingly common, especially in building projects, to bring in professional fund-raisers or canvassing directors from outside the membership.

When the Macedonians gave "beyond their ability," they were exercising risk-taking faith. This is more important than whether it corresponded to a particular amount they had promised. Whether one uses the faith promise approach or not, God honors prayer, dependence, and generosity. If we don't set an exact amount, we may find that God still abundantly provides.

(I address two relevant issues—financial integrity and accountability in the Church and parachurch, as well as the use of ministry funds for buildings—in appendixes A and B.)

Pastors' Salaries

Pastors are paid to free them for ministry. "Anyone who receives instruction in the word must share all good things with his instructor" (Galatians 6:6). Paul calls this the minister's "right of support" from the church (1 Corinthians 9:3-12). He says, "The Lord has commanded that those who preach the gospel should receive their living from the gospel" (1 Corinthians 9:14). Furthermore, "The elders who direct the affairs of the church well are worthy of double honor, especially those whose work is preaching and teaching. . . . 'The worker deserves his wages'" (1 Timothy 5:17-18). Being paid more than he needs gives the pastor the opportunity to live as an example to the flock, most of whom—in America and Western nations—have considerable discretionary income. On hearing of his salary raise, one pastor told his elders, "This is much more than I need to live on." The elders responded, "Yes, we know. We want to see what you do with it."

I have no sympathy for churches that deliberately underpay their pastors, forcing them to find ways to supplement their income. It's different, of course, when a church genuinely can't afford to pay a pastor. Many pastors have gladly worked part-time jobs on the side to serve smaller churches, and I don't mean to imply this is always inappropriate. However, it creates significant challenges.

Pastors and lay leaders should work side by side in financial matters. David High compares businessmen in the church to kings and pastors to priests. He argues that both have important roles but the two should not be confused:

> Priests without kings chase provision to their own hurt. Kings without priests try to generate vision many times to their own hurt. . . . Today we have churches full of frustrated kings, sitting in pews with their arms folded, listening to frustrated priests who have heard from God but don't have the money to make it happen. . . . Many good, godly men have destroyed themselves and their ministries when they felt they had to become fund-raisers. Once they start chasing money, something twists inside and their message and ministry begin to ring hollow.[5]

Pastors and Outside Income

Because I served as a pastor, my heart is in the local church. A number of my closest friends are pastors. I respect and deeply appreciate pastors. What I am about to say comes neither from cynicism nor suspicion. It is intended for the protection of both pastors and churches.

The Lord decried the fact that priests and prophets alike were corrupted by money (Micah 3:11). Peter reminds church leaders to be "shepherds of God's flock . . . *not greedy for money*, but eager to serve" (1 Peter 5:2, italics mine). He insisted that no money-lover was qualified to be a church leader (1 Timothy 3:3). In his ministry, Paul was so committed to avoid even the appearance of loving money that he often supported himself (1 Corinthians 9:18).

I recently read an interview with a pastor. When asked about his opulent home (with its own bowling alley), his response was, "God doesn't want all his children in coach. He wants some of them in first class." But when those in coach are paying for the pastor to ride in first class, it creates a distinctly different model than the "eager to serve" pastor advocated in Scripture.

Even at age eighty-two, Oral Roberts was still talking about shiny new cars and saying, "God wants us to prosper. And if we prosper, our people will prosper. If the pastor doesn't prosper, the people won't have the faith to prosper."[6] Consider the contrast between this prosperity model and the servanthood model of our Lord: "For even the Son of Man did not come to be served, but to serve, and to give his life as a ransom for many" (Mark 10:45).

Paul warns Titus about ministers "ruining whole households by teaching things they ought not to teach—and that *for the sake of dishonest gain*" (Titus 1:11, italics mine). These passages I've quoted constitute a biblical mandate to pastors and Christian leaders, and their boards and constituents, to take great pains to protect leaders and ministries from unnecessary temptations toward greed, financial impropriety, and possible scandal.

Serious problems develop when pastors are paid much more or much less than the average person in the church. Disparity can have an adverse effect on both pastors and parishioners. Years ago the tendency was for pastors to be underpaid, requiring them to neglect their calling to find other sources of income or tempting them and their families toward envy or resentment. Pastors who are underpaid—I mean, when the congregation can afford to pay them more—tend to be underappreciated, taken for granted, and sometimes patronized as "the poor pastor," who is in fact kept poor by the church. Unfortunately, this remains true of many pastors today.

However, the tendency now in many large churches, especially with senior pastors, is just the opposite—it is to pay them as if they were company CEOs, tempting them to feel more important than the people they shepherd, setting them up, often unintentionally, to "lord it over" the flock. Note the contrast in 1 Peter 5 between pastors being "greedy for money" and "eager to serve." When a pastor encourages people to tithe and give generously in freewill offerings—which he should do as part of preaching the whole counsel of God—and his income is far more than theirs, people wonder, *How can he understand our financial struggles when he lives in a house that nice and makes all that money?* Sometimes this situation arises from the tendency to fill church boards with successful businessmen, instead of a cross-section of the congregation. This skews the average salary levels of board members and inclines them to pay pastors far above the church average.

I have many good friends who are senior pastors, devoted to God and the ministry. Many of them handle money well. I'm not questioning their hard work or integrity. I'm questioning instead the market that's been created for pastors of large churches, who may make several times what other pastors on staff do, even those working harder with fewer vacations and less opportunity for outside income.

Sometimes pastors are offered what amounts to bribes to get them to leave their churches. I know a pastor of a large church who declined an invitation to become a candidate for an even larger church, saying he believed it was God's

> **Serious problems develop when pastors are paid much more or much less than the average person in the church.**

will that he stay with his present congregation. But the other church persisted, inviting him to fly out for a visit on a private jet. They wooed him and offered him an enhanced financial package, eventually persuading him to leave his church after all. (Apparently, God's will was negotiable.)

Many churches became accustomed to doing special favors for their pastors when they were grossly underpaid. Clergy discounts were routinely offered, and in some places still are. Pastors were given free places to stay on vacation and other freebies—sometimes even cars. But today, when many pastors are paid adequately, the same favors are extended by habit. The IRS allows pastors to have tax-exempt housing allowances that save them thousands of dollars annually. I was very grateful for this exemption when I was a pastor, and I'm in favor of seeing it continue. My point is only that the old stereotype of the underpaid pastor isn't always true—for which I'm extremely glad. Yet I've heard pastors who are making good salaries still talk as if they're underpaid.

Some pastors receive outside pay for speaking engagements and writing books. This may be fine. But are paid members of the church staff using church equipment and time to do the typing, research, and events scheduling for which the pastor is being paid by outsiders? This situation sets up a temptation that pastors don't need—the lure to say yes to out-of-town engagements and add-on projects in order to make money on the side without decreasing their regular pay from the church. These opportunities sometimes create ethical conflicts of interest that wouldn't be tolerated in the business world. (If you're paid by IBM to write software, can you then sell it to others and keep the profits? Anyone can do work on the side—but can you market work for which you've already been paid by your employer? And can you take time away from your desk to teach seminars and be paid for them?)

How much time is the pastor expected to invest in local church ministry each week? Forty hours? Fifty hours? More?

I believe that pastors and church boards should set clear parameters concerning the time and money involved in the pastor's outside speaking and writing. These parameters should be fair to both pastor and church. How much time is the pastor expected to invest in local church ministry each week? Forty hours? Fifty hours? More? This should be mutually agreed upon, so the pastor knows when his church time and personal time begin and end.

Can a pastor write a book in which he draws from a message he gave to his church? Of course. But when the pastor speaks and writes in his nonvacation time, for which he is already receiving a church salary, is it ethical for him to receive book royalties and speaking honorariums for the same work hours? What message does it send if a pastor is paid by the church while writing a book, then is also paid by the book publisher, and then is paid again when he delivers the material at a conference that takes him away from his church? Is this really in the pastor's or church's best interests? (Ironically, when it comes time to set salaries, the board may reason, "He's become very well known through his books and conferences—he deserves to have his salary increased, whereas our lesser-known pastors don't qualify for a merit raise.")

Sometimes these ethical dilemmas discourage a pastor because he wrestles with his conscience. This happened when I tried to write my first book when I was still a pastor. Every hour I spent on the book was one more hour I wasn't available to the church. I was writing in the middle of the night to avoid a direct conflict, but that kind of a schedule took its toll. For several subsequent book projects, I requested one- or two-month unpaid leaves of absence, allowing me to focus on writing the book with no conflict of interest and no double pay. Most pastors want to do the right thing—and they want to know they're doing the right thing.

When a pastor accepts a speaking invitation, he receives an honorarium on top of his regular salary. For a book contract, he may receive tens of thousands of dollars, perhaps a hundred thousand dollars or more, upon signing. For a full-time author, this may be business as usual, but for a pastor or parachurch leader, it may present a serious temptation for personal advancement partially at the expense of his church. If the board and church want and encourage him to write and speak, that's fine—but clear guidelines should be set so that no one misunderstands.

If an unpaid leave isn't used, an alternative might be to schedule a daily writing time (say, from 6:00 to 8:00 A.M.) before the pastor's church duties begin. In this case, the book royalties could go to the pastor, because he's writing on his own time. If the church decides to sponsor the writing project, the pastor might be allowed to write during regular office hours at his normal salary, with the royalties going to the church.

A church might grant a pastor a certain number of outside speaking engagements to be done on church time, with honorariums going to the church, or they might allow the pastor to keep the honorariums if they want to compensate for underpaying him. Pastors and boards should discuss how much time is appropriate for a secretary paid by the church to type books, articles, and materials for conferences, and to make related phone calls, if the proceeds from these activities will not go to the church. Examining various company policies for comparable arrangements might be advisable.

I offer these suggestions not to make life more difficult for pastors but to make it easier. It isn't that I distrust pastors. Rather, I desire to protect them and their churches from temptation, impropriety, and the appearance of impropriety. When things are unclear, people always talk. If people don't understand the pastor's working arrangement, especially as it relates to writing and outside speaking and seminars, if it isn't perfectly clear and in writing, then staff and church members are always tempted to gossip—which is in no one's best interest.

FINANCING AND FUND-RAISING IN OTHER MINISTRIES

If Philippians 4:19 is true ("My God will meet all your needs . . ."), why do so many Christian organizations constantly publicize their financial woes?

"Please be sensitive to God—send us your contribution," pleads a radio and television preacher. "We must receive $300,000 by the end of the month or we'll have to close our doors!" (Yet when only $100,000 comes in, the doors stay open. And it never seems to occur to anyone that God might want to close the ministry's doors.)

Hudson Taylor, a pioneer missionary to China, said, "God's work done in God's way will never lack God's supply." If a work is constantly in want of money, always begging for donations, either it's not God's work or it's not being done in God's way. Money is not an organization's greatest asset. God is. Godly people and the goodness of the cause are additional assets. If a ministry has the right God, the right people, and the right cause, then the finances should also be right.

Should Needs Be Made Known?

Some "faith missions" don't believe that specific needs should be made known. Instead, they say, God should be trusted to move people's hearts to give. I understand and respect this position. However, it should be balanced with what Paul says in 2 Corinthians 1:8: "We do not want you to be uninformed, brothers, about the hardships we suffered in the province of Asia." His missionary team informed their supporting churches about their trials and needs. He saw other believers as participating in his ministry through their prayers (2 Corinthians 1:11). It's difficult to pray effectively when the facts aren't known. The same is true of giving. Most often, I give in response to a known need—but someone first has to inform me of it. Paul didn't manipulate people when he shared a need, nor did he make them feel that without their giving God would not provide (Philippians 4:10-19). Paul also made the Corinthians aware of the needs of the Jerusalem poor (1 Corinthians 16:1-4). Then he went one step further to encourage them to take an offering for that need, to be distributed by his ministry team. He moved from information to persuasion, but never to manipulation.

The abundance of ministries in our society produces a competition for donor funds. For the leaders of these ministries it creates a sense of urgency—an unspoken philosophy that "we must get these funds before someone else does." Some organizations come up with a new enemy each month, requiring huge amounts of money to combat, giving people a reason to choose them because their cause is more urgent. To undercut this sense of competition and to remind everyone that God has only one team, I recommend that ministries give away a percentage of their assets to support other ministries. In kingdom work, we all win or lose together, and we should rejoice at the gains of every Christ-centered ministry.

As ministries have grown and technology has developed, quality promotional materials are more easily produced—in stark contrast to the products of ditto machines and offset printers that were prevalent decades ago. Some ministries now produce full-color reports with stunning photographs and layout and design that is comparable to those of America's top businesses. This isn't necessarily wrong. But what if the money spent on slick, expensive publications was instead spent on the actual work of the ministry? If a television program costs $100,000 to produce and $200,000 to purchase the airtime—and then results in $400,000 in contributions to the ministry—is it a success? The ministry may come out $100,000 ahead, but in proportion to the $300,000 investment, can the expense be justified? What would donors think if they knew that three out of every four dollars given merely paid back the organization for what it spent to produce the invitation to give?

> I recommend that ministries give away a percentage of their assets to support *other* ministries.

Support Raising

Many missionaries say that support raising is the part of their work they dread. Ironically, some of those who are most effective in doing the actual work of ministry are least effective in raising funds. The best approach to support raising involves prayerfully presenting the ministry, sharing the facts, and extending the opportunity to form a partnership. When it goes beyond that into "selling yourself," with follow-up contacts pressing for a commitment, support raising loses its innocence. Churches and missions organizations need to become actively involved on behalf of their missionaries so they do not have to become something they aren't—and shouldn't be.

As a pastor, I came to believe that the raising of personal support had gotten out of hand. Support is one thing, but the "support mentality" is another. I've talked with men attending seminary who expected the church to pay their way. Their assumption was that if they were doing anything for God, his people should pay for it. But who pays an engineer, a physical therapist, or a nurse to get their training? They take a job, work extra hours, and make sacrifices. If God provides another way, they gladly accept it, but they don't assume that someone owes them a free ride. Why should a seminary student be less willing to sacrifice for his sense of calling than those going into other professions? If he's working hard and needs help, the body of Christ may well get involved. But he shouldn't live in expectation of it.

George Müller's Guidelines

George Müller was a nineteenth-century Englishman who founded orphanages that cared for thousands of homeless children. He was known for not soliciting funds or sharing facts and figures, but believing God would provide for every need of the ministry. For reasons they couldn't explain, the hearts of people were often moved at particular times—the exact times they were needed—to give funds or provisions for the orphanages. The following are George Müller's fund-raising guidelines. Although I don't believe the first guideline is universally valid (as I've mentioned above), I think the others should be prayerfully considered by any church or ministry:

1. No funds should ever be solicited. No facts or figures concerning needs are to be revealed by the workers in the orphanage to anyone, except to God in prayer.
2. No debt should ever be incurred.
3. Money contributed for a specific purpose should never be used for any other purpose.
4. All accounts should be audited annually by professional auditors.
5. No ego-pandering by publication of donors' names with the amount of their gifts; each donor should be thanked privately.
6. No names of prominent or titled persons should be sought for the board or to advertise the institution.
7. The success of the institution should be measured not by the numbers served or by the amounts of money taken in, but by God's blessing on the work, which is expected to be in proportion to the time spent in prayer.[7]

Fund-raising will never rise above the level of character exhibited by Christian leaders, who are not to be lovers of money nor benders of truth for financial gain (1 Timothy 3:3, 8). We must not be "greedy for money" (1 Peter 5:2). Christian leaders and pastors need to take a strong stand for godly fund-raising, not asking, "What are other ministries doing?" but, "Lord, what do you want us to do?"

Using Pressure to Raise Funds

In 1995, a charity called the Foundation for New Era Philanthropy declared bankruptcy, unveiling a fraudulent financial scheme that had taken more than $350 million from hundreds of individuals and charitable organizations. The victims had been convinced to deposit money with New Era because the foundation supposedly had a group of wealthy anonymous donors who would match the deposits and double them within six months. The operation was a pyramid or Ponzi scheme. There were no anonymous donors.[8]

More than two hundred evangelical Christian organizations lost money in the New Era scandal, including relief organizations, colleges, denominations, and local churches. Fortunately, more than 85 percent of the money was eventually recovered. But the scam revealed a disturbing financial desperation among evangelical organizations.

I'm the director of a small nonprofit organization. We receive support from donors. But because my book royalties are assigned to the ministry and we distribute them to others, we give away a large proportion of the amount we receive. You might ask, "Then why not just pay your own way and not take donations?" Because we want and need prayer, partnership, and accountability. We don't keep a large amount of money in savings because we desire to use and give the money we're entrusted, not stockpile it. I understand that many organizations have times of particular financial need, because we've had some ourselves. When we do, I go back to the seventeen financial principles I wrote when we started our ministry in 1990. The first principle is as follows:

> Eternal Perspective Ministries belongs to Jesus Christ. EPM staff are
> privileged to be his servants (1 Corinthians 3:6-7). EPM will exist only
> as long as God wants it to. If it becomes evident that his purpose for
> EPM is finished, we will close our doors. The sun does not rise or set on
> this ministry. It is simply a tool at God's disposal (2 Timothy 2:21), for
> him to use as—and as long as—he chooses.[9]

When EPM's financial inflow dropped two years ago, we decided to close our ministry office on Fridays and lay off our most recently hired employee. When our revenues increased again, we realized that being closed on Fridays had saved money without significantly hampering our ministry. Through the shortage, we discovered a better way of operating, and we've continued it ever since. Not everything that requires more money is progress, and not all progress means spending more money. Sometimes it means spending less.

Ministries need to learn not to panic at financial crises. Speaking of "all kinds of trials," Peter says, "These have come so that your faith—of greater worth than gold, which perishes even though refined by fire—may be proved genuine and may result in praise, glory and honor when Jesus Christ is revealed" (1 Peter 1:6-7). Who brings financial struggles to our ministries? The default answer, judging by fund-raising letters, is "Satan, to destroy God's work and make us less effective." But the better answer, based on this passage, is "God, to accomplish his work and make us more effective through deepened character and greater dependence on him." We should not focus only on what measures will get us out of a financial crisis, but what God is wanting to teach us while we're in the thick of it.

Gifts and Premiums as Fund-Raising Tools
A "premium" is a book, tape, picture, or anything else offered in exchange for a contribution to an organization. If the premium offer is coupled with a request

for money, it's a means of motivating the recipient to give. It may also be a genuine way of saying thank you, but normally it wouldn't be given if not for an anticipated financial benefit.

Some of my own books have been offered as premiums, and I'm thankful to see them get into people's hands. Certainly, utilizing premiums can greatly increase giving revenues, but there are some cautions we should consider.

When a ministry says that a book is worth $15 when it actually costs them $3, it may be misleading. It would be more accurate to say, "If you bought this book in a store it would cost $15." Care should especially be taken when the organization prints its own materials and names its own prices. A ministry may offer a "$59 Bible" that costs only $4 to produce. Is this honest?

Donors who give in response to a premium offer may be buying two things: a material object and a rebate (in the form of a tax deduction for charitable giving). Of course, there's nothing wrong with buying a book or getting a tax break. But it's a problem if there's an illusion that this arrangement constitutes real giving.

When churches and ministries offer to display donors' names if they give a certain amount, they're appealing to people to give for the wrong reason. Givers who seek earthly rewards, whether in the form of material things or recognition, get their temporal reward but lose their eternal one. Jesus says, "They have received their reward in full" (Matthew 6:2).

Perhaps we should contact ministries we believe in and indicate our commitment to ongoing financial support without receiving anything in return. Maybe we should tell them, "Please keep the gifts—we'd prefer God's reward later to your reward now."

A HISTORY OF EVANGELICAL FUND-RAISING

In the early 1900s, evangelicals walked away from liberal churches and started new congregations from scratch financially.[10] Over the next several decades, as American prosperity increased, so did evangelical resources. Fortunately, this prosperity has helped to fund kingdom projects. Unfortunately, greater resources inevitably create temptations toward careless stewardship.

"Wycliffe Bible Translators in 1934 debated whether to hold its first training program in a rent-free barn or lavish $5 a month on a vacant farmhouse."[11] The point isn't that the cheapest plan is always the best—sometimes it clearly isn't—but that when resources were more limited, ministries naturally were more frugal.

In *More Money, More Ministry: Money and Evangelicals in Recent North American History*, Larry Eskridge and Mark A. Noll document that the most influential figure in determining early evangelicalism's approach to funding ministries was George Müller—as well as Hudson Taylor and Amy Carmichael, who adopted Müller's ideas.[12]

Many North American evangelical ministries, especially foreign missions agencies, embraced Müller's practices, which include the seven fund-raising guidelines I listed earlier. "They resolved never to take on debt and never to ask directly for funds, in order to prove God's existence to an unbelieving world."[13] As a result, by the early twentieth century many Christians believed it was morally wrong for a ministry to make its needs known or to ask for money. But evangelist D. L. Moody changed this picture dramatically:

> Like Müller and those who imitated him, Moody avoided debt and plowed publication royalties back into his enterprises. But unlike Müller, Moody was bold as the winter wind when it came to asking for money. He regularly and enthusiastically buttonholed America's corporate barons to ask for large gifts, and spent much of his time personally signing thousands of typed "begging letters" sent to potential supporters.[14]

Both fund-raising methods had their strengths and weaknesses, but Moody's approach eventually eclipsed Müller's. Between 1970 and 1992, the amount Americans donated to nonprofit organizations rose from $16 billion to $105 billion.[15] The early evangelical commitment to avoid debt eventually dissipated as debt became more prevalent in the secular realm.

MODERN FUND-RAISING TECHNIQUES

Most evangelical ministries, including Christian colleges, aggressively pursue givers. An entire industry has been built around Christian fund-raising. Once upon a time, a fund-raising letter writer discovered that a thoughtful "P.S." generated more revenue. The rest is history. Because ministry directors aren't necessarily the best fund-raisers, professional copywriters moved from writing the P.S. to writing entire letters. They soon discovered that as effective as postscripts were, writing in the margins worked even better. Exclamation points worked, but boldface type worked even better. Underlining worked—and red underlining was even better. Then came yellow highlights. If a new ink is invented that changes colors while a person is reading, it will be the next hot innovation.

Some evangelical mailings are disguised to appear as if they came from the IRS or a bank. Others are made to look like telegrams or FedEx deliveries. The idea is to overcome the potential donor's resistance to bulk mail. I've received U.S. bulk mailings made to appear as if they're from foreign countries. Some organizations don't put their name on the return address, or they put on an assumed name, knowing the recipient might not open the envelope if he knows what the contents really are. In other words, these mailings are based on *deception*. If Jesus calls Satan "the father of lies," what do deceptive mailings say about a ministry? If it has tried to deceive readers on the outside of the envelope, why wouldn't it deceive them on the inside?

I once received a registered-mail notification, requiring that I drive five miles to the post office to sign for it. When I arrived to claim my presumably important mail, I was handed a mass-mailing piece with the usual red underlining that had been sent to thousands of people on the ministry's mailing list.

What would donors think if they knew that some organizations don't write their own fund-raising letters?

It was a plea to give because funds were desperately needed (yet at least tens of thousands of dollars—sent at ten times the bulk-mail rate—had been spent to send it registered mail). We let this organization know that we wouldn't reward trickery by sending support.

What would donors think if they knew that some organizations don't write their own fund-raising letters? They hire outside groups—experts at getting the highest giving return for the dollar—to do it for them. In a magazine article, Samaritan's Purse is cited as "one of the few Christian aid agencies that [doesn't] use a professional advertising agency to create their direct-mail materials."[16] When someone who's not part of a ministry is drafting its fund-raising letters, the potential for inaccuracy inevitably increases.

Eskridge and Noll point out how an emphasis on fund-raising can skew an organization's priorities:

> In the end, evangelical entrepreneurs, and their constituencies . . . convince themselves that the successes of the organization are a sign of God's approval, and that any decline of the organization would mean a setback to God's work in the world. So they spend their time and energies building and growing their organizations. Growth requires more money; more money means more ministry. In the worst cases, means and ends become reversed, and entrepreneurs and administrators do ministry in order to grow. In the best cases, more ministry means more people who become newly aware of the great gift God has given them, and who then, in gratitude, reach into their own pockets so that others might also know.[17]

A *Christianity Today* article criticizes organizations that overuse the word *urgent*:

> "Urgent" letters make some people wonder just how important the need may be. We know that it will take days or weeks for our donation to reach its destination. If the need is really that urgent, it is being paid for with existing agency funds.[18]

In other words, often the money sent from donors won't go to the need itself, but to replenish ministry accounts depleted to make those needs known. To some that's a hairline distinction, to others it's critical. In a letter to the editor of *Christianity Today*, Richard Stearns, president of World Vision

U.S., responds to the criticism of organizations that "create a false sense of urgency":

> The decisions to use words like urgent to underline key phrases in an appeal letter, or to include a painful photograph of a child in need can have life and death consequences. An appeal that raises an additional $10,000 can feed 100 children for five months or inoculate 500 children against the five deadly childhood diseases. These are the true ethical consequences of the debate over fund-raising language and tactics. Critical needs justify urgent appeals as long as those appeals are honest and fully accurate. If a building is on fire, one does not send a subtle memo to alert the occupants; one pulls the fire alarm.[19]

Stearns raises an important point. Are we more distressed at the materials that draw attention to the fact that children are dying than we are by the reality that children are dying? Are we concerned about fund-raising ethics but not the ethics of letting children die? How calm and measured a tone do we expect from those committed to rescuing children from starvation? Our criticisms of relief fund-raisers should be tempered by confessing our own indifference to the plight of the needy. It's reasonable for us to expect documented facts, accurate statistics, sound reasoning, and quotes in context. It's not reasonable for us to expect dispassionate appeals from those with a God-given passion to feed the hungry and reach the lost before they die.

FUND-RAISING DECEPTIONS

For years I taught a Bible college ethics class. If I were to teach it again, I would add a section called Ethics in Christian Fund-Raising. The Evangelical Council for Financial Accountability says it receives more complaints about fund-raising than any other issue.[20]

Some people are bothered by the "waste" of frequent mailings from Christian organizations. If a donor sends a modest gift to an organization, that gift may be canceled out by the frequent mailings he receives over the course of a year. On the other hand, organizations will say they're obligated to repeat their message to remind people to pray and to give. Experience has shown that if they don't send mailings, they won't receive funds—and perhaps not much prayer either—for the kingdom causes they support.

Personalization increases donations. But what about those fund-raising letters underlined by hand, giving the impression of a personal letter? Envelopes and postscripts often are handwritten to give the same impression. Handwritten notes in the margins create the illusion of a personal touch. Some people—especially the elderly, who are unfamiliar with modern technologies—are fooled by such practices. Isn't a greeting that says "My dear friend" disingenuous when the recipient is someone the writer has never seen or heard of?

Can God be honored by a fund-raising appeal that knowingly deceives some of its recipients?

When a letter is signed by someone, shouldn't it be fair to assume he actually wrote the letter? Isn't that the point of using a signature in the first place? Yet in many organizations, the CEO—or whoever signs the letter—doesn't write it at all. In some cases, he never even sees it. If it isn't written by an outside company, then his assistant or another staff member in the fund-raising department—likely someone he barely knows—writes it. Shouldn't that be acknowledged? Perhaps the CEO should say, "Our donor relations director, Diane Meyer, wrote the following letter, which I concur with and believe is important for you to read." If it sounds strange to credit someone unknown to the recipients, is it because we've become desensitized by pretending prominent people are writing letters they really aren't?

A Christian brother, whose sincerity I don't doubt, tried to sell me on simulated handwriting, a touch that would distinguish our mailings, making the recipients feel as if I personally handwrote each of them. But of course I would not be personally handwriting each of them! My use of this technology would be an attempt to deceive. Why are we trying to flatter people by making them think we're giving them personal attention that we're not?

"Everybody does it." No, they don't. But even if they did, deception doesn't become moral just because it's widespread.

What about envelopes that say "You've won" or "Check enclosed," when in fact the recipient has won nothing and what's enclosed isn't a real check? How can people who profess to worship a Christ who is "full of grace and truth" practice this kind of deception? What example are we setting for our children? We tell them "don't lie" and "don't take credit for someone else's work." Then we turn around and do those things in Christian ministries.

What would you think if you found out your son's friend had written a paper, but your son turned it in with his name on it, taking credit for someone else's work? You'd be shocked. You'd insist that your son confess his deception to the teacher and take the appropriate punishment. Yet this is routinely done in Christian ministry—people put their names on articles and letters they didn't write. What's the difference?

What about using stock pictures of a mother and child that aren't the same mother and child mentioned by name in the letter? What if the touching story in the letter didn't actually happen in the country that the letter is about? Or what if it happened under another ministry, not the one sending the letter? What if it happened twelve years ago? Wouldn't the reader assume the picture was of the people being talked about, that the events had actually happened in the place and under the ministry the letter refers to, and that they had happened recently, at least within the last year? If the reader would assume these things but they are not true—and no effort is made to correct those natural assumptions—isn't that deception?

A letter may not claim that all funds received will go to help these particular poor people in this particular village in India. However, if the letter is about these people, the donor will want to help them. If the funds will be used by the ministry for other purposes, this should be made clear.

Donor intent is paramount. If an appeal is made to "feed the hungry," but the donor's gift goes to support the building of a field office for the famine relief organization, there's a gap between belief and reality. The organization may justly argue that the building of this facility will result in the feeding of many hungry people. However, honesty demands that the donor be told that's where the funds are going. If it's a good cause, explain why. But don't leave false impressions. The goal isn't just acquiring funds but communicating truthfully.

Ministries should practice the golden rule by asking, "What have I not included in this letter that a donor would want to know before making a decision about giving to this cause?" The ability to put oneself in the place of donors is one reason that ministry staffers should themselves be generous givers. The reason some ministry fund-raisers don't think like givers is that they're not givers.

The Red Cross lost its credibility when it collected far more money than it could actually distribute after the September 11 terrorist acts in New York City. The money was spent, but not where donors intended it. Ethics demands that if extra money will be used for other purposes, the ministry must say so. If it doesn't, and any funds cannot be used as donors intended, the organization should offer donors the opportunity to take back their contributions.

The use of matching funds or challenge grants has a legitimate role in motivating givers. "For every hundred dollars given to the ministry, an anonymous donor will contribute another hundred dollars, matching up to three million dollars." Such an approach is effective. But it raises a temptation. If major donors make an outright gift commitment, should a ministry ask them to make it a challenge gift instead? No, because their intent was to give it all to the ministry anyway. The funds are already committed, they are not at risk, and therefore saying that other donors' gifts will be doubled by matching is not accurate.

The goodness of the cause cannot be divorced from the goodness of the ministry's presentation of the cause. Dishonesty ultimately backfires, but even if it doesn't, it is still wrong.

> If an appeal is made to "feed the hungry," but the donor's gift goes to support the building of a field office for the famine relief organization, there's a gap between belief and reality.

261

CONCERNS WITH TELEMARKETING

Many ministries have turned to telemarketing to raise funds. One argument against telemarketing is its association with intrusive phone calls that put kingdom ministries on the same level with phone companies begging people to change service providers. The strongest argument for telemarketing is that it works—it brings in money. However, lotteries, embezzlement, bank robberies, and pyramid marketing schemes may also bring in money, but we wouldn't want to use those methods for fund-raising.

My friend Barry Arnold, a missions pastor, has served on the board of a major mission. He shared with me the following insights on telemarketing:

1. Telemarketing is a very expensive way to raise money. The first 20 cents of every dollar contributed goes directly to the telemarketing company. The ministry's normal overhead rate of about 15 percent has to be added beyond that. Therefore, only 65 cents of each dollar given through telemarketing is available to fund programs. Telemarketers generally take for their "fee" 40 to 60 cents of every dollar contributed. I would have less of a problem with telemarketing if donors were told, up front, what percentage of their gift was going to the telemarketer. But of course that never happens.

2. Telemarketing violates basic biblical principles of giving and financial stewardship:

- Telemarketing pressures people to give before they've had time to carefully evaluate their total financial situation. (According to 2 Corinthians 9:7, NKJV, the giver should "purpose in his heart.")
- Telemarketing denies donors the opportunity to pray, get godly counsel, discuss a gift with a spouse, or search the Scriptures before deciding on an amount (2 Corinthians 9:7).
- The telemarketing script ignores the Holy Spirit's role in the exercise of the gift of giving (Romans 12:8) and his quiet prompting toward freewill giving.
- Telemarketing relies on the combined elements of surprise and guilt to produce donations. One would have to strain to visualize the "cheerful giver" described in 2 Corinthians 9:7 holding the phone. (See also 2 Corinthians 9:5.)
- Telemarketing is a human-to-human "sales agreement" that may rob the giver of an eternal reward (Matthew 6:2-3).
- Telemarketing may result in greater bondage on the part of donors who contribute by credit card as the telemarketing script urges (Proverbs 22:7; Romans 13:7).

CONCERNS WITH DONOR CONFERENCES

I mentioned previously an invitation from a ministry active in Third World countries that was offering a luxurious stay at an exclusive resort in the Bahamas. I have in front of me an invitation from another organization to which our ministry made a one-time contribution of $5,000. The invitation is for a two-week luxury cruise visiting seven countries. The ship stops at three ports where there are brief opportunities to observe ministries. It offers veranda rooms starting at $2,899. There are a number of extra charges listed, not to mention airfare to get to the port.

In today's mail I received an invitation from another major evangelical ministry to a gathering called "Realities of the World's Children in the Twenty-First Century," centering on the plight of poor children. Enclosed is a picture of where the conference will be held—a gorgeous hotel sitting on a lake, described as "a world class destination . . . a beautiful resort with a blend of casual elegance, superb service, and world-class recreation. Throughout your stay, winding walkways will lure you through stunning displays of lush fountains and manicured courtyard gardens. . . . The resort offers breathtaking golf courses, smashing tennis facilities, a wonderful spa with staff to pamper you." Then there's the dinner cruise on a boat that's no less than "exquisite." True, some people are already taking such trips. So, why shouldn't ministries offer them in a way that can stretch people's vision for ministry? A great deal of money will likely be contributed by those going on these cruises and staying in these luxury hotels. Does the end justify the means?

Isn't there something fundamentally inappropriate about using a facility steeped in luxury for a conference concerned with helping dying children, when the costs for the weekend, if spent on helping children instead, would keep thousands alive? Isn't feeding into the allure of excessive lifestyles a problem rather than a solution? How can we wish our supporters would forgo luxuries to support kingdom causes, then turn around and offer them luxuries to support kingdom causes? Why are we appealing to—and justifying—something in donors that Christ may be seeking to overcome in them? (And in us?)

It's appropriate for ministries to express sincere gratitude for acts of generous giving. What seems inappropriate is pampering these givers to motivate them toward further giving. (There's also the effect on those in the ministry who start living a rich lifestyle vicariously through their donors.) Are expensive tours, chartered fishing trips, and exotic vacations necessary?

I sometimes speak at donor events in very nice surroundings, realizing that Paul said, "I have become all things to all men" (1 Corinthians 9:22). He also said, "I know what it is to be in need, and I know what it is to have plenty. I have learned the secret of being content in any and every situation, whether well fed or hungry, whether living in plenty or in want" (Philippians 4:12). There are many wealthy people who need to be reached with the liberating truth of joyful giving. To reach them, we must go where they are or invite them where they will come. Yet, perhaps we are doing a disservice to many by assuming we must have the nicest possible accommodations to win their attendance at a conference, when if we focused on the opportunity to use money for God's kingdom they might come just as willingly—and perhaps more so.

Shouldn't we teach donors through our words and deeds that God is their rewarder, not us? The giving of good books and helpful gifts can be appropriate, but churches and ministries should be careful not to overshadow the biblical reasons for giving.

Shouldn't we teach donors through our words and deeds that God is their rewarder, not us?

Ministries should not allow donors to determine policy. One mission was offered the free use of a beautiful luxury ship to take its donors up and down the coast of Africa so they could see their work among the poor. Fortunately, the ministry president saw that this would be inappropriate. But anything that a donor offers to pay for—including weekends in extravagant resorts—can be tempting. "We can't really refuse something if it's offered us, can we?" The answer is "Yes, we can." And in some cases we certainly should.

Just as donors need to speak up and challenge ministries to spend their money more carefully, ministries with long-term relationships with donors earn the right to gently challenge them. Certainly we should not allow some donors' expensive tastes to change how the ministry operates. Churches and ministries should offer mature spiritual leadership rather than follow the agendas set by wealthy donors.

A delightful twenty-two-year-old woman came to me. She had suffered a disfiguring accident, followed by dozens of painful surgeries. Then she became wealthy through an insurance settlement. In a newspaper interview, she was asked, "What will you do with the money?" She said she wanted to support Christian ministries. In tears, she told me of the phone calls that followed from ministries and a Christian college. Suddenly everyone wanted to take her to lunch. Then she told me she'd been serving on the board of an evangelical mission. I asked her, "Do you think they'd have asked a twenty-two-year-old to be on the board if you weren't wealthy?" She sobbed and said, "Since the money came in, I don't know who really cares and who just wants to use me."

Many donors have become cynical toward churches and ministries, believing that they are being courted only because of their wealth. Unfortunately, sometimes it's true. (What more effective way to ensure significant giving than to put a wealthy person on the board?) Many ministries and a fair number of local churches do it, but courting big donors seems like the favoritism of the rich that Scripture explicitly condemns (James 2:1-5).

RELATIONSHIPS BETWEEN MINISTRIES AND DONORS

Psychiatrist and lecturer Dr. Roy Menninger said,

> Having money to give away and the power to decide to whom to give
> it is intoxicating, and foundations can be irritating examples of the

"narcissism of the righteous." . . . We all need to be aware of some of the darker sides of human views of money and of giving and receiving, if we are to keep from exploiting the power position of the donor or the dependent position of the seeker.[21]

Ministry representatives and donors should conduct their interactions in a way that's biblical and honest. Communication should be open, and false expectations should be avoided. We should commit ourselves to no game playing, hidden agendas, or unfounded assumptions.

Donors should understand and respect the ministry's representatives and not take advantage of them from a power position. Donors and ministry representatives are both God's slaves, his errand boys and girls. Both should be humble and transparent. Ministry representatives who constantly pump up donors, telling them how important and wonderful they are, forfeit the right to complain when donors turn around and act in a way that's self-important. If you want someone to act humbly, feeding his pride isn't the best strategy. We shouldn't tempt donors toward the very things from which God seeks to deliver them—including pride (craving recognition and status), control, independence, and materialism.

Ministry staffers can fall into the trap of ingratiating themselves and flattering donors. This is manipulative and explicitly violates Scripture: "A lying tongue hates those it hurts, and a flattering mouth works ruin" (Proverbs 26:28); "He who rebukes a man will in the end gain more favor than he who has a flattering tongue" (Proverbs 28:23). Flattery never serves the interests of the person we're flattering—it serves only our interests. Any relationship with a donor is unhealthy if a ministry leader or a pastor will not raise concerns about character or choices. Withholding the truth in the interests of not losing someone's support is a disservice to the donors and to the Lord. Instead, we should speak the truth in love (Ephesians 4:15).

Some donors see through flattery and don't appreciate it, whereas others soak it up. Sometimes, genuine and healthy friendships develop in this context, but most donors aren't looking for more close friends.

Someone told me he'd called a well-known leader on a matter of some urgency. A few weeks had gone by and the leader hadn't called him back. He said, "I'm used to calling the ministries we support and having everyone know my name. People step out of meetings to take my calls. Now I know how people feel when they're waiting for me to return their calls."

This lesson in humility was healthy. It's one reason I'm grateful to be part of a ministry that both receives substantial gifts and also grants them. I know what it's like on both sides.

I've suggested to ministry representatives that they send us no-frills information letting us know about strategic projects. I will read these. There is no need for me to go on fishing trips or sightseeing tours or even regular lunches. If I spent my days and nights having dinner, traveling, and vacationing with people from all the organizations we support, I would have no time to write books and therefore would have much less to give to kingdom causes. Once I explain my perspective, most ministry representatives understand. I've found the majority to be gracious and kingdom-minded.

Ministry representatives shouldn't presume to know whether it's God's will for a donor to give to a project. Likewise, donors shouldn't presume to know God's will for exactly how the money should be used once it's given. When giving, we need to truly release funds into the care of stewards we trust.

PAID CELEBRITY ENDORSEMENTS FOR MINISTRIES

One of the most disturbing recent fund-raising developments is paid celebrity endorsements of charities given at conferences and concerts. A speaker or musician might give an appeal for a ministry's child sponsorships. For every child sponsored as a result of the appeal the performer receives $25 to $50. (In the secular world, this is called a kickback.)

A pastor's wife attending a popular conference heard a speaker strongly endorse a ministry that works with needy children. On a hunch, the pastor's wife asked the speaker afterward if she or the organization had been paid an endorsement fee. "Of course," the speaker replied.

If someone is *paid* money by a ministry for asking an audience to *give* money to that ministry, it doesn't qualify as a heartfelt endorsement.

Speakers have been paid as much as $10,000 for a single large-event endorsement. Someone learned at a ministry board meeting that the organization was "negotiating" with a popular musician to get his endorsement. "What's there to negotiate?" he asked. "Either someone believes in this ministry and is willing to give his money and time and name to it, or he doesn't." If someone is *paid* money by a ministry for asking an audience to *give* money to that ministry, it doesn't qualify as a heartfelt endorsement. It seems more like a bribe or a payoff.

Satan is a master at twisting good things and perverting acts of grace and kindness into profit-seeking ventures. It's commendable when speakers or musicians believe in a mission so much they would sacrifice to support it. It's wonderful that they'd take an offering for that ministry. But to be paid for doing so—to take for themselves *any* amount of money given by those intending it to go to help poor children—is unethical. (If the audience knew, they would be heartsick and perhaps angry. God *does* know. Is he heartsick? angry?)

I know a fine group of young musicians who were approached by a major missions organization asking them to promote its ministry. The mission offered them a 20 percent cut of all funds collected at their concerts. Suppose the lead singer made the following public statement: "Eighty percent of tonight's offering will go to feed the hungry in Haiti; the other 20 percent will go to us as payment for bringing this to your attention." If the truth were divulged, people would be able to act in light of it. But most ministries, musicians, and speakers wouldn't agree to such a disclosure. Why? Because it would look bad for everyone. But if it *looks* bad, isn't that because it *is* bad? If those involved would be embarrassed by disclosure, isn't that an indication it shouldn't be done in the first place? I think that veteran ministry leaders should be ashamed of themselves for putting this kind of temptation in front of young Christian musicians. They need examples of integrity, not offers that would compromise their integrity.

I have no problem with a ministry asking to present its vision to a speaker or group and then asking them to pray about calling attention to their cause. I have major problems with offering them a percentage of "the take" (once known as the offering). Unless this is done with full disclosure, unless clear verbal or printed recognition is made of this financial arrangement, the offering is a deception. Anything less than full disclosure to potential donors constitutes fraud. Such arrangements will inevitably promote abuse, and sometimes lead to public scandal. Consider the temptation to overstate or misrepresent needs or to speak with artificial enthusiasm for the poor, while thinking of the larger kickback they will get for doing so. Our enemies dish out enough temptations without us dispensing them to our friends. Think of a Christian speaker appealing to people to give to starving children, knowing what the audience doesn't—his personal wealth will increase directly in proportion to what he says and how well he says it.

Imagine your pastor asking the congregation to dig deep and give to a mission to plant churches and give medical aid to the needy in rural Columbian villages. Hearts are moved. The church takes an offering and $50,000 is given. Praise God! Now imagine it's a week later, and a church board member mentions that the pastor was paid $10,000 for making the plea and only $40,000 actually went to the mission. How would you respond? It may sound absurd— but that's exactly the deal arranged by some Christian ministries with musicians.

Some say, "We don't publicly disclose this arrangement, because even though we know it's right to spend money to raise money, people would get the wrong idea. They'd misunderstand." The real danger isn't that people would misunderstand—it's that they would *understand*. If they understood that part of the offering was going to the celebrity, not to the cause, they would see it for what it is, and probably not support it. (If I believed in the cause and knew of these arrangements, I would send my check directly to the organization, so more would go to needy children instead of to the celebrity. Shouldn't I be given the information to allow me to make that choice?)

Taking an offering should be an opportunity to serve the needy, not a means to make money off the cause of the needy. The only way to know one's motives are right in making the appeal is not to profit from the arrangement. Those in ministry should seek to serve, not to be served. (Isn't that what ministry is about?) They should look for the right organization to support—which would presumably not be the one that offered them the kickback.

"But speakers are paid an honorarium—what's the difference?" The difference is that people assume the speaker is being paid. If you attend a seminar, it's understood that part of the cost goes to the speaker. If you pay for a concert, it's understood that the funds go to the music group. No one's being lied to or misled. But in the case of paid celebrity endorsements, people *are* being misled. Poll those attending and you'll find that most believe the speaker or musician is voluntarily endorsing the ministry because God has touched his heart by it. The audience has no clue that the first several thousand dollars given, or a percentage of the total, goes not to the cause but to the speaker or musician.

The ministry may argue, "It costs money to make money. If we put a full-page ad in a magazine, or if we produce an infomercial, it will cost us a higher percentage of what's given than if we pay 20 percent to a music group. If people realize it's okay to spend money to advertise in a magazine, why isn't it okay to pay to get the endorsement of a speaker or music group?"

The operative word is "realize." Everyone knows that it costs money to put an ad in a magazine. But unless it's explicitly disclosed, they have no clue that a speaker or music group is being paid for its endorsement.

"But the poor get more help than if we didn't do this." Who says we have to choose between misleading people and helping the poor? Believing that honest fund-raising can't be productive is an insult to God and his people. Personally, I believe that speakers or musicians who are endorsing a ministry and receiving nothing in return should make this clear. Doing this would be a great example to other speakers and musicians and would reassure the audience (who might otherwise become cynical as they learn about deceptive practices). Best of all, the speaker or musician's reward would then come not from the ministry but from the Lord. We're not to do things for those who can benefit us, but for those who can't—and then God himself will reward us in heaven (Luke 14:12-14).

Buying and Selling the Spiritual

Opportunism and attempts to buy and sell the spiritual are not new. Simon Magus was the first entrepreneur to see "money" written all over ministry:

> When Simon saw that the Spirit was given at the laying on of the apostles' hands, he offered them money and said, "Give me also this ability so that everyone on whom I lay my hands may receive the Holy Spirit."

Peter answered: "May your money perish with you, because you thought you could buy the gift of God with money! You have no part or share in this ministry, because your heart is not right before God. Repent of this wickedness and pray to the Lord. Perhaps he will forgive you for having such a thought in your heart." (Acts 8:18-22)

What makes us think that God has changed his opinion of attempts to profit under the veil of ministry? Every church and ministry leader should ask, "What are we doing that would make us embarrassed or uncomfortable if people knew it?" As I write this, I am asking myself that very question concerning our own nonprofit ministry. If we think of something—and I just did—isn't that a good indication we should stop it now?

Donors should ask the ministries they support whether they are paying to get celebrity endorsements or are spending their funds in some way other than it appears. If the answers aren't ethically and biblically satisfactory, donors should say that until the ministry's policies change, they can no longer in good conscience support them and must give their money to ministries that are operating at a higher level of integrity. For everyone's sake, including their own, ministries need to be held accountable by their supporters—and so do Christian musicians and speakers.

> What makes us think that God has changed his opinion of attempts to profit under the veil of ministry?

We should be stimulating each other to love and good deeds, setting ethical examples, raising the bar for each other, not lowering it. Jesus will examine the motives of our hearts—including our truthfulness and the sincerity of our words spoken on behalf of the poor and in support of kingdom ministries (1 Corinthians 4:5). If we have given to the needy for their good and God's glory, he will commend us. If we have taken from them for financial gain, he will not.

Imagine standing before Christ someday and hearing him say, "I tell you the truth, whatever you did for one of the least of these brothers of mine, you did for—yourself!"

THE ETHICS OF GHOSTWRITING

Ghostwriting is when someone else writes a book that is credited to a celebrity as if he or she wrote it. The usual rationale for this practice is that because the real writer's name isn't well-known and marketable, the book won't sell unless it's released under the celebrity's name.

This is so commonly practiced that many Christian publishers, authors, and celebrities see no ethical problem with it. Some of these people are sincere in their beliefs—I know because I've talked with them. I have great respect for my publishers, and many others too, but all of us, including me, naturally become desensitized. Sometimes those of us who are on the inside of publishing—including authors, agents, and publishers—fail to see what those on the outside immediately recognize as unethical.

I'm not talking about the legitimate process of coauthoring, in which authors invest varying levels of work and expertise into the writing. Nor am I talking about books that, after being written, need substantial editing provided by the publisher. By ghostwriting, I'm talking about when the actual writer's name is not on the cover, or when a person's name is on the cover (even as a coauthor with the real writer) who did little or nothing to write the book.

I know of cases where the celebrity didn't write a word and only skimmed through the book for the first time late in the editing process. Is this honest?

Consider what this practice does to immature believers who are athletes, musicians, or public figures made prominent through tragic or newsworthy events. "Here's the offer: We will make you a lot of money, and you will get to take credit for doing something you really didn't do." We feed their ego, and set them up for deception and pride, which is bound to cause them to fall (Proverbs 16:18). They're under enough temptation already—why do we feel compelled to add to it by making the false claim that in addition to everything else they're writers?

If we teach them it's okay to lie by taking credit for a book they didn't write, why should we be shocked if we discover they lied when they claim to have graduated from a college they didn't, or to have fought in a war they didn't, or to have done a job they didn't? Isn't it ironic that Christian publishers would consider it an ethical breach if they discovered an "author" gave them a résumé containing false information, when the same publisher has knowingly led the public to believe this person wrote a book he or she really didn't write? Which is the bigger lie?

Nothing is more uncomfortable than hearing an interview with those who are asked about their experiences writing a book they didn't write. Their temptation is to pretend and cover up the truth. Sometimes they pretend long enough that they convince themselves they're writers, becoming better liars all the time.

Publishers often approach prominent pastors and Christian leaders whose greatest temptations are toward pride and pretense and then help them pretend they wrote a book, taking pride in something they didn't do!

Putting musicians, writers, speakers, and others on pedestals goes way beyond healthy respect for role models. It borders on idolatry. Arguably it's not good for anyone, but certainly it's not good for the young, the immature, and those already struggling with pride, pretense, money loving, and other temptations that are only fed by "I wrote a book" celebrity status.

Ask the average person what it means when a name is on a book cover, and they'll tell you it means the person actually wrote it. That's what book buyers believe. Hence, the book is sold to them under false pretenses. I've been told "the ghostwriter knows what he's agreeing to, and if he doesn't need to see his name on the book, that's up to him." But the question isn't what the ghostwriter or celebrity believes, it's what the potential book-buyer believes. Ghostwriters may receive far greater royalties than if they were known as the book's true author. They may have a vested interest in the falsehood just like everyone else involved.

Why not tell the truth on the cover, saying who *really* wrote the book and leaving off the names of any who didn't write it? The answer is simple: "It wouldn't sell as well." If the response is that "the book is just as good or better than if the celebrity wrote it," that may well be true, but people should be allowed to decide that for themselves, shouldn't they? How dare we mislead and deprive readers of accurate information about who actually wrote the book they are considering buying? This isn't just patronizing and insulting, it's downright dishonest. Why do we imagine this is any different than withholding information about the used car we're trying to sell, for fear that if we told the truth people wouldn't buy it? Is our goal just to sell books, or to honor Jesus?

The same principle applies to columns and articles—including those in many ministry and Christian college publications—that are not actually written by the Christian leaders listed as authors. Some college presidents never write their own articles in school publications, yet their names are always attached to them. If students at the same college put their name on papers written by someone else, this would be grounds for dismissal. So why is it all right for the president to do it? Similarly, ministry fund-raising letters signed by the president or CEO frequently aren't written by him.

In 1990, a scandal occurred involving Milli Vanilli. The singing group's name became a cultural synonym for dishonesty and hypocrisy simply because the people doing the singing for their recordings weren't the ones getting credit for it. So why is this recognized as being wrong, but it's somehow considered acceptable to take credit for a book, article, or letter someone else wrote? A class-action suit was filed against Milli Vanilli and their recording company, and purchasers of *Girl You Know It's True* were given the opportunity to request a rebate for fraud damages. Are readers of books that are not written by their stated authors entitled to a rebate for exactly the same reasons?

Someone could argue that the real singers sounded better than Milli Vanilli. But the point is that the whole thing was a lie, and customers were outraged by it. It's ironic that Christians would stoop to ethics that even most non-Christians, who don't believe what the Bible says about truth, would immediately recognize as wrong.

Isn't it reasonable for both Christians and non-Christians to be able to buy a Christian book with the confidence that the person identified on the book and publicized as the author actually *wrote* it?

"But ghostwriting is a well-established practice." Many things are well-established practices, but that doesn't make them right. I've seen people heart-sick, disillusioned, and angry when they discover that various popular Christian books weren't written by the person whose name is on the cover. We who supposedly esteem the truth so highly should be the last ones to participate in such deceit.

Every argument I hear for ghostwriting is pragmatic. *Of course* people make money by ghostwriting. People also make money from prostitution, theft, and drug dealing. The real question is not whether ghostwriting is *profitable* but whether it is *moral.* I never hear people offering biblical and ethical justifications for it, only practical ones. Why? Perhaps because there simply is no biblical justification for it.

There's sometimes a fine line between ghostwriting and celebrity books written "with" others. Writing a book about people, with their cooperation, is certainly fine, as long as there's no pretense or false impression about who did the writing. But when the cover puts the celebrity's name first, followed by "and" or "with" the true writer, the implication is that the celebrity did most or much of the writing. If, in fact, the "author" did nothing more than grant interviews, answer questions, pass on a few pages of a journal, or supply a recorded speech, then he or she isn't the author and shouldn't be promoted as such.

If this isn't a book *by* Celebrity X but *about* Celebrity X, that's fine—but shouldn't this distinction be made clear by listing the real author's name exclusively on the cover? The celebrity can still be emphasized as the subject of the book, but not as the author. The writer shouldn't pretend to be a world-class athlete or movie star, and the celebrity shouldn't pretend to be a writer. Sometimes the "name" person is a celebrity author who can write but didn't write the book. If the celebrity didn't write it but just supplied some suggestions or advice, he or she belongs on the acknowledgments page, not the cover. Ask yourself, "Given the amount of work the celebrity actually contributed to writing the book, if the name wasn't well-known, would it be on the cover?" If the answer is no, then the ethics are clear—the celebrity's name shouldn't be on the cover as author.

I believe Christian ghostwriting is a scandal waiting to explode. If we in the Christian community don't clean up our act soon, we're going to face widespread loss of credibility. What a tragedy if *60 Minutes* were to expose a practice we should never have tolerated. Can't you see an interviewer holding up a book and asking well-known Christian authors, "Did you *really* write this book?" Envision the neatly edited scenes of embarrassment, head-hanging, evasions, rationalizations, and reports that "so-and-so author and publisher wouldn't return our calls."

This could be a major setback for Christian publishers and authors at the very time that Christian books have made unprecedented inroads into the mainstream culture. We need to confess, repent of, and change our policies—and stop being driven by money-love and ego building.

If we're not telling the truth about who wrote the book—on the cover, in large print—why should people believe what's inside the book, in small print?

FALSE ADVERTISING BY CHRISTIAN COLLEGES

Many Christian colleges routinely print doctrinal statements in their catalogs that are not believed or taught by some or even many of their professors. The academic vice president of a major Christian liberal arts college confided to me, "If Christian parents actually knew what their children are being taught in our classrooms, they would pull them out of college tomorrow." And, I would add, they'd never give another dime to that college.

If Christian colleges told the truth in their promotional materials, some would read like this: "Thirty-four percent of our faculty believe in the inerrancy of God's Word. Twenty-one percent of our science teachers believe the biblical account of creation. No one in our psychology department believes in the doctrine of original sin. Two out of our three sociology teachers are proabortion and defenders of homosexual lifestyles. The director of our philosophy department is an agnostic. The head of our Bible department hasn't attended church for ten years because he doesn't believe in organized religion."

Why not be honest and admit this publicly? The answer is simple: So Christian parents will keep paying to send their students there, and so the college's major Christian donors will keep sending money. I am a great believer in Christian higher education. But the doctrinal statements published by many Christian colleges, including some at which I've spoken, are simply false advertising (also known as lying). Much of the motive for this dishonesty boils down to money.

FEES FOR CHRISTIAN SPEAKERS

In Judges 8:22-27, we see a remarkable account of a man with a right perspective who does not crave power but makes what appears to be just a small concession. The Israelites say they want Gideon to rule over them because he is their hero who saved them from Midian. But Gideon says, "I will not rule over you, nor will my son rule over you. The Lord will rule over you" (Judges 8:23). But then he makes a request, that they would each give him an earring—just that much and no more—from their share of the plunder. The weight of the gold rings came to about forty-three pounds. Gideon made the gold into an ephod, which he placed in his hometown.

"So what?' we might think. "That's a small price for people to pay. They wouldn't even miss it. And Gideon certainly earned it." But the verse ends with this sentence: "All Israel prostituted themselves by worshiping [the ephod] there, and it became a snare to Gideon and his family" (Judges 8:27).

The hero Gideon is transformed from a man of perspective to a man as shortsighted as the kings of the heathen nations. "There's nothing wrong with gold earrings and a beautiful ephod, and nothing wrong with a man being rewarded for faithful leadership." Yet somehow it all turned into something terribly wrong. It became a snare to Gideon and his family, and led Israel to idolize a cheap substitute for God rather than worship the true God. Gideon, his children, and the nation paid a terrible price. I believe that some Christian speakers are in serious danger of making the same mistake today.

I attended a ministry fund-raising event where the speaker made a point of saying, "I believe in this ministry so much I'm going to give 10 percent of my honorarium back." What he didn't mention was that his fee for this thirty-minute speaking engagement was $5,000. So he gave $500, but walked away with $4,500. Of course, it's his prerogative to set a fee and the organization's prerogative to pay him that. (Although those attending the fund-raiser would likely give less if they knew the first forty-five gifts of $100 would be negated by the speaker's fee). But for the speaker to imply he was making a financial sacrifice for the ministry's cause—or that he was there because he believed so much in the ministry—was misleading.

In *Fresh Wind, Fresh Fire,* Jim Cymbala comments:

> I am dismayed at the contracts required by some contemporary Christian musical groups. To perform a concert at your church, the stated fee will be so much (in either four or five figures) plus round-trip airfare—often in first class, not coach. Every detail of the accommodations is spelled out, down to "sushi for twenty persons" waiting at the hotel, in one case. All this is done so that the group can stand before an inner-city audience and exhort the people to "just trust the Lord for all your needs."[22]

I, too, am dismayed at fees charged by Christian speakers to come "serve the Lord and his people" for a single weekend. I don't mean to say that all fees are wrong, although I personally think it's better to leave honoraria in the hands of those who are extending the invitation to speak. But when Christian speakers are charging ten to thirty thousand dollars to represent the Lord, isn't something wrong?[23] Some will say, "We should charge what the market demands," and, "Shouldn't Christians be able to make money like non-Christians do?" and, "Don't muzzle the ox that treads the grain." Well, yes, but how much grain can one ox tread in a single evening?

A Christian physicist has the right to make as much money for his lecture on thermodynamics as any other scientist. But when you are billed as a *Christian* speaker and the supposed objective is representing Jesus, when words such as "ministry" and "serving" and "testimony" are used to promote the event, isn't that a little different? Would it affect people's attitudes to hear that the speaker demanded a fee of $10,000?

Isn't ministry about something more than what the market demands? What about Christian conferences that are marketing extravaganzas and ministries that offer their own Visa cards so they can receive a percentage on each purchase? Have we gone too far?

It may not be wise for everyone, but my practice is never to charge a speaking fee and to leave honoraria completely voluntary. I've received everything from no honorarium to several thousand dollars. When someone extending an invitation asks for estimates or guidelines, my assistant and I politely decline to give numbers. When organizations start to tell me what honorarium they're willing to give, I tell them I'd rather not know. This is not because I'm so spiritual but exactly the opposite: It's because I want to be influenced by the leading of God's Spirit in deciding where to speak, and I don't trust myself to remain uninfluenced by the money. I want to reduce the temptation of going somewhere to ostensibly "serve" God and his Church when in fact I'd be going for the financial payoff.

THE CHRISTIAN CELEBRITY SYNDROME

Ron Blue and Company manages financial assets exceeding two billion dollars. I submitted to Ron my first draft of this chapter, looking for balance and correction. I expected him to encourage me to tone down my concerns about everything from fund-raising to ghostwriting to speaker fees to celebrity endorsements. He surprised me by saying "I totally agree. Don't tone it down."

> If we would be ashamed or embarrassed by full disclosure of our finances—everything from our salaries and all other sources of income to our proportion of giving—it's an indication we should be living differently.

Ron shared his observations of troubling financial ethics in some churches and nonprofit organizations. He expressed a deep concern for what he called the "Christian celebrity" phenomenon that leads to serious abuses, many of them financial, which he's in a unique position to see. Ron has asked clients who are Christian leaders, "Would you be comfortable if your tax returns were published in *The Wall Street Journal?*" His point is that if we would be ashamed or embarrassed by full disclosure of our finances—everything from our salaries and all other sources of income to our proportion of giving—it's an indication we should be living differently. If we would be embarrassed for other people to know the truth, shouldn't we be concerned about God, whose standards are much higher and who does know the truth?

In A.D. 400, Jerome warned the church, "Shun, as you would the plague, a cleric who from being poor has become wealthy, or who, from being nobody has become a celebrity."[24] In the early church, leaders led by a model of sacrifice and generosity, not by privilege and accumulation. Unfortunately, the modern evangelical culture—including the publishing and music industries—is generating Christian celebrities and lavishing them with wealth they're often unprepared to handle.

This isn't sour grapes. In doing many book signings and media and speaking events, I've had at least a taste of what it's like to be treated as a celebrity. It's fine to respect and appreciate someone's writing, but some people treat me better than I deserve. I do not believe that these people are trying to dishonor God. And I personally know a number of people known as Christian celebrities who genuinely seek to honor God. I'm as vulnerable as anyone to sliding down the slippery slope of pride, succumbing to flattery, and gradually coming to think that I deserve special attention, recognition, and material indulgences.

I take no pleasure in addressing these issues. I hope it will serve Christ's body by initiating some much needed self-examination, dialogue, and reform.

WHAT TO LOOK FOR WHEN GIVING TO A MINISTRY

As stewards, we should invest wisely in eternity. This means we must give intelligently, based on an accurate appraisal of those to whom we entrust God's money. In other words, we need to do our homework before we give. This might include asking our pastors for advice, carefully examining a ministry's publications (including financial statements), meeting with a ministry representative, visiting an office or the mission field and observing the work, or consulting with others in a position to know more intimately what a particular ministry is really like.

Reading an organization's literature is a good start, but it isn't enough. A ministry's publications will present the organization in the most positive light. There will be stories of conversions, revivals, and changed lives—but you'll almost never hear about failures, infighting, immorality, or misappropriation of funds. There are many ministries that I deeply respect, but I've come to appreciate them by taking a closer, more personal look at them.

Every organization has legitimate overhead and "home office" expenses. But some are unnecessarily high. Others have been known to spend well more than half of incoming gifts for further fund-raising efforts, especially when buying expensive television spots. Some devote their greatest energies and resources not to meeting needs but to selling themselves to the public, cultivating donors, and competing for available funds. Others are sincere but are culturally insensitive, have poor contacts or distribution methods in foreign countries, and sometimes are attempting short-term solutions that contribute to long-term problems. For example, some local farmers in the Third World have been put out of business by deliveries of free food from relief organizations. The farmers have worked all year to grow their crops only to see their food go to waste and their efforts go unrewarded because no one will buy food when they can get it for free. Consequently, the farmers lose their incentive and no longer grow food, thus ensuring the crisis will get worse and creating an endless dependence on the outside world. A sensitive relief organization (and there are some excellent ones) will work toward encouraging rather than discouraging local workers and the local economy, with a goal not only of immediate famine relief but ongoing famine prevention.

There are certain characteristics to look for in any ministry you might choose to support. I've written an article titled "Nineteen Questions to Ask Before You Give to Any Organization," which is available on our ministry's Web site.[25] Here are the basic questions, without the elaboration I've included in the article:

1. Am I fulfilling my primary giving responsibility to my local church?
2. Are there things about this ministry that make it uniquely worth investing in?
3. Have I not only read the literature from this ministry, but talked with others who know it close up but have no vested interests in it?
4. Have I considered a ministry or vision trip to see and participate in what this ministry is actually doing on the field?
5. Does the ministry's staff demonstrate a servant-hearted concern for those to whom they minister?
6. Do the organization's workers demonstrate a sense of unity, camaraderie, and mutual respect? (Ask employees, "For what reasons have people left this organization in the last few years?")
7. Have I talked directly with people at the "lower levels" of this ministry, not just executives and PR people? How do they feel about the ministry?
8. Is this ministry biblically sound and Christ-centered? Do people call upon the Lord Jesus to ask his guidance and the Holy Spirit's empowerment to do their work?
9. What kind of character, integrity, purity, and humility is demonstrated by the ministry leaders?
10. What kind of accountability structures (just using the word accountability isn't enough) does the organization have?
11. If this is a secular or semi-Christian organization rather than a distinctively Christian one, why would I give to it rather than to another?
12. How clear are this organization's goals and objectives, strategies, and tactics, and how effective are they in carrying them out?
13. Is this organization teachable and open to improvement to become more strategic?

14. Am I certain I've gotten an objective view of this ministry, or have I seen only the positives without the negatives? (Ask them, "What are your weaknesses?")
15. What ethics and what view of God and people are demonstrated in this organization's fund-raising techniques?
16. How much money does the organization spend on overhead expenses and fund-raising, and how much in actual ministry to people?
17. Does this ministry show a clear understanding of cross-cultural ministry factors and local conditions and how the flow of money may affect them?
18. Does this organization speak well of others and cooperate with them?
19. Is this ministry pervaded by a distinctly eternal perspective?

I realize these questions may sound like they arise out of suspicion. But the more worthy an organization is, the more it will welcome examination. Asking these questions is always to the benefit of the best ministries, because they'll stand up under scrutiny. Other ministries would take such questions very seriously if they found more potential donors asking them.

Of course, no organization is perfect. We support organizations that we know have certain weaknesses. If you've had problems with a ministry, the solution is never to give less. It is to find some good organizations—not perfect ones—and give more than ever. If you wait to give until you find the perfect ministry, you'll never give. Far better to risk giving than to withhold giving. But the good news is this: There are many fine trustworthy Christian ministries.[26] You may give to them with the confidence that you're making a true eternal investment.

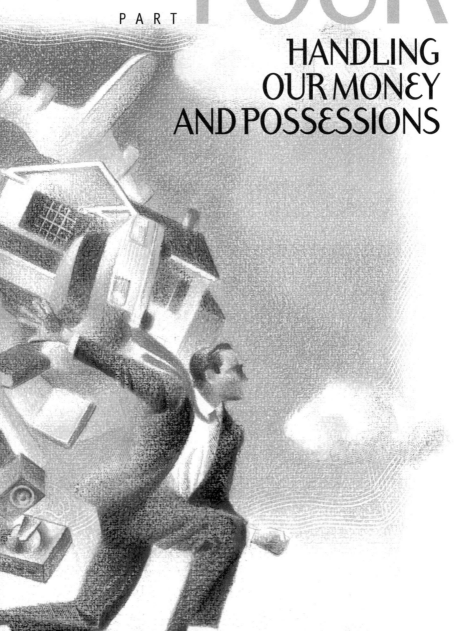

FOUR

HANDLING OUR MONEY AND POSSESSIONS

CHAPTER 16

Making Money, Owning Possessions, and Choosing a Lifestyle

Can a man be poor if he is free from want, if he does not covet the belongings of others, if he is rich in the possession of God? Rather, he is poor who possesses much but still craves for more.   TERTULLIAN

I do not believe one can settle how much we ought to give. I am afraid the only safe rule is to give more than we can spare. In other words, if our expenditure on comforts, luxuries, amusements, etc., is up to the standard common among those with the same income as our own, we are probably giving away too little. If our charities do not at all pinch or hamper us, I should say they are too small. There ought to be things we should like to do and cannot do because our charitable expenditure excludes them.   C. S. LEWIS

How different our standard is from Christ's. We ask how much a man gives. Christ asks how much he keeps.
ANDREW MURRAY

Do we have the right to earn or to keep large amounts of money? Does Scripture call all disciples to surrender their possessions and "live by faith"? Is it okay for a Christian to be wealthy? Is it Christ-honoring to live comfortably? Should we live "simply"? These and related questions are the focus of this chapter.

GOD'S WAY TO EARN MONEY: WORK
Only governments and counterfeiters *make* money. The rest of us have to earn it, inherit it, win it, or steal it. Work is the God-ordained means for contributing to society, finding fulfillment, and meeting material needs so we can provide

for our families (Proverbs 20:4; 1 Timothy 5:8). In God's ideal plan, every person is a worker. Regardless of age, ability, or handicap, nearly everyone can make a meaningful contribution to family and society through work—even if it's unpaid or very simple.

Scripture emphasizes work as the primary means of making money to meet material needs:

> He who works his land will have abundant food, but he who chases fantasies lacks judgment. (Proverbs 12:11)

> The sluggard craves and gets nothing, but the desires of the diligent are fully satisfied. (Proverbs 13:4)

> All hard work brings a profit, but mere talk leads only to poverty. (Proverbs 14:23)

> Make it your ambition to lead a quiet life, to mind your own business and to work with your hands, just as we told you, so that your daily life may win the respect of outsiders and so that you will not be dependent on anybody. (1 Thessalonians 4:11-12)

> For even when we were with you we gave you this rule: "If a man will not work, he shall not eat." (2 Thessalonians 3:10)

> Our people must learn to devote themselves to doing what is good, in order that they may provide for daily necessities and not live unproductive lives. (Titus 3:14)

God gives us skills we should develop in order to do our work well (Exodus 35:10, 30–36:1). Christians see God as their main employer: "Whatever you do, work at it with all your heart, as working for the Lord, not for men, since you know that you will receive an inheritance from the Lord as a reward. It is the Lord Christ you are serving" (Colossians 3:23-24).

Employees are to work hard and well, realizing that even if their employer doesn't reward them, God will (Ephesians 6:5-8). Employers are to pay decent wages (Deuteronomy 24:14-15; Jeremiah 22:13; James 5:4-5). Christians in business should set fair prices and use honest scales (Deuteronomy 25:13-16; Proverbs 16:8; Proverbs 20:10). Believers will tell the truth—the whole truth—when they sell a car, house, product, or service. They know that God is watching and will hold them accountable for how they conduct their business (2 Corinthians 5:20).

PRIVATE OWNERSHIP OF PROPERTY

What should we do with the money we earn? Do we have the right to own land and have possessions? The command "Thou shalt not steal" proves that property can belong to one person and not to another (Exodus 20:15). God commands us not to covet our neighbor's house, wife, servant, ox, donkey, "or anything that belongs to your neighbor" (Exodus 20:17). The Law lays out strict rules for the protection of private property, requiring restitution for property violations (Exodus 21–22). The right to private property ownership was so ingrained in Israel that not even the king had the right to take land belonging to another (1 Kings 21:1-3, 16, 19).

Nevertheless, God told the people, "The land is mine" (Leviticus 25:23). As a reminder of this fact, a farmer's field had to be left unplowed and unused every seventh year (Exodus 23:11). Although land could be bought from others, when Jubilee came every fiftieth year, parcels of land were restored to the families from which they came (Leviticus 25:8-17). When land was sold, the transaction price was determined by how many years remained until Jubilee. In a sense, then, the land wasn't sold at all but merely leased. "What he is really selling you is the number of crops" (Leviticus 25:16).

When land was sold, the transaction price was determined by how many years remained until Jubilee.

Every seventh year was the year of release, when all debts were canceled (Deuteronomy 15:1-3). This practice prevented permanent indebtedness and servitude. Even in the sixth year, people were to lend generously to the needy, knowing the loan would probably be a gift because of the upcoming year of release. To deny a loan for that reason was to "harbor a wicked thought." By giving generously, the people of Israel would assure themselves of God's reward (Deuteronomy 15:9-11).

The year of release and Jubilee were designed to avoid permanent and hopeless poverty. In effect, they also put a limit on a person's wealth—or at least on one's ability to make wealth at the long-term expense of others by accumulating their land. Jubilee signaled a fresh start for both the poor and the rich—neither would spend a lifetime in extreme wealth or extreme poverty.

In the New Testament, the norm was to share one's property generously. Of course, this didn't negate the private ownership of property, because it was only what one privately owned that he could voluntarily give.

LIFESTYLES IN THE GOSPELS AND EPISTLES

Some Christians consider the apostles' lifestyles as normative. But there was a striking difference between the itinerant ministry of Jesus and the apostles, as seen in the Gospels, and the settled communities of Christians reflected in the Epistles.

Jesus called certain people to leave everything. In Acts 2–4 we see radical action in light of the great needs created by the Jews attending Passover in Jerusalem. But in the Epistles we see established communities much like ours today. These Christians were to have a radical attitude toward money and possessions as they lived with their families in their homes and operated businesses. They were told to "lead a quiet life," "work with your hands," and "not be dependent on anybody" (1 Thessalonians 4:11-12).

Christians needed steady employment to provide for their families. Paul said they were not to be idle wanderers or parasites but should "settle down and earn the bread they eat" (2 Thessalonians 3:12).

The challenge for such disciples was to maintain a "pilgrim mentality." They were to use their roots and ties to glorify God, not to become complacent or immobilized. They were to be content where they were yet open to God's direction should he lead them elsewhere.

Lifestyles in the Gospels

Some writers and preachers regularly speak out in magazine articles, books, and sermons against the lukewarmness and materialism of today's Christians. Much of what they say is accurate, but they commonly make two mistakes. First, they cite passages from the Gospels while ignoring the Epistles, even though the Epistles demonstrate the form that churches took after Christ's ascension, after the Holy Spirit was sent to indwell his people. Because the Church wasn't born until after the events recorded in the Gospels, we must look to the Epistles to draw balanced conclusions about normative Christian lifestyles.

The second mistake is failing to deal with the larger context of the Gospels themselves, quoting only isolated texts that tell people to give away everything. Some might get the impression that Christians who retain any possessions cannot be true disciples. But a careful reading of the Gospels gives us a perspective confirmed in the Epistles. All disciples are to have the same perspective concerning money and possessions, but there are two kinds of disciples when it comes to the matter of private ownership. An overview of the Gospel of Mark shows us this distinction.[1]

Jesus called his first four disciples to leave their fishing business to follow him (Mark 1:16-20). Abandoning their possessions was part of answering the call, because Christ's ministry was itinerant, requiring almost constant travel, mostly on foot. To follow Christ, the disciples simply had to leave their boats and nets. The central point isn't that they left their boats, but that they followed Jesus. Leaving behind their major possessions was simply the inevitable by-product of their new mission.

But even these apostles didn't irreversibly divest themselves of all possessions. Just ten verses after they've left their nets, they went to "the home of Simon and Andrew," where Simon's mother-in-law lived, presumably with his wife and children as well. The Gospels repeatedly refer to Jesus and the disciples traveling by boat on the Sea of Galilee. Most likely, the boat belonged to one of the fishermen-turned-apostles. This assumption is substantiated by the fact that

Peter and the others were back in a boat fishing again within days of Christ's death (John 21:1-3).

Peter says to Jesus, "We have left everything to follow you!" (Mark 10:28). He doesn't say, "We have *sold* everything," though they may have liquidated many of their possessions (Luke 12:32-33). When Jesus hung on the cross, "he said to his mother, 'Dear woman, here is your son,' and to the disciple [John], 'Here is your mother.' From that time on, this disciple took her into his home" (John 19:26-27).

This means that after three years of following Jesus, John still had a home. Furthermore, we know that he *continued* to have a home in later years, because "from that time on he took her into his home." Even if it belonged to his extended family, it's regarded as John's home. Jesus' mother presumably lived there until she died.

The apostles represented God's call to traveling missionary work. Such work necessitates leaving behind major possessions that would tie people to a location and prohibit their ability to go where Jesus called them. (Nevertheless, most missionaries will settle in their foreign communities, where they will own certain possessions.)

A Second Kind of Disciple

Levi the tax collector represents the second kind of disciple—one who utilizes possessions for kingdom causes, rather than giving them away. "[Jesus] saw Levi son of Alphaeus sitting at the tax collector's booth. 'Follow me,' Jesus told him, and Levi got up and followed him" (Mark 2:14). We're not told that Jesus commanded Levi to sell his possessions and give to the poor. In the very next verse, Jesus and the disciples are at a dinner party in Levi's house, along with many other tax collectors and "sinners." Levi's house was used to introduce people to Jesus. Given his profession and the number of people at the party, it was undoubtedly nicer and larger than the average house.

Although large crowds followed Jesus, he chose only twelve apostles (Mark 3:13-19) to join him in his itinerant ministry, traveling and preaching. Others from the crowd also followed Jesus. They weren't chosen as apostles but served as disciples. When they weren't with Jesus, where did these "disciples but not apostles" go? Where else but back to their families, homes, fields, livestock, and jobs. Just as Jesus had for many years served God working as a carpenter and living in a house on a piece of land, so these others served God as they raised their families, and lived and worked in their own communities. Clearly, the majority of Christ's followers never divested themselves of all their possessions, nor were they expected to.

When Jesus chose the twelve, others undoubtedly would have been delighted to be chosen. They may have been disappointed at having to return to their houses and jobs to serve Christ in a "normal" life. But it was his choice, not theirs. We must not regard God's calling as second class. The call to leave all possessions for itinerant ministry was always the exception, never the rule.

After Jesus healed the Gerasene demoniac, "the man who had been demon-possessed begged to go with him" (Mark 5:18). Here we have a man not only willing but eager, nearly desperate, to leave all else behind and follow Christ. The next verse is significant: "Jesus did not let him, but said, 'Go home to your family and tell them how much the Lord has done for you, and how he has had mercy on you.'" Although Christ called the apostles to *leave* their homes,

Both callings served the same purpose: glorifying God and furthering his kingdom.

he instructed this man to *go* to his home. Indeed "he did not let him" adopt the lifestyle of the apostles. Christ insisted that God's kingdom could be better served if this man made his home his base of operation.

Was this an inferior calling? Judge by the results: "So the man went away and began to tell in the Decapolis how much Jesus had done for him. And all the people were amazed" (Mark 5:20). Christ called him not to leave everything behind, but instead to settle into his community—with all that implies as to shelter, possessions, and vocation—and to use his home and possessions to further the kingdom.

There were two callings—one to leave behind family and possessions, and the other to go back to them. But both callings served the same purpose: glorifying God and furthering his kingdom.

Jesus sent the twelve disciples out in pairs and told them not to take any food or money with them. They were to stay in houses and be fed by those who were receptive to their message (Mark 6:8-11). Again we see the two types of disciples. Traveling missionaries take nothing except what facilitates their travels (a staff, sandals, and the clothes on their back). The other is the "settled-in" disciple who provides shelter, food, and supplies for traveling missionaries. In order for the first type of disciple to survive and succeed, the second type of disciple must possess and provide. In order for some not to have possessions or permanent homes, and not to generate income, others must have possessions, homes, and incomes to care for themselves *and* the traveling missionaries.

God may occasionally change his specific instructions to those who are called to a traveling lifestyle. In Luke 22:35-36, Jesus tells the apostles that his earlier orders about what they were not to carry no longer applies. They are now to take with them a purse, a bag, and even a sword.

A Disciple's Eternal Values

In a probing call to discipleship, Jesus says,

> If anyone would come after me, he must deny himself and take up his cross and follow me. For whoever wants to save his life will lose it, but whoever loses his life for me and for the gospel will save it. What good

is it for a man to gain the whole world, yet forfeit his soul? Or what can a man give in exchange for his soul? (Mark 8:34-37)

The number of economic terms Jesus uses is striking: *save, lose, gain, forfeit, give,* and *exchange.* All disciples of Christ receive a radical call as to how they should view and handle their money and possessions. Whether they're called to leave possessions behind for kingdom purposes or to retain ownership for generous kingdom purposes, their eyes should be set on receiving gain in the next world more than this one. Today's money and possessions will be of no use when our souls are laid bare before the Creator. On that day, money and possessions will be seen either to have facilitated our mission or to have hindered it.

In Mark 10 we meet a rich young man who asks Jesus what he can do to inherit eternal life. At first, Jesus tells him to keep all the commandments. When the man replies that he has kept the commandments since his youth, Jesus tells him to leave everything and follow him (Mark 10:17-31). This is a crucial lifestyle passage, because some consider Christ's command here as a universal call so that those who don't follow it are not true disciples.

After the man tells Jesus that he's kept the commandments, "Jesus looked at him and loved him" (Mark 10:21). Christ cared about this rich man, and he discerned the inner workings of his heart. Based on this appraisal, Jesus issues a particular call. He makes a more sweeping financial demand than ever before—more than he had made to any of the disciples outside of the twelve, and perhaps more than he'd asked of some of the twelve. "'One thing you lack,' he said to the rich young man. 'Go, sell everything you have and give to the poor, and you will have treasure in heaven. Then come, follow me'" (Mark 10:21).

Jesus actually gives the man five commands: *go, sell, give, come,* and *follow.* Knowing the state of the man's heart, Christ issues the specific commands he knew were best.

There are two common errors in interpreting this passage. One is to conclude that Christ always calls his disciples to sell their possessions, give all to the poor, and go out as missionaries of faith, supported by the rest of the Christian community. But if this were true, there would be no "rest of the Christian community." We would all own nothing, have no place to stay, no way to travel, and no means of support.

The other error, more common and equally serious, is to conclude that God *never* calls his disciples to sell all and give to the poor. I spoke earlier of a young man in our church whose Bible study group talked him out of selling his house and giving all the money away, when he sensed God leading him to do so. I've found this to be a common experience among Christians, one that we should make every effort to correct.

When actress Lisa Whelchel was eighteen, starring in the popular *Facts of Life* television show, she heard a Christian speaker talk about thousands of starving children in Haiti. In her book, *The Facts of Life and Other Lessons My Father Taught Me*, she writes, "My eyes were opened to what a privileged life I lived and how totally unaware I was of what was going on in the rest of the world. I was profoundly moved and convicted."

When the service was over, she went to the front, sobbing, dropped her Rolex watch and her diamond and emerald ring into the speaker's coat pocket and asked him to sell them and give the money to help the poor. Whelchel went home full of conviction:

> I could easily live on 10 percent of my salary. I decided to sell my condominium and rent a nice apartment. It wasn't necessary for a single girl to live in a three-bedroom, two-story condo. And I certainly didn't need to be driving around in a Porsche. Selling the car and buying a moderate car would free up thousands of dollars. I had money invested in real estate across the country. If I sold it, the money would feed tens of thousands of children. It was a no-brainer. My zeal was strong. I knew that I had heard from God and that I was doing the right thing.

Unfortunately, those close to Whelchel thought her response was extreme, the product of fleeting guilt feelings. They told her it was "irrational." As clear as God's leading seemed, she says, "My resolve began to break down under the weight of their arguments, which seemed full of logic and wisdom. Eventually I abandoned the call, closed my eyes, and returned blindly to living a life that seemed to make sense."

She then tells the rest of the story:

> Less than ten years later, all that money was gone anyway. A chunk of it had been invested in a high-rise office building in Pittsburgh that went belly-up. Another significant portion was in Texas land that dried up during the oil crisis and was eventually foreclosed upon. When I got married, I sold my condo and bought a house during the California real estate boom in the 1980s, only to give it back to the bank three years later when the bottom fell out of the market. *The Facts of Life* was canceled, and I spent all the cash I had making payments on everything for as long as I could. At twenty-eight, I was broke.

Whelchel concludes, "[God] was trying to get me to invest my money in heaven, where it would be safe, but I thought it was too risky to take him at his word."[2]

I know a man who gave millions of dollars away one year when advisors thought he shouldn't. The next year, 80 percent of his holdings were gone. He told me, "I only wish now I'd given away a lot more."

Even if the financial numbers we deal with are much lower, the same principles apply to all of us. Why do we assume that God no longer calls "normal" Christians to give away most or all of what he has entrusted to them? And who do we think we are trying to talk people out of taking radical steps to follow Jesus?

Today there are still two kinds of disciples—one who gives up his income and possessions to further the cause in full-time ministry, and one who earns an income to generously support the same cause. (We should be careful not to discourage one another from either of these callings.)

There is not, however, a third kind of disciple, who does whatever he or she feels like with money and possessions and fails to use them for the kingdom. Such people are common today, but by New Testament standards they are not disciples.

A LIFESTYLE OF HOSPITALITY

Hospitality is commanded in Scripture (Romans 12:13; 1 Timothy 5:10; 1 Peter 4:9). Obedience to this command assumes that Christians have houses, beds, chairs, food, drink, medicine, and other provisions to share with travelers and the needy. John commends Gaius for his hospitality to "the brothers, even though they are strangers to you," then adds, "You will do well to send them on their way in a manner worthy of God. It was for the sake of the Name that they went out, receiving no help from the pagans. We ought therefore to show hospitality to such men so that we may work together for the truth" (3 John 5-8). By making available his material resources, one type of disciple can "work together for the truth" with the other.

Just because they have different lifestyles, one kind of disciple is no more spiritual than the other. Mary of Bethany, arguably the most devoted of all Christ's disciples, lived in a large house with considerable possessions, which she and her family regularly made available to the twelve. Judas Iscariot, on the other hand, "left all" to follow Christ.

Paul and his traveling ministry team were deeply grateful for the hospitality that facilitated their ministry (Acts 28:7; Romans 16:23). Without the support of those disciples called by Jesus to have and share possessions, those called to leave possessions behind couldn't carry out their mission.

In light of this distinction between the two types of disciples, what are we to do with Luke 14:33? "In the same way, any of you who does not give up everything he has cannot be my disciple." Does "give up" mean give away? It cannot, if we consider Christ's injunction that even the twelve should have sandals, staffs, and cloaks, and that other disciples should go back to their homes and provide food and housing. Clearly, some of Christ's disciples were relatively well-off people who retained their ownership of property and financially supported him (Luke 8:1-3).

Giving up everything must mean *giving over* everything to kingdom purposes, surrendering everything to further the one central cause, loosening our grip on everything. For some of us, this may mean ridding ourselves of most of

289

our possessions. But for *all* of us it should mean dedicating everything we retain to further the kingdom. (For true disciples, however, it cannot mean hoarding or using kingdom assets self-indulgently.)

DETERMINING A GOD-HONORING LIFESTYLE

Regarding our attitude toward wealth, Jesus gave commands. Regarding our possessions and lifestyle, he gave us principles. Jesus did not hand us a checklist of what we can and cannot own, and how we can or cannot spend money. Jesus didn't say just one thing about money and possessions. He said many things. They aren't random clashing noises, but a carefully composed melody and harmony to which we must carefully listen as we develop our lifestyles. If Jesus gave us a checklist, we would not have to depend prayerfully and thoughtfully on him to guide us into the kind of lifestyle that pleases him. On the one hand Christ says, "Do not store up for yourselves treasures on earth" (Matthew 6:19). On the other hand Paul gives the following instructions:

> Command those who are rich in this present world not to be arrogant nor to put their hope in wealth, which is so uncertain, but to put their hope in God, who richly provides us with everything for our enjoyment. Command them to do good, to be rich in good deeds, and to be generous and willing to share. In this way they will lay up treasure for themselves as a firm foundation for the coming age, so that they may take hold of the life that is truly life. (1 Timothy 6:17-19)

Note that Paul doesn't say what he easily could have: "Command those who are rich to stop being rich." The implication is that there is legitimate diversity in the amount of money and possessions held by Christians. Most early Christians weren't people of high social standing (1 Corinthians 1:26-29). "The brother in humble circumstances ought to take pride in his high position" (James 1:9). That "high position" was their position in Christ as God's heirs (Romans 8:17). Believers who lived in humble circumstances weren't second class but of equal importance and value (1 Corinthians 12:21-23). As a result of persecution, some believers lost their possessions and social status and became poor (Hebrews 10:34).

Other believers were well-to-do, which explains why Paul can address those he calls "rich" in the church. One of the first converts was the Ethiopian eunuch, who was "an important official in charge of all the treasury of Candace, queen of the Ethiopians" (Acts 8:27). He was a wealthy man with a huge sphere of influence. Cornelius had great political power and wealth. Mary, Martha, and Lazarus had a large home, as did Mary the mother of Mark, who had servants and in whose house "many people" gathered to pray (Acts 12:12). As the church spread before there were church buildings, meetings took place in the sizable homes of the more wealthy believers.

Priscilla and Aquila, accomplished tent makers, were people of means. Not only did a church meet in their house (1 Corinthians 16:19), they were able to leave their home in Rome, travel to Corinth, buy or rent another home (the one in which the church met), and rebuild their business. When they traveled with Paul, they likely did so as self-supported missionaries.

Pastors should encourage the poor not to be intimidated by more affluent church members and also not to pass judgment on them. They should likewise encourage the more affluent not to marginalize or look down on the less affluent, because God hates partiality (James 2:1-9). This is why pastors should not flatter the wealthy, and why ministries should reevaluate how they court donors. They should not cater to people's desire for recognition or to meet in luxurious accommodations.

There's no room for making wealth a source of security, or for lacking generosity or hospitality, or for an unwillingness to share. Still, Paul leaves a door open for Christians to be "rich in this present world"—but only if they carefully follow the accompanying guidelines related to their open-handed use of that wealth. The rich are not told they must take a vow of poverty. They are told essentially to take a vow of generosity. They are to be rich in good deeds, quick to share, and quick to part with their assets for kingdom causes. In doing so, they will lay up treasures in heaven.

Who are these "rich," and how rich are they? Nearly everyone reading this book is rich, both by first-century standards and by global standards today. As of 2002, two-thirds of all countries had a per capita income less than 10 percent of America's.[3]

If you made only $1,500 last year, that's more than 80 percent of the people on earth. Statistically, if you have sufficient food, decent clothes, live in a house or apartment, and have a reasonably reliable means of transportation, you are among the top 15 percent of the world's wealthy. If you have any money saved, a hobby that requires some equipment or supplies, a variety of clothes in your closet, two cars (in any condition), and live in your own home, you are in the top 5 percent of the world's wealthy.

A youth pastor told me, "You can't really talk to kids about giving, because they don't have any money." One look at their cars, clothes, video games, concerts, movies, fast food, visits to Starbucks, and so on clearly says otherwise. In fact, even without counting the possessions that Mom and Dad buy for them, the average Christian teenager in America has $1,500 disposable cash income—far more than most adults in the world.

> Pastors should encourage the poor not to be intimidated by more affluent church members and also not to pass judgment on them.

We must lay aside our illusions and realize that when Scripture speaks of the rich it is not talking about "them" but "us." Those we think of as rich today are really the megawealthy. But it is us, the rich, to whom Paul is speaking. The concession to rich Christians immediately follows a sobering warning of what awaits those who desire to get rich (1 Timothy 6:9-10). If we are rich (and we are), we aren't necessarily living in sin. But we are certainly under great temptation to sin. And most rich people succumb to that temptation.

We say, "There's nothing wrong with wanting to be rich." God says, "People who want to get rich fall into temptation and a trap and into many foolish and harmful desires that plunge men into ruin and destruction" (1 Timothy 6:9). We say, "There's nothing wrong with being eager to get rich." God says, "One eager to get rich will not go unpunished" (Proverbs 28:20). We say, "The rich have it made." Jesus says, "It is hard for a rich man to enter the kingdom of heaven" (Matthew 19:23).

Jesus speaks of the "deceitfulness of wealth" (Mark 4:19). The psalmist warns, "Though your riches increase, do not set your heart on them" (Psalm 62:10). As we saw in chapters 3 and 4, the dangers of materialism are far-reaching. We should not think that we're immune to the value-changing nature of wealth: "To suppose, as we all suppose, that we could be rich and not behave the way the rich behave, is like saying we could drink all day and stay sober."[4]

Although many will volunteer to bear them, riches do create burdens. Wealth is a relational barrier. It keeps us from having open relationships. The wealthy say, "I don't know if people like me for who I am or only because of my money." (Of course, there's a solution to this: *Give the money away and then you'll find out!*)

The wealthy are always trying to get out from under their tax burden. But to reduce estate taxes you must reduce your estate. Once again, giving solves the problem. In fact, every downside to wealth is immediately canceled out through giving. The man tired of being poor may not easily find alternatives, but the man tired of being rich can solve his dilemma through giving. Indeed, giving is the only antidote to materialism.[5]

Tricia Mayer has held a variety of marketing and business management positions at Microsoft. She wrote me:

> I've seen a generation of young people become wealthy in a very short period of time. I've also seen people lose their wealth through the "dot-com" demise and recession, and watched firsthand as people who put their security in wealth have been devastated. I've observed a lot about how money affects people in direct correlation with the values they place on it. Money is a blessing, but it is also a burden when we're given more than we need. Giving produces freedom 100 percent of the time—freedom from the bondage of things, freedom to receive more from

God, and freedom to be a conduit of blessing to others. Christians who have freely given their time, money, and themselves are the people who have changed eternity for themselves and countless others.

We all have our own call from God. We shouldn't be preoccupied with God's plan for others. Nor should we make comparisons. When Peter pressed Jesus concerning his plans for John, the Lord responded, "What is that to you? You must follow me" (John 21:22). There are some things that no Christian should do—such as hoard money, live in opulence, or fail to give generously. But there are other things that some Christians can freely do that others cannot (or choose not to do), such as own land, a home, a car, a business, go on certain vacations, or spend money in other ways.

"Money is a blessing, but it is also a burden when we're given more than we need. Giving produces freedom 100 percent of the time."

How much money and how many possessions can we safely keep? Enough to care for our basic needs and some wants, but not so much that we are distracted from our central purpose or that large amounts of money are kept from higher kingdom causes. Not so much that we become proud and independent of the Lord (Deuteronomy 8:13-14). Not so much that it distracts us from our purpose or insulate us from our sense of need to depend on God (Matthew 6:26-29).

Those who *want* to get rich set themselves up for spiritual disaster. Those who *happen* to be rich, simply as a result of circumstances, hard work, or wisdom, have done nothing wrong. They need not feel guilty—*unless* they withhold their riches (which are really God's) from his work, or their lifestyles are self-centered and excessive. According to author John Piper, "The issue is not how much a person makes. Big industry and big salaries are a fact of our times, and they are not necessarily evil. The evil is in being deceived into thinking a $100,000 salary must be accompanied by a $100,000 lifestyle. God has made us to be conduits of his grace. The danger is in thinking the conduit should be lined with gold. It shouldn't. Copper will do."[6]

Solomon suggests it can be unwise to remain rich: "Give me neither poverty nor riches, but give me only my daily bread. Otherwise, I may have too much and disown you and say, 'Who is the Lord?' Or I may become poor and steal, and so dishonor the name of my God" (Proverbs 30:8-9). Giving is the safety valve that releases the excess pressure of wealth.

ASKING THE HOLY SPIRIT FOR LIFESTYLE GUIDANCE

There is, of course, a subjective aspect to asking God's leading in our lifestyles and giving. But it's certainly not all subjective. We mustn't forget that he's already given us his leading in the form of Scripture. There's an objective nature to Christ's command not to lay up treasures on earth but in heaven. There's an objective nature to Paul's statement of why God entrusts riches to us—so we can help those who have too little (2 Corinthians 8:14-15) and be generous on every occasion (2 Corinthians 9:10-11). The Holy Spirit teaches us by reminding us of Christ's words (John 14:26). This isn't some vague, mystical, gut-level feeling, but revealed truth.

We can ask God about whether we should buy a nice, new, and unnecessary car. In the absence of an angel appearing and saying no, we typically assume that God's answer is yes. But if we read Matthew 6 and 2 Corinthians 8–9, the answer is clear. If we took these verses seriously, we might require an angel to appear and say yes before we would buy the unnecessary car rather than give God's money to help the poor and reach the lost. (Is this decision really as difficult as we sometimes make it?)

Whenever we have excess, giving should be our natural response. It should be the automatic decision, the obvious thing to do in light of Scripture and human need.

We dare not trust our instinctive promptings, which tend to be self-serving, leading us to rationalizations. Too often we imagine we are asking God's Spirit for guidance, when actually we are relying on our culture-driven values. No wonder our decisions end up looking suspiciously like everyone else's.

WHY LIVE MORE SIMPLY?
There are thousands of ways to live more simply. We can buy used cars rather than new, modest houses rather than expensive ones. We don't have to replace old furniture just for appearances. We can mend and wear old clothes, shop at thrift stores, give up recreational shopping, use fewer disposables, cut down on expensive convenience foods, and choose less expensive exercise and recreation. Some of us can carpool, use public transportation, or a bike instead of a car or second car. But these are things few of us will do unless we have clear and compelling reasons.

We should live more simply—and give more generously—because heaven is our home.
I talk about heaven in nearly all my books, fiction and nonfiction. We've lost sight of our citizenship in heaven, and it's hurt us in countless ways. In fact, the single greatest deterrent to giving—and to living more simply—is the illusion that this world is our home.

Suppose your home were in France and you were visiting the United States for eighty days, living in a hotel. Furthermore, suppose there's a rule that says you can't take anything back to France on your flight home, nor can you ship anything or carry back money with you. But while you're in America, you can earn money and send deposits to your bank in France. Question: Would you fill your hotel room with expensive furnishings and extravagant wall hangings? Of course not. Why? Because your time in America is so short, and you know you can't take it with you. It's just a hotel room! If you're wise, you'll send your treasures home, knowing they'll be waiting for you when you arrive.

We're only on earth for approximately eighty years—or sixty or forty or less. In the big picture, that's not much more than eighty days. Scripture says, "Each man's life is but a breath" (Psalm 39:5). Life here is like vapor breathed out on a cold day. Here one moment, gone the next. We're here on earth on a short-term visa. It's about to expire! Don't spend too much time and money and energy on your hotel room when instead you can send it on ahead.

We should live more simply—and give more generously— because it frees us up and shifts our center of gravity.

Copernicus sparked a revolution when he proved that the sun doesn't revolve around the earth. Giving will spark a Copernican revolution in the lives of Christians who understand that life doesn't revolve around the things of earth. In giving, we surrender our possessions to their proper center of gravity: God. Life no longer revolves around houses and land and cars and things. It revolves around God's kingdom in heaven. By giving, we relocate our treasures from earth to heaven. Giving—and the simpler living that results when we give— breaks us out of Money's orbit and sets up for us a new center of gravity, in heaven.

Giving and simpler living loosen the grip of materialism on our lives. Giving away what we don't need is the greatest cure for affluenza. How can we expect to embrace the Christian experience of Paul, Luther, Wesley, Müller, Carmichael, Taylor, and a host of others without also embracing their attitude toward possessions and the simpler lifestyle it fostered?

We should live more simply—and give more generously— because we're God's pipeline.

As we discussed in an earlier chapter, Christians are God's delivery people, through whom he does his giving to a needy world. We are conduits of God's grace to others. Our eternal investment portfolios should be full of the most strategic kingdom-building projects to which we can disburse God's funds. If we forget that we're God's stewards—his delivery drivers—it's like FedEx or UPS forgetting that what they carry in their trucks doesn't belong to them. When that happens, deliveries grind to a halt and people don't get what they need.

God comes right out and tells us why he gives us more money than we need. It's not so we can find more ways to spend it. It's not so we can indulge ourselves and spoil our children. It's not so we can insulate ourselves from needing God's provision. It's so we can give and give generously (2 Corinthians 8:14; 9:11).

We should live more simply—and give more generously—
because of the reward we'll receive in heaven and the joy it will bring us.

If I choose a smaller house here on earth and invest the savings in God's kingdom, God will give me eternal treasures in heaven that will make a big house on earth seem utterly trivial. Why settle for an expensive necklace now when by selling it and giving the money to meet needs it could contribute to an imperishable treasure in eternity?

We should live more simply—and give more generously—
because of the dire spiritual need of the world.

Suppose God wanted to reach the world for Christ and help an unprecedented number of suffering people. What might you expect him to put in the hands of his delivery people? Unprecedented wealth to meet all those needs and reach all those people? Well, he's done it, hasn't he? The question is, what are we doing with it?

John Piper makes this observation:

> Three billion people today are outside Jesus Christ. Two-thirds of them have no viable Christian witness in their culture. If they are to hear— and Christ commands that they hear—then cross-cultural missionaries will have to be sent and paid for. All the wealth needed to send this new army of good news ambassadors is already in the church. If we, like Paul, are content with the simple necessities of life, hundreds of millions of dollars in the church would be released to take the gospel to the frontiers. The revolution of joy and freedom it would cause at home would be the best local witness imaginable.[7]

We should live more simply—and give more generously—
because of the world's dire physical needs.

"[Agabus] stood up and through the Spirit predicted that a severe famine would spread over the entire Roman world. (This happened during the reign of Claudius.) The disciples, each according to his ability, decided to provide help for the brothers living in Judea. This they did, sending their gift to the elders by Barnabas and Saul" (Acts 11:28-30).

Here is the biblical pattern for giving: See a need, give to meet it. Giving according to our ability means living on less than God has entrusted to us. If he has entrusted us with a great deal, as he has most people reading this, it means living on far less so we can deliver the excess to the needy. That way they will not have too little and we will not have too much—exactly what God intends, according to 2 Corinthians 8:14.

"Live simply that others may simply live." Of course, there is not necessarily a direct correlation between my simple living and someone else being rescued from starvation or reached with the gospel. There's only a correlation if I use the resources I've freed up to feed the hungry and reach the lost. My ability to give while living simply assumes I will continue to make a decent wage. If I quit my job and go off to pursue simple living for simple living's sake, spending what little I earn on myself, what good does that do for anyone else?

In fact, if I try to make only enough money for my family's immediate needs, it may violate Scripture: "He who has been stealing must steal no longer, but must work, doing something useful with his own hands, that he may—"

That he may what? Have just enough to live on? No, "that he may *have something to share with those in need*" (Ephesians 4:28, italics mine). We should work not only to care for our families and because it's healthy, but also so that we can take the excess income and use it to help the needy.

Even though earning just enough to meet the needs of my family may *seem* nonmaterialistic, it's actually selfish when I could earn enough to care for others as well. The point of "living simply" is not so we can say no to money, but so that we can *use* money to say yes to God.

NEW MODELS OF SIMPLIFIED GENEROUS LIVING

After feeding the five thousand, Jesus told his disciples, "Gather the pieces that are left over. Let nothing be wasted" (John 6:12). If ever waste wasn't an issue, you would think it would be when the provision was miraculously provided! We should remember Christ's words, "Let nothing be wasted," when we look in our refrigerators and garbage cans and garages. Can you imagine the disciples sitting in a small circle and Jesus multiplying the loaves and fish in their midst until they are buried under piles of it while the multitudes go hungry? Unthinkable, isn't it? God provides excess not so it can be stored up but so it can be distributed to the needy.

> God provides excess not so it can be stored up but so it can be distributed to the needy.

Every local church also needs examples of other churches that are positive models of living simply and giving generously (2 Corinthians 8:1-2). When thousands of churches are giving more than half of their income to feed the hungry and reach the lost, when they are as excited about giving to the poor as they are about their building projects, the attitude will become contagious and the world will see God's grace at work. When the world—and other Christians—see the freedom of such living, they'll be drawn to it.

What keeps us from living on less? It's not just our love for things, it's our fear of loneliness or abnormality. If simple living were the norm in our churches, it would be much easier to live simply ourselves. But we don't want to be left out or seem weird. We need examples to follow, models of simpler lifestyles that we can observe firsthand to convince us it's really possible—and desirable. We need to see people we respect, people like us who choose to live differently. A mandate to "live simply" won't do it. It's easier to follow foot-prints than to follow orders. If most people in the church have new cars, beau-tiful homes, hot tubs, and cutting-edge entertainment centers, it's hard to remember these aren't what the church is here for.

One Christian told me, "When I look at the Bible, I get really convicted to change my lifestyle. But then I look around at all the other Christians who live like I do and I end up saying, 'It must be okay—everybody else lives this way too.'"

Most people assume that anyone who lives below the typical standard of living simply can't afford to buy any more. If they could, they would, right? Why not? It never occurs to them that some people might be choosing to live way below their means. This is why we must risk being transparent in order to learn from each other.

To turn the tide of materialism in the Christian community, we desper-ately need bold models of kingdom-centered living. Despite our need to do it in a way that doesn't glorify people, we must hear each other's stories about giv-ing or else our people will not learn to give. (See appendix E, "Should Giving Always Be Kept Secret?")

I believe that churches, Bible colleges, Christian liberal arts colleges, and seminaries should develop courses—preferably requirements, but at least elec-tives—not just about budgeting or personal financial planning but thorough biblical studies of stewardship and giving. The Christian community should be filled with people who set a cap on their lifestyles, giving away everything above that amount. We need to draw a line and stop accumulating beyond it. Give away everything else. That isn't even sacrificial giving, it's just giving ac-cording to our ability. Simple as it is, the models are so few and far between that people don't even conceive of how it could work.

"I guess I must be stupid," one person told me, "to think of downsizing our house and selling the second car and giving it to missions. I thought God was in it, but when I mentioned it to my Christian friends, they all gave me a blank stare." We need to hear each other's stories in order to raise rather than lower the bar for each other.

John Wesley's perspective was changed as a result of something that hap-pened to him while at Oxford. Consider the following story:

> [Wesley] had just finished buying some pictures for his room when one of the chambermaids came to his door. It was a winter day and he noticed that she had only a thin linen gown to wear for protection against the cold. He reached into his pocket to give her some money for a coat, and found he had little left. It struck him that the Lord was not pleased with how he had spent his money. He asked himself:
> "Will Thy Master say, 'Well done, good and faithful steward?' Thou

has adorned thy walls with the money that might have screened this poor creature from the cold! O justice! O mercy! Are not these pictures the blood of this poor maid?"

Perhaps as a result of this incident, in 1731 Wesley began to limit his expenses so he would have more money to give to the poor. He records that one year his income was £30, and his living expenses £28, so he had £2 to give away. The next year, his income doubled, but he still lived on £28 and gave £32 away. In the third year, his income jumped to £90; again he lived on £28, giving £62 away. The fourth year, he made £120, lived again on £28, and gave £92 to the poor.

Wesley preached that Christians should not merely tithe, but give away all extra income once the family and creditors were taken care of. He believed that with increasing income, the Christian's standard of giving should increase, not his standard of living. He began this practice at Oxford and he continued it throughout his life. Even when his income rose into the thousands of pounds, he lived simply and quickly gave his surplus money away. One year his income was slightly over £1,400; he gave away all save £30. He was afraid of laying up treasures on earth, so the money went out in charity as quickly as it came in. He reports that he never had as much as £100 at one time.

When he died in 1791, the only money mentioned in his will was the miscellaneous coins to be found in his pockets and dresser drawers. Most of the £30,000 he had earned in his lifetime he had given away. As Wesley said, "I cannot help leaving my books behind me whenever God calls me hence; but, in every other respect, my own hands will be my executors.[8]

John Wesley's royalties at one time gave him what today would be an annual income of $160,000. Yet he lived like someone today might at an income of $20,000. Sound radical? Why? Isn't it perfectly in keeping with Scripture? "Your plenty will supply what they need. . . . You will be made rich in every way so that you can be generous on every occasion" (2 Corinthians 8:14; 9:11). Perhaps you'll never be as radical as Wesley—I'm certainly not, but his example inspires me and makes me reevaluate my lifestyle and giving.

It helps a great deal to discuss these matters and make changes together with like-minded people who understand and support our commitment to change. This is one reason I highly recommend that you discuss the issues of this book with others, including your immediate family.

Once when I preached a message on money, some friends in our church took radical steps to increase their giving. Nanci and I realized they were applying my message with more trust and abandon than we were. As a result, we were challenged to further increase our own giving.

"Spur one another on toward love and good deeds" (Hebrews 10:24). How often, instead, do we lull each other into complacency and materialism?

Dixie Fraley, cofounder of the Orlando-based Foundation Forum, told me about friends of hers. She said, "They're such an example of the art of giving. Every year we try to outgive each other!" Why not? Isn't that spurring one another on? Don't we need to help each other raise the bar of giving so we can learn to jump higher? Shouldn't we be asking, "How can we spur each other on to greater and greater giving?"

"But we don't want to compare each other's giving." Yet Paul tells the Corinthians about the Macedonians' giving, saying he was making this comparison to challenge their own giving (2 Corinthians 8:8). Isn't it time we revoke our policy of silence and begin helping each other reevaluate our lifestyles and giving?

SIMPLE LIVING OR STRATEGIC LIVING?

During World War II when fuel was precious, billboards routinely asked motorists, "Is this trip necessary?" Every resource used for individual convenience was one less resource available for the nation's central concern: winning the war. Today, we're engaged in a great spiritual battle that requires great resources (Ephesians 6:12). Spending money on our own private concerns leaves less for the kingdom's central concern. We should ask, "Is this thing necessary? Does it contribute to my purpose in being here on this earth? Is this item an asset or liability to me as a soldier of Christ?"

The American church, taking its cue from our culture, has adopted a peacetime mentality. Consequently we live a peacetime lifestyle. But Scripture says we're at war. We should make sacrifices commensurate to this crisis, that we may win the war. Ralph Winter uses the term "wartime lifestyle."[9] We might also call it a "strategic" lifestyle. I find that description more helpful and precise than "simple" lifestyle. If I'm devoted to "simple living," I might reject a computer because it's modern and nonessential. But if I live a wartime or strategic lifestyle, the computer may serve as a tool for kingdom purposes. My computer is serving that purpose as I'm writing this book. Likewise, a microwave oven might free up our time to engage in kingdom causes. Simple living may be self-centered. Strategic living is kingdom centered.

Ralph Winter makes an intriguing proposal:

> The essential tactic to adopt a wartime lifestyle is to build on a pioneer mission perspective and do so by a very simple and dramatic method. Those who are awakened from the grogginess and stupor of our times can, of course, go as missionaries. But they can also stay home and deliberately and decisively adopt a missionary support level as their standard of living and their basis of lifestyle, regardless of their income.

This will free up an unbelievable amount of money—so much, in fact, that if a million average Presbyterian households were to live within the average Presbyterian minister's salary, it would create at least two billion dollars a year. Yet that happens to be only one-seventh of the amount Americans spend on tobacco. But what a mighty gift to the nations if carefully spent on developmental missions![10]

Of course, a wartime mentality can be taken to such an extreme that we feel it's unfaithful to enjoy any possessions, pleasures, or special activities. I'm thankful that in the midst of his command that the rich be generous, Paul tells them to put their hope in God, "who richly provides us with everything for our enjoyment" (1 Timothy 6:17). Even in wartime, it's important to have battle breaks. Soldiers need rest and recreation. Life isn't just utilitarian. There's nothing wrong with spending money for modest pleasures that renew and revive us, especially considering that our battle will last a lifetime.

I'm grateful to have fun possessions, such as a bicycle and tennis racket. They aren't necessary; yet they contribute to my physical and mental health. Our family spends money on vacations that aren't "necessary," yet they bring renewal and precious relationship-building opportunities. My wife and I sometimes go out to dinner, enriching our relationship and renewing our vigor to return to life's battles. We can give away much or most of our income yet still have breathing room for legitimate recreational spending.

If I have a wartime mentality, I won't look at my income as God's call to spend more, but rather as his provision to invest more in the cause. I might determine to live on a certain amount of money each year, an amount that allows some room for discretionary or recreational spending. All income beyond that I will give to God's kingdom purposes. (For the most part, Nanci and I have done this for the last twelve years, and we have never regretted it.) If he provides twice the amount of money I've designated for my living expenses, then I'll give away 50 percent of my income. If he provides four times that much, I'll give away 75 percent. If he provides ten times that much, I'll give away 90 percent. If my income decreases or family needs increase, the percentages will change, but our standard of living doesn't have to.

Too often we assume that God has increased our income to increase our standard of living, when his stated purpose is to increase our standard of giving. (Look again at 2 Corinthians 8:14 and 9:11).

I might determine to live on a certain amount of money each year, an amount that allows some room for discretionary or recreational spending. All income beyond that I will give to God's kingdom purposes.

Suppose a woman desires to go to work when the children are grown. Suddenly the family has a second income. Nearly always this second salary produces a higher standard of living. (Expenditures rise to meet income.) But why? One income has been sufficient until this point. If the cause of Christ is so worthy, why not devote the entire second income to it?

If you have a full-time job with an adequate income and also do other things that earn money (in my case, write books and receive money for speaking), why not give away 100 percent of that extra income to the Lord?

Do such proposals seem strange? If so, why? Have we forgotten that all Christ's disciples are committed to using their money and possessions to further his kingdom? Have we distanced ourselves so far from the battlefield that our peacetime lifestyle has left us comfortable and complacent, unfit for battle and indifferent to the battle's eternal stakes?

GOD LOVES RICH PEOPLE—ENOUGH TO TELL THEM THE TRUTH

When Jesus interacted with the rich young ruler, he "looked at him and loved him." When you love someone, you act in his best interest. What Jesus says next is 100 percent loving: "One thing you lack. . . . Go, sell everything you have and give to the poor, and you will have treasure in heaven. Then come, follow me" (Mark 10:21).

Jesus isn't giving the man an ultimatum because he doesn't care about him. He is making an offer of treasures far beyond anything the man had even dreamed of. Jesus isn't telling him, "You shouldn't care about treasures." He is saying, "You care about short-term treasures you can't keep. I'm offering you long-term treasures you'll never lose. I'm not telling you to turn away from treasures—I'm telling you to embrace the right treasures, the ones that really matter, the ones that will last forever."

But what is the young man's response? "At this the man's face fell. He went away sad, because he had great wealth" (Mark 10:22). He wasn't willing to give up perishable earthly treasures for heavenly treasures that will never perish. With sadness, Jesus says to his disciples "How hard it is for the rich to enter the kingdom of God! . . . It is easier for a camel to go through the eye of a needle than for a rich man to enter the kingdom of God" (Mark 10:23, 25).

At this, "the disciples were even more amazed, and said to each other, 'Who then can be saved?'" Jesus assures them that although it wasn't humanly possible, God could save a rich man too. Then Peter says, "We have left everything to follow you!" Instead of rebuking him for thinking of himself, Jesus says, "I tell you the truth, . . . no one who has left home or brothers or sisters or mother or father or children or fields for me and the gospel will fail to receive a hundred times as much in this present age (homes, brothers, sisters, mothers, children and fields—and with them, persecutions) and in the age to come, eternal life" (Mark 10:29-30). Both short-term rewards and eternal rewards await any who will follow Christ's call to put all our money and possessions—which really aren't ours and which can neither satisfy nor last—into his hands.

"A biblical lifestyle will necessarily recognize itself as being in opposition to the prevailing values and lifestyle of its culture. It is informed by a different view of reality."[11] This view of reality isn't harsh or austere, but exciting and joyful. It need not lead to asceticism or bare-bones living. Neither should it lead to condemnation of Christians who have bigger incomes or feel greater liberty to possess more than we do. Rather, it emphasizes the riches of God's eternal kingdom. Those who hold such a view are sincerely grateful for the refreshing pleasures and helpful possessions of this life. They simply realize how fleeting it all is: "We look not at the things which are seen, but the things which are not seen; for the things which are seen are temporal, but the things which are not seen are eternal" (2 Corinthians 4:18, NASB).

Regardless of what material things surround us, this view of reality remains focused on the ultimate pleasure of possessing Christ. Our Lord is pleased when we live in a way that draws attention to the greatest pleasure and possession of life—the Person who made us (and for whom we were made) and the place he's making for us (and for which we were made).

CHAPTER 17

Debt: Borrowing and Lending

Their property held them in chains . . . chains which shackled their courage and choked their faith and hampered their judgment and throttled their souls. They think of themselves as owners, whereas it is they rather who are owned: enslaved as they are to their own property, they are not the masters of their money but its slaves. CYPRIAN

God opposes usury and greed, yet no one realizes this because it is not simple murder and robbery. Rather, usury is a more diverse, insatiable murder and robbery.
MARTIN LUTHER

A man jumped off a twenty-story building. Onlookers were terrified, but the man seemed perfectly calm. As he plummeted by the window of a fifth-story apartment, he looked at the wide-eyed occupant and said, "Everything's all right so far."

This apocryphal story reminds me of the attitude many people take toward debt in its early stages: "Everything's all right so far." But what happens to most debtors later is equivalent to what happened to the man when he finally reached the ground.

The average American family devotes one-fourth of its spendable income to outstanding debts.[1] Since 1945, consumer debt in the United States has multiplied thirty-one times. The IRS calculates that the average filer spends ten times more paying off interest on debts than he gives to charitable causes.

If all evangelical Christians were out of debt, hundreds of millions of dollars would be freed up for God's kingdom. Our families would be stronger, because financial pressures caused by indebtedness are major factors in more than half of divorces.

We speak with disdain of politicians not limiting their spending to available revenues. But our national debt is an extension of the same irresponsible mentality many of us demonstrate in our own lives.

Home mortgages, auto loans, and credit cards all seem normal to us, but debt is an aberration that evokes severe warnings from God's Word. We must take a closer look at debt to understand the serious problem it poses.

THE NATURE OF DEBT

Credit is a grant to pay later for what's received now. Interest is the fee that the creditor receives and the debtor pays for his grant. Whenever a person goes into debt, he obtains money he hasn't earned. In exchange for the money or possessions he presently receives, he mortgages his future time, energies, and assets.

One hundred years ago, debt was regarded as an earned privilege for the few. Now it's seen as an inalienable right for all. Borrowing has become an integral part of our lives. Why do I receive mailings nearly every week telling me that $5,000 or $10,000 or $20,000 has already been approved for me and to receive it I need only send in the enclosed agreement? Why do banks and credit companies repeatedly beg me to borrow from them, listing dozens of ways I could use the money? Why are people so anxious to lend me money? The answer is simple—they want me to borrow because they will profit greatly from my debt.

Why does a credit card statement showing you owe $500 say that you only need to pay $35 this month? Because the creditors don't want the debt repaid in full. If most people paid the full amount at the end of the month, the lenders would go bankrupt. They must get you to borrow, then pay back less than you owe for a long enough period of time that the money you pay them in interest is enough to make their profits.

Our self-centered, debt-centered economy is like those electronic bug-zappers. They emit a light attractive to insects that blissfully fly right into the trap, only to be killed.

"That's a cool-looking stereo. And what a great sale! I don't have any cash, but that's no problem . . . here's my Visa."

ZAP!

WHAT DOES SCRIPTURE SAY ABOUT DEBT?

Proverbs sounds the alarm against debt (Proverbs 1:13-15; 17:18; 22:26-27; 27:13). Those in debt are warned to get out as soon as possible (Proverbs 6:1-5). Debt is bondage: "The rich rule over the poor, and the borrower is servant to the lender" (Proverbs 22:7).

The *New American Standard Bible* translates Romans 13:8 as follows: "Owe nothing to anyone." This would appear to prohibit debt. The New International Version reads, "Let no debt remain outstanding." This translation allows debt but only under conditions that it be paid off as soon as possible.

Hudson Taylor and Charles Spurgeon believed that Romans 13:8 prohibits debt altogether. However, if going into debt is always sin, it's difficult to understand why Scripture gives guidelines about lending and even encourages lending under certain circumstances (see appendix C, "Lending Money, Charging Interest, and Co-signing a Loan.") If debt is always sin, then lending is aiding and abetting sin, and God would never encourage it.

We shouldn't normally borrow and should always pay off debt as soon as possible.

Being in a position to lend money to others is a blessing, whereas being the borrower is a curse (Deuteronomy 28:44-45). Unless there's an overwhelming need to borrow, it's unwise for God's children to put themselves under the curse of indebtedness. At the very least, Romans 13:8 proves we shouldn't normally borrow and should always pay off debt as soon as possible. The common practice of borrowing monthly and making partial payments violates this principle.

"The borrower is servant to the lender" doesn't absolutely forbid debt, but it's certainly a strong warning. God says we're not to be servants of men (1 Corinthians 7:23). How can we be fully free to serve God when we're indentured to human creditors?

The Mosaic Law reflects a strong connection between debtors and slaves. Both debts and slavery were canceled in the year of Jubilee. More often than not, the person was a slave because he was a debtor (Deuteronomy 15:2, 12). Unable to pay back debts, he was sold into slavery. Few sights are more pathetic than the well-meaning person who goes further and further into debt, one day waking up to realize he's a lifelong slave.

Nehemiah tells of a terribly desperate time in Israel's history:

> Others were saying, "We are mortgaging our fields, our vineyards and our homes to get grain during the famine." Still others were saying, "We have had to borrow money to pay the king's tax on our fields and vineyards. . . . We have to subject our sons and daughters to slavery. Some of our daughters have already been enslaved, but we are powerless, because our fields and our vineyards belong to others." (Nehemiah 5:3-5)

In a time of famine, the ultimate act of despair was to mortgage fields, vineyards, and homes. Clearly, such things should never be done under normal circumstances. Yet today, in the most affluent society in human history, it's routine for people to mortgage fields, vineyards, and homes! Many wealthy people borrow every year to pay their taxes. Those who appear to be powerful "are powerless, because our fields and our vineyards belong to others."

Debt is an extreme measure, resorted to in times of national crisis. Yet today it's so normative that Christians routinely undertake it without prayerful consideration and counsel. "Everybody else does it—why not me?" Debt is increasingly common for the young. American 18- to 25-year-olds, including college students, have an average unpaid credit card balance of $1,700.[2]

Scripture discourages debt. It condemns the misuse of debt and the failure to repay debts (Psalm 37:21; Proverbs 3:27-28). If we take God's Word seriously, we should avoid debt. In those rare cases where we go into debt, we should make every effort to get out as soon as possible (2 Kings 4:1; Matthew 5:25-26; 18:23-24). The question isn't, "Why not go into debt?" but why? Unless the answer is extraordinarily convincing, we shouldn't do it.

SOME INITIAL QUESTIONS BEFORE GOING INTO DEBT

The best credit risks are those who won't borrow in the first place. The worst credit risks are those who always think they need to borrow. Without a firm conviction against going into debt, people will inevitably find the "need" to borrow. Those with convictions against borrowing will always find ways to avoid it. (In other words, they'll choose to spend less money.) The more you're inclined to go into debt, the more probable it is that you shouldn't.

The basic question is this: Is the money I will be obligated to repay, and the bondage it will create, worth the value I'll receive by getting the money or possessions now?

When it comes time for me to repay my debt, what new needs will I have that my debt will keep me from meeting? Or what new wants will I have that will tempt me to go further into debt?

After warning against the dangers of indebtedness, several Christian books offer examples of cases when borrowing is appropriate. These exceptions include purchasing a house or a business, going to college, and even buying cars and furniture. Others make exceptions for so-called secured loans, those backed by collateral, including houses or cars that could be sold if the debtor can't pay. Typically, we rationalize that our particular situation is one of these exceptional cases. But we should never go into debt unless there are compelling reasons. If we think our situation is an exception, we should seek out several wise counselors to see if they agree. (I emphasize "wise" to discourage you from seeking counsel from someone who believes that debt is normative.)

DEEPER QUESTIONS ABOUT DEBT

Before we incur a debt, we should ask ourselves some basic spiritual questions: Is not having enough resources to pay cash for what I want God's way of telling me it isn't his will for me to buy it? Is it possible that this thing may have been God's will but I don't have the resources to buy it because of past unwise decisions? If a lack of wisdom has put me in a position where I can't afford to buy something, wouldn't I do better to learn God's lesson by forgoing it until—by his provision and my diligence—I save enough money?

The "debt mentality" involves six key assumptions:

- We need more than God has given us.
- God doesn't know best what our needs are.
- God has failed to provide for our needs, forcing us to take matters into our own hands.
- If God doesn't come through the way we think he should, we can find another way. Abraham tried this approach, which proved dishonoring to God (Genesis 16:2).
- Just because today's income is sufficient to make our debt payments, tomorrow's will be too.
- Our circumstances won't change—our health will be good, we'll keep our present job, our salary will keep up with inflation, and God won't direct us to another job with a lower salary or lead us to increase our giving.

It's one thing to trust God to provide for our present needs (Matthew 6:33). It's another to presume upon him by dictating (via a decision to incur debt) the terms of his future provision. By choosing to go into debt, we twist God's arm to provide not only for our needs, but also our wants.

Do we believe God knows best what our needs are? Debt spends money we don't have. So isn't our decision to go into debt proof that we believe we need more than God has given us? If we don't have the resources to buy something, and if we feel such need for it that we're borrowing to get it, aren't we saying God has failed to meet our needs?

If God knows best, and if he knows what we need, then why hasn't he provided sufficient funds? Is he encouraging us to pray for provision rather than take things into our own hands by borrowing? In this age where we seem unwilling to wait for anything, does God want us to learn what it means to "wait on the Lord" (Psalm 27:14; Isaiah 30:18)?

Some say, "I'll just fill out the loan application. If it goes through, I'll take that as a sign God wants me to borrow the money." But just because a lender is willing to give us a loan doesn't mean God approves of our decision to borrow the money, any more than a clerk's willingness to sell us a lottery ticket would indicate that God approves of gambling.

MORE QUESTIONS ABOUT DEBT

Before we go into debt, we should ask ourselves the following questions:

1. Is debt our way of getting around depending on God? (Why trust God to provide when we can get a loan?)
2. Is debt our means of short-circuiting the God-created means of acquisition—including work, saving, planning, self-discipline, patience, and waiting for divine provision?

3. What message are we sending to God when we go into debt rather than live on what he has provided? What are we really saying when we take out a loan? How does it reflect on our view of God? What are we saying about his sovereignty, goodness, wisdom, or timing?

4. What effect will going into debt today have on our ability or willingness to tithe and give voluntary offerings tomorrow?

5. What effect will today's decision to go into debt have on tomorrow's freedom to follow God wherever he wants us to go?

6. By taking out a loan that commits us to make payments over a number of years, are we presuming upon God? (Certainly, if we will require more income to make the payments, we're presuming on God. We may "know" that we'll receive a promotion and pay raise in September, but God hasn't guaranteed it. Plans change, companies go out of business, and employees fail to get "certain" promotions.)

7. Although our income today might be enough to make debt payments over the next twenty years, is it right to assume that we'll continue to generate the same level of income? (Many people's income increases over the years, but many others' decreases. Many incur increased financial commitments beyond their control, such as health-related expenses or caring for an elderly relative. People get laid off. Has God promised that can't happen to us?)

8. Are we mortgaging the future to pay for the whims of the present? Are we mortgaging God by supposing to commit him to pay off something he may disapprove of?"

9. Is debt our way of getting around depending on God? of circumventing prayer, patience, and waiting on God to provide?

10. If we "must" go into debt to provide for our "needs," is it because our "needs" are really wants in disguise? Have we spent so much money on our wants that there's not enough left for our needs? Have we robbed God and forfeited his financial blessing by failing to give him the firstfruits?

11. Have we really exhausted all other avenues to avoid going into debt? Have we given up expensive activities, hobbies, and memberships, and liquidated valuable possessions? (Often, we think we have no choice but to go into debt, when in fact we're making many unnecessary choices that drive us toward it.)

One of the strongest arguments for not going into debt is that we're not God. We're not sovereign, omniscient, or omnipotent. James 4:14 warns that we cannot know what will happen tomorrow. And if we don't know and cannot control all that the future holds, how can we be sure that we can pay off new debts? We can be certain that God will provide for our basic material needs if we seek first his kingdom (Matthew 6:25-34), but where does the Bible promise that God will provide for all the debts we incur through our own greed, impatience, or presumption? If we are seeking first his kingdom, will we put ourselves in bondage to debt?

WHAT ABOUT BORROWING TO BUY A HOUSE?

Many financial counselors put home mortgages in a different category from other debts. One reason is that the loan is secured by the house's equity. If financial crises arise and the payments can't be made, the home can be sold and the equity—which is the current sale value of the house minus the amount still owed on the mortgage—can be regained. A case can certainly be made for borrowing to buy a reasonably priced house instead of renting. Although rental rates on houses may increase as much as 3 to 6 percent annually, the payments on a straight thirty-year mortgage remain constant throughout the life of the loan. Unless the economy slumps, or the house is located in an area with a depressed economy—and let me emphasize that both sometimes happen—the value of the house may also increase at 3 to 6 percent (or more) annually.

Unfortunately, many aspiring homeowners end up buying a house that's out of their range. One common formula for figuring out what's affordable is that the purchase price of a home shouldn't be more than two-and-a-half times the family's gross annual income. (But only count the income of the primary breadwinner—God may lead a wife and mother to quit her job for the benefit of the children. Housing decisions based on two incomes often prove disastrous, creating temptations to neglect parental responsibilities.)

The monthly payment for a home mortgage, including taxes and insurance, shouldn't be much more than people are willing to pay for rent. Most of the monthly mortgage payment goes for interest, but there are tax deductions that will reduce the net cost. Money paid for rent isn't tax deductible and doesn't build equity; on the other hand, people always spend more on fixtures and decorations when they buy. So, borrowing for a home is sometimes wise and sometimes not.

Not all debt is the same. I'm sympathetic to farmers, accident victims, the unemployed, abandoned spouses, and others who find themselves in situations where, after prayer and evaluation, debt seems the best or only alternative. In such cases we need to trust God to help us get back out of debt as soon as possible.

Trust is believing God will take care of our basic needs. When we go into debt, however, we usually don't do it to meet our needs but to fulfill our wants. We all need shelter, but do we need a particular house in a certain neighborhood? We all need food, but do we need to eat out? We need clothes, but do we need those with designer labels?

Often we define our wants as needs. Through debt we unconsciously try to maneuver God into a position where he's obligated to "provide" in the form of our future payments. In a blasphemous role reversal, we set up the rules of the game and then expect God to play by them. Assuming the role of Master, we demote God to the obedient genie, who exists to underwrite our causes and fulfill our agendas. In such cases debt is not merely unwise, but evil.

WHEN DEBT IS ESPECIALLY DANGEROUS

God sometimes disciplines us by making us face the consequences of unnecessary debt. When we go into debt for illegitimate reasons, we go on our own. God isn't party to our decision, and he isn't obligated to fulfill our financial commitment.

> It's our intention never to go into debt again. If we do, it will only be after carefully calculating the cost.

We bought our house in 1978 with a large down payment. Although we signed a thirty-year contract at a good interest rate, we increased the size of our payments in order to pay the loan off in thirteen years. By getting out of debt as soon as possible, we minimized both the amount and the duration of our indebtedness. Only two months after our last payment, our income was drastically decreased. With no house payment, we were able to get by on much less. Although we're convinced our original decision to borrow for a home purchase was right, it's our intention never to go into debt again. If we do, it will only be after carefully calculating the cost. Although we don't believe that debt is always wrong, we've frequently witnessed disastrous consequences of unwise indebtedness.

1. Debt is especially dangerous when a possession's resale value is less than what is owed.

Most purchases are high-depreciation items, including cars, clothes, and furniture. As soon as we buy such things, we typically cannot turn around and sell them without a significant loss. (The moment you sign your name on a contract to buy a new car, you lose thousands of dollars that you cannot recoup.) If we buy an asset that can definitely be resold at or above its original cost, we can at least get out of the debt by surrendering the asset. The steeper the depreciation, the greater the risk in a purchase and the greater our presumption in incurring debt.

Who can know which assets will appreciate? For years, many people in our area thought that houses always appreciate—yet many had to sell their homes during economic downturns for less than they paid. God and his principles are certain. The economy is not.

2. Debt is especially dangerous when it tempts us to violate our convictions.

A Christian couple at our church assumed a large home mortgage that depended on both their incomes. When the wife became pregnant, they realized that to keep the house they'd have to violate their convictions against leaving their child in a day-care center while the mother worked.

Whenever we make lifestyle decisions that tempt us to violate our convictions, the consequences are severe. This couple should never have put themselves in that situation. But they could have recognized their error, asked God's forgiveness, and taken whatever losses were necessary to get out of bondage and into housing affordable for a single income. Instead, they opted to provide a beautiful house for their children to grow up in while robbing them of something far more important—the presence of their mother. In seeking a higher standard of living, this couple ended up sacrificing a higher standard of life. They and their children (now grown) paid a terrible price.

3. Debt is especially dangerous when we're tempted to rob our primary creditor (God) to pay our secondary creditors (people).

Some Christians give nothing to God, while others reduce their giving to make monthly payments on conveniences. I've heard people say that it would be a "poor witness" not to pay their bills. They suppose that God would have them pay their creditors rather than give him the firstfruits. One Christian financial counselor routinely advises people not to give anything to God unless they are completely out of debt. (Some have received this advice from Consumer Credit Counseling Service, a service I otherwise recommend.)

If we're faithful in our giving to God, only then can we look to him for help in finding the resources to pay others. God says when his people give him tithes and freewill offerings, he will "throw open the floodgates of heaven and pour out so much blessing that you will not have room enough for it" (Malachi 3:10). Isn't that exactly what people need if they want to get out of debt? Not giving is never a financial solution—it's a source of financial problems. God tells his people that because they spent money on themselves that they should have given to him, he put holes in their purses (Haggai 1:2-11). Jesus says that with the measure we give to God it will be given back to us (Luke 6:38). The more serious our financial problems, the more critical it is that we do what God says will result in his provision—give!

> If we're faithful in our giving to God, only then can we look to him for help in finding the resources to pay others.

A creditor may say, "Nobody should give to their church until they pay me off." But the firstfruits aren't owed to the Church, they're owed to God. Those who put God first are nearly always more responsible money handlers. Ultimately, they will pay off their human creditors. If creditors see that someone is making disciplined lifestyle choices, they will usually respect his or her commitment to give.

God will not eliminate the consequences of our unwise decisions. If by giving to God we can no longer afford to make payments on a loan, then we need to liquidate our assets, take losses where we must, and cut spending to a minimum to eliminate the payments. But we should never rob God—not for any reason, and certainly not to compensate for our self-indulgence!

4. Debt is especially dangerous when our monthly payments leave us little freedom to respond to the Holy Spirit's promptings to give generously to meet others' needs.
I'm speaking of freewill giving, above and beyond the tithe. Life brings numerous opportunities to meet others' needs. This may involve giving cash, buying someone groceries, or taking them out to lunch. If our indebtedness leaves us unable to respond to God's promptings, we've robbed ourselves and others of blessings.

5. Debt is especially dangerous when it restricts our freedom to respond to the Holy Spirit's call to move or change.
God might desire to relocate us or change our job. How deeply rooted are we? How dependent are we on our current income level? How irreversibly committed are we to the possessions we've amassed and the financial obligations they entail? Are we so deeply obligated to maintaining a debt-oriented lifestyle that we can't escape from it?

If God called you today to go to the mission field, how long would it take you to free yourself from your financial responsibilities in order to follow him? If God directed you today to go to Asia to share the gospel, or to go to Africa to work as a carpenter or serve as a nurse, how would you respond? Would you dismiss the thought because your debts demand a monthly income that immobilizes you?

Does it seem impossible for you to pull up stakes in response to God's leading because debt has driven the stakes so deep? Has your borrowing robbed you of a pilgrim mentality? Has your indebtedness so deafened you to God's voice that you wouldn't even hear his call to pull up stakes?

THE CONSEQUENCES OF DEBT
What are some of the consequences of a debt-laden lifestyle?

1. Debt lingers. The new boat is fun for a while, but two years later, when it's sitting in storage, the motor needs repair, and the kids don't want to ski anymore, we're still paying for it.

2. Debt causes worry and stress. Stress experts say that the bigger a person's mortgage (or any debt), the bigger the stress. Debt is a serious enemy of mental health.

3. Debt causes denial of reality. We drive our bank-financed cars, running on credit card gas, to open a department-store charge account so we can fill our savings and loan-funded homes with installment-purchased furniture. We're living a lie and hocking the future to finance it. When creditors call, many people won't answer, believing that somehow they can go right on spending money they don't have. One day it catches up—but by then integrity, relationships, and credibility have been ruined.

4. Debt leads to dishonesty. "The check's in the mail" isn't funny when you've heard it repeatedly from a Christian brother who is enslaved to debt—and now to dishonesty. Some people lie on credit applications, not revealing debt for fear they'll be disqualified for further loans. Others desperately resort to criminal acts to try to keep up with their debt payments.

5. Debt is addictive. There are striking comparisons between debtors and drug addicts. The way out of both addictions can be very difficult. Those in debt with one income will almost always go into debt with two incomes, just as they will if the one income is doubled. Ninety-eight percent of the time debt is an internal problem, not an external one. It isn't a matter of insufficient funds but insufficient self-control.

6. Debt is presumptuous. Scripture says the just shall live by faith. The borrower, however, lives by presumption. Undertaking any debt is a gamble that our future income will be sufficient to make payments. The Bible says we don't know what a day may bring forth and we should not presume (Proverbs 27:1).

7. Debt deprives God of the chance to say no or to provide through a better means. God can give us direction either by providing funds or withholding them. When we borrow, we eliminate that second option and thereby blur God's leading. If we really need something, there are alternatives to debt. One of them is to accumulate savings that will allow us a margin on which to draw when needed. But if the money for a need isn't there, our first course should be to seek provision from God, not the banker (John 14:13-14).

8. Debt is a major loss of opportunity. Our loss isn't simply the interest we're paying. Our true loss is the difference between the money we're losing and the money we could have earned with it. Worse yet, debt is a loss of opportunity to invest in eternity. Perhaps the greatest tragedy of debt is that it results in diminished giving, loss of opportunity to help others, and loss of eternal rewards.

9. Debt ties up resources and makes them unavailable for the kingdom of God. Whenever we've taught on giving at our church, many people say: "Now that I understand God's principles of giving, I'd love to double or triple our giving, or even more. But we're so strapped with debt, it's just impossible." Past unwise decisions inhibit present and future generosity. The solution is not to shrug our shoulders helplessly, but to give as much as we can now and commit ourselves to get out of financial bondage so we can give more in the future.

ILLUSIONS ABOUT DEBT

Our desire to have certain things clouds our thinking and leads us to rationalize by going into debt. Here are some of our primary illusions:

1. "The money we borrow is ours." In fact, borrowed money belongs to us no more than a lawnmower we borrow from a neighbor. We must return borrowed money as surely as we must return a borrowed car.

2. "The amount we borrow is the amount we'll end up paying back." We will end up paying back far more than we borrow. If we buy a $200,000 house with a $20,000 down payment, borrowing $180,000 at 7.25 percent on a thirty-year contract, our $200,000 house will actually cost $442,000. So why call it a $200,000 house when we're actually paying well over twice that much?

3. "Borrowing actually saves us money because of the tax benefits." If we're in the 20 percent tax bracket, whenever we spend $100 on deductible interest (not all interest is deductible), then that means we've saved twenty dollars, right? Wrong. We haven't saved $20; we've spent $80.

When we bought our home, we were advised to take out the longest term loan possible because of the great tax savings generated by deductible interest. When I looked it over, I realized that desiring to pay more interest in order to get tax savings was like giving someone $100 in exchange for $20, then bragging that I'd come out $20 ahead. Of course, those in higher tax brackets receive a larger "rebate" on their interest. But this doesn't change the deficit nature of debt. When we're in debt, we're under obligation. Our desire should be to pay *less* interest over time, not more.

4. "It's foolish to pay back a loan that has lower interest than your money can make somewhere else." This is the philosophy of "using other people's money." Although it may appear to be valid on paper, it overlooks a critical element. Debt is a real burden, not an imaginary one. Removing debt is removing a burden. As long as we owe money, we're a servant. Someone else has a hold on our assets. There's a great mental and spiritual release when we get out of debt. Scripture says we must let no debt remain outstanding (Romans 13:8). It doesn't add "unless we can get higher interest on our money somewhere else."

I can't adequately describe the freedom we experienced by paying off our house early twelve years ago. Even if we could have made more money in another fashion, getting out of debt was tremendously liberating. It also helped immeasurably in facing the major financial challenge that followed only a few months later. We had no way of knowing what was coming, but God did.

THE LURE OF HOUSES AND CARS

Owning a home is not a God-given right—and it may or may not be a wise financial choice. People are fond of saying, "Renting is like pouring money down the drain." Not so. When you rent, you get what you pay for—a place to live! It's also incorrect to say that buying a house always pays off. Often it does, but not always.

Even when a home is appreciating in value it has hidden costs that renters don't have to pick up. A monthly house payment doesn't include the cost of replacing the door, fixing the plumbing, hiring someone to clean the sewer line, fixing the broken garage door, or rebuilding the sagging deck. Nor does it include having to repair or replace the refrigerator, hot-water heater, or dishwasher.

On the other hand, rental property repair expenses have to be paid for somehow, and because the landlord isn't in business to lose money, he passes on those costs to the renter in the form of higher rental rates. If the decision is made to buy instead of rent, make certain the house is in good condition and see that repairs and improvements are budgeted. Most homeowners find that the growing equity in a house, through debt retirement and property value appreciation, more than compensates for repairs and replacement costs. On the other hand, people spend more discretionary income on houses. Often they become more reluctant to move and less flexible to God's leading to go overseas or serve elsewhere.

If you do buy a house, be sure it's well within your budget.

If you do buy a house, be sure it's well within your budget. Don't allow a real estate agent to show you houses above your budget. Anything you look at will become a temptation and cause dissatisfaction with what you can actually afford.

We have an unlimited capacity to rationalize overspending on houses and cars. Studies in The Wall Street Journal prove that it's far less expensive to maintain a used car than buy a new one. "The cheapest car anyone can ever own is always the car they presently own," and "The longer a car is driven, the cheaper it becomes to operate."[3]

Yet when we get the "car bug," we make irrational decisions. A man "on a tight budget" tried to explain how he'd made a wise decision buying a brand-new car that got forty miles per gallon to replace his old paid-for car (still running fine) that got only twenty-five miles per gallon. This man had committed himself to paying $270 per month in order to "save" $30 per month. He was coming out $240 per month behind. Given the high depreciation on his new car, by the time he was finished with his payments it would be worth little more than his old, fully depreciated car. Yet his desire for the new car was so strong it overrode all reason, convincing him he'd made a wise "investment."

CREDIT CARDS

Seventy-five thousand people each day in the United Sates receive approval for Visa and MasterCard credit cards. For many, it's a turn into a downward spiral. Finance companies trip over themselves in their attempts to persuade consumers to get another credit card. They give prizes just for filling out an application form. How easy is it to get credit in America? One man with an income of $27,000 owns more than 800 credit cards. His credit line is $9 million per month.

In 1996, USA Today claimed that the average American household owed

$4,010 in credit card debt.[4] (This included households that didn't own any credit cards.) In 2000, "The American Credit Counselors Corporation estimated the average American credit card holder owes $13,000 to credit card companies." The National Association of Colleges and Employers reports that 22 percent of college students owe more than $7,500 on credit cards.[5]

Credit cards facilitate impulse buying, which is nearly always unnecessary and self-indulgent. When using credit, consumers buy more, buy what they don't need, and pay more for it. Why? Because credit cards lie to us—they make us think we have money when we really don't.

> **Considering that only a century ago it was generally considered a sin for Christians to go into debt, it's amazing that credit cards have been so widely accepted in the Christian community.**

Considering that only a century ago it was generally considered a sin for Christians to go into debt, it's amazing that credit cards have been so widely accepted in the Christian community. Christian ministries and increasing numbers of churches accept credit card donations. Many Christian colleges sponsor their own credit card for alumni, encouraging them to use it regularly because a small amount of money from each purchase is "given" to the college by the credit card company.

Like being handed the controls of a deadly weapon with a hair trigger, many people are propelled by their credit cards into irresponsible debt that entails exorbitant interest, often 15 to 20 percent annually. (And even when it's under 10 percent, it adds up quickly.) The person with a $2,000 balance (at 19.5 percent interest) is told he can pay just $75. But he doesn't realize that the first $32.50 of that $75 is interest. He goes right on charging "sale" items and digging an ever deeper hole.

If you carry a $7,000 balance on an 18 percent credit card and pay the 2 percent minimum payment each month, you'll end up paying more than $20,000 for that $7,000. All those things you bought at half price? They may cost you three times what you think they did.

Some people use credit cards for the convenience, paying off the full amount owed on every statement, so they don't ever pay interest costs. We do this ourselves, and in twenty-five years we have never paid any interest. This approach has advantages, but it also has drawbacks. Citibank calculates that a consumer using a credit card will buy 26 percent more than he would if he were carrying cash, even if he pays it all off without interest charges. The convenience of having a credit card is also a liability—its very convenience constitutes temptation.

Here are some simple rules for using credit cards:

- Never use your credit cards for anything except budgeted purchases.
- Pay off your credit cards every month.

- The first month you have a credit card bill you cannot pay in full, destroy the card and don't get another one.

Even if you pay the full amount when due and avoid interest charges, if it's psychologically easier for you to lay down a credit card than to part with cash, you shouldn't own a credit card. If you determine to carry a credit card and say, "I won't use it except for emergencies when I would have used cash anyway," you may minimize the drawbacks. But keep an eye on your spending. For many people, the only solution to credit card abuse is plastic surgery—cut the card in half.

CHURCHES AND DEBT

Many churches spend more on interest payments than on world missions. Debt ties the church's hands. If attendance drops, the economy suffers, or giving dips, then pastors or missionaries must go unpaid. The building completed eight years ago, already needing repairs, keeps demanding those monthly payments, mostly going to interest.

Scripture mentions three major building programs. Each was financed directly by up-front giving. There were no tabernacle bonds, no borrowing, no pledges—just straightforward giving. People gave more than enough and had to be restrained from giving to the tabernacle (Exodus 36:6-7). Notice the terms "willing heart," "whose heart stirred him," "whose heart moved him," and "everyone who could" (Exodus 35:5–36:2).

The same was true in building the temple. Three times in a single passage it says that the people "offered willingly" (1 Chronicles 29:6, 9, 17).

We see the same thing hundreds of years later when the temple needed to be rebuilt. "Everyone whose heart God had moved" made "freewill offerings" (Ezra 1:5-6). They "gave freewill offerings" and "according to their ability they gave" (Ezra 2:68-69). The words *freewill offering* and *offered willingly* appear repeatedly (Ezra 7:16).

In each of these three building projects, the work didn't begin until it was obvious that the project could be completed without borrowing.

There are no New Testament examples of church building construction, but Jesus clearly states that *any such project should only be undertaken with the certainty of having sufficient funds for completion:*

> Suppose one of you wants to build a tower. Will he not first sit down
> and estimate the cost to see if he has enough money to complete it? For
> if he lays the foundation and is not able to finish it, everyone who sees
> it will ridicule him, saying, "This fellow began to build and was not able
> to finish." (Luke 14:28-30)

Many argue that church buildings cannot be constructed debt free. But this argument would be far more believable in the relative poverty surrounding Old

Testament building projects. Do we really believe that God could empower poor Israelites to do what Christians cannot do today?

Lack of money to support the work of a church is usually rooted in a lack of conviction among church members. To borrow money without addressing this reality is a terrible mistake. Countless churches have gone deeply into debt over ill-advised building projects. Horror stories abound of buildings that were never finished, or buildings that, when finally finished, have sanctuaries that are mostly empty because the church split or dissipated under financial pressure. When a church overextends itself financially, it inevitably spends more time during services trying to persuade people to give to the building fund. This changes the focus from worshiping Christ, studying the Scriptures, and meeting the needs of the community to concerns about buildings, mortgages, and money. Typically, before it's all over, people start leaving the church. In contrast, churches that build debt-free—and yes, many have done it—almost always tell great success stories.

Addressing the subject of debt, Hudson Taylor said:

> It is really just as easy for God to give beforehand. He prefers to do so. He is too wise to allow His purpose to be frustrated for lack of a little money; but money wrongly placed or obtained in unspiritual ways is sure to hinder blessing.
>
> And what does going into debt really mean? It means that God has not supplied your need. You trusted Him, but He has not given you the money; so you supply yourself, and borrow. If we can only wait right up to the time, God cannot lie, God cannot forget: He is pledged to supply all your need.[6]

A pastor of a debt-free church said, "If you get a loan, your congregation never has to trust God, they just trust the bank. And when it's all over, they look around and say, 'Look at what the bank built.' When they say, 'Praise God for what he did,' there's an asterisk beside it. But when you build debt-free and say, "Praise God,' there's no asterisk. It's all God's doing."[7]

According to Jeff Berg and Jim Burgess in The Debt-Free Church, when a ministry borrows money, it incurs the following set of risks:

- Becoming the slave of a lending institution
- Becoming a slave to big givers
- Becoming trapped by financial pressure
- Becoming mired in an endless cycle of borrowing
- Losing flexibility to respond to ministry opportunities.[8]

In the Old Testament building projects, future ministry was paid for with present money. But churches that borrow pay for present ministry with future money. In each biblical instance, the people didn't merely promise to give, they actually *gave* the funds before construction began or as they were needed. Why can't—or why shouldn't—we do the same?

Early in our own church's history, we discovered that if people aren't inclined to give significantly toward a project, it's an indication that their hearts aren't in it. And if people's hearts aren't in a project, it shouldn't be undertaken. It's healthy to stretch our faith, but a church's building projects should never exceed its convictions. (That's why I think it's normally a mistake to seek outside funding for a building project. The church should undertake only what it's willing to give itself to.)

With "pay as you go" building projects, offerings gauge the hearts of the people. When borrowing, leaders often find out too late—the hard way—that people aren't behind the project. And some are no longer part of the church.

The Church should model for its people wise stewardship that avoids presumption and financial bondage.

"But unless you're already rich, you can't build a house or a church building or go into business without borrowing money." Not true. At every income level, there are many examples of debt-free churches and families.[9] Although they're in the minority, there are also many businesspeople, Christian and otherwise, who have saved up money for years in order to go into business debt-free. Unlike their competitors, they're able to ride out economic ups and downs because they're not saddled with debt. They don't use other people's money to grow and expand too fast, only to find they've overextended themselves so they wind up filing for bankruptcy.

With discipline, purpose, and patience, a business can be started and maintained without debt—and so can a church building project. Likewise, the average individual who buys a lower-priced house with a down payment of 10 percent could have most of the house paid for by diligently saving for six or seven years, and all of it paid for by saving for twelve—with interest working for him instead of against him. The problem isn't lack of resources but lack of discipline and patience.

Although the New Testament doesn't give an account of fund-raising for a building project, Acts 4:32-35 shows how the Church responded to other needs—they gave immediately. As a result, "there were no needy persons among them" (Acts 4:34). Later, the poverty-stricken Macedonian church followed this same model to send money to feed the hungry in Jerusalem (2 Corinthians 8:1-5).

New Testament Christians had far less than we have, but by giving generously and sacrificially they fully met every need. Although there were many moneylenders, both in Old Testament and New Testament times, we don't see a single example of the Church (or Israel) borrowing money to accomplish God's work. Why do we believe—or, why do we *assume*—that with our relative material abundance the Lord would have us resort to measures unheard of in biblical times?

SOME BENEFITS OF NOT BORROWING FOR CHURCH BUILDINGS

- Creates a greater dependence upon God
- Allows God to show his faithfulness
- Teaches the importance of sacrificial giving (2 Corinthians 8:1-5)
- Teaches people to avoid debt and bondage
- Testifies to the world about the reality of the gospel (Philippians 2:15; 1 Peter 2:9, 12)
- Promotes biblical fund-raising by simply presenting the ministry need and trusting God to provide through the generous giving of his people (1 Corinthians 16:1-2)
- Sets a financial example for believers (1 Timothy 3:4-5, 12)
- Helps guard ministries from hard economic times (Proverbs 22:27)
- Allows flexibility for a church to respond to ministry opportunities[10]

IS BORROWING AN ACT OF FAITH?

Strangely, going into debt for building projects is often portrayed as an act of great faith—the greater the debt, the greater the faith. The Bible suggests the opposite. It's not faith to test God's provision with presumption. It's not faith to depend on a lending institution instead of on God's supernatural provision. Some would say, "It takes faith to pay back a loan." If this were true, then the proper conclusion would be, The larger the loan and the less collateral, the greater the faith. But such a viewpoint violates every biblical caution about borrowing, as well as Christ's explicit warning not to begin building when you lack the required resources (Luke 14:28-30). Notice he doesn't say the man who undertakes a building project without sufficient funds to complete it is "a man of faith." Instead, he describes him as an object of ridicule.

> When churches borrow, they obligate God to provide in the future what he has not made available in the present. That's not faith, but presumption.

Another common argument is this: "When you wait until you have the means to proceed to build, that's not walking by faith—it's walking by sight." This perspective ignores the biblical examples of building and God's method of advancing ministries. When churches borrow, they obligate God to provide in the future what he has not made available in the present. That's not faith, but presumption. Greater risk does not always indicate greater faith. Sometimes it indicates faith in ourselves—or laziness, if we're unwilling to give money in advance in order to experience the fruit of a debt-free building project.

Finally, the Scripture passages about building the tabernacle and the temple demonstrate God's way of fund-raising for building prospects: Start the building when the money is in hand.

Churches and ministries should be careful when they teach from the passages that deal with Israel's three building projects. God revealed that he wanted Israel to undertake these projects, but these texts do not prove that God is in favor of *every* building project. They simply show a model for how to fund and build the projects that God approves. There is no biblical basis on which to conclude that God endorses or opposes a particular church building project. Churches and their leaders should seek God's direction and ask his wisdom before undertaking a building project (James 1:5).

Leaders must be careful not to misappropriate passages of Scripture—such as the story of the two spies who had faith and the ten who did not (Numbers 13:1–14:45)—to prove that a building project is God's will and that those who question it are questioning God. To treat specific projects, as if God himself has passed them down from Mount Sinai, is to invite disunity in the church family.

I *do* believe that God sometimes—in fact, often—leads churches to construct buildings. Buildings can be part of an effective ministry strategy. (For more on this subject, see appendix B, "The Use of Ministry Funds for Buildings.")

GETTING OUT OF DEBT

Scripture makes it clear that if we've borrowed money, whether for good reasons or bad, it's our responsibility to pay it back as soon as possible (Proverbs 3:27-28; Matthew 5:25-26). To not repay a debt is to join ranks with the wicked (Psalm 37:21). Bankruptcy—no matter how legal it may be—is normally not a moral option. I know people of integrity who have come out of bankruptcy proceedings with the legal right not to pay back a dime to others, but who, as a matter of conscience, have dedicated themselves to paying it back anyway over the next decade or more. I believe God is honored by this.

If you are in debt, two questions are relevant: How did you get into debt, and how can you get out? The reason the first question is important is to help you make future decisions. If you've gotten into debt unwisely, you should do more than get out of debt; you should also recognize that you've made wrong choices and commit yourself not to repeat them. Debt isn't the main problem; it's a symptom of a more basic problem—greed, impulsiveness, and lack of discipline. This is what we must bring before God.

How to Get out of Debt

Here's a ten-step process to help you get out of debt:

1. Repent. Acknowledge that you've taken your cues from the world, not God. Change your mind and your actions regarding money, things, needs, wants, giving, saving, spending, and debt. "Do not conform any longer to the pattern of this world, but be transformed by the renewing of your mind. Then you will be able to test and approve what God's will is—his good, pleasing, and perfect will" (Romans 12:2).

2. Immediately give God the firstfruits. When we give to God the first and best of our income, we say in effect to him, "I recognize your ownership and trust you to bless my obedience."

Never rationalize disobedience. It's self-contradictory to seek God's blessing on your finances while putting yourself under his curse by withholding the tithe and offerings he has directed you to give. More than anything, you need his blessing to get out of debt.

Don't just gradually increase your giving until it gets up to a tithe, any more than you'd gradually stop robbing banks. Stop robbing God *now*. (You might also ask him if he wants you to start paying back what you've robbed him of in the past.) Please God in this way and he will bless you, even if it involves making significant lifestyle changes.

3. Incur no new debts. Operate on this principle: "If I can't afford it now, it isn't God's will now."

4. Systematically eliminate existing debts. Draw up a careful budget. Make a specific plan to get out of debt. Seek wise financial counsel. Liquidate unnecessary assets. It won't happen overnight, but with a good plan and determination you can and will get out of debt.

5. Perform plastic surgery on your credit cards. If the card is a temptation, destroy it. The exception is if you always make full payment when due (so you never pay interest) *and* it is no easier for you to put down the card than to put down cash. Warning: Remember the studies showing that those who use credit cards—even if they pay them off monthly—usually spend more than if they only use cash. Watch out for the illusion that using the card isn't really spending.

6. Stop rationalizing your debt habit. Houses and cars are the strongest temptations for some, whereas for others it is furniture, clothing, or electronic equipment. Recognize your weakness and don't let it master you. When it comes to houses, remember this: The Carpenter from Nazareth is making the perfect home for you in heaven (John 14:2-3). It's not here and now, it's then and there! Instead of moving up to a bigger and better house, is it possible that God wants you to use his money here and now to send ahead building materials for his construction project in heaven? (Matthew 6:19-21).

7. If debt seems the best or a necessary choice, go slowly and prayerfully. Get objective financial counsel from good stewards (Proverbs 15:22). Seek financial wisdom only from those who have proven financially wise.

8. Learn the difference between saving and spending. Saving is when you have more money than when you started; spending is when you have less. If you buy an $80 sweater on sale for $30, how much money do you save?

Most people would say $50. Wrong. You don't *save* anything. You *spend* $30. Far too many people have "saved" themselves into financial bondage.

9. List your debts and, if necessary, contact your creditors. Establish a schedule that's workable within your budget to repay your creditors. By comparing the different interest rates on your debts, prioritize your debt reduction, paying off most quickly those with the highest interest.

If your debt is beyond your ability to pay at prescribed levels, explain your plan of repayment to your creditors. Normally they will welcome your plan, because they're often faced with bankruptcies in which they receive little or nothing. Eliminate smaller debts and consolidate your remaining debts in order to pay as few bills as possible. Liquidate unnecessary assets and use the funds to reduce debts. You may be able to move into less expensive housing, get a cheaper car, sell the boat or RV, and convert other unused or unneeded items to cash.

In this process, it's usually important to get wise counsel. We typically get into financial trouble acting on our own, so we shouldn't expect to get out of it the same way. You may receive wise counsel from a friend, a counselor, or a church leader. In some areas you can contact the Consumer Credit Counseling Service, which offers debt counseling at no cost. (But I'll say it again—if you're advised not to give or tithe until you're out of debt, reject this counsel. Remember, robbing God isn't a solution, it's a big part of the problem.)

10. If you've done everything else and it still seems insufficient, consider ways to increase your income in order to eliminate your debts.

If you are already working full-time, more work isn't a long-term solution. Still, a second job or household business may be a temporary necessity to reverse the consequences of past decisions.

Be patient. It may have taken you five, ten, twenty, or thirty years to get into the financial situation you're in. It can't be reversed overnight. However, by following these guidelines, you'll be well on your way out of bondage. You'll also start to experience the freedom of being able to respond generously to needs and eternal investment opportunities. This will bring to you the joy of giving and God's grace and blessing that come with it.

FINANCIAL PRINCIPLES TO LIVE BY

- Nothing is a good deal unless you can afford it.
- Before you take matters into your own hands, God wants an opportunity either to provide your needs or to show you that they aren't really needs.
- Just because you can afford something doesn't mean God wants you to get it.
- Increased income doesn't necessarily mean that God is saying spend

more. More often, his real message is give more (2 Corinthians 8:14; 9:10-11).

Years ago, some friends of ours went deeply into debt to purchase a nice house. At a time when the average house payment was $500, they were making payments of $880 per month—in addition to the never-ending hidden costs of home ownership. For years they experienced great financial bondage. They despaired because they wanted to give freely to needs that God laid on their hearts, but the house left them no money. Finally they made a difficult and courageous decision: They walked away from the house, took their losses, swallowed their pride, and found housing they could afford. Immediately they experienced God's blessing. And after renting for several years, they saved up enough money to buy a home they could afford.

> All I have needed Thy hand hath provided—
> Great is Thy faithfulness, Lord, unto me!

We sing it, but do we mean it? Our lifestyle of debt tempts us and allows us to pursue what God hasn't provided and doesn't intend for us. Will we take the hard but liberating steps to get ourselves out of debt's grip and into the only hands in which we're safe—God's?

There remains one debt to which all our money and possessions must be unreservedly committed, yet which we can never retire: "Let no debt remain outstanding, except the continuing debt to love one another" (Romans 13:8). Origen, the Church father, put it this way: "The debt of love is permanent, so we must pay it daily and yet always owe it."

CHAPTER 18

Saving, Retiring, and Insuring

Make as much as you can, save as much as you can, and give as much as you can.   JOHN WESLEY

Earthly goods are given to be used, not to be collected. Hoarding is idolatry.   DIETRICH BONHOEFFER

Billions of dollars each year are poured into savings accounts, retirement funds, and insurance policies. Are these wise places for Christian stewards to place their God-entrusted funds? Is it unspiritual to have these things? Is it irresponsible not to have them? Are they morally neutral? Can they be used well or poorly depending on amounts and attitudes? Do savings and insurance pose dangers to us? Are there biblical principles that can help us evaluate them? In this chapter, we'll seek to answer each of these questions.

SAVING

Saving in the Scriptures

The purpose of savings is to set money aside for the future. By forgoing expenditures now, we preserve resources for later. "In the house of the wise are stores of choice food and oil, but a foolish man devours all he has" (Proverbs 21:20). The wise anticipate future needs while the foolish consume their resources, not considering the future.

"Go to the ant, you sluggard; consider its ways and be wise! It has no commander, no overseer or ruler, yet it stores its provisions in summer and gathers its food at harvest" (Proverbs 6:6-8). Even ants know there will be no food in winter unless it's stored during the summer. Only a shortsighted person would fail to store up provisions (money, food, or supplies) for upcoming times of predictable need.

By God's inspiration, Joseph devised a careful savings plan in light of an upcoming famine in Egypt (Genesis 41:25-57). For seven years the Egyptians stored a large portion of the harvest. When the seven years of famine came, they drew on their stores of grain. The nation was able to care for itself—and provide for others as well.

Saving Today

Sometimes our future needs aren't as predictable as in these biblical examples. Nurserymen or carpenters may have seasonal incomes and must discipline themselves to save for the lean months. But most of us receive a regular paycheck. Even for those with steadier incomes, it seems wise to set aside funds to allow for both anticipated and unanticipated expenses—but most people don't. Although we live in the most affluent society in human history, eighty-five out of one hundred Americans have less than $250 in available savings when they reach age sixty-five.[1] That means, without counting retirement funds, that a person who has worked from age twenty has managed to save less than six dollars per year. If the reason for this lack of savings was faith in

The average American family is three to six weeks away from bankruptcy.

God and a conviction that we shouldn't hang on to resources but give them to meet others' needs, then we'd be in the company of the poor widow of Mark 12 and the Macedonian Christians of 2 Corinthians 8. But the reason typically isn't our trust in God. It's usually self-indulgence, presumption, and lack of foresight and discipline. God doesn't bless a lack of savings for those reasons.

In the event of a lost job or unexpected major expense, the average American family is three to six weeks away from bankruptcy. Yet in other countries with far lower incomes, people have learned to save enough to provide for future needs. To be shortsighted is to invite poverty. To feast now without regard to future famine is to manage our resources poorly and presume upon God or others to bail us out.

We must learn not only to weigh our expenditures in light of their immediate value but their ultimate cost. Money needlessly spent is a double loss. Not only is it gone, but its *potential* for earnings is also gone. Had we set it aside, it *could* have been multiplying on earth through savings or in heaven through giving.

It's wise to give first, save second, and spend last. Otherwise, we will spend everything and have nothing to give or save. We'll also set ourselves up to fall into debt when true needs arise.

Saving is a discipline that develops authority over money. Instead of letting money take us wherever our whims incline, we take control.

Reasons for Saving

After I give the firstfruits to the Lord, I can take money off the top of my paycheck to save for future purposes. I might save for a family vacation or a remodeling project. I'm not saving without purpose, but for a specific cause.

Long-term savings are a way of using years of plenty to prepare for years of lack, as Joseph did. Anticipating retirement, I might set aside money to supplement an income reduction in the future. Or I might systematically save for my children's college education, which could be ten years away.

There are also many poor reasons for saving. Some save out of greed. Others save because they're misers. Others save out of fear. They're anxious about the future. By stockpiling money, they insulate themselves from God, no longer depending on his provision and protection.

We can't say, "Saving money is biblical" or "Saving money is unbiblical." It may be either, depending on the reasons and the alternatives.

The Dangers of Hoarding

Hoarding is saving taken to an extreme. It's accumulating assets for no purpose other than to ward off future disaster, or to provide wealth for many years to come. The classic example of hoarding is the rich fool, who says:

> I will tear down my barns and build bigger ones, and there I will store all my grain and my goods. And I'll say to myself, "You have plenty of good things laid up for many years. Take life easy; eat, drink and be merry." (Luke 12:18-19)

God then says, "You fool! This very night your life will be demanded from you. Then who will get what you have prepared for yourself?" Jesus promises, "This is how it will be with anyone who stores up things for himself but is not rich toward God" (Luke 12:20-21).

When we read about the rich fool, our first mistake is in thinking we're not really rich. Bill Gates, Ted Turner, and Warren Buffet are rich. We're just lower upper class, or middle class, or lower class. Because we know so many people who are wealthier than we are, we think we're not rich. But we're wrong. Even most lower-class Americans have access to benefits and luxuries—including medical care, indoor bathrooms, running water, food, microwave ovens, radio, television, reading materials, sports equipment, and financial assistance from government, churches, and charities—that the richest people in Bible times never dreamed of. By global standards, even the poorest Americans are easily in the upper 20 percent of the world's wealthy. By historical standards, anyone with a house, indoor plumbing, and enough to eat is certainly rich.

Our second mistake in reading about the rich fool is in assuming we're not fools. We act as if the rich fool was terribly different than we are. In fact, he was living out the American dream, reflected in television commercials, movies, and conversations. He was storing up wealth to rely on in the future while enjoying his favorite recreational pursuits in the present. God calls this man a fool because when his life is suddenly over, his obituary shows that he's been rich toward himself but not toward God.

What will happen to the billions of dollars in the savings accounts, real estate holdings, insurance policies, stock market portfolios, and retirement plans of western Christians? Christ suggests we should be "rich toward God" rather than "store up things" for ourselves. Why? Because by giving freely to God, we store up things in another world where they'll matter and last. Meanwhile, we'll also honor God and help our neighbors. If we fail to do this, we are exactly the same as the rich man—we are *fools*.

Is it inconsistent to say that saving for possible short-term needs can be wise, whereas saving vast sums for decades ahead can be foolish? It may appear to be, but I'm attempting to balance what Scripture says about both. We can't ignore all the verses in Proverbs that laud saving, yet we also can't ignore Christ's scathing appraisal of the rich fool. It may not be easy to find a balance—in fact, personally I find it very difficult—but that's the position Scripture puts us in. The solution is not to focus on one group of Scriptures while ignoring others, but to affirm both and seek to honor both, even when we find it difficult.

Hoarders imagine themselves as wise. Jesus says they're anything but wise. They're fools. Hoarding is an attempt to completely cover our material bases so that God becomes unnecessary. Rather than responsibly taking steps for future provision while trusting in God's sovereignty, we assert our own sovereignty by hoarding.

A common goal of hoarders is to achieve "financial independence." But from whom do we wish to be independent? God? Our family? Christian brothers and sisters? I certainly favor independence from the government or parents, in the sense that I earn my own living. There's a kind of dependence that's terribly unhealthy. But isn't there a kind of independence that's equally unhealthy?

"Whoever trusts in his riches will fall, but the righteous will thrive like a green leaf" (Proverbs 11:28). When we stockpile riches for every conceivable scenario, aren't we trusting in our riches rather than in God? The clear teaching of the New Testament is that we are to be *channels* of money and possessions, not storehouses. Whatever role that saving has in our lives, it should always be secondary to giving. And it must never be a substitute for trusting God.

Should We Save for Possible Disasters?

Some Christians believe that everyone should store up years of water, food, and even ammunition for our families. One author says that believers should secure passports now in order to be prepared to flee the country during a nuclear holocaust. Certain Christian financial counselors encourage us to invest in diamonds, art, and antiques to hedge against various economic catastrophes that may be ahead. One Christian resource suggests placing assets in offshore tax havens and Swiss bank accounts. Numerous advisers emphasize gold, claming it's the ultimate answer to future security.

When evidence suggested that the Y2K bug would likely create weeks of economic turbulence, it seemed reasonable to acquire extra supplies, including food and water. It turned out to be a false alarm. But it also served as a test—where were people's hearts? How much did they store up and for whom? Would we have been willing and eager to share with neighbors and others in need?

In early 1999, countless mainstream magazines and newspapers contained Y2K articles citing the likelihood of a temporary loss of electricity in various parts of the country. Believing that I should provide for my wife and daughters, I decided to buy a generator. After paying for it, though, I felt uneasy. Why was I providing this for myself and my family regarding *possible* future hardship when that same money could deliver people in other places from actual present hardship? I considered people around the world who on their best day have greater need than we might have on our worst day. Convicted, I gave the generator to a mission to Native Americans, who could make good use of it even after Y2K was long gone.

I don't mean that it's faithless to lay something aside in the face of a likely shortage. It may just be good planning, especially if the money's not wasted. Someone who had extra food stored for Y2K could go ahead and eat it afterward and not have wasted money. (It certainly isn't more spiritual to have money in the bank or stock market than canned food on a shelf.)

But there's a difference between conscientious planning for the future and hoarding or survivalism. Does the same Christ who said we should look to the birds and the lilies and trust our heavenly Father to provide for our futures, and that we are to lay up treasures in heaven and not on earth, really want us to stockpile gold bullion and store up years of freeze-dried food in a bomb shelter? Does that really sound like what Jesus would call us to do?

> A common goal of hoarders is to achieve "financial independence." But from whom do we wish to be independent? God? Our family? Christian brothers and sisters?

Our own retirement accounts—which are quite small by American standards but large by nearly every other measure—contain a combination of mutual funds, precious metals, and other investments. I don't believe these are inherently wrong. But they can become dangerous. When we amass wealth to protect ourselves against imminent doom, where is our faith? Yes, extremely difficult times may be ahead. (With much of the world already experiencing such things, why would we think it couldn't happen to us?) Prudent foresight can be wise. Realism and good planning should characterize God's children. Panic and hoarding should not.

I remember the reactions of people during past shortages of gasoline, sugar, and other supplies. One man, storing drums of gasoline in his garage, said, "I have to get as much as I can before the hoarders get it!" If economic catastrophe does come, will it be a time that draws Christians together to share every resource we have, or will it drive us apart to hide in our own basements or mountain retreats, guarding at gunpoint our private stores from others? If we faithfully use our assets for his kingdom now, rather than hoarding them, can't we trust our faithful God to provide for us then?

Here's what James says to the wealthy stockpilers in the church of his day:

> Now listen, you rich people, weep and wail because of the misery that is coming upon you. Your wealth has rotted; . . . your gold and silver are corroded. Their corrosion will testify against you and eat your flesh like fire. You have hoarded wealth in the last days. . . . You have lived on earth in luxury and self-indulgence. (James 5:1-5)

James doesn't suggest that these people could avoid future tribulation by hoarding their wealth. On the contrary, it was their hoarding and self-indulgence that assured them of God's coming judgment. Far from being the solution, hoarding is part of the problem!

The book of Exodus contains a graphic lesson against hoarding. When God provided manna from heaven to meet the needs of his people, he told them they'd have just enough for each day. They shouldn't try to store it up. But Israel had its hoarders. They determined to save up in case God didn't come through. But God made the stored manna foul, filling it with worms (Exodus 16:16-20). Their savings may have seemed to reflect good planning; but they were stockpiling, and God would not bless it.

God will provide for his obedient, responsible, and wise children who seek first his kingdom (Matthew 6:33). Any savings, retirement, insurance, or survival plan that diverts our attention from God also undermines our dependence on him.

Distinguishing Saving from Hoarding

Saving is a means of not presuming upon God. Hoarding is a means of replacing God. Saving can avoid presuming upon others to assume responsibility for our future needs. Hoarding is a self-absorbed commitment to independence from others who could help us if we're in need, just as we can and should help others.

Here's another lesson we can learn from the ants: The more hostile the climate, the larger the anthill, because more storage space in needed. The milder the climate, the smaller the anthill. Why? Because ants only store for the coming winter, not for a decade of winters.

When I save, I lay something aside for future need. If I sense God's leading, I will give it away to meet greater needs. When I hoard, I'm unwilling to part with what I've saved to meet others' needs, because my possible future needs outweigh their actual present needs. Hence, I fail to love my neighbor as myself.

The difference between saving and hoarding isn't simply the amount but the attitude. Nonetheless, there's a vast difference between saving five hundred dollars or a few thousand dollars for a "rainy day" and saving a quarter of a million dollars that could last a rainy decade. Some lay up enough to survive a stormy century! In seeking to provide for our future needs, we should not neglect those who are currently needy. Our plenty will supply what they need (2 Corinthians 8:14).

"God pours out his choicest blessings on those who are anxious that nothing shall stick to their hands. Individuals who value the rainy day above the present agony of the world will get no blessing from God."[2]

Saving for Retirement

Most people must pay Social Security taxes and thereby save for retirement. Many have pensions and retirement plans through their employer. Financial counselors speak of the three-legged stool of retirement—Social Security, employee retirement programs, and individual savings (often through Individual Retirement Accounts and other investments).

We must ask the same question about our retirement savings as all savings. Is this reasonable planning, exercising foresight as Proverbs commends? Or is it an alternative to trusting God, a backup in case God doesn't come through? How is maintaining a generous retirement plan fundamentally different from the rich fool storing up for his later years to live out his life in comfort and security? We know what Jesus thought of that man's retirement plans (Luke 12:16-21). Why should we assume he thinks differently about ours? We should study this passage and compare our attitudes, behavior (including giving), and plans for the future to that man's, and ask how different we are from him. If there's no difference, obviously we need to change something.

How much is reasonable to save for retirement? At what point does responsible saving cross the line and become greedy hoarding? What would happen if I took part, most, or all of the funds I would otherwise put into retirement and invested them in God's kingdom? Financial counselors would tell me that I would be "jeopardizing my retirement years." Might God say I would be "enhancing my eternal years"? If I waste the money, spend it, or am just a poor planner, that's one thing. But will God really fail me if I invest these funds in his kingdom in an honest effort to obey his words in Matthew 6:19-21 and many other passages?

I agree with Larry Burkett's assessment of the saving-for-retirement obsession:

Retirement planning so dominates the thinking of Christians who have sizable incomes that they overkill in this area enormously. The fear of doing without in the future causes many Christians to rob God's work of the very funds he has provided. These monies are tucked away in retirement accounts for twenty to forty years. God's Word does not prohibit but rather encourages saving for the future, including retirement (Proverbs 6:6-11; 21:20), but the example of the rich fool, given by the Lord in Luke 12:16-20, should be a clear direction that God's balance is "when in doubt—give; don't hoard."[3]

We are to love our neighbors as ourselves. If we or our children were hungry, would we take something out of our retirement program to feed them? If so, why wouldn't we consider doing this for our neighbor's children? Are we truly obeying the command to love our neighbor as ourselves if we're storing up money for potential future needs when our neighbor is laboring today under actual present needs?

Are we truly obeying the command to love our neighbor as ourselves if we're storing up money for potential future needs when our neighbor is laboring today under actual present needs?

I realize this is a troubling and threatening question. Believe me, it bothers me to ask it. Although my retirement savings account may be small by American standards, it's still enough to keep many people alive and reach many people with the gospel. Nanci and I decided a while back to take out some retirement funds and give them to God's kingdom. But we still have a significant amount left. Some day we may give more of it away, or none of it, or all of it. I don't know. But I do know we must ask God, because it belongs to him, not us.

I know missionaries who so believed in their work training young believers in Europe that they cashed out their retirement funds and gave them all to the ministry. Many Christians would shake their heads and say, "How foolish." But if God commended the widow for giving away her last two pennies, wouldn't he commend these missionaries who—even without retirement savings—have many more financial resources than the widow could have dreamed of? Isn't their action consistent with Christ's promise that if we "seek first the kingdom of God and His righteousness . . . all these things shall be added to you"? (Matthew 6:33, NKJV) Were these missionaries fools—or are we?

The rich fool never had the opportunity to use the money and possessions he stockpiled for himself. Will our own excess funds hoarded for the future one day become as filled with worms as Israel's hoarded manna? We don't know whether Christ will return in our lifetime. But he certainly will return in the lifetime of some Christians. We also know this: All money stored in retirement funds, savings, insurance policies, houses, real estate, and personal possessions will become eternally useless the moment Christ returns. If the countless billions of dollars now invested in earthly accounts were freed up and poured into helping the needy and fulfilling the great commission, what eternal impact might result?

Five minutes after we die, we'll know exactly how much we should have given rather than kept. But then it will be too late. Why not spend the rest of our lives closing the gap between what we'll know we should have given then and what we *are* giving now?

Can Any Resource Remain "Untouchable"?

The goal of much retirement planning is to provide a regular monthly interest income sufficient to meet all our needs without ever touching the principal that generates the interest. This way it's impossible to outlive our money.

I met with a man who inherited a million dollars and wanted to invest it in God's kingdom. A Christian financial counselor told him, "Whatever you do, just give away the interest earnings, but never the principal. Remember, the principal is always untouchable."

I told him I couldn't know exactly how God would lead him, but I was certain about one thing: He dare not tell God that the principal was *untouchable.* Who are we to declare any resource off-limits to the One who provided it and owns it? The principal is God's as much as the interest. Furthermore, he knows how to make an eternal impact with the principal as well as the interest. And he also knows how to take care of our needs without a million dollars in the bank!

If we have a large amount of money, God may desire for us to give it away all at once. Or perhaps he will lead us to give more gradually from the principal, so it steadily decreases over the years. But when it comes to money above and beyond our needs—and especially when it's more than we would reasonably need in the future—the assumption should surely be that we ought to give it now rather than later. The window of opportunity to give may close in ten years, six months, or next week.

How Much Is Enough?

Using that three-legged stool as a symbol of retirement planning, I don't feel right asking God to hold up the stool if I haven't made an effort to put on a leg or two. Yet I also don't feel right taking everything into my own hands, leaving no material needs for God to provide and no need for me to trust him or pray for his provision in the future. How can we meaningfully pray, "Give us this day our daily bread," when we own the bakery?

Many financial counselors would tell me I'm not laying up nearly enough for retirement. But when I read Scripture, I wonder if I'm laying up too much. I live in this tension and I suppose it will never be resolved. But I also know that whatever posture I take with financial planning, I must leave room—a great deal of room—for God. It's him, not a retirement fund, in whom I should trust.

The rich fool took matters into his own hands. He planned for his retirement but not his walk with God. He never consulted with the Creator of the universe as to what he should do with his money for the rest of his life. I don't want to be a poor fool by not planning for the future. But I also don't want to be a rich fool by overplanning for it. Above all, I want to make plans for the right future, the eternal one. I want to ask how each investment will be paying off not just thirty years from now, but thirty million years from now.

Many of us have accumulated not only financial reserves, but also valuable possessions. At any time, not only our savings but also our other material assets should be considered fair game for divine distribution. We should be especially quick to evaluate luxury items. Antiques, art, coins, and other collections may be of great (but only temporary) financial worth. They could be used for strategic purpose in the kingdom of God—but not when they're lying in a safe, behind a locked display, or hanging on a wall.

Is God calling us to liquidate some of these items and invest them in his kingdom? Are we willing to seek his will in diligent prayer and biblical meditation? If anything we have is off-limits to God, if it's not fair game for prayerful dialogue, then let's be honest about it—we aren't stewards, we're embezzlers. We aren't serving God, we're playing God. If we consider "our" retirement funds off-limits to God, we're acting as owners, not stewards. When we ask God's direction for our lives, we need to lay everything on the table.

Charles Spurgeon writes:

> Christians often look to man for help and counsel, and mar the noble
> simplicity of their reliance upon their God. . . . If you cannot trust God
> for temporals, how dare you trust Him for spirituals? Can you trust Him
> for your soul's redemption, and not rely upon Him for a few lesser
> mercies? Is not God enough for thy need, or is His all-sufficiency too
> narrow for thy wants? . . . Is His heart faint? Is His arm weary? If so,
> seek another God; but if He be infinite, omnipotent, faithful, true, and
> all-wise, why gaddest thou abroad so much to seek another confidence?
> Why dost thou rake the earth to find another foundation, when this
> is strong enough to bear all the weight which thou canst ever build
> thereon? . . . Let the sandy foundations of terrestrial trust be the choice
> of fools, but do thou, like one who foresees the storm, build for thyself
> an abiding place upon the Rock of Ages.[4]

Is saving large amounts of money for retirement as essential as we're constantly told? Reading 2 Corinthians 8:3-15, can you pick up a hint about the need or the wisdom of saving up money for retirement? The Macedonian Christians had virtually no material things, yet they gave beyond their means to the point of leaving themselves impoverished. If they didn't need to think of tomorrow, why do we—with all our material wealth—need to be so concerned about storing up earthly treasures for thirty years from now?

We may legitimately use retirement programs for a good purpose, but are they not just one more tool the Provider can use for his own good purposes? God—not our IRA or 401(k)—is the source of our future well-being. The truth is, we really don't need retirement programs. I'm not saying we can't use them or shouldn't have them—but, as God's children, we don't need them. Our brothers and sisters in other ages didn't have retirement programs, and neither do most Christians today in other places. Yet they've found God absolutely sufficient to meet their needs.

How much retirement savings is really enough? Once again, we must consider the available alternatives to invest in eternity. It's not an overstatement to say that if even one-fourth of the funds tied up today in the retirement programs of all Christians were made available to churches and Christian ministries, world missions could be propelled forward in unprecedented ways. This isn't just because of the value of the money, but because along with the giving of such treasure would go the giving of hearts and the corresponding prayer and commitment that God could use to reach the world.

> If even one-fourth of the funds tied up today in the retirement programs of all Christians were made available to churches and Christian ministries, world missions could be propelled forward in unprecedented ways.

Society in general (and financial advisors in particular) appeals constantly to our fears and insecurities. One wealthy widow told me of several friends whose husbands also have died who are sitting on large fortunes. She said, "Whenever we discuss whether we should give more, before you know it we get into the 'bag lady syndrome'—talking as if unless we have millions stashed away, we're going to end up out on the streets." Ironically, giving isn't a cause for insecurity but a cure for it, because it turns our hearts toward the only One worthy of complete trust, and it fulfills the conditions of seeking first his kingdom so that we can depend on him to provide for us materially as well (Matthew 6:33).

How much is too much? I can't answer the question for you. I have a hard enough time trying to figure it out for myself. But I do know that each of us should ask ourselves the question. We should also shut out the distracting noises of the world, tune our ear to God's Word, and quietly listen for his answer. And we should listen to the voices that bring a balance of biblical principles, not to those who blindly follow the lead of popular culture rather than taking a serious look at what the Bible teaches.

Retirement from What and for What?

Where did we get our concepts about retirement? What do we read in Scripture about saving up for retirement? Try doing a Bible study on the subject—I guarantee you, it won't take long! How many people in other places and times in history have been able to even consider the option of retirement or of saving up money to last twenty-plus years? Typically, we see financial planning from a cultural perspective, not a biblical one.

When it comes to the "retirement dream," we must ask, "Whose dream is it?" It may be the American dream—but is it God's? For some people, retirement has replaced the return of Christ as the "blessed hope," the major future event that we anticipate.

When a man retires at sixty-five, studies show his chances of having a fatal heart attack immediately double. Our minds and bodies weren't made for an arbitrary day of shutdown. Nowhere in Scripture do we see God calling healthy people to stop working. Of course, it's perfectly legitimate to work without pay. It's your option to give labor to ministry and volunteer work rather than to your present job. But as long as God has us in this world, he has work for us to do. The hours may be shorter, the work different, the pay lower or nonexistent. But he doesn't want us to take still-productive minds and bodies and permanently lay them on a beach, lose them on a golf course, or lock them in a dark living room watching game shows.

If you've saved for retirement and no longer need to work for pay, then work for God, the church, the poor, or underprivileged children. And don't forget the great opportunity you have to become a self-supported missionary for two or five or ten or twenty years. If you're still here, God isn't done with you. In fact, your most fruitful years of ministry may be ahead. That's true whether you're in a retirement home or anywhere else. God has a unique ministry for you here and now. Don't kill time, any more than you would burn money. Instead, invest it in eternity.

Christian Foundations: Saving, Investing, and Giving

Never has there been so much wealth in the hands of Christians. And never have there been so many Christian foundations.[5] Foundations are nonprofit organizations that make grants to charitable organizations and ministries, including schools and the arts. Foundations are professional grant makers. They have their own capital or assets, enhanced by earned interest and sometimes supplemented by gifts. One major foundation advisor says, "Small donors are the engine that runs God's kingdom. They provide the bulk of the support, but rarely more than $1,000 per person per year. They provide the prayer support. They provide the encouragement to the individuals within the organization. And they provide financial stability to an organization."[6]

Christian foundations maintain a certain amount of interest-generating capital, which is given away, often annually. Usually, the principal is kept intact. Sometimes foundations give away the legal minimum of 5 percent annually, meaning that their principal grows each year rather than diminishes. Hence, the foundation's assets often get bigger each year. (Or when the stock market declines they can significantly shrink.) Individuals, families, or corporations can set up foundations. Often, they are directed by paid professionals who decide how much to give, who should receive it, and how it should be distributed. Foundations often do what individuals can't. They take on risky ventures outside of a ministry's usual means of operating, ventures that may have great kingdom payoffs.

Many wealthy people who want to involve their children in the family giving see foundations as a way to do that. People used to create foundations to last forever. Lately, however, more and more people are creating foundations that will distribute the principal value of the fund within fifteen or twenty-five years of the grantor's death. This approach ensures that the fund will be administered by people who knew the grantor and his or her wishes, and it avoids the tragically common situation in which grantors long ago set up foundations to support Christian colleges that have since become at best nominally Christian and sometimes even anti-Christian.

Some wealthy Christians, instead of creating foundations, are doing their giving directly during their lifetime. They are doing this within an estate planning process that reduces their estate as they get older and leaves behind much less than they might have.

In some cases, foundations bring to the table not only money, but also expertise. They can offer wisdom as they work with ministries that may not be accustomed to receiving large gifts or carrying out large, independently funded projects.

Christian foundations have done much good—and God certainly leads his people to different decisions. However, all who are considering setting up a foundation should ask themselves the following questions.[7] They are equally pertinent to all of us—even on a smaller scale—who have savings, retirement plans, real estate, and other investments that we think or hope we will one day give to God's kingdom.

1. How much is our self-worth tied up in our net worth? How important is the recognition and status we get from gift recipients? Is holding on to funds in a foundation a way of gaining recognition? (If so, then we are not really giving, we are purchasing power and status under the guise of giving.) If we gave everything away, would organizations stop courting us? Are we willing to live with that?

2. Does putting money into a foundation allow us control we're

unwilling to give up? Is our decision to place significant assets into a foundation an egocentric attempt at giving us the best of two worlds—being givers, yet still having wealth and power? By setting up a foundation, are we attempting to one day control our accumulated wealth from beyond the grave?

3. Why has our sovereign God entrusted today's Christians with greater financial resources than at any time in history? Is it to possibly meet needs twenty or thirty years from now or to definitely meet needs today?

The first church in Jerusalem didn't hold back resources as a hedge against possible future needs. Instead, they used their resources to meet present, actual needs (Acts 2:44-45; 4:34-35). If the Jerusalem church had held on to more of its assets, it might have needed less help from others later. Yet God provided the excess to meet others' present needs, allowing others to help when the time came for future needs (2 Corinthians 8:14-15). Why should we hold on to what we don't need when God says the reason it has been entrusted to us is for distribution to the needy? (2 Corinthians 9:11).

Does one generation have the responsibility to evangelize the world and feed the poor in the next generation? Or does each generation have the responsibility to reach and care for its own? Doesn't the God of providence know how much is needed when? If we take much of what he has provided now and save it to meet future needs, will there be a shortfall in meeting present needs? If the world is full of lost and dying people now, is it appropriate to defer our present giving in order to possibly reach lost and dying people twenty years from now? Given the present urgency, shouldn't we assume that God has provided today's resources for today's needs? And shouldn't we trust him to provide for future needs when the time comes? John Wesley said, "He who governed the world before I was born shall take care of it likewise when I am dead. My part is to improve the present moment."

The New Testament pattern is clear—Christians gave to meet actual, present needs as they arose. We see no example of them holding back wealth for possible future needs.

4. Doesn't endlessly perpetuating a foundation guarantee that the bulk of the fortune will go up in smoke at Christ's return? Wouldn't more be accomplished for the kingdom by giving away a larger percentage of the capital now or by having a phase-out plan that culminates in giving away all the assets, not just a portion of them?

5. Some would argue that many ministries aren't prepared to receive large amounts of money all at once. But distributions can be spread out among dozens of worthy ministries, so that none receives more than it can handle. If a foundation's assets are exceptionally large,

maybe they should be phased out over a period of years. But if the needs are real and the opportunities are current, doesn't the weight of evidence suggest that we should distribute our assets rather than holding them? Shouldn't we assume that giving now is the best course of action, and that postponing our giving should be the exception, not the rule?

6. If God gave us the ability to make money, why should we leave to others much of the responsibility for giving it away? Are we sure that after we die the next generation will have the same priorities we have?

Even if we completely trust our grown children—as Nanci and I certainly do—aren't there better ways of teaching them about giving than leaving behind a large fortune for them to gradually give away after we die? When our daughters were teenagers, we delegated to them the responsibility of choosing ministries to receive funds from our book royalties (which are owned and distributed by our ministry). Once we designated $10,000 for each to give, and they made phone calls and checked information on the Internet, learning about eternal investment possibilities and drawing their hearts toward various ministries. We did it again soon after they were married. They and their husbands had the joy of giving away another $10,000 of royalties—in this case earned from a novel they wrote with me.[8]

But how much does it really help grown children to develop a heart for giving and missions by putting them on the foundation board so they can give away "our money" for the rest of their lives? Shouldn't they first learn to give by watching our example of distributing money rather than holding on to it, and then by actually giving away money that God chooses to entrust to them through their own labor? (Vicarious giving only goes so far.) What better model of giving can we show our children than giving today?

7. Is it really better to give the interest on five million dollars for twenty years than to give the five million dollar principal the first year? If we hang on to the money, do we really believe that Wall Street can outperform the God who promises 10,000 percent interest on money given to him?

8. Do you really want to take upon yourself and lay upon your children the unnecessary burdens of wealth distribution, when you could easily give the money away instead?

Frederick T. Gates, who was John D. Rockefeller Sr.'s chief philanthropic advisor, said this of Rockefeller: "Neither in the privacy of his home, nor at the table, nor in the aisles of his church, nor during business hours, nor anywhere was he secure from insistent appeal. . . . He was constantly hunted, stalked, and hounded almost like a wild animal." Although few of us have wealth like the Rockefellers, many of us know what it's like to be pursued by others—including many fine ministries—trying to convince us to support them.

If you're holding on to money today with the thought that you'll have more to give later, you're kidding yourself.

Thoughts on Postponed Giving

Referring to the ruined temple, God says, "These people say, 'The time has not yet come for the Lord's house to be built'" (Haggai 1:2). He then asks, "Is it a time for you yourselves to be living in your paneled houses, while this house remains a ruin?"

On the priority scale, are we putting God's kingdom work first, or are we mainly just building our personal kingdom? God rebuked Israel for procrastinating about funding his work by saying "the time has not yet come." Meanwhile they were aggressively funding their own projects, such as building and furnishing their nice, paneled houses.

They didn't say, "We won't rebuild the temple." They intended to do it—eventually. But they said, "This isn't the time."

Many Christians make similar statements. We intend eventually to give generously to God's kingdom—later, after we take care of more pressing things. (Things centered around ourselves.)

If you're holding on to money today with the thought that you'll have more to give later, you're kidding yourself. The economy may fail, you may become dependent on the money you've held on to, and your heart will stay on earth with your money instead of following it to heaven. Nongivers remain nongivers until the moment they give. Intending to give eventually is radically different than actually giving.

God links Israel's financial problems to their failure to give toward doing God's work: "Give careful thought to your ways. You have planted much, but have harvested little. You eat, but never have enough. You drink, but never have your fill. You put on clothes, but are not warm. You earn wages, only to put them in a purse with holes in it" (Haggai 1:5-6). It's not that God always withholds material blessing from nongivers. He may provide the same amount for givers and nongivers, but for a giver it will go much further. For a nongiver, money—no matter how much—disappears, as if put in a purse with holes in it.

God says, "'You expected much, but see, it turned out to be little. What you brought home, I blew away. Why?' declares the Lord Almighty. 'Because of my house, which remains a ruin, while each of you is busy with his own house'" (Haggai 1:9). We think we come out ahead by not giving. But God says exactly the opposite. He says the nongiver puts a curse on himself. God says, "Because of you the heavens have withheld their dew and the earth its crops. I called for a drought on the fields and the mountains, on the grain, the new wine, the oil and whatever the ground produces, on men and cattle, and on the labor of your hands" (Haggai 1:10-11).

Postponed giving is usually postponed obedience, and postponed obedience is disobedience. Charles Spurgeon had something to say about this:

> Churlish souls stint their contributions to the ministry and missionary operations, and call such saving good economy; little do they dream that they are thus impoverishing themselves. Their excuse is that they must care for their own families, and they forget that to neglect the house of God is the sure way to bring ruin upon their own houses. Our God has a method in providence by which He can succeed our endeavors beyond our expectation, or can defeat our plans to our confusion and dismay; by a turn of His hand He can steer our vessel in a profitable channel, or run it aground in poverty and bankruptcy. It is the teaching of Scripture that the Lord enriches the liberal and leaves the miserly to find out that withholding tendeth to poverty. In a very wide sphere of observation, I have noticed that the most generous Christians of my acquaintance have been always the most happy, and almost invariably the most prosperous. I have seen the liberal giver rise to wealth of which he never dreamed; and I have as often seen the mean, ungenerous churl descend to poverty by the very parsimony by which he thought to rise. Men trust good stewards with larger and larger sums, and so it frequently is with the Lord; He gives by cartloads to those who give by bushels. Where wealth is not bestowed the Lord makes the little much by the contentment which the sanctified heart feels in a portion of which the tithe has been dedicated to the Lord.[9]

INSURANCE
The Nature and Implications of Insurance

Insurance is a guarantee against loss. By purchasing an insurance policy for a comparatively small price, the purchaser is assured of recovering from a large loss, should it occur. Possessions or people can be insured. Houses, cars, buildings, boats, collections, weapons, books, businesses, and almost anything else can be insured—even the hands of professional musicians or the careers of athletes. Common forms on people are medical, disability, and life insurance.

There are obvious benefits to insurance. For an affordable amount, someone can avoid considerable losses. If theft, fire, accident, disease, or death occurs, people are very happy they have insurance. If these things don't occur, they should be happier still. They're glad to have bought the insurance just for the peace of mind.

Laws require minimum liability insurance for automobiles. There are regulations for deeds, permits, and loans requiring fire insurance on houses. In such cases, insurance isn't an issue. We should simply obey the law (Romans 13:1-7).

Are there any biblical principles suggesting that insurance has disadvantages? One is a loss of our perceived need to trust in God. Scripture teaches that God desires to develop our character through trial and losses. If everything—other than items of sentimental value—is restored when a house burns down or a catastrophe strikes, we're saved much heartache. But are we also "saved" of the need to trust a sovereign God?

If my car gets hit, its replacement is guaranteed. If I get sick, the doctor and hospital will be paid. If I stay sick, my family will receive a full income. If I die, my family will be taken care of for many years. Of course, the mental and emotional loss may be substantial, but if my insurance policies are sufficient, there's no such thing as significant material loss. The situation is airtight—so airtight, in fact, that God's provision may appear unnecessary.

Corporation and Community Insurance

It used to be that people had to trust God to provide for the medical bills when they got sick. If they stayed sick, they and their family had to depend on God, family, and the Christian community for support materially and personally. A person who was injured and could no longer work was helped by his family, church, neighbors, and community. His "insurance" was his own participation in the community. People cared, helped, and prayed. God worked through these personal relationships to meet not only material but emotional and spiritual needs. If someone died, others came forward to help care for the family. With insurance, all that changed. But is the change for the better?

One hundred years ago, if a house burned down, neighbors and church members rallied and gave of their assets of time and money and helped to rebuild. (You've seen it in the movies, among the Amish, or on *Little House on the Prairie*, right?) But now the insurance company takes care of that. Friends, neighbors, and church members may feel bad and offer brief emotional support, but then they return to their own lives, barely affected and minimally involved with their suffering neighbors.

Today, someone who is injured is compensated by unemployment insurance, worker's compensation insurance, or disability insurance. Because they are "taken care of," other people don't get involved.

To distinguish between these two sources of care, let's call the contractual insurance issued by an insurance company "corporation insurance," and let's call the spontaneous provision issued by a community, whether geographical or spiritual, "community insurance." History has demonstrated that as corporation insurance becomes prevalent, the role of community insurance is minimized and ultimately nearly eliminated. If a person has sufficient corporation insurance, there's little or no perceived need for community insurance.

The demise of community insurance is not only a problem with corporation insurance but also with the endless number of government programs that dole out money without providing the holistic care that happens naturally in a network of established relationships. The fault lies not only with the government or with the providers of corporation insurance, but also with the members of the community, who fail to realize that they're still needed. Insurance not only pushes people away from supporting relationships, it also steps into the void created by people turning away from relationships.

Regardless of who is at fault, a tragic erosion of community, church relationships, and commitment has occurred. The natural events of life that once drew people together no longer do so. Because everything's taken care of, people seldom become meaningfully involved in each other's lives.

"But can't God work through an insurance company like he can work through a church or community?" God can work through anything. But he desires to work through people in personal ways, not simply through a huge, impersonal pool of assets that issues computer-printed checks from one part of the country to another.

I know insurance agents who are exceptionally kind, compassionate, and helpful. They might go beyond the call of duty in carrying out their jobs. But they may not be church members, and often they aren't even neighbors of their clients. Even if they are, the money they distribute isn't theirs; it's the corporation's. It has been paid (not lovingly contributed) by a million people who don't know, or care to know, each other.

Health Insurance

We can look at health insurance in several ways. First, when we consider the exorbitant medical costs of our society, it seems dangerous and irresponsible not to have health insurance. After all, if everyone else is paying to have health insurance, why should an extended family, church, or society be expected to pick up the tab for someone who could have bought health insurance but chose not to?

Our ministry provides health insurance, and I'm grateful for it. Even if it wasn't provided, I'd probably choose to have it. Although I've been moved to this decision by the stark reality of escalating health-care costs and stories of cases that have resulted in hundreds of thousands of dollars in medical bills, I believe the situation is not ideal.

What *would be* ideal? A Christian community that is spontaneously self-insured. I don't mean a situation where everyone signs contracts and pays premiums to the church, nor one where the church acts as an insurance company in a formal way. I mean a relationship in which the church takes responsibility

345

to care for its members who are ill or disabled, just as it did in the first century and always did until recent history—when society started providing alternatives to church care.

Whether a large benevolence fund is maintained or special offerings are taken as needs arise, the church should be there to meet needs. The church, not the insurance industry, is the body of Christ. Jesus said that the gates of hell would not prevail against the Church—not insurance companies. God can provide however he wishes. But his ideal plan is to provide through his church.

What *would* *be* ideal? A Christian community that is spontaneously self-insured ... in which the church takes responsibility to care for its members who are ill or disabled, just as it did in the first century and always did until recent history.

Consider what would happen if the massive sums that Christians pay in insurance premiums were instead given voluntarily to churches. Much of this money could be passed on immediately to the cause of reaching the world for Christ and feeding the hungry. The rest could be accumulated, if this seemed the best way, and saved at a significant rate of interest. As needs arose, the money could be drawn upon. Perhaps the same results could be accomplished through special offerings.

Several churches could join together within a community. Apart from the potential financial advantages of such an arrangement, God's people would be acting as God's people—united in ministry and personally involved in the lives of the needy. God would be seen to work through them, just as he did in the early Church.

I'm told that Amish communities function in this way. I've heard of a few churches that operate on this basis, although I've never seen one firsthand. The problem for a small church would be the possibility of a massive hospital bill, but larger churches—or a community of churches working together—would have a broader base of support, thereby greatly reducing the individual risk.

Since 1993, Christian Care Ministry has had a program called Medi-Share, a self-regulated group with more than forty-five thousand members from thirteen different denominations. Members, including many health care professionals, share each other's medical bills on a not-for-profit basis. This alternative to insurance allows many households to save thousands of dollars each year and has helped members in all fifty states pay tens of millions of dollars in medical bills. Although it cannot guarantee coverage, the group claims no eligible treatment has ever gone unpaid.[10]

Medi-Share is not an insurance company, but a lower cost alternative requiring a $150 annual fee plus a monthly sharing in actual member costs. (It also covers catastrophic bills up to $5 million, for expenses exceeding $50,000, through an insurance policy.) One of Medi-Share's purposes for existing is stewardship: "Most members are able to significantly cut their annual medical expenses, leaving them with more income for giving to the Lord's work."[11] The organization also educates and encourages healthy lifestyles, and denies coverage for morally objectionable procedures such as abortions.

Although our family is not yet part of such an arrangement, I believe there's much to be said for this type of organization. Instead of always accepting society's status quo, we should ask God to show us more biblical alternatives.

Life Insurance

Life insurance is actually death insurance, because it's payable upon the death of the insured. The major purpose of life insurance is to replace the provider's income. If you've ever sat through an insurance sales presentation, you know that the agent will explain how you must have a certain amount of insurance in order for your dependents to be taken care of at your present standard of living (allowing for inflation) for another five, ten, or twenty years after your death. Typically, the agent will summarize the results on a computer printout, suggesting a huge amount of coverage requiring large insurance premiums.

But where does God fit into all this? If a man dies tomorrow, it seems reasonable in this economy to have a moderate amount of funds designated to care for many of his family's basic needs. On the other hand, to supply them with a huge chunk of money to be appropriated over the next fifteen years until his children are grown, and another thirty years until his wife may die, seems like too much. If life insurance is appropriate, its purpose should be to provide for a family for a season, not to protect them against any and every eventuality, and certainly not to profit them by their loved one's departure.

I've had distraught unemployed men tell me that due to their large life insurance policies they're worth more to their family dead than alive. One of them seriously contemplated suicide for this exact reason. Something's terribly wrong when a man's most effective avenue of material provision for his family is his own death.

When I die, I don't want the church to say, "Randy was a good provider—all his wife's needs are taken care of." I want them to realize that my wife does have needs and will continue to have them. Yes, I may have seen to some of her ongoing material needs through a house, some savings, some retirement funds, and a modest life insurance policy. But she'll need the ongoing help and support and wisdom and counsel and encouragement of the church, just as my children would have when they were younger. In fact, at some point my loved ones might need material help as well. Would that be so terrible? Isn't it okay to sometimes need help from others in Christ's body?

Time and time again, I've seen Christians keep their distance from hurting brothers and sisters because they believe the insurance company, government, hospice, or some benevolence organization is taking care of them. When it comes to caring for their needy, even some of the pseudo-Christian cults put evangelicals to shame.

Life insurance agents don't account for many things that could and probably will happen over the next five, ten, or twenty years. Not the least of these, I hope, would be my wife's remarriage. Of course, this isn't certain, and it might take several years. (And I'm grateful she hasn't already picked someone out!) I believe it's often unhealthy for a woman to bring a large amount of money into a second marriage. Although many men have failed to provide life insurance that would have been a big help to their wives, many others have provided so much that it actually works against them. (For instance, children can be hurt when they are lavished with many possessions and vacations that the family couldn't afford when Dad was alive.)

Our children need to know that God is the One who will meet their needs. Having enough insurance to be responsible is one thing. But playing God by factoring in every conceivable future scenario, and thereby overinsuring, is another.

Would Jesus have bought an insurance policy if one had been available? How about the apostles? If not, why not? If so, what kind and how much?

Is Insurance God's Tool or a God Substitute?

The greatest danger of insurance is that it easily undermines our dependence on God. I must carefully evaluate my motives when it comes to buying insurance. Is it a God-given means of provision? Or is it an end-run that makes trust obsolete and God unnecessary? The more prone I am to trust in insurance, the more likely it is that I should have less, not more.

The kings of Israel paid tribute to foreign powers, the kings of Egypt and Syria. Isaiah condemned them for trusting in worldly powers rather than God (Isaiah 30:1-2). Is dependence upon the worldly power of insurance corporations an act of independence from the God who promises to provide for those who trust him? Is collective insurance a financial equivalent to the Tower of Babel? Is it a God-substitute? Are we using insurance, savings, and our retirement plan as a horizontal means to gain our family's financial security without having to look vertically to God? Is it a way to hedge our bets in case God doesn't come through? Is insurance a means by which faith becomes obsolete and God unnecessary? If our financial bases are covered, do we really have to depend on God?

Here's the bottom line question: Is insurance a legitimate tool of God or an illegitimate substitute for him? Is it a provision or an idol? These questions can only be answered in our hearts, but we need to ask them.

Would Jesus have bought an insurance policy if one had been available?

(As it was, when Jesus died, he entrusted his mother to the care of the apostle John.) How about the apostles? If not, why not? If so, what kind and how much? Because no parallels to the kinds of insurance policies we buy today are mentioned in Scripture, it's impossible to prove that insurance is right or wrong. Some would consider insurance as a legitimate way of providing for their family. Others see it as a lack of dependence on God. The sin of presumption could be committed in either case.

Our own choice has been to use insurance sparingly. Naturally, we buy insurance when it's legally required. When we owned cars (the ministry owns them now), we didn't carry collision insurance, because it cost more than the cars were worth. Before it became part of our compensation package, we chose high-deductible, low-cost health insurance. We've never had disability or mortgage insurance. Our ministry provides a life insurance policy. (Normally, with a few exceptions, term insurance makes more financial sense than whole life.)

In short, we do have insurance—more than some, less than others. We want to be responsible, yet leave plenty of room for God. We also want to be able to use the money for God's kingdom that would otherwise go to pay additional premiums.

I'm not trying to set a standard for others to follow. Everyone must measure his or her own situation and convictions. Nanci and I have no debt, and our children are now grown and married. Our parents are either deceased or financially independent. There are many factors to consider when making an insurance decision. Sometimes I think we should have a little more insurance; other times I think we should have less. This tension is healthy. As we continue to grow in Christ, we continue to evaluate. But we are determined to follow his lead as best we can discern it.

Why Worry?

"Seek first his kingdom and his righteousness, and all these things [what you eat, drink, and wear] will be given to you as well" (Matthew 6:33). Unlike the pagans who "run after all these things" and "worry about tomorrow," believers are told to follow Christ, live a radical life of faith, and trust God to provide (Matthew 6:25-34). In this passage, Jesus says that God cares for the birds. Yet birds aren't created in God's image. Christ didn't die for birds. The Holy Spirit doesn't indwell birds. Birds won't reign with Christ. But we will! So Christ asks his disciples, "Are you not much more valuable than they?" (Matthew 6:26). If he takes care of the less valuable creatures, will he not take care of us, who are far more valuable?

Of course, the birds provide for their immediate future through labor— building nests and obtaining food for their young. But they don't maintain one nest in the mountains and another at the beach. Neither do they fill their cellars with freeze-dried worms. Birds do the work that God created them to do; they sing when they work, they don't hoard, and they instinctively trust their Creator to take care of them. Should we who know God's grace do any less?

Contrast this with a life-insurance pitch that preys upon the anxieties that Jesus told us we're not to have. (Not all insurance agents take this approach— many are honest and not manipulative). Jesus says, "Accept my sovereignty and goodness, and you won't have to worry about tomorrow. Trust me." The agent says, "Buy our policy and you won't have to worry about tomorrow. Trust me." We must ask whether God offers adequate coverage. And does he have the resources to back up the offer?

> **All of us trust in something. The more dependable the object of our trust, the less we need to worry.**

All of us trust in something. The more dependable the object of our trust, the less we need to worry. The stock market isn't God, *The Wall Street Journal* isn't the Bible, your asset manager isn't your priest, and financial experts aren't prophets. (Prophets were put to death when their prophecies didn't come true!) That doesn't mean the stock market is bad, but it does mean it's not trustworthy. It may do well for a day, a month, a year, or even a few decades. But because the stock market is uncertain, it can only produce anxiety when it becomes the object of our trust. God is the only totally trustworthy object. Therefore, he's the only one who cannot betray our trust.

Why is this truth so hard for us to accept? If we believe that God can create us, redeem us, and bring us through death to spend eternity with him, why can't we take him at his word when he says he'll provide for our material needs?

If God calls on you today to share your resources with another, you must not say, "I can't, Lord, because I don't know where my own provisions are coming from." Yes, you *do* know where they're coming from. They're coming from God. You may not know the form this provision will take, but you do know the Source. Like the poor widow who had no cash reserves, you know that God will take care of you, even if there are no visible resources.

If God has control of everything, and God takes care of his children, and God gives everything necessary to those who walk with him; and if you are his child, and you are walking with him—why worry? Worrying never helps anything anyway—but has hurt plenty.

The Bottom Line: Dependence

In each of the matters dealt with in this chapter—saving, retirement, and insurance—the issues are the same. Do these instruments reduce or increase our sense of dependence on God? Do they reduce or increase our flexibility and openness to God's direction? Considering what money spent on these things would do if invested in God's kingdom now, is this money being well utilized?

If we don't have savings or retirement funds or insurance, is it because we're consciously trusting God and giving substantially to meet others' needs? Or is it because we're lazy, undisciplined, and irresponsible? God honors the sacrificial pilgrim of faith, but he does not honor the lazy fool. God wouldn't have been pleased with the rich fool for squandering his money rather than hoarding it. Either way he would've failed to invest his assets in God's kingdom. There's sometimes a fine line between faith and foolishness.

Remember the missionary family who took their retirement savings and poured everything back into the mission? I suggest that God looks very differently at these people than at the Christian who spends his money on short-term indulgences with no thought of saving for upcoming needs or providing for his family's future. Both may have nothing at a given stage in life, but God's voluntary obligation to the one is much different than to the other. To those who seek first his kingdom and sacrificially give of their assets to his kingdom, he promises to provide materially (Matthew 6:32-33; Philippians 4:19).

No matter how much it clashes with the prevailing opinion, we can't afford to dismiss William MacDonald's exhortation:

> Reserves are crutches and props which become a substitute for trust in the Lord. We can't trust when we can see. Once we decide to provide for our future, we run into these problems. How much will be enough? How long will we live? Will there be a depression? Will there be inflation? Will we have heavy medical bills?
>
> It is impossible to know how much will be enough. Therefore we spend our lives amassing wealth to provide for a few short years of retirement. In the meantime, God has been robbed and our own life has been spent in seeking security where it cannot be found.
>
> How much better it is to work diligently for our current necessities, serve the Lord to the maximum extent, put everything above present needs into the work of the Lord, and trust him for the future.[12]

We may choose to have savings accounts, retirement funds, and insurance policies. But if we do, let's be careful to have only enough to avoid presuming on God but never enough to avoid trusting him.

CHAPTER 19

Gambling, Investing, and Leaving Money

Avoid sin rather than loss. RICHARD MATHER

If you wish to leave much wealth to your children, leave them in God's care. Do not leave them riches, but virtue and skill. For if they have the confidence of riches, they will not mind anything besides, for they shall have the means of screening the wickedness of their ways in their abundant riches. JOHN CHRYSOSTOM

GAMBLING

When I wrote the original version of this book in 1988, I saw no need to give much attention to gambling. Times have changed!

Recently I was on a long bike ride when I stopped at a convenience store to buy bottled water. The store was filled—ten people in line in front of me. I couldn't figure out why. Suddenly the manager announced, "The machine's broken. We can't sell any more Lotto tickets." Within seconds all ten people in front of me walked out the door. "Can I help you?" the clerk called, while I was still standing fifteen feet away.

State governments spend hundreds of millions of dollars annually persuading people to buy lottery tickets. They advertise the top prize but don't reveal the astronomical odds; instead they give the odds of winning the lowest prize. Lotteries are a government-controlled version of the old inner-city numbers games that targeted those most vulnerable to get-rich-quick schemes. In the past, the government prosecuted numbers running as a criminal act. Perpetrators went to jail. Now government itself is the perpetrator. When you consider that 43 percent of callers to the 1-800-GAMBLER national hotline are addicted to lottery gambling, it quickly becomes apparent that the state, which is supposed to protect its citizens, has become an agent of their destruction.[1]

A generation of young people is growing up believing that gambling is innocent, normal fun that pays off—despite the fact that gambling spawns poverty, family breakdowns, crime, drug use, alcohol abuse, joblessness, and suicide.

Ads for the Illinois lottery, posted on billboards in Chicago's poorest neighborhood, read, "This could be your ticket out." It's the worst ethics—and an offense to God—to tempt the poor to squander what little money they have. Dispensing false hope exploits the poor.

Many Christians have followed this same path of irresponsibility and addiction. Christian leaders are hesitant to speak out against it for fear of sounding legalistic or hurting feelings. Yet the destructive nature of gambling is so significant that failing to address this issue is the same as failing to shepherd people who need guidance.

There's a difference between reasonable risks and gambling. Gambling is a shortcut to God's created pattern of working to earn money. In gambling, wealth isn't distributed on the basis of work, service, or personal need, only by chance.

Pastor Barry Arnold began a message on gambling this way:

> If you had the option of participating in an activity that would incontrovertibly and directly contribute to increased crime: thefts, robberies, embezzlement, bankruptcies, child abuse, domestic violence, and suicide, would you go ahead and participate in that activity?
>
> If there was a *possibility* that the entertainment you chose today could—fifteen years from now—destroy your daughter's marriage and contribute to her conviction for writing bad checks; if your entertainment might result in your son's incarceration for embezzlement, or lead him to abandon his children, would you go ahead and choose that entertainment, or would you do something else?
>
> Americans gamble more money each year than they spend on groceries. Five to eight percent of American adolescents are already addicted to gambling; 75 percent of pathological gamblers admit to having committed at least one felony to support their habit; 18 percent of people housed by inner-city missions are homeless as a result of gambling; police chiefs across the country warn that wherever gambling is introduced, even in small towns, crime follows.[2]

Ironically, many churches use gambling, such as bingo and raffles, for fundraisers. Instead of offering people alternatives to addictions, these churches unwittingly invite people to develop them.

Although it's true that some people are able to gamble without losing control, others are extremely vulnerable to the addictive nature of gambling—and there's no way to tell ahead of time who those people will be. No one expects to become a statistic, but the whole gambling industry is designed to snare addicts.[3] And the recovery rate is notoriously low. Gamblers Anonymous claims that less than 10 percent of compulsive gamblers who have gone through treatment are able to resist returning to gambling.

The gambler's ambition is to win. But winning comes at the expense of others. Jackpots are built from other gamblers' losses. Gambling thrives on the gullible, undisciplined, and lazy. Coffers are filled with revenues from people who should have used their money for constructive purposes. Ironically, the state ends up doling out support funds to many of the same people who buy lottery tickets. Try explaining that gambling is innocent fun to a child who hasn't eaten for two days because his parents are spending grocery money on lottery tickets and casinos.

States are notorious for pointing out all the good they're doing with lottery money—helping schools, improving neighborhoods, protecting an endangered species. How about protecting families endangered by gambling? People don't gamble to improve schools and help the elderly—so let's quit pretending. The state exploits its citizens' character flaws, then pats itself on the back for all the good things it does with the money. Instead of slinking away in shame for exploiting the weak, we claim the moral high ground for doing so.

As a bumper sticker says, "The lottery is a tax on people who are bad at math." The chances are greater of being struck by lightning than of winning a multimillion-dollar lottery. But even if a gambler ends up winning, he or she has violated God's means of provision. It's hard and wise labor that brings financial profit (Proverbs 14:23).

One of the great ironies of gambling is that the vast majority of people lose money, and the few who win find that money doesn't make them happy—and it may even ruin their lives. A 1999 study reported that "six months after winning the lottery, you are likely to be no happier than if you had been paralyzed in a car crash."[4] As the winner of 6.5 million British pounds put it, "I've got the pool, the mansion, the Jag . . . but all my lotto win has brought me is misery. . . . Soon you realize you have as many troubles when you are rich as when you haven't two pennies to rub together."[5]

God is jealous of our affections, demanding that he alone be the focus of our worship (Exodus 20:3-5). To trust in gambling is idol worship. Only Jesus should be our master (1 Corinthians 6:12). Gambling offers false hope. Scripture tells us to put our hope in God (Psalm 42:5, 11). God tells us to work for a living, not play the odds and seek shortcuts to wealth (Proverbs 28:19-20). God is sufficient to supply all our needs (Philippians 4:19).

> One of the great ironies of gambling is that the vast majority of people lose money, and the few who win find that money doesn't make them happy—and it may even ruin their lives.

355

Jesus says our heart always follows our treasure (Matthew 6:21). When we lay down money for gambling, our heart is drawn into gambling. Scripture warns us against covetousness (Deuteronomy 5:21) and calls us to contentment (Philippians 4:11-12). Gambling feeds the former and prevents the latter.

We're commanded to love our neighbors (Matthew 22:39). Taking advantage of the weaknesses of others for the hope of gain is the opposite of loving your neighbor. In gambling, one person's gain is many people's loss.

Nevertheless, many Christians view gambling as innocent fun. Perhaps it would help to apply the reward test. God will reward his children for working hard at any honest job, earning money, using it wisely, and sharing it generously. Can you picture standing at the judgment seat and Jesus rewarding you for gambling? (If not, does that tell you something?)

INVESTING
Investments and Biblical Principles
Although gambling violates biblical principles, there are other actions in life that involve risk but are still legitimate. Scripture doesn't directly teach that we should invest, but it does provide illustrations of investing, including real estate ventures (Proverbs 31:16). Jesus speaks illustratively of investing in such a way as to gain financial returns (Matthew 25:14-29; Luke 19:12-26). This suggests that he approves of wise investments, and it certainly indicates he doesn't forbid investing. His injunctions to invest in eternity, by laying up treasures in heaven rather than on earth, puts in perspective our earthly investments but does not preclude them.

Investing doesn't simply bring profits to the investor (sometimes it doesn't even do that). It also profits the business in which we have invested. A Christian should avoid investing in any enterprise that makes its profit from people doing what they shouldn't. For example, in most cases I believe people shouldn't take out a second mortgage on their home. Consequently, for me to invest in high-yield second mortgages would be an attempt to profit from others' poor decisions. I would not feel right doing that.

Mutual funds, today's most common investments, distribute their investors' money in a wide range of companies, some of which do things with the money that a Christian wouldn't condone. Can we in good conscience invest money when even a small portion of it goes to underwrite abortions or fund the tobacco and alcohol industries? There's a difference of course—abortion is always wrong, whereas tobacco and alcohol consumption are not inherently wrong, but often prove unwise and destructive. The point is, there are more basic questions than whether or not an investment makes money. It's challenging to examine exactly where investment money goes in a mutual fund. But we're God's money managers. Isn't it reasonable for him to expect us to invest his money in companies that don't help fund ungodliness?

Values-Based Investing

Churches and ministries often welcome every gift, regardless of how it was earned. Likewise, many Christians don't evaluate the source of their investment income. God operates by a different standard: "You must not bring the earnings of a female prostitute or of a male prostitute into the house of the Lord your God to pay any vow, because the Lord your God detests them both" (Deuteronomy 23:18).

God *does* care where the money comes from. Often a church or ministry can't know the source of its contributions. The biblical principle applies primarily to the giver of the gift, not the recipient. But when pastors and leaders know that something has come from a source displeasing to God, they should address the issue, both for the sake of the donors—and those whose lives are affected by their choices—and the church or ministry. If this standard applies to the source of incoming funds, surely it applies even more to where we choose to put our money.

"Socially responsible investing" pioneer Amy Domini established ethical criteria that matched her liberal perspective to eliminate investments in offending companies. Over an eight-year period, the stock market performance of the companies chosen exceeded that of the Standard & Poor's 500 index. Of course, even if they hadn't, conscience should prevail over pragmatism. I cite this example because many evangelical Christians shrug their shoulders and say, "It's too difficult to monitor investments; and besides, values-based investing would produce poor returns." But if people who believe in environmental concerns, and those who oppose nuclear power and weapons production (which include some Christians) have strong enough convictions not to invest in such things, shouldn't those of us who oppose abortion, pornography, anti-Christian bigotry, and the marketing of sex and violence to children also have the fortitude to put our money where our morals are?

Consider Ephesians 5:1-11, which culminates in the command, "Have nothing to do with the fruitless deeds of darkness, but rather expose them." How can we justify investing in companies that market the fruitless deeds of darkness? Isn't funding evil a clear violation of the warning against establishing an unequal yoke with darkness (2 Corinthians 6:14-18)?

This certainly isn't easy to track when there are so many companies with so many names. Most Christians would think it was wrong to invest in *Playboy* magazine. But the Houston-based Internet company Telescan specializes in data retrieval tools that it uses in partnership with *Playboy's* Web sites.[6] But who would know that if they saw Telescan on a long list of companies invested in by their mutual fund?

Hewlett-Packard supports Planned Parenthood, the nation's largest abortion provider. Rick's Cabaret International (NASDAQ symbol: RICK) is a public company self-described as a "premier adult nightclub offering topless entertainment." In *Putting Your Money Where Your Morals Are,* Scott Fehrenbacher lists many objectionable companies that mutual funds invest in. Among these are Tenet (NYSE symbol: THC), the second-largest chain of hospital facilities in the nation, including some of which perform for-profit, elective abortions; and American Express (NYSE Symbol: AXP), which uses shareholder funds to actively promote homosexual causes.[7]

Many mutual funds invest in Disney, which owns ABC, ESPN, and A&E, as well as film studios Miramax, Touchstone, and Hollywood Pictures. Miramax has produced films overflowing with gratuitous heterosexual and homosexual sex, rape, and murder. *Pulp Fiction* and *Priest* mock Christians and are among the most offensive movies in the last decade—and they're Disney products! Peter and Rochelle Schweizer, in their book *Disney: The Mouse Betrayed,* document what many call pedophilia in Disney's Miramax film *Kids.*[8]

Sometimes refusing to do business with a company may accomplish more than selling shares. A financial counselor wrote the following note to me:

> When I find that a company such as Levi opposes basic Christian values, I can sell my shares, but if this drives the price down, the market will find it is attractively priced, and shares will be bought to bring it back to its original level. On the other hand, I could choose not to buy Levi products. This action does have a direct impact on their profitability. Granted, I do not buy enough pairs of jeans in one year to force them out of business, but I can probably convince enough of my friends to make their purchases elsewhere resulting in lower profits. If Levi's profitability is down, then their value has dropped, and they will become a much less attractive investment. It could even reach the point that the "pagan" marketplace shuns the stock because there are more attractive stocks available, which often leads to a change in senior management—hopefully someone with better values.
>
> Unfortunately, as Christians we tend to become selectively aware of certain organizations, then transfer our economic support to other organizations we have no way of researching. What do the other companies that make jeans support? What are their corporate practices? Do they give benefits to same-sex partners, and do they support Planned Parenthood? Do I know? How much time should I devote to research?

These questions are valid, but they should motivate us to give *more* thought to this issue, not less. Regardless of whether we'll drive down a company's value by selling shares, we are still accountable for where we put God's money. For instance, those who own certain Fidelity mutual funds (which includes many Christians) have unknowingly helped support the government of Sudan, a genocidal regime that has systematically enslaved and persecuted Christians for decades. Various Christian denominations have invested in Talisman Energy, a huge Canadian oil company that does 25 percent of its business with Sudan. Vanguard and the state of New York were among those who divested themselves of Talisman after antislavery groups lobbied them. I hope by the time you read this it's no longer true, but as of 2002, Fidelity still owned millions of shares in Talisman. I joined many others in addressing my concerns to Fidelity:

> I'm writing to protest Fidelity's investment in Talisman Energy—and your unwillingness to address the consequences of this investment.
>
> Talisman is a major financial partner with the Sudanese government, a regime that Congress calls "genocidal." The money you invest in Talisman enables the Sudanese government to launch vicious slave raids against black civilians in southern Sudan. Government forces gang-rape women and girls, and have abducted thousands into bondage and attempts at forced conversion to Islam.
>
> Talisman compounds the problem by filling Sudan's war coffers with oil profits and by creating one more reason to clear the oil-rich land of southern Sudan. For this reason, many prominent funds have divested from Talisman—including TIAA-CREF, Vanguard, and the State of New York.
>
> But Fidelity has failed to follow suit, and is now one of the largest shareholders in Talisman. You argue that Fidelity cannot take responsibility for the actions of companies in its portfolio. But if this were another time in history, would Fidelity invest in Southern cotton plantations or Nazi munitions factories? I hope not.
>
> I encourage Fidelity to divest immediately from Talisman. If you do not, I'll have no choice but to discourage those in my circle of influence from having any relationship with Fidelity.

Scott Fehrenbacher persuasively argues that it's wrong for Christians to invest God's money in music that promotes murder and rape (e.g., by funding gangsta rap), blatantly immoral movies, blood-spattering video games, pornography, nude dancing bars, abortion, alcoholism, and tobacco addiction.[9] Some companies, including the large conglomerate that owns MTV, actively engage in trashing Christian beliefs and morals. That we would invest God's money in companies sponsoring anti-Christian philosophies and activities seems unthinkable. Yet it happens every day.

The average Christian whose retirement program is in mutual funds or stocks managed by others has no clue where God's money is actually going. Mutual funds serve to separate the investor from the companies invested in.

The Mennonite Mutual Aid Association has well over a billion dollars invested in the MMA Praxis Growth Fund. Yet "more than 30 percent of the fund's assets were invested in companies involved in abortion or pornography and companies that specifically promoted homosexuality with their internal policies."[10]

Values-based investing isn't a new concept:

> As early as the 1800s, the Quakers withdrew from business relationships and partnerships involved in the slave trade. In the 1920s, churches and denominations in America chose to actively screen their money from being invested in "sin stocks," defined then as belonging to companies that manufactured products related to alcohol, tobacco, and gambling.[11]

Some of our retirement funds are invested in a company whose guiding principles state that they "avoid investing in companies that are involved in practices contrary to Judeo-Christian principles," in particular abortion and pornography.[12] Some years this particular fund has underperformed the Standard & Poor's 500, and in others it has outperformed it. We have stayed with it in the low-performing years because we believe in its commitment to never fund what dishonors Christ.

The average Christian whose retirement program is in mutual funds or stocks managed by others has no clue where God's money is actually going.

It will not be easy, but if we are God's stewards we should take responsibility to investigate—and choose carefully—where we put God's money. I confess that some of the mutual funds we're invested in may include immoral holdings, because I don't have the time or expertise to do this research and have only acted on information I've received. Most of us need to rely on others for this. The question is, who are these others, and how can we receive accurate information from them on these matters?

If enough Christians would adopt a values-based approach, we might see a shift in priorities among some mutual funds or brokerages, so we could more wisely entrust them with our investments. But even if we're the only ones to do this, our stewardship responsibility is to God, and he is the one who will ultimately evaluate and reward us.

How Much Risk Is Appropriate?

Some mutual funds are conservative, striving for steady, consistent growth. Others are more volatile, with greater potential for growth and for loss. What level of risk should we take with God's money?

Scripture teaches an investment principle of steady plodding as opposed to hasty speculation. "The plans of the diligent lead to profit as surely as haste leads to poverty" (Proverbs 21:5). Investors who are eager to get rich with high-yield, high-risk investments are setting themselves up for loss and disillusionment.

"He who gathers money little by little makes it grow" (Proverbs 13:11). Many Christians aren't content to gather money little by little. Consequently, they've lost a great deal of money—not to mention sleep—on investments they felt certain would make them wealthy.

The higher the potential return of any investment, the higher its risk. I saw a prospectus that promised investors their money would be multiplied ten times in a one year period—a 1,000 percent return! Now, why would this company in effect pay 1,000 percent interest for investors' money if it could get a bank loan for less than ten percent interest? The answer is that the proposition was so risky (or illegitimate) that no bank would touch it. (Remember, banks thrive on loaning money. When they refuse to lend, there are good reasons.)

Every investment involves risk. Farmers take risks when they plant their seed. They're uncertain of the weather and the market for their crop. They have no guarantee that their crop won't be lost in a tornado or insect plague or that their barns won't burn. Life involves risks. Some risks are necessary, reasonable, and well worth taking. Others are not.

Is Investing Gambling?

Not all risk-taking is gambling. But if the risk becomes great enough, it crosses the line. The stock market certainly involves risk. Yet for some it's a reasonable place to invest, especially if they choose their stocks carefully. Of course, no matter how careful we are it's possible to lose a great deal of money, even all of it. Every decade or so, the market takes a huge dip that should remind us we cannot count on a steady upward movement. Some people are comfortable investing venture capital in young, emerging companies, taking more risk with the possibility of greater returns. (Also, by underwriting young companies, these investors arguably provide a valuable service to society.) Such risk taking requires a certain kind of personality—one that's not prone to worry.

Those who invest in the stock market must be patient and detached enough so that investments don't become their primary focus, distracting them from their single-minded purpose as Christ's followers. Any Christian whose heart and happiness go up and down with the stock market has no business investing there. But because our hearts will follow our treasures (Matthew 6:21), worry-free investing doesn't come naturally.

Occasionally, I've invested small amounts of money. Fifteen years ago when I was a pastor, I put six hundred dollars in a particular computer company.

> **Many Christians aren't content to gather money little by little. Consequently, they've lost a great deal of money— not to mention sleep—on investments they felt certain would make them wealthy.**

361

Three months later it had tripled in value. I decided to sell it one morning and take the profits. As I was about to make the call, the phone rang. Someone from our church was in the hospital. I needed to get there immediately. I spent the whole day with one of our church families. The next morning when I called to sell the stock, I discovered that in one day the value of the shares had dropped dramatically. My visit to the hospital had cost eight hundred dollars.

Fortunately, I was able to realize that God was in that hospital call. Ministering to a needy family was far more important than the money. I didn't need to worry about the "loss." I was still four hundred dollars ahead (although the same principle would apply if I'd lost it all). The point is that it was God's money, not mine. He wasn't going to worry about it—why should I?

If we invest, we must understand and be comfortable with risk. When we evaluate whether or not to invest, we need to look not only at the money, but also at the amount of time, energy, and emotional attachment required. Sometimes, money is the smallest cost of investing.

A Christian financial counselor told me about a land investment he made with his brother. First, he described the difficulty of making the payments. Then he told of all the time and energy it took to develop the land, which he found himself constantly thinking about. The venture put tremendous stress on his family, making his wife ill. Finally the tensions of partnership destroyed his relationship with his brother. They'd been close prior to the purchase but remain distant to this day. My friend said, "It looked like a great investment, but the price we ended up paying was enormous."

Some investments work like a dream. Others, like this one, turn out to be a nightmare. We must always count the cost, even potential costs that aren't so obvious when the investment-dream adrenaline is flowing.

Why Am I Investing?

Nothing is an investment unless it's likely to bring profit. Furthermore, you must intend eventually to exchange it for that profit. Otherwise, it's just a purchase. So, for example, apart from rare exceptions we do not "invest" in a wedding ring," or "invest" in a car, or "invest" in a mountain cabin. If we intend to keep these items, they aren't investments, they're purchases.

Financial advisor Larry Burkett cites four basic bad reasons for investing:

- greed (1 Timothy 6:9)
- envy (Psalm 73:3)
- pride (1 Timothy 6:17)
- ignorance (Proverbs 14:7).[13]

Investments shouldn't be motivated by fear and insecurity, because God promises to provide for our material needs. If you're investing merely to enhance your personal kingdom, not God's, your reason for investing is biblically unsound. You're being rich toward yourself and not toward God (Luke 12:21). If you're investing to multiply assets that can eventually provide for your family, the needy, and ministry purposes, those can be good motivations. Many foundations and individuals invest some principal and give earnings to kingdom causes. But we must ask ourselves whether God is a qualified investor. If I gave him not only the interest but also the principal, couldn't he multiply it in the lives of others better than I could—or a mutual fund manager?

Once we have given money away, it is safely in God's hands. As long as we keep it, however, even with the best intentions, there's a possibility it will leave us or we will leave it before we can give it away. Many Christians have discovered this truth the hard way through downturns in the stock market, company takeovers, and corporate bankruptcies. Many people have prospered in their investments and have increased their giving as a result. And that may be exactly what God wants. Nevertheless, the surest, most risk-free way to invest in eternity isn't by making earthly investments; it's by doing what the poor widow did—giving now to God's kingdom.

Guidelines for Investing

Never risk money you can't afford to lose. Never make uninformed or hasty investment decisions. Never make any major financial decision without counting the possible financial, mental, emotional, and spiritual costs. Remember that someone with millions of dollars in investments may be in greater bondage than someone with no investments at all.

If we're poor stewards, we first need to learn basic financial responsibility, including how to give and how to get out of debt. Sadly, some people who are heavily into investments are also deeply in debt, including credit-card debt. For these people, there's a surefire proposal that will earn them a guaranteed 12, 15, or 18 percent return at no risk. All they have to do is take the money they might put in investments and instead pay off their credit cards. It makes no sense to seek potentially profitable investments while incurring substantial losses due to debt.

AVOID DISASTROUS INVESTMENTS. The typical get-rich-quick scheme offers tremendous profit at minimal risk. Usually it involves an unprecedented opportunity, a breakthrough in an area you know little about. This might be real estate in another part of the country, a new microchip that will revolutionize the computer industry, or a discovery that will cure cancer.

Typically, a friend (who heard about them from a cousin, whose brother-in-law is a financial wizard and says this is the next Microsoft) brings these investments to your attention. He's usually sincere and genuinely believes he's helping you out. The person selling the deal makes you feel like he's doing you a favor by allowing you this incredible opportunity. He emphasizes that you must make your decision within the next few days. You're impressed when this knowledgeable person assures you, "This is a great investment opportunity." (Have you ever heard someone trying to sell something by calling it "a lousy investment opportunity"?)

A Christian investment firm held a seminar at a nearby Christian college. They presented a surefire investment opportunity too good to pass up. A couple in our church got on the bandwagon, as did many others. They took out their entire savings and invested it. Not long afterward, the Christian investor and his Christian company disappeared with everyone's Christian money. The most tragic thing about this story is that it's so common. I've heard the same story, with different names and places, over and over again.

When we were in a small group Bible study with five other couples, our discussion one evening turned to money. One couple shared in tears that they'd lost their entire retirement savings in a bad investment. Another couple said that they had invested in condominiums that never materialized and lost nearly all their money. The next couple told of their huge losses from an investment. A fourth couple then shared they'd co-signed for a loan to a respected Christian businessman, whom they were sure would make good on it. He didn't make good on it, and they became responsible for the debt. Years later, this man was generating a tremendous salary and living in affluence, yet he hadn't paid them back a dime and probably never would.

Here were four Christian couples out of a group of six who had independently experienced disastrous financial situations. It wasn't the losses themselves that were most striking, but the heavy toll they had taken on the couples' hearts and minds, their relationships, and their marriages. As we studied the Scriptures that night, we were struck by the huge diversion of money, time, and energy that could have been invested in God's kingdom. How easily lost are treasures entrusted to men and how forever secure are those entrusted to God (Matthew 6:19-21).

Losses from unwise investments seem even more common in the Christian community than outside it. Losses from unwise investments seem even more common in the Christian community than outside it. I attribute this to the "spiritual credibility" that people project simply by calling themselves Christians. Who would believe that a Christian—who leads in prayer, quotes the Scriptures, and addresses an audience under the roof of a church or Christian college—would lie, cheat, and steal? (Or at best, be a fool?) Because such things are more expected in the secular world, people are sometimes more suspicious, cautious, and less gullible.

It's particularly tragic when pastors and Christian leaders become involved in get-rich-quick investments. In their sincerity, perhaps even thinking of kingdom gains, they influence others to become involved. One pastor took a second mortgage on his house to invest in a project headed by a church member. Following the pastor's example, other families became involved. Within a year, all the money had been lost. Another pastor spoke openly of the opportunity to invest in a particular invention of a local Christian that was sure to make tremendous profits. Many people followed, thinking that if the pastor was involved it must be all right. Once again, all the money disappeared.

Of course, not every investment in which money is lost is dishonest. An investment can be completely honest but unwise. Likewise, it's possible for an unwise investment to beat the odds and make money or a wise investment to end up losing money.

There's an unfortunate myth that if our hearts are right God will automatically bless us, even if our heads are empty when it comes to sound business principles. We must be careful not to presume upon God's favor and expect him to bail us out of unwise decisions. P. T. Barnum said, "There's a sucker born every minute." Often, it seems, those suckers can be found in the Church.

Some people wrongly assume that there are laws to protect them against bad investments. However, because many bad investments are entirely honest, and even some dishonest ones are legal, this is simply not true. At best, an illegal scheme may end up in the prosecution of those responsible. Rarely do investors get their money back.

OBTAIN WISE FINANCIAL COUNSEL. David said, "I will praise the Lord, who counsels me" (Psalm 16:7). "Your statutes are my delight; they are my counselors" (Psalm 119:24). Ultimately, we can get the best financial counsel from God's Word. If we do, we'll often find it gives us perspectives dramatically different from those of human counselors—secular and Christian. The many scriptural principles dealt with in this book are far more important than independent counsel from me or others, regardless of their financial experience. Still, there's a great deal to be gained from seeking wise counsel:

- Wisdom is more precious than rubies, and nothing you desire can compare with her. (Proverbs 8:11)
- The way of a fool seems right to him, but a wise man listens to advice. (Proverbs 12:15)
- Plans fail for lack of counsel, but with many advisers they succeed. (Proverbs 15:22)
- Listen to advice and accept instruction, and in the end you will be wise. (Proverbs 19:20)
- The quiet words of the wise are more to be heeded than the shouts of a ruler of fools. (Ecclesiastes 9:17)

These passages make it clear that we should seek a number of counselors, not just one, when we're making important decisions. The point isn't just quantity, but quality—they must be truly wise. Because wisdom begins with fearing God (Proverbs 9:10), usually these counselors should be Christians who are walking with God and living by his principles. The counsel of the ungodly must not be our standard (Psalm 1:1). Having weighed the Scriptures and the counsel of others, we should ask God for wisdom. He promises to give it to those who seek it (James 1:5).

It's much easier to find a Christian financial counselor than a biblical financial counselor. Financial advisors should be evaluated not only by their professed faith but also by their knowledge of Scripture, grasp of finances, track record, character, and skills.

It's usually best to receive investment advice from fee-based financial counselors, rather than salespeople paid by commission. It's extremely difficult for financial counselors to give objective advice when they have specific products to sell. For them to recommend alternatives that would be better for you but earn them less money—or no money—is more than you can reasonably expect. Usually they won't try to cheat you, but they will naturally narrow the options to the alternatives that earn them money. (After all, selling particular investment opportunities is what they do for a living.) They have a vested interest in persuading you to make a decision to their advantage, which may not be to yours. That's another reason why wise counsel should be sought from more than one person (Proverbs 11:14; 24:6).

Studies demonstrate that many "no load" mutual funds (those with no sales commission) perform as well as "load" funds, which may charge a front-end fee of 5 percent or a back-end fee of 3 percent that goes to the sales representative. With a 5 percent front-load fund, your investment must increase by 5 percent just to break even. Only then can you begin to earn money. Look at it this way: If two runners are racing 100 meters and one is given a five-meter start, which one is more likely to win? A no-load fund, on the other hand, doesn't put you behind from the start. That's great for you, but not for your advisor, who will receive no commission. In a fee-based arrangement, you will more likely get good advice not tied to any particular product, you will pay for guidance only as you receive it, and the fee will typically be much less than a commission.

It's also important to seek spiritual counsel from people who can advise you where to put your money to work in God's kingdom. Once again, however, you must be aware of vested interests. Two wealthy women approached me and asked if I would advise them periodically about which Christian ministries to support. They told me about bad experiences they'd had with ministries that had obtained their names as "wealthy donor prospects" and pressured them to give. The only way I could advise these women with integrity was to make sure I had nothing to gain from them. I established a simple ground rule: I would be glad to advise them, but they weren't to do anything for my material benefit, not even buy lunch for me. Only when we eliminated the possibility of any vested interest on my part did I feel they could trust me—and I could trust myself.

Once you have received counsel, the decision is yours. If you doubt the wisdom or rightness of investing in something, you shouldn't proceed, because "everything that does not come from faith is sin" (Romans 14:23).

CONSULT YOUR MARRIAGE PARTNER. Discuss matters carefully with your spouse before making an investment or any financial commitment. "A prudent wife is from the Lord" (Proverbs 19:14). Many unwise decisions have been made by husbands acting on their own. Either they say nothing to their wife or they ignore her reservations, which should have been seen as a message from God to slow down, pray, and think more carefully. The long-term consequences are severe when a couple is divided on financial decisions. There will always be blame when there's not agreement.

Four out of five married women will one day be widows. Because a wife will survive her husband 80 percent of the time, it's essential that he include her in major financial decisions.

Men, if you were to die today, would your wife know what to do with your family's finances? Does she have access to and understand the will (or trust), bank accounts, investments, and insurance policies? Financial ignorance is one more pressure she won't need.

One of the best gifts a husband can leave his wife is instructions (both oral and written) about what she will need to know about their finances if he dies before she does. He should also arrange for someone trustworthy to serve as her advisor if needed. (The more financial arrangements that can be determined in advance, including prepaid funeral arrangements, the better.)

LEAVING MONEY BEHIND
Inheritance

By far the most significant transfer of wealth in human history is taking place today as America's World War II generation passes money and possessions to its heirs. How much has this generation amassed in pensions, savings, stocks, insurance policies, and real estate? Estimates vary between seven and ten trillion U. S. dollars.[14] If estate transfers continue at their present rate (they may or may not), by 2015 more than 14 trillion dollars will have passed from parents to children.

Even a modest middle-class estate—consisting of land, a house, furnishings, retirement funds, savings, collections, and other valuables—is often worth half a million dollars and sometimes much more.

"A good man leaves an inheritance for his children's children" (Proverbs 13:22). In Old Testament times, passing on ownership of the land to children and grandchildren was vital. Without it, succeeding generations couldn't do their farming or raise livestock. Many people lived at a subsistence level. Most were too poor to buy land. With no inheritance they could end up enslaved or unable to care for their parents and grandparents, who normally lived on the property with them until they died.

Today in America, however, things are very different. Inheritances are usually windfalls coming to people who live separately from their parents, have their own careers, are financially independent, and already have more than they need. Most often they aren't carrying on the family business, or if they are, they don't need a windfall in order to continue doing so. They have dependable sources of income generated by their own work, skills, saving, and investing. When such people inherit a farm, house, or other real estate, what becomes of it? Typically, they liquidate the asset or use it as a further source of income. They do not need the land or the money. Having it will simply mean increasing their standard of living, sometimes dramatically.

Inheritances are usually windfalls coming to people who . . . already have more than they need.

Hebrew firstborn sons were legally entitled to a double portion of inheritance (Deuteronomy 21:17). If a man died without sons, the inheritance went to his daughters, if no daughters to his brothers, if no brothers to his nearest relatives (Numbers 27:1-11). Ultimately land could not be lost to a family line, as it reverted to them in the year of Jubilee, when all debts were canceled.

In those days, daughters often remained in their father's home, or they lived with their husbands, enjoying the benefits of his land. A father's inheritance did not normally go to his daughters, most likely so as not to interfere with their husbands' responsibility to provide for them. As a father of daughters, I consider it important not to leave money that would interfere with my sons-in-law's responsibility to provide for my daughters. How dare I take away from them the character-building privilege and divine calling of working hard to care for their families? Many well-meaning parents have caused serious marital conflicts by leaving money to their grown children. Money that's "his" and "hers" divides the marriage and fosters an unhealthy independence. Married couples who inherit wealth should not keep it separate from each other.

Those who cite Scripture to prove that parents should leave an inheritance to children typically do not follow Scripture's guidelines of leaving to sons only, a double portion to the firstborn, and so on. It seems inconsistent to say that an inheritance should be left because the Bible says so, but then to turn around and do it very differently than the Bible directs. A better approach is to understand the reasons for inheritance, then see these not as rules to be legalistically obeyed but as underlying principles that we should seriously weigh.

In a society with such affluence and opportunity as our own, I believe that in most cases Christian parents should seriously consider leaving the bulk of their estate to churches, parachurch ministries, missions, and other kingdom purposes, leaving only a small portion to their children. Our children should work hard, plan, and experience the joy of trusting God. Let God decide how much to provide for our adult children. The money we've generated under God's provision doesn't belong to them—it belongs to him.

New Testament principles and examples suggest we shouldn't strive to leave a large estate in the first place. If we do, it's evidence we've hoarded God's provision rather than shared it. John Wesley made a great deal of money on his books, as well as some hymns. Yet at his death his estate was worth only £28.

Wesley was left with so little, not because of poor planning but good planning; not because he had squandered it, but because he had generously given it to the cause of Christ. Wesley's stated goal had been to have as little left as possible when he died. At the end of his life, he wrote in his journal, "I left no money to anyone in my will, because I had none."[15] What a contrast to Christians who die with vast estates that could have been invested in the kingdom all along as God provided the assets!

Scripture commands us to give. Jesus commends the poor widow not for storing up coins and designating them to the temple in her will but for giving them. He doesn't say to the rich young man, "Leave your estate to the poor"; he says, "Sell all you have and give to the poor." God doesn't call all of his followers to do this. But he does call us to give, and primarily now—before we die, not after.

To Whom Do We Leave God's Money?

No matter how much we give away before we die, all of us will leave behind some money and possessions. (Even John Wesley left those twenty-eight pounds!) We have the responsibility to choose now where those assets will likely do the most good. This is a decision on which we shouldn't procrastinate. Seventy percent of Americans die without a will. And many who do have a will would do well to revise it radically after reevaluating biblical principles and considering the facts about inheritances today.

An enormous amount of wealth is being passed on to people who are totally unequipped to manage it. Anyone can spend money—precious few can handle it biblically. It's irresponsible to pass on money and assets to anyone—including adult children—who have demonstrated that they're incapable of handling it faithfully with eternity in mind. We shouldn't give substantial funds to those not mature enough to handle it any more than we would hand over an unlimited supply of candy to a five-year-old.

If we don't follow a policy of biblical money management, disastrous things can happen. We can lose the opportunity to invest God's assets in his kingdom. We can do irreparable damage to our children. If we leave our grown children a large estate, the best thing that can happen is that they and our grand-children use it wisely in a character-building, eternity-impacting way. The worst things that could happen are far more numerous: It may damage their character, take away their incentive to work, make them presumptuous, under-mine their trust in God, tempt them to live in luxury, damage family relation-ships, and waste God's resources, just to name a few. When Ron Blue addresses this, he asks three questions about wealth transfer:

1. What are the best and worst things that can happen?
2. How serious are they?
3. How likely are they to occur?

People often testify that their time of greatest blessing was when they were younger and had much less to live on. They say that's when they developed character, discipline, self-control, and trust in God. How ironic that these same people pass on large amounts of money to their children, robbing them of what could have been their greatest time of blessing and character development.

An estate is typically put in trust until children reach a certain age. Children know the money is coming, and by then any hope of a normal life is gone. In most cases, though, both parents don't die while children are minors. The in-heritance typically comes sometime between the children's twenties and sixties.

Rather than leave an inheritance, some choose to give large amounts of money to their children now. Some buy nice homes for newly married chil-dren—which only pressures them to adopt a lifestyle commensurate with their new neighborhood. Shouldn't we instead entrust our adult children to the Lord, pray for them, help financially when there's a real need, but never lavish money on them that can encourage inappropriate or premature lifestyle choices?

Multimillionaire Andrew Carnegie said, "The almighty dollar bequeathed to a child is an almighty curse. No man has the right to handicap his son with such a burden as great wealth. He must face this question squarely: will my for-tune be safe with my boy and will my boy be safe with my fortune?"[16]

Carnegie's second question is haunting. For many years I've had the op-portunity to speak to and interact with wealthy believers, and I've been struck by the heartbreaking stories I've heard about the devastating effects of receiving a large inheritance. In *The Legacy of Inherited Wealth*, written by two wealthy heir-esses, seventeen adult heirs recount the blessings and curses of their inherited wealth. Their stories suggest that the curses far outweigh the blessings. Al-though these people tried to find the bright side of inherited wealth, they were much more convincing when talking about the dark side. Frustration, anger, doubt, insecurity, and resentment—all tied to growing up wealthy or becom-ing wealthy through inheritance—repeatedly surface. If you are considering leaving significant wealth to your children—or are raising your children in affluence—you should read *The Legacy of Inherited Wealth*. It may convince you to change your strategy. At the very least it will alert you to the land mines of passing on wealth to children in our culture.[17]

I used to believe that the strongest argument against passing along wealth to our children is the many needy people who could be helped if the money were given away. But in addition to the lost opportunity to do good that is represented by inherited wealth, I now see the significant harm that often is done to the heirs. This is true not only of the very wealthy, which I've already mentioned, but also of the transfer of middle-class wealth.

Regardless of whether a person is eighteen, thirty-eight, or fifty-eight, the anticipation of receiving significant amounts of money (or actually receiving it) can tempt one to quit work or slack off and become accustomed to having and doing whatever he or she pleases. If a person wasn't irresponsible before, he or she likely will be now. (The younger one is when inheriting wealth, the more serious the damage.) Unearned wealth magnifies old temptations and produces many new ones. It makes people unproductive and lazy, robbing them of character, judgment, and initiative.

> The almighty dollar bequeathed to a child is an almighty curse. No man has the right to handicap his son with such a burden as great wealth.
>
> ANDREW CARNEGIE

Inherited wealth tends to make people unhappy, greedy, and cynical. And who needs to work hard when there's all that money? New temptations often lead to addictions. Giving money to a careless spender is like throwing gasoline on a fire. And nothing divides siblings more quickly than a large inheritance. Leaving more to God's kingdom and less to financially independent children is not only an act of love toward God, but also toward them.

Consider the words of some people who knew a bit about handling wealth:

Frederick T. Gates (John D. Rockefeller Sr.'s advisor): "Your fortune is rolling up, rolling up like an avalanche! You must distribute it faster than it grows! If you do not, it will crush you, and your children, and your children's children."

Cornelius Vanderbilt: "Inherited wealth is as certain death to ambition as cocaine is to morality."

Henry Ford: "Fortunes tend to self-destruction by destroying those who inherit them."[18]

And, of course, God says, "An inheritance quickly gained at the beginning will not be blessed at the end" (Proverbs 20:21).

Nanci and I knew a couple who had finished their missionary training and were soon to be headed to the mission field, when suddenly the wife inherited significant wealth from an uncle who had no children. They were excited, thinking they could now become self-supporting missionaries. When they asked my advice, I said that I thought they needed the accountability and prayer support that would come with having financial supporters. I advised them not to go out independently. Instead, I suggested they give away the great majority of the money, thanking God for the opportunity to invest in eternity. Then they could move forward, undistracted, with their plans for the mission field.

In the end, they did what the majority would do—they kept most of the money. The wife opened her own account, because the money was really "hers." Over the next several years, their relationship took a nosedive: their children suffered from overindulgence; terrible accusations were made; and the marriage ended in a messy divorce. Obviously, the money wasn't the only problem, but it certainly had a huge negative impact on this family. What seemed to be a blessing—what could have been a blessing if they had given most of the money away—proved to be a curse.

I've heard Ron Blue ask, "Do you know any examples of wealth transferred successfully to the third and fourth generations?" As a financial advisor, Ron is in a position where he would see how families transfer their wealth, but he's at a loss to come up with more than one or two examples.

If heirs succeed after receiving an inheritance, they'll never know if they could have made it on their own by working hard and trusting God. The family money will always make them question their own competence, as well as God's provision.

Christian parents who are still convinced that they should leave great wealth to their children should consider the following strategy: Entrust your children with a small amount of your estate while you're still alive. Based on how they handle these funds, you may develop convictions about how much money—or how little—to leave to them when you're gone. Only those who prove faithful with a little should be entrusted with a lot (Luke 16:10). If the little bit you give them now hurts them a little, you can be certain that giving them a lot later will hurt them a lot.

We should not transfer wealth to our children unless we've successfully transferred wisdom to them. Without wisdom, wealth will not only be wasted, it will damage our children—100 percent of the time. I'll make a statement that may seem incredible, but I firmly believe it. If I were the devil and I wanted to ruin a group of Christians, I'd try to get their parents to leave them large amounts of money. That's how much I'm convinced of the dangers and temptations of unearned wealth. Everything I've learned over the years has convinced me that, in most cases, children who inherit wealth would have been far better off if the money had been put in a burn pile and torched. I don't recommend that strategy, but I seriously believe the statement is true.

Fortunately, we don't have to burn our money or ruin our children's lives. Instead, we can give more money away while we're alive, and leave most of what's left to churches and Christian ministries. As Ron Blue says, "Do your givin' while you're livin', so you're knowin' where it's goin'."

What's Fair or What's Right?

No matter how much a couple intends to leave to their children or grandchildren, most say, "To be fair, we have to leave the same amount of money to each." If every child or grandchild is equally spiritual, an equally good steward, and living in equal circumstances, then equal inheritance is appropriate. However, there may be significant differences in our descendents' stewardship, attitudes, abilities, obligations, health, and needs, any of which may call for leaving them differing amounts. We should love our children and grandchildren equally, but that doesn't mean we should treat them the same.

To leave a substantial amount of money to a child whom you know is wasteful or wayward is to fund his or her sin and sorrow. If you wouldn't pay a drug dealer, hire a prostitute, waste money gambling, or give it to an anti-Christian cult, why would you leave money to someone who will likely use it for those same purposes? I believe it's immoral to leave money to people who have demonstrated that they are morally incapable of handling it in a Christ-honoring way.

A young man preoccupied with fairness says to Jesus, "Teacher, tell my brother to divide the inheritance with me" (Luke 12:13). Jesus warns him, "Watch out! Be on your guard against all kinds of greed; a man's life does not consist in the abundance of his possessions" (Luke 12:15). He then tells the parable of the rich fool who had hoarded his assets and was about to die, which culminates in God asking the rich man, "Then who will get what you have prepared for yourself?" (Luke 12:20).

When it comes to leaving an inheritance, the question isn't what's fair, but what's right. The real issue is this: Will your children *need* your money and will they *use* it wisely? If the answer to the first question is no, you shouldn't feel compelled to leave it to them. If the answer to the second question is no, you should feel compelled *not* to leave it to them. If the answers differ from child to child, you should establish the terms of distribution accordingly.

Much of this evaluation process—and the potential hurt feelings that might arise over differences in inheritance—can be avoided by giving and leaving to God most of what he has entrusted to us.

I have seen families devastated by fighting over an inheritance. Relationships between siblings have been ruined permanently because, "It isn't fair. He got cash and I got stuck with a house I can't sell," or "She took that antique chair I wanted," or "Where was she when Mom was ill?" or "It isn't fair that he got as much as I did when he doesn't even have a family to care for." This kind of bickering and whining over things that didn't belong to them in the first place is not only disgusting, it's also largely avoidable with a little forethought, communication, and a clearly written will.

Parents can choose objects of personal meaning to leave to each family member and give the rest to God's kingdom. The less left to the children, the less there is to fight about. Of course, the kind of people who would fight over what belonged to their deceased parents probably wouldn't use these assets to God's glory. No amount of money would appease or change them. Indeed, it would only provide fuel for their vices. Such children need prayer and guidance. What they certainly do not need is more money.

Family Conferences about Inheritance

If parents decide to give most or all of their estate to God's kingdom, they should explain their plans to their children. This will prevent false expectations and free their children from later resentment and present guilt feelings stemming from what they might imagine they have to gain by their parents' death. Even though they know they shouldn't, grown children commonly find themselves thinking about and looking forward to all the money and possessions that will be theirs when their parents die. Some go into debt now because they know (or think they know) they're going to win a virtual lottery when their parents die. The sooner these attitudes are defused, the better.

I recommend either having a family conference or writing out in detail what your plan is, then asking each adult child to get back to you with his or her response. I was with two wealthy parents and their son, who was in his early twenties, as they discussed how much they should give away and how much they should leave to him. It was uncomfortable at first, but because he was a godly young man, he gave them freedom, acknowledging it was their money, not his, and encouraging them to give generously and not feel they needed to leave it to him.

We've had similar discussions with our daughters, who are spiritual women whom we fully trust. Nanci and I intend to leave them enough to be of modest assistance, but not enough to change their lifestyles or undercut their need to plan and pray with their husbands and depend on them to provide. We've communicated this and they understand and agree with our plan to give most of our estate to God's kingdom. Our daughters and their husbands are some of the most kingdom-minded and financially responsible people we know. But it's God's money, not ours, and not theirs. It's up to him, not us, to entrust them with whatever wealth he deems appropriate. He knows the right amount for them to handle. We don't. We don't want to tinker with his design for their lives by passing on money he wants us to manage and distribute.

Look at it this way: Suppose you had a money manager, whom you'd put in charge of all your financial assets. (Some readers do have such a person.) Now, suppose your money manager died. What would you think if you found out he left all your money to his children? That would be unthinkable, right? Why? Because when a money manager dies, the money goes to the owner, not to the money manager's children. The logic should be obvious if we're serious when we say that God is the owner—and if we're not serious, we'd better admit it now and realign our thinking with the Bible's!

At a Generous Giving conference, Dois Rosser and his daughter Cindy told the story of when Dois and his wife called their grown children together for a special gathering.[19] He explained they wouldn't be receiving much of an inheritance, because he planned to use most of it to construct buildings for poor churches around the world. Dois's daughter said her father was nervous because he didn't want his children to think he didn't love them.

How did the children respond? Cindy said, "Dad and Mom always lived that way. They taught us a strong work ethic. We knew we needed to use our own gifts well. Inheritance was a no-brainer for us. We didn't feel disenfranchised. A model of generous living is my great inheritance from my parents, and I celebrate that more than I can tell you. If there's anything I want my children to have, it's a heart of generosity. Mom and Dad modeled for us that it didn't belong to any of us but to God."

The organization started by the Rosser family's wealth in 1988, International Cooperating Ministries, has since built more than 1,100 church buildings in seventeen countries, along with six training centers, a seminary, and a graduate school.[20] Not only the Rossers, but also their children and grandchildren have rejoiced, participated in, and benefited from what God has done through investing the family wealth in eternity. This decision was in everyone's best interests—including all those people in the seventeen needy countries!

What would you think if you found out that your money manager left all your money to his children?

Family members who respond negatively to a decision to leave money to the cause of Christ instead of them demonstrate a character that proves they're unqualified to inherit in the first place. Committed Christians will be the first to say, "That's wonderful, Dad and Mom. Go for it! And thanks for being a great example to us."

A wealthy man told me that he had sat down with his sons and daughters and their spouses and explained he was giving away most of his wealth. Whatever was left at his death, he said, would be going to Christian ministries. The family said they understood. Afterward his son-in-law took him aside. The young man said, "Thank you—now I know it's really up to me to provide for your daughter."

This young man had likely believed up until then that anything he did to provide for his family would pale in comparison to what his father-in-law would eventually leave them. Suddenly, he was exactly where God wanted him—in the primary position of responsibility for his family.

Paul says that God gives some of us "plenty" so we can give to those with less, so they won't have "too little" and we won't have "too much" (2 Corinthians 8:14-15).

When I ask people if their children really need more money, parents will nearly always reply no.

"What would you hope your children would do with the inheritance?" I ask.

"Well, it would be great if they gave it away to those who really need it."

"But if God has entrusted the money to you, and giving it away is what you know is right, then why don't you do that?"

If you want your children's counsel as to where to give it, ask them now so you can take it into account as you write or revise your will, or liquidate assets to give away. (Why not ask them to recommend some worthy recipients you can designate in the will?)

Even the most godly children may not give away most of what they inherit. They reason, "Dad and Mom left this for us, so I guess they intended for us to use it on ourselves." I heard someone say he felt compelled to spend his inheritance, to honor his parents' wishes!

No one loves and trusts their children more than Nanci and I. But our love and trust has been demonstrated in ways that make insignificant what we leave them in our will. It's time to break with our culture's patterns of undiscerning inheritance. By establishing a new model for stewardship, we can help our children and our churches think in terms of eternity. Perhaps in another few generations what seems so radical to most of my readers now will seem self-evident. Wouldn't that be great?

Many of the world's multimillionaires have left massive inheritances, but also a heritage of greed, self-indulgence, betrayal, adultery, arrogance, snobbery, and self-centeredness. On the other hand, countless Christians have left no material inheritance to their children, but a godly heritage of character and spiritual values. Such a heritage is infinitely more valuable than a large inheritance. Many adult children who have received a great monetary inheritance resent their parents. Most who have received a great spiritual heritage praise God for their parents.

The Will

The execution of your will according to your instructions is the final outworking of your stewardship on earth. A valid, written will is the only instrument by which you can ensure that your intentions will be carried out.

More than three out of ten Americans will die before retirement. Ten of ten will die eventually. Yet seven out of ten Americans die without a will. When there's no will, the courts make important decisions that most people would want to have made themselves—including who the children's guardians should be and exactly where the assets should go. Some people write their own will, but even attorney-drawn wills are inexpensive considering the vital purpose they serve. The most costly alternative is no will at all.

Once written, wills should be periodically updated. When our children were small, our will designated one-third of the estate to be divided between our children, held in trust by their designated guardians, mentioned by name in the will. (Obviously, we'd asked the guardians in advance, so this wouldn't be a surprise.) The bulk of this money would likely go to their college education, if that was the path they chose. Another third was left directly to their guardians to be used as they saw fit in caring for the entire family, including their own children. (This was to anticipate and avoid the problems with the "new kids" having greater resources than the old.) The final third was designated to our church, a tenth of the estate for the church's general fund, and the rest to be distributed to world missions under the direction of our elders.

After our girls got married in 2001, we revised the will to leave a modest designated gift amount to our daughters and their husbands and our (possible) future grandchildren. All the rest is designated to our church, world missions, famine relief, street children, prison ministries, and various other ministries.[21] Of course, if family needs or circumstances change again, we can revise our will accordingly.

Is Leaving Money the Same as Giving Money?

Leaving an estate to the church, Christian ministry, or a foundation isn't really "giving," at least not in the full sense. Giving is a choice to part with what we could have kept. But when we die, we have no choice but to leave it. Keeping it isn't an option. I believe that God will graciously grant us rewards in heaven for what we do and give before we die—not for what others do with what we've left behind after we die (even if it's by our instructions).

We might be impressed to hear that someone left millions of dollars to God's kingdom. But to die with that much money might indicate that the person had been withholding it from God. (I'm not the judge.) It might demonstrate an unwillingness to trust God while still facing life's uncertainties. I say this to suggest we shouldn't regard leaving money in our will as true generosity.

"It is appointed for men to die once, but after this the judgment" (Hebrews 9:27, NKJV). We receive reward for what we actually do on earth. Leaving instructions for what others are to do after we leave with what we once managed isn't the same as giving it away while we're still here. Death isn't your best opportunity to give; it's the end of your opportunity to give. God rewards acts of faith done while we're still living.

Death isn't your best opportunity to give; it's the end of your opportunity to give. God rewards acts of faith done while we're still living.

I've discovered that this concept is difficult for some to grasp, so let me try to elaborate. Suppose I leave in my will a written request for my friend Steve to say "I forgive you" to someone who wronged me. That may seem like a nice gesture, but wouldn't God want me to trust him enough to offer that forgiveness myself while I'm still here? If God would reward me for leaving behind such a request (he's certainly free to do as he pleases), surely he'd have rewarded me more for actually doing it rather than having someone else do it on my behalf. Right?

To put it in a biblical context, would Jesus have celebrated to the same degree the action of the woman who gave away her last two coins if she had died that day and left those two coins to the temple charity in her will? I don't think so. Sure, he would be pleased that she left them in her will as opposed to wasting them or leaving them for ungodly purposes, but I don't think her reward would have been comparable, because her action would have required neither faith nor sacrifice.

Certainly, untold millions have benefited from gifts made by the Maclellan Foundation and the DeMoss Foundation, among others. Many will testify to that, and I've seen the fruit myself. But had all the available money been given away during the lifetime of the founders to help feed people and spread the gospel, their testimonies would have been equally strong, wouldn't they? True, there's much more presently in foundations because it *wasn't* all given away in someone's lifetime or even at the death of the founder. Much interest has been earned on the principal. But remember, God could have been multiplying the smaller amount given away years ago, at what amounts to 10,000 percent interest (Matthew 19:29).

Is it possible that God entrusts the amount he knows is needed for each generation and that we shouldn't save money to do the kingdom work of future generations? (Especially since when Christ returns, all the hundreds of millions of dollars sitting in foundations, benevolence funds, accounts, and estates will become worthless?)

The question is how much we should leave behind, and how long we should postpone giving what we could give today. Much good has been accomplished with money designated in wills to churches and Christian ministries. But just because something is a good thing doesn't mean it is the *best* thing. It might be better to give away some or even most of our assets while we're still living and can exercise trust in God and apply wisdom in our decisions about where to give the money.

Before buying something he intended to give, King David insisted on paying full price. "I will not take for the Lord what is yours, or sacrifice a burnt offering that costs me nothing" (1 Chronicles 21:24). God rewards sacrifice and faith. Giving is choosing to part with something, whereas leaving is merely controlling the destination of what we can't keep anyway. Because we've held on to these treasures until the last possible moment—literally until our last breath on earth has been taken—leaving them behind doesn't seem like an open-handed gesture worthy of great reward.

It's certainly possible we'll be rewarded for making a choice to leave money to a worthy cause when we die. But I can't see biblical proof of that. We do know that Scripture doesn't say, "Test me in this by leaving your assets after you die and see if I won't open the floodgates of heaven." It does say that of our current giving. It doesn't say, "Leave and it will be left to you in the measure you leave." But it does say, "Give and it will be given to you in the measure you give."

Giving and leaving are two different things. Giving is voluntarily parting with an asset; leaving is more like being robbed. In a sense, death is like a thief who takes our assets from us quickly, completely, and without warning. Suppose someone stole a million dollars from my bank account and gave it to feed the hungry. Now, arguably, the million will do just as much good that way as if I'd willingly given it myself. Would I be rewarded? No. Even if I managed to convince the thief as he walked out the door to use my money for some good causes, no one would consider me to have engaged in an act of giving.

Jesus had a different will for Peter than for John—and he has a unique will for each of us. Thomas Maclellan and Art DeMoss and their families have certainly done much good for Christ's kingdom, as they have followed Christ's particular leading for them through the foundations that bear their names. His leading for others—taking into account the same biblical principles and dealing with fewer or more assets—may be very different.

Delaying giving as a strategy for future kingdom building is risky. We could hold on to assets out of fear of letting go or unwillingness to surrender control to the Lord. As long as money lies within our grasp, there's not only the danger that we'll lose the assets, but also that we'll change our minds or be seduced by the status, prestige, and recognition of controlling (or having our name attached to the distribution of) what belongs to God.

King David said, "I have never seen the righteous forsaken or their children begging bread" (Psalm 37:25). Why? Because their parents left them so much money or they passed on such great wealth to their children? No, it's because "they are always generous and lend freely" that "their children will be blessed" (Psalm 37:26).

In A.D. 390, John Chrysostom said this to Christian parents: "If you wish to leave much wealth to your children, leave them in God's care. Do not leave them riches, but virtue and skill."

CHAPTER 20

Battling Materialism in the Christian Family

"If it had grown up," she said to herself, "it would have made a dreadfully ugly child: but it makes a rather handsome pig, I think." And she began thinking over other children she knew, who might do very well as pigs.
LEWIS CARROLL, *ALICE'S ADVENTURES IN WONDERLAND*

There are only three ways to teach a child. The first is by example, the second is by example, and the third is by example. ALBERT SCHWEITZER

In Zambia, a man buys a new suit and a motorcycle. Meanwhile, his wife and children suffer from malnutrition. His youngest child starves to death before his eyes. If he hadn't bought the suit or if he sold the motorcycle, he could feed his family for a year.

Across the Atlantic in the United States, a man chooses to work twenty hours of overtime per week while his wife takes on a job to increase their already large income. They eat in the best restaurants, belong to an elite club, and clothe their children in the latest fashions. They give their daughter an expensive horse for her twelfth birthday and their son a new car for his sixteenth. Their children have computers, stereos, and expensive ski equipment. The parents plan to send their children to the most prestigious colleges. Dad doesn't have the time for personal talks, family devotions, or church. In fact, the children rarely see their father for more than a few minutes each day, but they know his checkbook is always there.

Two countries, two men, two materialists more similar than we think. The first man will stand before God and give an account for the precious wife and children he allowed to suffer and die rather than surrender the prestige and pleasure of his things. The second man will give an account for another deadly form of abuse—his spiritual neglect of his family, whose deepest needs he sacrificed on the altar of his own lust for money, possessions, and status. He will answer for rearing his children in an overindulgent environment that has so warped their values they will likely never recover.

On the day of judgment, no thinking person would want to stand in either man's shoes.

MATERIALISM IN THE CHRISTIAN HOME

Scripture states that it's the responsibility of parents to provide for their children. For Christians to choose not to provide for their children or other needy relatives is to deny the faith and become worse than an unbeliever (1 Timothy 5:8). Likewise, it's the responsibility of grown children, not the state or an insurance company, to take care of their parents and other relatives in their old age or illness (Mark 7:10-12; 1 Timothy 5:8, 16).

Jesus rejects any "spiritual" attempts to excuse a failure to provide materially for one's family (Mark 7:9-13). When there are loved ones who need our help, God calls us to give to him *and* to them. Christ was not too busy dying for the sins of the world to take the time and concern to entrust his mother's welfare to one of his own apostles—who from that point forward made sure her needs were cared for (John 19:26-27).

AFFLUENZA

It's one thing to provide for our children. It's another thing to smother them with possessions until they turn into self-centered materialists. An alarming number of children from Christian homes grow up grasping for every item they can lay their hands on. Children raised in such an atmosphere—which includes most children in America—are afflicted with a killer disease, called *affluenza*:

> Affluenza is a strange malady that affects the children of well-to-do parents. Though having everything money can buy, the children show all the symptoms of abject poverty—depression, anxiety, loss of meaning, and despair for the future. Affluenza accounts for an escape into alcohol, drugs, shoplifting, and suicide among children of the wealthy. It is most often found where parents are absent from the home and try to buy their children's love.[1]

Consider the typical American Christmas. When the annual obstacle course through crowded malls culminates on the Big Day, what's the fruit? We find a trail of shredded wrapping paper and a pile of broken, abandoned, and unappreciated toys. Far from being filled with a spirit of thankfulness for all that Christmas means, the children are grabby, crabby, picky, sullen, and ungrateful—precisely because they've been given so much.

We love our children. So do their grandfathers and grandmothers, aunts and uncles, cousins and friends. All of us seem to think that love is measured by giving things. We say it isn't so, but we go right on acting as if it were. Our children aren't battery operated. Their deepest needs are spiritual, mental, and emotional, and these needs cannot be met by flashing lights and dollhouses. This sometimes dawns on us, but we soon forget. Another Christmas, another birthday, and again we immerse our children in things. In doing so, we mentor them in a perspective on life directly at odds with the Scriptures we seek to teach them at home and in church.

Things we would have deeply appreciated in small or moderate amounts become unappealing or even revolting in excessive amounts. As a man who has gorged himself at a banquet finds the thought of food repulsive, one glutted with material things loses his regard and respect for them. Eventually he doesn't care what happens to them. The prevalent disrespect of children for their possessions and those of others is a direct result of overindulgence.

When we mistake the giving of material things for the sharing of grace, we do a great disservice to our children. Children who grow up getting most of what they want have a predictable future. Unless they learn to overcome their upbringing, they'll misuse credit, default on their debt, and be poor employees. They'll function as irresponsible members of their family, church, and society. They'll be quick to blame others, pout about misfortunes, and believe that their family, church, country, and employer—if they have one—owes them. Having counseled numerous such adults, I'm convinced that many of them are this way because their sincere but misguided parents overindulged them.

Parents who spoil their children out of "love" should realize that they are performing acts of child abuse. Although there are no laws against such abuse—no man-made laws, anyway—this spiritual mistreatment may result in as much long-term personal and social damage as the worst physical abuse.

One Christian counselor advised parents that if they didn't give their children as many material possessions as their friends did, it would turn them against the Christian faith. Where does someone come up with such a distorted perspective? Certainly not from God's Word.

Many Christian families today are held back from following God's call to a more simple or strategic lifestyle because they don't want to deprive their children of material advantages. Meanwhile, they deprive their children of countless spiritual and eternal advantages.

If you decided to move to a remote mission field, your children might not have organized athletics, school dances, a nice bicycle, or a car—but the spiritual benefits could be enormous. As Christian parents, we must learn to choose what's best on earth (for ourselves and our children) in light of heaven's value system. Our concern should be for an eternal standard of living. This kind of perspective is contagious within a family. An eternal value system is the greatest heritage we can give our children.

On the principle that gratifying a desire needlessly only tends to increase it, John Wesley asked the following questions of well-intentioned parents:

- Why should you purchase for them more pride or lust, more vanity, or foolish and hurtful desires?
- Why should you be at further expense to increase their temptations and snares, and to pierce them through with more sorrows?[2]

PARENTS AS MODELS

Everything learned in life, from coping methods to table manners, is learned in families. Families are the heart and soul of society. The home, not the school, is the primary place of learning. In the home, character is built, habits are developed, and destinies are forged.

If you decided to move to a remote mission field, your children might not have organized athletics, school dances, a nice bicycle, or a car—but the spiritual benefits could be enormous.

Every good financial perspective and habit encouraged in this book is developed best by parental modeling. Children learn most effectively not only from what we say, but what we do. Our actions speak louder than words—sometimes so loudly that our children can't hear a word we're saying. Training our children about money and possessions begins at birth. For better or worse, we are their tutors, every hour of every day. Consciously or unconsciously, we continually train them, engraving our values in them as if drawing with a stick in wet cement. Albert Schweitzer puts it this way: "There are only three ways to teach a child. The first is by example; the second is by example; the third is by example."[3]

Many years ago, when my daughters were two and four, I took them out for breakfast. On our way back to the car, I was surprised to see that both of them had toothpicks in their mouths. Then I reached to my own mouth and found that I too had a toothpick. Unconsciously, as a matter of habit, I had picked up that toothpick on the way out of the restaurant. My little girls, who at the time probably didn't know what a toothpick was for, had climbed up on the counter and imitated my action.

I recalled that when I was a child, my father often had a toothpick in his mouth. To this day, even when I have no need of one at all, I often take a toothpick when I leave a restaurant. And here were my own children doing the same. This is the essence of parenthood. Children imitate everything we do, whether important or unimportant, healthy or unhealthy. Sometimes our children will fail to listen to us. Rarely will they fail to imitate us.

Although I wasn't raised in a Christian home, and although my mother became the spiritual inspiration to our family when she came to Christ after I did, I thank God for a father who never bought what he couldn't afford, didn't waste money, chose his investments carefully, and did not—although he was generous—let me have everything I wanted. He didn't always set out to teach me these habits, but his example made an indelible impression on me.

COMMUNICATION BETWEEN MARRIAGE PARTNERS

What do we do if our spouse feels insecure because of the amount of money we want to give to the Lord? This is a journey that husbands and wives need to go on together. One partner may have the gift of giving, and the other may have the gift of being stretched!

When there are special offerings at church, Nanci and I each come up with a figure and then we compare numbers. Normally, we go with the higher figure. Years ago, one of us consistently came up with the higher number. But now it's different. Sometimes one of us comes up with the higher amount; sometimes it's the other.

I'm commonly asked the following question: "What should I do? I want to tithe and give voluntary offerings, but my husband's not a Christian and says no. It makes it awkward for me and the children."

My own mother was in this position from the day she came to Christ until the Lord took her home twelve years later. First Peter 3:1-6 says that a wife is to be submissive, even to her unsaved husband. You shouldn't give money that your husband has explicitly forbidden you to give. If you would truly give if you could, God will still reward your heart attitude.

If you make a separate income, you can tell your husband that you believe God wants you to give and it would be wrong not to. He may relent begrudgingly, but in time he may see the blessings of giving. Even if you don't have an income, ask your husband if he would allow you to begin giving something, perhaps $60 per month. Tell him you're willing to reduce your discretionary spending—and sacrifice—in order to free up money to give.

Tell him what Scripture says in Malachi 3:10 and Luke 6:38 about God's promise to bless and his challenge to test him to see what happens when we give. Ask him if he would agree to your giving like this for at least one year (or six months, or three). Then at the end of that time, you'll decide together if you're better or worse off. If you're better off—or even if he admits there's no discernable difference—you're in a good position to ask to increase the giving amount so you can enjoy more of God's blessing. A person can indirectly receive the blessings that God gives to his or her spouse (1 Corinthians 7:14).

Because this is one issue in which God invites us to test him, ask God to prove himself to your spouse. Some have found—by being gently persistent about giving, even if at a lesser amount than they would have chosen—that instead of giving becoming the divisive issue they imagined, it was actually the first step in their partner coming to Christ. If your spouse is a Christian, you have the right, based on his or her profession of faith, to take a stronger position to encourage him or her to follow Christ with you in this area. Of course, you must still be respectful.

You can cultivate a spirit of giving in your children. Although my non-Christian father didn't like the fact that I gave as a new Christian, he acknowledged that I had a right to give because it was money I had earned. Whether young or older, children can be freed from materialism through giving.

If you had no other reason for giving, doing it for your children would be reason enough. Breaking the bonds of materialism in your life—through generous giving and moderate lifestyle choices—will prove to be one of the greatest gifts you can give your children.

NO SUBSTITUTE FOR YOU

Giving gifts to children is often a substitute for giving them personal attention. Many children receive a playhouse, then a train set, then skis, then a motorcycle, then a car, all to compensate for the fact that their parents—often their father especially—are not available to spend time with them. Anything we give our children is a poor substitute for ourselves.

I spoke with a Christian man who loves his wife and five children and wants the best for them. He works hard so they can have a beautiful house, lots of things, and enough money for the children to go to college. In fact, he works so hard that the last three years he hasn't had time to go on vacation with his family! This man's children are growing up with plenty of material things. Tragically, they're also growing up without a father.

It's the time we spend with our children that will leave lasting impressions—not the money we've given them. Our children will not remember what we did for them nearly as much as they will remember what we did with them.

Nearly 40 percent of American children are being raised by single parents. Some of the best parents I know are single parents, but one of their greatest temptations—often subconscious—is trying to compensate for their children's loss of parental attention by giving them more and more material things. When there's a divorce and the noncustodial parent becomes a Disneyland Daddy (or a Magic Mountain Mommy), there's a tendency for parents to try to outdo each other in giving material things. The real loser is the child, who grows up glutted with things but starving for love and discipline.

CHANGING CHRISTMAS

Can we change the pattern of materialism in our homes? Certainly. Take Christmas, for example. We can buy far less. We can hand make presents, set a budget, and buy presents in advance to avoid the unnerving jostling through stores.

Any change is good if it helps us to focus on Christ rather than on ourselves. We can visit shut-ins or take food to the needy—to focus on giving rather than receiving.

My wife often staged a "Happy Birthday Jesus" party for our girls and their friends. Each child brought one gift personally made for Jesus. (After all, whose birthday is it?) One year, a few nights before Christmas, our family sat around a candlelit table holding hands. Then each of us shared what we appreciated about the Lord. After praying together and singing Christmas carols, we went around and shared what each of us appreciated about each other. It was an unforgettable evening.

By taking our focus off the human receiver and putting it on the divine giver, Christmas can become a symbol of God's giving heart rather than people's grabbing hands.

If a child receives four presents, the gifts can be spread out on each of the four days before Christmas. On Christmas night, after reading Scripture and singing carols, each giver can present his or her gift in turn to the recipient. In the quietness and simplicity of the celebration, we can pray and express our gratefulness to God for his greatest of all gifts, the Lord Jesus. By taking our focus off the human receiver and putting it on the divine giver, Christmas can become a symbol of God's giving heart rather than people's grabbing hands.

This is only a beginning. You may wish to make more radical changes in your Christmas. One November, when our missions pastor told our church about needy Christians in Sudan, family after family spontaneously decided to forgo Christmas presents and give to the church in Sudan. My family was among them, and it was a wonderful Christmas, made better by the knowledge that we'd given to what matters instead of exchanging more stuff we didn't need. But even if you still exchange presents, you can make Christmas different. Don't be victimized by the world's materialism. Worship Christ in simplicity.

TEACHING YOUR CHILDREN ABOUT MONEY

"Train a child in the way he should go, and when he is old he will not turn from it" (Proverbs 22:6). Deuteronomy 6:6-9 describes the training process as both formal and informal. We are to "teach" our children and "talk" about the principles of Scripture as occasions arise throughout the day. Often, the informal discussions will open a door for the formal instruction, and vice versa.

Every experience your children have with money is a teaching opportunity. Some lessons they will learn the hard way. If they put their tongue on a lightbulb once, they'll probably never do it again. Children who lose or ruin their favorite possession through carelessness will learn a valuable lesson. So do those who see the joy in another's eyes as a result of something they've given. Often, parents can help by verbalizing a lesson. But there's no substitute for our children's own experiences and the impressions they leave, both pleasant and painful.

When we're alert to life, endless teaching opportunities emerge. When our daughters were small, they often went with us to our bank's "money machine" located in a supermarket. They saw us put in the card. Out came money. It all looked so easy. One time I explained that we weren't going to do something because we didn't have enough money. One of the girls said, "Just go to the money machine and get some more." This was an opportunity to discuss exactly what money is, how we must work to earn it, and that there's not an infinite amount of it available. We must take the time and effort to explain, especially in those teachable moments when a child's interest is piqued. You don't have to be eloquent—just take a stab at it. The kids will get it.

Often, we have no idea how deeply we affect our children by our casual, offhand comments. One night, when one of my daughters was seven years old, she prayed, "Dear Lord, I thank you so much that we are not too rich or too poor." This pleased me but also surprised me—where did it come from? As I thought about it, I remembered that probably six months earlier I had shared briefly with her a verse in Proverbs: "Give me neither poverty nor riches" (Proverbs 30:8). I applied it to a situation we saw while driving somewhere. I had long since forgotten that conversation. Obviously, my daughter hadn't.

OUR CHILDREN'S OTHER TEACHERS

Society is much more aggressive than we are in teaching our children about money. For an educational experience, spend just one Saturday morning watching cartoons and children's programs. Take special note of the commercials. Advertising goes straight to the kids, inundating them with a materialistic perspective and subtly encouraging them to manipulate their parents into buying trendy products.

Although many parents, including me, are concerned about the wrong sexual values taught by television, equally dangerous are the wrong material values. More Christian parents are now teaching their children what God says about sex. I applaud this. But we need to give equal attention to teaching them what God says about money and possessions.

We can develop our children's discernment and decision-making skills by asking them on the spot what an advertisement is saying and what its purpose really is. Ask them, "How important do you think these things are to God?" and "How would they improve your character or spiritual life if you owned them?" Don't dismiss these ads as silly—discuss them with your children. Only with dialogue and training can they learn to discern the faulty underpinnings of society's insistent materialism.

One night, my daughters asked me to play the popular board game called The Game of LIFE. I had seen and heard about it but had never played it. Someone had loaned the game to the girls, and they had been playing it on and off for a few days before they decided to teach Dad how to play. As the game progressed and I started to catch on, I was amazed at how accurately it reflected our society's materialistic mind-set. One of my girls was disappointed when she landed on a space that made her a teacher rather than a doctor or a lawyer—despite the fact that in real life she wanted to be a teacher! Why the disappointment? Because it meant she would receive a lower salary for the rest of the game. And money, after all, is what LIFE (and, for many people, life) is all about.

The Game of LIFE, like life itself, presents the choice of whether we should have children. But because there's a minimum amount of money—but no minimum amount of children—required to win the game, my girls were consistently choosing money over children. When I chose children instead of money, they thought it was a bad move—never considering the personal implications if their mother and I hadn't made that same "bad move" in life! Choosing children might mean losing the game, and who plays a game with the intention of losing? Clearly, this little board game was not just reflecting values—it was instilling them!

This turned out to be an excellent teaching opportunity. Nanci and I shared with our daughters Scripture's infinitely higher regard for children than money. We shared how "winning" and "success" are very different in God's eyes than in the world's. I couldn't help but think of all the Christian parents who wouldn't dream of letting their children play with a Ouija board or watch sexually explicit videos but wouldn't think twice about letting them play LIFE (or its equivalent) without addressing its blatant materialism.

Surrounded by so much unbiblical instruction about money, we parents need strong allies. There's much that our churches can do to teach children, youth, and adults basic biblical principles of stewardship. Sermons, classes, special seminars, small-group discussions, parent support groups, family-oriented radio programs, books, and tapes—all these are potential avenues to challenge and equip parents to teach their children in this vital area. Parents and older students might benefit from reading and discussing portions of this book or my little book on giving, *The Treasure Principle*.

Because Jesus, the Master Teacher, spent so much time addressing money, Christian schools seem like a natural place to devote a study unit to money. What better context in which to explain what money is, what it does, what God says about it, and how to earn, give, save, and spend it. Older children could be taught subjects ranging from how to balance a checkbook to how the economy works. The class could create its own product, sell it at a school carnival, and give the profits to missionaries. This would point out the positive ways that wealth can be generated and the importance of using wealth generously and wisely. The same thing could be done by home-schooling families.

The possibilities are endless—but we must begin with a conviction of how important the subject really is.

The following chapter offers practical suggestions that parents can implement to teach their children the principles and practices of biblical stewardship.

FACING MORTALITY

Before leaving on trips, sometimes I said to my children, "I'm not expecting anything to happen, but remember, if it does, I'll see you again in heaven."

Mortality is a fact of life. What do we gain—and what do our children gain—if we pretend it isn't? I'm going to die. So are you. So are our children. We don't know when, but we do know it will happen—unless, of course, Christ returns in our lifetime. He will come again, but throughout the centuries he hasn't yet, even though countless people believed that he would return before they died.

> Mortality is a fact of life. What do we gain— and what do our children gain—if we pretend it isn't?

How many children—whether ten years old or forty— have been traumatized by the sudden loss of a parent? When Dad and Mom speak openly about the inevitability of death, it's a gift to their children. If Christian parents remind their Christian children that the worst that can happen in death is temporary separation, it's reassuring. Their relationship cannot be terminated, only interrupted. What will eventually follow—whether in hours, days, years, or decades—is a great reunion, wonderful beyond imagination.[4]

It's neither morbid nor inappropriate to speak of such things with your family. Denial of truth, not truth itself, is the breeding ground for anxiety. One of the greatest gifts you can bestow on your loved ones is the honest anticipation of reunion in the better world, the one for which we were made.

FIELD TRIP TO A DUMP

How can we teach our children the emptiness of materialism in a direct and memorable way? Try taking them to visit a junkyard or a dump. It can actually be a great family event. (The lines are shorter than at amusement parks, admission is free, and little boys love it.) Show them all the piles of "treasures" that were formerly Christmas and birthday presents. Point out things that cost hundreds of dollars, that children quarreled about, friendships were lost over, honesty was sacrificed for, and marriages broke up over. Show them the miscellaneous arms and legs and remnants of battered dolls, rusted robots, and electronic gadgets that now lie useless after their brief life span. Point out to them that most of what your family owns will one day be in a junkyard like this. Read 2 Peter 3:10-14, which tells us that everything will be consumed by fire. Then ask this telling question: "When all that we owned lies abandoned, broken, and useless, what will we have done that will last for eternity?"

RAISING GIVERS

We should be raising up a generation of givers, not keepers. But the next generation is growing up amid—and inheriting—vast wealth. They have no tradition of giving, no vision for investing in eternity, no sense that God's purpose for prospering them is not so they can live in luxury, but so they can help their churches, aid the poor, and reach the lost.

Every statistic I've seen indicates that the younger a person is in America (people old enough to have at least some resources), the less they tend to give—not less in *total* (that would be attributable to less income), but less in *proportion* to what they have. What an indictment on us as parents and churches that we are failing to train our children to give. The best thing we could do for them would be to instill in them the giving habit. Giving shouldn't be an add-on elective to the spiritual life; it should be a required course at the very core of life's curriculum. If our children don't learn about giving from us, then who will teach them?

> Train a child in the way he should go, and when he is old he will not turn from it. (Proverbs 22:6)

> Teach them to your children and to their children after them. (Deuteronomy 4:9)

> I have chosen him, so that he will direct his children and his household after him to keep the way of the Lord by doing what is right and just. (Genesis 18:19)

> What we have heard and known, what our fathers have told us. We will not hide them from their children; we will tell the next generation the praiseworthy deeds of the Lord, his power, and the wonders he has done. He decreed statutes . . . and established the law . . . which he commanded our forefathers to teach their children, so the next generation would know them, even the children yet to be born, and they in turn would tell their children. Then they would put their trust in God and would not forget his deeds but would keep his commands. (Psalm 78:3-7)

Many people who want their children to develop hearts for God overlook the one thing that Jesus explicitly says will move our children's hearts toward heaven: giving (Matthew 6:19-21). Children who are not taught to give—by their parents' example, family discussions, and personal guidance—are hamstrung in their ability to live for Christ. This generation must be shown the joy of giving and taught the discipline of giving. In order to enhance their giving, they must also be taught to avoid debt and control spending. Our duty to our children is clear: "Bring them up in the training and instruction of the Lord" (Ephesians 6:4). In the next chapter, I will address practical ways to help our children become givers.

In the movie *Chariots of Fire*, Olympian Eric Liddell says, "I believe God made me for a purpose . . . and when I run, I feel his pleasure." When our children give, they should feel our pleasure—and learn to feel God's pleasure too.

CHAPTER 21

Teaching Children about Money and Possessions

Sharper than a serpent's tooth it is to have a thankless child. WILLIAM SHAKESPEARE

The less I spent on myself and the more I gave to others, the fuller of happiness and blessing did my soul become.
HUDSON TAYLOR

This chapter is a practical follow-up to the last. It assumes that you are committed to teaching your children to be good and generous financial stewards.

LEARNING THE HARD WAY

Children learn by experience, both good and bad. Consequently, my wife and I occasionally allowed our daughters to make poor financial decisions, such as spending impulsively. This was hard for me. My impulse was to always explain to my kids why they should hang on to their money instead of wasting it on this little bauble or that sixty-second horsey ride. But I found that if it was always their parents' decision, even though they were reluctantly practicing obedience they weren't learning wisdom.

When we occasionally began letting them buy some of the things they wanted, they started learning for themselves, the hard way. When something of true value came along, they couldn't afford to buy it. Meanwhile, the little trinket they bought last month was lost, broken, or of no interest. Now they wanted to buy a book they could keep and read and share, but they couldn't because the money spent on the fleeting pleasures of plastic rings and colored stickers was gone forever.

We must be careful not to bail out our children by saying "Well, I guess you learned your lesson, so I'll get you what you want." On the contrary, the only way children will learn their lesson is by being allowed to face the consequences of their own unwise spending. If we can keep ourselves from interfering with the natural laws of life, mistakes can be our child's finest teachers.

When a child loses or breaks a toy, a parent who feels sorry for the child will often replace the toy with a new one. Meanwhile, the child is deprived of learning the way life functions. You must care for things, because there are consequences to having them lost or broken. If the consequences are removed, the wrong lesson is learned: "It's okay to be careless because you get what you want anyway." The wrong behavior is reinforced rather than corrected.

When a child loses or breaks a toy, a parent who feels sorry for the child will often replace the toy with a new one. Meanwhile, the child is deprived of learning the way life functions.

If a twelve-year-old squanders his lunch money, what should his parents do? Nothing. He must earn some more money, use the money he's saved, or go without lunch. The lessons of life are very simple and effective—if we will just stay out of the way!

"But what if it wasn't the child's fault—what if someone broke his toy or stole his money?" Aren't there many losses and misfortunes in life that aren't the fault of the person yet must be accepted and dealt with? A child whose toys are replaced and whose money is replenished by parents never learns the way life operates. He's not being prepared for the real world of stewardship.

Suppose your child wants a bicycle. You could get him a decent used bike in a garage sale for twenty dollars or even free if you checked around. But perhaps this isn't good enough for him. He wants a brand-new bicycle like his friends have. One way to teach him the cost of having nice things is to tell him that if he really wants it, you'll loan him the money at the going rate of interest. Work out a payment schedule with him, showing him how much this $100 bicycle will really cost him and how long it will take to pay it off.

At this point, he may back out of the deal. If so, good for him. But if he doesn't, let him go ahead. By the time he pays off the debt from miscellaneous chores—perhaps as much as six months down the road—he will never forget the cost of borrowing. By then a used bicycle—which is what his briefly beautiful bicycle is by now—will sound much more attractive. The lesson he learns can give him wisdom later when it comes to buying a car, a house, or anything else.

CHILDREN, WORK, AND MONEY

Nanci and I are pleased to see our daughters and their husbands consistently making wise and generous financial choices. We're grateful that both our sons-in-laws' parents helped instill this same kind of wisdom in them. That is an enduring legacy, and a precious one.

As parents, we should help our children learn to associate money with labor. Money and possessions do not fall out of the sky. They are earned through work—good, hard, and well-done work. We can encourage our children to work at tasks, make things, and sell them. We can teach them that work can be meaningful and fun as well as financially profitable.

A common mistake that parents make is to dole out money to children arbitrarily as life goes by. This teaches them to believe money has no cost, that it comes easily or automatically. As a result, they disassociate money from work. They begin imagining it's their right to have money even when they haven't worked for it. It's this faulty thinking that later puts able-bodied people on welfare. Although the government fosters this kind of handout mentality, the attitude itself is—tragically—usually learned at home.

Children will always appreciate bicycles, athletic equipment, and favorite clothes much more when they've worked for them. The child who receives a new car as a gift on his eighteenth birthday is going to have a very different value system than the one who works hard, saves up his money, and makes his own decision to buy an $,1800 car rather than a $12,000 car.

Although money should be associated with work, not all work should be associated with money. Children shouldn't always be paid for their chores. However, there are many "extras" that can legitimately be rewarded financially. There are jobs outside the home that children can take on as they grow older—including paper routes, washing cars, mowing lawns, and baby-sitting.

However we do it, it's important that we teach our children a work ethic. On the other hand, it's equally important that children learn to put work and other commitments in their proper place. When I was a youth pastor, I saw many teenagers suffer spiritually because they regularly missed church, youth group, and special retreats due to jobs, athletics, music, school activities, and other commitments. Although all these can be good, something's wrong when, as a result, a student misses vital opportunities to cultivate his or her spiritual life. Any young person who is encouraged or allowed by his or her parents to put other pursuits above ministry, fellowship, and the teaching of Scripture, will live out those same principles as an adult church member—if he or she isn't too busy making money to go to church at all.

SAVING

Children learn the value of money and the discipline of self-control through saving. If your bank doesn't permit small accounts, it's possible to put your children's money in your account and keep deposit and withdrawal ledgers between them and you. Pay them the same interest rate you are earning. They will be impressed to learn firsthand that saving money produces even more money. As soon as they have enough to open their own account, this is ideal.

Children need reasons and incentives to save. If they want a major item, say a telescope, help them develop a plan to save for it over a period of six months or a year. Perhaps they'll be able to save fifteen or thirty dollars a month. Help them think of jobs to accomplish this goal. If they stick with their plan to save money over a long period of time, buying that telescope won't be an impulsive decision. And once they've earned it, they'll be more likely to take good care of it.

Children should be shown how to save both for short-term and long-term purposes. They might be saving to go skating this weekend. Or they might be saving to buy a sleeping bag three months from now or have spending money on a major family vacation a year from now.

Many parents know what it's like to have teenagers go to costly school events. Kids may want to buy expensive dresses or rent tuxedos and go to fancy restaurants. Frustrated parents have told me that between the clothes and the dinner, it's common for such evenings to cost several hundred dollars.

Any parent who automatically picks up the tab for such events is doing the children a terrible disservice. If your teenagers believe that these events warrant that kind of money, they need to work for it themselves—months in advance, if necessary. Then and only then will they understand the cost. When working for something is the only alternative, it's amazing how many creative options young people can come up with and still have a great time, including borrowing nice clothes, using "old" clothes, and choosing a "cheap" place for dinner. Of course, if parents think nothing of spending huge amounts of money for a single evening out, their children will learn the same values.

We helped put our daughters through college, just as our parents helped us. However, I don't believe that parents should automatically pay for their children's entire college education. Sometimes they can't. But even when they can, in some cases it might be better if they didn't. When young people spend a year after high school working to earn money for college, they develop character and financial responsibility.

I don't believe that parents should automatically pay for their children's entire college education.

One family in our church promised to pay exactly half the cost of their children's college education. Their son went off to school and had a great time but failed three classes. So they modified their arrangement. He would have to pay all the tuition up front, then present his report card at the end of the term. At that time, they would reimburse him half the cost of all courses in which he achieved a C or better. These are wise parents who see the importance of incentive and responsibility. They understand what many parents don't— that the quality of a college education often improves dramatically when the student has a substantial part in paying for it.

I suggest a separate college savings account for the children into which both parents and children regularly contribute from the time the children are young. In some cases it's possible to do this under the federal government's Uniform Gift to Minors Act, so that the interest generated by this account is taxable on the children's income instead of the parents'. Usually this means that the taxes will be much lower or nonexistent, depending on the child's overall earnings.

Because some savings can be channeled into investments, children can also be taught about the stock market. When I was a grade-schooler, picking berries and harvesting cauliflower in the summer, my father encouraged me to take some of the money and invest it in stocks. This was very interesting and rewarding. Although I made a fair amount of money on the transactions, even if I hadn't it would have been well worthwhile. I came to understand at an early age how the stock market and our economy work. That knowledge has been very helpful ever since.

GIVING

The most fundamental lesson any child can learn about finances—even more important than saving—is the lesson of giving. As parents, we should teach our children to give. This is more than simply taking our own money and handing it to our child to put in the offering. In such cases the child isn't giving—she's simply delivering our gift. In order for it to really be giving, it must come from what actually belongs to the child.

We taught our daughters to tithe from the very earliest age. No matter where their income came from, even as a gift, 10 percent belonged to the Lord and it was untouchable. If Grandpa gave them ten dollars for Christmas, the question was never, "What can I do with ten dollars?" but "What can I do with nine dollars?"

I've read several sources that say emphatically, "Don't require your children to tithe." I disagree. That advice makes no more sense to me than to say, "Don't make your children wash their hands before a meal, or wear coats on a cold, windy day, or put away their toys, or go to church."

For those who say, "But giving must be from the heart, not imposed by someone else," I'd respond, "But giving is also a habit, and like all good habits it can and should be cultivated." There's no better way for a parent to cultivate giving than by making it one of the family's standard practices.

I know people raised on the tithe who would no sooner stop tithing than brushing their teeth. Tithing is so ingrained in their family that the children never express a desire to forgo it. It would be as unthinkable not to tithe as not to close the refrigerator door, not to turn off the faucet, or not to pray before a meal. Of course, keeping to a routine is no guarantee of spirituality. But the holy habit of giving is like the holy habits of Bible study, prayer, witnessing, and

397

hospitality. These things need to become part of our lifestyle. Those raised without these habits are at a great disadvantage trying to develop them as adults.

We first started giving our girls a salary of fifty cents per week when they were ages three and five. We called it a "salary" because they had to do certain tasks to receive it. "Allowance" often means regularly doling out funds with no commensurate responsibility. One nickel of that fifty cents was sacred, designated to the Lord. They'd often choose to give more than this, and we encouraged them to do so, reminding them that true giving starts after the tithe.

But when our daughters chose to give more, they did it fully aware that they'd worked for this money and that giving it away would leave them with less money to spend. We didn't intervene and reward them for their giving by compensating for what it cost them. To do so would have been to violate the essence of giving. We should let God reward as he wishes, in his time and his way, and not interfere.

Whenever one of the girls would say, "This week I want to give all my allowance," we were careful not to stifle her spirit by teaching her to be "reasonable." We wanted our children to give as their hearts were led. If this meant giving "unreasonably" as the widow of Mark 12 and the Macedonian believers of 2 Corinthians 8, then so be it. That would put them in good company! (In fact, no matter how much they give, our children will still live in unimaginable wealth compared to these Bible figures.)

When the girls were seven and five, I gave each of them three jars I'd labeled with their names and the designations "Giving," "Saving," and "Spending." I told them that every time they earned their salary (which was by then one dollar per week) they were first to put at least 10 percent into the Giving jar, then distribute the rest between the other two jars as they wished. But once they put money in the Giving jar, even beyond the tithe, it was dedicated to the Lord and they couldn't take it back. Every Sunday morning, they'd empty their Giving jar and take it to the offering box at church.

Once they put money in Saving, they weren't to take it out and spend it except for some upcoming special expenditure. However, they were free to transfer money from Saving or Spending to Giving, or from Spending to Saving. As the jars were lined up, it went like this: They could transfer money to any jar on the left, but never to a jar on the right.

I will never forget the night I explained this new system to my daughters. They were so excited they immediately took the money they already had and distributed it between the jars. They arranged the jars just right on their dressers and spent hours figuring things with pad and pencil while their dinner grew cold. My seven-year-old asked me to show her how to figure percentages on our calculator. She was writing on labels, completely on her own, "Giving: 20¢ a week," "Saving: 30¢ a week," and "Spending: 50¢ a week." For years, the use of these jars stimulated conversations about their money management. This simple system probably resulted in more financial education than anything else Nanci and I did.

Children can't learn money management unless they have money to manage and unless that money is earned by their effort. I can't overemphasize this point—parents who shovel out money according to the dictates of the moment are not teaching their children proper stewardship.

THE GIVING FAMILY

One man wrote to me, "My wife and I have taught our kids from the earliest days to be regular givers to God and his kingdom purposes. Our family has been blessed with four young adults who love Jesus, and I believe that our faithfulness in giving has contributed to that. God's returns are not always financial."

When I asked a group to share their giving stories, one man, Daniel J. Arnold, told me, "Giving to the glory of the Lord Jesus Christ and the expansion of his kingdom on earth has become the common purpose of our family, our co-mission. We test the will of God for us in prayer and come together in agreement on every gift. Giving enters us into a life of faith and trust in God." Like everything else in the home, stewardship is *caught* as much as taught.

I recommend that families get involved together in special missions projects. Family members can work together to financially support, pray for, and correspond with a missionary, a needy family, or an overseas orphan. Becoming aware of needs elsewhere reminds our children of the incredible abundance in America and our opportunity to share it with the needy.

If you're planning a major family vacation, why not visit a mission field? Combine the fun with the education and encouragement to church missionary families (provided it isn't an inconvenience to them). When Karina and Angela were eight and six, Nanci and I took them for two months visiting five of our church's missionary families in England, Austria, Greece, Egypt, and Kenya—all for less money than many Americans spend on a car. None of us will ever outlive the impact of the trip itself or the planning, working, praying, and saving for it. We first had the thrill of seeing God provide and then seeing his exciting work in those fascinating countries. We took the girls out of school for those two months, but they learned far more in the traveling than they would have in the classroom. This trip shaped them not only for life but for eternity.

> Becoming aware of needs elsewhere reminds our children of the incredible abundance in America and our opportunity to share it with the needy.

TEACHING OUR CHILDREN SELF-CONTROL

Few things we can teach our children are more valuable than the discipline of saying no. We must model delayed gratification and teach the discipline of avoiding expenditures when the money could accomplish a higher purpose by being given away, saved, or used more wisely. Self-control is one of the highest Christian virtues (Galatians 5:22-23; Titus 2:1-12).

A preacher told this story: "One day I asked the Lord, 'What's a million years to you?' God said, 'It's only a second in time to me, Son.' So then I asked, 'What's a million dollars to you?' God said, 'It's only a penny to me, Son.' So then I said, 'Okay, Lord, how 'bout you just give me a million dollars?' 'Sure, Son,' God replied. 'But you'll have to wait just a second.'"[1]

Sometimes we have to wait longer than we want—but that's what builds our character and self-control. Children need help to develop sales resistance. They are by nature impulsive spenders. Self-discipline doesn't come naturally. Every time we say no to our children about ice cream, candy, or a new toy, we can teach them something important:

- In order for things to be special, they must be the exception, not the rule.
- There are higher values than immediate gratification.
- There are better ways to use God's money than to follow our impulses.

Children raised this way will usually follow the same pattern of decision making when they're on their own. Self-control learned by children in one area carries over into others. Children who learn to say no to unnecessary purchases are much more likely to say no to immorality, alcohol, drugs, or shoplifting.

Children whose parents won't give them everything they want are invariably more content than their spoiled counterparts. They ask for things less often and when they do ask they're far more selective. When their parents say no, they can accept a no because they're aware that no amount of begging or badgering will get them their way. (It will only result in discipline.) Children who are used to getting whatever they want continually spend their time sharpening their skills for manipulating their parents.

Obviously, parents should sometimes say yes to their children's requests. In the context of good stewardship, giving to our children can teach the lesson of generosity, not indulgence. Tightfisted stinginess is as negative a model as indulgence. Balance is the key. Our goal isn't to be penny-pinchers obsessed with money and fretting over every expenditure but joyful, responsible, and generous stewards of God's abundance. The point of being careful with God's money is to free up more resources to be used for kingdom purposes. A wonderful side effect is that it also builds more Christlike character.

SPENDING

Children can learn to shop intelligently, looking around and not buying the first thing they see. We can teach them how to compare values and discover the best places to buy. To avoid impulsive spending, our family has a rule of not making major purchases unless we've considered it for at least several months. If we still want something four months later, it's no longer an impulsive expenditure.

I suggest less shopping for entertainment. Aimless wandering through malls and shopping centers produces unnecessary spending. It can breed discontent to look at all the latest models of things we don't need and can't afford anyway. I recommend a family "field trip" to a shopping center for a specific purpose—but not to buy something. Look at all the different things, then ask yourself and your children if they're really worth the cost in light of what else could be done with the money, especially to help others and invest in God's kingdom.

I walked through a shopping center one day, identifying the products in the stores that could be described as things I needed as opposed to things I might want. The result was more amazing than I anticipated. Other than a few items of food and the most basic clothing, the other 99.9 percent of the items were nonnecessities. When I took our girls on the same sort of tour, their job was to identify "need items" as opposed to "want items." They had a fun time and came home realizing how few needs and how many wants we have.

An effective way to teach children how to properly spend money is to show them how you spend it. By the time children are ten, perhaps even younger, they're old enough to be let in on the family budget.

One technique is to bring home an entire paycheck in one dollar bills (explain that to the bank teller). Or you could use play money to illustrate the same thing. Put the money in piles to show how much goes to what expenses monthly. This approach allows children to visualize where the family's money goes. It helps them compare what's expensive and what isn't, what's a priority and what's not.

Some things will surprise the children, and they'll ask you questions that are mutually enlightening. You'll probably reevaluate your budget and make some healthy changes. Comparing the amount you give away to the amount you spend on yourself may be particularly convicting.

Your children may see things from a responsible perspective for the first time. Children who have been told to turn off the lights when they leave a room or to shut the front door behind them suddenly understand when they see the stack of money that goes to pay the electric bill. Children may hear their parents' words, but until they visualize what they mean, the words don't really sink in.

Looking at your tax return helps gauge your spiritual perspective. For example, how much you spend on interest compared to how much you give says a lot about what you believe. Do you take a greater deduction for interest on debt than you do for your charitable giving? Show your children your tax return, not just for their instruction but for yours.

PROGRESSIVE RESPONSIBILITY

As parents, our ultimate purpose isn't simply to give our children food and shelter for the first twenty years of life. Our purpose is to one day present to the Lord, the church, and the world mature young adults who are good servants, good stewards, and good citizens.

As children grow up, they should gradually be weaned financially from their parents. Especially as they are nearing the end of high school, children should be progressively earning more money and accepting more responsibility for their finances. By the time they're ten, most children might have their own savings account. By twelve, they might have a part-time summer job. By sixteen, they could have their own checking account. By seventeen, they might be paying for their own transportation, recreation, and some of their clothing. Of course, this will vary a great deal according to family needs, preferences, work opportunities, and a child's development.

After they complete high school, as long as our children are still in their early twenties, it may be reasonable to provide their food and lodging. But we must discern when this stops being healthy and starts developing bad habits of dependence that will be hard to break when they finally have to function in the real world. We must also realize that what's good for one child may be bad for another.

The goal is to help our children become increasingly independent of us—which should lead to an increasing dependence on the Lord. Dependence isn't eliminated, it's simply transferred. As we entrust our children with more and more financial responsibility, we should find them becoming more and more financially trustworthy. As they prove themselves trustworthy, God will entrust more and more to them, as well.

Let me repeat for emphasis what I said earlier: We parents should not transfer wealth to our grown children unless we've first transferred wisdom. Without wisdom, passing on wealth won't just be wasted—it will damage our children 100 percent of the time.

REWARDS AS INCENTIVES

In chapter 9 we saw that God uses a system of positive reinforcement, both through granting short-term rewards and promising long-term rewards. Although God has built into each of us the need for incentives and motivation by reward, some parents don't follow his pattern with their children. Dr. James Dobson addresses the subject of rewards in *Dare to Discipline*:

> Adults are reluctant to utilize rewards because they view them as a source of bribery. Our most workable teaching device is ignored because of a philosophical misunderstanding. Our entire society is established on

a system of reinforcement, yet we don't want to apply it where it is needed most: with young children.[2]

The great success of Awana, Boy Scouts, Girl Scouts, and similar children's programs is largely due to their emphasis on achievement. This shows up in patches, badges, ranks, and other tangible rewards. Of course, like every good thing, this can be taken to an extreme. But because all children are created to mature through proper motivation, we must gear our training toward motivating them in the most effective ways toward the most healthy ends.

> The great success of Awana, Boy Scouts, Girl Scouts, and similar children's programs is largely due to their emphasis on achievement.

God rewards us for what we do, how we do it, and why we do it (1 Corinthians 4:2, 5). Because having a good attitude sometimes requires considerable work, we periodically rewarded our daughters in small material ways simply for their attitudes. But although attitude is always important, it's also appropriate to reward children for specific actions and tasks performed.

Of course, not all rewards are material. As God says "well done" to his faithful servants, so a parent's praise is a child's greatest reward. Our children's biggest smiles emerged when we commended them for their actions and attitudes. And when we did give a material reward, we often tied it to a relationship-building experience, such as a breakfast out with Dad or ice cream with the whole family. Our children knew they weren't earning our love. But they also knew it was possible to gain approval and other rewards through their faithful efforts. Without this training, they'd never know how to responsibly function in their families, vocations, or in their service for Christ, the ultimate Rewarder (Hebrews 11:6).

CHILDREN WHO SHARE

Most parents can identify with this lament: "We wish Jimmy knew how to share." Sometimes we're appalled and embarrassed by our children's displays of greed and possessiveness. We want them to learn to share—yet too often we don't provide them a model for sharing.

Most of us will buy a certain tool or kitchen gadget that we'll use only a few times a year, rather than borrow it from a neighbor. This decision does two things—it results in unnecessary expense and circumvents the development of a relationship with our neighbor that would be naturally cultivated by sharing resources. It also trains our children to think and live independently rather than interdependently.

What do our children learn when they hear us complain about the fact that we loaned someone our car and it was returned dirty or dented? They may have even heard us say, "That's the last time we'll ever loan our tent to the youth group." However, if we view our assets as really belonging to God, we'll be glad to loan our car or a tent, even though we realize it may come back a little bit worse for wear. But that's part of sharing. To learn true sharing, children must see us do it. We must not just talk about sharing. We must share.

Hospitality is one of the strongest ways we can teach our children. By opening our homes to others and being gracious hosts and hostesses, we teach our children both to share and enjoy the fruits of sharing. They see firsthand the value of encouraging other people and drawing close to them through the unselfish use of possessions. You might even look back with your children at some of the people to whom you've opened your home and wonder if, without knowing it, you've entertained an angel in disguise (Hebrews 13:2).

CHILDREN WHO ARE THANKFUL

"Sharper than a serpent's tooth it is to have a thankless child." Any parent who has one knows exactly what Shakespeare meant. In the midst of the abundance they've always known and with the sin nature they've always had, our children won't naturally be thankful. We must teach them thankfulness.

"Praise the Lord, O my soul, and forget not all his benefits" (Psalm 103:2). As parents we can lead the way by counting our blessings in front of the children and openly expressing our thankfulness to God for all he's done for us. We must be careful not to nullify this by complaining when things don't go our way. What do our children learn when they hear us say, "What a shame it had to rain today," or "This stupid car is always breaking down," or "That's the second year in a row without a raise"?

We often asked our daughters at night to identify a number of things they were thankful for that God had done for them that very day. At first this may be difficult, but in time it develops a sensitive eye to the ways God cares for us. At the top of this list of things to be thankful for is God himself, our loving Redeemer. Next are the family and friends and church he's given us.

Children can also give thanks for material things, for more than just toys—for a body that works, a bed to sleep in, a house to live in, for the air, sunshine, rain, the beauty of flowers and trees. They can give thanks for a country in which they're free to worship and share their faith. Giving thanks for all these things draws their hearts not to the things themselves but to the One who graciously provides them. The focus isn't on the gifts, but the Giver. Then even when the body hurts, the bed's hard, and the house is cold and creaky, there remains the constant assurance that God is still there and still faithful.

As children develop thankfulness for their food and other provisions, they can learn to see them not as "easy come, easy go" commodities but as personal provisions of a loving heavenly Father. Otherwise, in this throwaway society of paper plates, paper towels, plastic spoons, and disposables of every kind, it's hard to develop a proper appreciation for things.

The obstacles to thankfulness are many. Yet they must be overcome in our Christian homes, where we're to give thanks in all circumstances (1 Thessalonians 5:18). Never apologize for insisting that your children or grandchildren develop an old-fashioned habit of saying please and thank you. Children who aren't taught these basic courtesies are being failed by the adults in their lives.

LEAVING A LEGACY

Nothing will interfere more with our children's relationship with God—or even prevent them from having such a relationship—than a life centered on things. Our greatest legacy to our children is to help them develop their inner lives, their spiritual selves, their hearts for God. We must intertwine these lessons with the building of strong character, moral fiber, and rugged biblical values that can endure the beatings of a godless, materialistic society.

Although many parents will leave their children a big inheritance, we can leave them what really matters—a heritage of wisdom and generosity. They can then pass on this legacy to their own children and their children's children. Godly generations and an eternal impact can result from our simple acts of faithful stewardship—not only of money, but also of the children God entrusts to us.

Where Do We Go from Here?

> I continually find it necessary to guard against that natural
> love of wealth and grandeur which prompts us always,
> when we come to apply our general doctrine to our own
> case, to claim an exception.   WILLIAM WILBERFORCE

> The antagonism between life and conscience may be
> removed in two ways: by a change of life or by a change
> of conscience.   LEO TOLSTOY

In this concluding chapter, I will introduce some new ideas, but mostly I will pull together and summarize key points and principles that will serve as the basis for a final challenge.

One of the most remarkable articles on money I've read came from an unlikely source: novelist Stephen King, a writer better known for horror stories than theological insights. In a *Family Circle* magazine article, he breaks with the spirit of materialism by making a passionate argument for giving—not out of altruism but self-interest. Although he doesn't write from an eternal perspective, King intuitively realizes not only that giving is right, but also that it's smart. He doesn't acknowledge the glory of God, the good of others, or the giver's eternal rewards as higher reasons to give, but he nonetheless recognizes that giving packs a transcendent purpose and pleasure here and now:

> A couple of years ago I found out what "you can't take it with you" means. I found out while I was lying in a ditch at the side of a country road, covered with mud and blood and with the tibia of my right leg poking out the side of my jeans like a branch of a tree taken down in a thunderstorm. I had a MasterCard in my wallet, but when you're lying in a ditch with broken glass in your hair, no one accepts MasterCard.
>
> We come in naked and broke. We may be dressed when we go out, but we're just as broke. Warren Buffet? Going to go out broke.

Bill Gates? Going out broke. Tom Hanks? Going out broke. Steve King?
Broke. Not a crying dime.

All the money you earn, all the stocks you buy, all the mutual funds
you trade—all of that is mostly smoke and mirrors. It's still going to be
a quarter-past getting late whether you tell the time on a Timex or a
Rolex. . . .

So I want you to consider making your life one long gift to others.
And why not? All you have is on loan, anyway. All that lasts is what you
pass on. . . .

[This needy world is] not a pretty picture, but we have the power
to help, the power to change. And why should we refuse? Because
we're going to take it with us? Please.

Giving isn't about the receiver or the gift but the giver. It's for the
giver. One doesn't open one's wallet to improve the world, although
it's nice when that happens; one does it to improve one's self. . . .

A life of giving—not just money, but time and spirit—repays. It
helps us remember that we may be going out broke, but right now
we're doing okay. Right now we have the power to do great good for
others and for ourselves.

So I ask you to begin giving, and to continue as you begin. I think
you'll find in the end that you got far more than you ever had, and did
more good than you ever dreamed.[1]

Contrast Stephen King's perspective with that of a regular attender at my
church, who sent the following anonymous letter in response to a sermon on
giving:

I was never so disappointed in a service as I was Sunday. I have an
unbelieving friend that I got to come with me, and what were you
preaching about? Money! I can assure you she was not impressed!
And why money, when there are so many beautiful things to say?
You'd better reconsider such messages in the future. Leave money
to God, and he will handle everything, believe me. I love this church
and usually like the sermons, but that was terrible.

The writer signed off with the knife-turning flair so typical of anonymous letters: "A Christian who loves to go to church to hear the Word."

One of our other pastors preached that message, and I can objectively say it
was biblical and accurate. Many appreciated the message. But this person's reaction is sadly common. Some who imagine they "love to hear the Word" are
offended when taught what the Word actually says, when it threatens their
comfortable assumptions and lifestyles.

Is the solution to avoid a defensive reaction by avoiding the subject of money? No! If we're to proclaim "the whole will of God" (Acts 20:27), then our pastors and teachers must address this subject to which Scripture devotes so much attention.

When churches and parachurch organizations address the subject of giving, a frequent, fundamental mistake is tying the teaching to a specific project or need. We preach on giving because the offering is down or to kick off a building fund drive. Or we send a pamphlet on giving along with a letter that says our ministry or school will shut down if we don't receive $50,000 in the next four weeks. The result is that people view the instruction on giving merely as a fund-raising tool, a means to the end of accomplishing our personal or institutional goals. (Indeed, often that's just what it is.) I recommend scheduling messages on giving when there are no special pleas to give or special projects to give to.

In a society preoccupied with money and possessions, Christians will continually be exposed to wrong thinking and living. Certainly, we cannot expect the Christian community to take Scripture seriously unless pastors clearly teach and apply it.

I encourage readers to ask their pastors to address these subjects from the pulpit. Most pastors know this subject is important but feel self-conscious addressing it on their own initiative. They will welcome such an invitation. (This book could serve as a resource for them—in fact, some pastors have preached right through it.) Small groups and Sunday school classes need to discuss these issues.

Fellow Christians ought to disciple each other in financial stewardship. Young believers need to see biblical lifestyle principles embodied. Those who've learned the hard way about the bondage of debt need to warn others. Young couples need to hear their elders tell of their joy in giving, and how God has used it in their family. Husbands and wives need to be encouraged to discuss and act on these truths. (One step I took as a pastor was to assemble and distribute a booklet of financial testimonies by ten church families.)

My small book *The Treasure Principle: Discovering the Secret of Joyful Giving* is being widely used in churches, ministries, and Bible studies. Many churches have used the earlier edition of *Money, Possessions, and Eternity* in their small-group Bible studies. Crown Financial Ministries offers stewardship Bible studies for churches.

I challenge Bible colleges, Christian liberal arts colleges, and seminaries to develop courses centered on a biblical theology of stewardship and giving. We need much more than a class on budgeting and financial planning. We need a Bible-centered, Christ-centered theology of money and possessions that deals with critical issues every Christian should face.

RAISING THE BAR

I believe the Christian community should be filled with people who set caps on their lifestyles, giving away everything above that amount. Some call this "setting a finish line." That means if we make a predetermined amount of money or save a certain amount, that's it. We won't accumulate any more. We'll give away everything else. That isn't sacrificial giving, it's giving according to our ability. Yet, by most of our standards, it's so radical we may not know anyone who lives that way.

As we contemplate adjusting our lifestyle according to the needs we see around us, we should consider the example of John Wesley after his conversation with the young chambermaid (which I mentioned in chapter 16).

To turn the tide of materialism in the Christian community, we desperately need bold models of kingdom-centered living.

Perhaps as a result of this incident, Wesley preached that Christians should not merely tithe but give away all extra income once the family and creditors are taken care of. He believed that with increasing income, a Christian's giving, not his lifestyle, should increase. He began this practice at Oxford and continued it throughout his life. Even when his income rose to thousands of pounds, he lived simply and quickly gave away his surplus. He was afraid of laying up treasures on earth, so the money went out to charity as quickly as it came in.

Wesley's practice is in keeping with Scripture (2 Corinthians 8:14; 9:11). God allows us to put our names on his account and to determine our own salaries as his money manager. Many of us overvalue our service, paying ourselves too much. Wouldn't it be better to live on less and have God reward us, than live on more that God intended for higher purposes?

LEARNING FROM EACH OTHERS' EXAMPLES

In Romans 12:6-8, Paul lists seven spiritual gifts, including prophesying, serving, teaching, showing mercy, and giving. I'm convinced that of all these gifts, giving is the one least thought about and discussed. It's the gift buried deepest in the Western church. We regularly see the gift of teaching and know what it looks like. We hear testimonies about miraculous healings, restored marriages, successful parenting, and nearly everything else but giving. We know about prayer warriors and Bible students, but rarely do we hear stories of people who give most of their incomes to the Lord. If it's all right to be aware of and follow the lead of prayer warriors, why not giving warriors?

Of course, all of us are called to serve, show mercy, and give, even if we don't have those gifts. But I believe that in different times of history God has sovereignly distributed certain gifts more widely according to current needs and opportunities (such as the gift of mercy during plagues).

Suppose God wanted to fulfill his plan of world evangelization and help an unprecedented number of suffering people. What gift would we expect him to distribute widely? The gift of giving. And what might we expect him to provide to those to whom he's given that gift?—unprecedented wealth to meet all those needs and further his kingdom.

Look around. Isn't that exactly what God has done? The question is what are we doing with the wealth he's entrusted to us to reach the lost and help the suffering?

SHARING OUR GIVING STORIES

People respond best when they have tangible examples they can follow in their leaders and their peers (Numbers 7:3; 1 Chronicles 29:9; 2 Chronicles 24:10).

To turn the tide of materialism in the Christian community, we desperately need bold models of kingdom-centered living. We should glorify God, not people. But we must see and hear other giving stories or our people will not learn to give.

Scripture tells us to give but not in order to be seen by others (Matthew 6:1). That doesn't mean it's wrong to tell our stories. Certainly we should be careful to avoid pride, as in every other area. But Jesus also says, "Let your light shine before men, that they may see your good deeds and praise your Father in heaven" (Matthew 5:16). He commands us to let others see our good deeds, not so they'll praise us, but so they'll praise our Father. It all comes down to who gets the credit.

In fact, if I give out of a heart of joy, believing Christ's promise that it's more blessed to give than to receive, believing that I will get heavenly treasures for every earthly treasure I give away, it strips my giving of pride. Why would I be proud of doing what's in my best eternal interests? And if other people hear about my giving, why should I be proud? If I were thirsty and I found cold, clear water and told other people I was drinking it, would that be cause for pride? Cause for joy, yes, but not for pride.

Through an unfortunate misinterpretation of biblical teaching, we've hidden giving under a basket (see appendix E, "Should Giving Always Be Kept Secret?") As a result we're not teaching Christians to give. And they're lacking joy and purpose because of it.[2]

I mentioned earlier that when our missions pastor returned from Sudan, he told our church about the desperate need and opportunities to make a difference. People responded wholeheartedly. The fourth-grade class at our school raised thousands of dollars through work projects. A sixth-grade girl took the $50 she had saved up to play on a basketball team, and gave it to help Sudanese believers. One family had saved several hundred dollars to go to Disneyland. Their children asked if they could give the money to help persecuted Christians instead. Before long, people had given $60,000 to help in Sudan. We never took an offering. It was contagious, from the grassroots. People told their giving stories. And when they did, it thrilled and encouraged the body to give more.

King David told the people exactly how much he'd given to build the temple. The precise amounts of gold and precious stones contributed by the leaders were also made public. "The people rejoiced at the willing response of their leaders, for they had given freely and wholeheartedly to the Lord" (1 Chronicles 29:9). The people could rejoice only because they knew what their leaders had given. They could follow their leaders' example in giving only because they were aware of how much they had given. Unless we learn how to humbly tell each other our giving stories, our churches will not learn to give.

A SENSE OF DESTINY

The fact that you're reading these words is likely part of God's plan to change your life—and in turn, to change history and eternity. Sound like an overstatement? I don't think so.

Remember what Mordecai said to Esther: "If you remain silent at this time, relief and deliverance for the Jews will arise from another place, but you and your father's family will perish. And who knows but that you have come to royal position for such a time as this?" (Esther 4:14).

Is God calling you to be a more generous giver? Is he calling you to be a "generous giving" evangelist, sharing with others the liberating joy of giving?

Just as Esther was in a position of privilege, so is nearly everyone reading this book. Are you educated and literate? Do you have food, clothing, shelter, a car, and some electronic equipment? Then you are among the privileged, the world's truly wealthy.

Why has God entrusted you with the privilege of wealth? For just such a time as this. One ministry calls a group of its key donors "History's Handful." Is there an exaggerated sense of significance in this term? I don't think so. Giving to God's great causes is a calling and privilege that should infuse us with a sense of destiny.

It's no accident that you live in this time and place in history. Remind yourself again why the God of providence has entrusted you with so much: "Your plenty will supply what they need. . . . You will be made rich in every way so that you can be generous on every occasion" (2 Corinthians 8:14; 9:11).

Is that your destiny? Is God calling you to be a more generous giver? Is he calling you to be a "generous giving" evangelist, sharing with others the liberating joy of giving? What books does he want you to read? What studies does he want you to lead in your church? Whom does he want you to invite to which giving conference?[3]

Is God raising up a great army of givers today? If so, isn't the fact that he's entrusted us with so much wealth persuasive evidence that he's called us to be part of that army?

Many are praying the prayer of Jabez: "Bless me and enlarge my territory!" (1 Chronicles 4:10). Why not pray that prayer about your giving? Why not set a figure you can live on, then tell God that everything he provides beyond that amount you'll give back to him?

Years ago, Scott Lewis was challenged by Bill Bright to give one million dollars to help fulfill the great commission.[4] This amount was laughable to Scott—far beyond anything he could imagine, because his machinery business was generating an annual income of less than $50,000.

Scott had given $17,000 the previous year, but Bill challenged him to set a goal of giving $50,000 the next year. Scott was dumbfounded. How could he give away next year more than he made all this year? Yet he and his wife determined to ask God to provide enough to do it. And he did. Not many years later, they had given the full one million dollars, and they haven't stopped since. Their way of living didn't change much, but the amount of their giving did.

THE BURDEN OF PROOF

For many, their philosophy of finances seems to be, "As long as I have it, why not spend it?" A more biblical philosophy would be, "As long as I have it, why not give it?" The burden of proof should fall on spending, not giving. The question isn't, Why should we give? That's obvious. The question is, Why *shouldn't* we give? And how do our answers stand up to Scripture?

Given our abundance, the burden of proof should always be on keeping, not giving. Why would you not give? We err by beginning with the assumption that we should keep or spend the money God entrusts to us. Giving should be the default choice. Unless there is a compelling reason to spend it or keep it, we should give it.

Someone recently told me I ought to be careful not to go overboard by too much empasis on giving. He warned that it might lead to extremes and imbalance, and that people might start neglecting their family's material needs. I told him that as I look at my life and others, I see little danger of that happening!

Do we really believe we'll stand before Christ's judgment seat and hear him say, "I have this against you—you gave too much; you should have spent it on yourself instead!" Jesus never called someone a fool for giving too much and keeping too little. He did call someone a fool for keeping too much and giving too little (Luke 12:20-21).

As you read these words, America's prosperity may be continuing or it may be seriously eroding or showing mixed signals. We have no way of knowing how long prosperity will last. Why not give away the abundance while we still can? Why not give until our hearts are more in God's kingdom than in our remodeling project, business venture, dream vacation, or retirement plan? Why not ask God if he wants us to hold off building our dream house here, since our Bridegroom is already building our real dream house in heaven? Meanwhile we can use God's funds to build something that won't go up in smoke.

Paul exhorts the Corinthians to follow the example of the Macedonians: "Excel in this grace of giving" (2 Corinthians 8:1-7). Then he tells the Corinthians that others will be encouraged to follow their example (2 Corinthians 9:12-14). Individuals, families, and churches can establish beachheads of strategic lifestyle, disciplined spending, and generous, globally minded giving. By infectious example, we can claim more territory for Christ than we ever dreamed possible.

A revival of lavish giving and strategic living is a revival of grace empowered by God. As the body of Christ gets serious about learning and living out God's instructions concerning money and possessions, Christ's cause will be furthered and his person exalted.

GETTING SIDETRACKED FROM THE REAL ISSUE

Sometimes Christians get sidetracked from their central mission through illegitimate or secondary financial concerns. One example is the tax protest movement that now includes thousands of Christians across the country, many of whom use their church contacts to propagate their cause. Usually, they refuse to pay income tax, citing innumerable reasons why taxes are unjust and unconstitutional. They do this despite the fact that in a much more unjust society, Paul commanded the Roman Christians to obey their government and pay their taxes (Romans 13:1-7).

When asked about the tax to be paid to Caesar, Jesus turned the focus to something more important (Mark 12:13-17). The issue of paying taxes to Caesar is insignificant compared to a person's need to surrender his or her whole life to God. Jesus says the tax is to be paid, but he emphasizes that there are much higher things with which we should concern ourselves.

Taxes, like a thousand other subjects, are secondary issues to the true disciple. Although some taxation is certainly unreasonable and unfair, both Jesus and Paul said that paying taxes is a duty. We may object to the system, we may support legislation to change it, and we may actively lobby for tax relief, but we are still to pay our taxes. In any case, our concerns about unfairness must not become our focus.

GIVE IT NOW OR GIVE IT LATER?

People ask, "Should I give now, or should I hang onto it, hoping my investments will do well and I'll have more to give in a year or two?"

A relevant response is, "How soon do you want to experience God's blessing?" and "Do you want to be sure the money goes to God's kingdom or are you willing to risk that it never will?"

If we don't give now we run some real risks:

- **The economy may change and we'll have less to give.** God says we don't know what's going to happen tomorrow, and we certainly don't know how much money we're going to make (James 4:13-17). Countless investors have been absolutely sure about getting great returns on money that instead disappeared overnight.
- **Our hearts may change and we may not follow through with giving.** Zacchaeus said, "Here and now I give my possessions." If you procrastinate, the same heart that's prompting you to give today may later persuade you not to. Why? Because as a result of postponing giving, your heart's vested interests increase on earth and decrease in heaven.
- **Our lives may end before we've given what we intended.** I don't believe it's ever wrong to give now. With 10,000 percent interest (Matthew 19:29), God can produce far greater returns on money invested in heaven today than Wall Street or real estate ever can. When we stand before God, he won't say, "You blew it when you gave me all that money before the stock market peaked."

UP IN FLAMES

When the Lord returns, what will happen to all the money sitting in bank accounts, retirement programs, estates, and foundations? It will burn like wood, hay, and straw, when it could have been given in exchange for gold, silver, and precious stones (1 Corinthians 3:11-15). Money that could have been used to feed the hungry and fulfill the great commission will go up in flames.

When the Lord returns, what will happen to all the money sitting in bank accounts, retirement programs, estates, and foundations?

John Wesley said, "Money never stays with me. It would burn me if it did. I throw it out of my hands as soon as possible, lest it should find its way into my heart." Wesley's goal was to give so generously as to leave virtually nothing behind when he died. He achieved his goal. While it still had value, he traded in his "Confederate currency" for treasures in heaven.

Occasionally, I ask myself this troubling question: How much Confederate money will I have left when I die or Christ returns?

Have you ever played one of those card games where the winner is the one who runs out of cards first? At the end of the game, every card left counts against you. The American dream is to die with as many cards in your hand as possible. But maybe we've got it backwards. Maybe our strategy should be like John Wesley's—to not get stuck with all those cards at our life's end.

It's curious that the Church has become the most tightfisted at the very

415

time in history when God has provided most generously. There's considerable talk about the end of the age, and many people seem to believe that Christ will return in their lifetime. But why is it that expecting Christ's return hasn't radically influenced our giving? Why is it that people who believe in the soon return of Christ are so quick to build their own financial empires—which prophecy tells us will perish—and so slow to build God's kingdom?

DEPOSITING THIS LIFE IN ETERNITY'S ACCOUNT

When Hudson Taylor opened a bank account for the China Inland Mission, the application form asked for an asset list. Taylor wrote the following as the sum total of his assets: "Ten pounds and all the promises of God." Our greatest resources are spiritual, not material. They come from another world, not this one.

One morning I was at a restaurant when a frazzled woman blew through the door and loudly complained to her friend, "The wipers aren't working again on my Porsche, and the Audi's in for repairs. I've had it!"

I smiled but at the same time was saddened for this poor woman. (Yes, *poor* woman.) What a contrast to the believer with eternal perspective:

> I have learned to be content whatever the circumstances. I know what it is to be in need, and I know what it is to have plenty. I have learned the secret of being content in any and every situation, whether well fed or hungry, whether living in plenty or in want. I can do everything through him who gives me strength. (Philippians 4:11-13)

Paul doesn't say it is wrong to live in plenty, but that the same secret to contentment applies then as when we're in poverty. (Notice, too, that Paul had to *learn* contentment—that means it didn't come naturally for him.) Contentment isn't the product of material abundance; it results from our invisible resources in Christ. In the third century, Cyprian, bishop of Carthage, wrote this description of the affluent:

> Their property held them in chains . . . chains which shackled their courage and choked their faith and hampered their judgment and throttled their souls. . . . If they stored up their treasure in heaven, they would not now have an enemy and a thief within their household. . . . They think of themselves as owners, whereas it is they rather who are owned: enslaved as they are to their own property, they are not the masters of their money but its slaves.[5]

God keeps records of what we do with his money. At the moment we meet Christ—at our death or his return—all accounts will be frozen, all assets and expenditures opened for the Final Audit. And then it's God himself—the Owner, Manager, and Auditor of the Bank of Eternity—who will make eternal disbursements based on how our account reads after the last deposit has been made and the account finally closed.

C. T. Studd was a rich and famous English athlete who sold his entire estate, gave it away, and went to the mission field to serve Christ. He summed up the perspective that motivated him: "Only one life, 'twill soon be past. Only what's done for Christ will last."

WHO ARE WE FOLLOWING?

After Christ made some radical statements about money, "the Pharisees, who loved money, heard all this and were sneering at Jesus" (Luke 16:14). The Pharisees were the religious conservatives of their day. The lesson for us is that we may believe the Scriptures, defend them, be willing to die for them, and still be money lovers who reject and take offense at the radical teachings of Christ about money and possessions.

Our hymnbooks say a lot about following Jesus. Our pocketbooks say even more. What does it mean when God has entrusted Christians with greater wealth than in all human history, yet many are giving less to kingdom purposes than ever before? Surely it means we are following our culture, not our Christ.

G. Campbell Morgan, the famous preacher, said this:

The measure of failure on the part of the Church is the measure in which she has allowed herself to be influenced by the spirit of the age, because she has been untrue to the facts of her own life. We are sometimes told today that what the Church supremely needs is that she should catch the spirit of the age. A thousand times no. What the Church supremely needs is to correct the spirit of the age. The church in Corinth catching the spirit of Corinth became anemic, weak, and failed to deliver the message of God to Corinth. The church of God in London, invaded by the spirit of London, the materialism, militarism, sordidness, and selfishness of London, is too weak to save London. . . .

If the Church's failure is due to the fact that the spirit of the city has invaded the church, the Church's success is due to the fact that the Spirit of the Church invades the city. The Church of God always fails when she becomes conformed to the methods, maxims, and manners of the city. The Church of God always succeeds when, true to the supernatural nature of her life, she stands in perfect separation from the city. Only thus is she able to touch and help the city.[6]

> In the Western Church, affluence has dulled our senses. Although God's Word calls for our attention, we go right on mindlessly living out of sync with eternity's musical score.

417

In the Western Church, affluence has dulled our senses. Although God's Word calls for our attention, we go right on mindlessly living out of sync with eternity's musical score. We ad-lib our own rendition of the concert, while an audience of angels and saints shudders at our indifference to the Conductor's direction.

With or without us, God is moving. He is accomplishing his kingdom program. He is using the time, energy, skills, and material resources of his disciples all over the world to touch and change lives for all eternity. The question isn't whether God is moving. The question is whether we will choose to get on board. If we don't, everyone loses, not least of all us.

A HARD LOOK AT OURSELVES

William MacDonald, in his book *True Discipleship*, makes the following observations about the life of faith:

> God's will is that our lives should be "a perpetual crisis of dependence on him." We defeat his will in our lives when we lay up treasures on earth.
>
> The life of faith does not follow automatically when a person becomes a Christian. It requires deliberate action on his part. This is especially true in an affluent society. The believer must put himself in a position where he is compelled to trust God. . . . It is only as he gets rid of his reserves and other false supports that he can truly launch out into the deep.[7]

What are we to make of such words? Are they naive and irresponsible, or faithful and true? Does the answer depend on the condition of our heart? MacDonald continues:

> God pours out his choicest blessings on those who are anxious that nothing shall stick to their hands. Individuals who value the rainy day above the present agony of the world will get no blessing from God. . . .
>
> How utterly in keeping with this age of grace it is for us to sell our prized possessions—our diamonds and other jewelry, our original paintings, our antique furniture, our sterling silver, our stamp collections—and put the proceeds to work in the salvation of souls throughout the world.[8]

It isn't surprising that unbelievers would scoff at such a proposal. But isn't it revealing when professing disciples of Jesus Christ resent, resist, rationalize, and pontificate about why such a perspective is foolish or legalistic? Isn't the truth simply that we're far more comfortable with the world's teaching about money and possessions than with Christ's? Are we really so far removed from New Testament discipleship that what was once elementary to any true Christian is now foreign to us?

Why do we take consolation in celebrity Christians who judge success by the standards of the world? Why do we take our cues from people so conspicuously different than Jesus? Why do we listen to men who, had they lived in the first century, would have sold tickets to the feeding of the five thousand and charged a fee to watch the raising of Lazarus?

Shouldn't we just admit the obvious—that the New Testament call to discipleship, compassion, and giving leaves no room for the way many of us are thinking and living? Is it time to get beyond the theoretical stance of "I'd be willing to give up anything if God asked me to," and start actually giving up things in order to do what he's commanded us?

Where are the prophetic voices in churches decrying our self-centered affluence and indifference to global needs and calling us to a joyful generosity that exalts Christ, helps the hurting, and fills our souls to overflowing?

Is it unfair to ask whether Jesus, if he were living in America today, would spend $40,000 on a luxury car, given the staggering level of human needs and the eternal investment alternatives? If our answer is that Jesus wouldn't take such a step, then why would we who are called to "follow in his steps" (1 Peter 2:21) take such a step?

Tolstoy said, "The antagonism between life and conscience may be removed either by a change of life or by a change of conscience." Many of us have elected to adjust our consciences rather than our lives. Our powers of rationalization are unlimited. They allow us to live in luxury and indifference while others, whom we could help if we chose to, starve and go to hell.

If the preceding statement is offensive, isn't the truth it affirms even more offensive? We American Christians have a silent agreement with each other not to talk about such things. "Laying guilt trips" on each other is the modern unpardonable sin. But shouldn't we violate that agreement rather than postpone the discussion till the judgment seat of Christ . . . where we will find ourselves woefully ill-equipped to argue with the Judge?

We can avoid later judgment by correcting ourselves now: "If we judged ourselves, we would not come under judgment" (1 Corinthians 11:31).

If we fear appearing foolish by taking seriously the New Testament view of money and possessions, we should remind ourselves of what the Bible says about being fools for Christ (1 Corinthians 1:18-31; 4:8-13). The question is not *whether* we will be seen as fools—that part is certain—but *when* and *by whom* we will be seen as fools. Better to be seen as fools now in the eyes of other people—including other Christians—than to be seen as fools forever in the eyes of the Audience of One, whose judgment ultimately matters.

OUR ACCOUNTABILITY AS GOD'S MONEY MANAGERS

In ancient times, only eunuchs were entrusted with the king's harem. Other men could be ensnared by passions for beautiful women, but the eunuch could be near them without violating the king's trust. Christians are to be eunuchs in regard to money and possessions. We're not to be infatuated with them, led astray by them, or entangled with them. These material resources are a part of our daily lives; we deal with them and appreciate them for what they are. But they hold no captivating sway, no seductive hold on us.

Money and possessions are assets when they meet our basic needs, serve God's purposes, and allow us to focus on Christ and his kingdom as the objects of our desire. They become liabilities when they themselves become the objects of our desire.

Isn't it time we took inventory of our assets? What should we liquidate now while we still can, and where should we give it where it will make an eternal difference?

Speaking of financial stewardship, Jesus says, "From everyone who has been given much, much will be demanded; and from the one who has been entrusted with much, much more will be asked" (Luke 12:48). In all of human history, have the followers of God and Christ ever been entrusted with more than we have? Consequently, has there ever been a generation of believers of whom God will demand more?

I pointed out earlier that the person who works for forty years at $25,000 a year handles a million dollars in his or her lifetime. God entrusts a fortune even to those of us who think of ourselves as underprivileged. We will answer to him for what we've done with it (Romans 14:12). Where did it all go? What did we spend it on? What difference did it all make for eternity?

The early Church father John Chrysostom warned his fellow believers, "You have taken possession of the resources that belong to Christ and you consume them aimlessly. Don't you realize that you are going to be held accountable?"

Isn't it time we took inventory of our assets? What should we liquidate now while we still can, and where should we give the proceeds where they will make an eternal difference?

We must stop saying that Scripture is unclear on this subject. Yes, it leaves room for differences in lifestyle. But it leaves no room whatsoever for materialism, greed, envy, pride, selfishness, hoarding, irresponsible spending, unjustifiable debt, or indifference to the needs of the poor or the lost. When we try to justify any of these sins on the basis of "legitimate lifestyle differences," we fool ourselves and each other, but not God.

He has given us in Christ all the resources we need to obey him (2 Peter 1:3). If we are disobedient, it's not because we can't obey but because we won't. Charles Spurgeon had this to say about affluence in the Church:

> The Christian far oftener disgraces his profession in prosperity than in adversity. It is a dangerous thing to be prosperous. The crucible of adversity is a less severe trial to the Christian than the fining-pot of

prosperity. Oh, what leanness of soul and neglect of spiritual things have been brought on through the very mercies and bounties of God! Yet this is not a matter of necessity, for the apostle tells us that he knew how to abound. When he had much he knew how to use it. Abundant grace enabled him to bear abundant prosperity. When he had a full sail he was loaded with much ballast, and so floated safely.[9]

For some of us, it's time to drop to our knees and ask God's forgiveness for our self-indulgent lifestyles, our indifference to human need, and our shortsightedness about eternal issues. For others, it's time to joyfully move on in our process of enlightenment, applying more and more of the biblical principles we've examined. For each of us, it's time to commit or recommit ourselves to a life of obedient and exhilarating discipleship, with all that implies in the handling of God's money and possessions. It's time to turn our backs on the American dream of unlimited prosperity. It's time to trade in our short-term material dreams for the long-term kingdom dreams of the risen Christ.

I urge you to embrace Christ's invitation: "Give, and it will be given to you" (Luke 6:38). Then, when he gives you more, remind yourself why: "So that you can be generous on every occasion" (2 Corinthians 9:11). When you give, you'll experience his joy. When you give, you'll feel his pleasure.

Yesterday, I had a phone conversation with a man who recently read The Treasure Principle. He owns a profitable business and now believes for the first time that he knows why God has blessed him financially. It's not so he can drive nicer cars and live in a nicer house. It's to give it to build God's kingdom. As I told him about a dozen different missions groups, pro-life projects, prison ministries, and ways to help persecuted Christians, he was moved by all the wonderful investment options. He finished our conversation determined to liquidate more assets to dramatically expand his eternal investment portfolio. I wish you could have heard the excitement in his voice. He isn't a reluctant, guilt-ridden giver. He's a man who has been released from material bondage. He's thrilled to have finally gotten on board with what matters!

I invite you to join this brother in joyfully leveraging the assets that God has entrusted to you. Make an eternal difference. Send your treasures on to heaven, where they'll safely await you. When you do, you'll feel the freedom and sense the smile of God.

We dare not procrastinate obedience. Nothing is more fleeting than the moment of conviction. If we turn our backs on that moment, the next time may not come until we stand before our Lord—when it will be too late to reclaim a lifetime of squandered opportunities.

I've included at the end of this chapter a financial covenant with God that you may wish to make. I encourage you to read it thoughtfully and prayerfully. You may or may not have already made part of this commitment. You may wish to revise the wording to something you can fully affirm. But if you put your name to this covenant, I guarantee you'll never regret it.

COMING TO GRIPS WITH ETERNITY

The meager flame of this life will appear to be snuffed out by death, but on the other side it will rage to sudden and eternal intensity. In light of this knowledge, we must learn to "fix our eyes not on what is seen, but on what is unseen," living each day in the light of the long tomorrow (2 Corinthians 4:18). A. W. Tozer said, "Any temporal possession can be turned into everlasting wealth. Whatever is given to Christ is immediately touched with immortality."[10]

Martin Luther said, "I have held many things in my hands and I have lost them all. But whatever I have placed in God's hands, that I still possess."

God tells us to prepare for the long tomorrow by using our short todays to exchange earthly treasures for heavenly ones. In eternity we'll worship God with people of every tribe, nation, and language. We'll say thanks to them and they'll say thanks to us for acts of faithfulness done for Christ while we lived on earth. We'll tell our stories and listen to theirs, enjoying the warmth, sharing the joy, with our Lord the center of attention. What a privilege. Do you have trouble getting out of bed in the morning? If picturing scenes in heaven doesn't give you a purpose for living, I don't know what will!

Five minutes after we die we'll understand what's most important and what's been most important all along. We'll see with eternity's clarity. We can either take off the blinders now, while we still have our earthly lives to live, or wait for them to be taken off after death when it will be too late to go back and change what we've done on earth.

May what will be most important to us five minutes after we die become most important to us now.

A FINANCIAL COVENANT WITH GOD

I submit to the Lord God Almighty. I affirm his ownership of me and every aspect of my life. I declare that "my" money and possessions are actually his. I recognize that God is the owner of everything and I am his steward, a money manager for the assets he has entrusted to me.

As a symbol of my total submission to God, and as a beginning point for my commitment to giving, I set aside the tithe, the first 10 percent of everything, as holy and belonging exclusively to the Lord. I will return to him the whole tithe, being careful not to rob him and incur his curse. I will give back to him, through his church, the firstfruits of all he provides. I do this in obedience to him and in desire of his blessing. By faith, I take God up on his challenge: "Test me in this . . . and see" (Malachi 3:10). I ask him to show me it is far better to live on 90 percent with his blessing than 100 percent without it.

Having been set on the right course by the tithe, I embark on a lifelong adventure of Christian giving. Beyond the tithe, out of the 90 percent that God has entrusted to me, I will seek to give generous freewill gifts as I sense his leading. I recognize that God has entrusted wealth to me not so I can live like a king, but so I can be "generous on every occasion" (2 Corinthians 9:11). I recognize that I can rob God not only by withholding the tithe but by failing to give whatever offerings he may call upon me to give.

I pray that God will teach me to give sacrificially to feed the hungry, to reach the lost, to invest in worthy causes and ministries that submit themselves to Christ, and to use his funds wisely and biblically (2 Corinthians 8–9).

I commit myself to stay out of financial bondage, so I can be free to serve God single-mindedly. I acknowledge that I can't take earthly treasure with me when I leave this world, and I purpose to store it up instead as heavenly treasure—for Christ's glory and the eternal good of others and myself. Recognizing that heaven is my home and Christ is my Lord, I commit myself to seek his guidance and to do as he directs with his assets.

Signed: _____

Witness: _____

Date: _____

APPENDIX A

Financial Integrity and Accountability in Churches and Ministries

In 2 Corinthians 8, Paul advises the church at Corinth about the proper handling and distribution of church funds—and the need to do so in an above-board and accountable fashion. The Corinthians were collecting a substantial offering to be distributed to the poor in distant Jerusalem. Paul assures them that Titus, whom they knew to be a man of integrity, and another highly regarded man (unnamed in the text) had been "chosen by the churches to accompany us as we carry the offering" (2 Corinthians 8:19).

Paul also mentions a third Christian brother, a man with equally impeccable credentials, who would watch over the carrying of the funds. Titus and these two men, who were to join Paul and his group, formed a company to be trusted in handling and distributing the offerings (2 Corinthians 8:22-23).

Paul assures the Corinthians that his group would administer the funds "in order to honor the Lord himself and to show our eagerness to help" (2 Corinthians 8:19). Paul did not resent the direct participation of the other two character-approved men in this process of watching over the funds. On the contrary, he welcomed it. In fact, it is likely he initiated their involvement.

Any Christian leaders who resist financial accountability make themselves suspect. Leaders who put too much trust in themselves should not be trusted by others.

I spoke with a Christian leader who had been caught embezzling funds. His downfall came when he was in a personal financial crisis. Because of a lack of checks and balances, he was able to "borrow" money easily from an account that didn't belong to him. He rationalized that he would pay it back later. Many financial disasters could be avoided by setting up careful procedures that take into account our natural tendency to sin.

I know of a large church where all contributors' checks are stamped: "Pay to the order of Grace Church, or John Smith, pastor" (not real names). At best, this procedure generates suspicion. At some point, it will almost certainly present a serious temptation to this pastor. Someday, it may result in his downfall, heartache to the church, and damage to Christ's reputation. All unnecessary, if only proper precautions had been taken.

Paul says, "We want to avoid any criticism of the way we administer this liberal gift" (2 Corinthians 8:20). He went out of his way to include other character-approved men—both from inside and outside his own group.

Paul also says, "We are taking pains to do what is right, not only in the eyes of the Lord but also in the eyes of men" (2 Corinthians 8:21). Here are two important safeguards for preserving financial integrity and accountability:

First, we need to take pains to do what is right. A system of financial accountability may seem awkward, time-consuming, or a nuisance. At times it may seem unnecessary. But it is right, and therefore we must take pains to establish proper checks and balances.

Second, it's not enough for a leader to say, "My conscience is clear before the Lord." Our actions must be above reproach, "not only in the eyes of the Lord but also in the eyes of men." Whatever system of collecting and distributing funds we choose, it must involve awareness and accountability, with a plurality of character-approved men or women (preferably not chosen by each other but by a church or constituency). Although two character-qualified family members might appropriately sit together on a board, there's no place for the sort of nepotism that makes some organizations top-heavy with under-qualified relatives and childhood friends who look the other way instead of fostering accountability.

One of the most telling questions to ask in any church or ministry is this: Who has the courage and authority to tell the decision makers that what they are doing is unbiblical?

According to global missions researcher David B. Barrett, an estimated $16 billion was embezzled by the world's Christian churches in the year 2000, with an estimated $75 billion embezzled between 1980 and 2000. Barrett recommends that "Christians need to tighten up the scrutinizing of all funds holding their monies and to insist on all the accepted safeguards and controls and on all the strictest procedures."[1]

How financially transparent is a ministry? Do the leaders conceal salaries, expenditures, and sources of income? When they make bad decisions, do they admit and correct their mistakes or cover them up? Responsible kingdom investors should ask these questions, as part of the "Nineteen Questions to Ask before You Give to Any Organization" listed on pages 277–278.[2]

In light of the serious consequences of past carelessness, the leaders of every church and ministry should review the necessary steps they must take to be (and to appear) financially above reproach in the eyes of God *and* men—even if the steps are unprecedented and inconvenient.

ECFA AND OTHER ACCOUNTABILITY ORGANIZATIONS

The Evangelical Council for Financial Accountability (ECFA) was established in 1979. It comprises more than one thousand charitable, religious, and educational organizations that are qualified for tax-exempt, nonprofit status. The ECFA monitors its members, investigates alleged abuses, and issues public reports.[3]

The ECFA upholds "Seven Standards of Responsible Stewardship," including an orthodox doctrinal statement, a responsible board of directors, annual audits, and the avoidance of conflicts of interest.[4] The council requires every member organization to comply with twelve standards for fund-raising. These include communicating honestly, honoring of donor intent, and specific reporting on projects for which gifts are solicited. It also prohibits percentage compensation for fund-raisers and bars the principals of any organization from receiving royalties for any product used for fund-raising or promotional purposes.[5] The ECFA maintains that "good charities willingly answer tough questions" and has formulated a Donor's Bill of Rights.[6]

Certain ministries, including the one I direct, have legitimate reasons for not belonging to the ECFA. In our case, I'm the only full-time employee of our small ministry, and the cost of audits and other procedures to qualify for ECFA membership, which would be minimal to a larger ministry, is prohibitive for some small ministries. However, from the very beginning of Eternal Perspective Ministries, we have taken seriously the ECFA guidelines and have sought to comply with them voluntarily, even as a nonmember organization. (Our board and accountant carefully review our financial practices, and our books are open to those who inquire.)

Accountability to outsiders is important. But it must begin internally with wise and careful choices of leaders. It must include a commitment to plural leadership that does not leave one person, or one commanding individual surrounded by passive ones, in a position to embezzle, squander, or use funds for his or her personal benefit.

The spending patterns of some Christian organizations are exemplary. They are conscious of God's ownership of their assets and the fact that financial gifts have been given to them by other stewards who are sacrificing to further God's kingdom. These ministries spend their money carefully and thoughtfully with a view toward the purpose for which it has been given.

Other Christian organizations think nothing of providing expensive cars for their executives, booking first-class flights around the world, accommodating their staff in luxury hotels, and wooing donors at $200 dinners. Funds are contributed to ministries in good faith by people who assume they're being used carefully. Every organization needs staff members who are vocal advocates for the ministry's donors and beneficiaries.

Smart Money and *Forbes* magazines have issued annual "best in the nation" charity rankings. They've reduced their assessment criteria to three simplistic ratios, with various weightings to determine which charity is most efficient. However, the ratios are not the same for each publication, and even where they correspond, they are calculated or weighted differently.

Money magazine gives its own ratings, relying on calculated ratios and a grading system to identify those it considers most worthy of support. But such ratios can be misleading. For instance, the American Red Cross received more than $500 million in contributions following the September 11 terrorist attacks without spending very much on fund-raising. When they later admitted that only $100 million was going to victims' families, there was public outrage.[7] Yet when the Red Cross was rated against other charities, they scored very well—not because they were really more efficient but because they had received so much free public exposure.

Ministry Watch is a program of Wall Watchers, dedicated to comparing and ranking ministries, and giving information in areas that include efficiency and transparency.[8] Because its rating system is based on financial data derived from each organization's IRS Form 990 or audited financial statements, the playing field is theoretically level for every charity. However, there are many intangible qualities that cannot be measured by looking at financial data alone. Efficiency of operation, for example, is very different from effectiveness of mission.

In the nonprofit sector, it is very challenging to evaluate ratios and other numerical performance criteria. Although I applaud Wall Watchers and others for trying to hold ministries accountable, there is no substitute for personal interaction with a ministry to evaluate its mission, sense firsthand its heartbeat and vision, and assess its true accomplishments.[9]

Surveys indicate that 70 million people may be refraining from giving to nonprofit organizations because they don't know enough about them.[10] With 50,000 new charities emerging each year, accountability is critical. Still, donors must realize that some organizations that are ranked high by certain standards are not doing as vital or Christ-centered work as some that may be ranked lower.

The Use of Ministry Funds for Buildings

Are buildings a legitimate ministry expense? If so, what kinds of buildings and how many? Some churches have buildings that are worth little more than a typical private home of one of their members. Others have more than $100 million worth of land and buildings (and some parachurch ministries have even more). Can this extensive accumulation of material wealth be justified in the light of the world's needs?

In his book *The Golden Cow*, John White tells a story that reflects my own thoughts about buildings:

> Many years ago I stood one night in the rain, looking wonderingly at the walls of what was then the China Inland Mission headquarters in London. I had read many CIM books . . . and had been thrilled and quickened by the way God had supplied the mission's needs "through prayer to God alone." That night as I looked at the dirty but solid brick wall, I reached out my hand to touch it. It seemed like a holy thing. Not that the CIM was anything other than a human organization blessed and used by God. But to me the walls were an awesome and tangible monument to the reality of God's response to faith. It was as though God himself had put them there. "This is what God did," I said, glowing warmly, feeling the solidity of the wet bricks as awe stole over my whole body. "A solid monument to God's response to faith." There are many so-called monuments to faith around the world today. People would like us to believe that God raised them in answer to believing prayer. I don't think so. Many are monuments to human ingenuity, to public-relations know-how and clever advertising, to skill in milking Christian suckers. And because we would not need to depend on public-relations know-how and clever advertising if we truly believed in God, I suppose it is correct to say that the buildings of which I speak are monuments to unbelief rather than monuments to faith. We view them with understandable (but culpable) pride. We have made it. We need nothing. May God have mercy on us![1]

Spending money on buildings for ministries is inherently neither right nor wrong. In some cases, God is surely glorified through the financing, construction, and use of a building. In other cases, through massive indebtedness, disunity, extravagance, pride, and misuse God is dishonored.

I hear people criticize local churches for their buildings. "If that money had been given to the poor or used for missions, far greater things could be accomplished." This is sometimes true. On the other hand, by providing for a growing congregation's needs, a building can serve purposes of evangelism and edification, broadening and deepening the home base so that much more money, prayer, and personal involvement are ultimately given to missions and to the poor than otherwise would have been.

I've been on both sides of the building quandary. As a young believer, sitting in a congregation, I was uninspired by building projects. I thought my money could be better placed directly into missions, so I gave almost all of it to parachurch groups. I made much of the fact that the early Church had no buildings. I now see this to be a much less relevant argument, because God has put us in a different place and time than the first-century Church, with our own distinct needs and opportunities.

During my fourteen years as a pastor, my perspective changed. I saw not only the centrality of the local church, but also how buildings can be valuable tools that effectively facilitate ministry. Often it makes as much sense for a church to build a building as for a growing family to find a house that is adequate for its needs.

Over the years, our church buildings have been in constant use. Our twenty-year-old main building is used for worship on Saturday nights and Sundays, and for everything from weddings and funerals to basketball and school recess throughout the week. We've conducted Sunday school classes everywhere, including staff offices and storage rooms. Classrooms built for twenty sometimes house fifty, so we've kept building. Youth groups meet on different nights of the week, because there's insufficient room. Every classroom—and even a kitchen—has been used for our grade school. Without a doubt, this practical facility has greatly enhanced our ministry and our presence in our community.

Some years ago, we built a church office and ministry center. When we moved out of rented trailers into the office building, we found our communication and efficiency greatly enhanced, and we could better meet the needs of our people.

Yes, we could function without our buildings—just as a family could get by without their house by using tents or living at the neighbor's. We used rented facilities for the first five years of our church and did fine. Yet we found they prevented us from many significant ministries that our own buildings have allowed. I believe that these practical and attractive—but not extravagant—buildings have been a wise use of church funds and a true investment in eternity.

On the other hand, we must continually be careful that the construction of a building doesn't detract from our giving to meet needs and evangelize our community and the world. We must consciously battle the rationalizations that turn churches and organizations away from building Christ's kingdom to building their own. Certainly, something is desperately wrong when a church spends more money paying interest on its construction loans than on world missions. If missions spending declines during a building program, this reflects poorly on a church's priorities.

I don't believe that any church should spend millions of dollars on buildings without prayerfully considering whether it might be better to plant daughter churches instead. Of course, daughter churches need facilities too, but the freshness and vitality of a new work with new leaders is often a cost-effective alternative to expensive buildings, which sometimes cause a loss of ministry focus and can undermine the effective development of new church leaders.

Rick Warren, pastor of one of the largest churches in America, says this about church buildings:

> It is a serious mistake to think that everything the church does— worship, discipleship, ministry, evangelism, and fellowship—must be done within the four walls of a church building. In fact, I'm convinced that church buildings are a major barrier to exponential growth and that massive building programs are often a waste of money.
>
> Currently there are several dozen extremely large church buildings being planned and built in America, but I believe they are the last of the dinosaurs. History has proven over and over that future generations never fill the cavernous temples of previous generations. For instance, every time Spurgeon's Tabernacle was rebuilt (three times) it was downsized. The list of empty great cathedrals would be quite long. God wants to do something new in each generation. He blesses anointed people, not buildings.
>
> We also need to remember that the period of fastest growth for Christianity was during the first 300 years—when there were no church buildings at all. And today all of the rapidly exploding church-planting movements around the world are multiplying without having a physical church building.
>
> Buildings should be tools for ministry, not monuments. I've said repeatedly to our congregation that Saddleback will never build a building that could not be torn down if it prevented us from reaching more people. Churches should focus on building people, not building buildings! That's what being purpose-driven is all about. It's a people-building process. Build your people before your steeple.

Our resistance to building buildings has been one of Saddleback's values since its inception twenty-one years ago. One of the goals we set at Saddleback was to prove that you don't need to build a building in order to grow a church. That's why we waited until after our congregation was averaging more than 10,000 in attendance before we built our first building! I think we proved our point. Just because you are growing does not mean you should build a new or larger building. . . .

We enlisted and connected over 2,000 new people (who were not in any of our existing groups) into new Bible study groups in a single weekend. We would have never even considered numbers like that if we were trying to place them all on our campus.

I am absolutely opposed to building ANY size of facility that will only be used once or twice a week. It is poor stewardship of God's money to build a facility just because the pastor wants to speak to everyone at one time.

In fact, here's a little secret: Only pastors like really huge church services!

Normal people prefer more moderate-sized services, large enough to make the singing great, but not an overwhelming crowd. That's why I'd rather have a building of 200 and fill it with five services than have a 1,000-seat auditorium that is filled only once a week and then left empty the rest of the week. . . .

I encourage you to experiment and look for ways to reach and grow people faster and cheaper, without buildings. Don't let traditional methodology, or brick and mortar, or the lack of it, keep you from focusing on what matters most—changed lives![2]

To the extent that a church facility can be attractive and yet still functional and economical, I favor attractive buildings. I appreciate the desire to create a worshipful atmosphere. But worship doesn't require extravagance. Whether in the church or in a parachurch ministry, I believe that buildings should be built only as necessary, soundly but economically, and in such a way that they allow maximum ministry use, which means much more than one day a week.

Buildings present a danger of externalizing the church, making us forget that we—not the facilities we build—are God's dwelling place. Whenever the Church views worship facilities as Israel viewed the temple, she takes a dramatic step backwards.

Opulent edifices are often monuments to the ego of one man, organization, or congregation. Considering the opportunities to invest in eternity, reach the lost, and care for the poor—thereby bringing glory to the only One who deserves it—such buildings, in my opinion, have no place among God's people.

APPENDIX C

Lending Money, Charging Interest, and Co-signing a Loan

There are many possible motives for lending money. One is to meet another person's need; another is to profit from the loan by charging interest. Nothing is inherently wrong with lending. It's a mark of God's blessing to be in the position to make a loan (Deuteronomy 28:12). The righteous is one who gives and lends (Psalm 37:21, 26). God approves of the generous person who lends freely (Psalm 112:5).

In certain cases, lenders graciously forgave debt (Matthew 18:32-33). In Israel, every fifty years was the year of Jubilee, in which all debts were forgiven (Deuteronomy 15:1-3; Nehemiah 10:31).

Jesus states that when we lend we're not to expect repayment (Luke 6:34-35). However, the borrower is morally obligated to make the payment (Psalm 37:21). But we, in the spirit of giving, are to lend as we might give, expecting nothing in return. If we would force repayment, we shouldn't loan in the first place.

Built into the disciples' prayer is the well-known but seldom practiced phrase, "Forgive us our debts, as we also have forgiven our debtors" (Matthew 6:12).

The lender must evaluate the character of the borrower. To distribute money into the hands of a drug addict, compulsive gambler, or cultist is irresponsible. Furthermore, we should weigh whether a loan is what the prospective borrower really needs. Given the many dangers of debt, are we really helping other people by indebting them to us? Loaning money to bail out someone who is lacking financial discipline is like trying to put out a fire with gasoline.

We should calculate the effects of the loan on our relationships. Although we may imagine that lending money will endear people to us, experience often proves the opposite. One of the best definitions of a distant friend is "a close friend who owes you money." If someone irritates you and you wish never to see him again, give him a loan!

CHARGING INTEREST

In the Old Testament, stipulations governed borrowing and lending. Although collateral could be held, it was forbidden to hold an essential security, such as a garment needed for warmth on cold nights (Exodus 22:26-27; Deuteronomy 24:10-17).

Charging interest is the means by which a lender profits from a borrower. This was common practice in Babylon, Rome, and many ancient cultures. In Israel, interest could be charged to foreigners, but not as a means of exploitation (Deuteronomy 23:19-20). Loans to fellow Jews were always to be interest free (Exodus 22:25; Leviticus 25:35-37; Deuteronomy 23:20).

Whether interest is charged or not, there should be a spirit of graciousness in lending (Deuteronomy 15:8, 10). No one should take advantage of another person's misfortune. We must loan primarily to help the borrower, not to help ourselves. We're not even to take our brother to court to recoup our losses, because it's better to experience loss than to bring conflict with a brother before unbelievers (1 Corinthians 6:1-7).

Israel had a largely noninflationary economy. A lender's money was worth the same to him when it was returned as when he loaned it. Perhaps in an inflationary economy interest might be charged to match the inflation rate. But even if this isn't done, the gracious heart won't quibble about minor losses when his purpose in lending is to extend grace, not demand repayment.

Throughout church history, Christian teachers have taken a strong position against exacting usury on a loan in order to make personal profit. Whereas usury is thought of today as charging excessive interest, the word actually meant charging any interest. Ambrose, the fourth-century bishop of Milan, said, "If anyone commits usury, he commits robbery and no longer has life." John Calvin declared that professional moneylenders should be banned from the church. Martin Luther said, "After the devil there is no greater human enemy on earth than a miser and usurer, for he desires to be above everyone."[1]

Nevertheless, Jesus spoke without condemnation of gaining interest by deposit to a moneylender (Luke 19:23). Although this was a reference in a parable and doesn't necessarily imply approval, it seems unlikely he'd use something he believed was wrong as a positive illustration.

It appears that charging interest isn't wrong per se. It might be appropriate for lending institutions but not for individuals if they're loaning to fellow believers to help meet their needs. If interest is charged, perhaps it should be at no more than the current inflation rate.

There's a time to lend, a time to give, and a time to do neither. If the need isn't legitimate, I should neither give nor lend. If the need is legitimate, not the result of an unwise choice in which there's a lesson to be learned, I might give instead of lend. If, on the other hand, the need is real but a gift would contribute to someone's irresponsibility or loss of dignity, a loan might be the best solution.

I must be careful not to encourage my brother's indebtedness unless incurring the debt is absolutely necessary. The last thing a person in debt needs is more debt. When the needs are legitimate, a Christian policy ought to be to give freely. When the situation merits it, I may make a loan but only in the same helpful spirit as I would give a gift.

SIGNING FOR ANOTHER PERSON'S LOANS

Co-signing is assuming responsibility for the debts of another in order to assure a creditor that the borrower won't default on payment. If the person for whom I have co-signed doesn't make the payments, I become legally responsible for the entire liability.

Scripture is very clear about co-signing—we are told not to do it:

He who puts up security for another will surely suffer, but whoever refuses to strike hands in pledge is safe. (Proverbs 11:15)

Do not be a man who strikes hands in pledge or puts up security for debts; if you lack the means to pay, your very bed will be snatched from under you. (Proverbs 22:26-27)

In fact, if we have already put up security for our neighbor we're told that we should go to the creditor, humble ourselves, plead, and allow ourselves no sleep until we are freed from the obligation, like a gazelle from a hunter or a bird from a fowler's snare (Proverbs 6:1-5). To assume responsibility for the debt of another is to demonstrate poor judgment (Proverbs 17:18). If you doubt this teaching of Scripture, consider that no less than 50 percent of co-signers end up paying back part or all of the other person's debt![2]

When I sign for someone else, I am saying, "I will answer for all of this person's financial decisions, wise or unwise. I'm now legally and financially accountable for whatever he chooses to do."

If your desire is to help someone, give him the money outright, loan it to him—or offer him sound advice. More often than not, he shouldn't be going into debt in the first place. When someone asks you to co-sign, the best favor you can do—both for him and for yourself—is simply to say no.

Practical Guidelines to Control Spending

For many people, spending money is an addictive behavior similar to alcoholism or gambling. With compulsive spending, the true enemy lies within. We need to replace our preoccupation with short-term gratification and make our spending decisions from a long-term perspective. We must replace our self-indulgence with self-control, which is a fruit of the Holy Spirit (Galatians 5:23). "Like a city whose walls are broken down is a man who lacks self-control" (Proverbs 25:28). Without self-control on the inside, our lives are made vulnerable to innumerable assaults.

The following guidelines are designed to help you exercise self-control in spending. They can help you become a better steward of God's resources and free funds to use for kingdom purposes:

1. **Realize that nothing is a good deal if you can't afford it**. Paying $120,000 for a house that is worth $150,000 sounds like an excellent deal. Paying $80 for a pair of barely used skis that cost $400 new seems like a great deal. But if we can't afford them, it simply doesn't matter. It's always a bad choice to spend money on a "good deal" we can't afford.

2. **Recognize that God isn't behind every good deal**. Suppose we *can* afford it. Does that mean we should buy it? Self-control often means turning down good deals on things we really want because God may have other and better plans for his money.

3. **Understand the difference between spending money and saving money**. Saving is setting aside money for a future purpose. Money that's saved stays in our wallet or in the bank. It can be used for other purposes, including our needs or the needs of others. Money that's spent leaves our hands and is no longer at our disposal. As I said in chapter 17, if we buy an $80 sweater on sale for $30 and think we've just saved $50, we simply don't understand the concept of saving. Where is the $50 we think we saved? It doesn't exist. All we've done is spend $30. If we keep "saving" like that, we'll soon be broke!

4. **Look at the long-term cost, not just the short-term expense**. If we buy a nice stereo, we'll also end up buying a lot of CDs. If something breaks, we pay to get it

repaired. If we buy a new car, we fret about dents and buy insurance to fix them. If we acquire a "free" puppy, we immediately have to start spending $20 a month on dog food—and the next thing we know we're putting $1,200 into a fence and paying $400 to the veterinarian to stitch up its wounds from a dog fight. Over the course of a year or two, we may spend several thousand dollars on our free puppy. (As a dog lover, I speak from experience!) Count the cost in advance. Everything ends up being more expensive than it first appears.

5. Pray before you spend. When something's a legitimate need, God will provide it. How often do we take matters into our own hands and spend impulsively before asking God to furnish it for us? How often do we buy something—whether we consider it a "want" or a "need"—a week or a month before God would have provided it for free or at minimal cost, if only we'd asked him?

My friend wanted a good exercise bicycle. He even picked the exact model, a Tunturi with a retail price of $350. But instead of going out to buy it, he told me he was praying that God would provide him that exact bike. By not spending the money, he would have more to give. A few days later I was in a thrift store and was stunned to see a Tunturi bicycle, the exact model my friend wanted. It looked like it had never been used. I called my friend and he got the exact bicycle he had asked for, paying $25 instead of $350.

I did something similar when I finally gave up trying to purchase an original 1947 Time magazine with C. S. Lewis on the cover. I had bid for it on eBay a number of times, but it always moved out of my price range. One evening, having lost another bid, I thought, Lord, I'm wasting my time. I've asked you to help me win a bid, but I've never asked you to actually provide the magazine. It's a small thing, and I probably shouldn't want it this much. But I'm asking you for it. If you want me to have it, you're going to have to provide it at no cost.

I was virtually certain I'd never get it, but it felt good to surrender my desire to the Lord. Some time later, a person who'd read a few of my books, seeing how often I quoted C. S. Lewis, gave me the magazine! I couldn't believe it—until I remembered how I'd prayed for it. God graciously provided for me, at no cost, this thing I didn't need, but wanted. Had I bid enough money to get it earlier, I'd never have been so touched by God's answer to my prayer.

Often we either buy what we want or forgo what we want when there's a third alternative: ask God to provide it for us. If he doesn't provide it, fine—he knows best. But why don't we just give him a chance?

Waiting eliminates most impulsive buying. Many things that are attractive today hold no interest two months later. Look at garage sales and you get the picture. Setting a waiting period gives God the opportunity to provide what we want, to provide something different or better, or to show us that we don't need it and should use the money differently.

6. Examine every purchase in light of its ministry potential. Every time we spend money, we gain something and lose something. What we lose isn't merely money but what could have been done with the money if used in another way. When we spend $20—or $100 or $1,000—on something, we must weigh the value of these things against what the same money could have done if used another way—for instance, to feed the hungry or to evangelize the lost.

I don't say this to induce a guilt trip but to indicate the obvious—whenever money is used one way it prevents it from being used another. We must weigh and measure the various alternatives of how we use God's money. I sometimes choose to spend money on unnecessary things that still seem good and helpful. Sometimes I feel good about it; sometimes it seems questionable. Often, however, there's a clear line that I feel would be wrong for me to cross. For instance, I cannot justify spending thousands of dollars on jewelry when that same money could keep people alive or reach them with the gospel. I'm not saying it's wrong for anyone else to have nice jewelry. I'm saying that jewelry, like everything else, must be subjected to the scrutiny of conscience, the Holy Spirit, and God's Word. I'm sharing my convictions about my life and stewardship. You don't answer to me, but to God. None of us should impose our personal standards on others, but we should ask God to direct us when it comes to handling his money.

7. **Understand and resist the manipulative nature of advertising.** Responsible spending says yes to real needs and no to most "created" needs. We have far fewer needs than we believe. The temptation to overspend is immense. Advertising thrives on instilling discontent. Its goal is to create an illusion of need, to stimulate desire, to make us dissatisfied with what God has provided. People earn master's degrees in persuading us to buy things we don't need. Advertising enlarges our wants by telling us, "You need this car," "You won't be loved unless you wear these kinds of clothes," and "You won't have fun unless you use this product."

Advertising is seductive and manipulative. It programs us. We must consciously reject its claims and counter them with God's Word, which tells us what we really do and don't need. We should withdraw ourselves from advertising that fosters greed or discontent. That may mean less television, less flipping through sales catalogs and newspaper ads, and less aimless wandering through shopping malls.

8. **Learn to walk away from things you want but don't need.** Once I received a large, unexpected check. After giving a portion to the Lord, I still had $2,000 left. Before long, I was out looking at something I'd wanted but had never been able to justify. The price tag said $1,995. I examined it, comparison shopped, came back the next day, and seriously considered buying it. But in my heart there wasn't peace when I considered what that money could do for God's kingdom. Finally, I decided I shouldn't make the purchase. When I turned and walked away, something unexpected happened. I was suddenly filled with a deep sense

of relief and joy. I hadn't realized how this item had possessed me. To be free of it was the first blessing; to know the eternal difference the money would make was the second blessing. (I know godly people who own this same item— which I'm deliberately not identifying. You might have the same experience in regard to something I own but God doesn't intend for you to own.)

9. Realize that little things add up. Like water from a leaky faucet, money trickles through our hands. The little drips don't seem like much, but they add up to gallons. One dollar here and ten dollars over there; a hamburger here and a mocha there; video rentals and rounds of golf and extra tools and new clothes. These things may seem inconsequential, but they add up to hundreds of dollars per month and thousands per year that could be used for kingdom purposes. If a swimming pool is full of leaks, you can pump in more water, but it will never be enough until the leaks are fixed. We can take in more and more income, but until we fix the little leaks in our spending habits, we'll never be able to divert the flow of money for higher purposes.

10. Set up a budget and live by it. Imagine you entrust a large sum to a money manager, telling him to take out only what he needs to live on and then wisely invest the bulk of it on your behalf. A few months later, you call him to see how the investments are doing. Embarrassed by your call, he admits, "There are no investments. None of your money is left." Shocked you ask, "Where did it all go?" Sheepishly, your money manager responds, "Well, I can think of some expenses here and there, but for the most part I really can't say. There was this and that, and next thing I knew, it was all gone."

What would you think? How would you feel? How does God think and feel when at the end of the month nothing's left from the money he entrusted to us, and we don't even know where it went? If some of us ran a corporation and handled its money like we do God's, we'd go to prison!

"Be sure you know the condition of your flocks, give careful attention to your herds; for riches do not endure forever" (Proverbs 27:23-24). Flocks and herds are the rancher's basic units of wealth. God is saying, know what your assets are and know where they go.

We must get a grip on our management of God's assets. If we don't have well thought-out plans for what to do with God's money, rest assured that thousands of other people do have plans for it. If we don't harness it ourselves, others will end up with it and we'll end up having a garage sale.

Two practical steps can greatly help us get a grip on our spending: recording expenditures and making a budget. These steps will help us detect problem areas by clarifying our spending habits. They will foster a healthy dialogue about what we do with our money and help us develop careful spending habits. This will improve our mental and marital health because financial disorder is one of the leading causes of personal and familial stress.

For some, the most practical way to budget is the envelope system. When paychecks are cashed, the cash goes into envelopes with designations written on them: food, gas, garbage, entertainment, clothing, etc. If it's the tenth of the month and nothing's left in the entertainment envelope, no more movies or eating out. If we overspend in one area we must underspend elsewhere to compensate. (But if instead we spend the clothing money, it's going to catch up with us when we need to buy clothes.) The envelope system teaches us that there's a bottom to the well, that resources are limited. That's an invaluable lesson.

I recommend that you pick up one of the practical books on finances that deals with budgeting.[1] Such books show how to make a careful record of expenditures so you can find out where your money's going. Meanwhile, you can determine where you think it *should* be going. This will be the basis for your budget, which will include how much you've determined to give and to save and how much is available for spending.

Living on a budget will free up lots of money. I've met with families who follow a budget and do fine on an annual income of $18,000. I've met with others who make $20,000 a month and are always in financial crisis. It's not how much money we make, but how we handle it that matters.

Should Giving Always Be Kept Secret?

In chapter 16, I suggest that we share testimonies about giving in order to help the body of Christ grow in the grace of giving. I once objected to this type of disclosure—as many still do—because Jesus says, "But when you give to the needy, do not let your left hand know what your right hand is doing, so that your giving may be in secret. Then your Father, who sees what is done in secret, will reward you" (Matthew 6:3-4).

When he received an automated tax receipt from his church indicating he'd given no money the previous year, one man was outraged. He said he was obeying Scripture by not letting his left hand know what his right hand had given. *Giving was to be so secret*, he thought, *that even he shouldn't know how much he was giving.* A closer look at this passage, and the rest of Scripture, demonstrates this is not a valid interpretation.

In Matthew 6, Jesus deals with motives, something the religious elite often failed to examine. He starts with the broad category of "acts of righteousness," then moves to three such acts—giving, prayer, and fasting. This is not an exhaustive list. In their teaching, rabbis often spoke in groups of threes. Jesus could have added Bible reading, feeding the poor, or raising children. Today, we might include going on mission trips or attending a particular college or church. The idea is that any "act of righteousness" (or badge of spirituality) can accord us spiritual status in the eyes of others.

The most important verse, the one that sets up the entire passage, is the first: "Be careful not to do your 'acts of righteousness' before men, to be seen by them" (Matthew 6:1). The operative phrase is "to be seen by them." This is not a prohibition against others becoming aware of our giving, prayers, fasting, Bible study, feeding the poor, missions work, or church attendance. Rather, it's a command not to do these things in *order to* receive the recognition of men. Jesus continues, "If you do [that is, if you do good things to win human approval], you will have no reward from your Father in heaven." The problem isn't doing good things with reward in mind—*it's looking for the reward from men rather than from God.*

Then Jesus says, "When you give to the needy, do not announce it with trumpets, as the hypocrites do in the synagogues and on the streets, to be honored by men" (Matthew 6:2). Trumpet blowing may seem silly. There's no record that this was actually done. It seems to be satirical or humorous, a caricature of less obvious (to us anyway) things we do to get attention. But Christ's focus is the reason for which hypocrites draw attention to what they've done: "to be honored by men." Again, Christ's argument is not that our giving should never be seen, but only that we should never divulge or flaunt it in order to get human recognition. When that happens, "I tell you the truth, they have received their reward in full" (Matthew 6:5).

If we give in order to get men's praises, we'll get what we seek—college wings named after us, dinner invitations from heads of ministries, our names inscribed on pews or bricks, appointment to boards, or seeing our names on a plaque and in the newspaper. But in getting what we seek, we will lose what we *should* have sought—God's approval.

Let's look at the verses we started with: "So when you give to the needy, do not let your left hand know what your right hand is doing, so that your giving may be in secret" (Matthew 6:3-4).

This is a figure of speech. It's hyperbole, a deliberate overstatement, which would have been immediately clear to the hearers. That Christ's command cannot be literal is self-evident, because a hand lacks the ability to know anything, and the person's brain would inevitably know what both the right hand and the left hand were doing. There is no center of intelligence in one hand as opposed to the other, nor is there an ability for the brain to withhold information from one hand while disclosing it to the other. We aren't able to throw a switch so that we don't know we're giving or that we have given.

So what's Christ's point? Do your giving quietly, unobtrusively. Don't cough loudly just as you're giving. Don't slam-dunk your offering in the plate. Drop your check in the offering or send it in the mail without drawing attention to yourself. Fold the check. Keep the envelope sealed. Give in a spirit of humility and simplicity, as an act of worship. Don't give in order to get your name on a list. Don't give in a spirit of self-congratulation. Don't dwell on your gift, fixating on it, building a mental shrine to yourself. In other words, don't make a big production out of it, either in view of others or in the privacy of your own heart.

This verse cannot mean that we should—or even that we can—be unaware of our own giving, any more than we could be unaware of our praying, fasting, Bible reading, or evangelism. To suggest that it does would remove the discerning, thoughtful elements of giving, praying, fasting, and all other spiritual disciplines.

Can this verse mean it's always wrong for others to know that we've given? No. Acts 2:45 tells of Christians selling possessions and giving to the needy. Did other people know who had done this? In many cases, the answer would be obvious. These people knew each other—if you no longer had your prize camels, coat, or oxcart, people would figure out why. Acts 4:32-35 tells us about more people liquidating assets. Most names, which would mean nothing to us, aren't recorded, but they were surely known at the time.

But some givers were named even for our benefit. Acts 4:36-37 tells us that Barnabas sold a field and brought the money to the feet of the apostles. If Barnabas was looking for status and prestige, his motive was wrong. But it's certainly false to say that it was wrong for others to be made aware of his gift, because Scripture itself reveals it! Barnabas's act of generosity was commonly known among the believers and was publicly and permanently recorded in Acts.

Did public recognition tempt others to give for the wrong motives? Absolutely, as we see in the very next passage (Acts 5:1-11). Ananias and Sapphira gave for the wrong reasons. Then they lied to make their gift look better than it was. But the possible abuse of something doesn't nullify its legitimacy. The body of Christ can benefit from seeing open models of generous giving such as Barnabas's. The world can benefit from seeing the generosity of the Church as an attractive witness to the grace of Christ. The risks of disclosing a person's giving are sometimes outweighed by the benefits of disclosure.

Earlier in the same sermon, Jesus says, "Let your light shine before men, that they may see your good deeds and praise your Father in heaven" (Matthew 5:16). Here we are commanded to let men see our good deeds—and not to hide them. Giving is a good deed, isn't it? This passage and Matthew 6 balance each other. There's a time for giving to be seen, but only at the right time and for the right reasons.

We need to stop putting giving in a class by itself. If I give a message on evangelism, biblical interpretation, or parenting, I run the risk of pride. But it may still be God's will for me to share with the church what God has taught me in these areas. Paul speaks of himself as a model: "Follow my example, as I follow the example of Christ" (1 Corinthians 11:1). I could write books and do public speaking for the wrong reasons, even though I ask God that this wouldn't be the case. I could send e-mails with wrong motives, to seek man's approval, not God's. But I write books and speak and send e-mails anyway, partly because if we were to refrain from doing everything we could do with a wrong motive, we'd never do anything at all. (If your pastor only preached when there was no temptation to pride, he'd never preach.)

If Christ established a principle in Matthew 6:2-4 that other people should never know what someone gives, then the members of the early Church violated it in Acts 4:36-37. There's no way around it. Numbers 7 lists the names of donors to the tabernacle. First Chronicles 29 tells exactly how much the leaders of Israel gave to build the temple, then it says, "The people rejoiced at the willing response of their leaders, for they had given freely and wholeheartedly to the Lord" (1 Chronicles 29:9). Philemon 1:7 is likely a reference to Philemon's generous giving, and 2 Corinthians 8:2-3 is definitely a reference to the Macedonians' generous giving. As we seek to understand the meaning of Matthew 6:2-4, we must consider the full counsel of Scripture, as revealed in these other passages.

In Matthew 6, it's clear that whatever's true of giving is also true of praying and fasting. Jesus says in verse 6, "When you pray, go into your room, close the door and pray to your Father, who is unseen." He's swinging the pendulum away from the self-conscious, self-serving, image-enhancing prayers for which the Pharisees were notorious. But did he mean that all prayer must be private? No. Scripture has many examples of public and corporate prayer. Every time a pastor or worship leader prays in church, every time parents pray with their children, or husbands pray with wives, or families pray before dinner, or someone prays with the person being led to Christ, it demonstrates the falseness of the notion that it's always wrong to be seen or heard by others when you pray.

Jesus tells us to pray in secret, and God will reward us (Matthew 6:6). Yet gathering for group prayer is certainly important (Matthew 18:19-20). God wants us to pray secretly sometimes but not others. He wants us to give secretly sometimes but not others. It all comes down to the motives of our hearts and the purpose of disclosure.

Just as Matthew 6:6 doesn't mean it's always wrong to let others hear you pray, Matthew 6:3-4 doesn't mean it's always wrong to let others be aware of your giving. Because Jesus groups giving, praying, and fasting as the three acts of righteousness in this passage, whatever applies to one applies to the others.

When the poor widow gave, she gave publicly—Jesus could actually see the two coins. He used her as a public illustration (Luke 21:1-4). So, it was right that she gave in public, and it was right that people were told the exact amount of her gift. Her motives were right. The public disclosure did nothing to nullify her good heart.

Though confidentiality in giving records makes sense, it creates another temptation. Many believers take advantage of the veil of privacy by using it as a cloak for their disobedience in not giving. With all of today's talk about accountability, what are we doing in churches to hold each other accountable to generous giving? People may notice if you don't obey the command in Hebrews 10:25 to attend church, but how will they notice if you fail to give?

The body of Christ needs to let its light shine before men, and we need models of every spiritual discipline. We dare not let the risk of our pride keep us from faithfully disclosing God's work in this area of our lives. And if we must be silent to avoid our own pride, we should support others who can humbly testify to Christ's faithfulness in their giving.

God looks at the heart. He alone knows the real motives for our giving

(1 Corinthians 4:5). Scripture never says that a giver receives no eternal reward simply because others know about his gift. Donors could be known yet still have given to please God not men.

More than anything, what may force us to swallow our pride is talking about giving when it runs the risk of appearing that we're patting ourselves on the back. Our motive for not talking about our giving is not always humility. Sometimes it's fear, doubt and, yes, even pride. To vulnerably express to others where we are on our pilgrimage to generous giving can be an act of humility. We must always check our motives, but it certainly doesn't have to be an act of pride.

We shouldn't brag about our Bible study, prayer, evangelism, parenting, or giving, but neither should we cover it up. It's easier for people to follow footprints (what we do) than commands (what we say). If we aren't willing to openly and humbly discuss our giving, how can we expect to raise up givers? The church has plenty of examples of consumers—we need to see examples of givers. Hebrews 10:24 tells us to "spur one another on toward love and good deeds." We can only be spurred on by what we can see.

STUDY
GUIDE

MONEY,
POSSESSIONS,
AND ETERNITY

Why Is Money So Important to God?

Reading Assignment: preface, chapter 1

What does the Bible say about our money?

Why does the Bible devote so much attention to money and possessions?

How we relate to money and possessions is the story of our lives. What we need on this journey is a road map to help us understand God's perspective and to teach us to make eternally significant decisions. The key to our use of money and possessions is having a right perspective—an eternal perspective. In this lesson, we'll look at some key Scriptures to help us unlock God's view of our finances and economic goals.

Read and discuss the following passages of Scripture. (Depending on the number of people in the group, you can divide into subgroups of three or more, assigning each one a passage to study for ten to twelve minutes before reporting their answers back to the larger group. The reports should be limited to five minutes each.)

1. Luke 3:7-14. In this passage, John the Baptist forcefully exhorts a crowd of questioners about how to live—and how to give.

   a. Luke 3:11. Based on this verse, to whom do our possessions and wealth belong? How does our possession of wealth imply a responsibility apart from our own enjoyment?

   b. Luke 3:12-14. What special responsibilities do people have who work with money? What is the responsibility of everyone who is paid to work?

c. Based on Luke 3:7-14, what can we conclude about the money and possessions entrusted to us? What are the dangers of using them wrongly?

2. Luke 19:1-10. What principles about the proper use of money can we draw from the story of Jesus and Zacchaeus?

3. Matthew 19:16-30. In this passage, Jesus tells a rich man to take a radical step in regard to his wealth. What can we conclude about wealth and our willingness to depend on Christ?

4. Acts 19:18-20. In this passage, we see a radical response to ill-gained or inappropriate wealth. In what situations might new (or mature) Christians today be prompted to take such steps?

5. Acts 2:42-47. This passage records an example of true community in the context of Christian fellowship. What principles can we draw from this passage that will help us discover what God intends our attitudes and actions to be concerning money and possessions?

6. Acts 4:32-35. How should our gratefulness to God for our salvation prompt unusual generosity far beyond the requirements of Old Testament law?

In the following lessons, we'll be seeking to form a biblical view of God's plan for how we use our money and possessions to further his kingdom.

PRAYER: Lord, grant us a glimpse of your perspective about money, possessions, and eternity. Help us to understand your plan for us—and for all you've entrusted to us.

Asceticism and Materialism: Two Wrong Ways

Reading Assignment: chapters 2 and 3

Money is always evil.

Money is always good.

These two perspectives of money are equally incorrect. Still, we must examine them carefully to come to a biblical understanding of money and possessions. In this lesson, we'll consider two opposing worldviews: asceticism and materialism.

Read and discuss the following passages of Scripture. (Depending on the number of people in the group, you can divide into subgroups of three or more, assigning each one a passage to study for ten to twelve minutes before reporting their answers back to the larger group. The reports should be limited to five minutes each.) Each of the following passages sheds special light on the concept of asceticism, the idea that what's spiritual is good and what's physical is evil.

1. Proverbs 30:8-9. What does Scripture say about denying material goods? What kind of spiritual harm can asceticism cause?

2. Luke 7:36-50. What does Jesus say about the enjoyment and appreciation of material gifts? How are the spiritual values of love and forgiveness connected with a physical act of kindness in this story?

3. 1 Timothy 4:3-5. What are the keys to a proper use of the gifts we have been given?

4. 1 Timothy 6:17. How does this passage create a balanced alternative to materialism and asceticism?

5. Discuss other examples of misguided asceticism (from *Money, Possessions, and Eternity* or other sources). How do they differ from the wise balance of Scripture?

6. Luke 12:15. If asceticism isn't the answer to how we should treat material things, what about the opposite extreme: materialism? Jesus clearly warns against materialism: "Watch out! Be on your guard against all kinds of greed; a man's life does not consist in the abundance of his possessions" (Luke 12:15). What does this warning mean to you? How does it relate to your choices and priorities?

7. Luke 12:13-21. Read the parable of the rich fool and discuss the following statement: Greed isn't a harmless pastime; it's a serious offense against God. Just as one who lusts is an adulterer (Matthew 5:28), and one who hates is a murderer (1 John 3:15), so one who is greedy is an idolater (Colossians 3:5). What is it about greed that makes it idolatry? Use anecdotes from the book or other sources to illustrate.

8. Luke 16:19-31. Read the parable of the rich man and Lazarus and discuss the "doctrine of reversal": the fact that in eternity many people will find themselves in the opposite condition to what they experienced during their life on earth. Role-play a dialogue between a modern-day rich man (perhaps a CEO or financial advisor) and a "Lazarus" (a poor or homeless person). How should the doctrine of reversal affect our view of our present society?

PRAYER: *Lord, all things come from you, and your own do we give back to you.*

The Dangers of Materialism

Reading Assignment: chapter 4

Read the following passages of Scripture and discuss them in light of the following statement: *Materialism consists of the two things that God hates most—idolatry and adultery.* (Depending on the number of people in the class, you can divide into groups of three or more, assigning each group a passage to study for ten to twelve minutes before reporting their answers back to the class. The reports should be limited to five minutes each.)

1. Isaiah 57:3-9; Jeremiah 3:1-10; Ezekiel 16:1-48. The Old Testament prophets were quick to point out Israel's unfaithfulness, which was demonstrated by their turning to idols. In what ways have possessions become idols or "mistresses" to us today?

2. Ecclesiastes 2:1-11. Emptiness and meaninglessness are the fruit of unbridled materialism. What are some examples in our society of the emptiness produced by excessive greed? If possible, identify pictures in magazines that illustrate a loss of meaning. (Hint: The more "sophisticated" the magazine, the more ads you'll find for empty luxuries, shown by models with jaded expressions.) How was Solomon uniquely qualified to draw conclusions about materialism?

3. 1 Timothy 6:9-10. What does this passage say about a life devoted to money and possessions? What does it say about the effects of such a life on our faith in God?

4. Read and discuss the following quotes by five wealthy men. What strikes you about these statements?

John D. Rockefeller: "I have made many millions, but they have brought me no happiness."

W. H. Vanderbilt: "The care of $200 million is enough to kill anyone. There is no pleasure in it."

John Jacob Astor: "I am the most miserable man on earth."

Henry Ford: "I was happier when doing a mechanic's job."

Andrew Carnegie: "Millionaires seldom smile."

5. Isaiah 10:1-3; Jeremiah 5:27-28; 15:13; Hosea 12:8; Amos 5:11; Micah 6:12. Why is the righteous rich man such a rare phenomenon?

6. List adjectives or phrases to complete the following sentence: Materialism is_____.

(Ask each class member to contribute at least one word or phrase.)

PRAYER: Lord, grant us eyes to see the lure of money and possessions for what it really is—and to desire you more than ever.

Materialism, the Church, and the Gospel

Reading Assignment: chapters 5 and 6

In Micah 3:11, the Lord decries the fact that priests and prophets alike were corrupted by money. In 1 Peter 5:2, Peter reminds church leaders that they are to be characterized by an eagerness to serve, not a greed for money. Paul insists that no lover of money is qualified to be a church leader (1 Timothy 3:3). So, how did materialism creep into the church to do the damage it is currently doing?

Preachers of the gospel of materialism may think they're justified in connecting prosperity with the Christian life—but what's the true picture?

1. The following passages describe a link between material wealth and God's blessing. Read and discuss, then choose one key word from each passage.

Abraham—**Genesis 13:1-7;** Isaac—**Genesis 26:12-14;** Jacob—**Genesis 30:43;** Joseph—**Genesis 39:2-6;** Solomon—1 **Kings 3:13;** Job—**Job 42:10-17.**

2. Deuteronomy 15:10; Proverbs 3:9-10; 11:25; Malachi 3:8-12. What blessings are promised to those who give faithfully of their finances?

3. Deuteronomy 28. The Old Testament warns against the dangers of wealth. What curses will overtake those who don't obey God?

4. Psalm 37:35-36; Ecclesiastes 7:15; Luke 15:1-2; John 9:34. Christians are not the only ones who experience prosperity. Consider the Pharisees of Jesus' day. How do their lives show that prosperity does not imply spirituality?

5. Matthew 10:16-20; Mark 10:42-45; Luke 14:33; John 15:18-20; 2 Timothy 3:12; 1 Peter 5:9. According to these verses, will Christians always be prosperous?

6. Matthew 5:45; 19:23-24. What did Jesus teach about the doctrine of prosperity?

7. Philippians 1:29; 2:5-11; 3:7-8. What was the apostle Paul's view of prosperity?

PRAYER: *Father, grant us your peace concerning what you've provided for us, and help us use it to your glory.*

The Two Treasuries:
Earth and Heaven

Reading Assignment: chapter 7

Jesus always had two kingdoms in mind—two treasuries, two perspectives, and two masters. We can store up treasures either on earth or in heaven. What we value most—the temporal or the eternal—will determine what we do with God's money.

1. On what basis does Jesus argue against storing up treasures on earth? On what basis does he argue for storing up treasures in heaven? (Hint: On the basis of right versus wrong or smart versus stupid?) Why is this significant?

2. Agree or disagree: *Jesus says we shouldn't store up treasures for ourselves.* If you agree, explain why. If you disagree, revise the statement to make it accurate.

3. Why do we gain a vested interest in whatever we put our treasures into?

4. Matthew 6:21. According to Jesus, how can we develop more of a heart for the poor, the lost, suffering Christians, or others in the Church?

5. We will "invest" in whichever kingdom we choose. List various ways in which people invest in this world. Then list ways to invest in God's kingdom.

6. Matthew 13:44. What does it mean for Christians today to "sell all we have" to seek ultimate heavenly treasure? If someone in the group has read *The Treasure Principle* by Randy Alcorn, ask him or her to summarize the message of that book.

7. Philippians 3:7-11. What does Paul say about the treasure of this world? In what ways is Christ himself our treasure as Christians? In what sense are others our treasure? Is it right to consider eternal rewards our treasures?

PRAYER: *Lord, help us to learn how to relocate our treasures from earth to heaven.*

The Steward's Task

Reading Assignment: chapters 8 and 9

Webster's dictionary says that a steward is someone employed to manage domestic concerns; a fiscal agent; one who supervises the provision and distribution of funds. We are called to be stewards of God's estate, agents of our eternal spiritual welfare and the welfare of others. Read the section titled "The Lost Sense of the Eternal" (pages 108–109). Pray together David's prayer in Psalm 39.

1. Proverbs 24:12; Jeremiah 17:10; Acts 17:31; Romans 2:12-16; 1 Peter 4:5. What are some characteristics of God, our Master and Judge? What are the implications of these characteristics for our daily conduct?

2. Matthew 10:28; 13:40-42; 25:41-46; Mark 9:43-44; Luke 16:22-31. What words come to mind to describe the horrors of hell?

3. Revelation 5:11-13; 7:15; 19:9; 21:19-21; 22:5; Luke 22:29-30. What do these verses say about what awaits the believer after death? What words would you use to describe heaven?

4. Review the two charts on page 127. Are there degrees of reward in heaven? Discuss the relationship between regeneration and rewards. (This discussion will help summarize many of the points of chapter 9.)

5. Matthew 6:1-18. Discuss how the three disciplines of fasting, giving, and prayer can help us to forgo our own possessions, power, and pleasure in this life and accomplish higher purposes for God's kingdom.

6. Are possessions, power, and pleasure always bad, or can they be good? How can we prove from Scripture that they are sometimes good? Make a chart of Possessions—Power—Pleasure, listing things in each category that have their "down" side as well as an eternal up side.

PRAYER: *After listing as many items as possible under question 6, close in conversational prayer around the room, asking for wise stewardship of all these things.*

Stewards and Pilgrims

Reading Assignment: chapters 10 and 11

Stewardship is not a subcategory of the Christian life. Stewardship is the Christian life. What is stewardship? It is the use of all that God has entrusted to us: life, time, talents, money, possessions, family, and his grace.

1. Luke 16:1-13. Read the parable of the shrewd manager, often called the "unrighteous steward." See page 142 for several different interpretations of the parable. What do you think the passage means? What message do you get from it for your life?

2. Luke 16:10. Jesus says, "Whoever can be trusted with very little can also be trusted with much, and whoever is dishonest with very little will also be dishonest with much." What does this mean?

3. Luke 16:11-12, 17, 19. Identify the key word in each of these verses.

4. Matthew 25:14-30. Read the parable of the talents. How does this parable support the key ideas you listed in question 3?

5. Luke 19:11-27. Read the parable of the ten minas. What further insights into stewardship do we find here?

6. On one side of a chart write "The Master." On the other side, write "The Servant" or "Steward." In the appropriate places, list the "lessons concerning the master," found on page 147, and the "lessons concerning the servant," found on pages 148–149.

7. Read together the overall lessons from the stewardship parables on pages 149–150. Which of these lessons strikes you as being particularly significant at this point in your life?

8. Besides the two kingdoms, Scripture teaches us there are two covenants and two "countries" (this world and our heavenly home). Because we have not yet reached our true home, we are "pilgrims" on earth, a foreign country. Material things are valuable to pilgrims, but only as they facilitate their mission. If you are a Christian, what are the implications of the fact that heaven, not earth, is your home? How should that affect your giving and financial decisions?

9. Agree or disagree: *"In the truest sense, Christian pilgrims have the best of both worlds."* We have joy whenever this world reminds us of the next, and we take solace whenever it does not.

PRAYER: *Lord, help us to be faithful ambassadors as we serve you on this foreign soil, never forgetting that although we are headed home, we're not there yet.*

Tithing and Giving

Reading Assignment: chapters 12 and 13

The tithe is a tenth "of everything from the land, whether grain from the soil or fruit from the trees" (Leviticus 27:30). It belongs to the Lord, not to us. It applies to *everything*, not only to some things. It is holy, to be set apart and given to God, and used for no other purpose.

1. Malachi 3:8-10. Is it possible to rob God of what is rightfully his? Notice that Malachi makes reference not only to tithes but also to freewill offerings. Can we rob God by withholding offerings?

2. Genesis 14:20; 28:22; Deuteronomy 14:23. Notice how tithing began with Abraham and Jacob. What is the stated purpose of tithing?

3. Matthew 23:23; Luke 11:42. Jesus supported tithing, as shown in his dialogue with the Pharisees, but he expected more than outward obedience. What does Jesus say should accompany tithing?

4. What does the author mean when he says that tithing is the "floor" of giving and the "training wheels" of giving?

5. Acts 2:44-45; 4:32-37. The early Christians often went far beyond tithing to share all that they had. Does New Testament "grace giving" lower the Old Testament bar of tithing—or raise it? Why do you suppose the average American Christian gives only one-fourth as much as what was required of the poorest Israelite?

6. Look up each of the following passages and explain what it says about how we are supposed to give. Also, for each reference, explain the specific context and intent:

Mark 14:3-9; 1 Corinthians 16:2; 2 Corinthians 8:11; 2 Corinthians 9:7; 2 Chronicles 24:10; 2 Corinthians 9:7; 2 Corinthians 8:5; Mark 12:43-44; Acts 11:29; 2 Samuel 24:24; 2 Corinthians 8:3; Matthew 6:1, 4; James 2:1-5.

7. Go back to Malachi 3:8-10. Can you think of anywhere else in Scripture where God invites us to test him? God seems to be saying, "Would you just obey me and give me a chance to show you how I'll bless you?" Have you tested God with tithing and generous giving? If so, what have you learned? If not, what's keeping you from giving God a chance to show what he can do in this area?

8. Luke 6:38. What is Jesus saying? In light of this passage, how would you respond to someone who says, "God's promise to provide financially for givers was only intended for Israelites under the law"?

9. There is honest debate about whether tithing is a biblical or logical starting place for Christian giving, but there should be no debate about voluntary giving, which is clearly practiced in both the Old and New Testaments. Do you think many people need the training wheels of tithing to get them going on the bicycle of giving?

PRAYER: *God, grant us your grace to learn the practice and the joy of giving back to you.*

Giving–Reaching Out to the Needy

Reading Assignment: chapters 14 and 15

Caring for the poor is a major theme of Scripture.

1. Leviticus 19:9-10; Deuteronomy 15:10-11. Read aloud these admonitions from the Mosaic Law concerning provisions for the poor. Why are we to give to the poor? What do these verses tell us about God? What do these verses tell us about our situation on earth?

2. Luke 19:8; 10:36-37. If every person is our neighbor, as Jesus taught, what are the specific lessons we can learn from these verses? Compare them to **Proverbs 19:17; 22:9; 28:27**.

3. Luke 4:18-19. Jesus came to preach the gospel—the good news—to the poor, the blind, and the oppressed. Read aloud the parable of the banquet in **Luke 14:12-23**. How does this story parallel our situation today in which the needy seem more open to a gospel of help and hope?

4. How does our understanding of the parable of the banquet affect our personal responsibility of giving? In light of Christ's priorities, how do we evaluate the many good causes that constantly solicit donations? How can we use our understanding to help influence our church's giving to such funds?

5. Review page 254 and discuss some wise guidelines for Christians raising and using funds. Examine the list of qualities for evaluating a ministry or parachurch organization (see pages 277–278). Why is each of these important in relation to biblical teaching and standards?

6. As individuals, and as a church, how might we grade ourselves on our eternal perspective regarding life, ministry, and resources?

PRAYER: *Lord, grant us clarity of purpose, wisdom of action, and faithfulness in our giving.*

A Faithful Lifestyle

Reading Assignment: chapter 16

Do we as Christians have a right to earn large amounts of money? If we make a lot of money, do we have a right to hold on to it? Are we called to give up all of our wealth and "live by faith"? Is there such a thing as a "happy medium" lifestyle? Concerning these questions, Scripture gives us helpful guidelines for the making, using, and giving of what we possess.

1. Read and discuss the following verses. How does the wisdom of each verse apply to our lives today? **Proverbs 12:11; 13:4; 14:23; Ecclesiastes 9:10; 1 Thessalonians 4:11-12; 2 Thessalonians 3:10; Titus 3:14.** God's way for us to earn money is to work! But then what should we do with this money? Discuss the section on private ownership of property (see pages 282–283).

2. Mark 1:16-20. What Christian lifestyle is implied here?

3. Mark 2:14-15. How does this approach differ in its style of discipleship?

4. Mark 8:34-37. What do these verses say about our "cross," once we have determined what it is? Must following Christ in this radical way always affect our money and possessions?

5. Mark 10:17-31. Discuss the two common errors in interpreting this passage (page 287).

6. 1 Timothy 6:17-19. Must all wealthy people give up being rich? What must they do "on every occasion"?

7. According to Peter H. Davids, "A biblical lifestyle will necessarily recognize itself as being in opposition to the prevailing values and lifestyle of its culture. It is informed by a different view of reality." What does this mean?

PRAYER: *Thank you, Lord, for your true view of reality and the power to give and to serve you in keeping with that reality.*

Borrowing, Saving, Investing

Reading Assignment: chapters 17, 18, and 19

If you are using this study guide as part of a classroom curriculum, ask three students to read one of the assigned chapters and report to the class the main findings that the author presents about these important topics of financial accountability.

1. **Chapter 17:**
   a. What does Scripture say about debt?

   b. What are the most likely pitfalls for Christians, or for churches, facing a question of borrowing or lending?

   c. How could getting out of debt become a spiritual issue?

2. **Chapter 18:**
   a. When is saving good stewardship?

   b. What are the dangers of hoarding?

   c. What should be our view of retirement—our use of time and money in that period of life and our setting aside money for it? Is this an issue where it's not "all or nothing at all"? but striving to find a biblical balance?

d. Does a Christian really need insurance? Why or why not? In what cases is insurance a good idea, and in what cases might it be a bad idea?

3. Chapter 19:

a. Is gambling compatible with the Christian life? Is there really any harm in buying a lottery ticket or placing small bets at a casino?

b. What does Scripture teach about investments?

c. Should high-risk living be part of a Christian's life?

d. In the light of eternity, to whom does our wealth belong— us, our heirs, or God? Does this have implications for where God might want us to leave his wealth? What is the difference between Hebrew culture and ours when it comes to the meaning and impact of inheritance?

PRAYER: Lord, teach us day by day to value your entrustments (not gifts) of money and possessions, to be good stewards of what appears to be ours, and to be able to let go of it as you call us to do so.

Materialism in the Christian Family

Reading Assignment: chapter 20

Scripture states that it's the responsibility of parents to make basic material provision for their children. To neglect to provide for our families is to deny our faith and be judged worse than an unbeliever (1 Timothy 5:8). Jesus rejected any "spiritual" explanations of not caring materially for one's family (Mark 7:9-13).

1. In chapter 19, Randy Alcorn rejects the notion that Christians should normally leave large amounts of money to their adult children. He asks, "What would you think if your money manager died and left all your money to his children?" Do you agree or disagree that, more often than not, unearned income hurts rather than helps people?

2. Do you agree or disagree with this idea: *Parents should demonstrate their equal love for their adult children by leaving them equal amounts of money and possessions.*

3. Albert Schweitzer points out, "There are only three ways to teach a child. The first is by example, the second is by example, the third is by example." This is an overstatement—but how much truth does it contain? Give some illustrations in your life or that of your children or grandchildren.

4. The house you live in, the schools your children attend, the car you drive—all speak a message to your children. What is that message? Is it possible that they can send different messages depending on how you view and use them?

5. What is your lifestyle saying to your children about the importance you place on material things in relation to God's work and God's kingdom?

6. In what way does giving break the stranglehold of materialism?

7. What did you learn from your parents about giving? What did you teach—or are you teaching—your children about giving? If your children are older, what suggestions would you offer to parents of younger children when it comes to raising children to be givers?

PRAYER: Lord, open our eyes to what we find difficult to see—anything that could become an idol and turn us from your will. We ask this for our children's sake as well as our own.

The Bottom Line

Reading Assignment: chapter 21 and conclusion (and selected appendixes)

If you are using this study guide as part of a classroom curriculum, bring pens or pencils and plain white paper for your students for this class session.

1. Review chapter 21 and the conclusion.

a. What statements do you consider most significant?

b. Which statements do you disagree with?

c. What do these chapters make you want to do?

2. Ask each person to write a letter to their child(ren) or another person over whom they have responsibility or influence that summarizes the lessons about Christian financial responsibility. (Make it clear that no one will be required to read his or her letter aloud, so they are free to be as candid as possible with their advice and admonitions. However, you may want to allow time at the end of class—about fifteen minutes—for volunteers who want to share some of the conclusions they've reached and how they were able to share them in specific situations with their children.)

3. Ask groups to read their own letters to themselves silently (pretending they were written to them by a parent or mentor twenty or thirty years ago and supported by the example of a life of spiritual and financial accountability), and answer the following questions: How would your life be different if you had known these things? What can you still do to put some of these principles into practice?

4. Which appendix did you find most interesting? Choose one of the appendixes that you believe contains important material. Summarize it or pick an underlined section to read from to the group.

5. Read aloud the final section of the book, "Coming to Grips with Eternity," on page 422. Substitute this adapted prayer for the last two lines:

PRAYER: Lord, may what will be most important to us five minutes after we die become most important to us now.

Preface
1. Barna Research Group, June 5, 2001, www.barna.org.
2. Randy Alcorn, *The Treasure Principle* (Sisters, Ore.: Multnomah, 2001).
3. Crown Financial Ministries, www.crown.org, 800-722-1976.
4. "Dollars & Percents," *Stewardship Matters* (Christian Stewardship Association) 2, no. 1 (1998): 11.

Chapter 1: Money: Why Is It So Important to God?
1. Larry Burkett, "Good Financial Stewardship," *Religions & Liberty* (July–August): 1.

Chapter 2: The Weakness of Asceticism
1. Philip Yancey, *Money* (Portland, Ore.: Multnomah, 1985), 3.
2. Quoted by Leland Ryken, *Worldly Saints* (Grand Rapids, Mich.: Zondervan, 1986), 63.
3. Richard Foster, *Money, Sex, and Power: The Challenge of the Disciplined Life* (San Francisco: Harper & Row, 1985), 24–25.
4. Eugene Peterson, *Working the Angles: The Shape of Pastoral Integrity* (Grand Rapids, Mich.: Eerdmans, 1987), 9–10; and Dallas Willard, *The Spirit of the Disciplines: Understanding How God Changes Lives* (San Francisco: Harper & Row, 1988).
5. Tim Hansel, *When I Relax I Feel Guilty* (Elgin, Ill.: David C. Cook, 1981), 43.
6. Randy Alcorn, *In Light of Eternity: Perspectives on Heaven* (Colorado Springs, Colo.: WaterBrook, 1999).
7. Richard Foster, *Freedom of Simplicity* (San Francisco: Harper & Row, 1981), 52–73.
8. Ryken, 58.
9. Ibid., 61.
10. Ibid., 70.
11. Ibid., 61.
12. Holmes Rolston, *Stewardship in the New Testament Church* (Richmond, Va.: John Knox Press, 1950), 129–30.

Chapter 3: The Nature of Materialism
1. Al Gustafson and Robyn Johnson, "The Spiritual Measure of Money," *The Works* (summer 2000): 27.
2. Gwen Kinkead, "On a Fast Track to the Good Life," *Fortune* 7 April 1980, 74–84.
3. *Affluenza* was produced by KCTS/Seattle and Oregon Public Broadcasting, www.pbs.org.org/kcts/affluenza/show.html.
4. A. W. Tozer, *The Pursuit of God* (Harrisburg, Pa.: Christian Publications, 1958), 21–22.
5. *Merriam Webster's Collegiate Dictionary*, 10th ed., s.v. "materialism."
6. Michael S. Hamilton, "We're in the Money: How Did Evangelicals Get So Wealthy, and What Has It Done to Us?" *Christianity Today*, 12 June 2000, 36.

Chapter 4: The Dangers of Materialism
1. Herbert Schlossberg, *Idols for Destruction* (Nashville, Tenn.: Nelson, 1983), 88–89.

2. Aurelius Augustinus, *Confessions*, IX, 1.

3. Leland Ryken, *Worldly Saints* (Grand Rapids, Mich.: Zondervan, 1986), 62.

4. Blaise Pascal, *Pensées*, (thought #425), trans. W. F. Trotter (New York: E. P. Dutton, 1958), 113.

5. John Steinbeck, quoted in Richard Halverson, *Perspective*, 24 June 1987.

6. Thomas Carlyle, *On Heroes, Hero-Worship, and the Heroic in History* (1840), quoted in *Bartlett's Familiar Quotations*, 15th ed. (Boston: Little, Brown and Company, 1980), 474.

7. Quoted in Bruce Wilkinson, "Walk Thru Eternal Rewards" seminar and notebook (Atlanta, Ga.: Walk Thru the Bible Ministries, 1987).

8. Aaron Beck, *The American Journal of Psychiatry*, May 1985.

9. The actual figure on the test was $40,000, but that was in 1985. A closer current equivalent would be $50,000.

10. John Piper, *Desiring God* (Portland, Ore.: Multnomah, 1987), 156.

11. Adapted from Alexander Maclaren, *The God of the Amen* (New York: Funk and Wagnall, n.d.); cited by Steve Halliday & William Travis, in *How Great Thou Art* (Sisters, Ore.: Multnomah, 1999), 301.

12. David E. Neff, "Drunk on Money," *Christianity Today*, 8 April 1988: 15.

13. Ibid.

14. Randy C. Alcorn, *Christians in the Wake of the Sexual Revolution* (Portland Ore.: Multnomah, 1985), 153–54.

15. Piper, 157.

16. John Wesley, quoted in Charles Edward White, "Four Lessons on Money from One of the World's Richest Preachers," *Christian History* 19 (summer 1988): 21–22.

17. Randy Alcorn, *The Treasure Principle: Discovering the Secret of Joyful Giving* (Sisters, Ore.: Multnomah, 2001), 51.

Chapter 5: Materialism in the Church

1. Michael S. Hamilton, "We're in the Money: How Did Evangelicals Get So Wealthy, and What Has It Done to Us?" *Christianity Today*, 12 June 2000: 36.

2. Some good resources that have become available in the past several years (which, unfortunately, support my initial conclusions) include Athena Dean, *Consumed by Success* (Mukilteo, Wash.: WinePress Books, 1997) and *All That Glitters Is Not God: Breaking Free from the Sweet Deceit of Multilevel Marketing* (Mukilteo, Wash.: WinePress Books, 1998); Robert L. Fitzpatrick, *False Profits: Seeking Financial and Spiritual Deliverance in Pyramid Schemes and Multi-Level Marketing* (Lighthouse Point, Fla.: Herald Press, 1997); Amy Chen Mills, "Shaking the Money Tree," www.metroactive.com/papers/metro/10.03.96/cover/multilevel-9640.html; and Dean Van Druff, "What's Wrong With Multi-Level Marketing?" www.vandruff.com/mlm.html.

3. Many multilevel marketing operations now use the term *network marketing*, although their definitions of the term may vary. Because of these variations, I prefer to use the older term, *multilevel marketing*. In referring to multilevel marketing practices, I do not mean "pyramid schemes" based on the multilevel chain-letter approach where others are enlisted to send in their money in hope of rising to the top and receiving huge profits. Although there is a pyramid element to some multilevel sales companies, pyramids per se are illegal, whereas legitimate multilevel sales organizations are not.

4. Ruth Carter, *Amway Motivational Organizations: Behind the Smoke and Mirrors* (Winter Park, Fla.: Backstreet Publishing, 1999).

5. Gene A. Getz, *A Biblical Theology of Material Possessions* (Chicago: Moody Press, 1990), 27.

Chapter 6: Prosperity Theology: The Gospel of Wealth

1. John Piper, *Desiring God* (Portland, Ore.: Multnomah, 1987), 163–64.
2. John Wesley, quoted in Charles Edward White, "Four Lessons on Money from One of the World's Richest Preachers," *Christian History* 19 (summer 1988): 22.
3. "Quick Quotes on Money," *Christian History* 7 (1987): 2, 4.
4. Ibid.

Chapter 7: Two Treasuries, Two Perspectives, Two Masters

1. A. W. Tozer, "The Transmutation of Wealth," in *Born after Midnight* (Harrisburg, Pa.: Christian Publications, 1959), 106.
2. John White, *The Cost of Commitment* (Downers Grove, Ill.: InterVarsity Press, 1976), 47.
3. John Bunyan, as quoted in Bruce Wilkinson, "Walk Thru Eternal Rewards" seminar and notebook (Atlanta, Ga.: Walk Thru the Bible Ministries, 1987).
4. Randy Alcorn, *The Treasure Principle: Discovering the Secret of Joyful Giving* (Sisters, Ore.: Multnomah, 2001), 13.

Chapter 8: The Steward's Eternal Destiny

1. These include *Deadline* (Sisters, Ore.: Multnomah, 1993), *Dominion* (Multnomah, 1995), *Edge of Eternity* (Colorado Springs, Colo.: WaterBrook, 1998), and *Safely Home* (Wheaton, Ill.: Tyndale House, 2001).
2. Randy Alcorn, *In Light of Eternity: Perspectives on Heaven* (Colorado Springs, Colo.: WaterBrook, 1999), 2–3.
3. For material on heaven and eternal rewards, including common questions and answers, see "Eternity" on our Eternal Perspective Web site at www.epm.org.
4. Donald Gray Barnhouse as quoted in Bruce Wilkinson, "Walk Thru Eternal Rewards" seminar and notebook (Atlanta, Ga.: Walk Thru the Bible Ministries, 1987).

Chapter 9: The Steward's Eternal Rewards

1. John Bunyan, "The Resurrection of the Dead, and Eternal Judgment," http:// philologos.org/__eb-jb/Resurrection/dead05.htm.
2. I am indebted here to Bruce Wilkinson's "Walk Thru Eternal Rewards" seminar he gave to a small group at Western seminary in Portland, Oregon, in 1987.
3. John Bunyan, "Paul's Departure and Crown," www.johnbunyan.org/text/bun-paul.txt.
4. William Wilberforce, *Real Christianity* (Portland, Ore.: Multnomah, 1982), 65.
5. C. S. Lewis, *The Weight of Glory* (New York: Macmillan, 1980), 17–18, 3–4.
6. Richard Baxter, "The Saints' Everlasting Rest," in *The Practical Works of Richard Baxter* (Grand Rapids, Mich.: Baker, 1981), 39–40.

Chapter 10: The Steward and the Master

1. Ben Patterson, *The Grand Essentials* (Waco, Tex.: Word, 1987), 17.
2. Gene A. Getz, *A Biblical Theology of Material Possessions* (Chicago: Moody Press, 1990), 65–66.
3. Randy Alcorn, *In Light of Eternity: Perspectives on Heaven* (Colorado Springs, Colo.: WaterBrook Press, 1999).
4. Ray Boltz, "Thank You," Gaither Music/ASCAP, 1988.
5. C. S. Lewis, *The World's Last Night, and other essays* (New York: Harcourt Brace Jovanovich, 1952), 112–113.

6. John Wesley, quoted in Charles Edward White, "Four Lessons on Money from One of the World's Richest Preachers," *Christian History* 19 (summer 1988): 23.

7. Bill Mencarow, letter to Randy Alcorn, October 2001, used by permission.

Chapter 11: The Pilgrim Mentality

1. C. S. Lewis, *Mere Christianity* (New York: Macmillan, 1972), 118.

2. A. W. Tozer, "The World to Come" in *Of God and Men* (Harrisburg, Pa.: Christian Publications, 1960), 127, 129–30.

3. Lewis, *Mere Christianity* (New York: Macmillan, 1960), 120.

4. C. S. Lewis, *God in the Dock* (Grand Rapids, Mich.: Eerdmans, 1970), 150.

5. Lewis, *Mere Christianity*, 104.

6. C. S. Lewis, *The Last Battle* (New York: Macmillan, 1956), 172.

7. C. S. Lewis, *The Problem of Pain* (New York: Macmillan, 1948), 115.

Chapter 12: Tithing: The Training Wheels of Giving

1. The Barna Update June 5, 2001, www.barna.org.

2. Figures from the Internal Revenue Service, the Gallup Organization, and *Giving USA*, a publication if the American Association of Fundraising Counsel (AAFRC).

3. The Barna Update June 5, 2001, www.barna.org.

4. Os Guinness, *Doing Well and Doing Good: Money, Giving, and Caring in a Free Society* (Colorado Springs, Colo.: NavPress, 2001), 17.

5. Irenaeus, quoted in John David, *Your Wealth in God's World* (Phillipsburg, N.J.: Presbyterian and Reformed, 1984), 113.

6. *Dictionary of Christian Antiquities*, vol. 2, quoted in Fletcher Spruce, *You Can Be a Joyful Tither* (Kansas City, Mo.: Beacon Hill Press, 1966), 19.

7. *Dictionary of Christian Antiquities*.

8. Don McClanen, *The Tithe as Teacher: An Energizing Force* (Gaithersburg, Md.: Ministry of Money, 1980), 1–2.

9. McClanen, 3.

Chapter 13: Giving: Reciprocating God's Grace

1. P. E. Hughes, quoted in K. F. W. Prior, *God and Mammon* (Philadelphia, Pa.: Westminster Press, 1965), 17.

2. Justin Martyr, quoted in Virgil Vogt, *Treasure in Heaven* (Ann Arbor, Mich.: Servant Books, 1982), 85.

3. See Crown Financial Ministries' Bible studies on stewardship and giving, www.crown.org, 800-722-1976.

4. Karl Barth, *Church Dogmatics* (Edinburgh: T & T Clark, 1957), vol. 4.1, 41.

5. *Los Angeles Times*, 25 October 1990.

6. A. W. Tozer, *That Incredible Christian* (Harrisburg, Pa.: Christian Publications, 1964), 105.

7. Fred Smith Sr., "The Gift of Giving," The Gathering Newsletter 4, no. 3 (19 August 2000).

8. If you'd like a few business-card size summaries that state scriptural principles on giving, they're free on request from us at Eternal Perspective Ministries, 2229 E. Burnside #23, Gresham, Ore. 97030, 503-663-6481, info@epm.org. (Please send a self-addressed, stamped envelope.) Or see www.epm.org/givingcard.htm for ideas.

9. See Crown Financial Ministries' Bible studies on stewardship and giving, www.crown.org, 800-722-1976.

Chapter 14: Helping the Poor and Reaching the Lost

1. Claude Rosenberg Jr., *Wealthy and Wise: How You and America Can Get the Most out of Your Giving* (Boston: Little, Brown, and Company, 1994), 13–17.
2. Ralph Waldo Emerson, "Self-Reliance," in *Essays and Lectures* (New York: Library of America, 1983), 261–62.
3. See Ronald Nash, *Poverty and Wealth* (Westchester, Ill.: Crossway, 1986); John Jefferson Davis, *Your Wealth in God's World* (Phillipsburg, N.J.: Presbyterian and Reformed Publishing, 1984); Brian Griffith, *The Creation of Wealth* (Downers Grove, Ill.: InterVarsity Press, 1984); and R. C. Sproul Jr., *Money Matters* (Wheaton, Ill.: Tyndale House, 1985).
4. Os Guinness, *Doing Well and Doing Good: Money, Giving, and Caring in a Free Society* (Colorado Springs, Colo.: NavPress, 2001), 128.
5. Ibid.
6. Ibid.
7. John Wesley, quoted in Charles Edward White, "Four Lessons on Money from One of the World's Richest Preachers," *Christian History* 19 (summer 1988): 24.
8. For information about ministering to persecuted Christians, see www.epm.org/safelyhome.html and www.epm.org/persecuted.html.
9. Mike Galli, "Did You Know?" *Christian History* Issue 39 (Vol. XII, No. 3).
10. Jacques Ellul, *Money and Power* (Downers Grove, Ill.: InterVarsity Press, 1984), 151–52.
11. Mobilization Division, U.S. Center for World Mission, Pasadena, Calif., e-mail to author, 22 February 2002.
12. Elisabeth Elliot, *Through Gates of Splendor* (Wheaton, Ill.: Tyndale House, 1987), 176.
13. Eternal Perspective Ministries makes available a list of such organizations on our Web site: www. epm.org/orgs.html, or call 503-663-6481.
14. David Bryant, *In the Gap* (Ventura, Calif.: Regal, 1975), 13.

Chapter 15: Ministry Finances and Fund-Raising

1. Randy Alcorn, "Nineteen Questions to Ask Before You Give to Any Organization," www.epm.org/givquest.html.
2. John Chrysostom, quoted in *Christian History* 7, no. 2 (1987): 23.
3. Mel Rees, "Church Fund-raising," *Ministry* (July 1985): 4.
4. Garry Freisen deals with these and other possible weaknesses of the faith promise approach in his book *Decision Making and the Will of God* (Portland, Ore.: Multnomah, 1980), 361–67.
5. David R. High, *Kings & Priests* (Oklahoma City: Books for Children of the World, 1997), 26, 18.
6. Foster Church, "Legendary preacher enraptures audience," *The Oregonian*, n.d.
7. Eugene Habecker, "Biblical Guidelines for Asking and Giving," *Christianity Today* (15 May 1987): 34.
8. Ibid, 374–75.
9. To see all seventeen of our founding principles, go to www.epm.org/finance.html.
10. Michael S. Hamilton, "Money!" *Christianity Today* (22 June 2000): 38–43.
11. Ibid, 39.
12. Elisabeth Elliot, *A Chance to Die: The Life and Legacy of Amy Carmichael* (Old Tappan, N.J.: Revell, 1987), 153.
13. Larry Eskridge and Mark A. Noll, ed., *More Money, More Ministry: Money and Evangelicals in Recent North American History* (Grand Rapids, Mich.: Eerdmans, 2000), 105.

14. J. C. Pollack, *Moody: A Biographical Portrait of an Evangelist* (New York: Macmillan, 1963), 296–98.
15. Eskridge and Noll, 106.
16. Ken Waters, "The Art & Ethics of Fund-raising," *Christianity Today* (3 December 2001): 56.
17. Eskridge and Noll, 137–38.
18. Waters, 55.
19. Letter from Richard Stearns to the editor of *Christianity Today*, 3 December 2001. Mr. Stearns sent the author a copy of his full letter.
20. Some of the ethical questions raised here were prompted by a two-page ECFA handout entitled "Perceptions of Fund-raising Techniques," Winchester, Va., n.d.
21. Roy Menninger, speaking at 1981 Council on Foundations Annual Conference; cited from "Best Practices For Philanthropists," a paper provided by World Vision.
22. Jim Cymbala, *Fresh Wind, Fresh Fire,* (Grand Rapids, Mich.: Zondervan, 1997), 70.
23. Speakers arranged by fees at Christianspeakers.com.
24. "Quick Quotes on Money," *Christian History* 7 (1987): 2, 4.
25. Read the full article at www.epm.org/givquest.html.
26. Eternal Perspective Ministries is happy to recommend a wide variety of organizations—working in different ministries in various parts of the world—in which we firmly believe. We don't want your money, but we'll gladly help you contact the kinds of ministries in which you might have a special interest and who will use the funds you contribute to God's glory. See our listt at www.epm.org/orgs.html, or contact us at 503-663-6481, or 2229 East Burnside #23, Gresham, OR 97030.

Chapter 16: Making Money, Owning Possessions, and Choosing a Lifestyle
1. I am indebted here to Gregory L. Waybright, "Discipleship and Possessions in the Gospel of Mark" (Ph.D. diss., Marquette University, 1984).
2. Lisa Whelchel, *The Facts of Life and Other Lessons My Father Taught Me* (Sisters, Ore.: Multnomah, 2001), 57–60.
3. Global Mapping International, *GMI World* (winter 2002): 6.
4. L. P. Smith, quoted in David E. Neff, "Drunk on Money," *Christianity Today* (8 April 1988): 15.
5. Randy Alcorn, *The Treasure Principle: Discovering the Secret of Joyful Giving* (Sisters, Ore.: Multnomah, 2001), 56.
6. John Piper, *Desiring God* (Portland, Ore.: Multnomah, 1986), 166–67.
7. Ibid., 157.
8. Charles Edward White, "Four Lessons on Money from One of the World's Richest Preachers," *Christian History* 19 (summer 1988): 24.
9. Ralph Winter, "Reconsecration to a Wartime, not a Peacetime, Lifestyle," in *Perspectives on the World Christian Movement*, ed. Ralph Winter and Steven Hawthorne (Pasadena, Calif.: William Carey Library, 1981), 814.
10. Ralph Winter, "Penetrating the Last Frontiers," *Christian History* 7, no. 2 (1987): 30.
11. Peter H. Davids, "New Testament Foundations for Living More Simply," in *Living More Simply*, ed. Ronald J. Sider (Downers Grove, Ill.: InterVarsity Press, 1980), 51.

Chapter 17: Debt: Borrowing and Lending
1. Larry Burkett, *How to Use Your Money Wisely* (Chicago: Moody Press, 1986), 76.
2. Joshus Wolf Shank, "In Debt All the Way Up to Their Nose Rings," *U.S. News & World Report*, 9 June 1997.

3. Ron Blue, *Master Your Money* (Nashville, Tenn.: Thomas Nelson), 116, 118.

4. Christine Dugas, "Paying Off Cards Saves a Bundle," *USA Today*, 27 September 1996, sec. B, p. 7.

5. www.jobweb.com/Research/parents/studentpoll.htm.

6. Dr. and Mrs. Howard Taylor, *Hudson Taylor and China Inland Mission: The Growth of a Work of God*, vol. 2 (Singapore: Overseas Missionary Fellowship, 1918; reprint 1988), 54.

7. Mel Sumrall, personal interview, 27 May 1993.

8. Jeff Berg and Jim Burgess, *The Debt-Free Church* (Chicago: Moody Press, 1996), 54.

9. Ibid, 15–23.

10. This list adapted from an unpublished letter by Barry Arnold, 2001, and from *The Debt-Free Church*.

Chapter 18: Saving, Retiring, and Insuring

1. Ron Blue, *Master Your Money* (Nashville, Tenn.: Thomas Nelson, 1986), 13.

2. William MacDonald, *True Discipleship* (Kansas City, Kans.: Walterick Publishers, 1976), 97.

3. Larry Burkett, *How to Use Your Money Wisely* (Chicago: Moody Press, 1986), 26.

4. Charles Spurgeon, *Morning and Evening* (New Kensington, Pa.: Whitaker House, 2001): March 7, evening.

5. I am indebted to Tom McCallie of the Maclellan Foundation for some of this information on foundations.

6. From an e-mail from Tom McCallie, 3 January 2002.

7. I am indebted here to a paper written by Paul Eshleman, sent to me in 2001, entitled "Motivation for Giving"; also to Gary Latainer, for his article "Current Versus Deferred Giving: What Do the Scriptures Teach?" *Biblical Perspectives on Giving* (June 2001): 1.

8. Angela Alcorn, Karina Alcorn, and Randy Alcorn, *The Ishbane Conspiracy* (Sisters, Ore.: Multnomah, 2001).

9. Spurgeon, *Morning and Evening*, October 26, morning.

10. *The Christian Care Ministry*, P. O. Box 120099, West Melbourne, FL, 32912-0099, 800-374-2562, http://medi-share.org.

11. *The Christian Care Ministry Medi-Share Program 2001 Guidelines*, 8. www.biblicalhealthcare.com/pdf/2001guidelines.pdf.

12. MacDonald, 96–97.

Chapter 19: Gambling, Investing, and Leaving Money Behind

1. Ronald A. Reno, "Lotteries in the United States: A Brief Overview," prepared for the Gambling Impact Study Commission, *Citizen Link*, www.family.org.

2. Barry Arnold, "Odds Are, You Lose," a sermon preached at Good Shepherd Community Church, July 10–11, 1999. Full text available at www.epm.org/gambling.html.

3. Ibid.

4. Raj Persaud, "Forget It All," *The Independent* (London), 3 June 1999, 9.

5. Ibid.

6. Scott Fehrenbacher, *Putting Your Money Where Your Morals Are* (Nashville, Tenn.: Broadman and Holman), 50.

7. Ibid, 53.

8. Peter and Rochelle Schweizer, *Disney: The Mouse Betrayed* (Washington, D.C.: Regency, 1998), 112.

9. Fehrenbacher, *Put Your Money Where Your Morals Are*.

10. Ibid, 101.
11. Ibid, 88.
12. The Timothy Plan, www.timothyplan.com, 800-846-7526.
13. Larry Burkett, *How to Use Your Money Wisely* (Chicago: Moody Press, 1986), 66.
14. Os Guinness, *Doing Well and Doing Good: Money, Giving, and Caring in a Free Society* (Colorado Springs, Colo.: NavPress, 2001), 18.
15. Richard Foster, *Freedom of Simplicity* (San Francisco, Calif.: Harper & Row, 1981), 66.
16. Andrew Carnegie, quoted in Howard Dayton, *Your Money: Frustration or Freedom?* (Wheaton, Ill.: Tyndale House, 1979), 65.
17. Barbara Blouin and Katherine Gibson, *The Legacy of Inherited Wealth* (Blacksburg, Va.: Trio Press, 1995).
18. Guinness, 197–98.
19. Generous Giving Conference, 2 March 2002, Sarasota, Fla., www.generousgiving.org.
20. International Cooperating Ministries, 606 Aberdeen Rd, Hampton, Va. 23661, 757-827-6704, www.icmmbc.org.
21. If you'd like a list of ministries we recommend, visit our Web site: www.epm.org/orgs.html, contact us at info@epm.opg, or 503-663-6481.

Chapter 20: Battling Materialism in the Christian Family

1. David L. McKenna, "Financing the Great Commission," *Christianity Today* 15 May 1987: 28.
2. John Wesley, "The Use of Money," quoted in Charles Edward White, "Four Lessons on Money from One of the World's Richest Preachers," *Christian History* 19 (summer 1988): 23.
3. Albert Schweitzer, quoted in Malcolm MacGregor, *Training Your Children to Handle Money* (Minneapolis, Minn.: Bethany Fellowship, 1980), 111.
4. See Randy Alcorn, *In Light of Eternity: Perspectives on Heaven* (Colorado Springs, Colo.: WaterBrook, 1999).

Chapter 21: Teaching Children about Money and Possessions

1. Randy Alcorn, *Dominion* (Sisters, Ore.: Multnomah, 1996), 165.
2. James Dobson, *Dare to Discipline* (Wheaton, Ill.: Tyndale House Publishers, 1970), 56.

Conclusion: Where Do We Go from Here?

1. Stephen King, "What You Pass On," *Family Circle*, 1 November 2001, 156.
2. Randy Alcorn, "Is it wrong to let other know how much we give . . . ?" www.epm.org/giving.html.
3. I highly recommend the conferences put on by Generous Giving, www.generousgiving.org, 423-755-2399.
4. Randy Alcorn, *The Treasure Principle: Discovering the Secret of Joyful Giving* (Sisters, Ore.: Multnomah, 2001), 65–66.
5. Cyprian, quoted in Art Beals, *Beyond Hunger* (Portland, Ore.: Multnomah, 1985), 166–67.
6. G. Campbell Morgan, *Living Messages of the Books of the Bible* (Old Tappan, N.J.: Revell, n.d.), 120, 123.
7. William MacDonald, *True Discipleship* (Kansas City: Walterick Publishers, 1975), 92–93.
8. Ibid., 108.

9. Charles Spurgeon, *Morning and Evening*, February 10, morning, Christian Focus Publications, Scotland.

10. A. W. Tozer, "The Transmutation of Wealth," *Born after Midnight* (Harrisburg, Pa.: Christian Publications, 1959), 107.

Appendix A: Financial Integrity and Accountability in Church and Ministries

1. David B. Barrett, George T. Kurian, and Todd M. Johnson, *World Christian Trend* (Pasadena, Calif.: William Carey Library, 2001).

2. Randy Alcorn, "Nineteen Questions to Ask Before You Give to Any Organization," www.epm.org/givquest.html.

3. Evangelical Council for Financial Accountability, 440 West Jubal Early Drive, Suite 130, Winchester, VA, 22601; 800-323-9473; www.ecfa.org.

4. www.ecfa.org.

5. Ibid.

6. "The Giver's Guide" brochure, ECFA, Winchester, VA.

7. "Too Much 9/11 Giving," *Christianity Today*, 7 January 2002, 15.

8. Ministry Watch, www.ministrywatch.com.

9. At Eternal Perspective Ministries we're often asked for recommendations of what we think some of the best ministries are. Recognizing our own limitations, we're glad to share our opinion with those who ask. Contact EPM at info@epm.org, www.epm.org or 503-663-6481. We will never recommend you give to us, but only to others.

10. "Five-star Ratings of Faith-based Organizations Available at Ministrywatch.com," Press release, 30 May 2001.

Appendix B: The Use of Ministry Funds for Buildings

1. John White, *The Golden Cow* (Downers Grove, Ill.: InterVarsity Press, 1979), 65–66.

2. Rick Warren's Ministry Toolbox, Issue 66, 4 September 2002.

Appendix C: Lending Money, Charging Interest, and Co-signing a Loan

1. *Christian History* (1987), 7(2):18.

2. Howard Dayton, *Your Money: Frustration or Freedom?* (Wheaton, Ill.: Tyndale House, 1979), 50.

Appendix D: Practical Guidelines to Control Spending

1. Ron Blue, *Master Your Money* (Nashville, Tenn.: Thomas Nelson, 1997); Larry Burkett, *Debt-Free Living: How to Get Out of Debt (And Stay Out)* (Chicago: Moody Press, 2001); Larry Burkett, *Complete Financial Guide for Young Couples* (Wheaton, Ill.: Victor Books, 1989); and Howard Dayton, *Your Money Counts: The Biblical Guide to Earning, Spending, Saving, Investing, and Getting Out of Debt* (Wheaton, Ill.: Tyndale House, 1997).

TOPIC INDEX